OF ANY MIS TEXTBOOK

- Cover only the modules for a very technical perspective
- Omit any chapter you don't want—you can still cover the corresponding module
- Omit any module you don't want—it will not affect your ability to cover the chapters

Modules

XLM A: Careers in Business*

XLM B: Computer Hardware and Software

XLM C: Designing Databases and Entity-Relationship Diagramming

XLM D: (Skills Module) Decision Analysis with Spreadsheet Software

XLM E: Network Basics*

XLM F: Object-Oriented Technologies*

XLM G: Implementing a Database with Microsoft Access*

XLM H: The World Wide Web & the Internet

XLM I: (Skills Module) Building a Web page with HTML*

XLM J: (Skills Module) Building an e-Portfolio*

XLM K: Computer Crime and Forensics

*on StudentCD-ROM

Third Canadian Edition

MANAGEMENT INFORMATION SYSTEMS
for the Information Age

Stephen Haag
DANIELS COLLEGE OF BUSINESS

UNIVERSITY OF DENVER

Maeve Cummings
KELCE COLLEGE OF BUSINESS

PITTSBURG STATE UNIVERSITY

Donald J. McCubbrey
DANIELS COLLEGE OF BUSINESS

UNIVERSITY OF DENVER

Alain Pinsonneault
McGILL UNIVERSITY

Richard Donovan
McGILL UNIVERSITY

Toronto   Montréal   Boston   Burr Ridge, IL   Dubuque, IA   Madison, WI   New York
San Francisco   St. Louis   Bangkok   Bogotá   Caracas   Kuala Lumpur   Lisbon   London
Madrid   Mexico City   Milan   New Delhi   Santiago   Seoul   Singapore   Sydney   Taipei

McGraw-Hill Ryerson

Management Information Systems for the Information Age
Third Canadian Edition

ISBN: 0-07-095569-7

1 2 3 4 5 6 7 8 9 10   TCP   0 9 8 7 6

Printed and bound in Canada

Care has been taken to trace ownership of copyright material contained in this text; however, the publisher will welcome any information that enables them to rectify any reference or credit for subsequent editions.

Publisher: Nicole Lukach
Sponsoring Editor: Rhondda McNabb
Developmental Editor: Suzanne Simpson Millar
Associate Developmental Editor: Marcia Luke
Senior Editorial Associate: Christine Lomas
Marketing Manager: Charlotte Liu
Supervising Editor: Jaime Smith
Copy Editor: Rodney Rawlings
Senior Production Coordinator: Madeleine Harrington
Interior Design: Greg Devitt
Page Layout: Bookman Typesetting Co.
Cover Design: Greg Devitt
Cover Image: Digital Vision/Sara Hayward
Printer: Transcontinental Printing Group

Library and Archives Canada Cataloguing in Publication

Management information systems for the information age / Stephen Haag ... [et al.]. — 3rd Canadian ed.

Includes bibliographical references and index.
ISBN 0-07-095569-7

1. Management information systems—Textbooks.   2. Information technology—Management—Textbooks.   I. Haag, Stephen

T58.6.M34 2006   658.4'038'011   C2006-900239-8

STEPHEN HAAG is a professor in and Chair of the Department of Information Technology and Electronic Commerce in the Daniels College of Business at the University of Denver. Stephen is also the Director of the Masters of Science in Information Technology program and the Director of the Advanced Technology Center. Stephen holds a B.B.A. and M.B.A. from West Texas State University and a Ph.D. from the University of Texas at Arlington.

Stephen is the coauthor of numerous books including *Business Driven Technology* (with Amy Phillips and Paige Baltzan), *Interactions: Teaching English as a Second Language* (with his mother and father), *Information Technology: Tomorrow's Advantage Today* (with Peter Keen), *Excelling in Finance,* and more than 40 books within the I-Series. He has also written numerous articles appearing in such journals as *Communications of the ACM, Socio-Economic Planning Sciences, International Journal of Systems Science, Managerial and Decision Economics, Applied Economics,* and *Australian Journal of Management.* Stephen lives with his wife, Pam, and their four sons—Indiana, Darian, Trevor, and Zippy—in Highlands Ranch, CO.

MAEVE CUMMINGS is a professor of Information Systems at Pittsburg State University. She holds a B.S. in Mathematics and Computer Science, an M.B.A from Pittsburg State, and a Ph.D. in Information Systems from the University of Texas at Arlington. She has published in various journals including *Journal of Global Information Management* and *Journal of Computer Information Systems.* She serves on various editorial boards and is a coauthor of *Case Studies in Information Technology* and the concepts books of the I-Series, entitled *Computing Concepts.* Maeve has been teaching for 20 years and lives in Pittsburg, KS, with her husband, Slim.

DONALD J. McCUBBREY is a professor in the Department of Information Technology and Electronic Commerce and Director of the Center for the Study of Electronic Commerce in the Daniels College of Business at the University of Denver. He holds a B.S.B.A. in Accounting from Wayne State University, a Master of Business from Swinburne University of Technology in Victoria, Australia, and a Ph.D. in Information Systems from the University of Maribor, Slovenia.

Prior to joining the Daniels College faculty in 1984, he was a partner with a large international accounting and consulting firm. During his career as an IT consultant he participated in client engagements in the United States as well as in several other countries in the Americas and Europe. He has published articles in *Communications of the Association for Information Systems, Information Technology and People,* and *MIS Quarterly,* and coauthored the systems analysis and design text *Foundations of Business Systems.* He is an associate editor of the *Communications of the Association for Information Systems.* He is a cofounder and director emeritus of the Colorado

Software and Internet Association and lives in the Colorado foothills with his wife, Janis.

CANADIAN AUTHORS

RICHARD G. DONOVAN is a Faculty Lecturer and IS area coordinator in the Desautels Faculty of Management at McGill University. He holds a B.Comm. with a major in MIS and a concentration in Marketing, as well as a Certificate in Public Relations from the same university. In addition, Richard has a graduate diploma in Instructional Technology from Concordia University.

Prior to joining McGill full-time in July 1997, Richard Donovan worked at a top Canadian life insurance company for eight years, where he held positions such as Systems Consultant, Senior Training and Development Consultant, and as a production manager supervising a staff of 18. Since his arrival at McGill, he has won outstanding teaching awards and student life awards on 12 occasions.

While holding the position of Associate Dean of the Undergraduate Program from January 2001 to December 2004, Richard managed the growth of the program from 1750 students to 2250. He was responsible for ensuring the quality of the program, course content, and delivery. He continues to design and teach courses in the areas of IS and strategy, specializing in information systems, IT in business, and case analysis and presentation.

Richard also specializes in cost/benefit analysis of IT projects and the integration of IT into organizations, as well as instructional design, team facilitation, and presentation skills. He teaches executives at the McGill International Executive Institute and the Centre for International Management Studies (CIMS), and in McGill's MBA/Japan program.

ALAIN PINSONNEAULT is the Imasco Chair of IS and James McGill Professor in the Desautels Faculty of Management at McGill University.

He holds a Ph.D. from the University of California. Prior to joining McGill University in 1999, he was an associate professor at HEC-Montréal. Alain Pinsonneault has won numerous awards for both his research and teaching, including the prestigious Doctoral Award of the International Centre for Information Technology and MCI Communications in 1990, the Person of the Week of *La Presse* in 1991, most promising of HEC alumni in 1995, and the CDROM-SNI award for his innovative use of information technologies in teaching.

He has published numerous papers in journals such as *Management Science, MIS Quarterly, Information Systems Research, Organization Science, Journal of MIS, Small Group Research, Decision Support Systems, Journal of Electronic Collaboration,* and *European Journal of Operational Research.* He is a member of the editorial board of *MIS Quarterly, Organization Science,* and *Information Systems Research.*

ABOUT THE CONTRIBUTORS

PAIGE BALTZAN teaches in the Department of Information Technology and Electronic Commerce in the Daniels College of Business at the University of Denver. Paige holds a B.S.B.A. in MIS and Accounting from Bowling Green State University and an M.B.A. specializing in MIS from the University of Denver. Paige's primary concentration is on object-oriented technologies and systems development methodologies. Paige has been teaching at the University of Denver for the past five years. A few of the courses Paige teaches include Systems Analysis and Design, Telecommunications and Networking, Software Engineering, Database Management Systems, and The Global Information Economy. Paige is the coauthor of *Microsoft Word 2003* with Stephen Haag and James Perry. This book is part of the well-received I-Series from McGraw-Hill. Paige is also coauthor with Stephen Haag and Amy Phillips on the book *Business Driven Technology*.

Prior to joining the University of Denver, Paige spent three years working at Level(3) Communications as a technical architect and four years working at Accenture as a technology consultant specializing in the telecommunications industry. Paige lives in Lakewood, CO, with her husband, Tony, and daughters, Hannah and Sophie.

AMY PHILLIPS is a professor in the Department of Information Technology and Electronic Commerce in the University of Denver's Daniels College of Business. Amy has been teaching for more than 20 years—five years in public secondary education and fifteen years in higher education. Amy has also been an integral part of both the academic and administrative functions within the higher-educational system.

Amy's main concentration is database-driven Web sites, focusing on dynamic Web content, specifically ASP, XML, and .NET technologies. Some of the main core course selections that Amy teaches at the University of Denver include Analysis and Design, Elements of .NET, ASP.NET, and C#.NET. Her other publications include *Internet Explorer 6.0*, *PowerPoint 2003*, and (with Stephen Haag and Paige Baltzan) *Business Driven Technology*.

"CAREERS IN BUSINESS" CONTRIBUTORS

These are the people who offered great insight into the new Module A, "Careers in Business." No single person could have compiled information on the many business careers that appear in that Module. The contributor team includes:

- Dan Connolly (Hospitality and Tourism Management)
- David Cox (Finance)
- Kathleen Davisson (Accounting)
- Jeff Engelstad (Real Estate and Construction Management)
- Syl Houston (Management)

BRIEF CONTENTS

CONTENTS

Section Three: Moving Along

PREFACE

FLEXIBILITY

This third Canadian edition of *Management Information Systems for the Information Age* provides you the ultimate in flexibility, enabling you to tailor the content to the exact needs of your MIS or IT course. The nine **Chapters**, and 11 **Extended Learning Modules (XLMs)** can be presented in sequence, or you can choose your own mix of technical topics and business/managerial topics.

The nine chapters form the core of the material covering business and managerial topics, from strategic and competitive technology opportunities to the organization and management of information using databases and data warehouses. If you cover only the chapters and none of the Extended Learning Modules, the focus of your course will be MIS from a business and managerial point of view.

The Extended Learning Modules provide a technical glimpse into the world of IT, covering topics ranging from building an e-portfolio to computer crime and forensics. In addition, four are skills-oriented and make use of computer software such as Microsoft Excel and Access, as well as HTML and Web-based programming. If you choose only the modules and none of the chapters, the focus of your course will be the technical and hands-on aspects of IT.

Given these different approaches, you can easily select a course format that represents your own desired blend of topics. While you might not choose to cover the technologies of networks, for example, you might require your students to build a small database application. In that case, you would omit XLM E (Network Basics) and spend more time on XLM C (Designing Databases and Entity-Relationship Diagramming) and XLM G (Implementing a Database with Microsoft Access).

ORGANIZATION

This book is organized into three sections:

1. IT in Business
2. Developing and Using Technology Effectively
3. Moving Along

On the next page is a table of the chapters and the modules grouped into three sections. As you put your course together and choose the chapters and/or modules you want to cover, keep in mind the following facts about the plan of this book:

- You may cover any or all of the chapters as suits your purposes.
- You may cover any or all of the modules as suits your purposes.
- If you choose a chapter, you do not have to cover its corresponding module.
- If you choose a module, you do not have to cover its corresponding chapter.
- You may cover the sections in any order you wish.

Please note that XLMs A, E, F, G, I, and J are on the Student CD accompanying this textbook. Inside the text is an introduction to each, and your students must go to the CD for the full modules.

The unique organization of this text is aimed at giving you complete flexibility to design your course as you see fit:

SECTION ONE: IT IN BUSINESS	
CHAPTER 1: The Information Age in Which You Live: Changing the Face of Business **CHAPTER 2:** Strategic and Competitive Opportunities: Using IT for Competitive Advantage	**XLM-A:** Careers in Business* **Group Project Cases 1 to 5**

SECTION TWO: DEVELOPING AND USING TECHNOLOGY EFFECTIVELY	
CHAPTER 3: Systems Development: Steps, Tools, and Techniques **CHAPTER 4:** Databases and Data Warehouses: Building Business Intelligence **CHAPTER 5:** IT Infrastructures: Business-Driven Technology **CHAPTER 6:** Decision Support and Artificial Intelligence: Brainpower for Your Business	**XLM-B:** Computer Hardware and Software **XLM-C:** Designing Databases and Entity-Relationship Diagramming **XLM-D:** Decision Analysis with Spreadsheet Software (Skills Oriented) **XLM-E:** Network Basics* **XLM-F:** Object-Oriented Technologies* **XLM-G:** Implementing a Database with Microsoft Access (Skills Oriented)*, ** **Group Project Cases 6 to 13**

SECTION THREE: MOVING ALONG	
CHAPTER 7: Electronic Commerce: Strategies for the New Economy **CHAPTER 8:** Emerging Trends and Technologies: Business, People, and Technology Tomorrow **CHAPTER 9:** Protecting People and Information: Threats and Safeguards	**XLM-H:** The World Wide Web and the Internet **XLM-I:** Building a Web Page with HTML (Skills Oriented)* **XLM-J:** Building an E-Portfolio (Skills Oriented)* **XLM-K:** Computer Crime and Forensics **Group Project Cases 14 to 18**

*The complete text for this module is on the Student CD.
**Extended Learning Module G is a bonus module that you would typically cover in conjunction with Chapter 4 (Databases and Data Warehouses) and/or Extended Learning Module C (Designing Databases and Entity-Relationship Diagramming).

- **Management Focus**—By focusing on the chapters, your class will take on a managerial approach to MIS.
- **Technical Focus**—If hands-on, technical skills are more important, focus your MIS course on the Extended Learning Modules.

Organization—The Haag Advantage

The separation of content between the chapters and the modules is very simple. We can sum it up by saying:

- The **chapters** address what you want your students to **know**.
- The **modules** address what you want your students to **be able to do**.

The two combine to provide a well balanced repository of important information aimed at developing a prospective business professional equipped with both foundational knowledge and application experience, ready to take on today's highly competitive job market.

Each chapter and module contains full pedagogical support:

- Student Learning Outcomes
- On Your Own Projects
- Team Work Projects
- Summary: Student Learning Outcomes Revisited
- Key Terms and Concepts
- Short-Answer Questions
- Assignments and Exercises

The **chapters** focus on the *business and managerial* applications of MIS and information technology.

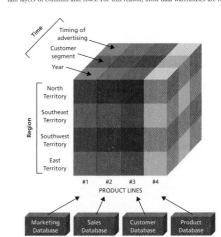

DATA WAREHOUSES ARE MULTIDIMENSIONAL In the relational database model, information is represented in a series of two-dimensional tables. Not so in a data warehouse—most data warehouses are multidimensional, meaning that they contain layers of columns and rows. For this reason, most data warehouses are really

Figure 4.8
A Multidimensional Data Warehouse with Information from Multiple Operational Databases

---

The **modules** focus on giving your students real *hands-on knowledge* they can apply in both their personal and their professional experiences.

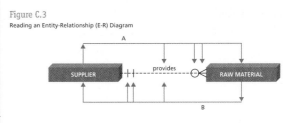

Figure C.3
Reading an Entity-Relationship (E-R) Diagram

Once you determine that a relationship does exist, you must then determine the numerical nature of the relationship, what we refer to as "minimum and maximum cardinality." To describe this, you use a | to denote a single relationship, a 0 to denote a zero or optional relationship, and/or a crow's foot (<) to denote a multiple relationship. By way of illustration, let's consider the portion of your E-R diagram in Figure C.3. To help you read the symbols and diagram, we've added coloured lines and arrows. Following the line marked A, you would read the E-R diagram as:

"A *Supplier* may not provide any *Raw Material* (denoted with the 0) but may provide more than one *Raw Material* (denoted with the crow's foot)."

Student Learning Outcomes and Summary

Student learning outcomes drive each chapter and module. We then summarize each chapter and module by revisiting the Student Learning Outcomes stated at its beginning. It's the old maxim:

1. Tell them what you're going to tell them.
2. Tell them.
3. Tell them what you've told them.

At the beginning of each chapter and module, you'll find a list of **Student Learning Outcomes**, providing your students with a road map of what they should learn and accomplish while reading a chapter or module.

CHAPTER SEVEN

STUDENT LEARNING OUTCOMES

BY THE END OF THIS CHAPTER, STUDENTS WILL BE ABLE TO:

1. Define and describe the two major e-commerce business models (business-to-business and business-to-consumer) as well as e-commerce and e-business.

2. Summarize Porter's Five Forces Model and how business people can use it to understand the relative attractiveness of an industry.

3. Describe the emerging role of e-marketplaces in B2B e-commerce.

4. Identify the differences and similarities among customers and their perceived value of products and services in the B2B and B2C e-commerce business models.

5. Compare and contrast the development of a marketing mix for customers in the B2B and B2C e-commerce business models.

Summary: Student Learning Outcomes Revisited

1. **Define and describe the two major e-commerce business models (business-to-business and business-to-consumer), as well as e-commerce and e-business.** *Business to business (B2B) e-commerce* occurs when a business sells products and services to customers who are primarily other businesses. B2B e-commerce is all about the commerce interactions among two or more businesses. *Business-to-consumer (B2C) e-commerce* occurs when a business sells products and services to customers who are primarily individuals. B2C e-commerce is all about the commerce interactions among a business and an end consumer.

2. **Summarize Porter's Five Forces Model and how business people can use it to understand the relative attractiveness of an industry.** Porter's *Five Forces Model* helps business people understand the relative attractiveness of an industry and includes the following five forces:
   a. *Buyer power.* High when buyers have many choices from whom to buy, and low when their choices are few.
   b. *Supplier power.* High when buyers have few choices from whom to buy, and low when their choices are many.
   c. *Threat of substitute products and services.* High when there are many alternatives to a product or service, and low when there are few alternatives from which to choose.
   d. *Threat of new entrants.* High when it is easy for new competitors to enter a market, and low when there are significant entry barriers to entering a market.
   e. *Rivalry among existing competitors.* High when competition is fierce in a market, and low when competition is more complacent.

3. **Describe the emerging role of e-marketplaces in B2B e-commerce.** An *electronic marketplace (e-marketplace)* is an interactive business providing a central market space where multiple buyers and suppliers can engage in e-commerce and/or other e-commerce business activities, such as sharing mission-critical information for the development of products and parts, collaborating on new ideas, and deploying infrastructure applica-

marketplace that connects buyers and sellers across many industries, primarily for MRO materials commerce. A *vertical marketplace* is an electronic marketplace that connects buyers and sellers in a given industry (e.g., oil and gas, textiles, and retail).

4. **Identify the differences and similarities among customers and their perceived value of products and services in the B2B and B2C e-commerce business models.** Customers in the B2C e-commerce business model are end consumers. They (1) exhibit greatly varying demographics, lifestyles, wants, and needs, (2) distinguish products and services by convenience versus specialty, (3) often shop for commodity-like and digital products, and (4) sometimes require a level of *mass customization* to get exactly what they want. Customers in the B2B e-commerce business model are other businesses. They (1) distinguish products and services by *maintenance, repair, and operations (MRO) materials* versus *direct materials*, (2) aggregate demand to create negotiations for volume discounts on large purchases, and (3) most often perform e-commerce activities within an e-marketplace.

5. **Compare and contrast the development of a marketing mix for customers in the B2B and B2C e-commerce business models.** A *marketing mix* is the set of marketing tools that your organization will use to pursue its marketing objectives in reaching and attracting potential customers. In B2B e-commerce, marketing mixes do not usually include broad and generic strategies that reach all potential businesses. Instead, marketing often occurs within the context of an e-marketplace. Once a contact has been made between businesses, the development of the relationship is still formal and often includes negotiations for pricing, quality, specifications, and delivery timing.

In B2C e-commerce, a marketing mix will include some or all of the following:
   a. Registering your site with a search engine.
   b. *Online ads* (small advertisements that appear on other sites), including *pop-up ads* (small Web

A **Summary** of these outcomes appears with the end-of-chapter elements per chapter/module, providing an invaluable tool for your students as they prepare to take an exam.

Case Studies

Opening Case

Each chapter begins with an opening case study, highlighting how an organization has successfully implemented many of that chapter's concepts.

CLOSING CASE STUDY TWO

USING INFORMATION TECHNOLOGY TO TRANSFORM A BUSINESS

The travel agency Colibri Tours, founded in 1988 and having its head office in Calgary, offers personalized tours to individuals and groups in Canada and Europe wanting to see western Canada and American sights such as the Grand Canyon, Yellowstone Park, and Alaska. It also provides value-added services: airport reception, travel programs for the elderly, sports activities, etc. Colibri has very successfully used information technology to transform its business, with annual sales just under $1 million.

Ms. Jacob, founder and president of Colibri Tours, turned to the Internet in 1998 in response to a signifi-

the agency's Web site (www.colibritours.com) and updates it, managed to locate a server specializing in tourism, enabling her to promote the site at a very affordable cost of $1800 per year. The site enables prospective customers to access itineraries, destination photographs, and road maps, all of which give the operation a dynamic character. Customized services are also offered to customers at a lower cost while maintaining profitability levels.

The Web site has enabled Colibri Tours to deal directly with consumers instead of wholesalers, while also attracting new wholesalers through the borderless ... y percent of its cus-
... reby changing the
... ty of the agency and
... d, due to the power
... es that transactions
... ed out quickly, and

DECISION SUPPORT AND ARTIFICIAL INTELLIGENCE
Brainpower for Your Business

CASE STUDY:
USING A BUSINESS INTELLIGENCE SOLUTION TO ACHIEVE GREATER FINANCIAL AND OPERATIONAL EFFICIENCIES

Black Photo Corporation (www.blackphoto.com), the largest photographic retailer in Canada, is a wholly owned subsidiary of Fuji Photo Film Canada Inc. It owns more than 180 retail locations specializing in photographic goods and services and on-site photo finishing production. Prominent vendors such as Pentax, Canon, Minolta, and Nikon supply the company. The company had an existing JDA enterprise solution, which did not provide adequate analytics or reporting, with a limited ability to assess inventory, sales margins, and demand trends in each store. "There was a need to see our data differently," says Tim Hammond, sen-
... d marketing

opment and implementation. Intellera used its retail sector knowledge, along with Cognos business intelligence applications, to provide Black Photo with a BI solution that was integrated very quickly into the existing JDA database: a "merchandising cube," which was designed in less than 60 days and which helped Black gain detailed exception reporting and analysis in more than 180 stores and the ability to see inventory in 3D perspective. The company could now measure and manage its inventory better. It could also now measure the performance of advertising campaigns in different geographical locations, and developed a flexible business intelligence infrastructure that could facilitate creation of additional "cubes" for other functional areas such as human resources and CRM.

The Intellera solution is used at every level in the company, from CEO to accountant. It has helped Black Photo achieve massive savings in

---

CLOSING CASE STUDY ONE

AN AUTOMATED DISTRIBUTION SYSTEM TO GAIN COMPETITIVE ADVANTAGE

Adidas-Salomon Canada Ltd. (www.adidas.ca), with its head office located in Concord, Ontario, has estimated 2004 sales of $216 million and has a distribution centre located in Brantford. Adidas-Salomon was created in 1997 when Adidas International (based in Germany) acquired Salomon Sports SA and Taylor Made. The Canadian product line, which originally had just Adidas athletic equipment, footwear, and sports apparel, now also has Salomon winter sports equipment and Taylor Made golf equipment. After the merger, the company was faced with the issue of moving much more inventory, and automating distribution became a necessity. Using this solution, the company has drastically reduced its distribution costs and gained a competitive advantage.

The key objectives of this automation at the new,

The ensuing combination of the TECSYS Warehouse Management System and the Psion Teklogix wireless data communications system has resulted in Adidas-Salomon Canada cutting distribution costs by half. Inventory levels are far more accurate, and the wireless devices makes the process less time-consuming. These benefits are ultimately helping Adidas-Salomon keep a step ahead of its competition by realizing benefits in cost control and operational efficiency. The new system has resulted in increased efficiency, and improved customer service and higher productivity at different levels. In 2004, Adidas-Salomon Canada received the 2004 Canadian Information Productivity Award of Excellence in the Mobile Solutions category in recognition of its innovative use of IT to solve business prob-

Closing Cases

To help your students apply what they have just learned, you'll find two closing case studies at the end of each chapter. Each case has a set of questions that are great for class discussion.

Team Work and On Your Own Projects

There are more than 50 Team Work and On Your Own projects spread throughout the text, in both the chapters and the modules. Many of these can be used as breakout exercises, and just as many can be assigned as homework.

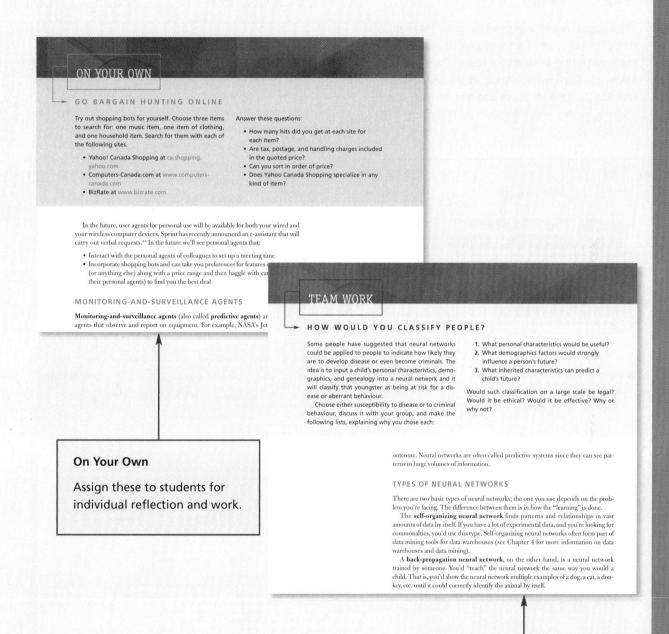

ON YOUR OWN

GO BARGAIN HUNTING ONLINE

Try out shopping bots for yourself. Choose three items to search for: one music item, one item of clothing, and one household item. Search for them with each of the following sites.

- Yahoo! Canada Shopping at ca.shopping.yahoo.com
- Computers-Canada.com at www.computers-canada.com
- BizRate at www.bizrate.com

Answer these questions:

- How many hits did you get at each site for each item?
- Are tax, postage, and handling charges included in the quoted price?
- Can you sort in order of price?
- Does Yahoo Canada Shopping specialize in any kind of item?

In the future, user agents for personal use will be available for both your wired and your wireless computer devices. Sprint has recently announced an e-assistant that will carry out verbal requests.[44] In the future we'll see personal agents that:

- Interact with the personal agents of colleagues to set up a meeting time
- Incorporate shopping bots and can take you preferences for features (or anything else) along with a price range and then haggle with ca their personal agents) to find you the best deal

MONITORING-AND-SURVEILLANCE AGENTS

Monitoring-and-surveillance agents (also called **predictive agents**) a agents that observe and report on equipment. For example, NASA's Jet

TEAM WORK

HOW WOULD YOU CLASSIFY PEOPLE?

Some people have suggested that neural networks could be applied to people to indicate how likely they are to develop disease or even become criminals. The idea is to input a child's personal characteristics, demographics, and genealogy into a neural network and it will classify that youngster as being at risk for a disease or aberrant behaviour.

Choose either susceptibility to disease or to criminal behaviour, discuss it with your group, and make the following lists, explaining why you chose each:

1. What personal characteristics would be useful?
2. What demographics factors would strongly influence a person's future?
3. What inherited characteristics can predict a child's future?

Would such classification on a large scale be legal? Would it be ethical? Would it be effective? Why or why not?

outcome. Neural networks are often called predictive systems since they can see patterns in huge volumes of information.

TYPES OF NEURAL NETWORKS

There are two basic types of neural networks; the one you use depends on the problem you're facing. The difference between them is in how the "learning" is done.

The **self-organizing neural network** finds patterns and relationships in vast amounts of data by itself. If you have a lot of experimental data, and you're looking for commonalities, you'd use this type. Self-organizing neural networks often form part of data mining tools for data warehouses (see Chapter 4 for more information on data warehouses and data mining).

A **back-propagation neural network**, on the other hand, is a neural network trained by someone. You'd "teach" the neural network the same way you would a child. That is, you'd show the neural network multiple examples of a dog, a cat, a donkey, etc. until it could correctly identify the animal by itself.

On Your Own

Assign these to students for individual reflection and work.

Team Work

These are designed for small groups of two to four. Many are great for in-class assignments.

Electronic Commerce and Group Projects

Electronic Commerce

These projects are designed to impart to your students hands-on, technological experiences, many requiring Web exploration. You'll find an Electronic Commerce project at the end of each chapter. To support these Online Learning Centre projects, we've provided links on the text's Web site at www.mcgrawhill.ca/college/haag.

Group Projects

At the end of each section, you'll find a list of Group Projects Cases, which are available on the Student CD. These require your students to use technology to solve a problem or take advantage of an opportunity. A quick warning to instructors: Some of these take an entire weekend to solve. Be careful not to assign too many at once.

Electronic Commerce

Getting Your Business on the Internet

Let's say you've decided it might be fun (and profitable) to establish a retail-oriented Internet-based business. You can use the one your team created in the previous Team Work project if it's appropriate or you can create a new one. You know that many such e-commerce businesses don't make it, but you'd like to be one that is successful. There are a lot of resources on the Internet that can help you with the tasks of selecting the right business in the first place, getting the site up and running, deciding who should host your site, marketing your site, understanding privacy issues, and obtaining the funds you need to pay your expenses until your business begins to show a profit. On the Web site that supports this text (www.mcgrawhill.ca/college/haa...) select "Electronic Commerce Projects"), we've provided direct links to many use... Web sites. These are a great starting point for completing this project. We also enco... age you to search the Internet for others.

► Electronic
Commerce Links

GROUP PROJECTS

CASE 8:
OUTSOURCING INFORMATION TECHNOLOGY

A&A Software: Creating Forecasts

Founded in 1992, A&A Software provides innovative search software, Web site accessibility testing/repair software, and usability testing/repair software. All serve as part of its desktop and enterprise content management solutions for government, corporate, educational, and consumer markets. The company's solutions are used by Web site publishers, digital media publishers, content managers, document managers, business users, consumers, software companies, and consulting services companies. A&A Software solutions help organizations develop long-term strategies to achieve Web content accessibility, enhance usability, and comply with national and international accessibility and search standards.

A&A Software has a ten-year history of approximately 1 percent in turnover a year and its focus has always been on customer service. With the informal motto of "Grow big, but stay small," it takes pride in 100 percent callbacks in customer care, knowing that its personal service has been one thing that makes it outstanding.

A&A Software has experienced rapid growth to six times its original customer-base size and is forced to deal with difficult questions for the first time, such as "How do we serve this many customers? How do we keep our *soul*—that part of us that honestly cares very much about our customers? How will we know that someone else will care as much and do as good a job as we have done?" In addition, you have just received an e-mail from the company CIO, Sue Downs that the number of phone calls from customers having problems with one of your newer applications is on the increase.

As customer service manager for A&A Software, your overriding goal is to maintain the company's reputation for excellent customer service, and outsourcing may offer an efficient means of keeping up with expanding call volume. A&A Software is reviewing a similar scenario of a major company, e-BANK, that outsourced its customer service in order to handle a large projected number of customers through several customer interaction channels. Although e-BANK had excellent people, it felt that its competencies were primarily in finance rather than customer service, and that it needed the expertise a customer-service-focused company could offer. e-BANK also discovered that it was cost-effective to outsource its customer service centre.

Additionally, the outsourcing approach was relatively hassle-free, since e-BANK did not have to set up its own CIC (customer interaction centre/call centre).

End-of-Chapter Elements

Key Terms and Concepts

ad hoc decision, 202
adaptive filtering, 226
artificial intelligence (AI), 211
artificial neural network
  (ANN), 218
back-propagation neural
  network, 220
buyer agent, 225
choice, 201
collaboration software, 206
collaboration system, 206
collaborative filtering, 225
crossover, 222
data mining agent, 228
decision support system (DSS), 202
design, 201
domain expert, 216
domain expertise, 216
expert system, 213

explanation module, 217
genetic algorithm, 222
geographic information system
  (GIS), 209
implementation, 201
inference engine, 216
intelligence, 201
intelligent agent, 224
knowledge acquisition, 216
knowledge base, 216

nonrecurring decision
  (ad hoc decision), 202
nonstructured decision, 202
personal agent, 226
predictive agent, 227
profile filtering, 226
psychographic filtering, 226
recurring decision, 202
robot, 212
rule-based expert system, 216

Short-Answer Que:

1. What are the four types of decisio
   this chapter? Give an example of e

2. What is a DSS? Describe its compor

3. What sort of a system would you u:
   wanted to work with your supplier:

4. What are three of the features tha
   software might have?

5. What is a geographic information s

6. How is information represented in
   information system?

Discussion Questions

1. Knowledge workers dominate today's business
   environment. However, many industries still need
   workers who do not fall into the category of
   knowledge workers. What industries still need
   skilled workers? Can you see a time when these
   jobs will be replaced by knowledge workers? Can
   you envision circumstances that would actually
   cause our economy to do an "about face" and
   begin needing more skilled workers than
   knowledge workers?

2. Consider today's economic environment—we
   have characterized it as the e.conomy, the "now"
   economy, the global economy, and the arriving
   digital economy. For each of these characterizations, identify why it's an effect causing the
   remaining three. That is, how is the "e" causing
   the "now," global, and arriving digital economies;
   how is the "now" economy causing the "e,"
   global, and arriving digital economies; etc.?

3. The three key resources in management informa
   tion systems (MIS) are information, information
   technology, and people. Which of these three
   resources is the most important? Why? The least
   important? Why?

4. Telecommuting, like all things, has a good and
   a bad side. What are some of the disadvantages

or pitfalls of telecommuting? How can these be
avoided?

5. As an information-literate knowledge worker for
   a local distributor of imported foods and spices,
   you've been asked to prepare a customer mailing
   list that will be sold to international cuisine
   restaurants in your area. If you do so, will you
   be acting ethically? If you don't consider the proposal ethical, what if your boss threatens to fire
   you if you don't prepare the list? Do you believe
   you would have any legal recourse if you didn't
   prepare the list and were subsequently fired?

6. How is your school helping you prepare to take
   advantage of information technology? What
   courses have you taken that included teaching
   you how to use technology? What software
   packages were taught? To best prepare to enter
   the job market, how can you determine what
   software you need to learn?

Assignments and Exercises

1. **PORTER'S FIVE FORCES MODEL AND YOUR SCHOOL.** To illustrate the use of Porter's Five Forces Model, let's
   apply it to your school. Assume that you are a school administrator and want to use Porter's Five Forces
   Model for evaluating your business program's competitive position in the marketplace. Is buyer power low or
   high? What are some options other than your school's program that students could choose? Is supplier power
   low or high? Who are your school's suppliers? Is the threat of substitute products or services low or high?
   What are possible substitutes to getting an education? Is the threat of new entrants low or high? What entry
   barriers exist? Is the rivalry among existing competition low or high? Who are your school's competitors?

2. **DEALING WITH THE GREAT DIGITAL DIVIDE.** The great digital divide addresses the concerns of many people
   that the world is becoming one marked by the "haves" and "have nots" with respect to technology—that is,
   the traditional notion of a "Third World" is now also being defined by the extent to which a country has
   access to and uses technology. Find out what, if anything, the United Nations is doing about this issue and
   express an opinion on whether you believe its efforts will be successful. Determine if there are organizations
   such as private companies or foundations that have the digital divide high on their agendas. For any such
   organizations you find, evaluate their efforts and express an opinion on whether they will be successful.
   Finally, search for a less developed country that is making significant local efforts to deal with the digital
   divide. If you can't find one, prepare a list of the countries you reviewed and briefly describe the conditions
   in one of them with respect to technology.

3. **RESEARCHING A BUSINESS-TO-BUSINESS E-MARKETPLACE.** Biz2Biz (www.biz2biz.com/marketplace) is a
   B2B e-marketplace. Connect to its site and do some looking around. What sort of marketing services does it
   provide through its Biz2BizCommunication program? What sort of services does it provide for creating and
   maintaining an electronic catalog? If you owned a business and wanted to join, what process would you have
   to go through? How much does it cost your organization to join Biz2Biz? What buyer tools does Biz2Biz

Each chapter and module contains complete pedagogical support in the form of:

- **Summary: Student Learning Outcomes Revisited.** These mirror the
  chapters Learning Outcomes.
- **Closing Case Studies.** Reinforcing important concepts with prominent
  examples from businesses and organizations (in chapters only).
- **Key Terms and Concepts.** With page numbers of where discussions of them
  are found.
- **Short-Answer Questions.**
- **Assignments and Exercises.** Problems designed to give your students the
  chance to apply key concepts.
- **Discussion Questions.** Challenging questions aimed at promoting an
  atmosphere of critical thinking in your classroom (in chapters only).

Changes for the Third Canadian Edition

The content changes for this third Canadian edition were driven by:

1. Instructor feedback regarding the second Canadian edition.
2. Instructor feedback on the fourth and fifth U.S. editions.
3. Changes in the business world.
4. Advances in the technology arena.
5. Changes made to competing texts.

We carefully sifted though all the competitive scanning information we could gather to create a third Canadian edition that builds on the great success of the previous one.

Throughout the text, you'll find new or updated opening cases, Global Perspectives, (now incorporating the second edition's Industry Perspectives boxes), Team Work and On Your Own projects, Closing Case Studies, Group Projects, and new or expanded coverage of such topics as business intelligence, customer relationship management, supply chain management, *n*-tier architectures, application service providers, and Web services. There is also a good balance of Canadian and international examples. We've provided all these content updates and new pedagogical features in a visually appealing, streamlined format.

We're pleased to have been able to respond to reviewer suggestions. Key improvements include:

- *New* **Extended Learning Module A**, "Careers in Business," including coverage of what IT skills your students need to learn to compete effectively in the job market.
- *Updated* **Extended Learning Module D**, "Decision Analysis with Spreadsheet Software," including coverage of 3D pivot tables.
- *Updated* **Chapter 5**, "IT Infrastructures."
- *Updated* **Chapter 7**, "Electronic Commerce," focusing on fundamental differences between business-to-business and business-to-consumer electronic commerce.
- *Updated* **Chapter 8**, "Emerging Trends and Technologies."
- *Enhanced* **Extended Learning Module G**, "Implementing a Database with Microsoft Access," including coverage of building input forms and making changes to reports.
- *Updated* **Extended Learning Module J**, "Building an E-Portfolio."

Student Supplements

Students using *Management Information Systems for the Information Age* are provided with robust media supplements created to provide tools for test preparation, teach MIS-related skills, connect students to real-world applications of MIS, and strengthen their understanding and enhance their abilities in MIS.

STUDENT CD-ROM

Electronic
Commerce Links

All copies of this text are packaged with a special CD-ROM that includes Extended Learning Modules A, E, F, G, I, and J, as well as 18 Group Projects.

When the CD-ROM icon appears in the margin of the text, the student can go to the text CD-ROM to access relevant data files, links, added content, or Skills Modules to enhance learning.

ONLINE LEARNING CENTRE (www.mcgrawhill.ca/college/haag)

Online
Learning Centre

The Online Learning Centre (OLC) follows the text chapter by chapter, with additional materials and quizzing that enhance the text and classroom experience. As students read the text, they can go online to take self-grading quizzes, link to hundreds of relevant Web sites, access videos, and work through related modules.

Software Skills & Computer Concepts

MISource provides animated tutorials and simulated practice of the core skills in Microsoft Excel, Access, and PowerPoint. MISource also animates 47 important computer concepts. Please contact your *i*Learning Sales Specialists for more information about this CD-ROM.

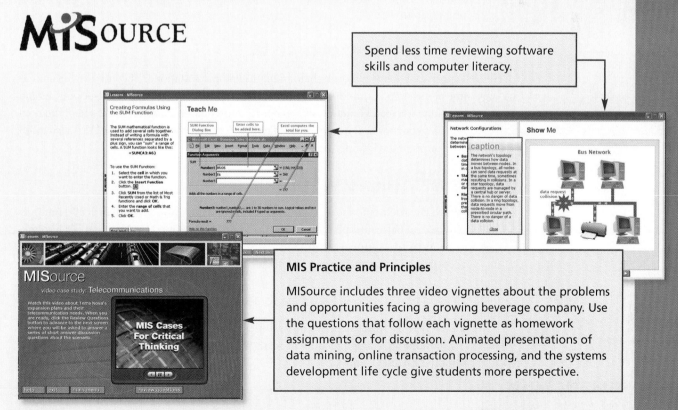

Spend less time reviewing software skills and computer literacy.

MIS Practice and Principles

MISource includes three video vignettes about the problems and opportunities facing a growing beverage company. Use the questions that follow each vignette as homework assignments or for discussion. Animated presentations of data mining, online transaction processing, and the systems development life cycle give students more perspective.

The Support Package for Instructors

We realize that no text is complete without a well-rounded and value-added support package. Ours is designed to ease your teaching burden by providing you with all the resources necessary for instructors.

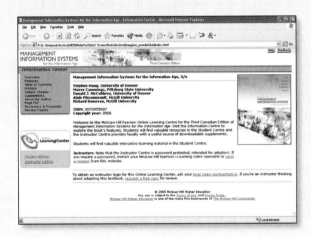

ONLINE LEARNING CENTRE (www.mcgrawhill.ca/college/haag)

The Online Learning Centre (OLC) contains a wealth of valuable information and supplements for both the instructor and the student, developed by Margaret Trenholm-Edmunds, from Mount Allison University.

Instructor's CD-ROM

This CD-ROM contains all the necessary instructor supplements fully adapted for this edition.

INSTRUCTOR'S MANUAL

Is provided to instructors to help prepare class presentations. Beyond proving an outline of the chapters/modules and discussions about the various projects, exercises and assignments, the IM includes Concept Reinforcement boxes to guide use of the textbook's pedagogy and modules, and facilitate class participation. The IM is also available through the Online Learning Centre.

COMPUTERIZED TEST BANK

Allows instructors to create their own tests, choosing from more than 1,000 multiple choice, true/false and fill in the bank questions. Developed by Margaret Trenholme-Edmunds, of Mount Allison University, the test bank items can also be selected according to topic and degree of difficulty.

POWERPOINT PRESENTATIONS

Developed by Anita Beecroft of Kwantlen College, have been adapted to reflect the 3rd edition and facilitate student learning in-class. These are also available on the Online Learning Centre.

VIDEOS

Videos are available to instructors using *Management Information Systems in the Information Age*, including CBC videos—all for situational analysis in the classroom. Contact your *i*Learning Sales Specialist for information.

WEBCT/BLACKBOARD

Content cartridges are available for the course management systems WebCT and Blackboard. These platforms provide instructors with user-friendly, flexible teaching tools. Please contact your local McGraw-Hill Ryerson *i*Learning Sales Specialist for details.

PAGEOUT

Visit www.mhhe.com/pageout to create a Web page for your course using our resources. PageOut is the McGraw-Hill Ryerson Web site development centre. The software, free to adopters, is designed to help faculty create an online course, complete with assignments, quizzes, links to relevant Web sites, and more—all in a matter of minutes.

PRIMIS CUSTOM PUBLISHING CASE OPTIONS

Through McGraw-Hill Ryerson's custom publishing division, Primis, instructors are able to select cases to accompany this text in a number of ways. Create your own case set, or browse the cases and make selections that correspond to the chapter material. Contact your McGraw-Hill Ryerson *i*Learning Sales Specialist for more information.

*i*LEARNING SALES SPECIALIST

Your *i*Learning Sales Specialist is a McGraw-Hill Ryerson representative who has the experience, product knowledge, training, and support to help you assess and integrate any of the above-noted products, technology, and services into your financial accounting course for optimum teaching and learning performance. Whether it's using test bank software, helping your students improve their grades, or putting your entire course online, your *i*Learning Sales Specialist is there to help you do it. Contact your *i*Learning Sales Specialist today to learn how to maximize all of McGraw-Hill Ryerson's resources.

*i*LEARNING SERVICES PROGRAM

McGraw-Hill Ryerson offers a unique *i*Services package designed for Canadian faculty. Our mission is to equip providers of higher education with superior tools and resources required for excellence in teaching. For additional information, visit www.mcgrawhill.ca/highereducation/iservices.

From the Authors

FROM RICHARD G. DONOVAN

As I look back on coauthoring this third edition, I see I could not have done it without the continued support of Alain Pinsonneault. His patience, dedication, encouragement, and professionalism are always appreciated. I would also like to thank Srihari Rao, our research assistant who provided invaluable support in this project.

Finally, I would like to dedicate this book to the three most important people in my life:

To Carmelina: You are The Love of My Life, My Very Best Friend and Number One Fan.

To Adamo and Justino: You continue to keep me young and proud.

FROM ALAIN PINSONNEAULT

Coauthoring a book such as this constitutes a major undertaking and demands a lot of work, but working with Richard Donovan also made it fun. Thanks, Richard. I would also like to thank Srihari Rao for his excellent work.

I dedicate this book to France, my wife whose love, friendship, and support energize my life, and to my three wonderful children, Alexe, Camille, and Loïc, who are my heroes.

Last, but certainly not least, we offer our gratitude to our reviewers. They contributed in countless ways to the development of the third Canadian edition. They include:

Guillermo Acosta, University of Guelph

Lorna Baltrusiunas, University of Windsor

David Bateman, St. Mary's University

Danny Cho, Brock University

Sylvia de Vlaming, Red River College

Marina G. Erechtchoukova, York University

Mary Furey, Memorial University of Newfoundland

Robert Goldstein, University of British Columbia

Michael A. Haughton, Wilfrid Laurier University

M. Gordon Hunter, University of Lethbridge

Terry L. Huston, University of Victoria

Yonghua Ji, University of Alberta

Norm Letnick, Okanagan University College

Francisco B. P. Moro, University of Windsor

David Parker, George Brown College

Robert Riordan, Carleton University

Stephen Rochefort, Royal Roads University

D. Rand Rowlands, George Brown College

Maryann Sullivan, Algonquin College

Janet Welch, Red Deer College

SECTION ONE

IT IN BUSINESS

CHAPTERS

EXTENDED LEARNING MODULES

GROUP PROJECTS

CHAPTER ONE

STUDENT LEARNING OUTCOMES

BY THE END OF THIS CHAPTER, STUDENTS WILL BE ABLE TO:

1. Define management information systems (MIS) and information technology (IT) and describe their relationship.

2. Validate information as a key resource and describe both personal and organizational dimensions of information.

3. Explain why people are the most important organizational resource, define their information and technology-literacy challenges, and discuss their ethical responsibilities.

4. Describe the important characteristics of information technology (IT) as a key organizational resource.

5. Define competitive advantage and illustrate the role of information technology in supporting operational excellence, major business initiatives, decision making, and organizational transformation.

6. Discuss the impacts information technology can have on your life.

Visit
www.mcgrawhill.ca/college/haag

Learning Centre

CASE STUDY:

INFORMATION TECHNOLOGY AT RITZ-CARLTON HOTELS HELPS STAFF DELIVER EXCELLENT SERVICE QUALITY

The Ritz-Carlton manages more than thirty luxury hotels across North America, Europe, Asia, Australia, the Middle East, Africa, and Caribbean. This chain of hotels has become synonymous with elegance and excellent customer service worldwide. About 95% of guests leave its hotels with the impression that they had a "memorable visit." It is the only hospitality organization which is a two-time recipient of the Malcolm Baldrige National Quality Award. Much of the secret to its success lies in its effective management of its knowledge workers in combination with Information Technology to track and fulfill customers' needs.

Each hotel in the chain includes one or two guest recognition coordinators. Their job consists of "preemptively" ensuring superior quality of service personalized to each guest according to his or her preferences. After receiving a list of incoming guests, they link up to the guest-history database. This "guest recognition system" includes the histories and preferences of more than half a million guests. The system is a Windows-based application accessible across a network spanning all of its hotels no matter where they are situated in the world. Guest recognition coordinators consult the system and then "tell the manager, and everyone else about VIPs and other guests who may have had previous difficulties coming in that day, as well as any other information on new high-profile guests. Maybe somebody likes chocolate or enjoys having dinner early. This is the time to pass that information along so we can be ready with a box of candy or early dinner time when the guests check in."

The "Ritz" realized that, although technology had to play a key role in providing this high a standard of service, its success crucially depended on getting all knowledge-workers involved. "We try to blend technology with a systematic approach in collecting information. It's important to inspire the staff to hunt for the information" explains Jonathan Campbell, former general manager at Ritz-Carlton in Kuala Lumpur, Malaysia. This consists of "active observation" by the hotel's knowledge workers. They discreetly watch hotel guests for particular individual behaviours which may be linked to individual preferences. For instance, a waiter at the Ritz in Montreal, Quebec may notice that a guest prefers one "sweet and low" and no milk with her tea. Immediately, this preference is jotted down as a "guest preference" on a "guest recognition pad" and then entered into the chain's worldwide system. Months later, if this guest ever finds herself ordering a tea in a Ritz-Carlton anywhere else in the world, the waiter will simply confirm whether she still prefers it with one "sweet and low" and no milk.[1]

Introduction

It is the **information age**—a time when knowledge is power. Today, more than ever, businesses are using information (and information technology) to gain and sustain a competitive advantage. You'll never find a business whose slogan is "What you don't know can't hurt you." Businesses understand that what they don't know can become an Achilles' heel and a source of advantage for the competition.

Think about your major. Whether it's marketing, finance, accounting, human resources management, or any of the many other specializations in a business program, you're preparing to enter the business world as a knowledge worker. Simply put, a **knowledge worker** works with and produces information as a product. According to *U.S. News & World Report* in 1994, knowledge workers in North America outnumber all other workers by a four-to-one margin.[2] Unfortunately, we couldn't find a more up-to-date reference for the same statistic, but we would imagine today that knowledge workers outnumber all other types of workers by at least a five-to-one margin.

Sure, you may work with your hands to take notes or use a mouse and keyboard to produce a spreadsheet, but what you've really done is use your mind to work with, massage, and produce more information (hopefully meaningful and useful information). Accountants generate profit and loss statements, cash flow statements, statements of retained earnings, and so on, some of which appear on paper. But you wouldn't say that an accountant produces paper any more than you would say Michelangelo was a commercial painter of churches.

In the information age, management information systems is a vitally important topic. Why? Because it deals with the coordination and use of three very important organizational resources—information, information technology, and people. Formally, we define MIS as follows:

> **Management information systems (MIS)** deals with the planning for, development, management, and use of information technology tools to help people perform all tasks related to information processing and management.

In that definition, you can find three key resources—information, information technology, and people. That is, people or knowledge workers use information technology to work with information. Indeed, if we were not in the information age, information technology would probably still be around but it wouldn't be nearly as important as it is today.

That's what this text is all about—management information systems or MIS. What you need to remember is that the sole focus of MIS is *not* technology. Technology is a set of tools that enables you to work with information. Pragmatically speaking, people and information are the most important resources within MIS, not technology. Of course, every organization today needs all three (and many others such as capital) to compete effectively in the marketplace. So don't think of this as a technology textbook, because it's not. You will read three very technology-focused chapters—Chapter 4 on databases and data warehouses, Chapter 5 on technology infrastructures, and Chapter 6 on decision support systems and artificial intelligence. But all the remaining chapters really focus on how people, information, and information technology work together to help an organization achieve a competitive advantage in the marketplace.

As we move forward in this chapter, let's first talk some more about today's exciting and dynamic market environment. Then, we'll explore information, people, and information technology as key resources. Finally, we'll address the specific roles and goals of information technology in both your life and the life of any business. It is these roles and

DELIVERING CUSTOMER VALUE

Toronto-based Celestica Inc. provides a broad range of services, including design, prototyping, assembly, testing, product assurance, supply chain management, worldwide distribution, and after-sales support and repair services. The company, which targets original equipment manufacturers (OEMs) in the computer and communications sectors, has a strong customer focus and considers investments in its supply chain strategy a critical differentiator in the marketplace.

The gradual withdrawal of OEMs from the manufacturing business and the takeover of same by suppliers such as Celestica, coupled with the tech boom in the 1990s, led to strong sales growth in the company. "As we scaled the business, we introduced new sites," says Steve Radewych, Celestica's Senior Director, SCM Americas. "That created more complex internal supply chains for us. We needed to collaborate within the walls of our own company. At the same time, we wanted to provide a global look and feel to our customers across the company, so no matter what site the customer engaged with, he would get the same capabilities and service."

Celestica has partnered with i2 Technologies, using i2 solutions to improve customer response time, decrease time-to-market, and improve communication through the value chain. Celestica today uses i2 Technologies' RHYTHM® solution to augment its global supply chain and integrate the supply chain planning processes of customers, component suppliers, and Celestica itself. The advanced planning software provides real-time product-demand information, and enables Celestica to execute a range of order decisions to provide cost-effective solutions to customers' manufacturing needs. It also enables all links in the supply chain to minimize turnaround time to changes in product demand, while maintaining optimal inventory levels.

The company continues to track technological developments in supply chain management and adopt other initiatives to deliver more value to customers. According to Andrew Gort, former Executive Vice-President of Global Supply Management for Celestica, the company "is committed to deploying flexible state-of-the-art technologies that expand customers' ability to be first to market globally."[3]

goals that drive our organization of this text. They also define the ways in which businesses today are gaining and sustaining a competitive advantage in the marketplace.

Today's Economic Environment

To be successful in business today, you have to understand and operate effectively within a dynamic, fast-paced, and changing economic environment. As you'll see later in this chapter, many businesses must undergo a sort of transformation just to stay in business and compete effectively. Other businesses remain highly competitive by continuing to innovate product and service characteristics. Whatever the case, today's economic environment is changing at a dramatic pace. As you enter today's economic environment, you must:

- Know your competition, an accomplishment sometimes known as *competitive intelligence*
- Know your customers, through tools such as customer relationship management (CRM)
- Work closely with your business partners, through tools such as supply chain management (SCM)
- Know how each and every part of your organization works together to provide its products and services

Throughout this text, we focus on all these, including many "best business practices" such as CRM and SCM and the technologies that support them. Right now, let's take an overall look at today's economic environment.

THE E.CONOMY

Electronic commerce is certainly the hottest topic in business today, and we've devoted all of Chapter 7 to it, as well as significant portions of other chapters (especially the next chapter). But what exactly is electronic commerce and what does it enable a business to do? Formally defined,

> **Electronic commerce** is commerce accelerated and enhanced by information technology, in particular the Internet. It enables customers, consumers, and companies to form powerful new relationships that would not be possible without the enabling technologies.

Electronic commerce will make winners out of some businesses and losers out of others. Indeed, most of the early dot-com companies are out of business today because of their failure to implement electronic commerce correctly. In short, you can't simply create a Web site and expect your customers to beat a virtual path to your door. You must still follow sound business principles and guidelines. That's why most of the early dot-coms failed. They ignored sound business principles and focused solely on the technology. That's a bad road to travel, and one that will undoubtedly lead to failure. Remember—information technology is indeed a key organizational resource, but it is only one of many.

Electronic commerce is giving rise to many new and innovative "best business practices," such as telecommuting and the virtual workplace (see Figure 1.1). Telecommuting and the virtual workplace go hand in hand:

> **Telecommuting** is the use of communications technologies (such as the Internet) to work in a place other than a central location.

> The **virtual workplace** is a technology-enabled workplace. No walls. No boundaries. Work anytime, anyplace, linked to other people and information you need, wherever they are.[4]

Figure 1.1

Telecommuting—Canadian Statistics[5]

Working from Home
31% of Canadians spend 20 hours or more working from home.
52% of Canadians find that the idea of working at home is either appealing or extremely appealing.
Benefits
68% of Canadians who telecommute report an improvement in overall quality of life.
57% of Canadians who telecommute report an improvement in finances.
60% of Canadians who telecommute report an improvement in standard of living.
36% of Canadians who telecommute report a positive impact on career advancements.
Telecommuting Leaders
Bell Canada: 5000 telecommuters
Canadian federal government: 5000 telecommuters
IBM Canada: 2300 telecommuters

Today, over 35 million people in North America telecommute, and that figure is expected to grow by 20 percent over the next several years. You may be participating in a form of telecommuting if you're taking this class via *distance learning*. Distance learning essentially enables you to learn in a virtual classroom without going to campus a couple of times of week. Of course, if you are participating in distance learning, your instructor is most probably participating in telecommuting as well. That is, he or she may be sitting at home right now sending you e-mails and leading class discussions in chat rooms.

Telecommuting is popping up in many business sectors—some make obvious sense and some may surprise you. For example, JC Penney has told its telephone service representatives who handle orders over the phone to go home and work there. In each home, JC Penney provides a computer, work space furniture, and a high-speed Internet connection. When you call the 1-800 number for JC Penney to order from its catalogue, your phone call is routed to the home of a telecommuter. The telephone service representative will answer the phone and use the Internet connection to record your order, inform you of a delivery time, and process your credit card. It makes sense when you think about it. If you're handling customer orders over the phone, all you really need is a computer with a connection to a database of product and customer information. You don't need to be sitting in a central office.

THE "NOW" ECONOMY

The "now" economy is one characterized by the immediate access customers have to the ordering of products and services. ATMs are an obvious and simple example. Using an ATM, you have access to your money any time of the day or night and just about anywhere in the world. You don't have to wait for your bank to open to cash a cheque or make a deposit. Business-to-consumer Web sites are also great examples. In the comfort of your home, apartment, or dorm, you can buy books from Amazon.com (www.amazon.com), make airline reservations (at www.aircanada.com for example, Air Canada's Web site), and purchase concert tickets from such sites as Ticketmaster (www.ticketmaster.com) or Admission (www.admission.com).

The truth is we've become a very impatient society. And we've come to expect businesses to provide us with products and services (or at a minimum the ability to order them) whenever and wherever we desire. Technology is certainly an integral facilitator here. **M-commerce**, the term used to describe electronic commerce conducted over a wireless device such as a cell phone or personal digital assistant, now gives you the ability to buy and sell stocks with your cell phone while driving down the road. And, using most Web-enabled personal digital assistants, you can bid on auctions at eBay or obtain up-to-the-minute weather forecasts.

A closely related concept is that of a wants-based economy. Some 30 years ago, people mainly purchased what they needed. Not so today. Consider these two examples. First, there's tennis shoes in which the heels light up with the pressure of each footstep. Now, how many people do you think really need tennis shoes with rear lights? Very few, if any, but if that's what they want, that's what they'll buy. A second example is that of dog bakeries, some of which even offer dog birthday cakes that range in price from $100 to $500. In reality, neither people nor dogs need to eat treats—some dog owners simply want to indulge their pets.

Why is it important to understand that you're in a wants-based economy? Because you will then realize that, while you can fairly easily forecast what your customers will need, you can't always predict what they'll want. So, the better you know your customers, the better you can determine what they might want.

I WANT IT!

Tennis shoes with lighted heels are just one of the many wants-based products that have recently surfaced. Take a walk around a mall, see how many wants-based products you can find, and then fill in the table below. Critically think about what information a business must know about its customers to identify potential buyers. Also, stay away from foods—we need very few actual food products, but our taste buds deserve variety.

Now that you've identified a few wants-based products, consider how technology could help you capture and process information relating to people who buy those products. Where would that information come from? Could you use technology to capture that information? Once you have the information, what technologies could you use to process that information?

Product	Price	Why People Want It	What Kind of People Buy It

THE GLOBAL ECONOMY

A **global economy** is one in which customers, businesses, suppliers, distributors, and manufacturers all operate without regard to physical and geographical boundaries.

Consider the table in Figure 1.2. It shows Canada's total import and export figures from 2001 to 2003 with its top trading partners. While foreign products and services are entering the Canadian market, Canadian companies are also selling their goods and services to a world market of over six billion people worldwide.

You must realize that most large businesses (and even many small businesses) operate as **transnational firms**—firms that produce and sell products and services in countries all over the world. This is a substantial career opportunity for you. Think of how much better your résumé would look if you could speak a foreign language or had knowledge in subjects related to all aspects of international commerce.

THE ARRIVING DIGITAL ECONOMY

Right now, we are in the information age. But we are seeing a transition into the digital age. When we do arrive there, the **digital economy** will be one marked by the electronic movement of all types of information, including physiological information such as voice recognition and synthesization, biometrics (your retina scan and breath for example), and 3D holograms. A hologram is a three-dimensional image projected into the air. If you've ever watched *Star Trek*, then you're familiar with the *holodeck*, a sophisticated technology-based device that allows people to have virtual experiences without the need for today's clunky gloves, headsets, and walkers (found in current virtual reality systems).

Again, we're not there yet. But we are definitely moving in that direction. A few short years ago, pay-per-view movies and sporting events in your home were only a vision of the future. Today, they are a reality and a part of the upcoming digital econ-

Figure 1.2

Canada's Trade and Investment over 2001–2003 (millions of Canadian dollars)[6]

	Exports of Goods and Services			Imports of Goods and Services		
	2001	*2002*	*2003*	*2001*	*2002*	*2003*
World	480,404	472,628	457,848	417,908	423,112	409,123
United States	387,108	382,101	364,753	296,400	295,734	279,866
EU-15	33,886	31,983	33,621	45,847	46,754	45,966
Japan	11,929	12,082	11,334	12,692	13,990	12,579
Rest of world	47,481	46,462	48,140	62,969	66,634	70,712

omy. This represents another substantial career opportunity for you. Don't limit your thinking to the digital movement of just words, numbers, graphs, and photos. Think outside the box and envision moving all types of information electronically. For a rich and thought-provoking discussion of the future digital economy, you might want to read Chapter 8. (This isn't a novel, so reading ahead won't ruin the rest of the story for you.)

Today's economic environment is indeed unique, exciting, and full of opportunities for you. Tomorrow's economic environment will be even more exciting and holds much promise for you in your career. Are you ready to help a business use technology to gain and sustain a competitive advantage?

Information as a Key Resource

Information is important for several reasons today, two of which we've already stated. First, information is one of the three key components of management information systems along with information technology and people. Second, as we have said, we are in the "information age," a time when knowledge is power. And knowledge comes from having timely access to information and knowing what to do with it.

DATA, INFORMATION, AND BUSINESS INTELLIGENCE

To understand the nature of information and exactly what it is, you must first understand another term—data. **Data** are raw facts that describe a particular phenomenon. For example, the current temperature, price of a movie rental, and your age are all data. **Information** then is simply data having a particular meaning within a specific context. For example, if you're trying to decide what to wear, the current temperature is information because it's pertinent to your decision at hand (what to wear)—the price of a movie rental, however, is not.

Information may be data that have been processed in some way or presented in a more meaningful fashion. In business, for instance, the price of a movie rental may be information to a checkout clerk, but it may represent only data to an accountant who is responsible for determining net revenues at the end of the month.

Business intelligence (BI) is information "on steroids," so to speak—knowledge about your customers, your competitors, your business partners, your competitive environment, and your own internal operations that gives you the ability to make effective, important, and often strategic business decisions. It enables your organization to extract the true meaning of information and take creative and powerful steps to ensure a competitive advantage. So business intelligence is much more than just a list of the products you sell. It might combine your product information with advertising strategy information and customer demographics information to help you determine the effectiveness of various advertising media on demographic groups segmented by location.

PERSONAL DIMENSIONS OF INFORMATION

As a knowledge worker, you work with and produce information. As you do, you can consider it from three points of view or dimensions—time, location, and form (see Figure 1.3).

THE TIME DIMENSION   The time dimension of information encompasses two aspects—(1) having access to information when you need it and (2) having information that describes the time period you're considering. The first really deals with timeliness. Information can in fact become old and obsolete. For example, if you want to make a stock trade today, you need to know the price of the stock right now. If you have to wait a day to get stock prices, you may not survive in the turbulent securities market. It's no wonder that over one-third of all stock transactions today occur over the Internet.

The second time aspect deals with having information that describes the appropriate time period. For example, most utility companies provide you with a bill that not only tells you of your current usage and the average temperature but also compares that information with that of the previous month and perhaps the same month last year. This type of information can help you better manage your utilities or simply understand that this month's high utility bill was caused by inclement weather.

THE LOCATION DIMENSION   The location dimension of information deals with having access to information no matter where you are. This simply means that you should be able to access needed information from an airplane, in a hotel room, at

Figure 1.3

Personal Dimensions of Information

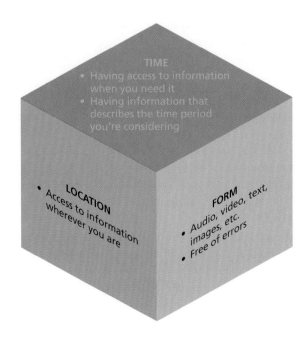

OVERCOMING LANGUAGE BARRIERS ON THE INTERNET

The Internet is certainly a technology that has eliminated geographical and location barriers. With almost one-sixth of the world's population having access to the Internet, "location, location, location" in the physical world is becoming less and less and less important.

However, now we have new issues to deal with, notably that of a language barrier. What happens if you connect to a site that offers information in a language you don't understand? How can you send an e-mail to someone in Japan who doesn't speak English?

One solution is language translation software. And one company leading the way in the development of language translation software is SYSTRAN. SYSTRAN Enterprise is a suite of software tools that enables you to, among other things, translate about 3700 words per minute, translate both e-mail and Web page content, and display Asian fonts.

Is it perfect? Not according to SYSTRAN's disclaimer, which says that although the software is designed to be as accurate as possible, "no automated translation is perfect nor is it intended to replace human translators. Users should note that the quality of the source text significantly affects the translations."

As you might expect, automated translation software has a particularly difficult time with idioms. When Kentucky Fried Chicken wanted to translate its slogan "finger-lickin' good" into Chinese, it came out as "eat your fingers off." Now, KFC wasn't using SYSTRAN's software, but this example does illustrate the difficulty of translating idiomatic expressions. Product names are another example. When General Motors tried to sell the Chevy Nova in South America, people didn't buy it. As it turns out, in Spanish *no va* means "it won't go." GM subsequently changed the name to Caribe for its Spanish markets.

By the way, you might want to try out the software at SYSTRAN's Web site (www.systransoft.com). There is a box into which you can type a phrase or sentence and choose the language into which you would like it translated.[7]

home, in the student centre of your campus, at work, or even driving down the road. Of course, because of the Internet you can be almost anywhere in the world and access almost any information you need.

To keep certain information private and secure while providing remote access for employees, many businesses are creating intranets. An **intranet** is an organization's internal "Internet" guarded against outside access by a special security feature called a *firewall* (which can be software, hardware, or a combination of the two). So if your organization has an intranet and you want to access information on it while away from the office, all you need is Web browser software, a modem, and the password that will allow you through the firewall.

The Canadian design company silverorange has created an award-winning intranet that you can demo at demo.silverorange.com. Employees can connect to the intranet and meet in online chat rooms, exchange documents, and discuss ongoing projects, even with employees located in remote geographical areas. While they are doing this, the firewall ensures that no one outside Silverorange.com can gain access to the intranet-based information.

THE FORM DIMENSION The form dimension of information deals with two primary aspects. The first is simply having information in a form that is most usable and understandable by you—audio, text, video, animation, graphical, and others. The second deals with accuracy. That is, you need information that is free of errors. Think of information as you would a physical product. If you buy a product and it's defective, you become an unsatisfied customer. Likewise, if you receive information that is incorrect, you're very unhappy as well.

For all these various information dimensions, be mindful that you provide your customers with information. Information you provide to your customers should be timely, describe the appropriate time dimension, accessible from anywhere, in the most usable form, and free of errors. Information is a valuable resource and also a commodity you provide to customers. Make sure they get it the way they want it.

ORGANIZATIONAL DIMENSIONS OF INFORMATION

Even if your choice in life is to be an entrepreneur and run your own business, you also need to consider various organizational dimensions of information. These include information flows, what information describes, information granularity, and how information is used (for either mainly transaction processing or analytical processing, which we'll discuss in an upcoming section).

INFORMATION FLOWS   Information in an organization flows in four basic directions—up, down, horizontally, and outward. To consider these flows, let's first briefly look at the structure of an organization. Most people view a traditional organization as a pyramid with four levels and many sides (see Figure 1.4). At the top is **strategic management**, which provides an organization with overall direction and guidance. The second level is often called **tactical management**, which develops the goals and strategies outlined by strategic management. The third level is **operational management**, which manages and directs the day-to-day operations and implementations of the goals and strategies. Finally, the fourth level of the organization comprises nonmanagement employees who actually perform daily activities, such as order processing, developing and producing goods and services, and serving customers. If you consider your school as an example, strategic management would include the chancellor, president, and various vice-presidents. Tactical management would include the deans. Operational management would include the department chairs and directors of academic programs. The final level would include instructors who are responsible for teaching the classes.

The *upward flow of information* describes the current state of the organization on the basis of its daily transactions. When a sale occurs, for example, that information originates at the lowest level of the organization and then is passed up through the var-

Figure 1.4

An Organization, Its Information Flows, and Information Granularity

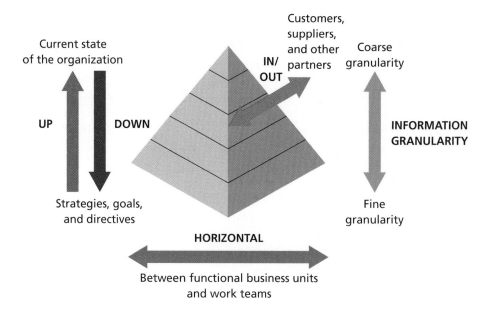

ious levels of management. Information gathered as part of everyday operations is consolidated by information technology and passed upward to decision makers who monitor and respond to problems and opportunities.

The *downward flow of information* involves the strategies, goals, and directives that originate at one level and are passed to lower levels. The *horizontal flow of information* is between functional business units and work teams. For example, at your school, various departments are responsible for scheduling courses. That information is passed horizontally to the registrar's office, which creates a course schedule for your entire campus (which may be online—timely and accessible from anywhere by you).

Finally, the outward and inward flows of information consist of information communicated to customers, suppliers, distributors, and other partners for the purpose of doing business. This (and its corresponding inward flow) is really what electronic commerce is all about. Today, no organization is an island, and you must ensure that your organization has the right information technology tools to communicate outwardly with all types of business partners. In a later section, and in more detail in Chapter 2, we'll discuss this outward flow of information within the context of creating business partnerships and alliances.

INFORMATION GRANULARITY   Figure 1.4 also illustrates another dimension of information—granularity. **Information granularity** refers to the extent of detail within the information. On one end of this spectrum is coarse granularity, or highly summarized information. At the other end is fine granularity, or information that contains a great amount of detail. As you might guess, people on the highest levels of the organization deal mainly with a coarse granularity of information, sales by year being an example. People on the lowest levels of the organization, on the other hand, need information with fine granularity. If you consider sales again, nonmanagement employees need information in great detail that describes each transaction—when it occurred, whether by credit or cash, who made the sale, to whom the sale was made, and so on.

So, when transaction information originates at the lowest level of an organization (with fine granularity), it is consolidated to a more coarse granularity as it moves up through the organization (the upward flow of information).

WHAT INFORMATION DESCRIBES   Another organizational dimension of information is what the information describes. Information can be internal, external, objective, subjective, or some combination of the four.

- **Internal information** describes specific operational aspects of the organization.
- **External information** describes the environment surrounding the organization.
- **Objective information** describes quantifiably something that is known.
- **Subjective information** attempts to describe something that is unknown.

Consider a bank that faces the decision of what interest rate to offer on a certificate of deposit. That bank will use internal information (how many customers it has who can afford to buy a CD), external information (what other banks are offering), objective information (what today's prime interest rate is), and subjective information (what the prime interest rate is expected to be several months down the road). As well, what other banks are offering is an example of not only external information (it describes the surrounding environment) but also objective information (it is quantifiably known).

As a general rule, people on the lowest levels of the organization deal mainly with internal and objective information (the price of a movie rental is an example). People on the highest levels of the organization, on the other hand, deal with all types of information.

MICHAEL DELL PREACHES IMMEDIATE INFORMATION ACCESS

We can all learn a lot from Michael Dell, CEO and founder of Dell Computer. In the mid-1980s, Michael couldn't even wait to get out of college to start his own direct-sales computer business. In the 20 years since he started the small operation in his dorm room, Dell Computer has definitely become the market leader, with over $49 billion in revenues in 2004.

Speaking to a group of entrepreneurs recently, Michael had this to say about the importance of timely information: "One of the great things about our business is that we have immediate information; we don't have to wait a week or a month. We get information every day, so that I know that yesterday we sold 77,850 computers. I know it by customer type, by product type, by geography, and what the mix was. So that immediacy of information is incredibly valuable to everything in our business, because it's changing very, very rapidly. We just continue to shrink the time and space and distance between our customers and our suppliers and make that as efficient as we can. We're down to about three to four days of inventory now. We get deliveries every two hours based on what we just sold. You take out the guessing."

That's a powerful set of statements; look closely at them. By having access to timely information, Dell Computer is able to carry only three to four days of inventory. That's remarkable when you compare it to the industry standard of about 45 days. Businesses in the technology sector cannot afford to carry 45 days' worth of inventory when you consider the rapid speed at which technology is changing.

Notice also that timely information takes out the guesswork for Dell. If your business is guessing to determine its next move, you won't be in business very long. Perhaps it's time to get timely information.[8]

People as a Key Resource

The single most important resource in any organization is its people. People (knowledge workers) set goals, carry out tasks, make decisions, serve customers, and, in the case of IT specialists, provide a stable and reliable technology environment so the organization can run smoothly and gain a competitive advantage in the marketplace. This discussion is all about you. You're preparing to be a knowledge worker.

INFORMATION AND TECHNOLOGY LITERACY

In a business environment, your most valuable asset is *not* technology but rather your *mind*. IT is simply a set of tools that help you work with and process information, but it's really just a *mind support* tool set. Technology such as spreadsheet can help you quickly create a high-quality and revealing graph. But it can't tell you whether you should build a bar or pie graph and it can't help you determine whether you should show sales by territory or sales by salesperson. Those are your tasks and that's why your business curriculum includes classes in human resources management, accounting, finance, marketing, and perhaps production and operations management.

Nonetheless, technology is an important set of tools for you. Technology can help you be more efficient and can help you dissect and better understand problems and opportunities. So, it's important for you to learn how to use your technology set. And it's equally important that you understand the information to which you're applying your technology tools.

A **technology-literate knowledge worker** is a person who knows how and when to apply technology. The "how" aspect includes knowing what technology to buy,

E-LEARNING: NOT JUST FOR SCHOOL

To become effective in your use of information, you can use technology to *learn*—not only about what certain information means—but more basically how to perform your work responsibilities better. Brink's Home Security recently implemented an *e-learning* management system to help (1) train its 2600 employees, (2) increase customer retention, (3) improve profits, and (4) reduce employee turnover.

Many of Brink's field personnel work nights and weekends installing home security systems. For them, instructor-led training classes in a central location (Brink's has a nationwide field workforce) created problems and simply didn't work.

The new e-learning management system helps managers develop customized online training modules and allows field personnel to access those modules 24 hours per day, seven days per week. The system even provides skills assessment and other forms of evaluation.

The total investment in the system for Brink's was $300,000. It expects to save $500,000 in the first three years as a result of replacing instructor-led classes with the e-learning modules. Brink's has already noticed that its better-trained field personnel have improved profit margins and increased customer retention.[9]

how to exploit the many benefits of application software, and what technology infrastructure is required to get businesses connected to each other, to name just a few. In this text and its accompanying CD, we have provided the following features to help you become a technology-literate knowledge worker:

- Extended Learning Module A: Careers in business
- Extended Learning Module B: Computer hardware and software
- Extended Learning Modules C and G: Designing databases and entity-relationship diagramming
- Extended Learning Module D: Decision analysis with spreadsheet software
- Extended Learning Module E: Network basics
- Extended Learning Module I: How to write HTML to create a Web site
- Extended Learning Module J: How to build an e-portfolio to advertise yourself on the Web

In many unfortunate cases, people and organizations have blindly decided to use technology to help solve some sort of business problem. What you need to understand is that technology is not a panacea. You can't simply apply technology to any given process and expect that process to instantly become more efficient and effective. Look at it this way—if you apply technology to a process that doesn't work correctly, then you'll only be doing things wrong millions of times faster. There are cases when technology is not the solution. Being a technology-literate knowledge worker will help you determine when and when not to apply technology.

Information-literate knowledge workers:

- Can define what information they need
- Know how and where to obtain that information
- Understand the information once they receive it
- Can act appropriately on the basis of the information to help the organization achieve the greatest advantage

Consider a unique, real-life example of an information-literate knowledge worker.

Several years ago, a manager of a retail store on the East Coast received some interesting information—diaper sales on Friday evening accounted for a large percentage of total sales for the week. Most people in this situation would immediately jump to the conclusion to make sure that diapers are always well stocked on Friday evening or run a special on diapers during that time to increase sales, but not our information-literate knowledge worker. She first looked at the information and decided it was not complete. That is, she needed more information before she could act.

She decided the information she needed was why a rash of diaper sales (pardon the pun) occurred during that time and who was buying them. That information was not stored within the store's computer system, so she stationed an employee in the diaper aisle on Friday evening who recorded any pertinent information to the situation (i.e., she knew how and where to obtain information). The store manager learned that young businessmen purchased the most diapers on Friday evening. Apparently, they had been instructed to buy the weekend supply of diapers on their way home from work. Her response was to stock premium domestic and imported beer near the diapers. Since then, Friday evening is a big sale time not only for diapers but also for premium domestic and imported beer.

The store manager's information-literate knowledge—her ability to define what information she needed, know how and where to obtain that information, and understand the meaning of the information once she received it—enabled her to determine that diapers and premium beer were complementary products for most young businessmen. Would you have made that connection? By the way, this is an example of a wants-based economic environment. While diapers are a very necessary product (just ask any parent), premium beer is a wants-based product.

YOUR ETHICAL RESPONSIBILITIES

Your roles as a technology-literate and information-literate knowledge worker extend far beyond using technology and information to gain an advantage in the marketplace for your organization. You must also consider your social responsibilities—this is where ethics becomes important. **Ethics** are the principles and standards that guide our behaviour toward other people. Ethics are different from laws. Laws either require or prohibit some sort of action on your part. Ethics are more of a matter of personal interpretation, and thus have a right and wrong outcome according to different people. Consider the following examples:

1. Copying software you purchased, making copies for your friends, and charging them for the copies
2. Making an extra backup of your software just in case both the copy you are using and the primary backup fail for some reason
3. Giving out the phone numbers of your friends and family, without their permission, to a provider of some sort of calling plan so you can receive a discount

Each of these is either ethically or legally incorrect. In the second example, you may have been ethically correct in making an extra backup copy (because you didn't share it with anyone), but according to most software licences you're prohibited by law to make more than one backup copy.

To help you better understand the relationship between ethical and legal acts (or the opposite), consider Figure 1.5. The graph is composed of four quadrants and you always want your actions to remain in quadrant I. If all your actions fall in that quadrant, you'll always be acting legally and ethically, and this in a socially responsible way.

In business, the question of ethics is an overriding concern because of the widespread use of IT to capture information. For example, if a business invests money to

E-MAIL: ELECTRONIC MAIL OR EXPENSIVE MAIL?

In February 1995, an employee at Chevron came across what he thought was an interesting and funny list—"25 Reasons Why Beer Is Better Than Women." He quickly logged into his e-mail and distributed the list to many people. The only problem was that one of the people who received the e-mail was a woman, and she was offended by it. What followed was a lot of legal mumbo jumbo and an eventual out-of-court settlement worth $2 million that Chevron had to pay to the offended employee—definitely an example of when e-mail becomes expensive mail.

Most people agree that the original sender should not have distributed the list. It was mail that was potentially embarrassing and offensive to some people and, therefore, should not have been distributed as a matter of ethics. What people don't agree on, however, is whether or not the company was at fault for not monitoring and stopping the potentially offensive mail. What are your thoughts? Before you decide, follow the accompanying diagram and consider the consequences of your answers.[10]

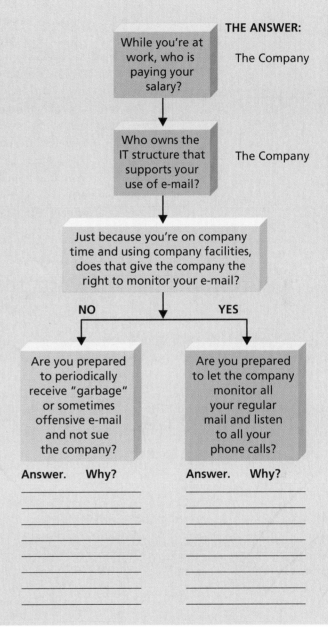

THE ANSWER:

While you're at work, who is paying your salary? → The Company

Who owns the IT structure that supports your use of e-mail? → The Company

Just because you're on company time and using company facilities, does that give the company the right to monitor your e-mail?

NO — Are you prepared to periodically receive "garbage" or sometimes offensive e-mail and not sue the company?

Answer. Why?
_____
_____
_____
_____
_____
_____
_____

YES — Are you prepared to let the company monitor all your regular mail and listen to all your phone calls?

Answer. Why?
_____
_____
_____
_____
_____
_____
_____

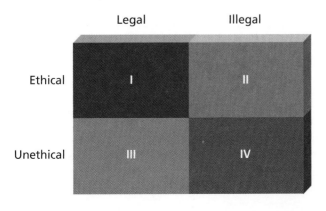

	Legal	Illegal
Ethical	I	II
Unethical	III	IV

Figure 1.5

Acting Ethically and Legally[11]

capture information about you as you make a purchase, does that information then belong to the business or do you still have privacy rights regarding its distribution?

Being socially and ethically responsible not only includes the actions you undertake yourself but also dealing with the actions of others, which may involve protecting yourself against cyber-crimes. Hackers are one group of people who commit cyber-crimes. A **hacker** is a very knowledgeable person who uses his or her knowledge to invade other people's computers. There are actually many types of hackers today—*white-hat hackers*, *black-hat hackers*, *crackers*, *hacktivists*, and *script bunnies*. Each has different motives and each is largely a different group of people. To protect yourself and your organization from their hacking, you need to understand who they are and what they do. We explore hackers in more detail in Chapter 9.

People, again, are the most valuable resource in any organization. People, like you as a knowledge worker, use IT to work with and massage information. The most successful people understand their information and information processing needs, and they understand the benefits of technology and know how to use technology to facilitate their working with information.

Information Technology as a Key Resource

Within management information systems (MIS), the third key resource is information technology. Formally defined, **information technology (IT)** is any computer-based tool that people use to work with information and support the information and information processing needs of an organization. So IT includes a cell phone or PDA that you might use to obtain stock quotes, your home computer that you use to write term papers, large networks that businesses use to connect to other businesses, and the Internet that almost one in every six people in the world currently use.

KEY TECHNOLOGY CATEGORIES

There are two basic categories of technology—hardware and software (see Figure 1.6). **Hardware** is the physical devices that make up a computer (often referred to as a *computer system*). **Software** is the set of instructions that your hardware executes to carry out a specific task for you. So, if you have a Nintendo GameCube, the GameCube box itself and the controller are hardware devices, while the games you play are software. Let's briefly look at hardware and software; for a more thorough discussion, read Extended Learning Module B.

TECHNOLOGY HARDWARE

All hardware falls into one of six categories—input devices, output devices, storage devices, telecommunications devices, CPU and RAM, and connecting devices. Here's a quick summary.

- An **input device** is a tool you use to capture information and commands; input devices include such tools as a keyboard, mouse, touch screen, game controller, barcode reader, and skimmer (used for swiping credit cards and the like).
- An **output device** is a tool you use to see, hear, or otherwise accept the results of your information processing requests. Output devices include such tools as a printer, monitor, and set of speakers.

Figure 1.6
Information Technology Hardware and Software

Description	Examples
Hardware: The Physical Devices That Make Up a Computer	
Input device—tool you use to capture information and commands	• Keyboard, mouse • Touch screen, game controller • Barcode reader, skimmer
Output device—tool you use to see, hear, or otherwise accept the results of your information processing requests	• Printer • Monitor • Set of speakers
Storage device—tool you use to store information for use at a later time	• Jump drive • Floppy disk • Hard disk • CD, DVD
Central processing unit (CPU)—the actual hardware that interprets the software instructions and coordinates how all the other hardware devices work together	• Pentium 4 • AMD Athlon XP Thunderbird
RAM (random access memory)—temporary memory that holds information, application software, and operating system software	• Many manufacturers make RAM that will fit in a variety of computers
Telecommunications device—tool you use to send information to and receive it from another person or location	• Telephone modem • DSL modem • Cable modem • Microwave • Satellite
Connecting devices—tools that connect devices to each other	• USB ports • Printer cord • Parallel and serial ports
Software—The Set of Instructions That Your Hardware Executes to Carry Out a Specific Task	
Application software—software that enables you to solve specific problems or perform specific tasks	• Word processing software • Payroll software • Spreadsheet software • Inventory management software
Operating system software—system software that controls your application software and manages how your hardware devices work together	• Windows XP • Windows 2000 • Windows Me • Mac OS • Linux • UNIX
Utility software—software that provides additional functionality to your operating system	• Antivirus software • Screensaver • Disk optimization software • Uninstaller software

- A **storage device** is a tool you use to store information for use at a later time. Output devices include such tools as a floppy disk, hard disk, CD, and DVD.
- A **telecommunications device** is a tool you use to send information to and receive it from another person or location. For example, if you connect to the Internet using a modem, the modem (which might be a telephone, DSL, cable, wireless, or satellite modem) is a telecommunications device.
- The **central processing unit (CPU)** is the actual hardware that interprets and executes the software instructions and coordinates how all the other hardware devices work together. Popular personal CPUs include the Pentium 4 and AMD Athlon XP Thunderbird. **RAM**, or **random access memory**, is temporary storage that holds the information you're working with, the application software you're using, and the operating system software you're using. Together, the CPU and RAM make up the "brains" of your computer.
- *Connecting devices* include such things as parallel ports into which you would connect a printer, connector cords to connect your printer to the parallel port, and internal connecting devices that mainly include buses over which information travels from one device such as the CPU to RAM.

That may be the shortest overview of hardware you've ever read. If you need more detail, please read the Extended Learning Module B on hardware and software.

TECHNOLOGY SOFTWARE

There are two main types of software—application and system. **Application software** enables you to solve specific problems or perform specific tasks. Microsoft Word, for example, can help you write term papers, so it's application software. From an organizational perspective, payroll software, collaborative software such as videoconferencing, and inventory management software are all examples of application software.

System software handles tasks specific to technology management and coordinates the interaction of all technology devices. Within system software, you'll find operating system software and utility software. **Operating system software** is system software that controls your application software and manages how your hardware devices work together. Popular personal operating system software includes Microsoft Windows XP, Microsoft Windows Me, Mac OS X (for Apple computers), and Linux (an open source operating system).

Utility software provides additional functionality to your operating system. It includes antivirus software, screensavers, disk optimization software, uninstaller software (for properly removing unwanted software), and a host of others. Again, in Extended Learning Module B we discuss software in greater detail.

DECENTRALIZED COMPUTING AND SHARED INFORMATION

All organizations use hardware and software to connect people to each other, reach out to customers, distributors, suppliers, and business partners, and to provide a reliable and stable computing environment for smooth operations. Because so many people perform so many different tasks within a business environment, the concepts of decentralized computing and shared information are very important (see Figure 1.7).

Decentralized computing is an environment in which an organization splits computing power and locates it in functional business areas as well as on the desktops of knowledge workers. This is possible because of the proliferation of less expensive, more powerful, and smaller systems including notebooks, desktops, minicomputers, and servers. The Internet is a great example of a decentralized computing environment. You use your computer or perhaps cell phone or PDA to access the information and services of host computers on the Internet. In this case, your computer is called a *client computer*, while the host computers are referred to as *server computers*.

Shared information is an environment in which an organization's information is organized in one central location, allowing anyone to access and use it as they need to. Shared information enables people in the sales department, for example, to access work-in-progress manufacturing information to determine when products will be available to ship. At your school, the registrar's office can access the information within the financial aid office to determine how much of your tuition bill is covered by a scholarship or loan. To support shared information, most businesses organize information in the form of a database. In fact, databases have become the standard by which businesses organize their information and provide everyone access to it. We've devoted all of Chapter 4 to databases as well as data warehouses, tools for organizing information to support decision-making tasks.

Now that we've provided you with a brief overview of information technology, let's look specifically at the roles and goals of information technology in any business. IT is an essential enabler of business operations. In the information age, all businesses need technology as tools for working with information.

Figure 1.7

Decentralized Computing and Shared Information

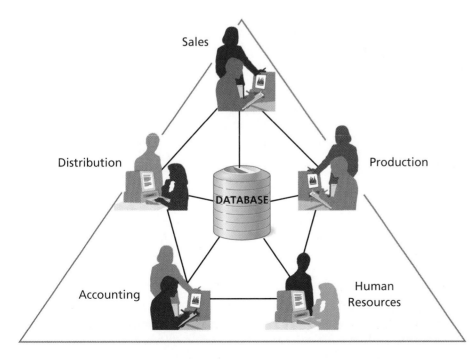

Roles and Goals of Information Technology

The roles and goals of information technology are many and varied. Here we introduce you to six important roles and goals. And we will constantly refer back to these throughout the chapter. So they're not only important to learn so you can do well on an exam; they will also help you better organize your view of technology within an organization. The six major roles and goals of information technology include (see Figure 1.8):

1. Increase employee productivity
2. Enhance decision making
3. Improve team collaboration

Figure 1.8

The Roles and Goals of Information Technology

Goal	IT Tool Examples	Business Benefits Examples
1. Increase employee productivity	• OLTP (online transaction processing) • TPS (transaction processing system) • CIS (customer-integrated system)	• Reduce time • Reduce errors • Reduce costs • Enable customers to process their own transactions
2. Enhance decision making	• OLAP (online analytical processing) • DSS (decision support system) • GIS (geographic information system) • EIS (executive information system) • AI (artificial intelligence) • Data warehouses	• Generate alternatives • Recommend solutions • Drill down through information
3. Improve team collaboration	• WSS (workgroup support system) • Groupware	• Manage knowledge within the organization • Support geographically dispersed teams • Facilitate communications • Develop applications quickly
4. Create business partnerships and alliances	• IOS (interorganizational system) • EDI (electronic data interchange)	• Manage supply chains • Share expertise and intellect • Enable B2B e-commerce
5. Enable global reach	• Internet • Translation phones	• Take advantage of a cheaper/larger workforce • Advertise locally made • Tap into global intellectual expertise
6. Facilitate organizational transformation	• Just about any technology you can name, depending on its use	• Stay competitive • Offer new customer interfaces • Enter new markets

4. Create business partnerships and alliances
5. Enable global reach
6. Facilitate organizational transformation

INCREASE EMPLOYEE PRODUCTIVITY

The original and still most fundamental role of information technology is to increase productivity. In short, because of its great speed and ability to store and process massive amounts of information accurately, IT can greatly reduce the time, errors, and costs associated with processing information in a variety of ways.

For example, if you have an automated payroll system, it can process payroll sheets and generate cheques more quickly than if you were doing it by hand. If your employees can submit time cards and expense reimbursement sheets electronically as opposed to submitting handwritten documents, then the likelihood of an error occurring is reduced. And when you decrease processing times and errors, you decrease costs. When you use technology to process transaction information, it's called **online transaction processing (OLTP)**—the gathering of input information, processing that information, and updating existing information to reflect the gathered and processing information.

IT systems such as our payroll example are called transaction processing systems. A **transaction processing system (TPS)** processes transactions that occur within an organization. Today, we pretty well accept these as rather dull and mundane. But your customers see them differently. If your TPSs don't process information correctly or don't work at all because of a computer outage, your customers may choose to do business with one of your competitors. Indeed, if you call an airline to make a reservation and you're informed that the computers don't work and your reservation cannot be processed, you may call another airline.

A vitally important hybrid of a TPS is a customer-integrated system. A **customer-integrated system (CIS)** is an extension of a TPS that places technology in the hands of an organization's customers and allows them to process their own transactions (see Figure 1.9). ATMs are a good example of a CIS. ATMs provide you with the ability to

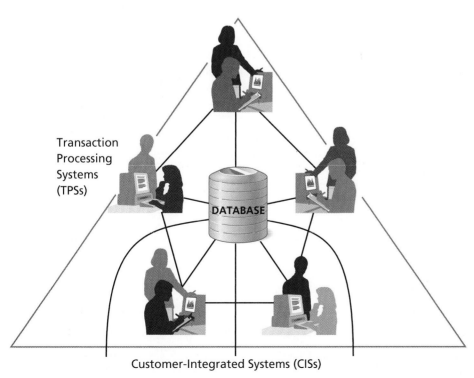

Transaction Processing Systems (TPSs)

DATABASE

Customer-Integrated Systems (CISs)

Figure 1.9

Transaction Processing and Customer-Integrated Systems

do your own banking anywhere at anytime. What's really interesting is that ATMs actually do nothing "new," but they give you greater flexibility in accessing and using your money. CISs further decentralize computing power in an organization by placing that power in the hands of customers.

The Web is full of examples of customer-integrated systems. When you use any Web site that allows you to order and pay for products and services, you're using a CIS. Customer-integrated systems are the new popular IT system today. You can use a CIS to scan your groceries, pay for fuel at the pump instead of going inside, and perhaps even register for classes online. When you enter the business world, first make sure your transaction processing systems work correctly and all the time. Then, try to convert them to customer-integrated systems. It's a win-win situation for your organizations and your customers.

ENHANCE DECISION MAKING

The counterpart to online transaction processing is **online analytical processing (OLAP)**—the manipulation of information to support decision making. And IT can definitely play a significantly role here. Some decisions are easy to make. If you're deciding what to wear to school, you'll look at today's weather forecast and decide whether to wear shorts and a T-shirt or perhaps a sweatshirt and pants. However, deciding what to major in or which job to accept upon graduation is much more difficult. Likewise, in business, deciding how many inventory units to reorder is relatively simple, while deciding where to build a new distribution centre is not.

Technology to support decision making falls into one of two general categories—(1) those that help you analyze a situation and then leave the decision entirely up to you including decision support systems, executive information systems, and geographic information systems and (2) those that actually make some sort of recommendation concerning what to do. The first category includes such IT tools as decision support systems, executive information systems, and geographic information systems. For example, an **executive information system (EIS)** is a highly interactive IT system that allows you to first view highly summarized information and then choose how you would like to see greater detail, which may alert you to potential problems or opportunities. In Figure 1.10, you can see three graphs which might appear in an EIS. The first one of the left shows sales by year. By clicking on a particular, year, you can then view sales by territory for that year. Then, by clicking on a particular territory, you can view sales by product line for that territory within a given year. These types of IT systems really offer you just great speed in massaging information, developing alterna-

Figure 1.10

Drilling Down with an Executive Information System

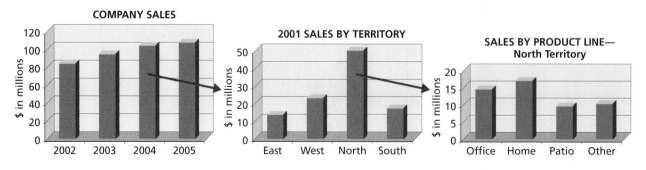

tives, and viewing information from various perspectives. However, they do not make recommendations concerning what you should do.

The second category includes technologies in the area of artificial intelligence. **Artificial intelligence (AI)** is the science of making machines imitate human thinking and behaviour. For example, a **neural network** is an artificial intelligence which is capable of learning to differentiate patterns. Your credit card company probably uses a neural network to monitor your card use and identify potential fraud if someone else happens to steal your card and attempt to use it. In this instance, the neural network has been fed every single credit card transaction you've performed, and it's developed a pattern of how, when, and why you use your card. Then, when a transaction occurs that doesn't fit the pattern of your profile, the neural networks alerts someone that your credit card may have been stolen.

We explore technology support for decision making throughout this text and specifically in Chapter 6.

IMPROVE TEAM COLLABORATION

Teams would certainly be characterized as a "best business practice" today. The adage "Two heads are better than one" does hold true. Of course, teams in the business world are often composed of more than two people with many being spread all over the globe, and that's why information technology plays such an important role in team collaboration. Collaboration-enabling technologies such as chat rooms, the Internet in general, and workgroup support systems are all fundamental to the success of a team.

A **workgroup support system (WSS)** is a system designed specifically to improve the performance of teams by supporting the sharing and flow of information. The foundation of any workgroup support system is **groupware**—the popular term for the software component that supports the collaborative efforts of a team. Popular groupware suites include Lotus/Notes Domino, Microsoft Exchange, Novell Group-Wise, and NetSys WebWare.

Groupware contains software components for supporting the following three team functions:

1. Team dynamics—communications among team members and the facilitation and execution of meetings. Specific technologies that support team dynamics include group scheduling software, electronic meeting software, videoconferencing software, and whiteboard software.
2. Document management—a **group document database** that acts as a powerful storage facility for organizing and managing all documents related to specific teams. Most group document database employ multiple levels of security, allowing some teams to access the information of other teams. In these databases, you can store and search information of all kinds—text, graphs, images, audio clips, and even videos.
3. Applications development—facilities that allow a team to develop unique applications quickly, so the teams can literally "get to work."

All of these technology-based tools and many more enable teams to work effectively, even when their members are geographically dispersed. Teams, as you'll learn in later chapters, are vitally important to the success of any organization. But concepts such as the virtual workplace and telecommuting are almost contradictory to the success of teams. If you consider even further that today's economy is a global one, any given team may be composed of people all over the world. In this case, technology, and specifically groupware, is an essential enabler of team innovation.

SPAR AEROSPACE LAUNCHES INFORMATION-SHARING INTRANET

Spar Aerospace, with its major sites in Brampton, Ontario and Sainte-Anne-de-Bellevue, Quebec has opted for an intranet solution to facilitate information sharing between different business units. Each site is dedicated to different product lines (i.e., telerobotics/Canadarm in Ontario and satellites/satellites subsystems in Quebec). Before intranets were introduced, collaboration was difficult. Each site maintained different libraries focused on specific disciplines and on serving the needs of a specific client base. Document sharing between sites was complicated because of incompatible document formats. In early 1995, Spar's management realized that the Internet and the World Wide Web allowed the sharing of numerous files of various formats. Consequently, the company decided to adopt an "internal Internet" solution—as Spar's management called it. The goal became to implement an integrated system giving employees companywide accessibility to the libraries' collections and to other useful information.

Today, when users within the Spar firewall type "biblio.spar.ca," a graphical menu appears offering a choice between the Ontario or the Quebec site. Clicking on either of these links leads the user to a listing of all information available at that site. Furthermore, conferencing capabilities have been added enabling engineering staff at either site to share various data and exchange project information with others.[12]

We'll talk more about the technologies that support team collaboration throughout this text and especially in Chapter 6. Your career opportunity lies in learning how to work effectively in a team environment. Many of your classes in school will probably require that you work in teams; the reason is because teams are such an important part of the business world.

FACILITATE MAJOR BUSINESS INITIATIVES

Each and every business contains unique and strategically sensitive expertise and intellect. Wal-Mart, for example, is a premier retailer of home and family products such as clothing. Vanity Fair, on the other hand, is a premier manufacturer of clothing including Lee and Wrangler jeans. So these two organizations have created a strong and highly successful business partnership.

When a customer buys a pair of Wrangler jeans at a Wal-Mart store on a Wednesday, for example, that information is sent that night to Vanity Fair, via computer of course. If Vanity Fair has a replacement pair in stock, it's immediately sent out on Thursday and arrives at Wal-Mart on Saturday. Three days for inventory replenishment is an outstanding feat, and would not be possible without the use of technology.

But speed isn't the only advantage. Vanity Fair's market-response system also takes the guesswork out of reordering and provides retailers with only the best-selling styles and lines. Vanity Fair's extended market response system will even analyze the sales databases of retailers and determine groups of products—for instance, matching jeans, shirts, and jackets—to help retailers forecast ideal inventory supply levels. As you can see, business partnerships and alliances enable each participating organization to tap into the intellectual capital of the other participating organizations.

This type of business partnership is enabled by interorganizational systems and is form of business to business (B2B) e-commerce. An **interorganizational system (IOS)** automates the flow of information between organizations to support the planning, design, development, production, and delivery of products and services. A typical IOS includes **electronic data interchange (EDI)**—the direct computer-to-computer transfer of trans-

FINDING BUSINESS PARTNERS AND ALLIANCES ON THE WEB

Like any other type of business, no dot-com on the Web can be an island. Indeed, dot-coms have determined that they must develop business partners on the Web. These partnerships manifest themselves in many different ways. One such way is through a **banner ad**—a small ad on one Web site that advertises the products and services of another business, usually another dot-com.

Visit the Web and go exploring. Find five Web sites on which banner ads appear. Which Web sites did you find with banner ads? For what business was each ad? Did you find any Web sites with more than one? If so, which sites? Now wait a day and visit the same five sites. Did any of the banner ads change? If so, why do you think they changed?

action information contained in standard business documents, such as invoices and purchase orders, in a standard format. In short, EDI replaces paper documents with digital records exchanged between business partnerships' computers. R. J. Reynolds uses EDI to order materials from its suppliers. In doing so, R. J. Reynolds has been able to cut order processing costs from $75 per order (using paper) to only 93 cents using EDI.

EDI is becoming so important that most large businesses won't do business with your business if you don't support EDI. For example, General Motors will only order raw materials and parts from suppliers who support EDI capabilities.

Another important concept related to EDI is electronic funds transfer (EFT). EFT allows organizations to complete the full transaction without physically sending anything, including the payment. So EDI supports the electronic transfer of information such as sales invoice, and EFT supports the electronic transfer of the monies to pay the sales invoice amount. Just as EDI is becoming a common business practice, so is EFT. Think about filing your income tax returns electronically. It doesn't make much sense to file the paperwork and then still have to send a personal cheque or receive a refund cheque from the federal government.

ENABLE KNOWLEDGE MANAGEMENT

Another important initiative that many businesses are implementing today deals with managing the knowledge within the organization. "Knowledge," in this case, refers to your organization's *know-how*—the expertise your organization uses to run itself, make important decisions, and set its strategic direction. Knowledge management deals with almost every type of knowledge in your organization, including how processes work, failed and successful attempts at reengineering, and the strategies your organization uses to target customer segments. In the case of the targeting strategies, the information your organization uses to make decisions is referred to as *business intelligence*; the actual decisions themselves and the strategies are knowledge.

It is also possible to have a *knowledge management (KM) system*—an IT system that supports the capture, organization, and dissemination of knowledge (i.e., know-how) throughout an organization.

ENABLE GLOBAL REACH

As we've already stated, you can characterize today's operating environment as one of a global economy. Because of technology, you now have the ability to market your products and services in countries all over the world and develop partnerships and alliances (which we just discussed) with other businesses throughout the globe. Not only can you do this, you *must* to be successful in the long run. Think about Honda cars for a moment, considered by most people to be manufactured in Japan, its "country" headquarters. Honda actually produces more cars outside than inside Japan. Not only that—Honda exports more cars from the United States than General Motors, Ford, or Chrysler.

A business can gain significant advantages by enabling global reach through technology. It can take advantage of a cheaper and larger workforce; many businesses in North America locate their back-end office functions (accounting and the like) in Ireland for this reason. It can also tap into the intellectual expertise of a workforce in another country. Many North American software publishers actually write and produce much of their software in such countries as India and Pakistan.

To operate effectively using global reach, businesses must use technology to overcome the barriers of time and location. One simple example is language translation software for mobile phones. ECTACO provides downloadable software that turns any Smartphone into a translation tool. Wherever you are—at home or on the move—the software's dictionary provides prompt bidirectional word translation.[13] There are also utilities on the Web that translate Web pages from one language to another.

To also operate effectively using global reach, you must consider the culture of other countries. **Culture** is the collective personality of a nation or society, encompassing language, traditions, currency, religion, history, music, and acceptable behaviour, among other things. For example, in many countries around the world workers take extended breaks at lunch well into the afternoon hours. So you shouldn't schedule a virtual team meeting during those particular hours. It's a simple example, but it does illustrate the fact that you have to consider the culture, in this case the work hours, of your various team members.

FACILITATE ORGANIZATIONAL TRANSFORMATION

And last, but certainly not least, information technology plays a critical role in facilitating organizational transformation. Organizational transformation is necessary to respond to the ever-changing needs (and wants) of today's marketplace. But organizational transformation doesn't have to be like going from a cocoon to a beautiful butterfly (one of nature's most dramatic and wonderful transformations). Businesses today can undergo a transformation by simply changing the way they deliver their products and services.

Consider Blockbuster Video—it has recently undergone one transformation (renting video games as opposed to just movies) and is in the middle of another. Blockbuster has created a business partnership with many cable TV services. Through a cable TV service, Blockbuster is now offering pay-per-view movies. So you don't have to go to a Blockbuster store to rent a video—you can order it from the comfort of your own home for about the same price. Not only that, once you order a movie, you can typically watch it several times within 24 hours.

This transformation for Blockbuster lies in changing how it delivers its products to you. Even more importantly, Blockbuster realizes that pay-per-view movies is the wave of the future, not going to a store to rent a video. Don't be surprised if, in ten years, you can't find a local video rental store. Of course, technology played a key role in Blockbuster's transformation. Without enabling network technologies and large servers that digitally store videos, Blockbuster would have no way of offering pay-per-view service.

Every business today must be willing to change, sometimes in minor ways but often in dramatic and "knee-breaking" ways. Just ask the folks at Kmart. At one point in

NOKIA—FROM PAPER, TO RUBBER, TO CELL PHONES AND TELECOMMUNICATIONS

The Nokia Company began over 150 years ago as a producer of paper. In 1967, the Nokia Corporation was formed, through a merger of the Nokia Company (paper), Finnish Rubber Works (rubber), and Finnish Cable Works (telecommunications cables).

As Nokia moved through the remainder of the 1960s, all of the 1970s, and into the 1980s, it saw huge possibilities in the wire-free telephone market. By transforming itself and focusing its energies in that area, Nokia produced the original and first hand-portable telephone in 1987.

You probably know the rest of the story. Today, Nokia is regarded as the premier innovator and manufacturer of cell phones. And it hasn't forgotten its past. For example, while producing rubber as a

primary product, Nokia was the first to manufacture and sell brightly coloured rubber boots (you might as well be in fashion while as work). So it's no surprise that Nokia innovated the multicoloured, clip-on facias that literally made cell phones an overnight fashion sensation.

Businesses don't have to go out of business just because the products they manufacture are no longer needed in our society. If your business finds itself in a shrinking market, be bold and innovative. Undertake some sort of dramatic organizational transformation. Nokia went from a premier manufacturer of rubber boots to the world's leading provider of cell phones in less than 15 years. That's a rather dramatic organizational transformation, wouldn't you say?[14]

time, it was considered to be a premier discount retailer. But it failed to transform itself to meet the changing desires of the market, and Kmart filed for bankruptcy in 2002.

In many instances, business transformation may be about deciding what information technology facilities and services to keep in house and what facilities and services to outsource. The organization may choose to outsource many of its IT operations and focus solely on its core competencies. In this case, the services of an applications service provider can be utilized. An **application service provider (ASP)** supplies application software (and, often, related services such as maintenance, technical support, and the like) over the Internet that would otherwise need to reside on its customers' in-house computers.

As we study business transformations in this text, you'll learn about some information technologies, including enterprise software and object-oriented technologies. As you learn about them, don't focus too much on the technology itself. Instead, focus on how businesses can use those technology to enable organizational transformation.

ETHICS, SECURITY, AND PRIVACY

As we close this first chapter, let's turn our attention back to ethics and a couple of new topics—security and privacy. We cannot stress enough how important it is for you to be ethical in your use of information and information technology. Even if you're not breaking the law, "shady" ethical acts can have a great impact on other people, and serious consequences for you. As a general rule of thumb when developing your ethical position, we encourage you to follow one simple rule: Do unto others as you would have them do unto you.

Unfortunately, you can't expect everyone to follow that rule, so much so that you must be vigilant in protecting yourself, your information, and your technology tools. As we said earlier, the easy power of information tools today increases the odds they will be misused by some people too, and not to guard your organization against bad actors out there is almost unethical in itself. You're probably familiar with viruses and worms, special types of software designed to do damage to your information and technology tools. You may also encounter **spyware** (also called **sneakware** or **stealthware**), software that comes hidden in free downloadable software and tracks your online movements, mines the information stored on your computer, or uses your computer's CPU and storage for some tasks you know nothing about. Spyware can invade your privacy, collect information about you, and send it—via the Internet—to an organization that might later sell that information.

Perhaps the greatest threat today (and on the horizon) to your personal safety in cyberspace is identity theft. **Identity theft** is the forging of someone's identity for the purpose of fraud. If you become a victim of identity theft, the "thief" will steal and use your credit cards, driver's licence, and numerous other forms of identification. In today's IT-based and often virtual world, the thief has only to steal the information associated with those forms of identifications, not the actual documents themselves.

In 2003, financial losses from identity theft were estimated to be approximately $100 billion in the United States and $300 billion worldwide. Those are astounding numbers, but they pale in comparison to what many experts were predicting for 2005—$1.8 trillion in the United States and almost $5 trillion worldwide.[15]

It is crucially important that you protect yourself, your information, and your technology tools. For starters, below are a few things to keep in mind (there are many more):

- Keep your antivirus software up to date.
- Use only secure Web sites when submitting personal or financial information.
- Never give out your personal information to enter a contest on the Internet.
- Change your passwords frequently and intersperse capital letters and digits in them.
- Never assume that everyone has the same ethical standards you do.

Summary: Student Learning Outcomes Revisited

1. **Define management information systems (MIS) and information technology (IT) and describe their relationship.** *Management information systems (MIS)* deals with the planning for, development, management, and use of information technology tools to help people perform all tasks related to information processing and management. *Information technology (IT)* is any computer-based tool that people use to work with information and support the information and information-processing needs of an organization. IT is one of the three key elements, along with people and information, of management information systems.

2. **Validate information as a key resource and describe both personal and organizational dimensions of information.** Information is one of the three key elements within MIS. We are in the

"information age," a time when knowledge is power. Information is the foundation for business intelligence. The personal and organizational dimensions of information include:

- Personal
  - *Time.* Access to information when you need it and information that describes the time period you're considering
  - *Location.* Access to information no matter where you are
  - *Form.* Information in a form that is most usable and understandable and information that is free of errors
- Organizational
  - *Information flows.* Up, down, horizontal, and inward/outward
  - *Granularity.* The extent of detail within information

- What information describes. *Internal* (specific operational aspects), *external* (the surrounding environment), *objective* (quantifiably known), and *subjective* (something unknown)

3. **Explain why people are the most important organizational resource, define their information and technology-literacy challenges, and discuss their ethical responsibilities.** People are the single most important resource in any organization, setting goals, carrying out tasks, and making decisions.

   - *Technology-literate knowledge workers* are people who know how and when to apply technology.
   - *Information-literate knowledge workers* (1) can define what information they need; (2) know how and where to obtain that information; (3) understand the information once they receive it; and (4) can act appropriately based on the information.
   - Most important, knowledge workers must be ethical. *Ethics* are the principles and standards that guide our behaviour toward other people.

4. **Describe the important characteristics of information technology (IT) as a key organizational resource.** Information technology is a set of tools you use to work with information. All technology is either *hardware* (the physical devices that make up a computer) or *software* (the set of instructions that your hardware executes).

5. **Define competitive advantage and illustrate the role of information technology in supporting operational excellence, major business initiatives, decision making, and organizational transformation.** A *competitive advantage* is providing a product or service in a way that customers value more than what the competition is able to do.

   - *Operational excellence.* The use of technology for efficiency (doing things right, in the least amount of time, with the fewest number of errors, and so on)
   - *Major business initiatives.* The use of technology to support initiatives such as customer relationship management, enterprise resource planning, sales force automation, and supply chain management
   - *Decision making.* The use of technology tools—such as decision support systems, executive information systems, and artificial intelligence (AI)—to (1) help you analyze a situation and/or (2) make some sort of recommendation concerning what to do
   - *Organizational transformation.* The use of technology to enable your organization to evolve and transform itself into new modes of operation, market segments, and so on

6. **Discuss the impacts information technology can have on your life.** Technology is everywhere in the business world. For your career, you need to learn to use technology tools specific to your job and industry and personal productivity tools. You also need to protect yourself, your technology, and your information in cyberspace. The issues of security and privacy are vitally important.

CLOSING CASE STUDY ONE

YOU AND YOUR INFORMATION

In the opening case study and throughout the chapter, you read about how pervasive and invasive technology is in your life today. No matter what you do or where you go, your information travels with you and is eventually captured and stored by a number of organizations. Many people simply accept this fact and think little beyond it. In this all-encompassing information and IT environment, let's consider two issues—trust and accuracy. As you'll see, they are related.

First, answer (with a simple yes or no) the questions below, which pertain to your everyday life.

1. Do you keep a paper record of all your long-distance phone calls—when you placed them by date and time, to whom, and the length—and then compare that list to your monthly phone bill?

   Yes ☐   No ☐

2. Do you meet with the meter reader to verify the correct reading of your water, gas, or electricity usage?

Yes ☐ No ☐

3. As you shop, do you keep a record of the prices of your groceries and then compare that record to the register receipt?

Yes ☐ No ☐

4. Do you frequently ask to see your doctor's medical record on you to ensure that it's accurate?

Yes ☐ No ☐

5. When you receive a tuition bill, do you pull out your calculator, add up the amounts, and verify that the total is correct?

Yes ☐ No ☐

6. Have you ever purchased a credit report on yourself to make sure your credit information is accurate?

Yes ☐ No ☐

7. Have you ever called the police department to verify that no outstanding traffic violations have been inadvertently assigned to you?

Yes ☐ No ☐

8. Do you count your coin change when you receive it from a store clerk?

Yes ☐ No ☐

9. Do you verify your credit card balance by keeping all your credit card receipts and then matching them to charges on your statement?

Yes ☐ No ☐

10. Do you keep all your paycheque stubs to verify that the amounts on your T4 form at the end of the year are accurate?

Yes ☐ No ☐

To how many of those questions did you answer yes? To how many did you answer no? More than likely, you answered no to almost all the questions (if not all of them). What does that say? Well, basically, that you trust organizations to keep accurate information about you. The real question is "Is that necessarily the case?"

Now answer the set of questions below, which relate to the level of confidence organizations have in the accuracy of information you give them.

1. When interviewing with potential employers, do they take your word that you have a college degree?

Yes ☐ No ☐

2. If you deposit several cheques into your chequing account at once, does the bank trust you to correctly add the amounts?

Yes ☐ No ☐

3. When you register for a class that has a prerequisite, does your school assume that you have actually taken the prerequisite class?

Yes ☐ No ☐

4. When you make a deposit at an ATM and enter the amount, does the bank assume that you entered the correct amount?

Yes ☐ No ☐

5. When you're buying a house and negotiating a loan, does the bank assume that the price you're paying for the house is correct and not inflated?

Yes ☐ No ☐

6. When insuring your car, does the insurance company assume that you have a good driving record?

Yes ☐ No ☐

7. When you apply for a parking permit at your school, does it assume that the car belongs to you?

Yes ☐ No ☐

8. When you file your taxes, does the Canada Customs and Revenue Agency assume that you've reported all your income over the past year?

Yes ☐ No ☐

The answer to each of those questions is probably no. And what does that say about the extent to which organizations trust you to provide accurate information? In this instance, it may not be strictly a matter of trust. Organizations today can't afford to have dirty information—information that's not accurate. Because organizations base so many of their decisions on information, inaccurate information creates a real problem that may equate to inefficient processes and lost revenue.

So, on the one hand, you're probably very trusting in your assumptions that organizations are maintaining accurate information about you; on the other, organizations don't really trust you to provide accurate information.

Questions

1. Should you really trust organizations to maintain accurate information about you? In many instances, is it even worth your time and energy to verify the accuracy of that information?

2. What other examples can you think of in which you simply trust that your information is accurate? What other examples can you think of in which specific organizations don't assume that you're providing accurate information?

3. What sort of impact will cyberspace business have on the issues of trust and accuracy? Will it become easier or more difficult for cyberspace business to assume that you're providing accurate information? Will you trust cyberspace business to maintain your information more accurately than traditional organizations?

4. What are the ethical issues involved in organizations sharing information about you? In some instances it may be okay and in your best interest. But what if the shared information about you is inaccurate? What damage could it cause? What recourse do you have, if any?

5. It's a real dilemma—most people think that credit card offerers charge extremely high interest rates. But how many people do you know who actually go through the process of calculating their average daily balances, applying the interest rates, and then verifying that the interest charged on their accounts is correct? Why do people complain that they are being charged excessive interest rates and then fail to check the accuracy of the interest calculations?

6. What about the future? As more organizations maintain even more information about you, should you become more concerned about accuracy? Why or why not?

CLOSING CASE STUDY TWO

USING INFORMATION TECHNOLOGY TO TRANSFORM A BUSINESS

The travel agency Colibri Tours, founded in 1988 and having its head office in Calgary, offers personalized tours to individuals and groups in Canada and Europe wanting to see western Canada and American sights such as the Grand Canyon, Yellowstone Park, and Alaska. It also provides value-added services: airport reception, travel programs for the elderly, sports activities, etc. Colibri has very successfully used information technology to transform its business, with annual sales just under $1 million.

Ms. Jacob, founder and president of Colibri Tours, turned to the Internet in 1998 in response to a significant increase of $40,000 in promotional costs and to a rise in related costs. A changing market scenario, with the rise of wholesalers in Europe and North America and the need to assure them of guaranteed tour departures, also prompted the company to seek a new way of doing business. Ms. Jacob, who personally built

the agency's Web site (www.colibritours.com) and updates it, managed to locate a server specializing in tourism, enabling her to promote the site at a very affordable cost of $1800 per year. The site enables prospective customers to access itineraries, destination photographs, and road maps, all of which give the operation a dynamic character. Customized services are also offered to customers at a lower cost while maintaining profitability levels.

The Web site has enabled Colibri Tours to deal directly with consumers instead of wholesalers, while also attracting new wholesalers through the borderless reach of the Internet. Eighty percent of its customers are now individuals, thereby changing the company's positioning. The visibility of the agency and its services has increased manyfold, due to the power of search engines. Colibri ensures that transactions through the Web site are carried out quickly, and follows up by telephone where required. The agency also sees to it that visitors are personally greeted at the airport, countering the impersonal nature of the Internet. Prices are never put up on the site, which avoids competition from hotels providing last-minute discounts, and also circumvents having to explain differences between rates offered to wholesalers and those offered to individual customers.

The Web site has completely altered the way Colibri Tours does business, with facilities such as the Web-based travel reservation form increasing productivity by 30 percent. Cost savings have been achieved to the tune of $40,000 per year due to lower-cost transactions. Very significantly, while 80 percent of business was earlier generated by promotions through wholesalers' trade fairs, the same percentage of business is now generated online.

Questions

1. Using the organizational dimensions of information framework presented in Figure 1.4, describe the different dimensions that the Colibri Tours Web site enables.

2. Colibri now uses the information collected on the Web site to personalize its interaction with clients arriving at the airport. While this can add value to service, list at least three ethical and privacy issues that such a usage of personal data raises.

3. Could Colibri Tours establish a partnership with other organizations and buy additional personal information to tailor its service to clients? How do you feel about this?

4. Figure 1.8 lists the roles and goals of information technology in organizations. What are the key benefits of using the Web as Colibri does to interact with clients? For example, how can the Web increase employee productivity? How can it enhance decision making? How can it help in transforming organizations?

5. Overall, what is your view of today's information age? Are we better off because we have access to a wealth of information, including personal information? Should organizations such as Colibri exploit their information for all it's worth? Should they consider your feelings?

Key Terms and Concepts

application service provider, 29
application software, 20
artificial intelligence (AI), 25
banner ad, 27
business intelligence (BI), 9
central processing unit (CPU), 20
culture, 28
customer-integrated system (CIS), 23
data, 9
decentralized computing, 20
digital economy, 8
electronic commerce, 6
electronic data interchange
    (EDI), 26
ethics, 16
executive information system
    (EIS), 24
external information, 13
global economy, 8
group document database, 25
groupware, 25
hacker, 18
hardware, 18

identity theft, 30
information, 9
information age, 4
information granularity, 13
information technology (IT), 18
information-literate knowledge
    worker, 15
input device, 18
internal information, 13
interorganizational system
    (IOS), 26
intranet, 11
knowledge worker, 4
management information systems
    (MIS), 4
m-commerce, 7
neural network, 25
objective information, 13
online analytical processing
    (OLAP), 24
online transaction processing
    (OLTP), 23
operating system software, 20

operational management, 12
output device, 18
RAM (random access memory), 20
shared information, 21
software, 18
spyware (or sneakware;
    stealthware), 30
storage device, 20
strategic management, 12
subjective information, 13
system software, 20
tactical management, 12
technology-literate knowledge
    worker, 14
telecommunications device, 20
telecommuting, 6
transaction processing system
    (TPS), 23
transnational firm, 8
utility software, 20
virtual workplace, 6
workgroup support system
    (WSS), 25

Short-Answer Questions

1. How does a knowledge worker differ from other types of workers?

2. What is management information systems (MIS)?

3. What is electronic commerce?

4. How are telecommuting and the virtual work-place related?

5. How is today's economy wants-based?

6. What will follow the information age?

7. What is the relationship between data and information?

8. What are the personal dimensions of information?

9. What are the three levels of management in an organization?

10. What is information granularity? How does it differ according to the levels of an organization?

11. What is the difference between internal and external information?

12. What are the two basic categories of information technology (IT)?

13. What are the six categories of information technology (IT) hardware?

14. How are decentralized computing and shared information related to each other?

15. What are the six roles and goals of information technology?

Assignments and Exercises

1. **SURVEYING THE GLOBAL ECONOMY.** Visit a local store in your area that sells clothing and perform a small survey. Pick up ten different pieces of clothing (shoes, shirts, pants, belts, etc.) and note the country in which they were made. Do your results support or contradict our assertion that we now live in a global economy? Why?

2. **FINDING TRUST IN TRUSTE.** TRUSTe (www.truste.org) is an organization on the Web that has created specific guidelines for the use of your private information by Web sites to whom you offer it. If a site adheres to all of TRUSTe's guidelines, that site can then display the TRUSTe logo. That way you know you're private information is protected. TRUSTe has four main guidelines or principles that Web sites displaying its logo must follow. Connect to TRUSTe. What are the four guidelines? Are any or all of these guidelines important to you as an individual? If so, which one or ones and why? Should the government require that all Web sites follow these guidelines or a similar set? Why or why not?

3. **REPORTING ON INTERNET STATISTICS BY BUSINESS SECTOR.** NUA (www.nua.ie) claims to be the world's leading resource for Internet statistics and trends. Connect to NUA and choose one of the business sectors located along the left side of the page. Pick a specific article discussing that particular business sector and prepare a short report for class. Which business sector did you choose? What was the focus of the article you chose? Did some of the statistics surprise you? Considering that you might be interested in working in a business sector on which NUA tracks Internet statistics, would you find NUA's site useful in preparing to go into that business sector? Why or why not?

4. **LEARNING ABOUT AN MIS MAJOR.** Using your school's catalogue of majors and courses (or the catalogue of another school), briefly outline what classes you would have to take to major in management information systems (MIS). Do any of the courses mention specific technology tools such as Java or Oracle? If so, which technology tools are listed? Now, do some searching on the Internet for salaries in the MIS field. What did you find? Does this particular major appeal to you? Why or why not?

5. **REVIEWING THE 100 BEST COMPANIES TO WORK FOR.** Every year *Fortune* magazine devotes an issue to the top 100 best companies to work for. Find the most recent issue of *Fortune* that does this. First, develop a

numerical summary that describes the 100 companies in terms of their respective industries. Which industries are dominant? Pick one of them (preferably one for which you would like to work) and choose a specific highlighted company. Prepare a short class presentation on why that company is among the 100 best to work for.

6. **REDEFINING BUSINESS OPERATIONS THROUGH IT INNOVATION.** Many businesses are building customer-integrated systems (CISs) as a way of redefining their operations through the use of information technology. We discussed several in this chapter, with the most notable and obvious example probably being that of banks offering ATMs. Identify how each of the eight types of businesses below are using technology to offer customer-integrated systems. As you describe a CIS for each type, be sure to include what advantages you receive as a customer. Also, describe how you would have to interface with each type of business if it did not offer a CIS.

- Airlines
- Grocery stores
- Phone companies
- Hotels
- Fuel stations
- Utility companies
- Cable TV providers
- Universities and colleges

Discussion Questions

1. Knowledge workers dominate today's business environment. However, many industries still need workers who do not fall into the category of knowledge workers. What industries still need skilled workers? Can you see a time when these jobs will be replaced by knowledge workers? Can you envision circumstances that would actually cause our economy to do an "about face" and begin needing more skilled workers than knowledge workers?

2. Consider today's economic environment—we have characterized it as the e.conomy, the "now" economy, the global economy, and the arriving digital economy. For each of these characterizations, identify why it's an effect causing the remaining three. That is, how is the "e" causing the "now," global, and arriving digital economies; how is the "now" economy causing the "e," global, and arriving digital economies; etc.?

3. The three key resources in management information systems (MIS) are information, information technology, and people. Which of these three resources is the most important? Why? The least important? Why?

4. Telecommuting, like all things, has a good and a bad side. What are some of the disadvantages or pitfalls of telecommuting? How can these be avoided?

5. As an information-literate knowledge worker for a local distributor of imported foods and spices, you've been asked to prepare a customer mailing list that will be sold to international cuisine restaurants in your area. If you do so, will you be acting ethically? If you don't consider the proposal ethical, what if your boss threatens to fire you if you don't prepare the list? Do you believe you would have any legal recourse if you didn't prepare the list and were subsequently fired?

6. How is your school helping you prepare to take advantage of information technology? What courses have you taken that included teaching you how to use technology? What software packages were taught? To best prepare to enter the job market, how can you determine what software you need to learn?

7. Consider the ATM system now in place worldwide. How does it address your personal dimensions of time, location, and form? Besides just tracking what transactions you've completed using an ATM, what other information might your bank want to know and use concerning your use of the system?

8. Information granularity changes according to the level of an organization. Consider your school, the classes it offers, and the number of students who register in those classes. What sort of information exhibiting coarse granularity would people at the highest levels of your school want to know? What sort of information exhibiting fine granularity would people at the lower levels of your school want to know? As a consumer (student), do you need fine or coarse information? Or perhaps both?

9. In addition to using neural networks to monitor credit card fraud, the same companies also use neural networks to determine whether you are a credit risk. By feeding in thousands of credit card applications, the neural network develops a pattern of who is and isn't creditworthy. Basically, the neural network compares your credit application to past ones and makes a recommendation. How do you feel about that? Should you be given or denied a credit card on the basis of what others have done (or failed to do)? Why or why not?

10. Many schools use groupware to offer distance learning classes. Instead of going to class, you communicate with your instructors and classmates via technology. Would you like to take distance learning classes? What are the advantages? Can you learn as much without going to class and personally interacting with your instructor and classmates? What might be some of the disadvantages of distance learning? Is there a happy medium? How about going to school for only one class session per week and then attending the other virtually via technology? Good or bad idea?

11. We often say that hardware is the *physical* interface with a technology system while software is the *intellectual* interface. How is your hardware your physical interface with your computer? How is your software your intellectual interface with your computer? Do you see technology progressing to the point where we may no longer distinguish between hardware and software and thus no longer perceive differing physical and intellectual interfaces?

Electronic Commerce

Using the Internet as a Tool to Find a Job

Electronic commerce is a great new business horizon. And it's not "just around the corner" any more. Electronic commerce is already here and businesses all over the world are taking advantage of it. Today, information technology can help you land a job. You can use your knowledge of IT and IT itself to help you find potential employers, place your résumé in their hands, locate summer internships, and learn the art of selling yourself during the interview and negotiation process. How? By simply cruising the Internet and using online job database and service providers as well as accessing information about how to prepare for an interview (among other things).

Are you taking advantage of the Internet to find a job? If you're not, we'd like to help you by introducing you to just a few of the thousands of Web sites that can help you find a job. In this section, we've included a number of Web sites related to finding a job through the Internet. On the Web site that supports this text (www.mcgrawhill.ca/college/haag), select "Electronic Commerce Projects." Here, we've provided direct links to all these Web sites as well as many, many more. These are a great starting point for completing this Real HOT section. We would also encourage you to search the Internet for others.

Electronic Commerce Links

JOB DATABASES

There are—quite literally—thousands of sites that provide you with databases of job postings. Some are better than others. Some focus on specific industries; others offer postings only for executive managers. For the best review of job Web sites, connect to two different places. The first is the 100 Top Network (www.100.com, choose "Career"). The second is the Career Resource Homepage at www.careerresource.net. This site provides the most comprehensive list of the available job Web sites such as Monster.ca. There, you'll find a list of over 1000 job Web sites.

Think for a moment about the job you want. What would be its title? In which industry do you want to work? In what part of the country do you want to live? What special skills do you possess? (For example, if you're looking for an accounting job, you may be specializing in auditing.) Is there a specific organization for which you would like to work?

Connect to a couple of different databases, search for your job, and answer the following questions for each database.

A. What is the date of last update?

B. Are career opportunities abroad listed as a separate category or are they integrated with domestic jobs?

C. Can you search for a specific organization?

D. Can you search by geographic location? If so, how? By province? By city? By postal code?

E. Does the site provide direct links to e-mail addresses for those organizations posting jobs?

F. Can you apply for a position online? If so, how do you send your résumé?

G. Can you search by a specific industry?

CREATING AND POSTING AN ELECTRONIC RÉSUMÉ

**Skills Module 4
E-Portfolio**

Most, if not all, job databases focus on two groups—employers and employees. As a potential employee, you search to find jobs that meet your qualifications and desires. Likewise, employers search job databases that contain résumés so they can find people (like you) who meet their qualifications and desires. In this instance, you need to build an electronic résumé (an *e-résumé* or *e-portfolio*, which we discuss in Skills Module 4 on the CD-ROM accompanying this text) and leave it at the various job database sites as you perform your searches. That way, organizations performing searches can find you.

Almost all the job database sites we've listed give you the ability to create and post an electronic résumé. Visit two new job database sites (different from those you visited to find a job). In each, go through the process of creating an e-résumé, posting it, and making some sort of modification to it. As you do, answer the following questions for each of the sites.

A. Do you have to register as a user to build an e-résumé?

B. Once a potential employer performs a search that matches your e-résumé, how can that employer contact you?

C. What valuable tips for building a good e-résumé are available?

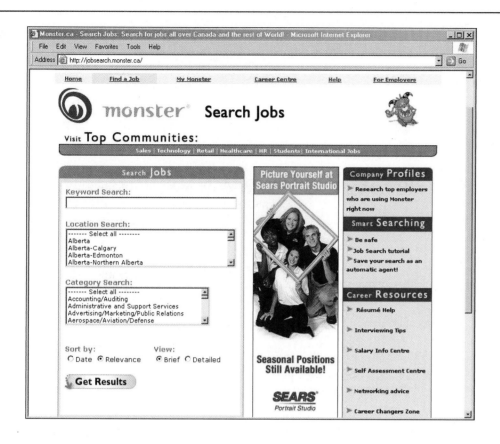

D. Once you build your e-résumé, can you use it to perform a job search?

E. When you modify your e-résumé, can you update your existing e-résumé or must you delete the old one and create a new one?

F. How many key terms concerning your qualifications can you include in your e-résumé?

G. For what time frame does your e-résumé stay active?

SEARCHING NEWSPAPERS THE NEW-FASHIONED WAY

One of today's most popular ways to find a job is to search the classified sections of newspapers. Every Sunday (if your library is open) and Monday you can visit your local library and find a gathering of people searching through the classified sections of the *National Post*, *Globe and Mail*, and *Halifax Chronicle Herald* in hopes of finding a job. Most of these people are attempting to find a job in a specific geographic location. For example, a person looking in the *Halifax Chronicle Herald* is probably most interested in finding a job in Nova Scotia or the Maritimes.

And as you might well guess, newspapers are not to be left off the Internet bandwagon. Today you can find hundreds of online editions of daily newspapers. And the majority of these provide their classified sections in some sort of searchable electronic format. Pick several newspapers, perform an online search for a job that interests you at each newspaper, and answer the following questions.

A. Can you search by location/city?

B. Can you search back issues or only the most recent issue?

C. Does the newspaper provide direct links to Web sites or provide some other profile information for those organizations posting jobs?

D. Does the newspaper provide direct links to e-mail addresses for those organizations posting jobs?

E. Is the newspaper affiliated with any of the major job database providers? If so, which one(s)?

LOCATING THAT ALL-IMPORTANT INTERNSHIP

Have you ever noticed that a large number of jobs require experience? That being the case, how does someone gain such experience through a job when experience is required to get the job? As it turns out, that's always been a perplexing dilemma for many students, and one way to solve it is by obtaining an internship. Internships provide you with valuable knowledge about your field, pay you for your work, and offer you that valuable "experience" you need to move up in your career.

On the Online Learning Centre (www.mcgrawhill.ca/college/haag), we've provided you with a number of Web sites that offer internship possibilities. Visit a few of them. Did you find any internships in line with your career? What about pay—did you find both paying and nonpaying internships? How did these internship sites compare to the more traditional job database sites you looked at earlier? Why do you think this is true?

INTERVIEWING AND NEGOTIATING

The Internet is a vast repository of information—more information than you'll ever need in your entire life. During the job search process however, the Internet can offer you very valuable specific information. In the area of interviewing and negotiating, for example, the Internet contains over 5000 sites devoted to interviewing skills, negotiating tips, and the like.

Interviewing and negotiating are just as important as searching for a job. Once you line up that first important interview, you can still not land the job if you're not properly prepared. If you do receive a job offer, you may be surprised to know that you can negotiate such things as moving expenses, signing bonuses, and allowances for technology in your home.

We've provided Web sites for you that address the interviewing and negotiating skills you need in today's marketplace. Review some of these sites (and any others that you may find). Then, develop a list of dos and don'ts for the interview and a list of tips to increase your effectiveness during negotiation. Once you've developed these two lists, prepare a short class presentation.

GOING RIGHT TO THE SOURCE—THE ORGANIZATION YOU WANT

Today, many organizations are posting open positions on their own Web sites. Their idea is simple: if you like an organization enough to visit its Web site, you just might want to work there. For example, if you connect to Hbc at www.dealsoutlet.ca and buy clothes online, you might consider working there if the opportunity is right.

Choose several organizations that you'd be interested in working for. For each, connect to its Web site, look for job opportunities, and answer the following questions:

A. Are you able to find job opportunities?

B. How difficult is it to find the job opportunities?

C. Are positions grouped or categorized by type?

D. Is a discussion of career paths included?

E. How do you obtain an application form?

F. Are there international opportunities available? Do the job descriptions include a list of qualifications?

G. Are there direct links to e-mail addresses for further questions?

Go to the Online Learning Centre at www.mcgrawhill.ca/college/haag for quizzes, extra content, a searchable glossary, and more! Click on "Electronic Commerce Projects" for links to hundreds of Web sites.

Go to the text CD-ROM for data files, extra content, and Skills Modules on Microsoft Excel, Microsoft Access, HTML, and e-portfolios.

CHAPTER TWO

STUDENT LEARNING OUTCOMES

BY THE END OF THIS CHAPTER, STUDENTS WILL BE ABLE TO:

1. Describe supply chain management (SCM) systems, their strategic and competitive opportunities, the challenges businesses face in employing them successfully, and available IT support.

2. Understand customer relationship management (CRM) systems, their strategic and competitive opportunities, the challenges businesses face in employing them successfully, and available IT support.

3. Describe business intelligence (BI) systems, their strategic and competitive opportunities, the challenges businesses face in employing them successfully, and available IT support.

4. Explain integrated collaboration environments (ICE), their strategic and competitive opportunities, the challenges businesses face in employing them successfully, and available IT support.

5. Analyze how individual systems that work together in an integrated manner can give airline companies a competitive advantage.

LearningCentre

Using IT for Competitive Advantage

CASE STUDY:
ZARA: FASHION FAST FORWARD

At Zara's flagship apparel store in downtown Madrid, the store manager scans the racks holding the latest fashions. Quickly, she notes which items are selling well and which are not. Currently, leather items—particularly the short skirts—are selling briskly; so are the tailored jeans, the black sequined shirts, and the red and blue gabardine blazers.

Making her bet on which items will be next week's hot sellers, she pulls out her handheld computer and enters an order that is transmitted over the Internet to Zara headquarters in the northwestern Spanish town of La Coruña.

There, Zara's designers and product managers are deciding what to create. Every day they gather suggestions from the flagship store in Madrid and 790 other store managers worldwide. Importantly, however, they don't just want specific orders. They ask for and get ideas for cuts, fabrics, or even a new line.

After evaluating the store managers' input, the team in La Coruña decides what to make. Designers draw up the latest ideas on their computers and send them over Zara's Intranet to one of its nearby factories. Within days, the cutting, dyeing, stitching, and pressing begin. And in just three weeks, the clothes will hang in stores from Barcelona to Berlin to Beirut. Zara isn't just a bit faster than rivals such as The Gap, whose lead time is nine months. It's 12 times faster!

What sets Zara apart from its competitors is a computerized network that ties the stores to the design shops and company-owned factories in real time. The Zara model may be unique, but at its heart is a perfectly simple principle: in fashion, nothing is as important as time to market.

For years, apparel companies have manufactured their garments in lesser-developed countries in pursuit of lower costs. Zara decided against that. The company believed that the ability to respond quickly to shifts in consumer tastes would create far greater efficiencies than outsourcing to low-cost countries could. "The fashion world is in constant flux and is driven not by supply but by customer demand," says one of the company's executives. "We need to give consumers what they want, and if I go to South America or Asia to make clothes, I simply can't move fast enough."

Once the company decided it would have the world's most responsive supply chain, the pieces of its operating model fell logically into place. Zara has a twice-a-week delivery schedule that not only restocks old styles but brings in entirely new designs; rival chains tend to receive new designs only once or twice a season. "It's like you walk into a new store every two weeks," noted one prominent retail industry executive. The advantages of world-beating time to market, according to Zara, more than offset manufacturing costs that run 15 to 20 percent higher than those of its rivals. For example, Zara almost never needs to absorb inventory writeoffs to correct merchandising blunders. And the company maintains steady profit margins of 10 percent—in line with the best in the industry.[1]

Introduction

Recent studies have shown that as competition intensifies in almost every industry, companies must develop innovative products and business processes to survive and thrive, and that information technology (IT) is a powerful tool to help them do so.[2] In this chapter, we discuss some of the most important IT applications businesses are using today:

- Supply chain management (SCM)
- Customer relationship management (CRM)
- Business intelligence (BI)
- Integrated collaboration environments (ICE)

We also discuss the competitive advantages that businesses can achieve by integrating their IT applications so that they operate in a holistic manner. We begin with supply chain management, an application many companies consider an absolute necessity for the smooth functioning of their daily operations.

Supply Chain Management

Dell Computer's supply chain management system is the envy of the industry. Its direct sell model gives the company a huge advantage over any competitor still using a traditional model of selling through retailers. Traditional PC manufacturers build PCs and ship them to wholesalers, distributors, or directly to retailers. The PCs sit on the retailers' shelves or in a warehouse until you come in and buy one. If you took a look at a typical distribution chain you will see that there are too many PCs in inventory. A **distribution chain** is simply the path followed from the originator of a product or service to the end consumer. Holding on to inventory in a distribution chain costs money, because whoever owns the inventory has to pay for it as well as pay for the operation of the warehouses or stores while waiting for someone to buy it.

Dell's model is different. It sells computers directly from its Web site so there is no inventory in its distribution chain. Dell has enhanced its supply chain as well. It uses i2 supply chain management software to send orders for parts to suppliers every two hours, enabling it to manufacture and deliver exactly what its customers want with little or no inventory in its supply chain.[3]

The differences between Dell's "sell, source, and ship" model and the traditional "buy, hold, and sell" model are illustrated in Figure 2.1.

WHAT ARE SUPPLY CHAIN MANAGEMENT SYSTEMS?

For a company the size of General Motors, with operations all over the world and tens of thousands of suppliers, supply chain management and IT-based supply chain management systems are critical necessities to ensure the smooth flow of parts to GM factories. As we discussed in Chapter 1, **supply chain management (SCM)** tracks inventory and information among business processes and across companies. A **supply chain management (SCM) system** is an IT system that supports supply chain management activities by automating the tracking of inventory and information among business processes and across companies.

Most large manufacturing companies use just-in-time manufacturing processes, which ensure that the right parts are available as products in process move down the assembly line. **Just-in-time (JIT)** is an approach that produces or delivers a product

Figure 2.1

Buy-Hold-Sell Versus Sell-Source-Ship

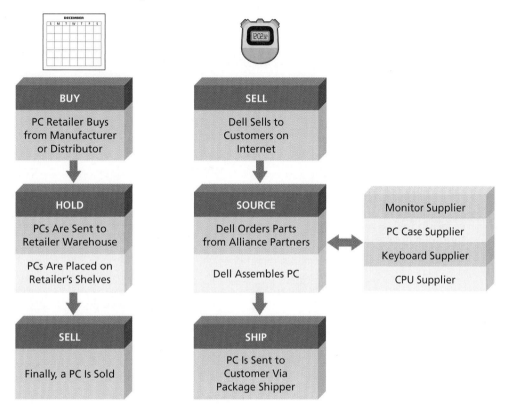

or service just at the time the customer wants it. For retailers, like Target, this means that products customers want to buy are on the shelves when customers walk by. Supply chain management systems also focus on making sure that the *right number* of parts or products are available, not too many and not too few. Too many products on hand means that too much money is tied up in inventory and also increases the risk of obsolescence. Too few products on hand is not a good thing either, because it could force an assembly line to shut down or, in the case of retailers, lose sales because an item is not in stock when a customer is ready to buy.

While modern supply chain management systems focus on assuring that the right amount of inventory is available when needed, they also encompass other essential functions such as selecting suppliers and monitoring their performance. For example, it does GM no good to have the right number of component parts on hand if their quality is so poor that they cause problems on the assembly line. As a consequence, many companies monitor the quality of parts received from their suppliers and, if quality is below expectations, either work with suppliers to improve their quality or put them on notice that they will not get any more of the company's business unless quality improves.

Managing logistics is another important process in modern supply chain management systems. **Logistics** is the set of processes that plans for and controls the efficient and effective transportation and storage of supplies from suppliers to customers. Many companies now have suppliers located in all parts of the globe. Coordinating logistics to be sure that parts reach their intended destination at the lowest cost is a critical and complicated part of supply chain management systems. A sample supply chain management system is illustrated in Figure 2.2.

Figure 2.2
A Sample Supply Chain Management (SCM) System Infrastructure

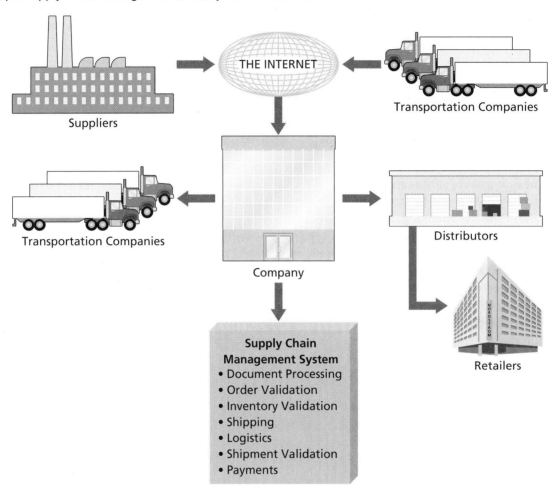

STRATEGIC AND COMPETITIVE OPPORTUNITIES WITH SUPPLY CHAIN MANAGEMENT

A well-designed supply chain management system chain helps a business by optimizing the following processes:

- *Fulfillment.* Ensuring the right quantity of parts for production or products for sale arrive at the right time
- *Logistics.* Keeping the cost of transporting materials as low as possible consistent with safe and reliable delivery
- *Production.* Ensuring production lines function smoothly because high-quality parts are available when needed
- *Revenue and profit.* Ensuring no sales are lost because shelves are empty
- *Spend.* Keeping the cost of purchased parts and products at acceptable levels

Cooperation among supply chain partners for mutual success is another hallmark of modern supply chain management systems. For example, many manufacturing companies share product concepts with suppliers early in the product development process. This lets suppliers contribute their ideas on how to make high-quality parts at a lower cost.

PERDUE TALKS TURKEY

Most folks have all they can handle on Thanksgiving Day to serve up one turkey for their family feast. The managers and employees of Perdue Farms have to move more than 1 million turkeys across the United States at Thanksgiving-time.

This task is a whole lot more manageable since Perdue invested some $20 million in a Manugistics (www.manugistics.com) supply chain management system. Using the SCM system's forecasting software and supply chain planning applications, Perdue finds it much easier to deliver the right number of turkeys to the right stores at just the right time. According to Don Taylor, Perdue's CIO, "As we get to November, we have live information at our fingertips."

Because getting turkeys from the farm to your local supermarket is a race against time, Perdue uses its SCM logistics module to be sure the turkeys arrive in fresh condition. Each of Perdue's trucks is equipped with a global positioning system that enables Perdue's dispatchers to know each truck's location at all times. If a truck has mechanical trouble en route, another truck is dispatched to rescue the turkeys and speed them on their way. Perdue uses a variety of technologies to keep in touch with customers, including telephone, e-mail, and videoconferencing. Some retailers have computer systems that communicate with Perdue's systems, allowing Perdue to track sales of its turkeys with real-time information obtained from in-store checkout scanners. "We're always looking for new technologies as they come along to see what makes sense for us," says CIO Taylor. When Thanksgiving rolls around, Taylor will give thanks for his SCM system for making his job a bit easier and for getting turkeys fresh to his retail customers' tables.[4]

In the retail industry, several companies recently completed a successful pilot study to demonstrate the practical feasibility of a process innovation called collaborative planning, forecasting, and replenishment.[5] **Collaborative planning, forecasting, and replenishment (CPFR)** is a concept that encourages and facilitates collaborative processes between supply chain partners. One of the techniques used in CPFR is to have retailers share sales information they obtain from store checkout scanners with manufacturers on a daily basis. This gives manufacturers more current and accurate information with which to schedule production. Excess inventory is eliminated from manufacturers' warehouses, distribution centres, and retail store shelves. Stockouts are reduced, as are total costs in the supply chain. The winners are the companies in the supply chain who use CPFR (their sales are higher) and the customers who shop at the retail outlets (the prices they pay are lower because of the cost savings produced by CPFR).

CHALLENGES TO SUCCESS WITH SUPPLY CHAIN MANAGEMENT

To be successful with supply chain management, you can learn from the experiences of companies who have achieved business benefits with SCM. A recent survey noted the following four key issues:

1. High-level executives must recognize the importance of supply chain management to the company's success.
2. You must work closely with your company's customers and suppliers to build world-class business processes.
3. Your supply chain management should be innovative in the way it integrates with internal IT systems as well as with the IT systems of key customers and suppliers.

EVEN NATIONS CAN GAIN A COMPETITIVE ADVANTAGE WITH IT

Using IT for competitive advantage is not restricted to companies. Singapore is a well-known example that a nation can use IT for competitive advantage as well.

As a small island nation with few natural resources, Singapore concluded some time ago that its most valuable resource was its people. The government decided that the wave of the future was IT, and that it should invest in training a cadre of IT workers and focus on becoming what they called the "Intelligent Island." Singapore subsequently became renowned for the way it used IT to speed up the flow of goods through its port facilities by replacing cumbersome paperwork processes with e-commerce techniques.

On its Web site, the Singapore Economic Development Board (SEDB) invites companies to "Plug into one of the best business environments in the world. Big or small, new or established, this is where you can inno-

vate and create, grow and globalize. Be part of the Singapore success story!"

As evidence of its continuing efforts, the SEDB recently recognized 17 Singapore-based companies for their success in harnessing Internet technologies for their supply chain management systems by presenting them with the eSupply Chain Management (eSCM) Certificate. Each company met the standards set by the eSCM Assessment Program sponsored by the Singapore Manufacturers Federation with the support of several government agencies. The goal of the eSCM program is to improve the SCM capabilities of Singapore companies by benchmarking their performance against world-class practices, and thereby help to ensure that Singapore maintains its position as a leader in the use of information technology for competitive advantage.[6]

4. You must continuously adapt your supply chain management strategies and systems as market needs change.[7]

Problems with supply chain management often arise because individual areas *within* a company do not communicate effectively with each other. One well-known example of this is the case of Volvo, which in one year made too many green cars and was not able to sell them. So, when the inventory of green cars started to build up, the sales and marketing staff at headquarters offered incentives to dealers in the form of price reductions. When the supply chain managers saw the resultant rise in the sale of green cars, they doubled their production of green cars. As a result, Volvo dealers again had more green cars on their hands than they knew what to do with until someone figured out that poor communication between sales and production was causing the problem.[8]

IT SUPPORT FOR SUPPLY CHAIN MANAGEMENT

The solution for a successful supply chain management system includes either purchasing sophisticated software with Web interfaces or hiring a third-party Web-based application service provider who promises to provide part or all of the SCM service. An **application service provider (ASP)** supplies software applications (and often related services such as maintenance, technical support, and the like) over the Internet that would otherwise reside on its customers' in-house computers (see Figure 2.3). Knowledge workers query the SCM software for information or to order inventory. The SCM software connects to potential suppliers, distributors, and transporting companies to determine where to purchase the inventory and the best way to have the inventory delivered. The SCM system also performs such functions as order validation, message validation to potential suppliers and distributors, inventory routing and validation, and electronic payments. While the SCM software market was pioneered

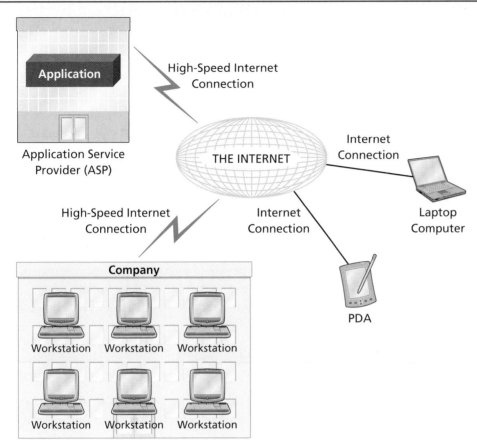

Figure 2.3

A Sample Application
Service Provider (ASP)
Infrastructure

by specialist companies such as i2 and Manugistics, it is now dominated by enterprise software providers SAP, Oracle, and PeopleSoft.[9]

Customer Relationship Management

Wells Fargo Bank's customer relationship management system tracks and analyzes every transaction made by its 10 million retail customers at its branches and ATMs, and through its Web-based online banking systems. It has become so good at predicting customer behaviour that it knows what customers need before many of them even realize they need it. Wells Fargo's system collects every customer transaction and combines it with personal information provided by the customer. The system is able to predict tailored offerings that will appeal to individual customers (a money-saving second mortgage, for example), at just the right time. As a result, Wells Fargo sells four additional banking products or services to its customers in contrast to an industry average of 2.2.[10]

Another example is the American Cancer Society, which depends on donations from the public to carry out its educational and service programs. It recently installed a Siebel eBusiness CRM application (www.siebel.com/ca) to better target members of its donor base to include planned giving. Terry Music, National Vice-President for Information Delivery, notes, "Our donor base contains many individuals who, through their wills or other financial instruments, are able to make substantial gifts to our cancer fighting efforts. With our CRM system, we are able to target them as a contained group within our fundraising efforts."[11]

LOOKING FOR OPPORTUNITIES CLOSE TO HOME

You don't have to be a part of a traditional for-profit organization to get into the habit of looking for ways to improve how customers are treated. Not-for-profits and governmental agencies can serve people better and also gain benefits for themselves from the way they use IT. For example, see if you can come up with ways that one of the local governmental bodies in your region, such as a city, county, or state, could get a competitive advantage from the way it uses IT to serve you as a citizen. Take the customer's perspective (yours). For example, how complicated is it to get your driver's license renewed? How difficult is it to get information on various governmental services? Can you pay a traffic ticket online with your credit card or do you have to mail in a cheque? If you feel a traffic ticket was issued unfairly, are you able to dispute it online or do you have to go to some office downtown and stand in line?

Once you have evaluated a local Web site, go to unpan1.un.org/intradoc/groups/public/documents/aspa/unpan013018.pdf. This site picked the best city Web sites in the world as of mid-2003. How does your local site compare with some of the sites on the list? What suggestions can you come up with to improve the customer service your local site provides to the citizenry?

WHAT ARE CUSTOMER RELATIONSHIP MANAGEMENT SYSTEMS?

What do you think is the primary driver for your organization? If you said the *customers*—congratulations, you are correct. Without customers, a business couldn't exist; and so, many businesses' primary goal is to increase customer satisfaction.

Acquiring and retaining customers are the basic objectives of any organization and, as a result, customer relationship management systems has become one of the hottest IT systems in business today. A **customer relationship management (CRM) system** uses information about customers to gain insights into their needs, wants, and behaviours in order to serve them better. Customers interact with companies in many ways, and each interaction should be easy, enjoyable, and error-free. Have you ever had an experience with a company that made you so angry you changed companies or returned the product? It's not uncommon for a customer to change companies after having a negative experience. The goal of CRM is to limit such negative interactions and provide customers with positive experiences.

CRM systems typically include such functions as:

- Sales force automation
- Customer service and support
- Marketing campaign management and analysis

It's important to note that CRM is not just software. It is a total business objective which encompasses many different aspects of a business including software, hardware, services, support, and strategic business goals. The CRM system you adopt should support all these functions and should also be designed to provide the organization with detailed customer information. In many cases, companies begin with a sales force automation application and then progress to the other two functions. **Sales force automation (SFA) systems** automatically track all the steps in the sales process. The sales process contains many steps including contact management, sales lead tracking, sales forecasting and order management, and product knowledge.

Some basic SFA systems perform sales lead tracking or listing potential customers for the sales team to contact. They also perform contact management, which tracks all

Figure 2.4

General Motors' Purchase Funnel[12]

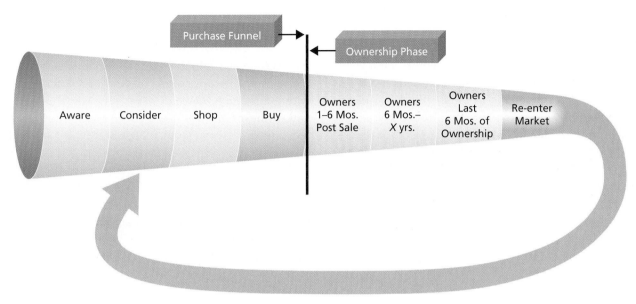

the times a salesperson contacts a potential customer, what they discussed, and the next steps. More sophisticated SFA systems perform detailed analysis of the market and customers and can even offer product configuration tools enabling customers to configure their own products (see Figure 2.4).

STRATEGIC AND COMPETITIVE OPPORTUNITIES WITH CUSTOMER RELATIONSHIP MANAGEMENT

One of the results of CRM is competitive advantage through achieving superior performance in CRM functions, in particular:

- Devising more effective marketing campaigns based on more precise knowledge of customer needs and wants
- Assuring that the sales process is efficiently managed
- Providing superior after-sale service and support through, for example, well-run call centres

Successful CRM systems provide a competitive advantage for your organization versus your competitors. All of the classic goals of CRM—treating customers better, understanding their needs and wants, tailoring offerings in response—are likely to result in the buyer choosing your product or service instead of the competition's. However, attempting to predict the amount or degree to which the CRM-enabled organization will gain market share can be a difficult task. Certainly, it is something that can be measured after-the-fact, thus allowing your organization to understand the true results of better CRM on customers' buying decisions. But predicting the degree of gain in market share and then forecasting a net result in terms of incremental revenues is difficult. One way to measure the benefits of CRM systems, according to one expert, is to place the benefits into two principal categories, revenue enhancers and cost cutters.[13] Examples of revenue enhancers and cost cutters are shown in Figure 2.5.

HOW CONTINENTAL AIRLINES CREATES HIGHLY LOYAL CUSTOMERS

According to Gordon Bethune, Chairman and CEO of Continental Airlines, the airline industry is getting so impersonal it's becoming like mass transit. Continental's strategy to differentiate itself from other airlines is to reestablish the concept that "if you pay more, you get more." Continental uses technology to identify its best customers, those who generate 10 percent of the company's revenue. Continental's CRM software identifies them as CO, which stands for "costars." The software tracks each touch point with the company and enables employees to recognize the costars by name. Costars receive extra attention even though they may be sitting in the coach section on a particular flight. The software even provides flight attendants with information on which beverage a costar prefers, and all beverages are free. Continental employees put a special tag on costars' bags and their bags are unloaded first.

Even so, Bethune recognizes that Continental's first obligation is to have its planes leave and arrive on time and get all its customers to their destinations safely. CRM can't do this for the company. What CRM does, however, is assure that the company's costars are given the special attention they have earned.[14]

CHALLENGES TO SUCCESS WITH CUSTOMER RELATIONSHIP MANAGEMENT

While many CRM systems provide substantial business benefits, other CRM projects are considered less than successful. As a matter of fact, a recent Gartner Group study found that 40 percent of companies surveyed hadn't made an investment in CRM—and that more than 50 percent of those that had saw the installations as failures.[15] Despite the fact that so many CRM software installations fail, and that some companies haven't even given them a try, a company that does its homework beforehand can look forward to a successful installation.

One analyst listed some of the most common reasons why CRM installations are less than successful:

- *The company's goals are too broad.* Too often a CRM initiative tries to encompass everything that should be done to attain the vision of a customer-centric com-

Figure 2.5

Example Revenue Enhancers and Cost Cutters

Revenue Enhancers	Cost Cutters
• Increase sales effectiveness	• Decrease cost of sales
• Add new customers at a higher rate	• More time to sell, less time on administration
• Offer new products/services	• Decrease cost of service
• Provide a better customer experience	• Cost per service interaction
• Increase revenue per customer	• Transition to more self-service
• Sell more of current products/services	
• Improve customer retention	

pany. While there is nothing wrong with having this vision, companies need to realize that the vision is more easily achieved with a series of small, tactical steps rather than with one giant leap forward.

- *Strategies are too generic.* CRM strategies must be business-specific. The CRM industry—analysts and consultants as well as vendors—have been saying that every company can use technology the same way to gain the same results. The truth is that each company needs a solution tailored to its unique requirements.
- *Implementations are often too software-centric.* Technology can and should play a role in enhancing customer relationships—but a supporting role, not a leading one. Software should support the specific CRM processes each company needs to get real business benefits.[16]

One widely held view is that CRM is the most important step your firm will take, because it is all about the most important asset your company has: the customer. True enough. It is important to remember, however, that CRM is not only a technology, but also a set of processes and people and skills. There must be a fit. This is true with any IT application, of course.

IT SUPPORT FOR CUSTOMER RELATIONSHIP MANAGEMENT

Figure 2.6 illustrates a sample CRM infrastructure. The **front office systems** are the primary interface to customers and sales channels; they send all the customer information they collect to the database. The **back office systems** are used to fulfill and support customer orders and they also send all their customer information to the database. The CRM system analyzes and distributes the customer information and provides the organization with a complete view of each customer's experience with the

Figure 2.6

A Sample Customer Relationship Management (CRM) System Infrastructure

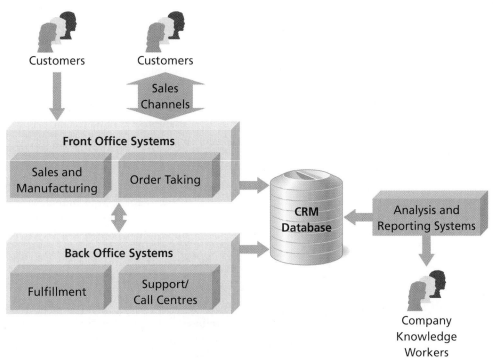

business. Many systems available today offer CRM functionality. Some of the big providers of these packages are Clarify, Oracle, SAP, and Siebel Systems. Clarify and Siebel are also some of the most prominent SFA software providers; others are Salesforce.com and Vantive. Salesforce.com was the first company to offer CRM using an ASP model and others have since followed suit.

Business Intelligence

FiberMark North America, a manufacturer of specialty packaging and paper, could not easily retrieve business intelligence from its expensive transaction processing systems. "We were desperate to get good information quickly," said Joel Taylor, Director of IS. Taylor spent less than $75,000 on QlikView — BI software from QlikTech (www.qliktech.com), which grabs FiberMark's information from its transaction processing systems and stores it in a readily accessible database.

Now, instead of printing 1000-page monthly sales reports for each of FiberMark's 29 salespeople, the salespeople can access business intelligence from the corporate intranet. "With a very short training cycle [15 minutes], they're up and flying," says Taylor. "They print four pages, not 1000." He stated the system paid for itself in nine months in saved paper and related costs alone. More important, though, salespeople and executives can get the specific, up-to-date business intelligence they want whenever they want it.[17]

WHAT ARE BUSINESS INTELLIGENCE SYSTEMS?

As was mentioned in Chapter 1, **business intelligence (BI)** is knowledge about your customers, competitors, business partners, and competitive environment, and about your internal operations—knowledge that gives you the ability to make effective, important, and often strategic business decisions. **Business intelligence (BI) systems** are the IT applications and tools that support the business intelligence function within an organization. The objective of BI is to improve the timeliness and quality of the input for decision making by helping knowledge workers to understand:

- The capabilities available in the firm
- The state of the art, trends, and future directions in the markets
- The technological, demographic, economic, political, social, and regulatory environments in which the firm competes
- The actions of competitors and the implications of these actions[18]

As illustrated in Figure 2.7, business intelligence encompasses both internal and external information. Some business people treat competitive intelligence as a specialized branch of business intelligence. **Competitive intelligence (CI)** is business intelligence focused on the external competitive environment. There is even an organization for people who specialize in competitive intelligence called the Society for Competitive Intelligence Professionals (SCIP). Visit its Web site at www.scip.org to find out more about its activities, programs, and publications.

Business intelligence has information as its foundation. Most often, it is information collected from various sources within

Figure 2.7

Building Business Intelligence

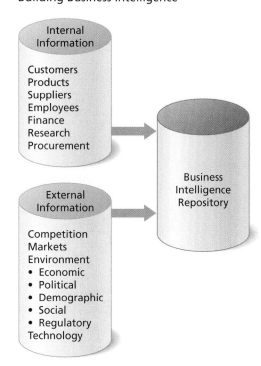

IBM AND FACTIVA JOIN FORCES TO TRANSFORM GLOBAL CONTENT BUSINESS

IBM and Factiva, a Dow Jones and Reuters Company, recently agreed to codevelop text analytics solutions built on the IBM WebFountain platform.

IBM's WebFountain is a mining and discovery tool that extracts trends, patterns, and relationships from massive amounts of information stored on proprietary databases, Internet pages, and newsgroups. Factiva's first application on WebFountain will offer an independent, external view of a company's reputation by analyzing information from a comprehensive collection of information sources. The resulting analysis will provide a view on relevant business issues, show new industry trends, and disclose relationships. Using this information, executives can gain new insights into the way that outsiders perceive their company or brand, see how perceptions change over time, and identify emerging issues associated with their company or brand. As Factiva subscribers, they will also be able to access the underlying sources from which the analysis was derived.

"It's the information that organizations don't know—outside their four walls and beyond the typical market research and outdated surveys—that can be the most critical for decision making, but until now, there was no single tool that could derive real intelligence from billions of pages," said Robert Carlson, IBM WebFountain Vice-President. "With WebFountain, customers can use the Internet's immense amount of data as a business tool, and Factiva's authoritative sources and classification expertise make the results even more powerful."

The IBM-Factiva partnership will allow executives tasked with enhancing a brand's image to gain insight, manage risk, and, perhaps most importantly, identify new business opportunities more quickly and cost-effectively than ever. "This is the next logical step toward giving people intelligence that they can act upon," said Clare Hart, President and CEO of Factiva. "Companies that can assimilate vast amounts of information and quickly determine market opportunities will emerge as leaders in today's extremely competitive environment. We expect this type of service to become a key business asset and a must-have for the most ambitious enterprises."[19]

an organization and from external sources as well. For example, as described in Chapter 1, information is collected from transaction processing systems and stored in various databases. A company may have databases for different applications, including separate databases for customers, products, suppliers, and employees, among many others. Such databases are necessary to support the processing of day-to-day transactions. On the other hand, they contain more detailed information than is needed to support most decisions that managers need to make.

To deal with this, most organizations summarize information from their various databases into a summarized data repository called a data warehouse. A **data warehouse** is a logical collection of information—gathered from many different operational databases—used to create business intelligence that supports business analysis activities and decision-making tasks. Often, a data warehouse is subdivided into smaller repositories called data marts for use by a single department within an organization. A **data mart** is a subset of a data warehouse in which only a focused portion of the data warehouse information is kept. For example, if an organization has a separate group that focuses on competitive intelligence, it may find it more effective to use its own data mart rather than the organization's data warehouse. Data warehouses and data marts are covered in Chapter 3.

Some of the tools used to derive business intelligence from data warehouses and data marts include the OLAP tools discussed in Chapter 1. They are discussed more thoroughly in Chapters 4 and 6. Other technical components of business intelligence include such tools as:

- Data mining
- Automated exception detection with proactive alerting and automatic recipient determination
- Automatic learning[20]

A **data mining tool** is a software tool you use to query information in a data warehouse. We discuss data mining tools in Chapters 4 and 6. Automated anomaly and exception detection is software that detects an unusual or unexpected condition, and proactively alerts the right person(s) that it has occurred. Some BI systems use artificial intelligence techniques to automatically learn and thus anticipate the kinds of business intelligence knowledge workers want and need. Artificial intelligence is discussed in detail in Chapter 6.

STRATEGIC AND COMPETITIVE OPPORTUNITIES WITH BUSINESS INTELLIGENCE

Business managers face many kinds of decisions ranging from routine decisions (such as whether to order additional stock) to decisions with long-range strategic implications (such as whether to expand into international markets). A survey by the Gartner Group of the strategic uses of business intelligence found that such uses were ranked by firms in the following order of importance:

1. Corporate performance management
2. Optimizing customer relations, monitoring business activity, and traditional decision support
3. Packaged standalone BI applications for specific operations or strategies
4. Management reporting of business intelligence[21]

Earlier, we mentioned that one of the primary purposes of BI is to improve the timeliness and quality of input to the decision process. Companies with well-designed BI systems available to their managers will find that their managers make better decisions on a variety of business issues. Higher-quality managerial decision making lets companies gain an advantage over their competitors who operate without the benefit of BI systems for their managers to use. BI systems provide managers with actionable information and knowledge:

- at the right time
- in the right location
- in the right form[22]

Despite the fact that the benefits of BI systems are self-evident, you will find that many companies today do not yet have them. One of the reasons for this is that knowledge of their value as a competitive tool is not widely understood by business managers. Another reason is that, in some cases, they have been installed in companies but not used effectively. Some of the challenges in using BI systems are discussed in the next section. (See Figure 2.8 for an illustration of how GM has integrated its various customer-facing systems with BI applications.)

CHALLENGES TO SUCCESS WITH BUSINESS INTELLIGENCE

As we discussed in Chapter 1, IT systems are of no value unless knowledge workers know how to use them effectively. BI systems are a great example of this. To ensure that BI systems have a high impact on business decisions, you must:

Figure 2.8

Aggregating Customer Touch Points at General Motors[23]

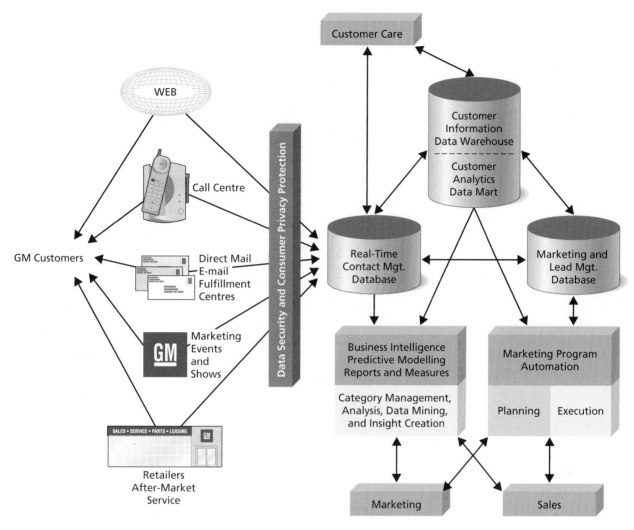

- Focus on using information provided by the BI systems to deal with an important business issue
- Provide the ability to customize BI information to each knowledge worker involved in the decision-making process
- Build discipline and precision into decision-making processes
- Recognize that knowledge workers must understand BI tools and know how to use them effectively
- Understand that many BI systems are complex systems and continually change as information provided them changes[24]

IT SUPPORT FOR BUSINESS INTELLIGENCE

While the World Wide Web is used to support BI systems in many firms, specialized software is at the heart of BI. In the past, a large number of companies built their own systems. Now the trend is toward buying packages. Gartner Research found that the number of firms that plan to manage their BI integration internally dropped from 49 percent in 2001 to 37 percent in 2002.[25] The reason for this change is that the traditional custom-design, build, and integrate model for BI systems takes too long (at least

IS HUGEHATS A GOOD INVESTMENT?

Assume that one of your teammates has a good friend named Brad, who is a born entrepreneur. Starting with lemonade stands when he was 11 and moving on to used golf balls and CDs, Brad always seemed to have a knack for "buying low and selling high." Brad has approached your teammates with an idea for an Internet business called "HugeHats." Brad has a larger-than-average-sized head and finds it hard to find hats that fit him. As a result, he thinks there is a large underserved market for people like him. He wants to start a company to sell large-size baseball and other types of hats over the Internet, but needs $20,000 to get started. He wants your team to borrow from your credit cards, if necessary, to invest in his venture. Brad has not done any formal analysis, but "just knows" this business will make all of you rich and that there is little, if any, competition. Your team tells him you will consider it but only after you gather some competitive intelligence to find out if this is a good idea or not.

Normally you would scan all the trade publications, talk to industry analysts, key participants in the indus-

try, and other retailers. For this exercise, however, you are artificially restricted to obtaining information from electronic sources.

Use the Internet to scan for similar sites, competitor news, and possible industry trends. Prepare a written summary of your findings followed by a recommendation as to whether your team should consider an investment in HugeHats. A good writeup will cover at least the following points:

- An assessment of the competition
- Evidence of your information search (at least six sources)
- A recommendation on whether to invest in HugeHats and, if so, how much
- Other points you believe to be relevant to the decision

Limit your writeup to three pages plus any attachments you wish to add.

---

six months) and costs too much ($2 to $3 million). Implemented quickly, specialized BI software packages can deliver immediate benefits and a quick return on a company's investment.[26]

A large number of firms are involved in aspects of the BI business. For example, several companies identified as companies to watch in the BI field are Aydatum, Brio Software Decisions, Cognos, Crystal Decisions, E-Intelligence, Hyperion, MicroStrategy, ProClarity, Siebel, and Spotfire.[27] One interesting feature of many BI software packages is a **digital dashboard**, which displays key information gathered from several sources on a computer screen in a format tailored to the needs and wants of an individual knowledge worker (see Figure 2.9).

Integrated Collaboration Environments

With 30,000 employees in more than 45 countries, Shell International Exploration and Production (SIEP, www.shell.com) is often presented with logistical challenges, particularly when it comes to sharing and transferring knowledge. The issue is exacerbated by the fact that SIEP is involved in different businesses such as exploration and refinement, and that employees typically migrate between jobs every three to four years.

SIEP used SiteScape's collaboration technology, Forum (www.sitescape.com), to form communities of practice (groups of experts who share information, insights, and advice about a common interest or practice) and to work toward global cooperation. "We hook up people who are working in related disciplines in Shell companies around the world so they can problem-solve and share learning and ideas," said Arjan

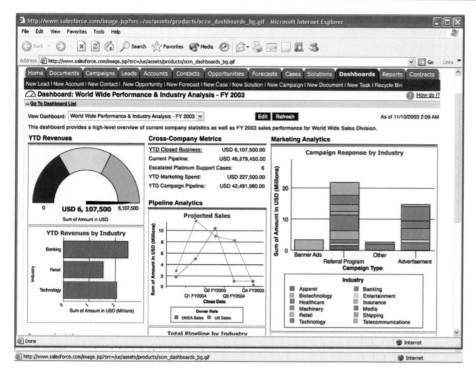

Figure 2.9

Sample Digital Dashboard

Van Unnik at Shell. "The big trick is to go further than connecting people in the same disciplines. We get excellent cross-fertilization of disciplines—for example, pipeline engineers and corrosion engineers sharing information and ideas, thereby coming up with better and more complete solutions—that's how we get great value."

During the five years of using Forum, SIEP created more than 100 such communities of practice, which included a few thousand members. To favour even greater cross-discipline fertilization, SIEP combined the 100 communities into 13 main communities of practice covering the main core oil businesses. Most SIEP employees spend between 30 minutes to two hours per week reading and sharing information, and at any given moment more than 15,000 are using the Forum regularly. The Forum has helped SIEP to:

- Improve communications for all project participants
- Improve project management
- Stimulate progress on different projects
- Provide greater leverage on the knowledge that exists in SIEP

In addition, the communities of practice have enabled people to access help 24/7. SIEP has been able to solve previously intractable problems, and has saved over $300 million a year.[28]

WHAT ARE INTEGRATED COLLABORATION ENVIRONMENTS?

Almost everything you do in your organization will be performed in a team environment. So improving team collaboration greatly increases your organization's productivity and competitive advantage. An **integrated collaboration environment (ICE)** is the environment in which virtual teams do their work. **Virtual teams** are teams whose members are located in varied geographic locations and whose work is supported by specialized ICE software or by more basic collaboration systems. A **collaboration system** is software specifically designed to improve the performance of teams by

Figure 2.10

An Integrated Collaboration Environment

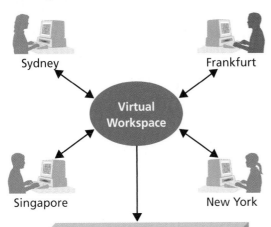

Sydney

Frankfurt

Virtual Workspace

Singapore

New York

ICE Support Technologies

Collaboration Software
Instant Messaging
Presence Awareness
Peer-to-Peer Software
Workflow Systems
Document Management Systems
Teleconferencing
Videoconferencing
Knowledge Management
Social Networking

supporting the sharing and flow of information. Integrated collaboration environments are supported by combinations of collaboration systems and other technologies as illustrated in Figure 2.10.

More and more, virtual teams are composed of people from your company's alliance partners as well. An **alliance partner** is a company your company does business with on a regular basis in a collaborative fashion, usually facilitated by IT systems.

Many companies first use e-mail and then move on to collaboration systems incorporating more advanced features such as giving employees access to each other's calendars, group scheduling, imaging, workflow systems, and document management systems. **Workflow** defines all of the steps or business rules, from beginning to end, required for a business process. For example, in order for a bank to process a loan application correctly, there are a specified series of business processes that must be performed by different knowledge workers. **Workflow systems** facilitate the automation and management of business processes. For example, all of the steps to process that loan application could be performed by a workflow system with the necessary documents updated and passed from knowledge worker to knowledge worker as electronic documents. Large companies produce millions of documents each month and they need to be organized and managed. A **document management system** manages a document through all the stages of its processing. It is similar to a workflow system except that the focus is more on document storage and retrieval. Banks, for example, retain copies of your cheques in electronic form and can produce a copy for you should you ever need one.

Companies will soon migrate to more sophisticated collaboration systems that utilize tele-, video-, and Web-conferencing in real time and that incorporate project management and workflow automation.

KNOWLEDGE MANAGEMENT Knowledge management systems are a variant of ICE. As was noted in Chapter 1, a **knowledge management (KM) system** is an IT system that supports the capture, organization, and dissemination of knowledge (i.e., know-how) throughout an organization. The objective of knowledge management systems is to be sure that a company's knowledge of facts, sources of information, and solutions are available to all of its employees whenever needed.

SOCIAL NETWORK SYSTEMS Social network systems are another, newer form of ICE. **Social network systems** are IT systems that link you to people you know and, from there, to people your contacts know. For example, if a salesperson at your company wants an introduction to an influential executive at another company, a social network system could find out if someone in your company has good enough connections to arrange an introduction. This is exactly the kind of question that might get a quick reply from the right kind of social network system. Figure 2.11 describes how social network systems work.

STRATEGIC AND COMPETITIVE OPPORTUNITIES WITH INTEGRATED COLLABORATION ENVIRONMENTS

The payoffs from collaboration can be huge. For example, while oil and gas exploration companies usually form joint ventures on large projects, they often do not

WALKING THE WALK

The IT industry is developing an international supply chain for software development. Although hardware manufacturing and assembly have been done offshore for years, moving software development to other countries in large amounts is a relatively new phenomenon. Most offshore development is moving to India, but it is also going to countries such as Bulgaria, China, Rumania, Russia, and Vietnam.

The development centre of Wipro Technologies, an Indian IT services giant, is located near Bangalore, India. Currently, about 6500 people work in several new buildings there, and by 2005 the campus is scheduled to have three times as many employees as it does today.

U.S. software firms are setting up captive development shops offshore. Smaller companies have done this for some time: for example, more than half of Agile Software's 200 developers work in India, Hong Kong, and southern China.

Bigger firms have joined the trend. In June 2003, SAP announced that it would double its workforce in India to 2000 within three years. Oracle plans to double (to about 6000) the workforce at its two Indian research centers, one of them in Bangalore. Microsoft and IBM both recently announced plans to expand their IT operations in India.

A programmer in Bangalore costs an American firm about one-quarter of what it would pay for comparable skills in the United States. Even when the extra infrastructure and telecommunications costs are added, savings from moving development offshore are still in excess of 30 percent. Technology, of course, makes it all possible. High-speed networks and collaboration software tools have made it cheaper and easier for geographically dispersed teams to function effectively.

Firms that develop software programs to facilitate such collaboration are among the offshore pioneers. Agile is one example; CollabNet is another. CollabNet offers a Web-based service that allows teams of programmers to coordinate their work, and it has recently bought Enlite Networks, another collaboration startup that develops many of its programs in India.[29]

collaborate on purchases of high-dollar-value commodities for the project. A recent survey estimated that the industry in the United States might realize up to US$7 billion in annual savings by using collaborative technologies and seeking more collaborative preferred provider relationships.[30]

There are many successful examples of knowledge management systems adding value. For example, in making the case for a knowledge system at Hewlett-Packard

LinkedIn is one of the best-known social network sites focused on business professionals. Here is a summary of the way its software works. It's a three-step process:

1. *Build your network*. You start out by asking people you know to sign up. After they do, they are encouraged to invite their friends and colleagues to join as well. That's how your network grows.

2. *Find the people you need*. Once you've built your network, it's easy to search it to find the people you need. It could be someone who could help you get a job, for example.

3. *Make a trusted contact*. Once you've located the person you want to reach, all you have to do is compose a message for her and send it via the network. When she receives it, she knows it came to her through a network of trusted friends and colleagues.

That's the way it works. For more details, check out LinkedIn's Web site at www.linkedin.com.

Figure 2.11

How Social Network Systems Work[31]

DO YOU WANT SPOKE POKING AROUND?

Assume that you and your teammates work in the accounting department at a large software company that sells CRM packages. Your company is in a highly competitive business and sometimes people wonder whether the company will survive. It has to compete against such big-name players as Seibel Systems and Salesforce.com, as well as scores of other companies.

Your company's management recently purchased a copy of Spoke (www.spoke.com), which we discuss briefly on the next page. Management announced to employees in every department of the company, including yours, that it needed help in getting new sales leads and that Spoke would help in the effort. You know that Spoke's application software searches the names and company affiliations stored in your e-mail contact list on your office computer's hard drive. It looks for companies the sales department is trying to reach, and if it finds one, refers the contact to someone in the sales department.

Suppose that Spoke finds a few likely companies in your contact list, or the contact list of one of your teammates, and that someone from the sales department gives you a call and asks you to arrange an introduction. Would you be willing to make an introduction, or do you feel it would be inappropriate? How do you feel about the Spoke software examining your contact lists whether you like it or not? Do you think a better way for employees to help the company get the additional sales it needs would be for employees to submit names of good prospects to the sales department rather than putting you in a position in which you might feel pressure to cooperate?

Prepare a team position statement on this issue for class discussion. You may find that your team cannot agree on a single position. In this case, team members may divide into two or more camps, each with a different opinion. In either event, be prepared to justify your position(s) for the class discussion.

(HP), John Doyle, the former head of HP Labs, is credited with saying, "If only HP knew what HP knows."[32] What he meant was that there was a huge amount of valuable knowledge in the brains and files (both paper and computer) of HP employees, and if it was shared and accessible to others, it could be useful in solving critical problems or lead to ideas for new products and services.

CHALLENGES TO SUCCESS WITH INTEGRATED COLLABORATION ENVIRONMENTS

Although gaining acceptance of integrated collaboration environments has not been a problem for most of their variants, it has been a problem for one of them—knowledge management systems.

Two academic researchers found that the reason lies not with knowledge management technologies, but in the lack of commitment and motivation by knowledge workers, professionals, and managers to use them.[33] Another observer sums it up this way:

- People don't realize how important the knowledge they possess actually is and therefore don't submit it to the knowledge repository.
- People believe that "knowledge is power" and are reluctant to share what they know with others.
- People don't have time to submit information. This can be a real problem and one where technology can help. By being closely tied to existing working practices, knowledge management applications transparently capture and store information back in the knowledge repository.[34]

Figure 2.12

A Comparison of ICE Software

Type	Basic Functions	Example	Web site
Collaboration	Real-time collaboration and conferencing	LiveMeeting	www.microsoft.com
Workflow	Business process management	Metastorm	www.metastorm.com
Document management	Enterprise content management	FileNet	www.filenet.com
Peer-to-peer	Desktop and mobile collaboration	Groove	www.groove.net
Knowledge management	Knowledge capture, organization, location, and reuse	IBM Knowledge Discovery	www-306.ibm.com/software/lotus/knowledge/
Social network	Leveraging your personal and professional network	Linkedin	www.linkedin.com

IT SUPPORT FOR INTEGRATED COLLABORATION ENVIRONMENTS

A comparison of ICE software is shown in Figure 2.12. Three ICE vendors dominate the market—IBM/Lotus, Microsoft, and Novell. Each incorporates "presence awareness" in the latest releases of their collaboration products. **Presence awareness** is a software function that determines whether a user is immediately reachable or is in a less-available status. Based on instant messaging (IM) technology, presence awareness is built into or will soon be included in all sorts of applications, from e-mail and CRM to knowledge management and social networking.

Groove and NextPage are both examples of a special kind of information-sharing software: **peer-to-peer collaboration software**, which permits users to communicate in real time and share files without going through a central server. The peer-to-peer filesharing feature in the collaboration software is combined with the ability to create and edit documents collaboratively and send and receive text and voice messages.

While scores of knowledge management software packages are available, social network software is relatively new. Still, there are several social network packages currently available, and more are becoming available every month. Some, such as Friendster.com and Tickle, focus on dating. Others, such as Tribe.net and Linkedin, focus on professional contacts. One of the more interesting and controversial social network packages is Spoke, which allows companies to mine their employees' computerized contact databases. Spoke searches employees' computer contact lists for contacts at other companies that can be used (with the employees' permission, of course) to arrange introductions for salespeople and thereby avoid cold calling.[35]

A View of the Integrated Enterprise

So far in this chapter, we've discussed four major categories of IT applications:

1. Supply chain management
2. Customer relationship management

IT BRIDGES THE LANGUAGE GAP

One of the challenges most companies face when they try to integrate their systems is that the same information within different applications is represented in different ways. For example, a product description in the manufacturing module of a company's ERP system might be ASIC GMAC6 620TBGA. Believe it or not, descriptions like this are not uncommon in the business world. And while manufacturing specialists and the computer applications they use can understand what such cryptic descriptions mean, other people and different computer applications can have problems. The same physical description of a product might be completely different in the company's CRM system, and customers and competitors probably label it as something completely different as well. Obviously, this creates a need for a solution that can standardize information descriptions so that they mean the same thing to different users and different computer applications. Otherwise, effective enterprise application integration will never occur, nor will companies be able to achieve effective application integration with third parties such as customers and suppliers.

Silver Creek Systems (www.silvercreeksystems.com) is a startup software company located in Colorado. It has a solution to offer companies who struggle with this problem. Silver Creek developed a software application capable of taking internal information (such as product information) and automatically transforming it, in real time, to the format needed by other applications within the company and in the formats needed by customers and suppliers. The software also has the capability to translate information into one of several widely used foreign languages at the same time. The features its software offers should go a long way toward easing the technical challenges of application system integration. Perhaps most important, however, is its language translation capability, which should make it easier for companies to customize their sales Web sites for doing business around the world.

3. Business intelligence
4. Integrated collaboration environments

When effectively deployed and utilized, applications such as these help businesses meet the challenges of an ever-changing competitive environment. One of the biggest challenges companies face today is to find ways to share information from different systems. When information is shared effectively, companies stand to gain many benefits in efficiency, effectiveness, and innovation. This is the concept of shared information that we discussed in Chapter 1.

To give you an appreciation of how much of what we have been discussing in this chapter can come together in a single industry, it's hard to think of a better example than the airline industry. The large airline companies in particular have given ample evidence over a number of years that they know how to integrate supply chain management systems, customer relationship management systems, business intelligence systems, and integrated collaboration environments for competitive advantage, as illustrated in Figure 2.13. The following discussion will show you how they do it.

AIRLINE RESERVATION SYSTEMS

The airlines really got started using IT in a significant way when American Airlines and United Airlines introduced the first airline reservation systems, SABRE and APOLLO. Airline companies that did not have their own reservation system, Frontier Airlines, for example, paid for the privilege of being a "cohost" on SABRE or APOLLO, which permitted its flights to be listed on the systems and available to travel agents. American and United got a tremendous competitive advantage from being the owners of the reservation systems. First, the systems were very profitable.

Figure 2.13

Integration of SCM, CRM, BI, and ICE in the Airline Industry

SCM	CRM	BI	ICE
• Spare parts	• Reservation systems	• Yield management	• Virtual team projects
• Fuel	• Frequent flyer programs	• Profitability analysis	• Knowledge management
• Food/beverages	• Consumer Web sites	• Competitive analysis	• Social networking
• Other supplies	• Check-in kiosks	• Cost management	• Competitive threat

Second, American and United had access to business intelligence on their own flights (e.g., which ones were filled to capacity, and which ones were taking off with too many empty seats). In addition, they had immediate access to competitive intelligence on other airlines, because it was all available in the reservation systems' databases. If Frontier wanted to have special competitive analyses prepared, it could request special reports, but it had to pay and wait for them.

FREQUENT FLYER PROGRAMS

When the airlines introduced frequent flyer programs, it was to increase the likelihood that their most valued customers, their frequent business travellers, would fly with them instead of the competition.

After frequent flyer programs came into being, with their mileage and other perks, air travellers saw that it made sense to concentrate their travel with a single airline in order to get free trips and upgrades. Frequent flyer programs are a great example of a successful customer relationship management system, because they collect, store, and use information about customers' behaviour, enabling airlines to offer more personalized customer service. For example, IBM is working with FinnAir applying complex business intelligence systems to increase frequent flyers' loyalty and reduce marketing costs. Eero Ahol, FinnAir's senior vice-president for business development and strategy, says that, so far, the technology has reduced marketing costs by 20 percent and improved response rates by 10 percent.[36] Much of the information needed to manage frequent flyer programs is collected from the airlines' reservation systems, which share it with the frequent flyer program's IT systems.

AIRLINE MAINTENANCE SYSTEMS

Have you ever been on an airplane that was getting ready to take off when all of a sudden the pilot announced that the flight would be delayed because of a "mechanical"? As the Chairman of Continental Airlines noted in the Global Perspectives box earlier in this chapter, the safety of an airline's passengers is its highest concern. If a faulty part is detected prior to takeoff, everyone waits until it is replaced. Airlines use up-to-date supply chain management systems to be sure they have the right replacement parts on hand when they are needed. By integrating their supply chain management systems with their business intelligence systems, airlines know how many air miles have been logged by each plane in their fleet. Information of this kind is used to predict how many spare parts should be stocked at each airport location. It is also used to schedule preventive maintenance. For example, certain parts may be replaced after specified time or mileage intervals whether or not an actual failure has occurred.

PUSHING THE STATE OF THE ART

It's good to get into the habit of noticing the ways that companies are using or not using IT effectively. You can start to build up your own catalogue of ideas for your organization. It's always good to use a state-of-the-art application and see if you can build on it to come up with something even better. Pick a company that you think is getting a competitive advantage from IT and try to suggest ways it could be improved. This is the time to let your imagination run free and to consider using some new and emerging technologies. If you like, you can read Chapter 8 to learn about emerging technologies.

YIELD MANAGEMENT SYSTEMS

A great example of a business intelligence system that can increase revenues is a **yield management system**, a specialized kind of decision support system designed to maximize the amount of revenue an airline generates on each flight. Basically, what such a system does is alter the price of available seats on a flight minute by minute as the date of the flight approaches, depending on the number of seats that have been sold compared to an estimate of what was expected. So if fewer seats have been sold, more low-cost seats are made available for sale. If more seats have been sold than what was originally estimated, fewer low-cost seats will be made available for sale. The objective is to have the airplane take off full at the highest possible average cost per seat, as illustrated in Figure 2.14. (Airlines would rather make at least some money on a low-cost seat than make nothing on an empty seat.) Yield management systems are the reason that an airfare you're quoted over the phone can be $100 higher when you call back an hour later. They're a good example of how business intelligence gathered from an airline's reservation system can be used to maximize revenues on each flight.

INTEGRATED COLLABORATION ENVIRONMENTS

As in all large corporations, employees at airline companies often work in teams. Airline companies, however, are much more likely to have employees based in many different locations. For example, United Airlines has its headquarters in Chicago, but headquarters employees may work with team members located in places like New York, London,

Figure 2.14

The Payoff from Yield Management

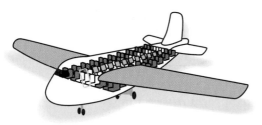

Average seat = $420
Yield = $50,400

120 seats occupied at average price of $420 per seat = $50,400 total yield for the flight

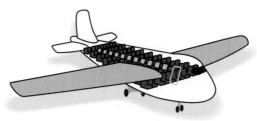

Average seat = $325
Yield = $65,000

200 seats occupied at average price of $325 per seat = $65,000 total yield for the flight

Frankfurt, and Sydney. So United Airlines, like other airline companies, uses some of the integrated collaboration environments we discussed earlier in the chapter, even though for an airline company there is no airfare to pay to bring team members together. Integrated collaboration environments, however, are an interesting competitive threat for airline companies as more and more companies adopt them. This is because companies will be able to avoid the cost and burdens on their employees (time away from their offices and families, for example) by using integrated collaboration environments to hold team meetings rather than flying employees to a central point for a face-to-face meeting.

Summing IT Up

Now that we've talked about some of the ways companies use IT for competitive advantage, we'll summarize four of the most important considerations you should keep in mind as you work to bring an IT-enabled competitive advantage to your organization. These include:

1. Competition is all around you.
2. IT competitive advantages are only temporary.
3. Be efficient *and* effective.
4. Push the state of the art.

First, remember that your organization is in a competitive environment. The reason we emphasize competitive advantage is that you and your competitors are both trying to attract and retain the same customers. Second, using IT for competitive advantage usually provides only a temporary advantage. This is because your competitors are forced to duplicate (or to better) what you have. This also means that your organization must be continually looking for ways to use IT for competitive advantage so you stay ahead of, or don't fall behind, the competition. That may sound like a lot of work, and a neverending cycle, but the reassuring reality is that there will be continuing opportunities for you to come up with creative IT solutions to business problems.

Third, remember that what you are trying to do is to make your organization both more efficient and more effective. This means that you should be applying IT to solving the most important business problems, as well as being more efficient generally. It's the difference between doing things right and doing the right things. You need to do *both*. Finally, if an IT system is going to give you a competitive advantage, it should push the state of the art. Do some research on what your competition does best and then try to surpass it. Don't let your imagination be limited by just considering technologies that are currently available or reject currently available technologies because they're too expensive. If you put artificial boundaries like these on candidate solutions, you may inhibit creativity unnecessarily. You can always bring an overly ambitious solution back to reality, but if you don't evaluate it, the opportunity will be lost.

Summary: Student Learning Outcomes Revisited

1. **Describe supply chain management (SCM) systems, their strategic and competitive opportunities, the challenges businesses face in employing them successfully, and available IT** support. A *supply chain management (SCM) system* is an IT system that supports supply chain management activities by automating the tracking of inventory and information among business

processes and across companies. Supply chain management systems can increase revenues, reduce costs, and increase customer satisfaction. The biggest challenge to their successful implementation is the lack of effective communication between individual areas within a company. Two well-known providers of SCM software are i2 and Manugistics. Dell Computer gets well-deserved recognition as well as competitive advantage from its IT-enabled SCM system.

2. **Understand customer relationship management (CRM) systems, their strategic and competitive opportunities, the challenges businesses face in employing them successfully, and available IT support.** *Customer relationship management (CRM) systems* use information about customers to gain insights into their needs, wants, and behaviours in order to serve them better. CRM is not just software but also a business objective that encompasses many different aspects of a business including software, hardware, services, support, and strategic business goals. CRM systems provide competitive advantage by increasing revenues, by cutting costs, and by treating your customers in ways that encourage them to choose your company over the competition. CRM system installations fail for many reasons, but chief among them is that companies focus on the software and fail to pay enough attention to business processes and acceptance by people within the organization. There are many CRM applications available. The two most prominent ones are Siebel Systems and Salesforce.com.

3. **Describe business intelligence (BI) systems, their strategic and competitive opportunities, the challenges businesses face in employing them successfully, and available IT support.** *Business intelligence (BI) systems* are the IT applications and tools that support the business intelligence function within an organization. Their objective is to improve the timeliness and quality of the input for decision making. Higher-quality managerial decision making is an important way companies gain an advantage over their competitors. The biggest challenge to the effective use of BI systems is that, in too many cases, knowledge workers do not know how to use them effectively. While the Web is used to support BI applications in some firms, specialized software is at the heart of BI, and there are many packages available. Brio Software Systems and Cognos are but two examples.

4. **Explain integrated collaboration environments (ICE), their strategic and competitive opportunities, the challenges businesses face in employing them successfully, and available IT support.** An *integrated collaboration environment (ICE)* is the environment in which virtual teams do their work. Virtual teams are teams whose members are located in varied geographic locations and whose work in ICEs is supported by specialized ICE software or by more basic collaboration systems. A *collaboration system* is software that is designed specifically to improve the performance of teams by supporting the sharing and flow of information. There are many varieties of collaboration systems including basic e-mail systems as well as *workflow systems*, *document management systems*, *knowledge management systems*, and *social network systems*. Companies can gain huge competitive advantages from collaboration systems through more effective coordination of the work of virtual teams and by fully utilizing available knowledge within their organizations. Knowledge management systems have been less successful than other forms of collaboration systems primarily because knowledge workers do not believe they add value to their work. ICE software combines collaborative tools focused on such virtual team activities as document management and workflow systems with network connectivity. Three ICE vendors dominate the market—IBM/Lotus, Microsoft, and Novell. Scores of KM software packages are available. Social network software is still quite new, but more packages are becoming available all the time.

5. **Analyze how individual systems that work together in an integrated manner can give airline companies a competitive advantage.** Large airline companies have long used information technology for competitive advantage. Airline reservation systems give the airlines business intelligence information on their flight activities as well as competitive information on other airlines who do not have reservation systems of their own. Their frequent flyer programs are great examples of customer relationship management systems, and now some airlines are using decision support systems to make them more effective. Airlines use supply chain management systems to ensure that spare parts are always there when needed. Finally, while airlines use integrated collaboration environments to support teamwork, at the same time the technology is a threat to their business because it has the potential to reduce the need for business travel.

AN AUTOMATED DISTRIBUTION SYSTEM TO GAIN COMPETITIVE ADVANTAGE

Adidas-Salomon Canada Ltd. (www.adidas.ca), with its head office located in Concord, Ontario, has estimated 2004 sales of $216 million and has a distribution centre located in Brantford. Adidas-Salomon was created in 1997 when Adidas International (based in Germany) acquired Salomon Sports SA and Taylor Made. The Canadian product line, which originally had just Adidas athletic equipment, footwear, and sports apparel, now also has Salomon winter sports equipment and Taylor Made golf equipment. After the merger, the company was faced with the issue of moving much more inventory, and automating distribution became a necessity. Using this solution, the company has drastically reduced its distribution costs and gained a competitive advantage.

The key objectives of this automation at the new, three-product-line Canadian distribution centre were to reduce picking errors and unit costs, and to improve inventory accuracy. The choice of the logistics system partner fell on TECSYS Inc. (www.tecsys.com), a North American Logistics Systems Integrator specializing in paperless logistics and e-fulfillment systems. Adidas-Salomon chose to implement TECSYS' Warehouse Management System (WMS), a multi-physical, multi-logical, full-function software solution with 11 different modules including receiving, put-away, picking, and shipping.

On the advice of TECSYS, Adidas-Salomon chose Psion Teklogix, with its specialized warehouse and distribution centre expertise, as the provider of the wireless data communications system for the distribution solution. In the new 28,000-square-metre automated distribution facility, mobile workers use around fifty 7025i handheld terminals with integrated scanners. The terminals have a memory-resident feature that prevents information loss in case workers walk out of range of the base stations or if a circuit goes down. There are four base stations throughout the distribution site, and the Psion Teklogix 9400 controller is hosted in Concord, giving a real-time interface between the WMS and the plant's workers. The 9400 is a key part of the mobile computing solution, providing excellent throughput and fast response times for the high-transaction site.

The ensuing combination of the TECSYS Warehouse Management System and the Psion Teklogix wireless data communications system has resulted in Adidas-Salomon Canada cutting distribution costs by half. Inventory levels are far more accurate, and the wireless devices makes the process less time-consuming. These benefits are ultimately helping Adidas-Salomon keep a step ahead of its competition by realizing benefits in cost control and operational efficiency. The new system has resulted in increased efficiency, and improved customer service and higher productivity at different levels. In 2004, Adidas-Salomon Canada received the 2004 Canadian Information Productivity Award of Excellence in the Mobile Solutions category in recognition of its innovative use of IT to solve business problems and derive greater benefit for all its stakeholders.

Questions

1. Undoubtedly, Adidas acquired Salomon Sports SA and Taylor Made for strategic business reasons. Was this facilitated by the use of IT? Why or why not?

2. The chapter discussed several examples of companies that have used IT for competitive advantage. Once the merger was finalized, how did Adidas-Salomon use IT to make this merger easier? What must they do moving forward to continue their success with the use of IT?

3. Was it a good idea to go with TECSYS Inc. to improve their inventory and distribution logistics? Could they have made another choice? If yes, what might this be?

4. One reason Adidas-Salomon partnered with TECSYS and Psion Teklogix was to keep a step ahead of the competition. How is this so? What must they do to continue to be a leader in this important IT area?

HOW INFORMATION TECHNOLOGY HELPED A SMALL BUSINESS GAIN COMPETITIVE ADVANTAGE

The Auberge de La Fontaine, located in Montreal, is a medium-sized inn with 21 rooms. It has enjoyed tremendous success by adopting an e-business strategy, which has enabled it to increase its clientele by 15 percent and reduce advertising and promotion costs significantly. It exemplifies one way a small business can grow and compete successfully with other inns.

The Auberge's e-business efforts started with its Web site in 1998, which was followed by a better one in 2000. This was complemented by simultaneous development of a database and a pricing system based on yield management, which uses mathematical modelling to adjust prices to demand. These two initiatives are the pillars of the Auberge's new strategy. Reservations are made by customers sending a form to the inn. While customers using search engines give the Auberge site most of its traffic, it attempts to use cross-referrals to the site through 380 links. The inn particularly relies on four cross-referral portals with similar levels of traffic: Bonjour Québec.com, B&B Select, Band &.com, and Worldres.

The inn's site (www.aubergedelafontaine.com) allows customers to see the rooms and also highlights the tourist and cultural attractions of Montreal, reducing promotional costs on brochures as well as telephone time with customers. The e-business model attracts the best customers, who plan vacations and make advance reservations, and American customers less sensitive to the higher average room rates presented online. Yield management also gives a more satisfactory pricing structure to customers. The Auberge's timely adoption of the Internet as a marketing tool was complemented by integrating its direct marketing experience into its database management operations and by targeting North American clientele who were already online shoppers.

The Auberge, having had a Web site since 1998, was ahead of most Canadian inns. This not only differentiated it from competitors, but also meant it needed a limited but focused investment. An initial attempt at grouping with fifteen other hotels revealed that only two were truly ready with a database and a Web site that allowed them to conduct customized electronic offers, showing how far ahead the Auberge was. The Auberge has used strategic tracking of other sites to ensure that the inn's site provides the most complete information among those in its category. The site provides such functionalities as a map, a currency converter, and information on tourist and cultural activities in Montreal, as well as links to important sites such as Tourisme Montréal and Bonjour Québec.com. The site is trilingual—in French, English, and Spanish—which helps the inn serve North American clientele better. Among the other competitive edges the site has enjoyed over the years is cross-referral across a large number of Web sites and visual appeal. The user-friendliness of the site is such that even those with minimal computer skills can use it effectively to make informed buying decisions.

The e-business model has not only increased the inn's clientele, but also the average revenue per room due to the ensuing cost savings in advertising and promotion coupled with the higher online booking rates. The investment in the model was recovered completely in six to eight months. The inn today gets over 19 percent of all reservations and 22 percent of room revenues through the Internet.[37]

Questions

1. The chapter discussed several examples of companies that have used IT for competitive advantage. Is there anything about the Auberge IT system that makes it a good example as well? If so, what characteristics of their IT system make this so?

2. The Auberge de La Fontaine, being a small entrepreneurial business, is faced with various obstacles when implementing an IT system. What are they? Do they make it easier or harder for a small business to overcome the challenges of implementing an IT system?

3. In Closing Case One, Adidas-Salomon implemented their IT system to keep a step ahead of the competition. Has the Auberge done the same

with their IT system? If yes, how and what do they need to do to continue? If no, why not, and what threats does this pose for the Auberge?

4. Has the Auberge had to change their business model by incorporating this new IT e-business system? Evaluate their success using as many elements of the supply chain management (SCM) model as you think are appropriate. What business intelligence can the Auberge gain from their IT system?

Key Terms and Concepts

alliance partner, 60
application service provider (ASP), 48
back office system, 53
business intelligence (BI), 54
business intelligence (BI) system, 54
collaboration system, 59
collaborative planning, forecasting, and replenishment (CPFR), 47
competitive intelligence (CI), 54
customer relationship management (CRM) system, 50

data mart, 55
data mining tool, 55
data warehouse, 55
digital dashboard, 58
distribution chain, 44
document management system, 60
front office system, 53
integrated collaboration environment (ICE), 59
just-in-time (JIT), 44
knowledge management (KM) system, 60
logistics, 45

peer-to-peer collaboration software, 63
presence awareness, 63
sales force automation (SFA) system, 50
social network system, 60
supply chain management (SCM), 44
supply chain management (SCM) system, 44
virtual team, 59
workflow, 60
workflow system, 60
yield management system, 66

Short-Answer Questions

1. What is a supply chain management (SCM) system? List three aspects of supply chain management that can give a business a competitive advantage.

2. What are the principal advantages of Dell's "sell, source, and ship" model over a traditional distribution chain?

3. What is a customer relationship management (CRM) system?

4. Why have many CRM and SFA systems been less than successful?

5. What is business intelligence? Why is it more than just information?

6. What is competitive intelligence? What is the relationship between competitive intelligence and business intelligence?

7. What is an integrated collaboration environment (ICE)?

8. Define virtual teams. Why are virtual teams so important in today's business world?

9. What is the purpose of knowledge management (KM) systems?

10. What are social network systems? How are they being used?

Assignments and Exercises

1. **COLLABORATION WORK.** In a group of three or more students, collaborate on a project to make a list of 100 music CDs or video DVDs. Classify them into groups. For example, if you choose DVDs, your categories might be adventure, comedy, classic, horror, musicals, among others. All communication about the project must be

electronically communicated (but not by phone). You might use e-mail, set up a Web site, use a chat room, use instant messaging, or use a collaboration e-room, if your school has that facility. Print out a copy of all correspondence on the project and put the correspondence together in a folder in chronological order. Was this task very different from collaborating face to face with your partners? In what ways was it better, in what ways worse? What additional problems or advantages would you expect if the people you were working with were in a different hemisphere?

2. **REAL-WORLD APPLICATIONS.** In the chapter we mentioned that many CRM installations have been less than successful. On the other hand, there are many satisfied users of CRM applications. Log on to the Internet and find at least three examples of companies who are getting real business benefits from their CRM systems. Prepare a report on the results they are getting and the way they achieved them. One place to start your search is at www.searchcrm.com. Another good source is the Web sites of CRM application software vendors Siebel and Salesforce.com (www.siebel.com and www.salesforce.com). At least one of your examples must be from a site other than the three mentioned.

3. **UNUSUAL APPLICATIONS OF GROOVE.** Groove is one of the best-known peer-to-peer collaboration software companies. It has a Web log (or "blog") on its Web site full of current information on the benefits of peer-to-peer collaboration software and the experiences of people who use Groove on team collaboration projects. Log on to Groove at www.groove.net and navigate to its blog. Find two examples of unusual ways people are using Groove and be prepared to summarize your findings in a class discussion. The more unusual the application the better.

4. **WAL-MART'S SCM SYSTEM.** Wal-Mart is famous for its low prices, and you may have experienced its low prices first-hand. At least, you have probably seen its motto, "Always Low Prices. Always." One of the biggest reasons Wal-Mart is able to sell at prices lower than almost everyone else is that it has a super-efficient supply chain. Its IT-enabled supply chain management system is the envy of the industry because it drives excess time and unnecessary costs out of the supply chain. So, because Wal-Mart can buy low, it sells low. As a matter of fact, if your company wants to sell items to Wal-Mart for it to sell in its stores, you will have to do business with it electronically. If your company can't do that, Wal-Mart won't buy anything from you. Log on to Wal-Mart's Web site (www.walmart.com), search for supplier information, and find out what Wal-Mart's requirements are for its suppliers to do business with it electronically. Prepare a brief summary of its requirements for presentation in class.

Discussion Questions

1. Do you think that your school would benefit from installing a customer relationship management (CRM) system? How might it benefit you as a student? How could it benefit your school?

2. Many companies believe the ASP model is the best way to use CRM. What are some of the disadvantages of the ASP model?

3. What advantages can you see for a manager to have a digital dashboard at her disposal? Are there any words of caution regarding the development and use of a digital dashboard she should hear from you before her company spends money on it?

4. If you were a member of a virtual team using collaboration software, would you want the presence awareness feature as part of the software? Why or why not?

5. As discussed in the chapter, Spoke software examines employees' e-mail contact lists searching for people at potential customer sites who may be known to employees. Do you think a company has an ethical obligation to notify employees it is going to use Spoke, or (because it will only search PC files on company-owned PCs) is it none of the employees' business?

6. Assume you are the chief financial officer (CFO) for a large company. Your company has hundreds of IT applications that have been installed over the years. Recently, the chief information

officer (CIO) proposed a project to install some new software that would enable the applications to share information easily. Develop a list of at least four questions for the CIO to answer to your satisfaction before you will consider supporting the project.

Electronic Commerce

Ordering Products and Services on the Internet

For most people, electronic commerce is all about business-to-consumer (B2C). On the Internet, you (as an individual consumer) can purchase groceries, clothes, computers, automobiles, music, antiques, books, and much more. If you want to buy it, there's probably an Internet site selling it. Even more, there are probably hundreds of Internet sites selling what it is you want, giving you the opportunity to shop for the best buy.

You can indeed find almost anything you want to buy on the Internet. However, you should carefully consider the person or organization from whom you're making the purchase. You want to be sure you are doing business with someone you can trust. This is especially true if you have to provide a credit card number to make the purchase.

→ **Electronic Commerce Links**

BOOKS AND MUSIC

Books and music make up one category of products you can readily find to purchase on the Internet. One of the most widely known and acclaimed Internet sites performing electronic commerce is Amazon.com (www.amazon.com). Amazon offers several million book and music titles for sale.

Of course, as with all products you buy on the Internet, you need to consider price and the amount you'll save on the Internet compared to purchasing books and music from local stores. Sometimes prices are higher on the Internet, and you can certainly expect to pay some sort of shipping and handling charges. We know that there are several sites that let you buy individual songs and download them to your computer in MP3 format, but for right now let's just focus on buying traditional CDs.

Make a list of books and music CDs that you're interested in purchasing. Find their prices at a local store. Next, visit three Web sites selling books and music and answer the following questions:

A. What are the books, CDs, or cassettes you're interested in?

B. What are their prices at a local store?

C. Can you find them at each Internet site?

D. Are the local prices higher or lower than the Internet prices?

E. How do you order and pay for your products?

F. How long is the shipping delay?

G. What is the shipping charge?

H. Overall, how would you rate your Internet shopping experience compared to your local store shopping experience?

CLOTHING AND ACCESSORIES

It might seem odd, but many people purchase all types of clothing on the Internet from shoes to pants to all kinds of accessories (including perfume). The disadvantage in shopping for clothes on the Internet is that you can't actually try them on and stand in front of the mirror. But if you know exactly what you want (by size and colour), you can probably find and buy it on the Internet.

Connect to several clothing and accessory sites and experience cyber-clothes shopping. As you do, consider the following.

A. How do you order and pay for merchandise?

B. What sort of description is provided about the clothing? Text, photos, perhaps 3D views?

C. What is the return policy for merchandise that you don't like or that doesn't fit?

D. Finally, is shopping for clothes on the Internet as much fun as going to the mall? Why or why not?

AUCTION HOUSES

Auction houses act as clearing stations at which you can sell your products or purchase products from other people in an auction format (essentially, consumer-to-consumer or C2C electronic commerce). eBay (www.ebay.ca), the most popular auction house, boasts millions of items for sale.

It works quite simply. First, you register as a user at a particular auction house. Once you do, you'll have a unique user ID and password that allow you to post products for sale or bid on other products. When the auction is complete for a particular product (auction houses set time limits that last typically from one to ten days), the auction house will notify the seller and the winning bidder. Then it's up to you and the other person to exchange money and merchandise.

So think of a product you'd like to buy or sell—perhaps a rare coin, a computer, a hard-to-find Beanie Baby, or a car. Connect to a couple of different Internet auction houses and answer the following questions for each:

A. What is the registration process to become a user?

B. Do you have to pay a fee to become a user?

C. Is your product of interest listed?

D. How do you bid on a product?

E. What does the auction house charge you to sell a product?

F. What is the duration of a typical auction?

G. Can you set a minimum acceptable bid for a product you want to sell?

H. How does the auction house help you evaluate the credibility of other people buying and selling products?

AUTOMOBILES

Another product category that you may not expect to find on the Internet is automobiles. That's right, on the Internet you can find virtually any automobile you'd be interested in purchasing—muscle cars, Jaguars, Rolls Royces, Hondas, and thousands more.

Try connecting to a few of these sites and browse for an automobile you'd like to own. As you do, think about these issues: What variety can you find (colour, engine size, interior, etc.)? Are financing options available? How do you test-drive a car for sale on the Internet? What happens if you buy a car and then don't like it? What about used cars? Can you trust people selling a used car on the Internet? How do you pay for a car, typically a relatively large purchase?

You can find a variety of sites that provide competitive pricing information concerning cars. Many of these sites are for all cars in general, not just those for sale on the Internet. One of the best sites is AutoSite (www.autosite.com). If you're ever shopping for a new or used car, you should definitely check it out.

Go to the Online Learning Centre at www.mcgrawhill.ca/college/haag for quizzes, extra content, a searchable glossary, and more! Click on "Electronic Commerce Projects" for links to hundreds of Web sites.

Go to the text CD-ROM for data files, extra content, and Skills Modules on Microsoft Excel, Microsoft Access, HTML, and e-portfolios.

EXTENDED LEARNING MODULE A

CAREERS IN BUSINESS

Student Learning Outcomes

By the end of this Module, students will be able to:

1. Identify the career field and business specialization in which you are interested.

2. Provide typical job titles and descriptions for your career field.

3. List and describe the IT skills you need to gain while in school.

Taking Advantage of the CD

In the business world, you need to be "a jack of all trades and a master of one." That means that you need to excel in a particular business functional area (or specialization), such as finance, accounting, marketing, or any of the other many business specializations. It also means that, while your expertise lies within one functional area, you need to be competent in all the other functional areas.

Think about majoring in marketing, for example. You need expertise in consumer behaviour, marketing strategies, branding techniques, and many other marketing-oriented concepts. But as a marketing analyst, you need other skills to be successful. You need knowledge of accounting and finance so you can put together a budget and monitor expenses. You need team and employee management skills so you can work effectively in a group and manage other people. You need knowledge of production and operations management so you can understand works-in-progress information and transportation optimization algorithms.

No matter what your career choice, you need knowledge of information technology tools that will allow you to perform your tasks more efficiently and effectively. This textbook isn't about trying to get you to major in information technology or choose MIS as a career. It's about informing you of the role of information technology and MIS in an organization and enabling you to select and use the right IT tools to carry out your tasks.

In this Module, we want to explore with you many of the career specializations in business, including

- Accounting
- Finance
- Hospitality and tourism management
- Information technology
- Management
- Marketing
- Production and operations management
- Real estate and construction management

At your school, there are probably departments devoted to providing degrees in these specializations. While titles and nomenclatures may differ (e.g., production and operations management is often called management science, operations research, statistics and operations technology, or some other variation), those specializations represent the major functional areas in a typical business.

After providing you with a brief introduction to each specialization, we include the following information:

- List of typical job titles and their descriptions
- IT tools you should focus on learning while in school
- Statistics concerning the job market

It is our hope that, after reading this Module, you will come to understand that IT and MIS are important no matter what your career choice. You may be taking this class because it's a required part of the business curriculum. It's required because, no matter what career you choose, you need knowledge of IT and MIS. This is similar to taking a human resources management class. While you may not be majoring in human resources management, you will at some time in your career have to manage people. Knowing how to manage them effectively is a career opportunity for you.

Take the time to pop in the CD that accompanies this textbook and read about careers in business.

SECTION ONE
GROUP PROJECTS

Taking Advantage of the CD

The following group projects are Cases that reflect the concepts and skills you've learned in Section One: IT in Business.

Case 1: Assessing the Value of Information
Trevor Toy Auto Mechanics

Case 2: Assessing the Value of Information
Affordable Homes Real Estate

Case 3: Executive Information System Reporting
Political Campaign Finance Consultants

Case 4: Building Value Chains
StarLight

Case 5: Strategic and Competitive Advantage: Analyzing Operating Leverage
Pony Espresso

SECTION TWO

DEVELOPING AND USING TECHNOLOGY EFFECTIVELY

CHAPTERS

EXTENDED LEARNING MODULES

GROUP PROJECTS

CHAPTER THREE

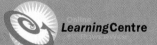

CASE STUDY:

AN ALTERNATIVE TO TRADITIONAL EDI FOR NEWARK ELECTRONICS

Newark Electronics, an American company with offices in Pointe-Claire, Quebec and in London and Mississauga, Ontario, is one of North America's leading distributors of electronic components. Initially, Newark Electronics was connected with most of its large suppliers via traditional electronic data interchange (EDI). However, the bulk of its trading partners remained SMEs unwilling, lacking the skills, or financially incapable to invest into traditional EDI systems. They saw traditional EDI as too expensive and complex to justify the convenience of sending and receiving documents electronically. Only 75 of its approximate 300 suppliers communicated with Newark via traditional EDI. This meant that Newark still needed to rely heavily on faxes, paper, and other various electronic communications to exchange purchase orders (POs), PO acknowledgements, and other important business information. Newark's low rate of acknowledged purchase orders indicated that something needed to be done. In early 2000, it stood at only 33 percent.

Newark wanted to garner the same efficiencies with its small suppliers that traditional EDI made possible with its larger ones. At the same time, Newark was sensitive to its smaller suppliers' concerns. They desperately wanted to avoid the high cost and complexity of traditional EDI solutions. Newark approached ADX—Advanced Data Exchange, a California-based company offering "Internet EDI"—a solution designed to bridge the EDI gap between big and small companies. Based on XML, ADX's Internet EDI represented a powerful, simple, and yet inexpensive alternative to traditional EDI. Users benefit from the advantages of traditional EDI but without its significant initial setup and maintenance costs. It enables companies to exploit the Internet and seamlessly consolidate various formats for exchanging documents. Businesses simply need to install the ADX Desktop Software onto their PCs and access the Internet. Activating the application places an Inbox/Outbox icon on the supplier's desktop similar to those found in many e-mail programs. Sending or receiving electronic documents is just as simple as sending or receiving e-mails. ADX translates the documents into the format that a recipient prefers and delivers them via the Internet to the recipient's inbox.

To date, Newark has managed to sign up most of its suppliers to the ADX option. Aside from Newark's low one-time investment of $27,550, suppliers were asked to pay less than $90 per month, on average, to exchange critical business information with Newark via the ADX software. Newark's PO acknowledgement rate has since increased from 33 to 94 percent and other benefits were also realized. Prior to adopting Internet EDI, the data entry tasks alone required four to six temporary clerical staff. With Internet EDI, these were no longer needed. Moreover, Newark's "mountain" of paper was drastically reduced, there were fewer stock outs, improved inventory control, and increased sales from improved fill rates resulting in more business for Newark's suppliers—well worth the average $90 monthly charge these were asked to pay. Overall, Newark realized an impressive 4428 percent three-year ROI and achieved first-year cost savings of more than $1.2 million.[1]

Introduction

Have you ever wondered why businesses build information systems or how a business knows when it's time to replace an old information system? Typically, new systems are created because knowledge workers request the systems in order to help them perform their work. For example, a marketing manager might request a system to produce product information and track customer sales information. A human resources manager might request a system to track employee vacation and sick days. Almost any position you take in a company today will require you to work with information systems because they are one of the most important parts of any business. Information systems supply the support structure for meeting the company's business strategies and goals. It's even common to find that a company's competitive advantage relies heavily on its information systems.

There are many factors that must come together in order to develop a successful information system. This chapter focuses on the *systems development life cycle (SDLC)*, a structured step-by-step approach for developing information systems (see Figure 3.1). Along with covering the SDLC, this chapter provides you with some of the primary activities you'll perform when building an information system. Many individuals make the mistake of assuming they won't benefit from learning about the SDLC because they're not planning on working in an IT department. These individuals are making a giant mistake. As a knowledge worker, or system end user, you and your work will definitely be affected by information systems and you'll be involved in many of the activities performed during the systems development life cycle.

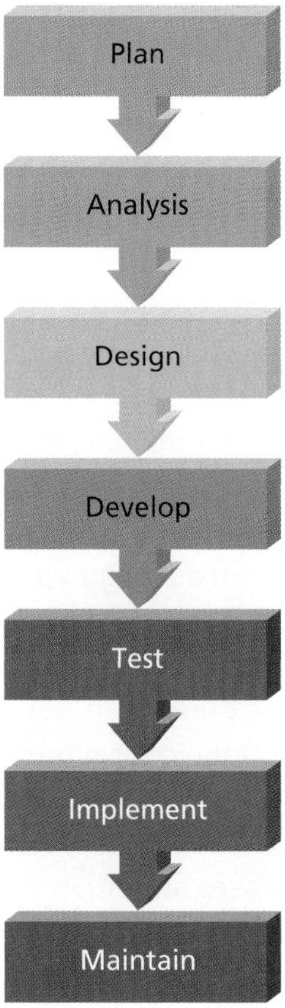

No matter what major you decide to pursue, be it accounting, marketing, or communications, you'll be involved in systems development. In fact, your involvement in developing systems is critical to the success of your company. Information systems that effectively meet your needs will help you be more productive and make better decisions. Systems that don't meet your needs may have a damaging effect on your productivity. Therefore, it's crucial you help your organization develop the best systems possible.

One way to ensure you develop successful information systems is to perform all seven phases in the SDLC. As we move through the SDLC in this chapter, we'll focus on how the overall process works, key activities within each phase, and what roles you might play. We don't expect to make you into a systems development expert. Students majoring in IT or MIS often take as many as seven courses that deal with a different aspect of systems development. However, even if you're not majoring in IT or MIS, and don't plan to be an expert, you'll still have systems development roles and responsibilities throughout your career.

Figure 3.1

The Systems Development Life Cycle

Plan

Analysis

Design

Develop

Test

Implement

Maintain

Insourcing and the Systems Development Life Cycle

The **systems development life cycle (SDLC)** is a structured step-by-step approach for developing information systems. There are literally hundreds of different activities associated with each phase in the SDLC. Typical activities include determining budgets, gathering business requirements, designing models, and writing detailed user documentation. The activities you, as a knowledge worker, perform during each systems development project will vary depending on the type of system you're building and the tools you use to build it. Since we can't possibly cover them all in this brief intro-

  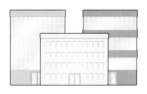 

Insourcing

IT Specialists Within
Your Organization

Selfsourcing

Knowledge Workers

Outsourcing

Another Organization

Figure 3.2

Insourcing, Selfsourcing,
and Outsourcing

duction, we have chosen a few of the more important SDLC activities that you might perform on a systems development project as a knowledge worker.

You have three primary choices as to who will build your system (see Figure 3.2). First, you can choose **insourcing**, which involves choosing IT specialists within your organization to develop the system. Second, you can choose **selfsourcing** (also called *knowledge worker development* or *end-user development*), which is the development and support of IT systems by knowledge workers with little or no help from IT specialists. Selfsourcing is becoming quite common in most organizations and is part of the overall concept of knowledge worker development or end-user computing. Third, you can choose **outsourcing**, which is the delegation of specific work to a third party for a specified length of time, at a specified cost, and at a specified level of service.

As we introduce you to the SDLC in this section, we'll focus on how the overall process works, key activities within each phase, roles you may play as a knowledge worker when *insourcing* a project, and opportunities you can capitalize on to ensure that your systems development effort is a success. The remaining sections of this chapter focus on how the SDLC changes when you selfsource and outsource your systems development efforts.

PHASE 1: PLANNING

The **planning phase** of the systems development life cycle involves determining a solid plan for developing your information system. The following are the three primary activities you'll perform during the planning phase:

1. *Define the system to be developed.* You must identify and select the system for development or determine which system is required to support the strategic goals of your organization. A **critical success factor (CSF)** is a factor simply critical to your organization's success. Organizations typically track all the proposed systems and prioritize them based on business impact or critical success factors. This allows the business to strategically decide which systems to build.

2. *Set the project scope.* You must define the project's scope and create a project scope document for your system development effort. The **project scope** clearly defines the high-level system requirements. Scope is often referred to as the "10,000-foot view" of the system or the most basic definition of the system. A **project scope document** is a written definition of the project scope and is usually no longer than a paragraph.

3. *Develop the project plan.* You must develop a detailed project plan for your entire systems development effort. The **project plan** defines the *what*, *when*, and *who* questions of systems development including all activities to be performed, the individuals, or resources, who will perform the activities, and the time required to complete each activity. The project plan is the guiding

Figure 3.3

A Sample Project Plan

ID	Task Name	Duration	Resource Names	May 26, '02	Jun 2, '02	Jun 9, '02	Jun 16, '02	Jun 23, '02	Ju
				S M T W T F S	S M T W T F S	S M T W T F S	S M T W T F S	S M T W T F S	S
1	**Planning**	**3 days**							
2	Set Scope	3 days	Scott	Scott					
3	**Analysis**	**8 days**							
4	Gather Business Requirements	8 days	Anne, Martha		Anne, Martha				
5	**Design**	**3 days**							
6	Model GUI	3 days	David			David			
7	**Development**	**2 days**							
8	Build Database	2 days	Logan			Logan			
9	**Testing**	**3 days**							
10	Write Test Condition	3 days	Martha				Martha		
11	**Implementation**	**1 day?**							
12	Install System	1 day?	Leigh				Leigh		
13	**Maintenance**	**6 days**							
14	Set Up Help Desk	6 days	Naomi						

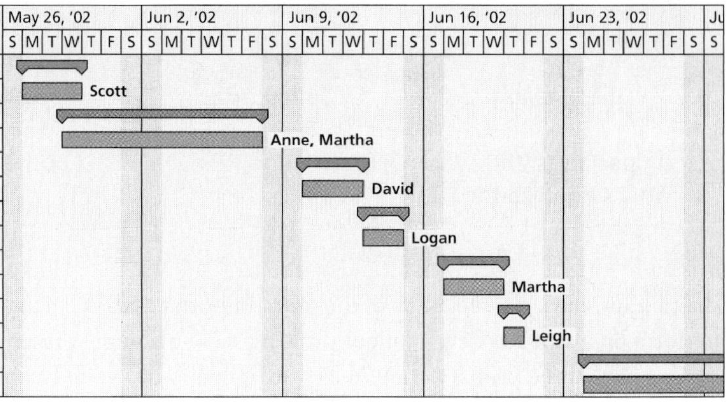

force behind ensuring the on-time delivery of a complete and successful information system.

To learn more about project planning and management, visit the Web site that supports this text at www.mcgrawhill.ca/college/haag.

YOUR ROLE DURING PLANNING   One of the most important activities knowledge workers undertake during the planning phase is defining which systems to develop. We can't stress the importance of this activity enough. Systems development focuses on either solving a problem or taking advantage of an opportunity. Your new system will be successful only if it solves the right problem or takes advantage of the right opportunity.

Developing the project plan is another critical activity in which you'll be directly involved. Figure 3.3 displays a sample project plan. A **project manager** is an individual who is an expert in project planning and management, defines and develops the project plan, and tracks the plan to ensure all key project milestones are completed on time. You must help the project manager define the activities for each phase of the systems development life cycle. The project manager is an expert in project management and you are the expert in the business operations; together the two of you will be able to develop a detailed project plan that meets everyone's needs.

KEY TO SUCCESS—MANAGE YOUR PROJECT PLAN   Continually monitoring and managing your project plan is key to successful systems development. The project plan is the road map you follow during the development of the system. There are many reasons why the project manager must continually review and revise the project plan including employees' vacations and sick leave, adding or removing activities, and changing time frames. Since the manager must continually update the project plan, it is considered a living document and you can expect it to change almost daily.

Carefully monitoring project milestones is a good way to ensure your project is on the path to success. **Project milestones** represent key dates by which you need a certain group of activities performed. For example, completing the planning phase might be a project milestone. If all your project milestones are completed on time, this is a good indication that your project is on schedule and will be successful. Also, when managing the project plan be sure to watch for scope creep and feature creep. **Scope creep** occurs when the scope of the project increases. **Feature creep** occurs when developers add extra features that were not part of the initial requirements. Closely monitoring scope creep and feature creep will also help ensure your project's success.

ANALYZING BUSINESS REQUIREMENTS

You have been hired to build an employee tracking system for a new coffee shop. Review the following business requirements and highlight any potential issues.

- All employees must have a unique employee ID.
- The system must track employee hours worked based on employee's last name.
- Employees must be scheduled to work a minimum of eight hours per day.
- Employee payroll is calculated by multiplying the employee's hours worked by $7.25.

- Managers must be scheduled to work morning shifts.
- Employees cannot be scheduled to work over eight hours per day.
- Servers cannot be scheduled to work morning, afternoon, or evening shifts.
- The system must allow managers to change and delete employees from the system.

PHASE 2: ANALYSIS

Once your organization has decided which systems to develop, you can move into the analysis phase. The **analysis phase** of the systems development life cycle involves end users and IT specialists working together to gather, understand, and document the business requirements for the proposed system. The following are the primary activities you'll perform during the analysis phase:

1. *Gather the business requirements.* **Business requirements** are the detailed set of knowledge worker requests that the system must meet to be successful. A sample business requirement might state, "the CRM system must track all customer sales by product, region, and sales representative." This business requirement states what the system must do from the business perspective.

   Gathering business requirements is similar to performing an investigation. You must talk to everyone who has a claim in using the new system to find out what is required. An extremely useful way to gather business requirements is to perform a joint application design session. During a **joint application design (JAD)** session knowledge workers and IT specialists meet, sometimes for several days, to define and review the business requirements for the system.

2. *Analyze the requirements.* Once you define all the business requirements, you prioritize them in order of business importance and place them in a formal comprehensive document, the **requirements definition document**. The knowledge workers receive the requirements definition document for their sign-off. **Sign-off** is the knowledge workers' actual signatures indicating they approve all the business requirements. Typically, one of the first major milestones in the project plan is the knowledge workers' sign-off on business requirements.

YOUR ROLE DURING ANALYSIS The most important role you'll play during the analysis phase is performing a detailed review of each business requirement and approving the analysis by signing off on the business requirements. One of the most common reasons why systems development efforts fail is because business requirements are either missing or incorrectly gathered during the analysis phase. For example, assume you're building a student registration system. What would happen if you documented the business requirement as "System must not allow students to add

THE TRUTH BEHIND BUSINESS REQUIREMENTS

The Standish Group International (www.standish group.com) reported that 31 percent of software projects are cancelled before they ever reach a customer's hands, and 53 percent ultimately cost at least 189 percent more than the original budget. North American corporations that do complete information system projects typically retain only about 42 percent of the features or business requirements that were originally proposed to the knowledge workers. Bad requirements are one of the primary causes for so many system failures. Business requirements are the detailed set of knowledge worker requests that the system must meet in order to be successful. They can include anything from basic functions to a knowledge worker's wish list of extreme functions.

Gathering clear and accurate business requirements is essential to delivering a successful system that meets your knowledge worker's needs. Learning how to gather business requirements has become such an advantage to organizations that there are now several different training programs and certifications a knowledge worker can pursue to ensure their success in this area. Microsoft Training and Certification Center offers several classes on gathering and analyzing business requirements. A knowledge worker can even become Microsoft-certified by passing the Analyzing Requirements and Defining Solution Architectures certification exam. The more knowledge workers know about gathering and analyzing business requirements the greater their chances are at developing successful systems for their company.[2,3]

classes"? This requirement is incorrect and should be "System must allow students to add classes." If you build a student registration system that doesn't allow students to add classes, it will be a complete failure.

The business requirements drive the entire system. If they are not accurate or complete, there is no way the system will be successful. You are the business process expert: that means you know how current processes and current systems work, and you know how things need to change. It's vitally important that you provide this information because the current system model will become the foundation for developing the new system model.

KEY TO SUCCESS—FIND ERRORS EARLY One of the key things to think about when you are reviewing business requirements is the cost to the company of fixing errors if the business requirements are unclear or inaccurate. An error found during the analysis phase is relatively inexpensive to fix; all you really have to do is change a Word document. An error found during later phases, however, is incredibly expensive to fix because you have to change the actual system. Figure 3.4 displays how the cost to fix an error grows exponentially the later the error is found in the SDLC.

PHASE 3: DESIGN

The primary goal of the **design phase** of the systems development life cycle is to build a technical blueprint of how the proposed system will work. During the analysis phase, end users and IT specialists work together to develop the business requirements for the proposed system from a logical point of view. That is, during analysis you document business requirements without respect to technology or the technical infrastructure that will support the system. As you move into design, the project team turns its attention to the system from a physical or technical point of view. That is, you take the business requirements generated during the analysis phase and define the

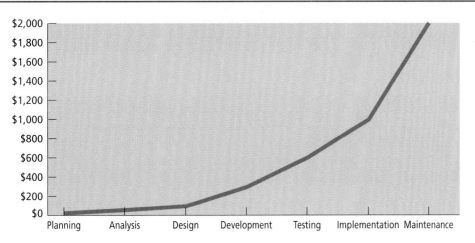

Figure 3.4

The Cost of Fixing Errors

supporting technical architecture in the design phase. The following are the primary activities you'll perform during the design phase:

1. *Design the technical architecture*. The **technical architecture** defines the hardware, software, and telecommunications equipment required to run the system. Most systems run on a computer network with each employee having a workstation and the application software running on a server. The telecommunications requirements encompass access to the Internet and the ability of end users to dial in remotely to the server. You typically explore several different technical architectures before choosing the final technical architecture.

2. *Design the system models*. **Modelling** is the activity of drawing a graphical representation of a design. You model everything you build including screens, reports, software, and databases. Many different types of modelling activities are performed during the design phase, including GUI screen design. The **graphical user interface (GUI)** is the interface to an information system. **GUI screen design** is the ability to model the information system screens for an entire system. You must decide many things when modelling a GUI, including the placement of items on the screen and the number of items contained in a drop-down list. You base your decisions on how and where to display menu items on whatever is easiest for the knowledge workers to use. If the menu items are positioned incorrectly, knowledge workers could waste a significant amount of time just searching.

YOUR ROLE DURING DESIGN During design, your role decreases as a business process expert and increases as a quality control analyst. IT specialists perform most of the activities during the design phase, but quality assurance is a key role for you. The IT specialists will develop several alternative technical solutions. It's your job to analyze each and ensure that the recommended solution best meets your business requirements. "Walk-thru" meetings are a key activity during the design phase. You'll be asked to formally sign off on the detailed design documents indicating that you approve of the proposed technical solution.

KEY TO SUCCESS—DETERMINE FUTURE REQUIREMENTS You typically explore several different technical architectures before choosing the final technical architecture. The final architecture must meet your needs in terms of time, cost, technical feasibility, and flexibility. One of the most important things to remember during the design phase is that your final architecture must not only meet your current system needs but also meet your future system needs. For example, you want to ensure that your database is large enough to hold the current volume of customers plus all the new customers you expect to gain over the next five years.

PHASE 4: DEVELOPMENT

During the **development phase** of the systems development life cycle, you take all your detailed design documents from the design phase and transform them into an actual system. This phase marks the point at which you go from physical design to physical implementation. The following are the two main activities you'll perform during the development phase:

1. *Build the technical architecture.* For you to build your system, you must first build the platform on which the system is going to operate. In the development phase, you purchase and implement equipment necessary to support the technical architecture you designed during the design phase.
2. *Build the database and programs.* Once the technical architecture is built, you initiate and complete the creating of supporting databases and writing the software required for the system. These tasks are usually undertaken by IT specialists, and it may take months or even years to design and create the databases and write all the software.

YOUR ROLE DURING DEVELOPMENT   IT specialists complete most of the activities in the development phase. Your role during this phase is to confirm any changes to business requirements and track the progress of tasks on the project plan to ensure timely delivery of the system. Constantly reevaluating the project plan during this phase helps you to determine if you'll be able to meet the final system delivery due date.

You cannot take a passive role during development. For example, you are still responsible for ensuring that the databases contain the information that supports your business requirements. So, you need knowledge of databases and the database design process. If you haven't already, we would encourage you to read Extended Learning Module C for additional information on designing and building databases.

KEY TO SUCCESS—TAKE ADVANTAGE OF CHANGING TECHNOLOGIES   Gordon Moore, cofounder of Intel Corporation, observed in 1965 that chip density doubles every 18 months. This observation, known as Moore's Law, simply means that memory sizes, processor power, and so forth all follow the same pattern over that period. Technology changes at an incredibly fast pace. It's possible to have to revise your entire project plan in the middle of a project because of a change in technology.

Many of the system examples we discuss in this chapter are small and easy to implement, such as a student registration system we alluded to above. These projects are great for discussion and initial understanding, but they're not indicative of real-world projects. Such projects have hundreds of business requirements, take years to complete, and cost millions of dollars. Technology changes quickly and you must be sure to take advantage of any new technologies that become available during your systems development effort.

PHASE 5: TESTING

The **testing phase** of the systems development life cycle verifies that the system works and meets all the business requirements defined in the analysis phase. Testing is critical. The following are the primary activities you'll perform during the testing phase:

WRITING TEST CONDITIONS

Your manager has asked you to test the cut-and-paste functionality for a word processing application. Write ten detailed test conditions using the template below. Be sure to think about cutting and pasting such things as different fonts, varying font sizes, bold and italic fonts, graphics, etc. Once you have completed your test conditions, estimate how many test conditions would be required to completely test the cut-and-paste functionality for Microsoft Word. We have provided a sample for you.

Test Condition Number	Date	Tester Name	Test Condition	Expected Result	Actual Result	Pass/Fail
21	5/27/2004	Hughes	Highlight text	Text highlighted	Text highlighted	Pass

1. *Write the test conditions.* You must have detailed test conditions to perform an exhaustive test. **Test conditions** are the detailed steps the system must perform along with the expected results of each step. The tester will execute each test condition and compare the expected results with the actual results to verify that the system functions correctly. Each time the actual result is different from the expected result, a "bug" is generated, and the system goes back to development for a "bug fix." A typical system development effort has hundreds or thousands of test conditions. You must execute and verify all of these test conditions to ensure the entire system functions correctly.

2. *Perform the testing of the system.* You must perform many different types of tests when you begin testing your new system. A few of the more common tests include:
   - **Unit testing** tests individual units or pieces of code for a system.
   - **System testing** verifies that the units or pieces of code written for a system function correctly when integrated into the total system.
   - **Integration testing** verifies that separate systems can work together.
   - **User acceptance testing (UAT)** determines if the system satisfies the business requirements and enables knowledge workers to perform their jobs correctly.

YOUR ROLE DURING TESTING IT specialists also perform many of the activities during the testing phase. Your involvement is still critical, as you are the quality assurance expert. You're directly involved with reviewing the test conditions to ensure the IT specialists have tested all the system functionality and that every single test condition has passed.

KEY TO SUCCESS—COMPLETE THE TESTING PHASE The first thing individuals tend to do when a project falls behind schedule is to start skipping phases in the SDLC, and the most common phase they skip is the testing phase. Failing to test the system can lead to unfound errors, and chances are high that the system will fail. It's critical that you perform all phases in the SDLC during every project. Try not to sacrifice testing time or your system may not work correctly all of the time.

PHASE 6: IMPLEMENTATION

During the **implementation phase** of the systems development life cycle you distribute the system to all the knowledge workers and they begin using the system to perform their everyday jobs. The two primary activities you'll perform during the implementation phase are:

1. *Write detailed user documentation.* When you install the system, you must also provide the knowledge workers with **user documentation** that highlights how to use the system. Knowledge workers find it extremely frustrating to have a new system without documentation.

2. *Provide training for the system users.* You must also provide training for the knowledge workers who are going to use the new system. You can provide several different types of training, and two of the most popular are online training and workshop training. **Online training** runs over the Internet or off a CD or DVD. Knowledge workers perform the training at any time, on their own computers, at their own pace. This type of training is convenient for knowledge workers because they can set their own schedule to undergo the training. **Workshop training** is held in a classroom environment and is led by an instructor. Workshop training is great for difficult systems for which knowledge workers need one-on-one time with an individual instructor.

YOUR ROLE DURING IMPLEMENTATION During implementation, you might attend training or help to perform the training. The system may have passed all the tests, but if the knowledge workers don't use the system properly, the system will fail. You must ensure that all the knowledge workers have the required training to use the system correctly.

GLOBAL PERSPECTIVES

CATA MONITORS IT SKILLS GAP

According to the Canadian Advanced Technology Association (CATA), an organization that has been monitoring the "IT skills gap," 88 percent of advanced technology companies in Canada believe they face a serious shortage in necessary technology skills and qualifications. Thus, as a student in information systems, your prospects for employment after graduation are very good. According to Robert Half Technology, more than a million North Americans may be employed in hi-tech jobs by the time you graduate, and demand is growing. These are well-paying jobs, with starting salaries ranging from $50,000 to $115,000 per year. The "IT skills gap" is most apparent in "core IT occupations," including computer science, electrical engineering, software design, and systems analysis. CATA estimates that in Ontario alone there will be openings for 56,000 new technology workers over the next five years.[5]

KEY TO SUCCESS—CHOOSING THE RIGHT IMPLEMENTATION METHOD You need to choose the right implementation method that best suits your organization, project, and employees to ensure a successful implementation. When you implement the new system, you have four implementation methods you can choose from:

- **Parallel implementation**. Using both the old and new system until you're sure that the new system performs correctly
- **Plunge implementation**. Discarding the old system completely and immediately using the new system
- **Pilot implementation**. Having only a small group of people use the new system until you know it works correctly and then adding the remaining people to the system
- **Phased implementation**. Implementing the new system in phases (e.g., accounts receivables, then accounts payable) until you're sure it works correctly and then implementing the remaining phases of the new system

PHASE 7: MAINTENANCE

Maintaining the system is the final phase of any systems development effort. During the **maintenance phase** of the systems development life cycle, you monitor and support the new system to ensure it continues to meet the business goals. Once a system is in place, it must change as your business changes. Constantly monitoring and supporting the new system involves making minor changes (e.g., new reports or information capturing) and reviewing the system to ensure that it continues to move your organization toward its strategic goals. The two primary activities you'll perform during the maintenance phase are:

1. *Build a help desk to support the system users.* To create the best support environment, you need to provide a way for knowledge workers to request changes. One of the best ways to support knowledge workers is to create a help desk. A **help desk** is a group of people who respond to knowledge workers' questions. Typically, knowledge workers have a phone number for the help desk they call whenever they have issues or questions about the system. Providing a help desk that answers user questions is a terrific way to provide comprehensive support for knowledge workers using new systems.

2. *Provide an environment to support system changes.* As changes arise in the business environment, you must react to those changes by assessing their impact on

MARRIOTT INTERNATIONAL

The hospitality services industry is highly competitive and it's difficult for any one organization in the industry to achieve a competitive advantage. When Marriott International, an international upscale hotel chain, set itself a strategic goal of becoming the world's leader in the hospitality services industry, it took an ingenious idea and transformed it into an information system with the help of Accenture, one of the world's leading outsourcing companies.

Accenture and Marriott teamed up to link Marriott's worldwide financial systems into a single service centre at one location. This allowed Marriott to leverage its operations to provide consistent, cost-effective services, making the organization quicker and more flexible, a competitive advantage that has helped Marriott leap ahead as one of the top worldwide hospitality service providers.[6]

the system. It might well be that the system needs to change to meet the ever-changing needs of the business environment. If so, you must modify the system to support the new business environment.

YOUR ROLE DURING MAINTENANCE During maintenance, your primary role is to be sure that all the knowledge workers have the support they require to use the system. You might be responsible for setting up a help desk or for developing change request forms for your users to fill out if they require a change to the system. Not only do you have to track the change requests but you also must verify that any changes requested for the system are worth performing. Changes cost money, especially once a system has reached the maintenance phase. You must carefully weigh each requested change for merit and monetary worth.

Selfsourcing and Prototyping

Throughout this text, we have elaborated on the concept of knowledge worker computing—knowledge workers taking an active role in developing and using their own systems to support their efforts in personal and workgroup environments. What we want to look at now is how you, as a knowledge worker, can go about developing your own systems, which we call *selfsourcing*. Recall that selfsourcing is the development and support of IT systems by knowledge workers with little or no help from IT specialists.

THE SELFSOURCING PROCESS

You can probably create many of the small knowledge worker computing systems in a matter of hours, such as customizing reports, creating macros, and interfacing a letter in a word processing package with a customer database to create individualized mailings. More complicated systems, such as a student registration system or an employee payroll system, require that you follow the formal SDLC process during development.

In Figure 3.5 we've illustrated the selfsourcing process and we've summarized the key tasks within some of the selfsourcing steps. As you can see, the selfsourcing process is similar to the phases in the SDLC. However, you should notice that the selfsourcing process includes *prototyping* (model building, which we'll discuss in detail

YOUR RESPONSIBILITIES DURING EACH STEP OF THE SDLC

As a knowledge worker, you're a business process expert, liaison to the customer, quality control analyst, and manager of other people. However, according to which step of the SDLC you're in, your responsibilities may increase or decrease. In the table below, determine the extent to which you participate in each SDLC step according to your four responsibilities. For each row, number the SDLC steps from 1 to 7, with 1 identifying the step in which your responsibility is greatest and 7 identifying the step in which your responsibility is the least.

	Plan	Analysis	Design	Develop	Test	Implement	Maintain
Business process expert							
Liaison to the customer							
Quality control analyst							
Manager of other people							

in the next section). This is key—when you develop a system for yourself, you will most often go through the process of prototyping. As you consider the key tasks in Figure 3.5, we would alert you to several important issues.

ALIGNING YOUR SELFSOURCING EFFORTS WITH ORGANIZATIONAL GOALS

When you first begin planning a system you want to develop, you must consider it in light of your organization's goals. If you're considering developing a system for yourself that's counterintuitive to your organization's goals, then you should abandon it immediately. Obviously, you don't want to build a system that reduces sales or decreases the number of customers. You have to consider how you spend your time building systems carefully, since you are busy and your time is extremely valuable. It's important to remember that developing a system through selfsourcing takes time—your time.

So, your first activity should always be to consider what you want to develop in conjunction with what your organization expects you to do.

DETERMINING WHAT EXTERNAL SUPPORT YOU WILL REQUIRE

Some selfsourcing projects may involve support from IT specialists within your organization. Your in-house IT specialists are a valuable resource during the process. Don't forget about them and be sure to include them in the planning phase. The chances of building a successful system increase greatly when you have both knowledge workers and IT specialists working together.

Figure 3.5

The Selfsourcing Process and Key Tasks in Selfsourcing

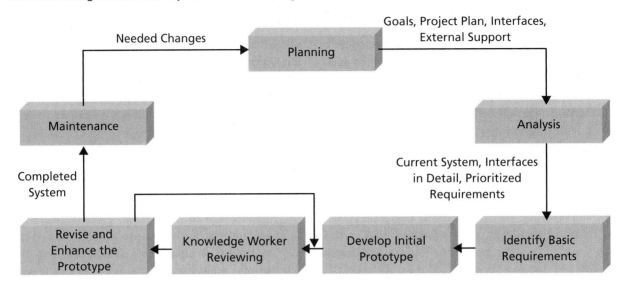

DOCUMENTING THE SYSTEM ONCE COMPLETE Even if you're developing a system just for yourself, you still need to document how it works. When you get promoted, other people will come in behind you and probably use the system you developed and might even make changes to it. For this reason, you must document how your system works from a technical point of view as well as create an easy-to-read operation manual.

PROVIDING ONGOING SUPPORT When you develop a system through selfsourcing, you must be prepared to provide your own support and maintenance. Since you are the primary owner and developer of the system, you're solely responsible for ensuring the system continues to function properly and continues to meet all the changing business requirements. You must also be prepared to support other knowledge workers who use your system, as they will be counting on you to help them learn and understand the system you developed. For example, if you develop a customer relationship database using Microsoft Access 2003, you must be prepared to convert it to Microsoft Access 2005 (or whatever the latest version happens to be) when it becomes available and your organization adopts it. The systems development process doesn't end with implementation: it continues on a daily basis with support and maintenance.

THE ADVANTAGES OF SELFSOURCING

IMPROVES REQUIREMENTS DETERMINATION During insourcing, knowledge workers tell IT specialists what they want. In selfsourcing, knowledge workers essentially tell themselves what they want. Potentially, this greatly improves the chances of thoroughly understanding and capturing all the business requirements, and thus the prospect of success for the new system.

INCREASES KNOWLEDGE WORKER PARTICIPATION AND SENSE OF OWNERSHIP No matter what you do, if you do it yourself, you always take more pride in the result. The same is true when developing an IT system through selfsourcing. If knowledge workers know that they own the system because they developed it and now

THREE QUESTIONS TO ASK WHEN SELFSOURCING

When developing your own system, ask yourself three questions to be sure you are on the right track. These three questions will help your team's organization and preparation. They also may help higher-level executives who aren't familiar with software development learn a few things about the process.

1. *Who are the intended users of the software?* If your development team doesn't know the answer to this question, go back to the analysis phase and do some more work on business requirements.
2. *What are the functional objectives of the project?* There will be a long list of features, functions, and capabilities that you must prioritize so your team can concentrate on the key ones. If your project manager can't list the top three functions without reference to paper, then he/she isn't in tune with what the project is all about.
3. *Which features should we build first?* Prioritize your development efforts and build the hardest pieces first. This will allow you to determine if you are going to be successful when building the entire system. If you can successfully build the hardest parts, then you should be able to create the remainder of the system.[7]

support it, they are more apt to participate actively in its development and have a greater sense of ownership.

INCREASES SPEED OF SYSTEMS DEVELOPMENT Many small systems do not lend themselves well to insourcing. These smaller systems may suffer from "analysis paralysis" because they don't require a structured step-by-step approach to their development. In fact, insourcing may be slower than selfsourcing for smaller projects.

PITFALLS AND RISKS OF SELFSOURCING

INADEQUATE KNOWLEDGE WORKER EXPERTISE LEADS TO INADEQUATELY DEVELOPED SYSTEMS Many selfsourcing systems are never completed because knowledge workers lack the real expertise with IT tools to develop a complete and fully working system. This might seem like no big deal, since the system couldn't have been that important if the people who needed it never finished developing it. But that's not true. Perhaps it was potentially a good idea. And if knowledge workers choose to try to develop their systems, they must spend time away from their primary duties within the organization. This diverted time may mean lost revenue for the company.

LACK OF ORGANIZATIONAL FOCUS CREATES "PRIVATIZED" IT SYSTEMS Many selfsourcing projects are done outside the IT systems plan of an organization, meaning there may be many private IT systems that do not interface with other systems and that contain uncontrolled and duplicated information. Such systems serve no meaningful purpose in an organization and can only lead to more problems.

INSUFFICIENT ANALYSIS OF DESIGN ALTERNATIVES LEADS TO SUBPAR IT SYSTEMS Some knowledge workers jump to immediate conclusions about the hardware and software they should use without carefully analyzing all the possible alternatives. If this happens, knowledge workers may develop systems whose components are inefficient.

TOSHIBA'S COIN-SIZE HARD DISK PROTOTYPE

Toshiba Corporation plans to begin sample production of a coin-size hard disk that can hold up to 3 GB of data. Currently, the smallest commercial hard disk in mass production have 1-inch platters. Toshiba's new drive contains a disk platter that is 0.85 inches in diameter and the entire drive is about the size of a coin. Toshiba demonstrated a prototype of the drive at the Consumer Electronics Show that took place in Las Vegas in January 2004. The company plans sample production beginning in the middle of 2004 and commercial production beginning as early as 2005.

According to data from market analysis company Coughlin Associates Inc., the market for 1.8-inch and smaller hard disk will grow exponentially over the next five years. The company estimates shipments of such drives will total 3.3 million drives in 2004 and grow to 23.7 million drives in 2008.[8]

LACK OF DOCUMENTATION AND EXTERNAL SUPPORT LEADS TO SHORT-LIVED SYSTEMS When knowledge workers develop systems, they often forgo documentation of how the system works and fail to realize that they can expect little or no support from IT specialists. All systems—no matter who develops them—must change over time. Knowledge workers must realize that anticipating those changes is their responsibility and making those changes will be easier if they document their system well.

Prototyping

Prototyping is the process of building a model that demonstrates the features of a proposed product, service, or system. A **prototype**, then, is simply a model of a proposed product, service, or system. If you think about it, people prototype all the time. Automobile manufacturers build prototypes of cars to demonstrate safety features, aerodynamics, and comfort. Building contractors construct models of homes and other structures to show layout and fire exits.

In systems development, prototyping can be a valuable tool for you. Prototyping is an iterative process in which you build a model from basic business requirements, have other knowledge workers review the prototype and suggest changes, and further refine and enhance the prototype to include suggestions. Most notably, prototyping is a dynamic process that allows knowledge workers to see, work with, and evaluate a model and suggest changes to that model to increase the likelihood of success of the proposed system.

You can use prototyping to perform a variety of functions in the systems development process:

- *Gathering requirements.* Prototyping is a great requirements gathering tool. You start by simply prototyping the basic system requirements. Then you allow knowledge workers to add more requirements (information and processes) as you revise the prototype.
- *Helping determine requirements.* In many systems development projects, knowledge workers aren't sure what they really want. They simply know that the current system doesn't meet their needs. In this instance, you can use prototyping to help knowledge workers determine their exact requirements.
- *Proving that a system is technically feasible.* Let's face it, there are some things to which you cannot apply technology. And knowing whether you can is often

unclear while defining the scope of the proposed system. If you're uncertain about whether something can be done, prototype it first. A prototype you use to prove the technical feasibility of a proposed system is a **proof-of-concept prototype**.

- *Selling the idea of a proposed system.* Many people resist changes in IT. The current system seems to work fine, and they see no reason to go through the process of developing and learning to use a new system. In this case, you have to convince them that the proposed system will be better than the current one. Because prototyping is relatively fast, you won't have to invest a lot of time to develop a prototype that can convince people of the worth of the proposed system is a **selling prototype**.

THE PROTOTYPING PROCESS

Prototyping is an excellent tool in systems development. Who uses prototyping and for what purpose determines how the prototyping process occurs. Most often, IT specialists use prototyping in the SDLC to form a technical system blueprint. In self-sourcing, however, you can often continue to refine the prototype until it becomes the final system. The prototyping process for either case is almost the same; only the result differs. Figure 3.6 illustrates the difference between insourcing and selfsourcing

Figure 3.6
Prototyping Steps for Insourcing and Selfsourcing

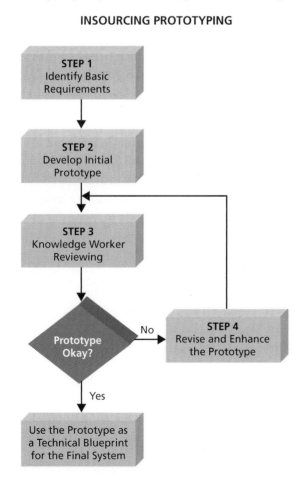

INSOURCING PROTOTYPING

STEP 1 Identify Basic Requirements

STEP 2 Develop Initial Prototype

STEP 3 Knowledge Worker Reviewing

Prototype Okay? — No → **STEP 4** Revise and Enhance the Prototype

Yes

Use the Prototype as a Technical Blueprint for the Final System

SELFSOURCING PROTOTYPING

STEP 1 Identify Basic Requirements

STEP 2 Develop Initial Prototype

STEP 3 Knowledge Worker Reviewing

Prototype Okay? — No → **STEP 4** Revise and Enhance the Prototype

Continue these steps until the prototype becomes the final system.

prototyping. Regardless of who does the prototyping, the prototyping process involves four steps:

1. *Identify basic requirements.* During the first step, you gather the basic requirements for a proposed system. These basic requirements include input and output information desired and, perhaps, some simple processes. At this point, you're typically unconcerned with editing rules, security issues, or end-of-period processing (e.g., producing W-2s for a payroll system at the end of the year).

2. *Develop initial prototype.* Having identified the basic requirements, you then set out to develop an initial prototype. Most often, your initial prototype will include only user interfaces, such as data entry screens and reports.

3. *Knowledge worker reviewing.* Step 3 starts the truly iterative process of prototyping. When knowledge workers first initiate this step, they evaluate the prototype and suggest changes or additions. In subsequent returns to step 3 (after step 4), they evaluate new versions of the prototype. It's important to involve as many knowledge workers as possible during this iterative process. This will help resolve any discrepancies in such areas as terminology and operational processes.

4. *Revise and enhance the prototype.* The final sequential step in the prototyping process is to revise and enhance the prototype according to any knowledge worker suggestions. In this step, you make changes to the current prototype and add any new requirements. Next, you return to step 3 and have the knowledge workers review the new prototype; then step 4 again, revision, and so on.

For either insourcing or selfsourcing, you continue the iterative processes of steps 3 and 4 until knowledge workers are happy with the prototype. What happens to the prototype after that, however, differs.

During selfsourcing, you're most likely to use the targeted application software package or application development tool to develop the prototype. This simply means that you can continually refine the prototype until it becomes the final working system. For example, if you choose to develop a simple CRM application using Microsoft Access, you can prototype many of the operational features using Microsoft Access development tools. Because you develop these prototypes using the targeted application development environment, your prototype can eventually become the final system.

That process is not necessarily the same when insourcing. Most often, IT specialists develop prototypes using special prototyping development tools. Many of these tools don't support the creation of a final system—you simply use them to build prototypes. Therefore, the finished prototype becomes a blueprint or technical design for the final system. In the appropriate stages of the SDLC, IT specialists will implement the prototypes in another application development environment better suited to the development of production systems.

THE ADVANTAGES OF PROTOTYPING

ENCOURAGES ACTIVE KNOWLEDGE WORKER PARTICIPATION First and foremost, prototyping encourages knowledge workers to actively participate in the development process. As opposed to interviewing and reviewing documentation, prototyping allows knowledge workers to see and work with working models of the proposed system.

HELPS RESOLVE DISCREPANCIES AMONG KNOWLEDGE WORKERS During the prototyping process, many knowledge workers participate in defining the require-

SSSSSSSSS . . . BUSTED!

Taggertrap, a prototype alarm warning system by Traptec, is activated by the ultrasonic sound of a graffiti artist's spray can. In the past, it has been almost impossible to catch graffiti vandals in the act. Now, thanks to Taggertrap, authorities are instantly alerted to acts of graffiti. The device has wireless sensors that can detect the sound of aerosol sibilance within 61 metres. Once it has detected the telltale sound, Taggertrap contacts the police via a cell phone and records the vandals with tiny DV cameras. Authorities receive the DV footage immediately via e-mail and dispatch personnel to the area. Early tests in San Diego caught over 20 graffiti vandals redhanded in a single day.[9]

ments for and reviewing the prototype. The "many" is key. If several knowledge workers participate in prototyping, you'll find it's much easier to resolve any discrepancies the knowledge workers may encounter.

GIVES KNOWLEDGE WORKERS A FEEL FOR THE FINAL SYSTEM Prototyping, especially for user interfaces, provides a feel for how the final system will look and work. When knowledge workers understand the look and feel of the final system, they are more apt to see its potential for success.

HELPS DETERMINE TECHNICAL FEASIBILITY Proof-of-concept prototypes are great for determining the technical feasibility of a proposed system.

HELPS SELL THE IDEA OF A PROPOSED SYSTEM Finally, selling prototypes can help break down resistance barriers. Many people don't want new systems because the old one seems to work just fine, and they're afraid the new system won't meet their expectations and work properly. If you provide them with a working prototype that proves the new system will be successful, they will be more inclined to buy into it.

THE DISADVANTAGES OF PROTOTYPING

LEADS PEOPLE TO BELIEVE THE FINAL SYSTEM WILL FOLLOW SHORTLY When a prototype is complete, many people believe that the final system will follow shortly. After all, they've seen the system at work in the form of a prototype. How long can it take to bring the system into production? Unfortunately, it may take months or years. You need to be sure that people understand that the prototype is only a model, not the final system missing only a few simple bells and whistles.

GIVES NO INDICATION OF PERFORMANCE UNDER OPERATIONAL CONDITIONS Prototypes very seldom take all operational conditions into consideration. This problem surfaced for the Department of Motor Vehicles of a U.S. state on the East Coast. During prototyping, the system, which handled motor vehicle and driver registration for the entire state, worked fine for 20 workstations at two locations. When the system was finally installed for all locations (which included more than 1200 workstations), the system spent all its time just managing communications traffic; it had absolutely no time to complete any transactions. This is potentially the most significant drawback to prototyping. You must prototype operational conditions as well as interfaces and processes.

LEADS THE PROJECT TEAM TO FORGO PROPER TESTING AND DOCUMENTATION You must thoroughly test and document all new systems. Unfortunately, many people believe they can forgo testing and documentation when using prototyping. After all, they've tested the prototype. Why not use the prototype as the documentation for the system? Don't make this mistake.

Prototyping is most probably a tool that you will use to develop many knowledge worker information systems. If you stick to the phases of the SLDC, have the correct resources, and learn how to make the most of your prototypes, you will be very successful in your career as a knowledge worker.

Outsourcing

Your final alternative is to *outsource*—that is, to choose external employees from another organization, or contractors, to develop a system. However, typically, large systems have both internal and external employees working on the development effort.

DEVELOPING STRATEGIC PARTNERSHIPS

The Outsourcing Research Council recently completed a study indicating that human resources (HR) is a top outsourcing area for many companies. Fifty percent of the companies surveyed said they were already outsourcing some or all of their payroll processing and another 38 percent said they were considering it.

Energizer, the world's largest manufacturer of batteries and flashlights, outsourced its HR operations to ADP, one of the top HR outsourcing companies. Energizer currently has more than 3500 employees and 2000 retired employees who all require multiple HR services. ADP provides Energizer with centralized call centres, transaction processing services, and Web-based employee self-service systems. Energizer's vice-president of human resources, Peter Conrad, stated, "ADP was clearly the most capable and offered the kind of one-stop shopping our company was looking for." For several of the systems provided by ADP employee usage topped over 80 percent in the first six months the systems were active.[10]

Energizer's choice of using ADP to develop its human resource system is an example of outsourcing. (Recall that *outsourcing* is the delegation of specific work to a third party for a specified length of time, at a specified cost, and at a specified level of service.) IT outsourcing today represents a significant opportunity for your organization to capitalize on the intellectual resources of other organizations by having them take over and perform certain business functions in which they have more expertise than the knowledge workers in your company. IT outsourcing for software development can take one of four forms (see Figure 3.7):

1. Purchasing existing software.
2. Purchasing existing software and paying the publisher to make certain modifications.
3. Purchasing existing software and paying the publisher for the right to make modifications yourself.
4. Outsourcing the development of an entirely new and unique system for which no software exists.

In these instances, we're not talking about personal productivity software you can buy at a local computer store. We're talking about large software packages that may cost millions of dollars. For example, every organization has to track financial infor-

1. Purchase existing software.

2. Purchase existing software and pay publisher to make certain modifications.

YOUR ORGANIZATION

4. Outsource the development of an entirely new and unique system for which no software exists.

3. Purchase software and pay publisher for the right to make changes yourself.

Figure 3.7
Major Forms of Outsourcing Systems Development

mation, and there are several different systems they can purchase that help them perform this activity. Have you ever heard of Oracle Financials? This is a great system your organization can buy that tracks all the organizational financial information. Building a financial system would be a waste of time and money since there are several systems already built that probably meet your organizational needs.

THE OUTSOURCING PROCESS

The outsourcing process is both similar to and quite different from the systems development life cycle. It's different in that you turn over much of the design, development, testing, implementation, and maintenance steps to another organization (see Figure 3.8). It's similar in that your organization begins with planning and defining the project

Figure 3.8
The Outsourcing Process

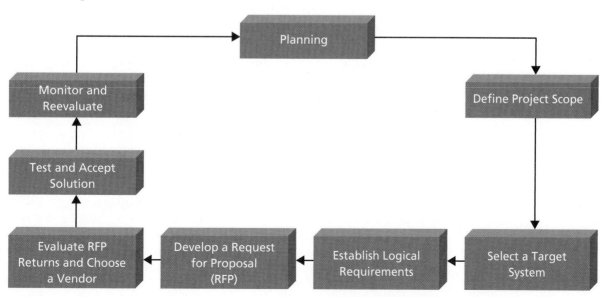

Planning

Monitor and Reevaluate

Define Project Scope

Test and Accept Solution

Evaluate RFP Returns and Choose a Vendor

Develop a Request for Proposal (RFP)

Establish Logical Requirements

Select a Target System

HOW MANY OUTSOURCING COMPANIES ARE THERE?

Assume your company is looking to outsource its payroll activities including calculating the payroll and generating the paycheques every month. Try searching the Internet to find different companies that offer this outsourcing service. Fill in the following table comparing the advantages and disadvantages of the different companies you find. Discuss which one you would choose and why.

Company Name	Advantages	Disadvantages

scope. It's during one of these phases that your organization may come to understand that it needs a particular system but cannot develop it in-house. If so, that proposed system can be outsourced. Below, we briefly describe the remaining steps of the outsourcing process.

SELECT A TARGET SYSTEM Once you've identified a potential system to develop by outsourcing, you still have some important questions to answer. For example, will the proposed system manage strategic and sensitive information? If so, you probably wouldn't consider outsourcing it. That is, you don't want another organization seeing and having access to your most vital information. If you're building an order entry system you might not want people to view your product prices, as they may be a significant part of your strategic advantage.

You should also consider whether the system is small enough to be selfsourced. If so, let knowledge workers within your organization develop the system instead of outsourcing it. On the other hand, if the proposed system is fairly large and supports a routine, nonsensitive business function, then you should target it for outsourcing.

ESTABLISH LOGICAL REQUIREMENTS Regardless of your choice of insourcing or outsourcing, you must still perform the analysis phase—especially the primary activity of gathering the business requirements for the proposed system. Remember that identification of the business requirements drives the entire system development; if the business requirements are not accurate or complete, there is no way the system will be successful. Regardless of whether you insource or outsource, you must still gather accurate and complete business requirements. If you choose to outsource, part of gathering the business requirements becomes your "request for proposal."

DEVELOP A REQUEST FOR PROPOSAL Outsourcing involves telling another organization what you want. What you want is essentially the logical requirements for a proposed system, and you convey that information by developing a **request for proposal (RFP)**, a formal document that describes in detail your logical requirements for a proposed system and invites outsourcing organizations (which we'll refer to as "vendors") to submit bids for its development. An RFP is the most important document in the outsourcing process. For systems of great size, your organization may create an RFP that's hundreds of pages long and requires months of work to complete.

It's vitally important that you take all the time you need to create a complete and thorough RFP. Eventually, your RFP will become the foundation for a legal and binding contract into which your organization and the vendor will enter. At minimum, your RFP should contain the elements listed in Figure 3.9. Notice that an RFP includes key information such as an overview of your organization, underlying business processes that the proposed system will support, a request for a development time frame, and a request for a statement of detailed outsourcing costs.

All this information is vitally important to both your organization and the vendors. For your organization, the ability to develop a complete and thorough RFP means that you completely understand what you have and what you want. For the vendors, a complete and thorough RFP makes it easier to propose a system that will meet most, if not all, your needs.

EVALUATE REQUEST FOR PROPOSAL RETURNS AND CHOOSE A VENDOR Your next activity in outsourcing is to evaluate the RFP returns and choose a vendor. You perform this evaluation of the RFP returns according to the scoring method you identified in the RFP. This is not a simple process. No two vendors will ever provide RFP returns in the same format, and the RFP returns you receive are usually longer than the RFP itself.

Figure 3.9

Outline of a Request for Proposal (RFP)

1. Organizational overview
2. Problem statement
3. Description of current system

   3.1 Underlying business processes
   3.2 Hardware
   3.3 Software (application and system)
   3.4 System processes
   3.5 Information
   3.6 System interfaces

4. Description of proposed system

   4.1 New processes
   4.2 New information

5. Request for new system design

   5.1 Hardware
   5.2 Software
   5.3 Underlying business processes
   5.4 System processes
   5.5 Information
   5.6 System interfaces

6. Request for implementation plan

   6.1 Training
   6.2 Conversion

7. Request for support plan

   7.1 Hardware
   7.2 Software

8. Request for development time frame
9. Request for statement of outsourcing costs
10. How RFP returns will be scored
11. Deadline for RFP returns
12. Primary contact person

Once you've thoroughly analyzed the RFP returns, it's time to rank them and determine which vendor to use. Most often, you rank RFP returns according to cost, time, and the scoring mechanism you identified. Again, ranking RFP returns is not simple. Although one vendor may be the cheapest, it may require the longest time to develop the new system. Another vendor may be able to provide a system quickly but without some of the features you have identified as critical.

Once you've chosen the vendor, a lengthy legal process follows. Outsourcing is serious business—and serious business between two organizations almost always requires a lot of negotiating and the use of lawyers. Eventually, your organization has to enter into a legal and binding contract that very explicitly states the features of the proposed system, the exact costs, the time frame for development, acceptance criteria, and criteria for breaking the contract for nonperformance or noncompliance.

OUTSOURCING HELP DESKS OFFSHORE

There are now two classes of help desk support customers—high-paying and low-paying. Today, vendors are tailoring support to the amount of money customers pay, and are transferring the lower-paying customers to offshore support sites. More and more companies, however, are finding that offshore help desks are causing their customers major problems.

Jim Miller, Chief Technology Officer at Creditex Inc., a Wall Street–based credit derivative trading firm, recently requested help with a Microsoft Exchange server that supports users in New York and London. The Microsoft help desk in India answered Jim's call and the technician on the other end of the line merely consulted online Microsoft knowledge-base articles, something Miller said he could have done himself. The technician told him that the only way to rectify the problem was to rebuild the whole machine and reinstall Exchange, an effort that Miller said would entail "a huge investment in time, the loss of significant data and e-mail down for an extended period of time."

Miller took a pass on the advice and asked the technician to place him back in the call queue, only to end up back in India four times. Finally, Creditex "escalated" its request for help to Microsoft support managers and finally received a call from a knowledgeable technician in Dallas who resolved the problem in 15 minutes.[11]

TEST AND ACCEPT SOLUTION As with all systems, testing and accepting the solution are crucial. Once a vendor installs the new system, it's up to you and your organization to test the entire system before accepting it. You'll need to develop detailed test plans and test conditions that test the entire system. This alone may involve months of running and testing the new system while continuing to operate the old one (the parallel method).

When you "accept" a solution, you're saying that the system performs to your expectations and that the vendor has met its contractual obligations so far. Accepting a solution involves granting your sign-off on the system, which releases the vendor from any further development efforts or modifications to the system. Be careful when you do this, because modifications to the system after sign-off can be extremely expensive.

MONITOR AND REEVALUATE Just like the systems you develop using the SDLC, systems you obtain through outsourcing need constant monitoring and reevaluation. You must continually evaluate and revise the project plan to ensure the system is going to meet its delivery schedule. In outsourcing, you also have to reassess your working relationship with the vendor. Is the vendor providing maintenance when you need it and according to the contract? Does the system really perform the stated functions? Do month-end and year-end processes work according to your desires? Does the vendor provide acceptable support if something goes wrong? These are all important questions that affect the success of your outsourcing efforts.

The most important questions, though, are: Does the system still meet your needs, and how much does it cost to update the system? In many instances, if the system needs updating you must contract with the original vendor. This is potentially one of the greatest drawbacks to outsourcing. When you outsource a system, you create a heavy dependency on a particular vendor to provide updates to the system, and such updates are expensive.

OFFSHORE OUTSOURCING

The recent trend in outsourcing is for organizations to outsource their IT functions offshore. **Offshore outsourcing** is using organizations from other countries to write

OUTSOURCING FREES CANADIAN NATIONAL ARTS CENTRE TO FOCUS ON ITS CORE COMPETENCIES

Ottawa's National Arts Centre, founded in 1969 as a Crown corporation, boasts three concert stages and more than 111,400 square metres of space. This Canadian landmark is one of the world's largest live-performance centres, hosting several classical and pop music concerts, English and French theatre plays, and art festivals every year.

In 1997, the centre decided to outsource its IT to Compaq, including all network management, system administration, bilingual help desk support, and on-site service. "Before Compaq came in, the IT infrastructure was semi-dysfunctional. . . . we had a very unstable network, inconsistent software on our desktops, outdated servers and PCs and no Internet access," says Richard Tremblay, director of administrative services. Over a period of 18

months, Compaq set up the Microsoft Windows NT Server network operating system, revamped the messaging system, provided access to the Internet, and installed nearly 200 new PCs running Microsoft Windows and the Office suite. Following a successful eight-month trial period, the centre signed on for a five-year outsourcing contract with Compaq covering support for all corporate applications and desktop software suites, and service for all desktops, servers, and communications devices.

Outsourcing simply made sense for the centre, because it allowed its people to focus on core competencies. "Our prime mission is to produce and stage live performances. We wanted to look at everything that was secondary to this mission and see if somebody else could do it better than we could," says Tremblay.[12]

code and develop systems. Stories about companies outsourcing work to India have been reported for years; however, it is becoming increasingly apparent that Romania, Bulgaria, Russia, China, Ghana, the Philippines, and dozens of other countries are also clamouring for and getting business from the United States. The value of IT services provided to U.S. businesses from offshore labour will double to US$16 billion in 2005 and then almost triple to US$46 billion by 2007, according to market research firm IDC.[13]

THE ADVANTAGES AND DISADVANTAGES OF OUTSOURCING

Making the decision to outsource is critical to your organization's success. Throughout this discussion of outsourcing, we've directly or indirectly described many of the advantages and disadvantages of outsourcing. What follows is a summary of the major advantages and disadvantages of outsourcing the systems development process in order to help you make this important decision.

ADVANTAGES   Your organization may benefit from outsourcing because it allows you to:

- *Focus on unique core competencies.* By outsourcing systems development efforts that support noncritical business functions, your organization can focus on developing systems that support important, unique core competencies.
- *Exploit the intellect of another organization.* Outsourcing allows your organization to obtain intellectual capital by purchasing it from another organization. Often you won't be able to find individuals with all the expertise required to develop a system. Outsourcing allows you to find those individuals with the expertise you need to get your system developed and implemented.

- *Better predict future costs.* When you outsource a function, whether systems development or some other business function, you know the exact costs.
- *Acquire leading-edge technology.* Outsourcing allows your organization to acquire leading-edge technology without having to acquire technical expertise and the inherent risks of choosing the wrong technology.
- *Reduce costs.* Outsourcing is often seen as a money saver for organizations. Reducing costs is one of the important reasons organizations outsource.
- *Improve performance accountability.* Outsourcing involves delegating work to another organization at a specified level of service. Your organization can use this specified level of service as leverage to guarantee that it gets exactly what it wants from the vendor.

DISADVANTAGES   Your organization may suffer from outsourcing because it:

- *Reduces technical know-how for future innovation.* Outsourcing is a way of exploiting the intellect of another organization. It can also mean that your organization will no longer possess that expertise internally. If you outsource because you don't have the necessary technical expertise today, you'll probably have to outsource for the same reason tomorrow.
- *Reduces degree of control.* Outsourcing means giving up control. No matter what you choose to outsource, you are in some way giving up control over that function.
- *Increases vulnerability of your strategic information.* Outsourcing systems development involves telling another organization what information you use and how you use that information. In doing so, you could be giving away strategic information and secrets.
- *Increases dependency on other organizations.* As soon as you start outsourcing, you immediately begin depending on another organization to perform many of your business functions.

Summary: Student Learning Outcomes Revisited

1. **List the seven steps in the systems development life cycle (SDLC) and associated activities for each step.** The *systems development life cycle (SDLC)* is a structured step-by-step approach for developing information systems. The seven steps and activities are as follows:
   1. *Planning.* Define system, set project scope, develop project plan.
   2. *Analysis.* Gather business requirements.
   3. *Design.* Design technical architecture, design system models.
   4. *Development.* Build technical architecture, build database and programs.
   5. *Testing.* Write the test conditions, perform testing.
   6. *Implementation.* Perform user training, write user documentation.

   7. *Maintenance.* Provide a help desk, support system changes.

2. **Describe keys to success you can use to help ensure a successful systems development effort.** This chapter provides you with several keys to success you can use to ensure your systems development efforts are successful. These include the following:
   - *Manage your project plan.* Continually monitoring and managing your project plan can ensure your project remains on track and all major project milestones are met.
   - *Find errors early.* The sooner you find errors in the systems development life cycle the less costly it is to correct the errors.
   - *Determine future requirements.* Establishing requirements for current as well as future needs

will help ensure that you do not outgrow your system.

- *Take advantage of changing technology.* Technology changes quickly and you must take advantage of any new technologies to ensure that your project is successful.
- *Complete the testing phase.* It's critical that you perform all phases in the SDLC during every project. Try not to sacrifice testing time or your system may not work correctly all of the time.
- *Choose the right implementation method.* You need to choose the right implementation method that best suits your organization, project, and employees to ensure a successful implementation. Implementation methods include parallel, plunge, pilot, and phased.
- *Work together.* It's important to build systems with both the knowledge workers and IT specialists working together because the knowledge workers are the business process experts and quality control analysts, and the IT specialists are highly skilled in designing, implementing, and maintaining the systems.

3. **Define the different ways you can staff a systems development project.** Insourcing, selfsourcing, and outsourcing are the three different ways you can staff a system development project. *Insourcing* uses IT specialists within your organization, *selfsourcing* uses knowledge workers, and *outsourcing* uses another organization. It is important to note that most large projects typically use insourcing, selfsourcing, and outsourcing all at the same time.

4. **List the advantages of selfsourcing.** When you selfsource a project you (1) improve requirements determination, (2) increase knowledge worker participation and sense of ownership, and (3) increase the speed of systems development.

5. **Describe prototyping.** *Prototyping* is the process of building a model that demonstrates the features of a proposed product, service, or system. A *prototype*, then, is simply a model of a proposed product, service, or system. If you think about it, people prototype all the time. Automobile manufacturers build prototypes of cars to demonstrate safety features, aerodynamics, and comfort. Building contractors construct models of homes and other structures to show layout and fire exits.

6. **Describe the five advantages of prototyping.** First, prototyping encourages active knowledge worker participation. Prototyping encourages knowledge workers to actively participate in the development process. As opposed to interviewing and the reviewing of documentation, prototyping allows knowledge workers to see and work with working models of the proposed system. Second, prototyping helps resolve discrepancies among knowledge workers. During the prototyping process, many knowledge workers participate in defining the requirements for and reviewing the prototype. The "many" is key. If several knowledge workers participate in prototyping, you'll find it's much easier to resolve any discrepancies the knowledge workers may encounter.

7. **Describe the outsourcing process and the current trend toward offshore outsourcing.** The outsourcing process includes selecting a target system, establishing logical requirements, developing a request for proposal (RFP), evaluating the request for proposal, choosing a vendor, testing and accepting the solution, and monitoring and reevaluating the solution. *Offshore outsourcing* is using organizations from other countries to write code and develop systems. Many companies are currently outsourcing IT work to India, Romania, Bulgaria, Russia, China, Ghana, the Philippines, and dozens of other countries.

SOME PROTOTYPES HIT, SOME MISS, AND SOME WE ARE JUST NOT SURE ABOUT

Pick up any copy of a technology magazine and you'll see loads of new prototypes anxious to hit the consumer market. Would you like to buy new mountain bike that is built without using any chains for only $5593?

How about some Smart Trading Cards? This alternative to cardboard baseball cards comes with a CPU where you can review highlights and listen to important personal statistics such as the leading skateboarder's number of broken bones. Unfortunately, these Smart Cards don't come with a stick of chewing gum, which was the big perk with the traditional baseball trading cards. A stick of chewing gum can no longer compare to a CPU. Especially considering the price for traditional baseball cards was 10 cents and the Smart Cards sell for $8 plus $20 for the card reader. With those kind of prices who cares about a stick of chewing gum?

How would you like a pair of snorkelling flippers that can change shape on the fly to help you adapt easily to your changing underworld environment?

The list of new prototypes goes on and on ranging from wristwatches with a digital compass to Wave Boxes, the first portable hydraulic whirlpool perfect for those city dwelling kayak fans.

But what do you think happens after you make a prototype? Chances are it will take one of two paths. On the first path, the prototype is a big hit and the product goes into mass production and is found in every Wal-Mart and Kmart in the country. On the second path, the prototype is unsuccessful and goes into storage for eternity. Only about 10 percent of product prototypes make it to the consumer market.

Every year, the online magazine *Wired News* presents the Vaporware Awards to the top ten most eagerly awaited technology products that never made it to consumers. As the technology industry continues to generate products that promise to revolutionize consumers work and personal lives, *Wired News* follows them from planning to delivery. For more information, visit www.wired.com.

In Ithaca, New York you can visit Robert McMath's museum of failed products, which he has been maintaining for over 30 years. Are you interested in purchasing edible deodorant, a nice can of aerosol toothpaste for kids, toaster eggs, a garlic cake? The list is endless, and for many of them you have to wonder what the inventor was thinking. (If anyone can tell us when or why you would eat garlic cake, we would be grateful.)

Building prototypes is the only way to determine if your product is going to be a hit or a miss. Understanding the prototyping process and the advantages and disadvantages covered in this chapter is important to your career as a knowledge worker, as you'll be working with information system prototypes and perhaps building some yourself.

Questions

1. Prototyping is an invaluable tool for systems development. Building a prototype allows knowledge workers to see, work with, and evaluate a model and suggest changes to the model. Refer back to the discussion on the cost of fixing errors or Figure 3.4. What do prototyping and this figure have in common? How can prototyping help you control your project budget and the cost of fixing errors?

2. Prototyping can be used in the analysis phase to help you gather business requirements. Throughout this chapter we discussed the importance of gathering solid business requirements. How can building a prototype help you gather solid business requirements on an information systems development project?

3. Listed above are many examples of prototypes. Use your creativity and business knowledge to generate an idea for a new product for a business or consumers. Or it can be a service that would help consumers perform their daily activities and activities. Write a brief paragraph describing your idea along with a picture of the product.

4. One of the disadvantages to building a prototype is that people tend to believe the final system will follow shortly. Why do you think this is so? If you were delivering a system prototype, how would you communicate to the system users that the real system would not be ready for another three years?

5. It is important to remember that communication is the primary key to deploying a successful prototype. When Planters Peanuts first started to market fresh-roasted peanuts, the product was a complete failure. Consumers continually confused the product with coffee beans and kept taking it home to grind it. The words "fresh-roasted" are probably what caused the product to initially fail. If you had been in charge, what could you have done to help consumers understand the product contained peanuts and not coffee beans?

THE STAMPEDE BARBEQUE RESTAURANT

The Stampede Barbeque Restaurant, located in Calgary, Alberta, has successfully been in business for 20 years. The restaurant specializes in barbeque chicken and beef and includes scrumptious side dishes of potato salad, coleslaw, and baked beans. Customers come from all around for a good old-fashioned barbeque dinner. On a Friday night you can expect the line to be out the door and the wait to be close to an hour. It is estimated that Shawn, the owner, serves over 500 barbeque dinners every day.

The restaurant is filled with 20 picnic tables with red-and-white tablecloths. There are a total of twelve wait-staff workers, five of whom have been working at the restaurant since it opened. Shawn cooks and prepares all of the special barbeque sauce himself along with three other cooks. The restaurant runs today just as it did 20 years ago. Shawn knows many of his customers by name. This is definitely part of the charm of the restaurant, but it is also one of its biggest problems. Everything in the restaurant is done manually, from taking orders to ordering inventory.

In 2001, Shawn's daughter, Carmen, graduated from college and came home to help run the family-owned business. She was amazed at how long it took to perform all of the manual processes required to run the business. Every night she manually counted all of the money in the cash register and compared it to the paper sales tickets that the wait staff filled out representing the customer orders. She also manually counted the inventory, from cans of beans to slices of cheese. Deciding what to order each day was a complete mystery to Carmen. Some days the restaurant sold tonnes of chicken dinners, and other days tonnes of beef dinners; there didn't seem to be any pattern. She continually found herself ordering too much of one item and not enough of the other. Every week she had to calculate the employee paycheques by reviewing each employee's cardboard handwritten time card. At the end of each month she calculated the sales tax reports. This was incredibly difficult, since the reports had to match all of the monthly paper tickets, of which there were close to 15,000.

Carmen quickly came to the conclusion that the restaurant had to be automated. Building an information system to support all of these manual processes would not only help the restaurant operate more efficiently, but also give Carmen more time to spend talking to and dealing with her customers. Carmen and Shawn decided to visit a local restaurant trade show to see what types of information systems were available. The show displayed all types of different restaurant systems. One used microwave frequencies that allowed the wait staff to send orders to a terminal in the kitchen using a type of PDA. Some systems could track sales for up to 20 years and generate sales forecasts based on anything from the day of the week to the weather. All of the systems produced daily sales reports and monthly tax reports. This feature alone would be a dream come true for Carmen, as this activity typically took her from two to three hours a day.

Carmen and Shawn are now overwhelmed by the number of restaurant information systems available.

Having no formal training with the SDLC or systems development, they are confused and frustrated with so many choices.

Questions

1. Shawn is not a believer in technology and he thinks the business works just fine the way it is. How would you convince him that an information system will help his business become even more successful? How can you explain to him that using the SDLC will help him successfully implement a new system?

2. Carmen realizes that she does not have the expertise required to choose a restaurant information system. She decides to ask you for help, since you have studied this type of information in college. How would you describe to Carmen the steps in the SDLC and how she can use them to choose and implement a system?

3. At the beginning of the project you develop a project plan to help guide you through the systems development effort. Carmen does not understand the plan or why you continually keep changing it. How can you explain to Carmen the benefits of developing a project plan and why it must be continually revised and updated?

4. Shawn has hired you to help choose and implement the system for the restaurant. From the information you already have about the restaurant, write five of the business requirements. Remember, writing clear and accurate business requirements is critical to the success of a project.

5. Some members of the wait staff have worked at the restaurant since it began. You're worried that they won't be receptive to using an automated system. How would you convince the wait staff that the new system will help them perform their jobs? Why is including them in the requirements-gathering activity critical to the systems development effort?

6. Thanks to your help, Shawn has successfully implemented a new restaurant system. The system is up and running and Shawn is extremely pleased with your work. You offer to spend an extra week writing user manuals and system documentation. Shawn declines your offer, as he does not see any benefit in these tools. How would you convince Shawn that documentation is critical to the continued success of his system?

7. At the restaurant trade show, Shawn and Carmen saw many different restaurant information systems that they could purchase. Research the Web to find two restaurant information systems that might have been at the show. Of the systems you found, which do you think you would choose and why?

Key Terms and Concepts

analysis phase, 85
business requirement, 85
critical success factor (CSF), 83
design phase, 86
development phase, 88
feature creep, 84
graphical user interface (GUI), 87
GUI screen design, 87
help desk, 91
implementation phase, 90
insourcing, 83
integration testing, 89
joint application design (JAD), 85
maintenance phase, 91
modelling, 87
offshore outsourcing, 104

online training, 90
outsourcing, 83
parallel implementation, 91
phased implementation, 91
pilot implementation, 91
planning phase, 83
plunge implementation, 91
project manager, 84
project milestone, 84
project plan, 83
project scope, 83
project scope document, 83
proof-of-concept prototype, 97
prototype, 96
prototyping, 96
request for proposal (RFP), 103

requirements definition
    document, 85
scope creep, 84
selfsourcing, 83
selling prototype, 97
sign-off, 85
systems development life cycle
    (SDLC), 82
system testing, 89
technical architecture, 87
test condition, 89
testing phase, 88
unit testing, 89
user acceptance testing (UAT), 89
user documentation, 90
workshop training, 90

Short-Answer Questions

1. What is the systems development life cycle (SDLC)?

2. What are the seven steps in the SDLC?

3. What is a critical success factor?

4. What is feature creep?

5. How does a project plan help the project manager do his/her job?

6. In what step in the SDLC do you define business requirements?

7. Why would a company outsource?

8. In what step in the SDLC do you build the technical architecture?

9. What is an activity performed in the design phase?

10. What is an activity performed in the testing phase?

11. How do online training and workshop training differ?

12. Why must you provide sign-off on the business requirements?

13. Will a project be successful if you miss business requirements?

14. What is selfsourcing?

15. What is a contractor?

16. Why would you build a prototype?

17. What is a selling prototype?

Assignments and Exercises

1. **SDLC AND THE REAL WORLD.** Think of the seven steps in the SDLC and try to apply them to one of your daily activities. For example, getting dressed in the morning would involve the following. First, you plan what you are going to wear. This will vary depending on what you are going to do that day and could include shorts, pants, jeans, etc. Second, you analyze what you have in your closet compared to what you planned to wear. Third, you design the outfit. Fourth, you get the clothes out of the closet and assemble them on your bed. Fifth, you test the outfit to ensure it matches. Sixth, you put on the outfit. Seventh, you wear the outfit throughout the day adjusting it as needed.

2. **HOW CREATIVE ARE YOU?** Congratulations! You've been appointed manager of the design team for Sneakers-R-Us. Your first activity is to design the GUI for the main system. The only requirements you are given is that the colours must be bold and the following buttons must appear in the screen.

   - Order Inventory
   - Enter Sales
   - Schedule Employees
   - Tax Reports
   - Sales Reports
   - Employee Vacation and Sick Time
   - Administrative Activities

   Create two different potential GUI screen designs for the main system. Provide a brief explanation of the advantages and disadvantages of each.

3. **REQUEST FOR PROPOSAL.** A request for proposal (RFP) is a formal document that describes in detail your logical requirements for a proposed system and invites outsourcing organizations (or *vendors*) to submit bids for its development. Research the Web and find three RFP examples. Briefly explain in a one-page document what the RFPs have in common and how each is different.

4. **UNDERSTANDING INSOURCING.** The advantages and disadvantages of selfsourcing and outsourcing are covered throughout this chapter. Compile a list of the different advantages and disadvantages of insourcing compared to selfsourcing and outsourcing.

5. **MANAGING THE PROJECT PLAN.** You are in the middle of an interview for your first job. The manager performing the interview asks you to explain why managing a project plan is critical to a project's success. The manager also wants to know what scope creep and feature creep are, and how you would manage them during a project. Write a one-page document stating how you would answer these questions during the interview.

6. **PROJECT MANAGEMENT.** Congratulations! You've been assigned the role of project manager for WakeUp Company. Your first project is to build an alarm clock. The project starts today and lasts for three months. You have the following resources available to work on the project.

   - Project manager (1)
   - Knowledge workers (3)
   - IT specialists (4)
   - Documentation experts (2)
   - Testing expert (3)
   - Extra experts (4)

   Your first activity is to develop an initial project plan with the above information. You must list the SDLC phases and associated activities, assign time frames to perform each activity, and finally assign a resource(s) to work on the activity.

7. **WHY PROTOTYPE?** You are in the middle of the design phase for a new system. Your manager does not understand why it's important to develop a prototype of a proposed system before building the actual system. In a one-page document explain what problems might arise if you went straight to developing the system.

8. **BUSINESS REQUIREMENTS.** Gathering accurate and complete business requirements is critical to the successful development of any system. Review the following requirements and explain any problems they might have.

   - The GUI must be red.
   - There should be three buttons labelled Start and Stop.
   - Buttons 1 through 8 are required for the calculator function.
   - There should be a text field for the user name and a button for the user password.

9. **WHY PROJECTS FAIL.** We've discussed five of the primary reasons why projects fail, but there are many more possible reasons. In order to be prepared for your role as a knowledge worker, research the Web to find three additional reasons why projects fail. Prepare a document explaining them and how you could prevent these issues from occurring.

Discussion Questions

1. Why is it important to develop a logical model of a proposed system before generating a technical architecture? What problems might arise if you didn't develop a conceptual model and went straight to developing the technical design?

2. If you view systems development as a question-and-answer session, another question you could ask is "Why do organizations develop IT systems?" Consider what you believe to be the five most important reasons organizations develop IT systems. How do these reasons relate to topics in the first five chapters of this book?

3. When deciding how to staff a systems development project what are some of the primary questions you must be able to answer in order to determine if you will insource, selfsource, or outsource? What are some of the advantages and disadvantages of each?

4. Your company has just decided to implement a new financial system. Your company's financial needs are almost the same as those of all of the other companies in your industry. Would you recommend that your company purchase an existing system or build a custom system? Would you recommend your company insource, selfsource, or outsource the new system?

5. Why do you think system documentation is important? If you had to write system documentation for a word processing application what would be a few of the main sections? Do you think it would be useful to test the documentation to ensure it's accurate? What do you think happens if you provide system documentation that is inaccurate? What do you think happens if you implement a new system without documentation?

6. What would happen to an organization that refused to follow the systems development life cycle when building systems? If you worked for this organization what would you do to convince your manager to follow the systems development life cycle?

7. Imagine your friends are about to start their own business and have asked you for planning and development advice with respect to IT systems. What would you tell them? What if their business idea was completely Internet-based? What if their business idea didn't include using the Internet at all? Would your answers differ? Why or why not?

8. What would happen to a systems development effort that decided to skip the testing phase? If you were working on this project what would you do to convince your team members to perform the activities in the testing phase?

9. Imagine you are working on a project and are getting ready to enter the development phase. Your boss suddenly decides to outsource the rest of the project and move you into another area. What are the advantages and disadvantages of this situation?

10. You are talking with another student who is complaining about having to learn about the systems development life cycle because he/she is not going to work an IT department. Would you agree with this student? What would you say to try to convince this person that learning about the systems development life cycle is relevant no matter where he/she works.

11. A company typically has many systems it wants to build, but unfortunately it doesn't usually have the resources to build all of them. How does a company decide which ones to build?

12. When you start working on a new system one of your first activities is to define the project scope. Do you think this is an easy activity to perform? Why is the project scope so important? Do you think everyone on the project should know the project's scope? What could happen when people on the project are not familiar with it?

Electronic Commerce

Finding Freeware and Shareware on the Internet

When you buy your first computer, software seems a secondary decision, since most computers come preloaded with software. But after a while you begin to feel a need for other software. However, even simply upgrading to the latest version of your existing software can make a real dent in your pocketbook. And after installing new software, you may find it simply doesn't meet your needs. That's when you notice that you can't return opened software, you can only exchange it for a new copy. So if it doesn't meet your needs you're out of luck with commercial consumer software.

Electronic Commerce Links

An alternative to commercial software that you might consider is shareware or freeware. Shareware is "try before you buy" software: users are permitted to try the software on their own computer system (generally for a limited time) without any cost or obligation; they then make a payment if they decide they want to keep using the software beyond the evaluation period. Freeware is software available at no charge to users for as long as they choose to use it.

USING YOUR COMPUTER FOR MORE THAN WORK

By far the most popular freeware/shareware applications are games. The quality of these titles is truly amazing for software that is free to download and begin playing immediately whenever you want. Shareware/freeware games are so numerous on the Internet that you'll often find games grouped by category: action/adventure, board, card, casino, educational, role-playing, simulation, sports, strategy and war, and word games.

When you're looking over the games available, remember that you should first ascertain whether the software is shareware or freeware. In some cases the Web site is not really clear on this issue. For example, some game descriptions make no mention of money, yet after you've downloaded the game it talks about registering your game for a price. At the other end of the spectrum you'll encounter traditional software that lists a price next to the description and requires a credit card to download and purchase, and often these games will describe themselves as shareware. Remember, though, true shareware permits you to download the software and try it for free; so in this case "shareware" is a bit of a misnomer.

Connect to the Internet and several sites that offer freeware and shareware games. Pick at least two games and download them. For each, answer the following questions:

A. Is a description of the game provided?

B. Are system requirements listed?

C. Can you tell if the game is freeware or shareware without downloading it?

D. Are any of the games you selected really commercial software that requires a purchase before you download the game?

E. If the game is shareware, how long may you use it before registration is required?

F. If the game is shareware, does the game cease to function after the free period? How can you tell without waiting that long?

G. How long does it take to download the game? Is it worth it?

ANIMATING YOUR COMPUTER SCREEN

Wander through most any office or even your school computer lab, and you'll see a variety of "screen savers" in action. Screen savers—the software that occupies your screen when the computer is unused for a period of time—are very common utilities. Sometimes they provide a beautiful scene with a recurring action. Others provide a different look every time they activate. Microsoft Windows includes several standard screen savers. In Windows 95 and beyond you'll also find desktop themes that do include a screen saver but go much further than that. In addition to providing software that activates when your computer is inactive, themes alter the look of the basic screen

you see when you are working. Borders, standard application icons, and even the cursor are changed with desktop themes.

Connect to a couple of different sites that offer screen savers. Download at least two screen savers and answer the following questions:

A. Is a description of the screen saver provided?

B. Is the screen saver available for other operating systems?

C. Can you tell if the screen saver is freeware or shareware without downloading it?

D. Do any of the screen savers include desktop themes for Windows?

E. Are any other screen savers or desktop themes available at the site?

F. Does the screen saver work as advertised?

PROTECTING YOUR COMPUTER INVESTMENT

Have you ever been frantically typing away, desperately trying to make an assignment deadline, when all of a sudden something goes wrong with your computer? If you're lucky the problem is easy to identify, so you correct it and go on with your work. Other times the solution eludes you. Most of the time these problems have nice logical explanations such as hardware or software conflicts or failures of some kind. In a few rare instances, the problem may have been caused intentionally—by a computer virus—a program which someone develops with malicious intent to harm an IT system.

So how does a computer virus get into your system? Anytime you download software, open a file attachment to an e-mail, or read a file off a diskette from another computer, you stand the chance of contracting a computer virus. And access to the Internet increases your opportunity to download files from many different sources. So on every computer it owns virtually every company installs antivirus protection software that scans new files for known viruses and purges them from the system. The catch is that traditional antivirus software can find only viruses it knows about. As new viruses come along, the software must be updated. The deviant minds that develop viruses seem to find more and better ways to infiltrate your system every day.

Connect to a site that allows you to download antivirus software, download it, and answer the following questions:

A. Is the antivirus software shareware, freeware, or traditional retail software?

B. What viruses does it detect?

C. Does the software remove the virus as well as detect it?

D. Are updates for the software available to detect new viruses? How often are they available? At what cost?

E. Does the software detect viruses not yet created? How does it do that?

F. Does the software site offer recommendations to reduce your chance of contracting a virus?

G. Does the site tell you what to do if you have already contracted a virus?

SEARCHING FOR FREEWARE AND SHAREWARE

So maybe the shareware/freeware software concept appeals to you. You'd like to be able to try the software before you buy. If you want software such as screen savers or antivirus software, you're in luck. Just look through the Web links on the Online Learning Centre (www.mcgrawhill.ca/college/haag).

But what if you want some shareware to help you compose music or keep track of your soccer team's schedule? Well, then you'll have to go searching. You could use a

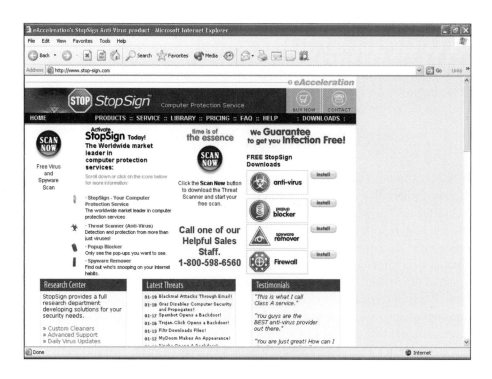

general-purpose search engine such as Yahoo! and type in "shareware" and "music" or "soccer." If you do this you will find a few shareware software titles to download.

But suppose those few titles don't meet your needs. Finding shareware/freeware titles can be daunting, for two reasons. First, currently there are over a million shareware and freeware titles available to you. Unless a search engine is designed specifically for this type of software, you'll probably miss many of these titles using a general-purpose search engine. Second, most shareware/freeware developers don't have their own Web sites. Since many don't develop their software as a business, they can't justify the cost of a site. To address both these challenges, Web sites have been created that maintain databases of thousands of shareware/freeware software titles. Most also include a search engine to help you navigate through these titles.

Find a site that maintains a database of freeware and shareware software. As you peruse it, answer the following questions:

A. How does the site group the software?

B. Can you search by operating system or platform?

C. Does the site provide descriptions of the software?

D. Can you search by file size?

E. Are screen captures from the software provided?

F. Are reviews and/or ratings of the software provided?

G. When was the last update of the site?

Go to the Online Learning Centre at www.mcgrawhill.ca/college/haag for quizzes, extra content, a searchable glossary, and more! Click on "Electronic Commerce Projects" for links to hundreds of Web sites.

Go to the text CD-ROM for data files, extra content, and Skills Modules on Microsoft Excel, Microsoft Access, HTML, and e-portfolios.

CHAPTER FOUR

STUDENT LEARNING OUTCOMES

BY THE END OF THIS CHAPTER, STUDENTS WILL BE ABLE TO:

1. Describe business intelligence and its role in an organization.

2. Differentiate between databases and data warehouses with respect to their focus on online transaction processing and online analytical processing.

3. List and describe the key characteristics of a relational database.

4. Define the five software components of a database management system.

5. List and describe the key characteristics of a data warehouse.

6. Define the four major types of data mining tools.

7. List key considerations in managing the information resource in an organization.

8. Identify the primary key field of a database.

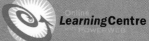

Online LearningCentre POWERWEB

DATABASES AND DATA WAREHOUSES
Building Business Intelligence

CASE STUDY:

CHRYSLER SPINS A COMPETITIVE ADVANTAGE WITH SUPPLY CHAIN MANAGEMENT SOFTWARE

According to John Kay, DaimlerChrysler's manager of electronic commerce, "Being able to get critical product information to our external suppliers as soon as it becomes available is a definite competitive advantage for all concerned." John is talking about Chrysler's Supply Partner Information Network (SPIN), a Web-based supply chain management system that increased productivity by 20 percent and reduced operating costs in the first year of its implementation.

The two technology tools critical to the success of SPIN, which already boasts over 3500 suppliers accessing and using it, are the Internet and databases. The Internet, of course, allows 24/7 access to SPIN by Chrysler's suppliers for providing parts, bidding on contracts, and submitting purchase invoices. The Internet also allows Chrysler to send to its suppliers, in real time, vitally important information updates on procurement requirements, strategy applications, and the like.

What's internal to SPIN is a powerful set of databases that track, organize, and maintain all of Chrysler's inventory, material requirements planning, work-in-progress, and supplier information. A database is a technology tool that enables you to organize vast amounts of information in the most logical way that suits your business needs. For SPIN to be successful, databases are an absolute necessity. As Jeremy Hamilton-Wright, the team leader in Chrysler's IS department, describes it, "SPIN supports everything from developing products to delivering parts and sending payments. SPIN works for all of Chrysler's different types of suppliers: production

suppliers, parts suppliers, and the suppliers that package parts."

All businesses today are using databases to organize and manage their information. Why? Because databases allow you to create logical relationships within your information. At Chrysler, for example, recall notices for a defective part or assembly are logically tracked back through the production process, including human operators and equipment, through database information. If Chrysler determines that the error didn't occur in the production process, it tracks information farther back through its databases to its inventory and suppliers.

Many organizations also use databases in support of their customer relationship management (CRM) strategies, another source of competitive advantage. Using CRM-enabled databases, organizations today can track customer purchases, purchases by credit card or cash, purchases by time of the day and day of the week, purchases by store location, and an array of customer demographics. All that information can then be logically organized in such a way that you could easily find the answer to the following question: "Which of our customers who have purchased over $1500 in the last six months at a store within a five-mile radius of their homes have a household income above $75,000 and no children?"

Answers to those types of questions are what we call *business intelligence*. Business intelligence helps you make sense of your information by allowing you to view it from different perspectives and ask insightful and thought-provoking questions. To support the creation of business intelligence, many organizations are taking information from their databases and creating data warehouses, another technology tool that supports the logical organization of information.[1]

Introduction

Imagine that you're the inventory manager for a multimillion-dollar firm and that you can accurately predict selling trends by the week, territory, salesperson, and product line. Imagine that you own an accounting firm and can accurately predict which and how many of your clients will file for tax extensions. Imagine that you're an accounts manager and can accurately determine creditworthy risks. Sound impossible? Not really—it's quite possible that you could make these predications with a 95 percent accuracy rate, or even higher.

How? Obviously your education has a lot to do with it. But so does access to and the ability to work with two resources that every organization owns today—information and business intelligence. *Access to* information and business intelligence implies that they are organized in such a way that you can easily and quickly get to them. *Working with* information and business intelligence implies that you have the right information processing tools. That's what this chapter is all about—organizing information and business intelligence and having the right tools to work them.

Throughout this chapter, we focus on (1) databases and data warehouses as methods for organizing and managing information and business intelligence and (2) database management systems and data mining techniques as IT tools you use to work with information and business intelligence.

Business Intelligence

"Business intelligence" sounds like a great term. But what exactly is it? **Business intelligence** is knowledge—knowledge about your customers, your competitors, your partners, your competitive environment, and your own internal operations. Business intelligence comes from information. It enables your organization to extrapolate the true meaning of information to take creative and powerful steps to ensure a competitive advantage. So business intelligence is much more than just a list of the products you sell. It would, for example, combine your product information with your advertising strategy information and customer demographics to help you determine the effectiveness of various advertising media on demographic groups segmented by location (see Figure 4.1).

Of course, business intelligence doesn't just magically appear. You must first gather and organize all your information. Then, you must have the right IT tools to define and analyze various relationships within the information. In short, knowledge workers such as you use IT tools to create business intelligence from information. The technology won't simply do it for you. However, technology such as databases, database management systems (DBMSs), data warehouses, and data mining tools can definitely help you build and use business intelligence.

As you begin working with these tools (which we'll discuss in great detail throughout this chapter), you'll be performing the two types of information processing we alluded to in Chapter 1—online transaction processing and online analytical processing. **Online transaction processing (OLTP)** is the gathering of input information, the processing of that information, and the updating of existing information to reflect the gathered and processed information. Databases and DBMSs are the technology tools that directly support OLTP. Databases that support OLTP are most often referred to as **operational databases**; inside these is valuable information that forms the basis for business intelligence.

Figure 4.1

Building Business Intelligence

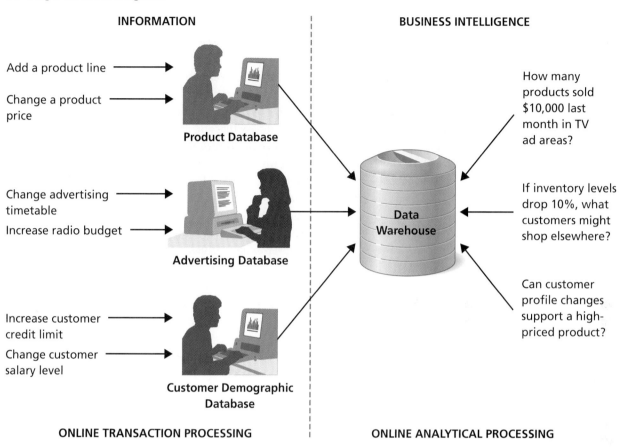

| INFORMATION | | BUSINESS INTELLIGENCE |

Add a product line ⟶ **Product Database**

Change a product price ⟶

Change advertising timetable ⟶ **Advertising Database**

Increase radio budget ⟶

Increase customer credit limit ⟶ **Customer Demographic Database**

Change customer salary level ⟶

Data Warehouse

How many products sold $10,000 last month in TV ad areas?

If inventory levels drop 10%, what customers might shop elsewhere?

Can customer profile changes support a high-priced product?

ONLINE TRANSACTION PROCESSING   ONLINE ANALYTICAL PROCESSING

Online analytical processing (OLAP) is the manipulation of information to support decision making. At Mervyn's, a former subsidiary of Target Corporation, OLAP is a must and a definite improvement over the way things used to work.[2,3] According to Sid Banjeree, "Mervyn's had people who spent hours pouring over shopping carts full of paper reports . . . to gather product information by units, by dollars, by a single store, by season, by region, and by ad zone. Now, those same people spend just a few seconds to perform the same tasks with OLAP and a data warehouse. As Sue Little, Mervyn's manager of merchandise planning and logistics systems, points out, "We're finally comparing apples to apples, and now we're spending only 10 percent of our time gathering data and 90 percent acting upon it, instead of the other way around."

A data warehouse is, in fact, a special form of a database that contains information gathered from many operational databases for the purpose of supporting decision-making tasks. When you build a data warehouse and use data mining tools to manipulate the data warehouse's information, your single goal is to create *business intelligence*. So data warehouses support only OLAP—they do not at all support OLTP.

As this chapter unfolds, we'll look specifically at (1) databases and database management systems and (2) data warehouses and data mining tools. Databases today are the foundation for organizing and managing information, and database management systems provide the tools you use to work with a database. Data warehouses are explosive, relatively new technologies that help you organize and manage business intelligence, and data mining tools help you extract that vitally important business intelligence.

The Relational Database Model

For organizing and storing basic and transaction-oriented information (eventually used to create business intelligence), businesses today use databases. There are actually four primary models for creating a database. The object-oriented database model is the newest and holds great promise—we'll talk more about the entire object-oriented genre in Chapter 5 and Extended Learning Module F. Right now, let's focus on the most popular database model—the relational database model.

As a generic definition, we would say that any **database** is a collection of data that you organize and access according to the logical structure of these data. In reference to the **relational database model**, we say that it uses a series of logically related two-dimensional tables or files to store data in the form of a database. The term **relation** often describes each two-dimensional table or file in the relational model (hence the name *relational* database model). A relational database is actually composed of two distinct parts: (1) the data itself—stored in a series of two-dimensional tables, files, or relations (people use these three terms interchangeably) and (2) the logical structure of the data. Let's look at a portion of an *Inventory* database to further explore the characteristics of the relational database model.

COLLECTIONS OF DATA

In Figure 4.2 we've created a view of a portion of an *Inventory* database. Notice that the *Inventory* database contains two files: *Part* and *Facility*. (In reality, it would contain many more files including *Orders*, *Distributors*, and so on.) A facility is simply a storage place for parts (similar to a warehouse). The *Part* and *Facility* files are related for two reasons. First, parts are stored in various facilities, so each file contains a common field—*Facility Number*. Second, you would use both files to manage your inventory, a common function in almost any business.

Within each file, you can see specific pieces of data (what we often call *attributes*). For example, the *Part* file contains *Part Number*, *Part Name*, *Cost*, *Percentage Markup*, *Distributor ID*, *Facility Number*, and *Bin Number*. *Bin Number*, in this case, describes the physical location of a given part in a facility. In the *Facility* file, you can see specific information including *Facility Number*, *Facility Name*, *Phone Number*, *Street Location*, and *Manager Number*. These are all important data that an inventory database would need to maintain. Moreover, you would need all this information (and probably much more) to effectively manage your inventory.

CREATED WITH LOGICAL STRUCTURES

Skills Module 2 Database Design— Access

Using the relational database model, you organize and access data according to its logical structure, not its physical position. So you don't really care in which row of the *Part* file 50' tape measures appear. You really only need to know that the *Part Number* is 1003 or—for that matter—that the name of the part is 50' tape measure. In the relational database model, a **data dictionary** contains the logical structure for the information. When you create a database, you first create the data dictionary. The data dictionary contains important information or logical properties about your information. The screen in Figure 4.2 shows how you can build the data dictionary for the *Part* file using Microsoft Access (a popular personal database package). Notice that the data dictionary identifies all field names, types (Currency for *Cost*, for example), sizes, formats, default values, and so on.

Figure 4.2

A Portion of an Inventory Database

Part Number is the primary key because of the key icon beside it.

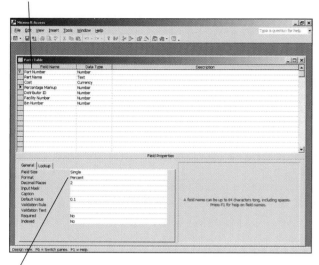

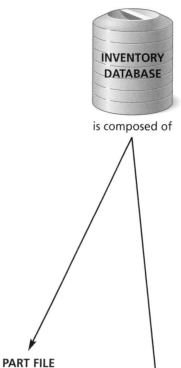

INVENTORY DATABASE

is composed of

For *Percentage Markup*, we defined its format as "Percent" and its number of decimal places as 2.

PART FILE

Part Number	Part Name	Cost	Percentage Markup	Distributor ID	Facility Number	Bin Number
1003	50' Tape Measure	$11.90	40.00%	10	291	2988
1005	25' Tape Measure	$9.95	40.00%	10	291	3101
1083	10 Amp Fuse	$0.07	50.00%	14	378	3984
1109	15 Amp Fuse	$0.07	50.00%	14	378	3983
2487	25 Amp Fuse	$0.08	50.00%	14	378	3982
2897	U.S. Socket Set	$29.75	25.00%	12	411	8723
3789	Crimping Tool	$14.50	30.00%	13	411	3298
3982	Claw Hammer	$9.90	30.00%	10	291	2987
4101	Metric Socket Set	$23.75	25.00%	12	411	4123
5908	6" Pliers	$7.45	25.00%	11	411	4567
6743	8" Pliers	$7.90	25.00%	11	411	4385

FACILITY FILE

Facility Number	Facility Name	Phone Number	Street Location	Manager Number
291	Pegasus	378-4921	3578 W. 12th St.	123456
378	Medusa	379-2981	4314 48th Ave.	234567
411	Orion	298-8763	198 Red Ln.	345678

This is quite different from other ways of organizing data. For example, if you want to access data in a certain cell in most spreadsheet applications, you must know its physical position—row number and column letter. With a relational database, however, you need only know the field name of the column of data (e.g., *Percentage Markup*) and its logical row, not its physical row. As a result, in our *Inventory* database example, you could easily change the percentage markup for part number 1003, without knowing where that data is physically stored (by row or column).

And with spreadsheet software, you can immediately begin typing in data, creating column headings, and providing formatting. You can't do that with a database. Using a database, you must first clearly define the characteristics of each field by creating a data dictionary. So you must carefully plan the design of your database before you can start adding data.

WITH LOGICAL TIES AMONG THE DATA

In a relational database, you must create ties or relationships in the data that show how the files relate to each other. Before you can create these relationships among files, you must first specify the **primary key** for each file—a field (or group of fields in some cases) that uniquely describes each record. In our *Inventory* database, *Part Number* is the primary key for the *Part* file and *Facility Number* is the primary key for the *Facility* file. That is to say, every part in the *Part* file must have a unique *Part Number* and every facility in the *Facility* file must have a unique *Facility Number*.

As well, when you define that a specific field in a file is the primary key, you're also stating that the field cannot be blank. That is, you cannot enter the data for a new part in the *Part* file and leave the *Part Number* field blank. If that were possible, you could potentially do it for more than one part. If so, you would have two parts with identical primary keys (blank), which is not possible in a database environment.

Again, this is quite different from working with spreadsheets. Using a spreadsheet, it would be almost impossible to ensure that each field in a given column (e.g., *Part Number* in the *Part* file) is unique. This points up the fact that, while spreadsheets work with data according to physical location, databases work with data logically.

If you look back at Figure 4.2, you can see that *Facility Number* also appears in the *Part* file. This creates the logical relationship between the two files and is an example of a foreign key. A **foreign key** is a primary key of one file that appears in another file. Now look at Figure 4.3. In it, we've added the *Distributor* file and the *Employee* file in the *Inventory* database. In doing so, we can illustrate two more examples of foreign keys.

Notice *Distributor ID* in the *Distributor* file—it is the primary key for that file. It also appears in the *Part* file—this enables us to track from whom we get our parts. So *Distributor ID* is the primary key in the *Distributor* file and also a foreign key that appears in the *Part* file. Now, take a look at *Employee Number* in the *Employee* file—it is the primary key for that file. And it also appears in the *Facility* file (as *Manager Number*). This enables us to track the manager for each facility. So *Employee Number* is the primary key in the *Employee* file and also a foreign key in the *Facility* file.

Foreign keys are essential in the relational database model. Without them, you have no way of creating logical ties among the various files. As you might guess, we use these relationships extensively to create business intelligence because they enable us to track the logical relationships between many types of data.

WITH BUILT-IN INTEGRITY CONSTRAINTS

By defining the logical structure of information in a relational database, you're also developing **integrity constraints**—rules that help ensure the quality of the data. For

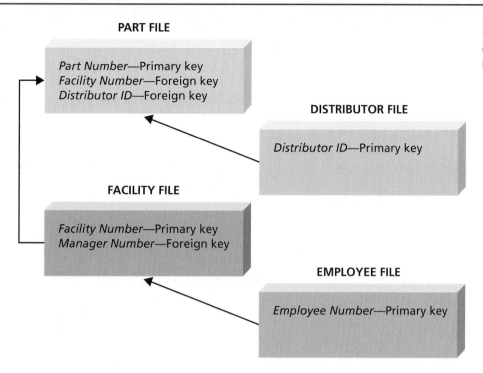

Figure 4.3

Creating Logical Ties with Primary and Foreign Keys

example, by stating that *Facility Number* is the primary key of the *Facility* file and a foreign key in the *Part* file, you're saying (1) that no two facilities can have the same *Facility Number* and (2) that a part in the *Part* file cannot be assigned to a facility number that does not exist in the *Facility file*. So, as you add a new part to the inventory, you must specify a facility in which it will be located that already exists in the *Facility* file. Likewise, you can't choose to eliminate a facility if parts are still assigned to it. This makes perfect sense. If you want to close a certain facility, you must first move all of the parts in it to a different facility.

Consumer Reports has rated the Ritz-Carlton first among luxury hotels.[4] Why? As outlined in the opening Case Study in Chapter 1, Ritz-Carlton has created a powerful guest preference database to provide customized, personal, and high-level service to guests in any of its hotels. Using a unique customer ID for you that creates logical ties to your various preferences, the Ritz-Carlton transfers your information to all the other hotels. The next time you stay in a Ritz-Carlton hotel, your information is already there and the hotel staff immediately knows of your desires.

For the management at Ritz-Carlton, achieving customer loyalty starts first with knowing each customer individually. To store and organize all this information, Ritz-Carlton uses a relational database, and employees use it to fill your every need (or whim).

Database Management System Tools

When working with word processing software, you create and edit a document. When working with spreadsheet software, you create and edit a workbook. The same is true in a database environment. A database is equivalent to a document or a workbook because they all contain information. And, while word processing and spreadsheet are the software tools you use to work with documents and workbooks, you use database management system software to work with databases. A **database management system (DBMS)** helps you specify the logical organization for a database and access and

PRIMARY KEYS, FOREIGN KEYS, AND INTEGRITY CONSTRAINTS

Let's consider the information that your school tracks for a class. In this instance, a class is a scheduled course. For example, your school may have FINA 2100—Introduction to International Financial Markets as a course. If it offers it in the fall, it becomes a class. Below, we've provided many pieces of information that your school probably tracks about the class. First, which is the primary key (put an X in the second column)? Second, for each piece of information, identify if it's a foreign key (a primary key of another file). If it is, write down the file name in the third column. Finally, in the fourth column for each piece of information, write down any integrity constraints you can think of. For example, can it be blank or must it contain something? Can it be duplicated across multiple records (classes)? If it's a number, does it have a specific range in which it must fall? There are many others.

Information	Primary Key?	Foreign Key?	Integrity Constraints
Department designation (e.g., FINA)			
Course number (e.g., 2100)			
Course name			
Course description			
Prerequisite			
Number of credit hours			
Lab fee			
Instructor name			
Room number			
Time of day			
Day of week			

use the information within a database. A DBMS contains five important software components (see Figure 4.4):

1. DBMS engine
2. Data definition subsystem
3. Data manipulation subsystem
4. Application generation subsystem
5. Data administration subsystem

The DBMS engine is perhaps the most important—yet seldom recognized—component of a DBMS. The **DBMS engine** accepts logical requests from the various other DBMS subsystems, converts them into their physical equivalent, and actually accesses the database and data dictionary as they exist on a storage device. Again, the distinction between *logical* and *physical* is important in a database environment. The **physical view** of information deals with how information is physically arranged, stored, and accessed on some type of storage device such as a hard disk. The **logical view** of information, on the other hand, focuses on how you as a knowledge worker need to arrange and access data to meet your particular business needs.

Figure 4.4

Software Subsystems of a Database Management System

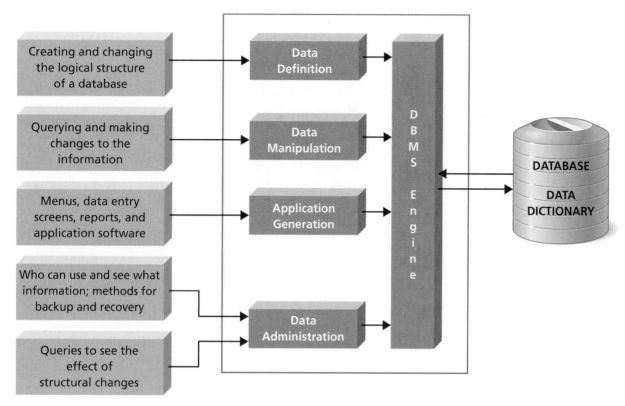

Databases and DBMSs provide two really great advantages in separating the logical from the physical view of data. First, the DBMS handles the physical tasks, so you, as a database user, can concentrate solely on your logical information needs. Second, although there is only one physical view of data, there may be numerous knowledge workers who have different logical views of the data in a database. That is, according to what business tasks they need to perform, different knowledge workers logically view data in different ways. The DBMS engine can process virtually any logical data view or request into its physical equivalent.

DATA DEFINITION SUBSYSTEM

The **data definition subsystem** of a DBMS helps you create and maintain the data dictionary and define the structure of the files in a database. In Figure 4.2, we provided a screen capture of the data definition subsystem using Microsoft Access. In that screen, we created the data dictionary and defined the structure of the *Part* file of our *Inventory* database.

When you create a database, you must first use the data definition subsystem to create the data dictionary and define the structure of the files. This is very different from using something like spreadsheet software. When you create a workbook, you can immediately begin typing in information and creating formulas and functions. You can't do that with a database. You must define its logical structure before you can begin typing in any information. Typing in the data is the easy part—defining the logical structure is more difficult. In Extended Learning Module C, we take you through the process of defining the logical structure for a database. We definitely

> Skills Module 2
> Database Design—
> Access

recommend you read that Module—knowing how to define the correct structure of a database can be a substantial career opportunity for you.

If you ever find that a certain file needs another piece of information, you have to use the data definition subsystem to add a new field in the data dictionary. Likewise, if you want to delete a given field for all the records in a file, you must use the data definition subsystem to do so.

As you create the data dictionary, you're essentially defining the logical properties of the data that the database will contain. Logical structures of data include the following:

Logical Properties	Examples
Field name	*Part Number, Bin Number*
Type	Alphabetic, numeric, date, time, etc.
Form	Is an area code required for a phone number?
Default value	If no percentage markup is entered, the default is 10%.
Validation rule	Can percentage markups exceed 100%?
Is an entry required?	Must you enter a *Facility Number* for a part, or can it be blank?
Can there be duplicates?	Primary keys cannot be duplicates, but what about percentage markups?

These are all important logical properties to a lesser or greater extent depending on the type of data you're describing. For example, a typical address might have a field name of *Customer Address* and a type of alphanumeric (allowing for both numbers and letters). Beyond those, the logical properties are not quite as important, with the possible exception of requiring that the field cannot be blank.

However, if you're describing something like *Percentage Markup* in our *Inventory* database, you'll want to define such logical properties as a default value and perhaps some sort of validation rule.

DATA MANIPULATION SUBSYSTEM

The **data manipulation subsystem** of a DBMS helps you add, change, and delete information in a database and mine it for valuable information. Software tools within the data manipulation subsystem are most often the primary interface between you as a user and the information contained in a database. So, while the DBMS engine handles your information requests from a physical point of view, it is the data manipulation tools within a DBMS that allow you to specify your logical information requirements. Those logical information requirements are then used by the DBMS engine to access the data you need from a physical point of view.

In most DBMSs, you'll find a variety of data manipulation tools, including views, report generators, query-by-example tools, and structured query language.

VIEWS A **view** allows you to see the contents of a database file, make whatever changes you want, perform simple sorting, and query to find the location of specific

TRACKING SHOE MOVEMENT WITH WIRELESS AND DATABASE TECHNOLOGIES

Managing your inventory is an important task and often a daunting one. Simply knowing where your inventory is scattered across multiple warehouses may often not be easy but it can certainly save you money. Consider Skechers USA, for example, a footwear maker in Ontario, California. It recently implemented a wireless tracking and database-enabled system to improve inventory management, which saves approximately $1 million annually.

When a shipment of shoes arrives from a Far East manufacturer (each box with 12 pairs of shoes), an employee uses a handheld scanner to verify its receipt.

Next, the employee logs the warehouse destination of each box. That information is all stored in a database. Then, at any time and from any location, an employee can determine the warehouse in which any given box of shoes is stored. This enables Skechers to efficiently schedule shipments out of its four different warehouse locations.

As Paul Galliher, VP of distribution, describes it, "We can now use logical pick paths and improve all the shipping processes with the proper documentation generated that allows us to see at which of our four buildings we can schedule a pickup."[5]

---

data. Views essentially provide each file in the form of a spreadsheet workbook. The screen in Figure 4.5 shows a view in Microsoft Access for the *Part* file of our *Inventory* database. At this point, you can click on any specific field and change its contents. You could also point at an entire record and click on the Cut icon (the scissors) to remove a record. If you want to add a record, simply click in the *Part Number* field of the first blank record and begin typing.

Notice, we've sorted the file in ascending order by *Part Number*. You can easily achieve this by clicking on the A→Z sort button in the view window. If you want to sort in descending order by *Percentage Markup*, simply point to any *Percentage Markup* field and click on the Z→A sort button. You can also perform searches within views. For example, if you wanted to find all parts that have the term "pliers" in the

Skills Module 2
Database Design—
Access

Sort using these
two buttons.

Find information
with the binoculars.

Figure 4.5
A View in Microsoft Access

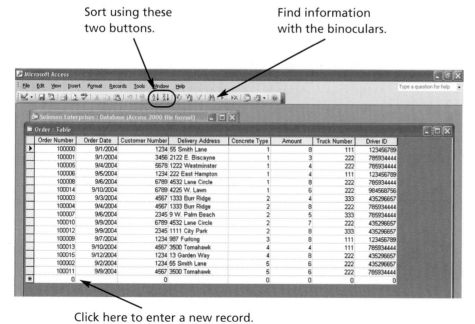

Click here to enter a new record.

Part Name field, simply point anywhere in that column, click on the "find text" button (the binoculars) and enter "pliers." Access will respond by highlighting each *Part Name* field where the word "pliers" appears.

As with most other types of personal productivity software, DBMSs support such functions and tasks as cutting and pasting, formatting (e.g., bolding a field), spell checking, hiding columns (just as you would do using spreadsheet software), filtering, and even adding links to Web sites.

REPORT GENERATORS   **Report generators** help you quickly define formats of reports and what information you want to see in a report. Once you define a report, you can view it on the screen or print it. Figure 4.6 shows two intermediate screens in Microsoft Access. The first allows you to specify which fields of information are to appear in a report. We have chosen to include *Part Number*, *Part Name*, *Cost*, and *Percentage Markup*. The second allows you to choose from a set of predefined report formats. Following a simple and easy-to-use set of screens (including the two in Figure 4.6) we went on to specify that sorting should take place by *Part Name* and that the name of the report should be "Part Report." The completed report is also shown in Figure 4.6. Notice that it only displays those fields we requested, that it's sorted by *Part Name*, and that the title is "Part Report."

Figure 4.6

Using a Report Generator

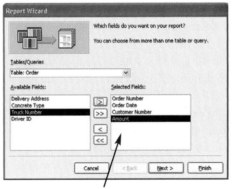
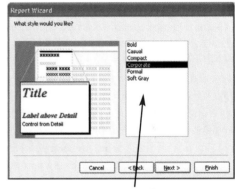

Selected fields from   Report formats
the *Order* file

CUSTOMER AND AMOUNT REPORT

Customer Number	Order Number	Order Date	Amount
1234	100000	9/1/2004	8
1234	100002	9/2/2004	6
1234	100006	9/5/2004	4
1234	100009	9/7/2004	8
1234	100015	9/12/2004	8
2345	100007	9/6/2004	5
2345	100012	9/9/2004	8
3456	100001	9/1/2004	3
4567	100003	9/3/2004	4
4567	100004	9/4/2004	8
4567	100011	9/9/2004	6
4567	100013	9/10/2004	4
5678	100005	9/4/2004	4
6789	100008	9/6/2004	8
6789	100010	9/9/2004	7
6789	100014	9/10/2004	6

A nice feature of report generators is that you can save a report format that you use frequently. For example, if you think you'll use the report in Figure 4.6 often, you can save it by giving it a unique name. Later, you can request that report and your DBMS will generate it, using the most up-to-date information in the database. You can also choose from a variety of report formats (we chose a simple one for our illustration). You can even choose report formats that create intermediate subtotals and grand totals, which can include counts, sums, averages, and the like.

QUERY-BY-EXAMPLE TOOLS   Query-by-example (QBE) tools help you graphically design the answer to a question. In our *Inventory* database, for example, "What are the names and phone numbers of the facility managers who are in charge of parts that have a cost greater than $10?" The question may seem simple considering that we have very few parts and even fewer facilities and managers in our database. However, can you imagine trying to answer that question if 100 facilities and 70,000 parts were involved? It would not be fun.

Fortunately, QBE tools can help you answer this question and perform many other queries in a matter of seconds. In Figure 4.7, you can see a QBE screen that formulates the answer to our question. When you perform a QBE, you (1) identify the files in which the information is located, (2) drag any necessary fields from the identified files to the QBE grid, and (3) specify selection criteria.

For names and phone numbers of facility managers in charge of parts with costs over $10, we first identified two files—*Part* and *Employee*. Second, we dragged *Part Number*, *Facility Number*, and *Cost* from the *Part* file to the QBE grid and dragged *Employee Name* and *Employee Phone Number* from the *Employee* file to the QBE grid. Finally, we specified in the Criteria box that we wanted to view only those parts with costs exceeding $10. Access did the rest and provided the information in Figure 4.7.

QBEs rely heavily on the logical relationships within a database to find information. For example, part 4101 has a cost exceeding $10. So, the QBE tool took the *Facility Number* from the *Part* file and found a match in the *Facility* file. It then used

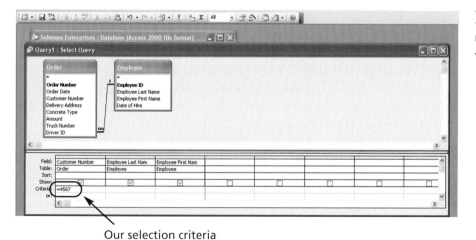

Figure 4.7

Using a Query-by-Example to Find Information

Our selection criteria

Customer Number	Employee Last Name	Employee First Name
4567	Evaraz	Antonio
4567	Robertson	John
4567	Robertson	John
4567	Robertson	John

FLOATING DATABASES ABOARD ROYAL CARIBBEAN CRUISE SHIPS

Databases are not a "landlocked" technology, as anyone at Royal Caribbean Cruises will tell you. With floating hotel-like structures that include restaurants, casinos, duty-free shops, and Internet cafes, Royal Caribbean has sophisticated database technologies aboard each ship. According to Thomas Murphy, Royal Caribbean CIO, "The technology is becoming so much more important in running a cruise ship. Customer satisfaction depends on it, but so does the basic operation of the ship."

Aboard a cruise ship, databases track everything including general customer information, customer complaints and inquiries, on-demand movie requests, Internet cafe use, shopping purchases, meal purchases, and pay-for-use services such as massages and haircuts. The system even tracks male customers according to what size of tuxedo they reserve. That information can be used again if the same passenger takes another cruise on a Royal ship.

Royal Caribbean is also planning to build a centralized land-based data warehouse. Each ship, as it records information in its database, will use wireless telecommunications technologies to upload information into the data warehouse. Service planners will then be able to better predict what types of services will be needed on future cruises. For example, by time of year and cruise destination, service planners will know what sizes of tuxedos to stock and approximately how many massages will be performed. (What fields of information would you have in a "massage" record?)

If you're on land and want to take a virtual tour of a Royal Caribbean cruise ship, you can do that. Just connect to Royal Caribbean's Web site (www.royal caribbean.com) and you can view estate rooms, eating facilities, spa facilities, and general entertainment areas. Of course, Royal Caribbean ultimately wants you to enjoy your virtual experience so much that you book a cruise.

But if you're not quite ready yet, the company would like you to leave some contact information at its Web site. It will then store that information in its database and, from time to time, send you some cruise information.[6,7]

---

the *Manager Number* in that matching record and performed another search of the *Employee* file to find another match. When it found a match, it then gathered the *Employee Name* and *Employee Phone Number*. Without the logical relationships correctly defined, this QBE query would never have worked.

→ SQL

STRUCTURED QUERY LANGUAGE **Structured query language (SQL)** is a standardized fourth-generation query language found in most DBMSs. SQL performs the same function as QBE, except that you perform the query by creating a statement instead of pointing, clicking, and dragging. The basic form of an SQL statement is:

SELECT ... FROM ... WHERE ...

After the SELECT, you list the fields of information you want; after the FROM, you specify what logical relationships to use; and after the WHERE, you specify any selection criteria. If you consider our QBE above of "What are the names and phone numbers of the facility managers who are in charge of parts that have a cost greater than $10?" the SQL statement would look like this:

SELECT Part.[Part Number], Part.Cost, Employee.[Employee Name], Employee.[Employee Number]

FROM Part, Employee

WHERE (((Part.Cost)>10));

DBMS SUPPORT FOR OLTP, OLAP, INFORMATION MANAGEMENT

In the table below, we've listed the various DBMS subsystems or tools. For each of these, identify whether it supports online transaction processing, online analytical processing, both online transaction and analytical processing, or the management of a database.

DBMS Tool	OLTP	OLAP	Both	Management
DBMS engine				
View				
Report generator				
QBE				
SQL				
Data entry screen				
DBMS programming language				
Common programming language				
Data administration subsystem				

Thoroughly introducing you to the syntax of SQL statements is outside the scope of this text and would easily require almost 100 pages of material. But you should be aware that SQL does exist. If you're majoring in IT or MIS, you'll undoubtedly take a course in SQL.

APPLICATION GENERATION SUBSYSTEM

The **application generation subsystem** of a DBMS contains facilities to help you develop transaction-intensive applications. These types of applications usually require that you perform a detailed series of tasks to process a transaction. Application generation subsystem facilities include tools for creating visually appealing and easy-to-use data entry screens, programming languages specific to a particular DBMS, and interfaces to commonly used programming languages that are independent of any DBMS.

As with SQL, application generation facilities are most often used by IT specialists. We recommend that you, as a knowledge worker, leave application generation to IT specialists as much as you can. You need to focus on views, report generators, and QBE tools. These will help you find information in a database and perform queries so you can start to build and use business intelligence.

DATA ADMINISTRATION SUBSYSTEM

The **data administration subsystem** of a DBMS helps you manage the overall database environment by providing facilities for backup and recovery, security management, query optimization, concurrency control, and change management. The data administration subsystem is most often used by a data administrator or database

LUFTHANSA WANTS YOUR COMPLAINTS

In a time when all airlines are seeking ways to gain passengers and their loyalty, Lufthansa is taking an approach like no other. Simply put, if you don't like something about your flight—the late departure/arrival, uncomfortable seats, hot meals that weren't hot, or anything else you care to complain about—Lufthansa wants to know about it.

This approach isn't to let you vent so that you'll feel better. Lufthansa takes every complaint and enters it into a database. The database, Oracle 9i, supports Lufthansa's COSMIC project—Customer Oriented Service Management Improvement in the Cabin. In any given month, Lufthansa employees enter 6000 to 7000 complaints about arrival/departure, boarding, meals, and other aspects of in-flight service. The system tracks such a level of detail that a complaint can even be recorded for a portion of food (e.g., your bread or meat) that you didn't feel was sufficient in size.

That many complaints may seem high, but consider that Lufthansa uses 14,000 cabin attendants to fly 45 million passengers each year to 350 different destinations in 94 countries. That means Lufthansa receives and records only one complaint per 650 passengers. That's good, but not good enough for Lufthansa.

Lufthansa uses Oracle's Discoverer data-mining tools to carefully sift through all the complaints. Lufthansa can easily categorize complaints by each outsourcing caterer. It uses that information to impose penalties on caterers who continually provide substandard food and beverages.

The Discoverer tool set has allowed Lufthansa to cut the time spent handling customer complaints by an amazing 70 percent. That not only saves money, but also increases customer loyalty and retention.

Soon, Lufthansa plans to create satellite links between its in-flight planes and the home office, which will allow cabin attendants to enter complaints on board a flight and have the complaints immediately analyzed.

Customer service is about providing exceptional service. But it's also about rectifying customer complaints. Using databases and tool sets that allow you to sift through and organize customer complaints, your organization can gain a competitive advantage, just like Lufthansa.[8]

administrator—people responsible for assuring that the database (and data warehouse) environment meets the entire information needs of an organization.

Backup and recovery facilities provide a way for you to (1) periodically back up information contained in a database and (2) restart or recover a database and its information in case of a failure. These are important functions you cannot ignore in today's information-based environment. Organizations that understand the importance of their information take precautions to preserve it, often by running backup databases, a DBMS, and storage facilities parallel to the primary database environment. In Chapter 3, we talked specifically about "contingency planning"—how to develop plans and strategies in the event of some sort of failure.

Security management facilities allow you to control who has access to what information and what type of access those people have. In many database environments, for example, some people may only need "view" access to database information, but not "change" access. Still others may need the ability to add, change, and/or delete information in a database. Through a system of user specification and password levels, the data administration subsystem allows you to define which users can perform which tasks and what information they can see. At car dealership JM Family Enterprises (JMFE), security management facilities are an absolute must because its technology is highly decentralized and includes users of mobile technologies.[9] JMFE's system supports encryption and passwords to protect databases, files, and many hardware resources. The system even supports automatic logoffs after a certain amount of time if users accidentally leave their system running.

SQL

Query optimization facilities often take queries from users (in the form of SQL statements or QBEs) and restructure them to minimize response times. In SQL, for example, you can build a query statement that might involve working with as many as ten different files. As you might well guess, when working with ten different files, there may be several different solutions for combining them to get the information you need. Fortunately, you don't have to worry about structuring the SQL statement in an optimized fashion; the optimization facilities will do that for you and provide you with the information you need in the fastest possible way.

Reorganization facilities continually statistics concerning how the DBMS engine physically accesses information. In maintaining those statistics, reorganization facilities can optimize the physical structure of a database to further increase speed and performance. For example, if you frequently access a certain file by a specific order, the reorganization facilities may maintain the file in that order to create an index that maintains the order in that file. What's really nice is that you don't have to be aware of the changes to your database with respect to physical locations—the DBMS engine will take care of it for you.

Concurrency control facilities ensure the validity of database updates when multiple users attempt to access and change the same information. This is crucial in today's networked business environment. Consider your school's online registration system. What if you and another student try to register for a class with only one seat remaining at the exact same time? Who gets enrolled? What happens to the person excluded? These are important questions, and once answered they must be defined in the database environment using concurrency control facilities.

Change management facilities allow you to assess the impact of proposed structural changes to a database environment. For example, if you decide to add a character identifier to a numeric part number, you can use the change management facilities to see how many files will be affected. Recall that *Part Number* would be the primary key for a *Part* file and that it would also be a foreign key in many other files. Some structural changes (such as adding a postal code extension) may not have much effect on the database, but others can cause widespread changes that you must assess carefully.

All of these—backup and recovery, security management, query optimization, reorganization, concurrency control, and change management—are vitally important facilities in any DBMS and thus any database environment. As a user and knowledge worker, you probably won't deal with these facilities specifically as far as setting them up and maintaining them is concerned. But how they're set up and maintained will affect what you can do. So knowing that they do exist and what their purposes are is important.

Data Warehouses and Data Mining

Suppose you, as a manager at Victoria's Secret, wanted to know the total revenues generated from the sale of shoes last month. That's a simple query, which you could easily implement using either SQL or a QBE tool. But what if you wanted to know "By actual vs. budgeted, how many size 8 shoes in black did we sell last month in the southeast and southwest regions, compared with the same month over the past five years?" That task seems almost impossible, even with the aid of technology. And, if you were actually able to build a QBE query for it, you would probably bring the organization's operational database environment to its knees.

This example illustrates the two primary reasons so many organizations are opting to build data warehouses. First, while operational databases may have the needed information, the information is not organized in such a way that lends itself to building business intelligence within the database or using various data manipulation tools. Second, if you could build such a query, your operational databases, which are probably already supporting the processing of hundreds of transactions per second, would seriously suffer in performance when you hit the start button to perform the query.

To support such intriguing, necessary, and complex queries to create business intelligence, many organizations are building data warehouses and providing data mining tools. A data warehouse is simply the next step (beyond databases) in the progression of building business intelligence. And data mining tools are the tools you use to mine a data warehouse and extrapolate the business intelligence you need to make a decision, solve a problem, or capitalize on an opportunity to create a competitive advantage.

WHAT IS A DATA WAREHOUSE?

A **data warehouse** is a logical collection of information—gathered from many different operational databases—used to create business intelligence that supports business analysis activities and decision-making tasks (see Figure 4.8). Sounds simple enough on the surface, but data warehouses represent a fundamentally different way of thinking about organizing and managing information in an organization. Consider the following key features of a data warehouse.

DATA WAREHOUSES ARE MULTIDIMENSIONAL   In the relational database model, information is represented in a series of two-dimensional tables. Not so in a data warehouse—most data warehouses are multidimensional, meaning that they contain layers of columns and rows. For this reason, most data warehouses are really

Figure 4.8

A Multidimensional Data Warehouse with Information from Multiple Operational Databases

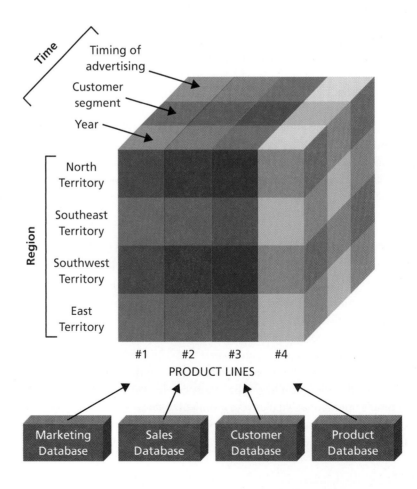

multidimensional databases. The layers in a data warehouse represent information according to different dimensions. This multidimensional representation of information is referred to as a *hypercube.*

In Figure 4.8, you can see a hypercube that represents product information by product line and region (columns and rows), by year (the first layer), by customer segment (the second layer), and by the timing of advertising media (the third layer). Using this hypercube, you can easily ask, "According to customer segment A, what percentage of total sales for product line 1 in the southwest territory occurred immediately after a radio advertising blitz?" The information you would receive from that query constitutes business intelligence.

Any specific sub-cube within the larger hypercube can contain a variety of summarized information gathered from the various operational databases. For example, the forwardmost and top left sub-cube contains information for the North territory, by year, for product line 1. So it could contain totals, average, counts, and distributions summarizing in some way that information. Of course, what it contains is really up to you and your needs.

DATA WAREHOUSES SUPPORT DECISION MAKING, NOT TRANSACTION PROCESSING In an organization, most databases are transaction-oriented. That is, they support online transaction processing (OLTP) and, therefore, are operational databases. Data warehouses are not transaction-oriented—they exist to support decision-making tasks in your organization. Therefore, data warehouses support only online analytical processing (OLAP).

As we just stated, the sub-cubes within a data warehouse contain summarized information. So, while a data warehouse may contain the total sales for a year by product line, it does not contain a list of each individual sale to each individual customer for a given product line. Therefore, you simply cannot process transactions with a data warehouse. Instead, you process transactions with your operational databases and then use the information contained within the operational databases to build the summary information in a data warehouse.

WHAT ARE DATA MINING TOOLS?

Data mining tools are the software you use to query information in a data warehouse. These tools support the concept of OLAP—the manipulation of information to support decision-making tasks. Data mining tools include query-and-reporting tools, intelligent agents, multidimensional analysis tools, and statistical tools (see Figure 4.9). Essentially, data mining tools are to data warehouse users what data manipulation subsystem tools are to database users.

QUERY-AND-REPORTING TOOLS **Query-and-reporting tools** are similar to QBE tools, SQL, and report generators in the typical database environment. In fact, most data warehousing environments support simple and easy-to-use data manipulation subsystem tools such as QBE, SQL, and report generators. Most often, data warehouse users use these types of tools to generate simple queries and reports.

INTELLIGENT AGENTS Intelligent agents utilize various artificial intelligence tools such as neural networks and fuzzy logic to form the basis of "information discovery" and building business intelligence in OLAP. For example, Bay Street financial analysts can use OLAP software called Data/Logic, which incorporates neural networks to generate rules for a highly successful stock and bond trading system.[10] Other OLAP tools, such as Data Engine, incorporate fuzzy logic to analyze real-time technical processes.

Figure 4.9

The Data Miner's Tool Set

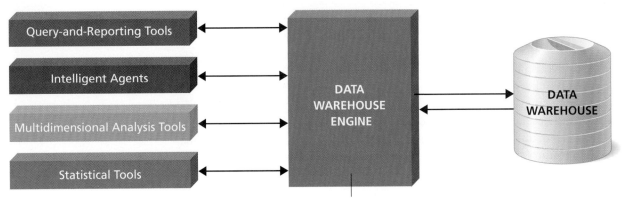

As in a DBMS, a data warehouse system has an engine responsible for converting your logical requests into their physical equivalent.

Intelligent agents represent the growing convergence of various IT tools for working with information. Previously, intelligent agents were considered only within the context of artificial intelligence and were seldom thought to be a part of the data organizing and managing functions in an organization. Today, you can find intelligent agents not only being used for OLAP in a data warehouse environment but also for searching for information on the Web. In Chapter 6, we'll explore artificial intelligence techniques such as intelligent agents.

MULTIDIMENSIONAL ANALYSIS TOOLS **Multidimensional analysis (MDA) tools** are slice-and-dice techniques that allow you to view multidimensional information from different perspectives. Within the context of a data warehouse, we refer to this process as "turning the cube." That is, you're essentially turning the cube to view information from different perspectives.

This "turning of the cube" allows you to quickly see information in different subcubes. If you refer back to the data warehouse in Figure 4.8, you'll notice that information by customer segment and timing of advertising are actually hidden. Using MDA tools, you can easily bring those to the front of the data warehouse for viewing. What you've essentially done is to slice the cube vertically by layer and bring some of the background layers to the front. As you do this, the values of the information are not affected.

STATISTICAL TOOLS Statistical tools help you apply various mathematical models to the information stored in a data warehouse to discover new information. For example, you can perform a time series analysis to project future trends. You can also perform a regression analysis to determine the effect of one variable on another.

Sega, one of the largest publishers of video games, uses a data warehouse and statistical tools to effectively distribute its more than $50+ million a year advertising budget.[11,12] With its data warehouse, product line specialists and marketing strategists "drill" into trends of each retail store chain. Their goal is to find buying trends that will help them better determine which advertising strategies are working best (and at what time of the year) and how to reallocate advertising resources by medium, territory, and time. Sega definitely benefits from its data warehouse, and so do retailers such as Toys "R" Us, Zellers, and Sears—all good examples of customer relationship management through technology.

A PERFECT MATCH—DATA WAREHOUSES, BUSINESS INTELLIGENCE, AND CUSTOMER RELATIONSHIP MANAGEMENT

Bank Hapoalim is Israel's largest bank, serving almost 2 million customers with a wide array of financial services and products. Bank Hapoalim's customer relationship management (CRM) focus is to offer superior customer care and unique financial services to maintain and expand its customer base.

As a part of this effort, Bank Hapoalim turned to Cognos, the world leader in business intelligence software and data warehouses. According to Tal Shlasky, data warehouse project manager at Bank Hapoalim, "We continue to devote our resources and energy to the individual customer in our quest to be more efficient and better suited to banking in the 21st century. Using an industry-leading solution like Cognos, we are doing just that. Cognos gives us an integrated view of the enterprise, allowing us to target customers based on their individual needs. Without a doubt, that capability gives us a competitive edge in the market."

To grow a customer base of 2 million, any organization needs data warehouses that support business intelligence.[13]

DATA MARTS—SMALLER DATA WAREHOUSES

Data warehouses are often perceived as organizationwide, containing summaries of all the information that an organization tracks. However, some people need access to only a portion of that data warehouse information. In this case, an organization can create one or more data marts. A **data mart** is a subset of a data warehouse in which only a focused portion of the data warehouse information is kept (see Figure 4.10).

Lands' End first created an organizationwide data warehouse for everyone to use, but soon found out that there can be "too much of a good thing."[14] In fact, many Lands' End employees wouldn't use the data warehouse because it was simply too big and complicated, and included information they didn't need. So Lands' End created several smaller data marts. For example, Lands' End created one for just the merchandising department. That data mart contains only merchandising-specific information and not any information, for instance, that would be unique to the finance department.

Because of the smaller, more manageable data marts, knowledge workers at Lands' End are making better use of information. If some of your employees don't need access to organizationwide data warehouse information, consider building a smaller data mart for their particular needs.

If you do choose to build smaller data marts for your employees, the data mining tools are the same. That is, data marts support the use of query-and-reporting tools, intelligent agents, multidimensional analysis tools, and statistical tools. This yields efficiency in an organization with respect to training. Once you've trained your employees to use any or all data mining tools, they can apply them to an organizationwide data warehouse or smaller data marts.

DATA MINING AS A CAREER OPPORTUNITY

Data mining represents a substantial career opportunity for you, no matter what your career choice. In the business world, you'll face numerous situations in which you need business intelligence to make the right and most effective decisions.

Fortunately, you don't have to be an IT expert to perform data mining. As you'll learn in Extended Learning Module D (Decision Analysis with Spreadsheet Software),

Figure 4.10

Data Marts Are Subsets
of Data Warehouses

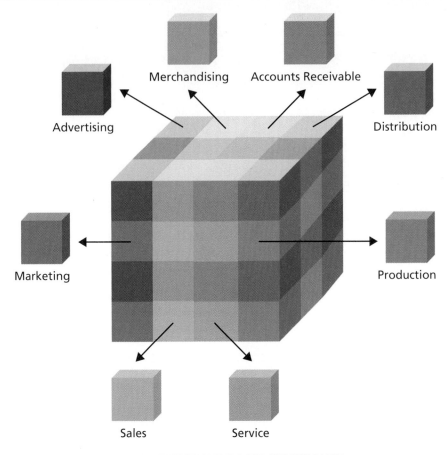

ORGANIZATION-WIDE DATA WAREHOUSE

you can actually use a spreadsheet tool such as Microsoft Excel to build a three-dimensional cube similar to the one in Figure 4.8. You can then use Excel's other decision support features to build a graph, perform a regression analysis, and "turn the cube" by bringing new layers of information forward. You can do the same with Microsoft Access, by building a three-dimensional cube (i.e., data warehouse) of information stored in a database.

Beyond personal productivity tools, you should consider learning how to use some data mining tools specific to the data warehouse environment. Some of the more popular ones are:

- Query and Analysis and Enterprise Analytic tools in Business Objects (www. businessobjects.com)
- Business Intelligence and Information Access tools in SAS (www.sas.com)
- ReportNet, PowerPlay, Visualizer, NoticeCast, and DecisionStream tools in Cognos (www.cognos.com)
- PowerAnalyzer tools in Informatica (www.informatica.com)

There are many, many others. You should have a look at your school's catalogue of courses in data mining—you may find them offered in the technology department, statistics department, and other departments. We recommend that at the very least you become acquainted with the following: SAS (the leading vendor in statistical software), Cognos (the leading vendor in data warehousing and data mining tools), and Informatica (the second-leading vendor in data warehousing and data mining tools).

FUTURE SHOP IMPLEMENTS DATA WAREHOUSING WITH THE HELP OF BURNTSAND INC.

With more than 100 stores, Future Shop (www.future shop.ca), Canada's largest and fastest-growing retailer of consumer electronic products, was having trouble making sense of the data it was collecting. Although customer and supplier data were being gathered at the operational level, they remained decentralized and were not synthesized and distributed to improve corporate decision-making. Future Shop contacted Burntsand Inc. (www. burntsand.com), a leading North American e-business solutions integrator, to provide them with a fast and reliable system to support their strategic and tactical business functions. They implemented a data warehouse to centralize all of Future Shop's data which were spread across several databases on different hardware platforms.

Today, Future Shop still gathers all of its crucial data from its decentralized systems, but now applies central business rules to standardize, clean, and unify the data, and then store them in its data warehouse. Bill Akam, Director of Strategic Programs at Future Shop, stated that "the business benefit of having all of our operational and strategic decisions aligned with one single unified set of data is creating efficiency and accuracy previously unachievable." According to Burntsand's former president and CEO Paul Bertin, the data warehouse now enables Future Shop "to develop a solid foundation for business intelligence, turning this data into useful information about their business and their customers. ... This use of the company's information asset allows Future Shop to positively impact their dealings and relationships with their suppliers and customers and gain a real competitive advantage."[15]

IMPORTANT CONSIDERATIONS IN USING A DATA WAREHOUSE

As with all types of technology, you can't simply implement a data warehouse and use data mining tools just because they're a "hot" set of technologies. Let your business needs drive your technology decisions. With respect to data warehouses and data mining tools, below are some questions to answer.

DO YOU NEED A DATA WAREHOUSE? If you ask most people in the business world if they need a data warehouse, they'll immediately say yes. But they may be wrong. Although data warehouses are a great way to bring together information from many different databases and data mining tools are a great way to manipulate that information, they're not necessarily the best technologies for all businesses. Why? For three reasons:

- Data warehouses and data mining tools are expensive. These are among the most expensive of all technologies, and your organization will devote considerable time in creating a data warehouse. Training in the use of data mining tools is also expensive.
- Some organizations simply don't need a data warehouse. You may find that you can easily extract necessary information to support decision making from operational databases. If so, don't use a data warehouse.
- Many IT departments suffer from supporting too many applications and application tools. As David Tanaka, a DSS manager at Hospital Health Plan Management Corp., points out, "Right now, we are support-strapped. If we introduce something like OLAP, we will have to give it a lot of support."[16] Technology and its use requires constant support. If you can't support it, don't implement it.

HOW UP TO DATE SHOULD DATA WAREHOUSE INFORMATION BE?

Information timeliness is a must in a data warehouse—old and obsolete information leads to poor decision making. Below is a list of decision-making processes that people go through for different business environments. For each, specify whether the information in the data warehouse should be updated monthly, weekly, daily, or by the minute. Be prepared to justify your decision.

1. To adjust class sizes in a university registration environment

2. To adjust radio advertisements in the light of demographic changes
3. To monitor the success of a new product line in the clothing retail industry
4. To adjust production levels of foods in a cafeteria
5. To switch jobs to various printers in a network
6. To adjust CD rates in a bank
7. To adjust forecasted demands of tires in an auto parts store

DO ALL YOUR EMPLOYEES NEED AN ENTIRE DATA WAREHOUSE? As we've already discussed, some of your employees may not need access to an organization-wide data warehouse. If this is the case, definitely consider building data marts. Data marts are smaller than data warehouses, and therefore more manageable and easier to access. The easier technology is to use, the more your users will take advantage of it.

HOW UP TO DATE MUST THE INFORMATION BE? Data warehouses contain information from other databases. From an operational perspective, it's important to consider how often you should extract information from those databases and update the data warehouse. "Instantaneously" is usually not feasible in most organizations because of communications costs and performance considerations. Some organizations take "snapshots" of databases every 30 minutes and update the data warehouse; others perform updates nightly or even weekly.

WHAT DATA MINING TOOLS DO YOU NEED? User needs should always drive what data mining tools are necessary—query-and-reporting tools, intelligent agents, multidimensional analysis tools, statistical tools, or some combination of the four. Whatever you choose, training is key. It's important for your organization to first make users aware of the capabilities of the entire data mining tool set. Then, once they decide on which tools are best, you'll need to provide training. If your users can fully exploit all the features of their chosen data mining tools, your entire organization will reap the benefits.

Managing the Information Resource in an Organization

As you prepare to enter today's fast-paced, exciting, and information-based business world, you must be prepared to help your organization manage and organize its information. After all, you will be a knowledge worker—a person who works primarily with information. Your organization will be successful, in part, because of your ability to organize and manage information in the way that best moves the organization toward its goals. Below is a list of questions to keep in mind. The answers to some are defi-

DO YOU WANT TO BE A CIO?

Regardless of your industry or business sector, one of the highest-paid IT jobs is that of chief information officer. According to *InformationWeek Research*'s 2004 National IT Salary Survey, managers in IT earn a median base salary of $90,000, while staffers earn a median base salary of $68,000. Those numbers sound pretty good, but compared to the median salary of CIOs ($122,000), they fall well short.

So what does it take to be a CIO? We know of two things for sure. The first is an intricate knowledge of how a business environment works; the second is an intricate understanding of how information technology can help a business work more efficiently and effectively. Those are givens.

If we were to offer a third requirement, we would say that the new generation of CIOs will come out of the data warehousing arena. Why? Because data warehousing specialists must understand the entire business in great detail, and they must know how to use information technology.[17]

nitely moving targets. As business and technology change, your answers may have to change as well.

WHO SHOULD OVERSEE THE ORGANIZATION'S INFORMATION?

In organizations today, you find chief executive officers (CEO), chief operating officers (COO), and chief financial officers (CFO), among others. You also find another title—**chief information officer (CIO)**, who is responsible for overseeing an organization's information resource. A CIO's responsibilities may range from approving new development activities for data warehouses and data marts to monitoring the quality and use of information within those data warehouses and data marts.

Two important functions associated with overseeing an organization's information resource are data and database administration. **Data administration** is the function in an organization that plans for, oversees the development of, and monitors the information resource. It must be completely in tune with the strategic direction of the organization to assure that all information requirements can and are being met.

Database administration is the function in an organization that is responsible for the more technical and operational aspects of managing the information contained in organizational databases (which can include data warehouses and data marts). Database administration functions include defining and organizing database structures and contents, developing security procedures, developing database and DBMS documentation, and approving and monitoring the development of databases and database applications.

In organizations of any great size, both functions are usually handled by a steering committee rather than a single individual. Steering committees are responsible for their respective functions and reporting to the CIO. It's definitely a team effort to manage most organizational resources—information is no different in that it needs careful oversight and management.

However, information is different from many "typical" organizational resources. For example, information is intangible, so it becomes extremely difficult to measure its worth or value. What dollar value would you attach to a customer record? Can a business realistically do that? The answer to the latter question is no. So, if you can't put a value on information, how can you know how much you should be spending on information technology tools? It is a difficult question to answer.

CRUD—DEFINING INFORMATION OWNERSHIP

One easy way to determine information ownership is to think in terms of CRUD—*c*reate, *r*ead, *u*pdate, and *d*elete. If you can create, update, and/or delete information, then in some way you own that information because you are responsible for its quality.

Here again, let's consider your school as an example and focus on your personal and transcript information. That information includes your student ID, name, address, phone number, GPA, declared major, declared minor (if you have one), and courses completed (this is your transcript).

For each of those pieces, first identify who has create, update, and delete privileges. There may be many individuals or departments that have these sorts of information privileges. If so, who is ultimately responsible for your personal and transcript information? Second, identify all the groups of people at your school who can only view your information.

Since information is intangible, it can also be shared by numerous people and not actually be "consumed." Money is different. If you have money in your department budget and spend it on travel, you can't very well use that same money for paying for employee education expenses. In a way, then, the intangibility of information is good because many people can use it. But, as we've alluded to many times, there are unique considerations in the security of information that do not exist for other organizational resources such as money.

HOW WILL CHANGES IN TECHNOLOGY AFFECT ORGANIZING AND MANAGING INFORMATION?

If there ever has been a moving target that businesses are trying to hit, it's most probably information technology. It seems that every day businesses are faced with new technologies that are faster, better, and provide more capabilities than the those of yesterday. Chasing technology in a business environment can be very expensive, and it is not what we would consider to be a best business practice.

What you have to remember is that technology is simply a set of tools for helping you work with information, including organizing and managing it. As new technologies become available, you should ask yourself whether those technologies will help you organize and manage your information *better*. You can't simply say, "A new technology is available that will allow us to organize and manage our information in a different way, so we should use it." The real question is whether that different way is better than what you're currently doing. If the answer is yes, you should seriously consider the new technology in the light of the strategic goals of the organization. If the answer is no, stay with what you've got until a tool comes along that allows you to do a *better* job.

One of the greatest technological changes that will occur over the coming years is a convergence of different tools that will help you better organize and manage information. Environment Canada's Ice Services (ice-glaces.ec.gc.ca), for example, is providing a combination of a data warehouse and Internet-based information resources seafarers can use.[18] This new system gathers ice charts stored on the Internet and logically organizes them in the form of a data warehouse. Using this new system, seafarers can obtain updated maps and charts that reflect changing ice conditions every four instead of twelve hours. Who knows? The *Titanic* might still be here today if this system had been available in 1912.

DO MOVIES AFFECT YOUR VIEW OF ETHICS?

Many movies today deal with ethical issues. It's not that movie producers make movies just so you'll think about your own ethics. But, if a movie does have within it an ethical dilemma, you'll want to discuss it with your friends. That, in turn, makes your friends want to pay to see the movie. It's a simple matter of providing the viewing public with a story that raises significant questions and encourages more people to see the movie.

Consider *Gattica*, a movie about the future. In its version of the future, a person's DNA determined his or her entire future. DNA was used to determine the type of job and whether the person would go to school. Of course, everyone's DNA was stored in a large central database that organizations and the government accessed often.

In one scene, a young woman met a young man at a nightclub. She was quite taken by him. So she stole a small strand of his hair and went to a nearby booth. The person working the booth analyzed the hair, accessed the young man's DNA, and provided the young woman with his complete biological profile. She used that information, of course, to determine whether to pursue a relationship with him.

Although it may seem like a rather outlandish view of the future, it does raise some important questions. Should we, as a society, be tracking that kind of information? If so, who should have access to it and for what reasons? Should you be able to pay (as the young woman did) to access someone else's medical information?

These are important questions that you cannot ignore. You may not have to deal with them right now, but you certainly will in the future. How will you respond?

IS INFORMATION OWNERSHIP A CONSIDERATION?

Information sharing in your organization means that anyone—regardless of title or department—can access and use whatever information he or she needs. But information sharing brings to light an important question—does anyone in your organization own any information? In other words—if everyone shares information, who is ultimately responsible for providing that information and assuring the quality of the information? Information ownership is a key consideration in today's information-based business environment. Someone must accept full responsibility for providing specific pieces of information and ensuring its quality. If you find out that wrong information is stored in the organization's data warehouse, you must be able to determine the source of the problem and whose responsibility it is.

This issue of information ownership is present in other management functions: if you manage a department, you're responsible for the work in the department as well as expenses and people. The same is true for information. If information originates in your department, you essentially own that information because you're providing it to those who need it and ensuring its quality.

WHAT ARE THE ETHICS INVOLVED IN MANAGING AND ORGANIZING INFORMATION?

Throughout this text, we address many ethical issues associated with information and information technology. Many of our discussions focus on your organization's societal obligations with respect to customers. Within the organization, those same issues are a concern. By bringing together vast amounts of information into a single place (a database or data warehouse) and providing software (a DBMS or data mining tools) that anyone can use to access that information, ethics and privacy become key concerns.

For example, as a manager of marketing research, should you be able to access the salaries of people in distribution and logistics? Should you be able to access medical profiles of those in accounting? Should you be able to access counselling records of those in manufacturing? The answer to some of these questions is obviously no. But how does an organization safeguard against the unethical use of information within the organization?

While most DBMSs provide good security facilities, it's far easier for someone within your organization to obtain information than it is for someone outside the organization. So what's the key? Unfortunately, we don't know the answer, and neither does anyone else. But it all starts with each person always acting in the most ethical way with respect to information. Ethics, security, and privacy will always be great concerns. You can do your part by always acting ethically. Remember, being sensitive to the ethics of other people is an important challenge that you must meet.

Summary: Student Learning Outcomes Revisited

1. **Describe business intelligence and its role in an organization.** Business intelligence is knowledge—knowledge about your customers, your competitors, your partners, your competitive environment, and your own internal operations. Business intelligence is much more than just a list of your products or to whom you've sold them. It would combine your product information perhaps with your advertising strategy information and customer demographics to help you determine the effectiveness of various advertising media on demographic groups segmented by location.

2. **Differentiate between databases and data warehouses with respect to their focus on online transaction processing and online analytical processing.** A database is a collection of data that you organize and access according to the logical structure of the data. Databases support both online transaction processing (OLTP) and online analytical processing (OLAP). Databases that support OLTP are often referred to as *operational databases*. These databases contain detailed data about transactions that have taken place. And using various data manipulation tools, you can query a database to extract meaningful information. A *data warehouse* is a collection of data—gathered from many different operational databases—used to create business intelligence that supports business analysis activities and decision-making tasks. Data warehouses support only OLAP, not OLTP.

3. **List and describe the key characteristics of a relational database.** The *relational database model* uses a series of logically related two-dimensional tables or files to store data in the form of a database. It is a collection of relations and integrity constraints. Key characteristics are:
   - A relation—composed of a set of records
   - Contain logical structures—you care only about the logical data and not about how it's physically stored or where it's physically located
   - Have logical ties among the data—all the files in a database are related in that some primary keys of certain files appear as foreign keys in others
   - Possess built-in integrity constraints—when creating the data dictionary for a database, you can specify rules by which the information must be entered (e.g., not blank, etc.)

4. **Define the five software components of a database management system.** The five software components of a database management system are:
   - *DBMS engine*. Accepts logical requests from the various other DBMS subsystems, converts them into their physical equivalent, and actually accesses the database and data dictionary as they exist on a storage device
   - *Data definition subsystem*. Helps you create and maintain the data dictionary and define the structure of the files in a database
   - *Data manipulation subsystem*. Helps you add, change, and delete information in a database and mine it for valuable information

- *Application generation subsystem*. Contains facilities to help you develop transaction-intensive applications
- *Data administration subsystem*. Helps you manage the overall database environment by providing facilities for backup and recovery, security management, query optimization, concurrency control, and change management

5. **List and describe the key characteristics of a data warehouse.** The key characteristics of a data warehouse are:
   - *Multidimensional*. While databases store information in two-dimensional tables, data warehouses include layers to represent information according to different dimensions
   - *Support decision making*. Data warehouses, because they contain summarized information, support business activities and decision-making tasks, not transaction processing

6. **Define the four major types of data mining tools.** The four major types of data mining tools in a data warehouse environment are:
   - *Query-and-reporting tools*. Similar to QBE tools, SQL, and report generators in the typical database environment
   - *Intelligent agents*. Utilize various artificial intelligence tools such as neural networks and fuzzy logic to form the basis of "information discovery" and building business intelligence in OLAP
   - *Multidimensional analysis (MDA) tools*. Techniques that allow you to view multidimensional information from different perspectives
   - *Statistical tools*. Help you apply various mathematical models to the information stored in a data warehouse to discover new information

7. **List key considerations in managing the information resource in an organization.** Key considerations in managing the information resource in an organization are:
   - Who should oversee the organization's information?
   - How will changes in technology affect organizing and managing information?
   - Is information ownership a consideration?
   - What are the ethics involved in managing and organizing information?

8. **Identify the primary key field of a database.** Before you can create relationships among files, you must specify the primary key for each file—the field that uniquely describes each record. In doing so, you are also stating the field cannot be blank.

CLOSING CASE STUDY ONE

WE'VE GOT OLTP COVERED; LET'S GO ON TO OLAP

In business environments today, you'll find rich, technically correct, and very supportive databases that meet transaction processing needs (OLTP or online transaction processing). But many of those same organizations have failed to implement the necessary technologies that support business analysis and decision-making needs (OLAP or online analytical processing). And it makes sense. It's far easier to implement a database for processing something like sales transactions than it is to provide the necessary technology tools and information that would support someone, for example, in determining where to build a new distribution centre.

So we've pretty well got OLTP covered. We need now to focus on OLAP. Consider these three companies and their efforts in supporting OLAP. They are not unique situations, nor are they bad ones. In fact, we would say that these are leading-edge companies because they are willing to acknowledge their problems, face them, and strive to do something about them.

EASTMAN CHEMICAL COMPANY

As Jerry Hale, CIO at Eastman, explains it, managers don't have easy access to the information they need to make effective decisions. He further explains that there is a variety of reasons for this problem—too much information is available, much of the information is in incompatible formats, and most of the decision support software is too difficult for managers to use. According to Jerry, "A high percentage of the data is there. The challenge is extracting it and presenting it in a way that's useful for managers to make decisions."

To combat such problems, Eastman is currently considering several alternatives. The first is to create a simple menu of reports from which managers can choose. And, upon choosing a specific report, managers will also have the ability to request to see the aggregated information in more detail. Eastman is also planning to incorporate external information into its data warehouse. This will allow managers to compare external information such as economic and chemical industry leading-indicator information to internal information such as production and forecasted demand. The goal, according to Jerry, is "to bring this to another level of access and ease of use." Sounds good.

TEXAS INSTRUMENTS

Texas Instruments faces equally difficult challenges. For example, it has a semiconductor fabrication plant in Kilby, Texas. That plant tests and manufactures new semiconductor products and streamlines the production and yield processes before manufacturing the chips at high volume. The plant tracks huge amounts of performance information from production equipment and prototype semiconductors. That information is then ideally used to make design and production decisions for the chips.

But, as Joe Lebowitz, TI's yield and product engineering director at the plant, explains it, the information needed to make those decisions must be pulled from multiple databases. One database contains semiconductor defect data, another database tracks and maintains process equipment history, and yet another database tracks and maintains electrical test data. As Joe describes it, "One of the big tasks at hand is tying those databases together and extracting the data we need."

Currently, several IT specialists do nothing all day except build data extraction programs and reports to provide managers with the information they need. And that time could be better spent making decisions instead of just extracting the information.

CIGNA CORPORATION

CIGNA Corporation, an employee benefits company with $18 billion in revenues, is actually half-pleased with its efforts to provide information that supports OLAP. According to Marc Bloom, CIGNA's insurance division business technology and information services director, "I think they get more than half of what they need." The challenge now is to get the other half.

Within the insurance division, managers make daily decisions on managing based on financial and operational information. This information primarily shows fluctuations in financial and operating metrics such as an increase or decrease in claims processing. Managers can receive this information in a variety of ways—through ad hoc facilities that allow them to build their own reports, though report templates already prepared by the IT staff, and though complete reports delivered to their desktop and notebook computers.

It really all depends on the skill set of the manager. As Marc explains it, "Everybody's got a different skill set. It's a question of having the right people and the right tools to access it, turning that data into useful information, and being able to do it quickly enough to make a timely decision."[19]

Questions

1. In your view, what is the single most important factor that hinders all organizations in general from providing good online analytical processing (OLAP) support? Why is it so much easier for organizations to provide good online transaction processing support (OLTP)?

2. Consider Eastman. According to Jerry, most of the decision support software is too difficult for managers to use. One identified solution is to provide a menu of predefined reports. Will that completely solve the problem? What other steps should Eastman take so that managers don't find the decision support software too difficult to use?

3. Now consider Texas Instruments. Its managers need information for decision making that resides in several different databases. One potential solution here is to build a data warehouse and extract the necessary information from the various databases. Will this solve the problem? Why or why not? If Texas Instruments does indeed build a data warehouse, what sort of training will its managers need? How can Texas Instruments convince its managers that learning how to use yet another technology tool will be beneficial?

4. Finally, consider CIGNA. According to Marc, CIGNA is halfway home in providing OLAP support. If you have only half the information you need to make a decision, how effective do you think you'll be? Can you expect to make the right decision 50 percent of the time if you have only 50 percent of the information you need? What if

you have 90 percent of the information you need? Will you be 90 percent correct in making your decisions? Why or why not?

5. Neil Hastie, CIO at TruServe Corp., describes most decision making in all types of businesses as "a lot of by-guess and by-golly, a lot of by-gut, and a whole lot of paper reports." That statement is not kind to managers in general nor IT specialists charged with providing the right people with the right technology to make the right decisions. What's the key to turning Neil's statement into a positive one? Is it training? Is it providing timely information access? Is it providing easy-to-use tools? Other solutions? A combination of several?

CLOSING CASE STUDY TWO

MINING DINING DATA

Restaurants, fast food chains, casinos, and others use data warehouses to determine customer purchasing habits and to determine what products and promotions to offer and when to offer them. Some of the leading data warehouse users include AFC Enterprises (operator and franchiser of more than 3300 Church's Chicken, Popeyes' Chicken and Biscuits, Seattle Coffee Company, Cinnabon, and Torrefazione outlets worldwide); Red Robin International (a 170-unit casual-dining chain); Harrah's Entertainment (owner of 26 U.S. casinos); Pizzeria Uno; and Einstein/Noah Bagel (operator of 428 Einstein's and 111 Noah's New York Bagel stores).

AFC ENTERPRISES

AFC Enterprises cultivates a loyal clientele by slicing and dicing its data warehouse to strategically configure promotions and tailor menus to suit local preferences. AFC's data warehouse helps it better understand its core customers and maximize its overall profitability. AFC tracks customer-specific information from name and address to order history and frequency of visits. This enables AFC to determine exactly which customers are likely to respond to a given promotion on a given day of the week.

AFC also uses its data warehouse to anticipate and manipulate customer behaviour. For example, AFC can use its data warehouse to determine that coffee is added to the tab 65 percent of the time when a particular dessert is ordered and 85 percent of the time when that dessert is offered as a promotional item. Knowing that, AFC can run more promotions for certain desserts figuring that customers will respond by ordering more desserts and especially more coffee (coffee is a high-margin item in the restaurant business).

RED ROBIN INTERNATIONAL

Red Robin's terabyte-size data warehouse tracks hundreds of thousands of point-of-sale (POS) transactions, involving millions of menu items and more than 1.5 million invoices. As Howard Jenkins, Red Robin's Vice-President of Information Systems, explains it, "With data mining in place, we can ask ourselves, 'If we put the items with high margins in the middle of the menu, do we sell more versus putting it at the top or bottom, [and if so], to whom and where?' We can also tell if something cannibalizes the sale of other items and can give the marketing department an almost instant picture of how promotions are being sold and used."

The placement of items on a menu is strategic business, just as the placement of promotional items in a grocery store can mean increased sales for one item and reduced sales for another. The job of finding the right mix is definitely suited to mining a data warehouse.

Using Cognos Business Intelligence, Red Robin now has measurable results of promotion and menu changes, makes better and more timely decisions, and has realized seven-figure savings in operational costs.

HARRAH'S ENTERTAINMENT

Harrah's Entertainment uses its data warehouse to make decisions for its highly successful Total Gold customer recognition program. Depending on their spending records, Total Gold members can receive free vouchers for dining, entertainment, and sleeping accommodations. Knowing which rewards to give to which customers is key.

John Boushy, Senior Vice-President of Entertainment and Technology for Harrah's, says, "We can determine what adds value to each customer and provide that value at the right time." Dining vouchers or free tickets for shows are awarded to day visitors, not sleeping accommodations. Customers who consistently visit a particular restaurant and order higher-end foods receive free dinners and cocktails, not vouchers for free (and cheaper) breakfasts.

PIZZERIA UNO

Pizzeria Uno uses its data warehouse to apply the 80/20 rule. That is, it can determine which 20 percent of its customers contribute to 80 percent of its sales and adjust menus and promotions to suit top patron preferences. These changes can often lead to converting some of the other 80 percent of Pizzeria Uno's customers to the more profitable 20 percent.

EINSTEIN/NOAH BAGEL

Einstein/Noah Bagel uses its data warehouse in real time to maximize cross-selling opportunities. For example, if data warehouse information reveals that a manager in a given store might be missing a cross-selling opportunity on a particular day, an e-mail is automatically sent out to alert managers to the opportunity. Salespeople can then respond by offering the cross-selling opportunity ("How about a cup of hot chocolate with that bagel since it's so cold outside?") to the next customer.[20,21,22]

Questions

1. Consider the issue of timely information with respect to the businesses discussed in the case. Which of the businesses must have the most up-to-date information in its data warehouse? Which business can have the most out-of-date information in its data warehouse and still be effective? Rank the five businesses discussed with a 1 for the one that needs the most up-to-date information and a 5 for the one that is least sensitive to timeliness of information. Be prepared to justify your rankings.

2. Harrah's Entertainment tracks a wealth of information concerning customer spending habits. If you were to design Harrah's Entertainment's data warehouse, what dimensions of information would you include? As you develop your list of dimensions, consider every facet of Harrah's business operations, including hotels, restaurants, and gaming casinos.

3. AFC Enterprises includes information in its data warehouse such as customer name and address. Where does it (or could it) gather such information? Think carefully about this, because customers seldom provide their names and addresses when ordering fast food at a Church's or Popeyes. Is AFC gathering information in an ethical fashion? Why or why not?

4. Visit a local grocery store and walk down the breakfast cereal aisle. You should notice something very specific about the positioning of the various breakfast cereals. What is it? On the basis of what information do you think grocery stores determine cereal placement? Could they have determined that information from a data warehouse or from some other source? If another source, what might that source be?

5. Suppose you're opening a pizza parlor in the town where you live. It will be a "take and bake" pizza parlour in which you make pizzas for customers but do not cook them. Customers buy the pizzas uncooked and take them home for baking. You will have no predefined pizza types but will make each pizza to the customer's specifications. What sort of data warehouse would you need to predict the use of toppings by time of day and by day of the week? What would your dimensions of information be? If you wanted to increase the requests for a new topping (such as mandarin oranges), what information would you hope to find in your data warehouse that would enable you to do so?

Key Terms and Concepts

Short-Answer Questions

1. What is business intelligence? Why is it more than just information?

2. What is online analytical processing (OLAP)? Why is it different from OLTP?

3. What is the most popular database model?

4. What is the role of a data dictionary in a database environment?

5. How are primary and foreign keys different? How are they the same?

6. What are the five important software components of a database management system?

7. What part of a DBMS helps you manage the overall database environment?

8. What is a data warehouse? How does it differ from a database?

9. What are the four major types of data mining tools?

10. What database tools are similar to data mining query-and-reporting tools?

11. What is a data mart? How is it similar to a data warehouse?

12. How often should you update information in a data warehouse?

13. What is the role of a chief information officer (CIO)?

14. How do the functions of data administration and database administration differ?

Assignments and Exercises

1. **FINDING "HACKED" DATABASES.** The Web site *The Happy Hacker* (www.happyhacker.org) is devoted to "hacking"—the breaking into of computer systems. When people hack into a system, they often go after information in databases. There, they can find credit card information and other private and sensitive information. Sometimes, they can even find designs of yet-to-be-released products and other strategic information about a company. Connect to *The Happy Hacker* and find an article that discusses a database that was hacked. Prepare a short report for your class detailing the incident.

2. **DEFINING QUERIES FOR A VIDEO RENTAL STORE.** Consider your local video rental store. It certainly has an operational database to support its online transaction processing (OLTP). The operational database supports such things as the adding of new customers, the renting of videos (obviously), the ordering of videos, and a host of other activities. Now, assume that the store also uses that same database for online analytical processing (OLAP) in the form of creating queries to extract meaningful information. If you were the store manager, what kinds of queries would you build? What answers would you be hoping to find?

3. **RESEARCHING DB2—A POPULAR BUSINESS DBMS.** IBM provides one of the most well-known DBMSs for the business world, called DB2. Connect to IBM's site (www.ibm.com) and search for "DB2." Read the product overview. What sort of data manipulation tools does it support? What sort of security management does it support? Does IBM claim that you can easily perform OLAP using DB2? If so, how and using what kinds of tools?

4. **CREATING A QUERY.** On the Web site that supports this text (www.mcgrawhill.ca/college/haag), we've provided the Inventory database (in Microsoft Access) we illustrated in this chapter. Connect to the site and download that database (choose "Chapter 4" and then "Inventory database"). Now create three queries using the QBE tool. The first should extract information from only one file (your choice); the second should extract information found in at least two files; the third should include some sort of selection criteria. How easy or difficult was it to perform these queries? Would you say that a DBMS is just as easy to use as something like word processing or spreadsheet software? Why or why not?

5. **CAREER OPPORTUNITIES IN YOUR MAJOR.** Knowledge workers throughout the business world are building their own desktop databases (often called end-user databases or knowledge worker databases). To do so, they must understand both how to design a database and how to use a desktop DBMS such as Microsoft Access or FileMaker (made by FileMaker). The ability to design a database and use a desktop DBMS offer you a great career advantage. Research your chosen major by looking at job postings (the Web is the best place to start). How many of those jobs want you to have some database knowledge? Do they list a specific DBMS package? What's your take on this—should you expand your education and learn more about databases and DBMSs? Why or why not?

6. **SALARIES FOR DATABASE ADMINISTRATORS.** Database administrators (DBAs) are among the highest-paid professionals in the information technology field. Many people work for 10 to 20 years to get a promotion to DBA. Connect to Monster.ca (www.monster.ca) or another job database or your choice and search for DBA job openings. As you do, select all locations and job categories and then use "dba" as the keyword search criterion. How many DBA job postings did you find? In what industries were some of the DBA job openings? Read through a couple of the job postings. What was the listed salary range (if any)? What sort of qualifications were listed?

Discussion Questions

1. Databases and data warehouses clearly make it easier for people to access all kinds of information. This has led to growing debates in the area of privacy. Should organizations be left to police themselves with respect to providing access to information, or should the government impose privacy legislation? Answer this question with respect to (1) customer information shared by organizations, (2) employee information shared within a specific organization, and (3) business information available to customers.

2. Business intelligence sounds like a fancy term potentially with a lot of competitive advantage rolled into it. What sort of business intelligence does your school need? Specifically, what business intelligence would it need to predict enrollments in the coming years? What business intelligence would it need to determine what curricula to offer? Do you think your school gathers and uses this kind of business intelligence? Why or why not?

3. Consider your school's registration database that enforces the following integrity constraint: to enroll in a given class, the student must have completed or currently be enrolled in the listed prerequisite (if any). Your school, in fact, probably does have that integrity constraint in place. How can you get around that integrity constraint and enroll in a class for which you are not taking nor have completed the prerequisite? Is this an instance of when you should be able to override an integrity constraint? What are the downsides to being able to do so?

4. When credit card companies make the decision of whether to issue you a credit card, they go through what is essentially a list of integrity constraints (such as your having a job for a given period of time) or rules. If you don't meet the integrity constraints, you're often denied a credit card. Put yourself in the shoes of a credit card company. What sort of integrity constraints would you follow? Would be willing to forgo any of them in certain situations? What would be the nature of those situations?

5. Some people used to believe that data warehouses would quickly replace databases for both

online transaction processing (OLTP) and online analytical processing (OLAP). Of course, they were wrong. Why can data warehouses not replace databases and become "operational data warehouses?" How radically would data warehouses (and their data mining tools) have to change to become a viable replacement for databases? Would they then essentially become databases that simply supported OLAP? Why or why not?

6. Information ownership in an organization is critical. It defines who has responsibility for the quality of the information. When was the last time you got the runaround from a business because no one seemed to know who or why some of your information was changed? As a customer, how did that make you feel? Were you inclined to find a substitute product or service (think back to Chapter 2)? Is it really that difficult of a task for an organization to clearly define who has responsibility for each and every piece of information? Why or why not?

7. Imagine that you work in the human resources management department for a local business and that many of your friends work there also. Although you don't personally generate payroll cheques, you still have the ability to look up anyone's pay. Would you check on your friends to see if they're earning more money than you? For that matter, would you look up their pay out of simple curiosity, knowing that you would never do anything with the information or share it with anyone else? Why or why not? People working at the IRS have been caught just curiously looking up the reported incomes of movie stars and other high-profile public figures. Is this acceptable? Why or why not?

8. As we discussed in the Global Perspectives "Do Movies Affect Your View of Ethics?," movies such as *Gattica* do play a role in our view of ethics. Make a list of the movies you've recently seen that raise ethical questions. Which questions do they raise? Did any of them, by chance, change your ethical views? Why or why not?

Electronic Commerce

Searching Online Databases and Information Repositories

The world of information is at your fingertips on the Internet. As you've already seen in the Electronic Commerce in Chapter 1, you can search the Internet for jobs and leave your résumé for employers to find. Almost any type of information you want you can find on the Internet.

Electronic Commerce Links

As you locate sites that provide information, you'll find many of them do so in the form of a database—a searchable grouping of information that allows you to find specific information by entering keywords and phrases. These words and phrases are in fact a kind of keys (similar to the primary and foreign keys we discussed in this chapter) that are used as matching criteria in a field of the database.

In this section, you'll explore a variety of information topics that you can find on the Internet. To help you, we've included a number of Web sites related to searching online database and information repositories. On the site that supports this text (www.mcgrawhill.ca/college/haag), we've provided direct links to all these other sites and many, many more. These are a great starting point for completing this Electronic Commerce section.

FINANCIAL AID RESOURCES

On the Internet, you can find valuable databases that give you access to financial aid resources as you attend school. These resources can be in the form of scholarships, money you don't have to pay back, and standard student loans. And there are a variety of financial aid lenders, ranging from traditional banks and the government to private parties wanting to give something back to society.

Find at least three Web sites that provide a financial aid database and answer the following questions for each.

A. Do you have to register as a user to access information?

B. Do you have to pay a fee to access information?

C. Can you build a profile of yourself and use it as you search?

D. Can you apply for aid while at the site or must you request paper applications that you need to complete and return?

E. By what sort of categories of aid can you search?

F. Does the site seem sincere in offering aid to you?

LIBRARIES

LexisNexis Butterworths is now completely on the Internet. Many libraries and other such sites even offer full books online for you to read. You may never have to go to the "physical" library again.

Think for a moment about a term paper you're currently writing or may have to write soon. What is the major topic? Now connect to a couple of different library sites and try to find some of the information you'll need. As you do, answer the following questions for each site.

A. What organization supports the site? Is the organization reputable?

B. Do you have to pay a subscription fee to access the information provided?

C. How good are the search capabilities?

D. How can you obtain printed versions of information you find?

E. Are you able to search periodicals? If so, how up-to-date are the issues?

F. Is finding information in libraries on the Internet easier or more difficult than finding information in a traditional library?

CONSUMER INFORMATION

Many consumer organizations also provide databases of information on the Internet. At those sites, you can read about the latest product reviews, search for new pharmaceuticals that cure diseases (or alleviate symptoms of them), and access safety information for products such as automobiles and children's toys.

Connect to several consumer organization sites and do some digging around. As you do, think about a product you're considering buying or perhaps have just bought. Is the information helpful? Is the information opinion only, completely factual, or a combination of the two? How important will this type of consumer information become as electronic commerce becomes more widespread on the Internet?

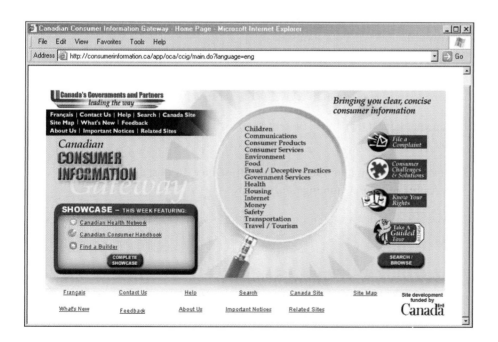

DEMOGRAPHICS

Recall from Chapter 1 that we characterized our economy today as "wants-driven." That is, a large portion of purchases are made on the basis of what people *want* and not necessarily what they need. This presents a real marketing and product development challenge.

For organizations focusing on meeting those wants or desires, the demographic makeup of the target audience is key. It's simple—the more you know about your target audience, the better equipped you are to develop and market products based on wants.

And you can find all sorts of demographic information on the Internet. Connect to a couple of different demographic-related Web sites and see what they have to offer. As you do, answer the following questions for each.

A. Who is the target audience of the site?

B. Who is the provider of the site?

C. Is the provider a private (for-profit) organization or a not-for-profit organization?

D. How often is the demographic information updated?

E. Does the site require that you pay a subscription fee to access its demographic information?

F. How helpful would the information be if you wanted to start a new business or sell various types of products?

REAL ESTATE

You can't actually live on the Internet, although some people may seem as though they want to try. But you can find real estate for sale and rent. You can find sites that take you through a step-by-step process for buying your first home, that provide mortgage and interest rate calculators, that offer financing for your home, and that even offer crime reports by neighbourhood.

Connect to several real estate–related sites and see what they have to offer. As you do, answer the following questions for each.

A. What is the focus of the site (residential, commercial, rental, and so forth)?

B. Does the site require you to register as a user to access its services?

C. Can you request that e-mail be sent to you when properties become available that you're interested in?

D. How can you search for information (by province, by postal code, by price range, by feature such as swimming pool, etc.)?

E. Does the site offer related information such as loans and mortgage calculators?

 Go to the Online Learning Centre at www.mcgrawhill.ca/college/haag for quizzes, extra content, a searchable glossary, and more! Click on "Electronic Commerce Projects" for links to hundreds of Web sites.

 Go to the text CD-ROM for data files, extra content, and Skills Modules on Microsoft Excel, Microsoft Access, HTML, and e-portfolios.

CHAPTER FIVE

STUDENT LEARNING OUTCOMES

BY THE END OF THIS CHAPTER, STUDENTS WILL BE ABLE TO:

1. Explain the relationship between the organization's roles and goals and the IT infrastructure.

2. List and describe factors that help increase employee productivity.

3. Explain system integration and how it enhances decision making.

4. List and describe different types of workflow systems.

5. List and describe IT infrastructure components that create business partnerships and alliances.

6. List and describe IT infrastructure components that enable global reach.

7. Assess why global reach is important, and identify how IT infrastructure can enable it.

WEB SUPPORT

- Online Magazines

- Online Movie Listings and Reviews

- Cooking from the Internet

Visit
www.mcgrawhill.ca/college/haag

LearningCentre

CASE STUDY:

MAKE THE CALL

How much time do you spend on the telephone each month? More importantly, how much is your monthly telephone bill? Do you want to make phone calls to anywhere in the world for free? If so, then all you need to do is make your phone calls over the Internet instead of using a traditional telephone service provider.

Originally, Internet telephony had a reputation of poor call quality, lame user interfaces, and low call-completion rates. With new and improved technology and IT infrastructures, Internet phone now offers similar quality to traditional telephone. Today, many consumers are making phone calls over the Internet by using *voice over Internet protocol* (VoIP). VoIP transmits over 10 percent of all phone calls and this number is growing exponentially.

If you want to make VoIP phone calls over the Internet, you need to find a vendor that offers these services, such as Skype at www.skype.com or Free World Dialup at www.freeworlddialup.com. VoIP works very similarly to e-mail: you simply send your call over the Internet in packets of audio tagged with the same destination. VoIP reassembles the packets once they arrive at their final destination.

There are many VoIP vendors. Each service works differently depending on the vendor's *IT infrastructure*—all the hardware, software, and telecommunications equipment that your organization employs to support its goals, processes, and strategies. Skype pairs P2P (point-to-point) technology with your PC's soundcard to create a voice service, which you can use to call other Skype users. Unfortunately, you can talk only to other Skype users. Vonage lets you place calls to any person who has a mobile or landline (regular telephone) number. Vonage sends the call over a cable or DSL connection via a digital-to-analog converter. A few providers even offer an adapter for a traditional handset that plugs right into your broadband modem. Which VoIP vendor would you prefer?

You can see how its IT infrastructure affects a company's product on service offering. Designing and building the correct IT infrastructure is critical to the success of any business. It can easily make or break a company.

At a more basic level, what do you think happens to a company that can't provide its knowledge workers Internet access at all—or whose provided access is extremely slow? A company must build an infrastructure that can handle all its current and future technological needs.[1]

Introduction

Because "IT infrastructure" means different things to different organizations at different times, it is difficult to formulate a definition that will encompass every possible meaning and satisfy everyone. For this reason, we have chosen the most basic and generic definition. An **IT infrastructure** includes the hardware, software, and telecommunications equipment that, when combined, provide the underlying technological foundation to support the organization's goals.

Organizations today can choose from literally thousands of different components to build their IT infrastructure. The components can include anything from software to strategic functions. Figure 5.1 provides a model of how the various components of an IT infrastructure support an organization's goals.

Just as your organization's goals dictate its structure, so they influence its IT infrastructure. For example, a flat structure has only a couple of managerial layers while a hierarchical one has many. If your organization has few hierarchial levels, it might be attempting to support the goal of information sharing. If your organization has a hierarchical structure, it might be attempting to support the goal of information privacy and security.

As a knowledge worker, you may be faced with questions regarding how the IT infrastructure can best support your organizational goals. You may be asked to make decisions regarding which type of components you want to purchase, and how you

Figure 5.1

How IT Infrastructure Supports the Organizational Goals

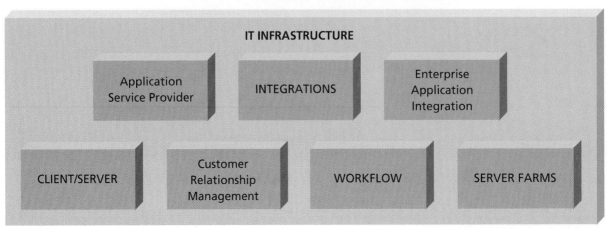

want to implement them. Of the many technologies available, how might you choose the ones that best meet your organizational needs?

This chapter discusses a few of the primary IT infrastructure components your organization can use to build a solid foundation that supports your organization. Enterprise application integration (EAI), customer relationship management (CRM), and enterprise resource planning (ERP) are just a few of the components we're going to discuss in the following pages. These components may not mean much to you now but, after reading this chapter, you'll have enough basic knowledge to understand how each works.

Organizational Goals and Strategies

Organizations spend a great deal of time determining primary goals, objectives, structures, and strategies. These critical components help your organization determine how it will operate in the marketplace, what its strategic directions or competitive advantages will be, and how it will achieve great success. A good IT infrastructure will support all of your organization's business and information needs.

Figure 5.2 lists the six primary roles and goals of information technology as we presented them in Chapter 1. It also provides a list of IT infrastructure components in support of each of the six. The remainder of this chapter walks you through each goal and related IT infrastructure components.

Figure 5.2

Roles and Goals of Information Technology and IT Infrastructure Components

Roles and Goals of IT	IT Infrastructure Components
Increase employee productivity	• Client/server network • Internet • Intranet • Extranet • Backup/recovery • Disaster recovery plan
Enhance decision making	• Integration • Enterprise application integration (EAI) • Enterprise application integration middleware (EAI middleware) • Storage devices
Improve team collaboration	• Documentation management systems • Enterprise information portals (EIPs) • Workflow systems
Create business partnerships and alliances	• Customer relationship management systems (CRM) • Sales force automation systems (SFA) • Electronic catalogue • Supply chain management systems (SCM)
Enable global reach	• Internet service provider (ISP) • Application service provider (ASP) • Collocation facilities • Server farms
Facilitate organizational transformation	• Enterprise resource planning (ERP) and enterprise software • Data warehouse • Infrastructure documentation

Increase Employee Productivity

Employees are the heart and soul of any organization. Without employees there simply wouldn't be an organization. Building an IT infrastructure that supports employee and customer needs should be one of the primary goals for any business. For example, every time a system crashes or fails, employees can't perform their jobs. Every time employees can't perform their jobs, the organization loses money. Employees are often sent home during system crashes, since there is no reason for them to sit around for hours without being able to work. For this reason alone, millions of dollars are lost each year due to system failures.

Building a solid IT infrastructure will reduce system failures, which increases employee productivity. The following IT infrastructure components support increasing employee productivity:

1. Client/server network
2. Internet
3. *n*-tier infrastructures
4. Backup/recovery
5. Disaster recovery plan

1. CLIENT/SERVER NETWORK

Building a client/server network is one of the best ways to ensure that the IT infrastructure supports employee productivity. In a **client/server network**, one or more computers are *servers* and provide services to the other computers which are called *clients*. The server or servers have hardware, software, and/or information that the client computers can access. Figure 5.3 is an example of a client/server network. You can see that several clients access a single server and a single printer. Almost all of the computer processing is performed on the server, which allows your organization to purchase **thin clients**—workstations that have only a small amount of processing power and cost less than a full-powered workstation. Purchasing thin clients can save your organization a tremendous amount of money when you consider that every single knowledge worker in the company needs a client station. A client/server network also allows your company to save money by purchasing a single printer that serves many individuals.

Prior to client/server networks, it was difficult for individuals to share information, applications, and hardware. For example, if a knowledge worker wanted to send a report out to several other knowledge workers he or she had to either manually copy the report several times or create several floppy disks containing the report. Using a client/server network, he or she can simply save the report on the server and other employees can directly access it or distribute it by e-mail. A client/server network also allows employees to share applications such as personal productivity software and hardware such as printers.

Review Extended Learning Module E for a detailed discussion of the many different types of client/server networks.

2. INTERNET

It's impossible to count the many number of ways the Internet makes an organization successful (or unsuccessful). Today, in the information age, most employees require an Internet connection in order to perform their jobs. The Internet allows employees to

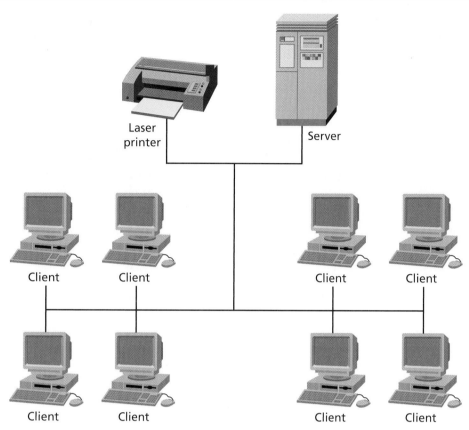

Figure 5.3

A Typical Client/Server
Network

send e-mail to customers, suppliers, and other employees all over the world for a fraction of the cost of a telephone call or surface mail. This advantage is referred to as **global reach**, the ability to extend a company's reach to customers anywhere there is an Internet connection, and at a much lower cost. Employees also receive the benefit of being able to search through volumes of information from organizations and libraries all over the world.

One of the biggest benefits of the Internet is the ability to place orders and receive information electronically. This method of ordering saves a company time and money, because customers no longer have to call the company to place an order.

Placing the ordering responsibility in the hands of the customer helps to decrease the number of incorrect orders. An order can be incorrect for several reasons, including a wrong address, size, or quantity. Every incorrect order costs the company money and hurts the company's relationship with the customer. The Internet can help alleviate some of the problems with incorrect orders, since the customer has taken on the majority of the ordering responsibility.

One thing to mention about the Internet is that it does not always increase employee productivity. Sometimes it can actually decrease employee productivity. The Computer Security Institute/FBI recently reported that 78 percent of companies have detected employee abuse of their Internet access privileges. The abuse included playing games, downloading movies, listening to music, gambling, trading stocks, e-mailing jokes, and even distributing critical company information. Employees also abuse the Internet by spending significant time sending personal e-mails to friends and family members. This sounds like a tiny problem but studies indicate that the amount of time employees spend abusing the Internet directly affects employee productivity.[2]

One of the decisions you'll make regarding your IT infrastructure is how you're going to design your Internet connections. Some companies implement full Internet access to all employees, while other companies provide full Internet access for only certain employees. Deciding which Internet infrastructure to develop will depend on employee needs and how much control the organization wants to have over how employees use the Internet.

3. *n*-TIER ARCHITECTURES

Personal computers (PCs) came out of isolation with the emergence of client/server networks. Basic client/server computing is a **2-tier architecture** since there are only two tiers—the client and the server. The server primarily supports data storage or access to peripherals such as printers, with limited access to application software. In a 2-tier infrastructure, the majority of the system logic and intelligence (application software) is located on the client PC. This can lead to information sharing issues, since the users must maintain the majority of the important corporate information on their PCs. This information, then, may not be accessible to all other employees. These types of networks do, however, have their place; as you read in Extended Learning Module E, you can set up a home network, which is essentially a 2-tier architecture.

You can address the problems of information and software sharing by moving to 3-tier, which moves the system logic and intelligence (and much of the information) from the clients to the server. A **3-tier architecture** contains clients, application servers, and data servers. The primary differences between 2-tier and 3-tier architecture are (1) the presence of the application servers for maintaining shared application software and (2) the presence of data servers for maintaining shared information.

Client/server networks, the Internet, and *n*-tier architecture considerations are central to any decision you make concerning your organization's IT infrastructure. We'll now spend the rest of this chapter focusing on other elements of IT infrastructures. Figure 5.4 displays these in three general categories:

1. Information views
2. Business logic
3. Data storage and manipulation

Figure 5.4

IT Infrastructure Components

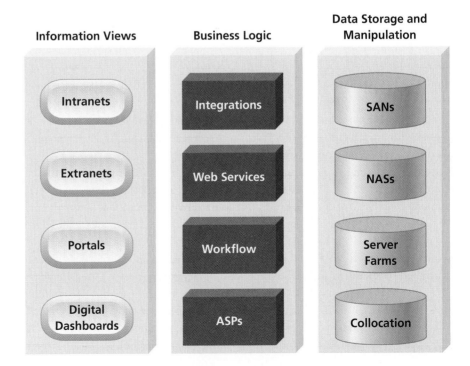

EMPLOYEE ABUSE OF THE INTERNET

The Internet doesn't necessarily increase productivity; in fact, employee abuse of the Internet can significantly decrease productivity. By some estimates, employees spend as much as six hours a day on the Internet playing games, gambling, buying stock, and sending personal e-mails.

Shawn Vidmar, IT director of an automotive dealership, has voiced concern over the problem at his company: "They obviously weren't doing their job. If they're trying to trade online and they're not doing their job, that's a problem. Productivity was being compromised, and I was worried about corporate liability. If somebody gets offended by an e-mail, they could go after the company."

Vidmar implemented new policies and employee education, and also decided to install Vericept Corporation's VIEW, a network abuse management system that tracks and analyzes network traffic. "Sending out an e-mail from here is like sending it out on Vidmar letterhead. I would hate to lose the business my grandfather started 60 years ago over a bad Internet joke," says Vidmar.[3]

4. BACKUP/RECOVERY

How many times have you lost a document on your computer because it crashed or lost electricity and you hadn't saved or backed up your work? How many times have you accidentally deleted a file you needed? **Backup** is the process of making a copy of the information stored on a computer. **Recovery** is the process of reinstalling the backup information after the information was lost. You can use many different media to do a backup of your organization's information, including tapes, disks, and even CD-ROMs. The importance of backups cannot be overemphasized.

How often should knowledge workers back up their files? The answer depends on your organizational goals. If your organization deals with large volumes of critical information, it might require daily backups. If your organization deals with small amounts of non-critical information, it only might require weekly backups. Deciding how often to back up is a critical decision for any organization.

5. DISASTER RECOVERY PLAN

Unfortunately, disasters—such as power outages, fires, floods, and even harmful hacking—occur all the time. Given that, your organization needs to develop a **disaster recovery plan**.

A good plan takes into consideration the location of the backup information. Many organizations choose to store backup information in an off-site storage facility, or a place separately located from the company and often owned by another company.

A good plan also considers the actual facility where knowledge workers will work. A **hot site** is a separate and fully equipped facility where the company can move immediately after the disaster and resume business. A **cold site** is a separate facility where the knowledge workers can move after the disaster but which does not have any computer equipment.

Your recovery plan should include a **disaster recovery cost curve** (see Figure 5.5), which charts (1) the cost to

Figure 5.5

Deciding How Much to Spend on Disaster Recovery

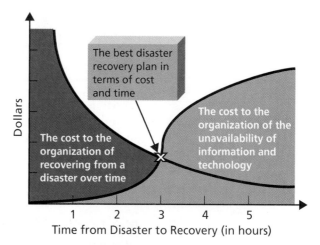

165

your organization of unavailability of information and technology and (2) the cost to your organization of recovering over time from a disaster. Where the two cost curves intersect is in fact the best recovery plan in terms of cost and time. Being able to quickly restore information and IT systems in the event of a disaster is a great way to provide a support structure that helps to continually increase employee productivity.

Information Views

The IT infrastructure components contained in the information views category are responsible for the presentation of information and receiving user events. These components include—but are not limited to—intranets, extranets, portals, and digital dashboards.

INTRANETS AND EXTRANETS

An **intranet** is an internal organizational Internet that is guarded against outside access by a special security feature called a *firewall* (which can be software, hardware, or a combination of the two). The primary characteristic of an intranet is that people outside the organization can't access it. Employees must have a user name and password to log on to a company intranet.

An intranet is an invaluable tool for presenting organizational information as it provides a central location where employees can find information. It can host all kinds of company-related information such as benefits, schedules, strategic directions, and employee directories. At many companies, every department has its own Web page on the company intranet for departmental information sharing. The advantages an intranet gives an organization are tremendous, and it should probably be a major component of your IT infrastructure.

An **extranet** is an intranet that is restricted to an organization and certain outsiders, such as customers and suppliers. Many companies are building extranets as they begin to realize the tremendous benefit of offering individuals outside the organization access to intranet-based information and application software such as ordering processing. When looking at the IT systems you're building, be sure to ask yourself, "What value could be added if employees, partners, vendors, and customers could access this system's information and processing capabilities?" If giving partners, vendors, and customers access to system information and processing helps your business, then you need to consider building an extranet. Finding new ways to present organizational information to and enable application software usage by external individuals is another important component of your IT infrastructure. We will discuss the important roles of intranets and extranets in Chapter 7.

PORTALS

"Portal" is a very generic term for what is in essence a technology that provides access to information. There are many specific implementations of portals, including enterprise information portals, collaborative processing enterprise information portals, and decision-processing enterprise information portals. These are discussed later in this chapter.

DIGITAL DASHBOARDS

Digital dashboards display key information gathered from several sources on a computer screen in a format tailored to the needs and wants of an individual knowledge

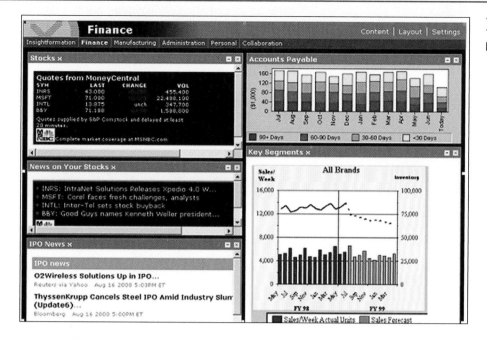

Figure 5.6

Digital Dashboard Example

worker. Digital dashboards commonly use indicators to help executives quickly identify the status of key information. Key information typically includes such things as critical success factors that you can monitor, measure, and compare. These fall within the realm of business intelligence, which we discussed in Chapters 1, 2, and 4.

Digital dashboards, whether basic or comprehensive, deliver results quickly. As they become easier to use, they will enable executives to perform their own analyses of business intelligence without inundating IT people with requests for special analysis, queries, and reports. They help managers view and react to business intelligence as it becomes available, which allows them to make decisions, solve problems, and change strategies quickly. Figure 5.6 displays an example of business intelligence presented in a digital dashboard.

FACTORS THAT INCREASE EMPLOYEE PRODUCTIVITY

AVAILABILITY Not all knowledge workers work from 9 to 5. It's not uncommon for a knowledge worker to arrive at work early, stay late, or work on the weekend to meet a deadline. For this reason, it's crucial that the IT infrastructure support the knowledge workers' varied schedules.

Availability is determining when your IT system will be available for knowledge workers to access. Some companies have IT systems available 24 hours a day, seven days a week. What happens if your employees need to work late, or during the weekend, and they can't because the information systems are unavailable? This would certainly lead to a decrease in employee productivity.

Another reason a company might support 24/7 system availability has to do with time zones. Imagine you work for a company based in Vancouver, B.C., and the company also has an office in London, England. When the London employees are finishing work, the Vancouver employees are just starting; since the same IT systems are worked on by the two sets of employees, they must be available round the clock. What happens if the company has global customers? Its system has to be available 24/7 in order to support the customers in different time zones.

ACCESSIBILITY Accessibility is determining who has the right to access different types of IT systems and information. What do you think might happen if all employees

IT COMPONENTS AND FACTORS

Supporting and increasing employee productivity is a primary goal for many organizations. In a group, review the list of IT infrastructure components and factors and rank them by their ability to increase employee productivity, 1 indicating the biggest impact and 12 the least impact.

IT Infrastructure Component/Factor	Ability to Increase Employee Productivity
Client/server network	
Internet	
Intranet	
Backup/recovery	
Disaster recovery	
Availability	
Accessibility	
Reliability	
Scalability	
Flexibility	
Performance	
Capacity planning	

have access to payroll information or bonus information? Payroll and bonus information is typically confidential, and at some companies you can be fired for having knowledge of or sharing this type of information.

Accessibility not only includes who can access information, but also how they can use it. "How" includes create, read, update, and delete, or what is often referred to as *CRUD* in the technology world. It's important that you define how each person can access information.

RELIABILITY Reliability ensures your IT systems are functioning correctly and providing accurate information. You might be surprised at how many times IT systems generate inaccurate or unreliable information. This can occurs for many reasons, including the information being entered incorrectly and the information becoming corrupted. Whatever the reason, if employees can't receive reliable information, then they can't perform their jobs.

Ensuring information is reliable is a critical and difficult task for all organizations. **Data cleansing** is the process of ensuring that all information is accurate. The more an organization can do to ensure its IT infrastructure promotes reliable information, the more money it will save by catching errors before they occur.

SCALABILITY Estimating how much growth your organization is expected to experience over the next few years is an almost impossible task. **Scalability** is a character-

INCREASE STUDENT PRODUCTIVITY

Congratulations! You've been appointed Student IT Infrastructure Leader, and your primary responsibility is to approve all designs for any new information systems. The school is planning to build six new information systems next year, in order to increase student productivity.

Your first assignment is to compile a list of three IT infrastructure components and factors that must be incorporated into any information system design. Along with the components/factors, provide a brief description of how each will increase student productivity. You can choose only three components for all six projects, so choose wisely.

istic of a system that indicates how much it can grow, or scale, as the organization and information needs grow. A number of factors can effect organizational growth, including market, industry, and the economy. If your organization grows faster than anticipated, you might find your systems experiencing all types of issues, such as running out of disk space or a slowing-down of transaction performance speed. To keep employees working and productive, your organization must try to anticipate growth and ensure that the IT infrastructure supports it.

FLEXIBILITY A single system can be designed in a number of different ways to perform exactly the same function. When you choose which design you want to implement, you must think about the system's flexibility, or the system's ability to change quickly. An inflexible system will cost your company money because it won't be able to handle market, business, or economic changes.

For example, say a company decides to expand its business into different countries and must add new languages and currencies to its IT system. The significant amount of time these modifications will take will cause the company to lose customers and sales. If the company had initially designed the system for this type of flexibility, it could have easily expanded the system to handle multiple languages and currencies.

PERFORMANCE **Performance** measures how quickly an IT system performs a certain process. A **benchmark** is a set of conditions used to measure how well a product or system functions. Many factors affect the performance of an IT system, ranging from the design of the system to the hardware that supports it, and performance directly effects knowledge worker productivity. If a system is slow, it will take knowledge workers twice as long to perform their jobs.

One of the most common performance issues you'll find occurs because of uncontrolled growth. For example, if business is booming and your company doubles the size of its order entry department, it must ensure the system functions exactly the same with twice as many users. If you used to have 50 order entry specialists and you now have 100, your IT systems might not function correctly due to the increased number of users.

CAPACITY PLANNING **Capacity planning** determines the future IT infrastructure requirements for new equipment and additional network capacity. It's cheaper for an organization to implement an IT infrastructure that considers capacity growth at the beginning than to try to upgrade equipment and networks after the system has already been implemented. Not having enough capacity leads to performance issues and hinders the ability of knowledge workers to perform their jobs. For example, if you have 100 workers using the Internet, and you purchase modems that are too slow and the network capacity is too small, your workers will spend a great deal of time just waiting to get information off the Internet. Waiting for a site to return information is not the most productive way for workers to spend their time.

Enhance Decision Making

Employees make decisions every day that effect the operations and ultimately the success of the business, as you will see in more detail in Chapter 6. To make smart decisions, employees must be completely informed of everything happening in and around your business. This is an incredibly difficult task, and it becomes more and more difficult as your business and its information requirements grow. The following IT infrastructure components can help:

- Integration
- Enterprise application integration (EAI)
- Enterprise application integration middleware (EAI middleware)
- Storage architecture

INTEGRATION

Typically, a business maintains separate systems for every department in the organization. Marketing might have its own pricing and market forecasting systems, sales might have its own sales and customer tracking systems, and accounting might have its own financial systems. Some organizations have hundreds of different systems operating across all departments. What types of problems do you think occur when an organization has so many separate systems?

What do you think might happen if your professor assigned 50 different textbooks for this course and based each lecture on information from all of them? It would be almost impossible for you to read all those books every time you prepared for class. You might even run into the problem of the different textbooks contradicting each other on certain topics or key terms. This is exactly what happens to an organization that has separate systems. Employees have a hard time making informed decisions because the information they need is stored across several different systems and sometimes conflicts.

Let's take a look at a customer address change example to demonstrate the problems that arise from having separate systems. If a customer moves and sends a change-of-address form to your company, this information must be entered into every single system where the customer address information is stored. Chances are some of the systems will be missed, and the customer now has different address information in different systems, or conflicting address information. How would an employee know which address is correct when trying to send a letter to the customer?

To alleviate this problem organizations build integrations. An **integration** allows separate systems to communicate directly with each other by automatically exporting data files from one system and importing them into another. Building integrations between systems helps your organization maintain better control of its information and helps quickly gather information across multiple systems.

Figure 5.7 shows an example of how your organization can integrate customer information systems. Every time new entries or changes occur, the information is inte-

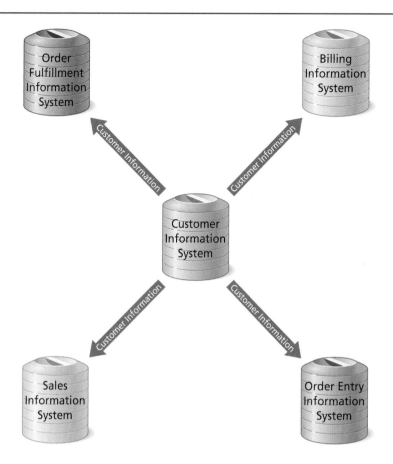

Figure 5.7

Integrating Customer
Information into
All Business Systems

grated, or automatically passed, to all of the other systems that maintain customer information. This eliminates the problem of having to enter the same customer information into multiple systems.

Integrations enhance employee's decision making by ensuring they have accurate and timely information. However, they are extremely hard and expensive to build and maintain, because you must find a way for systems that use different technologies to communicate. Integration issues also tend to increase exponentially as the number of systems in your company grows.

ENTERPRISE APPLICATION INTEGRATION (EAI)

Enterprise application integration (EAI) is the process of developing an IT infrastructure that enables employees to quickly implement new or changing business processes. EAI is a way of increasing business value by integrating not only business information but also business processes. Companies are investing in EAI to streamline business processes while keeping all organizational information integrated. It's important to understand that EAI is not something you can buy like a product or a development tool—it's something organizations try to accomplish. Most businesses are successful at accomplishing certain types of EAI—database EAI (sharing and copying information across databases) and system EAI (sharing information across multiple systems. The ultimate goal—*common virtual system EAI*, in which every business aspect comes together and they appear as a single unified system—is something almost every organization will attempt for many years to come. A few organizations will succeed, but most won't.[4]

ENTERPRISE APPLICATION INTEGRATION MIDDLEWARE

Enterprise application integration middleware (EAI middleware) allows organizations to develop different levels of integration from the information level to the business process level. EAI middleware simplifies integrations by eliminating the need for custom-built software. An organization can purchase an EAI package from a vendor that supplies a pre-built connector that translates and transfers information from one system to another. An EAI package saves your organization time and money, because system developers don't have to spend time custom-building interfaces between systems.

ActiveWorks, an integration product that focuses on business process integration of front-office customer and back-end business systems, is one of the primary EAI middleware packages available today. It was built by Active Software, founded in 1995.[5]

INFORMATION ARCHITECTURE

Informed decisions sometimes require reviewing past information as well as current information. Viewing historical information, or archived information, allows a company to perform detailed analysis on sales trends, customer trends, product trends, employee trends, etc. There is a wealth of knowledge in historical information.

So your IT infrastructure must define an *information architecture*, which describes in detail where and how information is stored, and usually includes the types and sizes of devices as well. Typically, historical information is stored on the same server as the current information. After a certain amount of time, it is *archived*—moved to a storage server—and in order to view it you must request that it be restored.

You also have to determine an appropriate cutoff date for archiving information. For example, if Bell Canada saved all billing information for every single customer throughout its history, it would need an incredible amount of space and most of the information would be outdated. You have to determine a cutoff date that makes business sense. If you make the cutoff date too soon, chances are you'll need frequent access to the archived information to answer questions and make decisions.

Improve Team Collaboration

Almost everything you do in your organization will be performed in a team environment. Very few tasks and assignments are performed individually in the working world. So improving team collaboration greatly increase your organization's productivity and should be a primary goal of your organization's IT infrastructure. **Collaboration software** allows people to work together. In Chapter 6, we will introduce you to many different types of collaboration software such as basic e-mail and group scheduling systems. Here we will cover three collaboration software components:

- Documentation management systems
- Enterprise information portals (EIPs)
- Workflow systems

DOCUMENTATION MANAGEMENT SYSTEMS

What do you think of when you hear the term "document"? The term can mean many different things to different people. A document can refer to any file that can be created and stored electronically including text, tables, forms, graphics, images, sound, video, etc.

3000 GAP STORES COMMUNICATING

The Gap Inc. has 3000 stores around the world, employing over 150,000 people who generated $16.3 billion in revenue in 2004. The company's primary goal is to achieve and maintain a 20 percent growth rate each year. To maintain this goal, The Gap needed to keep all of the employees connected with immediate access to real-time information by sharing information between several different legacy systems and new applications. The Gap chose to implement CORBA middleware to build the integrations between the different systems.

CORBA stands for "common object request broker architecture." The software allows programs at different locations developed by different vendors to communicate. Building an IT infrastructure based on CORBA integrations and the Internet allowed The Gap to exchange real-time sales, inventory, and shipping information among all of its information systems and employees. The new infrastructure allowed the company to send information to and from any IT system in the world, which increased employee and company performance.[6]

It's not uncommon to find 15 or 20 knowledge workers editing the same document. Large companies produce thousands of documents every month and they need to be organized and categorized. A **documentation management system** manages a document through its life cycle. The following are the primary functions of such a system:

- *Creation.* Allows knowledge workers to create different document types.
- *Modification.* Manages the integrity of a document as it's edited or modified by knowledge workers; otherwise known as *version control*.
- *Security.* Controls access to a document and only allows knowledge workers with appropriate access to view and edit the document.
- *Approval.* A document is sent to a particular knowledge worker for approval, similarly to a workflow system discussed in detail below.
- *Distribution.* Knowledge workers distribute documents via e-mail or the Web.
- *Archiving.* Saving a document in a storage facility with the ability to extract the document in the future.

A typical documentation management system contains a relational database management system where the texts of all documents are stored, and provides knowledge workers with the ability to perform full-text searches. Most systems allow businesses to capture data about paper documents, with one of the attributes being the document's location. If a knowledge worker requires a certain document to perform his/her job he or she can simply search the system for it.

ENTERPRISE INFORMATION PORTALS (EIPs)

Enterprise information portals (EIPs) allow knowledge workers to access company information via a Web interface. An EIP is similar to an Internet search engine such as Google, Yahoo!, or AltaVista, except the only information stored on an EIP is company information. Using an EIP, a knowledge worker can find and view enterprise-wide business information by performing a simple search.

An EIP is different from an intranet. Intranets are more like a corporate newsletter or static database of corporate information; an EIP is dynamic and serves as an electronic workspace for knowledge workers. EIPs provide personalized access to key information and applications and real-time notification of important new information

MANAGING MULTIPLE WEB SITES

Dow Corning Corporation develops and manufactures over 7000 products and services to customers all over the world. Every department in Dow Corning Corporation manages its own Web content.

When the company had a concern that the rush to publish information to the Web could cause the overall look and feel of the Web sites to suffer from a lack of consistency, it quickly realized it needed a documentation management system to ensure the consistency of its sites and company documentation while allowing experts in each department to contribute to the content.

Dow Corning decided to implement Documentum 4i eBusiness Platform, an e-business documentation management solution for creating, publishing, and managing Web site documentation. Documentum has an edit/quality control module that ensures that information posted on a site has been independently reviewed prior to release. With Documentum, Dow Corning increased customer satisfaction and employee productivity, and improved partner relationships.[7]

via e-mail. Critical information can also be presented in the form of graphics and charts that are continuously updated.

There are two primary categories of EIPs, collaborative processing and decision-processing. A **collaborative processing enterprise information portal** provides knowledge workers with access to workgroup information such as e-mails, reports, meeting minutes, and memos. A **decision-processing enterprise information portal** provides knowledge workers with corporate information for making key business decisions. EIPs are becoming increasingly popular in the workforce because of the amount of information sharing they provide for knowledge workers.

Both these categories of EIPs support integrated collaboration environments (ICEs), which we discussed in Chapter 2, and provide environments in which virtual teams do their work.

WORKFLOW SYSTEMS

Workflow defines all of the steps or business rules, from beginning to end, required for a process to run correctly. **Workflow systems** help automate business processes. Workflow systems help manage the flow of information through the organization whenever a process is executed. As a process is executed, a workflow system tracks where the information is and its status.

Let's take a look at how you could use a workflow system to help you complete a group project. The following are four steps you usually take when completing a group project:

1. Find out what information and deliverables are required for the project and when they are due.
2. Divide up the work among the group members.
3. Determine due dates for the different pieces of work.
4. Compile all the work into a single project.

One of the hardest parts of a team project is getting information passed around among the various team members. Often one group member can't perform his/her work until another group member has finished. Group members waste a lot of time waiting to receive information from another group member. This exact same situation

Enterprise information portals and workflow systems are great infrastructure components for improving team work and collaboration. You have just received an assignment to work on a group project with ten other students. The project requires you to develop a detailed business plan for a business of your choice. The types of activities you will need to perform include market analysis, industry analysis, growth opportunities, Porter's Five Forces analysis, financial forecasts, competitive advantage analysis, etc. For your project, determine the following:

1. How could you use enterprise information portals to share and post information within the group?
2. Why would you want to use an intranet—if so, what advantages would your team gain from using an intranet?
3. How could you use a workflow system to manage the tasks for the group members?

happens in the real world. You'll find the actual work is sitting idle waiting for an employee to pick it up to either fix it or continue working on it. Workflow systems help to automate the process of passing work around the organization.

A workflow system can automatically pass documents around to different team members in the required order. There are two primary types of workflow systems, messaging-based and database-based. **Messaging-based workflow systems** send work assignments through an e-mail system. The workflow system automatically tracks the order for the work to be assigned and each time it's completed it automatically sends the work to the next individual in line. If you used this type of workflow system to complete your group project it would automatically distribute the work to each group member via e-mail. Each time you finished a part of the project that needed to be sent to another group member the system would take care of this for you.

Database-based workflow systems store the document in a central location and automatically ask the knowledge workers to access the document when it's their turn to edit it. If you used this type of workflow system to perform your group project, the project documentation would be stored in a central location and you would be notified by the system when it was your turn to log in and work on your portion of the project.

Either type of workflow system will help improve teamwork by providing automated process support allowing knowledge workers to communicate and collaborate within a unified environment.

Create Business Partnerships and Alliances

With the growing popularity of performing business over the Internet, your IT infrastructure must support electronic business partnerships or your organization will not survive long in today's e-centric world. Creating business partnerships and alliances is a key strategy for any company that intends to be a serious player in the information age. There are four critical components to building a strong IT infrastructure to supporting these goals:

- Customer relationship management systems (CRM)
- Sales force automation systems (SFA)

- Electronic catalogue
- Supply chain management systems (SCM)

CUSTOMER RELATIONSHIP MANAGEMENT (CRM) SYSTEMS

Without customers a business couldn't exist. In fact, one important goal of any business is to increase customer satisfaction.

Keeping and retaining current and potential customers is one of the primary goals of any organization and customer relationship management has become one of the hottest buzzwords in businesses today. **Customer relationship management (CRM) systems** use information about customers to gain insights into their needs, wants, and behaviours in order to serve them better. Customers interact with companies in many ways and each interaction or experience should be enjoyable, easy, and error-free. Have you ever had an experience with a company that made you so angry you changed companies or returned the product? It's not uncommon for a customer to change companies after having a negative business experience. The goal of CRM is to limit these types of negative interactions and provide customers with positive business experiences.

It's important to note that CRM is not just software but also a business objective and encompasses many different aspects of a business including software, hardware, services, support, and strategic business goals. The IT infrastructure you create should support all of these aspects and must be designed to provide the organization with detailed customer information. Figure 5.8 is an example of a potential CRM system infrastructure. The **front office systems** are the primary interface to customers and sales channels; they send all of the customer information to the data warehouse. The **back office systems** are used to fulfill and support customer orders; they send all of the customer information to the data warehouse. The CRM system analyzes and distributes the customer information and provides the organization with a complete view of each customer's business experiences.

Many systems are available today that a company can purchase that offer CRM functionality; some of the big providers are Clarify, Oracle, SAP, and Siebel. Ensuring that your organization's IT infrastructure supports CRM is critical to your businesses success.

SALES FORCE AUTOMATION (SFA) SYSTEMS

The sales process includes many factors such as contact management, sales lead tracking, sales forecasting, order management, and product knowledge. **Sales force automation systems (SFA)** automatically track all the steps in the sales process. There are many SFA vendors, including Clairy, Siebel, Vantive, and Salesforce. Some basic SFA systems perform sales lead tracking or listing potential customers for the sales team to contact. They also perform contact management which tracks all of the times a sales person contacts a potential customer, what they discussed, and what are the next steps. More sophisticated SFA systems perform detailed analysis on market and customers and even offer product configuration tools where the customer can configure their own products.

One of the biggest problems organizations have when implementing SFA systems is developing the integrations. Sales, marketing, customer service centres, and customer billing are typically separate departments with separate systems. Often, these separate departments have communication problems that can hurt customer relationships. For example, a salesperson might talk to a customer and try to sell them a new

Figure 5.8

A Sample Customer Relationship Management (CRM) System Infrastructure

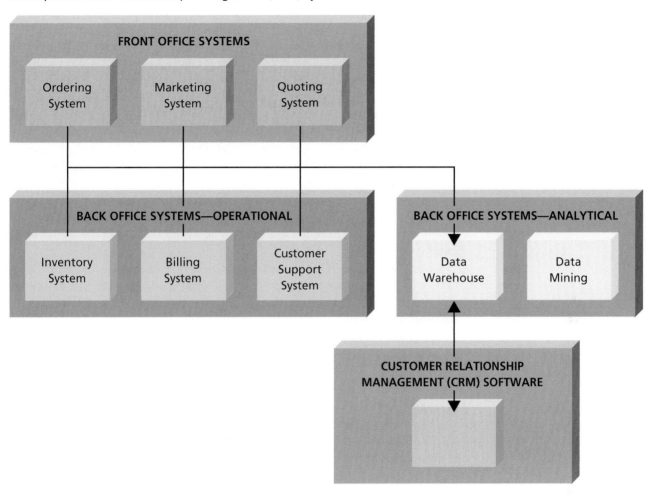

product without realizing the customer has been on the phone all day with another department in the company trying to resolve an issue with a current product. This is probably not the best day for the salesperson to approach the customer about additional products.

Getting separate departments to talk to each other electronically is a big challenge. An SFA system attempts to provide electronic communication between the sales systems alleviating such problems, as mentioned above. If the company had implemented an SFA system, the salesperson in the above example would already know that the customer had been talking to the company all day and even known exactly what problems the customer is experiencing. The salesperson could then approach the customer, help with the problems, and then try to sell additional products. SFA is an invaluable tool for increasing customer sales.

ELECTRONIC CATALOGUE

Providing an electronic catalogue is a great way to enable business partnerships and alliances. An **electronic catalogue** is designed to present products to customers or partners all over the world via the Web; it provides much more detailed information about products than paper catalogues, including real-time inventory status, photographs, product specifications, product instructions and safety procedures, video

FEDEX STREAMLINES SHIPPING

FedEx has become a master at supply chain management, using it to focus on building strong customer partnerships. FedEx has developed a tool, FedEx Ship Manager API, that can be downloaded for free off the Internet. The software allows customers to directly connect into FedEx's information systems when placing shipping orders and scheduling pickups.

This move gives FedEx an incredible competitive advantage. Customers now have complete control over shipping preparation, which helps to eliminate shipping errors since they enter the information directly. Customers can also monitor real-time shipping status right from their desk, which helps to increase employee productivity. FedEx has become a leader in the industry for its brilliant use of supply chain management.[8]

demonstrations, etc. Electronic catalogues even provide links to product reviews and industry information.

One of the biggest advantages of using an electronic catalogue is the search functionality. A customer can search the catalogue using a keyword, full text, line items, inventory levels, unit prices, etc. Giving customers such powerful search capabilities makes it easier for them to find a product especially if they know exactly what they want. Sometimes, however, the search functionality can make finding a product more difficult.

Let's assume you need to order new wastebaskets for your office. You simply open up a supplier electronic catalogue and type in the word "wastebasket." Unfortunately, your search returns 0 results. You then type in "trash bucket," "waste bucket," "trash bin," "garbage bin," and still nothing returns from your search results. You start to get a bit frustrated because you know this company sells office supplies and a wastebasket is a common office supply item. Finally you type in "garbage can," and several different types of wastebaskets appear on your screen.

This is one of the biggest issues with electronic catalogues, finding and associating all of the potential names for a given product. Everyone could potentially have a different name for a garbage can. If the company sells global products then it must also deal with offering the product in multiple languages. Trying to find all of the names and associating them with a given product is a critical and vital task to perform if the electronic catalogue is going to be successful.

Electronic catalogue software is available from many vendors, including Actinic, Harbinger, Mercado, and Requisite Technology. The software package already has the functionality of the catalogue aspects, and all a company has to do is input its own product information. Implementing an electronic catalogue is a huge advantage for any business, but of course it must be supported by the IT infrastructure.

SUPPLY CHAIN MANAGEMENT (SCM) SYSTEMS

Managing the supply chain is fundamental to the success of any business and controlling inventory is one of the largest problems facing businesses today. **Supply chain management (SCM) systems** track inventory and information among business processes and across companies. The primary goal of SCM is to reduce the amount of inventory a company must keep on hand by providing the company with a complete view into its suppliers to understand inventory levels and production capacity. SCM helps a company improve its operations and inventory tracking.

Figure 5.9

A Sample Supply Chain Management System (SCM) Infrastructure

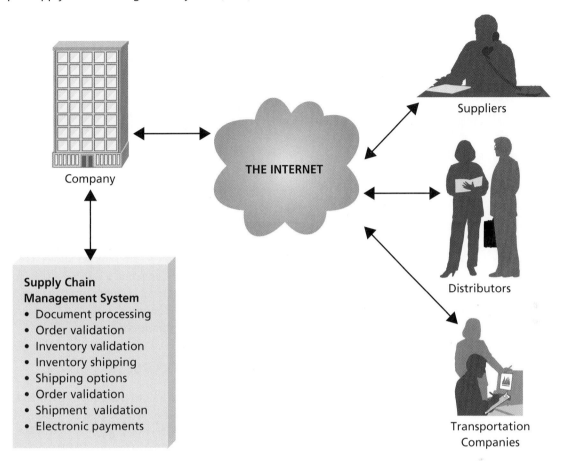

The solution for a successful supply chain management system includes either purchasing sophisticated software with Web interfaces or hiring a third-party Web-based application service provider that promises to provide part or all of the SCM service. Figure 5.9 provides an overview of how an organization's IT infrastructure can support SCM. The knowledge workers query the SCM software for information for ordering of inventory. The SCM software connects to potential suppliers, distributors, and transporting companies to determine where to purchase the inventory and the best way to have the inventory delivered. The SCM system also performs such functions as order validation, message validation to potential suppliers and distributors, inventory routing and validation, and electronic payments.

The two largest vendors of SCM systems include i2 and Manugistics. Dell Computer Corporation, one of the largest computer system companies in the world, recently implemented an i2 supply chain solution. Dell is a leader and innovator in Web-based sales and operation and is continually looking to set the industry standards for customer service, sales, and distribution. The company, undergoing enormous growth, decided to implement a SCM solution to help it manage its suppliers, distributors, transportation companies, and inventory. Dick Hunter, vice-president of manufacturing operations, has stated, "the supply chain solution from i2—and the processes we put around i2—is allowing us to move materials so fast around our supply chain that we're able to take advantage of lower-cost materials quicker and pass those lower-cost materials on to our suppliers. And that's allowing us to fuel our growth."[9]

Enable Global Reach

The IT infrastructure of your organization must be able to support global employees, suppliers, distributors, and most importantly customers. The primary tool used to help all of these individuals communicate globally is the Internet. The following are four of the primary global IT infrastructure components your organization must consider:

- Internet service provider (ISP)
- Application service provider (ASP)
- Collocation facilities
- Server farms

INTERNET SERVICE PROVIDER (ISP)

An **Internet service provider (ISP)** is a company that provides individuals, organizations, and businesses access to the Internet. There are hundreds of ISPs. Usually, ISPs have permanent and continuous connection to the Internet and sell temporary connection time to subscribers. This can be done either on a variable-price basis (e.g., the price depends on the number of hours you connect to the Internet) or on a fixed rate (e.g., a given cost per month, with unlimited connection time). How many of you use an ISP to connect to the Internet from your home computer?

APPLICATION SERVICE PROVIDER (ASP)

Outsourcing is the delegation of specific work to a third party for a specified length of time, at a specified cost, and at a specified level of service (the guarantee of perfect delivery). An **application service provider (ASP)** is a company that provides an outsourcing service for businesses software applications. Hiring an ASP to manage your organizations software allows you to hand over the storage, operation, maintenance, and upgrade responsibilities for a system to an ASP.

Companies can outsource application and infrastructure services. Application services include business functions such as payroll, accounting, intranets, and e-mail. Infrastructure services include large systems such as customer relationship management systems, enterprise resource planning systems, and customer service call centres.

Figure 5.10 represents how your IT infrastructure might support using an ASP. Your company gets access to the software through the Internet. The company knowledge workers can log on to the software from their offices, laptops, and sometimes cellular equipment depending on how the software works. The ASP stores, maintains, and upgrades the software ensuring security and backups of the data.

One of the most important agreements between the customer and the ASP is the **service level agreement (SLA)**, which defines the specific responsibilities of the service provider and sets the customer expectations. SLAs include such items as availability, accessibility, performance, maintenance, backup/recovery, upgrades, equipment ownership, software ownership, security, and confidentiality. For example, an SLA might state that the ASP must have the software available and accessible from 7 a.m. to 7 p.m. Monday through Friday. It might also state that if the system is down for more than 60 minutes the charge for that day of service will be waived.

Most industry analysts agree that the ASP market is growing rapidly. International Data Corp. estimates the worldwide ASP market will grow from around US$693.5 million in 2000 to US$13 billion by 2005. Zona Research (now the Sageza Group) reported in 2001 that 63 percent of the companies it surveyed are already using an ASP

Figure 5.10

A Sample Application Service Provider (ASP) Infrastructure

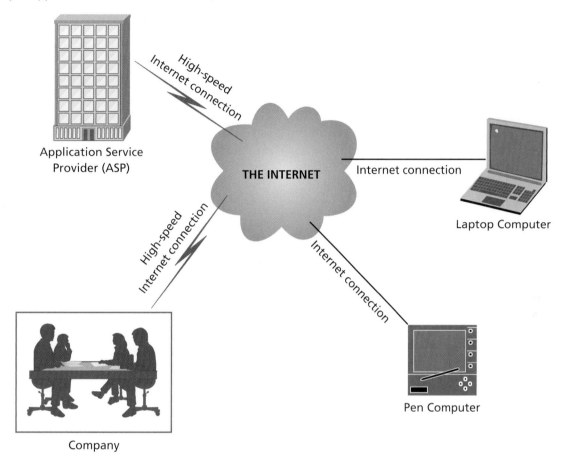

to access an average of two to six applications. As a knowledge worker, you'll find yourself working with ASPs and outsourced applications. You might even find yourself in the position of having to make the decision to outsource one of your business applications.[10]

COLLOCATION

Collocation (the word is variously spelled) is what happens when a company rents space and telecommunications equipment from another company, known as the *collocation vendor*. For example, if a company places a server that contains the company's Web site in a building owned by another company, the company has "collocated" its server with another company. Collocation facilities are typically warehouse-type buildings where hundreds of different companies can store computer hardware and software. If a company has a central office in Chicago and sales personnel in Chicago, Quebec City, and Hong Kong, the IT infrastructure must support all of the employees even if there is no central office in the town where they work. If a server is located in a collocation facility in Quebec City and Hong Kong, the sales personnel in these places can dial in to the server and be connected to the Chicago office's intranet and information systems. This saves the company a lot of time and energy because the alternative to this model would be to have the employees dial a long-distance number to the Chicago office or rent an office in each location to maintain the server. Renting space from a collocation facility is cheap and easy compared to setting up an entire office.

EURORESINS' UNIQUE STRATEGY

Euroresins is a leader in the European chemical products market. When it decided to outsource its IT department to IBM Global Services, the company wanted to minimize the costs and still be able to support the organization's IT infrastructure. The ASP model offered a perfect solution, and the company choose to partner with Multrix, one of the first ASPs in the Netherlands. Multrix provides applications along with a complete range of other services such as management, maintenance, security, and support.

Since outsourcing with Multrix, Euroresins has experienced significantly lower costs, better and more sophisticated services, and greater flexibility for adding services in different locations, something critical to doing business globally. The overall service is far better than the company could ever have built themselves.[11]

SERVER FARM

A **server farm** or **server cluster** is a location that stores a group of servers in a single place. A server farm provides centralized access and control to files and printers, and backups for each server. The advantage of a server farm is that if one server fails there are others that can perform the work and the knowledge workers don't experience any downtime. Server farms are often located in collocation facilities.

A **Web farm** is either a Web site with multiple servers or an ISP that provides Web site outsourcing services using multiple servers. For the most part you can use a single server to handle user requests for files on a Web site. For large Web sites you might require multiple servers.

Facilitate Organizational Transformation

Everything changes, and your organization must be ready to change whenever the economy, industry, technology, etc. changes. Being able to change quickly and easily is a huge advantage. The IT infrastructure has several critical components to help organizations change, including:

- Enterprise resource planning (ERP) and enterprise software
- Data warehouse
- Infrastructure documentation

ENTERPRISE RESOURCE PLANNING (ERP) AND ENTERPRISE SOFTWARE

Today, many organizations have come to realize that the development of a particular system without regard to the organization as a whole has serious disadvantages. To move toward a more holistic view, organizations are adopting the concept of enterprise resource planning and using enterprise software to develop all systems in a coordinated fashion. We first introduced enterprise resource planning systems in Chapter 4; we'll dive deeper into the topic here.

Enterprise resource planning (ERP) is the method of getting and keeping an overview of every part of the business (a bird's-eye view, so to speak), so that production, development, selling, and servicing of goods and services will all be coordinated to contribute to the company's goals and objectives. ERP may sound like a solid concept that all organizations should follow, but it just isn't that easy. In organizations of any size, seeing and understanding the whole corporate picture is difficult. To plan for all the resources needed for any initiative is even more difficult.

Further complicating the problem is that processes and IT systems are already in place supporting a particular business function, but perhaps not the organization as a whole. So just adopting ERP requires that most organizations undertake numerous reengineering efforts to ensure that the entire organization is operating as a single entity.

Enterprise software directly supports the concept of ERP. **Enterprise software** is a suite of software that includes (1) a set of common business applications, (2) tools for modelling how the entire organization works, and (3) development tools for building applications unique to your organization. Leading enterprise software vendors include SAP, Oracle, PeopleSoft, J. D. Edwards, Computer Associates, and Baan.

Figure 5.11 gives an example of how an organization could implement enterprise software. All of the information from the different departments is sent to the software, which maintains the data and can provide a holistic view of the organization. Once

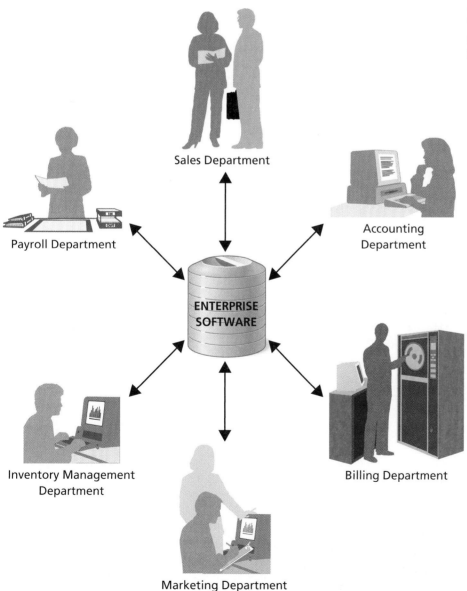

Figure 5.11

A Sample Enterprise Software Infrastructure

Sales Department

Accounting Department

Payroll Department

ENTERPRISE SOFTWARE

Inventory Management Department

Billing Department

Marketing Department

HOW ORLANDO SAVED 10,000 HOURS A YEAR

The Orlando, Florida city government has drastically improved its performance by implementing enterprise software. The city government has been using the J. D. Edwards ERP system since 1998. Today, over 400 Orlando government knowledge workers use it.

Rob Garner, comptroller, says, "All managers can view their budgets, drill down through multiple levels of financial information to individual transactions, and extract information and format it into any kind of report right from their desktops.

"Before implementing the system, we produced batch reports every month and shipped them to managers throughout city government. Now they don't have to rely on our IT department to generate financial information—they can get it themselves at any time, without having to ask anyone for it. We have redirected as much as 10,000 developer hours a year to supporting the needs of the user community."[12]

you use enterprise software to see the big picture, you can also use it to make changes to your organizational model and processes.

To use enterprise software effectively in support of ERP, your organization must first model its existing structure, divisions and departments, and processes, such as inventory procurement, accounts receivable, customer service, and so on. In parallel, it must also develop a model of all IT systems, how they work together, and perhaps how they conflict with each other. Armed with that information, your organization can then undertake the process of ERP to determine how best to streamline processes and develop the appropriate underlying IT systems that will support those processes through decentralized computing and shared information.

In the future, it looks as though enterprise software suites will replace **computer-aided software engineering (CASE) tools**—software suites that automate systems development. CASE tools were originally developed to support systems development, which focuses only on the development of a single system. Later, planning capabilities were added to some CASE tools, but it seemed to be more an afterthought than a well-defined plan. So CASE tools do not really require your organization to take a holistic view.

THE REALITY OF ENTERPRISE RESOURCE PLANNING AND ENTERPRISE SOFTWARE Although ERP and enterprise software sound almost too good to be true, many organizations are exploiting them. In spite of their tremendous advantages, however, many other organizations are either not using ERP and enterprise software or only partially implementing them. Some reasons for this are:

- *The existence of legacy systems.* **Legacy systems** are IT systems previously built using older technologies such as mainframe computers and programming languages such as COBOL. Legacy systems may work well in isolation but they tend to be very difficult to interface with when your organization develops new systems based on state-of-the-art technologies. Some organizations have invested literally billions of dollars in developing and maintaining legacy systems and they are not prepared to throw them away and switch to an ERP system.
- *The cost of ownership.* Enterprise software is among the most expensive software your organization can purchase, costing millions of dollars for a complete system. And after you purchase it, you have to customize it, which can easily cost millions of dollars more.

CHOOSING AN ERP VENDOR

Choose two of the leading enterprise software vendors (SAP, Oracle, PeopleSoft, J. D. Edwards, Computer Associates, and Baan) and, using the Internet, determine the primary differences between the two vendors' sys-

tems. Remember to think about the different IT infrastructure components mentioned in this chapter when you are performing your analysis.

- *The cost of reengineering.* Fundamental to the concept of ERP is business process reengineering. Let's face it—organizations that have evolved over time have inefficient, redundant, and incompatible processes. To rectify this, they must undergo numerous reengineering efforts. **Business process reengineering (BPR)** is the reinventing of processes within a business. Many people today characterize BPR as a "knee-breaking" initiative in which you completely disregard what you're doing in favour of processes that are streamlined and completely integrated. This, again, represents a huge expense, which some organizations are not willing to undertake.
- *The expertise needed.* Finally, to use enterprise software, your organization must provide extensive training to its IT staff. And each software suite requires expertise unique to that particular suite. Enterprise software vendors such as SAP and J. D. Edwards provide months and even years of training to your organization if you choose to purchase one of their suites. This expertise is in such high demand that you can actually become a certified developer using different enterprise software suites. If you do, your career will be long, prosperous, and full of money.

DATA WAREHOUSE

The promise of an ERP system is that one system could solve all of the information needs of the organization. ERP systems are great at capturing and storing data but they lack the ability to understand and analyze the data. Knowledge workers find themselves frustrated with ERP systems because they can't get the information they need from the system.

For this reason many businesses have implemented data warehouses along with ERP systems. The data warehouse consolidates the ERP information along with other sources of information in order to perform and support analysis. A data warehouse can help knowledge workers organize, understand, and analyze the information collected by the organization. This information is the true competitive advantage in the information age.

For detailed information on data warehouses, see Chapter 4.

INFRASTRUCTURE DOCUMENTATION

One of the keys to building a solid IT infrastructure is to ensure every component is well documented and the documentation is available to all company employees. A major issue for organizations today is the lack of system documentation. For example, assume you are building a data warehouse that must integrate with all of the ERP systems in the organization, but there isn't any documentation on how the ERP systems are designed and implemented. It'd be impossible for you to successfully integrate two systems.

IT Infrastructures and the Real World

Components of a solid IT infrastructure can include anything from documentation to business concepts to software and hardware. Throughout this chapter we have discussed many of these, including flexibility, scalability, client/server networks, supply chain management, and enterprise resource planning. It might seem like we have covered a great deal of material, but there are actually thousands of additional components that'll be important to building a solid IT infrastructure. Deciding which pieces to implement and how to implement them is becoming an almost impossible task as new products become available daily and businesses continually change. An IT infrastructure that meets your organizational needs today may not meet them tomorrow. Building an IT infrastructure that is scalable, flexible, available, accessible, and reliable is key to your organization's success.

As a knowledge worker you'll be responsible for approving the designs for the IT infrastructure for your systems. Remember to ask yourself the following questions before approving the designs:

- How big is your department going to grow? Will the system be able to handle additional users?
- How are your customers going to grow? How much additional information do you expect to store each year?
- How long will you maintain information in the systems? How much history do you want to keep on each customer?
- When do the people in your department work? What are the hours you need the system to be available?
- How often do you need the information backed up?
- What will happen to your system if there is a disaster? What is the recovery plan for your system?
- How easy is it to change the system? How flexible is it?

Ensuring your system designs answers each of these questions will put you on the path to building an IT infrastructure that will support your organization today and tomorrow.

Summary: Student Learning Outcomes Revisited

1. **Explain the relationship between the organization's roles and goals and the IT infrastructure.** An *IT infrastructure* includes the hardware, software, and telecommunications equipment that combined provide the foundation for the organizational goals, processes, and strategies. Organizational goals drive everything the organization does ranging from how it's structured to how it designs its IT infrastructure. For example, an organization can have many structures including flat or hierarchical. A flat organizational structure has only a

couple of managerial layers while a hierarchical organizational structure has many. If an organization has a flat structure it might be attempting to support the goal of information dissemination. If an organization has a hierarchical structure is might be attempting to support the goal of information secrecy and security.

2. **List and describe factors that help increase employee productivity.**
   - *Availability* is determining when your IT system will be available for knowledge workers to access.

- *Accessibility* is determining who has the right to access different types of IT systems and information.
- *Reliability* ensures your IT systems are functioning correctly and providing accurate information.
- *Scalability* is the process of building information systems that can grow, or scale, as the organization and information needs grow.
- *Flexibility* ensures the system is designed with the ability to quickly change.
- *Performance* measures how quickly an IT system performs a certain process.
- *Capacity planning* determines the future IT infrastructure requirements for new equipment and additional network capacity.

3. **Explain system integration and how it enhances decision making.** Many times an organization will have a separate and distinct system for each department. Some organizations end up with hundreds of different systems that do not communicate with each other. In order to help alleviate the problem of so many separate systems containing separate information, organizations build integrations. An integration allows separate systems to communication directly with each other by automatically exporting data files from one system and importing them into another system. Building integrations between systems helps the organization to maintain better control of its information and helps quickly gather information across multiple systems.

4. **List and describe different types of workflow systems.**
   - *Messaging-based workflow infrastructures* send work assignments through an e-mail system. The workflow system automatically tracks the order for the work to be assigned and each time it's completed it automatically sends the work to the next individual in line.
   - A *database-based workflow* infrastructure stores the document in a central location and automatically asks the knowledge workers to access the document when it's their turn to edit it.

5. **List and describe IT infrastructure components that create business partnerships and alliances.**
   - *Customer relationship management (CRM) systems* use information about customers to gain insights into their needs, wants, and behaviours in order to serve them better.
   - *Sales force automation (SFA)* is the process of automatically tracking all of the steps in the sales process.
   - *Electronic catalogues* are designed to present products to customers or partners all over the world via the Web.
   - *Supply chain management (SCM)* tracks inventory and information among business processes and across companies.

6. **List and describe IT infrastructure components that enable global reach.**
   - An *Internet service provider (ISP)* is a company that provides individuals, organizations, and businesses access to the Internet.
   - *Collocation* simply means that a company rents space and telecommunications equipment from another company, or a collocation vendor.
   - An *application service provider (ASP)* is a company that provides an outsourcing service for businesses software applications ranging from personal productivity programs to large enterprise-wide systems that would otherwise be located on the company's computers in the company's office building.
   - A *server farm* or *server cluster* is the name of a location that stores a group of servers in a single place.

7. **Assess why global reach is important, and identify how IT infrastructure can enable it.** With *global reach*, a company can interact with customers anywhere where there is an Internet connection, at much lower cost. Also, employees are able to search through information from organizations and libraries worldwide. Through global IT infrastructure components, chiefly Internet service providers, application service providers, collocation facilities, and server farms, the organization can support global employees, suppliers, distributors, and customers.

UNIVERSITY INFRASTRUCTURES

The year is 1982. Universities around the country are filled with students pursuing business degrees in accounting, marketing, management, and finance. The life of a student in 1982 is drastically different from the life a student in 2002. In 1982 only a couple of students had access to e-mail, none of the students had laptops, many of the students have never used a computer, and the idea of surfing the Internet was a concept students couldn't even understand. It's hard to believe that technology has come so far so fast.

Cheryl O'Connell graduated from university with a marketing degree in 1983. O'Connell says, "I remember all of my papers were either handwritten or typed on a typewriter; nobody had a computer. There were about 15 computers in the business school for all 3500 business students. The computers were in high demand and were primarily used for running statistical or spreadsheet programs, not word processing programs. I never dreamed that one day I would own a computer. The thought just never even crossed my mind."

In 1982 students didn't have access to e-mail, they weren't instant-messaging their friends, they had to use a dictionary to check their spelling, and they had to go to the library if they wanted to research a subject. If you had a conversation with one of these students and told them that in 20 years most students would own their own computers, they could automatically spell-check a 100-page paper in about ten minutes, and they could research libraries all over the world from their dorm rooms they would have told you that you were crazy.

In 1982 Apple Computer offered the Lisa computer, featuring 5-MHz 68000 microprocessor, 1 MB of RAM, 2 MB of ROM, a 12-inch black-and-white monitor, dual 5.25-inch 860-KB floppy drives, and a 5-MB hard drive. Its initial price was $10,000. In the same year IBM introduced the IBM PC-XT Model 370, with 8088 CPU, 768 K of RAM, a 360-K drive, and a 10-MB hard drive for $9000. Can you even imagine a 10-MB hard drive nowadays? A hard drive this small wouldn't even be able to handle one software package today.

In the 20 years since 1982 everything has changed. Over 90 percent of first-year students arrive on campus already owning or having personal access to a computer.

Today, one of the biggest selling features of a university is its IT Infrastructure. Offering Internet access to dorm rooms and supporting campus-wide wireless networks is quickly becoming a requirement for universities to offer its students.

Universities in general estimate that 30 percent of their network traffic is for e-mail, 40 percent is used to transfer files and downloads from the Internet, and 30 percent is everything else including games, instant messaging, and Web surfing.

A university's IT infrastructures are a strong factor students look at where they want to study. For this reason alone, it is critical that a university implement a solid IT infrastructure that meets the students' needs.[13,14]

Questions

1. Walking around your university, you probably see all kinds of technological gadgets that didn't even exist 20 years ago, including PDA's, cell phones, and wireless networks. How have these gadgets increased student productivity? How have they decreased it?

2. Does your university have a client/server network? If so, where are the clients located? Where is the server located? What kind of access do you have to the Internet? What type of activity do you think takes up the most capacity on the network?

   If your university does not have a client/server network, determine a design for the infrastructure to support one. Be sure to think about the factors that increase student productivity along with the IT infrastructure components. How big is your department going to grow? Will the system be able to handle additional users?

3. Imagine it's 2004 and your university has grown by 50 percent since 2002. How many students are now attending? Would the support departments such as accounting and human resources need to grow also as the number of students increases? What would happen to the university's IT infrastructure with the increased growth? What issues will the university encounter with its information

systems due to this unexpected growth? What could your university have done to help prepare for this kind of unexpected growth?

4. Your university has decided to implement an electronic catalogue for potential students to view when considering attending your school. What types of information would be saved in it? What would be three advantages of using an electronic catalogue instead of a paper brochure? What

would be one of the primary problems people would encounter?

5. Try to imagine what a university will be like 20 years from now. What types of new technological gadgets will drastically change the lives of students in the year 2022? How will student productivity be affected by the new gadgets? Use the Internet to see if you can find any articles on where universities are headed in the future.

CLOSING CASE STUDY TWO

TRANSFORMING THE ENTERTAINMENT INDUSTRY— NETFLIX

The online DVD rental pioneer Netflix is transforming the movie business with its unique business model, streamlined shipping strategy, and unique application infrastructure. Netflix is quickly becoming one of Hollywood's most promising new business partners and is experiencing staggering growth with over 1 million subscribers, which accounts for 3 to 5 percent of all U.S. home video rentals.

Typically, traditional video rental stores focus on major films and ignore older movies and smaller titles with niche audiences. Netflix is turning that idea upside down by offering a serious market for every movie, not just blockbusters. How? Netflix attributes its success to its proprietary software, called the Netflix Recommendation System, which constantly suggests movies you might like, based on how you rate any of the 15,000 titles in the company's catalogue. Beyond recommendations, Netflix has figured out how to get DVDs from one subscriber to the next with unbelievable efficiency with its corporate application infrastructure.

Netflix operates by allowing its subscribers to rent unlimited videos for $20 a month, as long as they have no more than three DVDs rented at a time. Currently there are more than 3 million disks in the hands of its customers at any given time, with an average of 300,000 DVDs shipped out of the company's 20 leased distribution centres daily. Netflix's unique application infrastructure allows it to track, monitor, and maintain detailed information on each of its disks, customers, and shippers. At any point in time the company can

tell you the exact location of each of its disks, a critical component for Netflix's business model.

To handle the rental logistics for its 5.5 million DVD library, the company created several proprietary applications. One of its most successful systems is its Web-based supply chain management system. The system works by having operators scan a barcode on every label for every single disk that arrives in its warehouses. The software then retrieves the name and address of the next person on the wait list for that DVD, prints out a label, and the disk is dropped back into the mail. The custom-built systems have allowed Netflix to slow hiring and reduce labour costs by 15 percent, and the vast majority of its DVDs never touch a warehouse shelf. On any given day, 98 percent of the 15,000 titles in Netflix's inventory are in circulation with its customers.[15]

Questions

1. Netflix makes the majority of its sales over the Internet. Having a great Web site and a solid IT infrastructure is critical to Netflix's business model. Do you think the company uses Web services to build its applications? Briefly describe what Web services are and how Netflix might use them to improve its business.

2. There are two primary types of EIPs: collaborative processing and decision processing. Explain the main difference between the two types.

Which type of EIP would you recommend Netflix implement? Why?

3. Describe the factors for supporting IT infrastructures and the importance of each to Netflix's IT infrastructure.

4. Netflix has hired you as its IT infrastructure expert. Netflix would like you to explain how a solid IT infrastructure can help the company support its primary goals. Netflix also wants you to explain what a 3-tiered architecture is and how it can help the organization.

5. Netflix has a massive amount of inventory that it must distribute around the country daily. Explain why a disaster recovery plan is critical to its business operations. Also, explain what might happen to Netflix if it lost all its customer information.

6. Netflix requires several different departments to make its business work. What types of systems do you think Netflix maintains in its different departments? Can you explain why Netflix would want to integrate the system information among its different departments?

Key Terms and Concepts

application service provider (ASP), 180
back office system, 176
backup, 165
benchmark, 169
business process reengineering (BPR), 185
capacity planning, 169
client/server network, 162
cold site, 165
collaboration software, 172
collaborative processing enterprise information portal, 174
collocation, 181
computer-aided software engineering (CASE) tools, 184
customer relationship management (CRM) system, 176
data cleansing, 168
database-based workflow system, 175

decision-processing enterprise information portal, 174
digital dashboard, 166
disaster recovery cost curve, 165
disaster recovery plan, 165
documentation management system, 173
electronic catalogue, 177
enterprise application integration (EAI), 171
enterprise application integration middleware (EAI middleware), 172
enterprise information portal (EIP), 173
enterprise resource planning (ERP), 182
enterprise software, 183
extranet, 166
front office system, 176
global reach, 163
hot site, 165

integration, 170
Internet service provider (ISP), 180
intranet, 166
IT infrastructure, 160
legacy system, 184
messaging-based workflow system, 175
performance, 169
recovery, 165
sales force automation system (SFA), 176
scalability, 168
server farm (server cluster), 182
service level agreement (SLA), 180
supply chain management (SCM) system, 178
thin client, 162
3-tier architecture, 164
2-tier architecture, 164
Web farm, 182
workflow, 174
workflow system, 174

Short-Answer Questions

1. What is an IT infrastructure?

2. What is a client/server network?

3. What is an intranet?

4. Why do you need a backup of information?

5. Why would you need to recover information?

6. What are two organizational roles/goals?

7. What are two IT infrastructure components that increase employee productivity?

8. What is enterprise application integration middleware?

9. What are integrations and how are they used to enhance decision making?

10. Why does a business need a disaster recovery plan?

11. What is customer relationship management?

12. What is sales force automation?

13. What is one advantage of using an electronic catalogue over using a paper catalogue?

14. What is supply chain management?

15. How can you use supply chain management to create business partnerships and alliances?

16. Why would a company implement documentation management software?

17. What is an ISP and how is it different from an ASP?

18. How can enterprise resource planning facilitate organizational transformation?

Assignments and Exercises

1. **AN EIP FOR YOUR COURSE.** Enterprise information portals (EIPs) allow knowledge workers to access company information via a Web interface. You have been asked to create an EIP for this course. Please answer the following questions in order to determine how the EIP should be developed:

   - What type of information would be contained on the EIP?
   - Who would have access to the EIP?
   - How long would information remain on the EIP?
   - What is the difference between a collaborative processing EIP and a decision processing EIP?
   - Which type of EIP would you implement and why?

2. **SPONSOR OF THE IT INFRASTRUCTURE.** In order to build a solid IT infrastructure you must have executive sponsorship. Your current boss doesn't understand the importance of building a solid IT infrastructure. In fact, your boss doesn't even understand what an IT infrastructure. First, explain to your boss what an IT infrastructure is and why it is critical for any organization. Second, explain each of the following organizational goals to your boss along with two related IT infrastructure components.

   - Increase employee productivity
   - Enhance decision making
   - Improve team collaboration
   - Create business partnerships and alliances
   - Enable global reach
   - Facilitate organizational transformation

3. **ARABIAN NIGHTS VIDEO.** Mackenzie Spencer is the director of IT infrastructure at Arabian Nights Video, a $100M video manufacturing plant. Internally, the company manages video manufacturing systems and a client/server network that serves more than 1000 knowledge workers. Mackenzie is reflecting on her decision to hire a third-party vendor (ASP) to implement the new inventory tracking system. Mackenzie has hired you as an ASP expert. On the basis of your vast knowledge of IT infrastructure components, what would be your advice to Mackenzie regarding the advantages and disadvantages of working with an ASP? What would you tell Mackenzie to include in the service level agreement with the ASP?

4. **IT INFRASTRUCTURE COMPONENTS AND THE REAL WORLD.** Throughout this chapter we have discussed several IT infrastructure components including client/server, reliability, integrations, electronic catalogues, etc. Pick two of the components discussed in this chapter and try to find business examples of how companies are using these components in the real world. We have also mentioned that there are thousands of additional components you can use to build an IT infrastructure. Try to research the Internet to see if you can find two additional IT infrastructure components that were not discussed in this chapter along with business examples of how businesses are using the components in the real world.

5. **CREATING THE IDEAL INFRASTRUCTURE.** As a knowledge worker you'll be responsible for approving IT system designs which ultimately affect your company's IT infrastructure and its abilities to achieve its goals. This

chapter has focused on many different IT infrastructure components including ERP, SCM, client/server, integrations, etc. Choose three of the different components discussed in this chapter and explain how you could use them to improve the IT infrastructure at your university. Be sure to think of current requirements as well as future requirements for the systems.

6. **THE COMPLETE IT INFRASTRUCTURE.** A document management system manages a document through its life cycle. The following table lists the document lifecycle phases in the first column. Explain what tasks a documentation management system would perform during each phase. Explain how you could use a documentation management system to help you work on a group project.

Document Lifecycle Phase	Tasks Performed	Group Project Tasks Performed
Creation		
Modification		
Security		
Approval		
Distribution		
Archiving		

7. Congratulations! You have been appointed Student Infrastructure Manager. Your first assignment is to approve the designs for the new on-campus Internet infrastructure. You're having a meeting at 9 a.m. tomorrow to review the designs with the student IT employees. In order to prepare for the meeting, you must understand the student requirements and their current use of the Internet, along with future requirements. The following is a list of questions you must answer before attending the meeting. Please provide your answer to each.

- Do you need to have a disaster recovery plan, if so what might it include?
- Does the system require backup equipment?
- When will the system need to be available to the students?
- What types of access levels will the students need?
- How will you ensure the system is reliable?
- How will you build scalability into the system?
- How will you build flexibility into the system?
- What are the minimum performance requirements for the system?
- How will the system handle future growth?

Discussion Questions

1. IT infrastructures often mimic organizational hierarchies. Define two different types of organizational hierarchies and how the IT infrastructure would be built in order to support them.

2. IT infrastructure components can include anything from software to strategic functions. After reading this chapter and learning about a few of the primary IT infrastructure components, explain why a company's IT infrastructure can include so many different components.

3. Organizations tend to spend a great deal of time determining their primary goals, objectives, structure, and strategies. Define your university's goals, and define the objectives, structure, and strategies that support these goals. Explain how your university's IT infrastructure supports its goals.

4. What is a client/server network? Does your university have a client/server network? How does its client/server network increase student productivity? How does its client/server network decrease student productivity?

5. Providing Internet access to employees is a great way to increase employee productivity. It's also a great way to decrease employee productivity, if the employees abuse their Internet privileges. What does it mean to have employees abuse the Internet? What can you do as a manager to prevent this? What would happen if all students in your university spent ten hours a day surfing the Net? Using the Internet, find two different types of network monitoring software that you would recommend your university purchase to deter abuse.

6. Imagine you are working for a large cookie manufacturing company. The company is 75 years old and just starting to implement technology to improve operations. Your direct manager has asked you to put together a presentation discussing integrations. In your presentation you must include definitions of integration, EAI, and EAI middleware. You must also explain each concept in depth along with a real-world example of how the concept will help your company become more successful.

7. What are the four major categories of EAI? Discuss each, along with an example of how the EAI could be used in your university. Also discuss two EAI middleware vendors. You can use the Internet to find more detailed information about EAI middleware vendors.

8. Customer relationship management (CRM) is the objective of managing the customer's relationship with the company through all the different customer business experiences. Supply chain management (SCM) tracks inventory and information

among business processes and across companies. What is the difference between these two IT infrastructure components? What do they have in common? Would a company implement both? If they did, why, and what would be the advantage of having both components?

9. Informed decisions sometimes require reviewing past information as well as current information. Research different types of storage devices and explain which type you would choose and why.

10. With the growing popularity of doing business over the Internet, creating business partnerships and alliances should become a primary goal for any organization's IT infrastructure. List two IT infrastructure components you could use to help a business create business partnerships and alliances.

11. A fellow student is trying to write a paper on third-party vendors for IT infrastructure components. Throughout this chapter we have discussed several different third-party vendors including ISPs, ASPs, collocation facilities, and server farms. Explain each one of these components to your fellow student along with a real-world example of each.

12. Enterprise resource planning (ERP) is the coordinated planning of all an organization's resources involved in the production, development, selling, and servicing of goods and services. Describe ERP and how an organization might benefit from implementing an ERP system.

13. IT infrastructures should support the creation of flexible and scalable IT systems that can quickly adapt to support new business requirements. Give an example of an IT infrastructure that is inflexible and not scalable and a barrier to supporting a changing business. Give an example of an IT infrastructure that is flexible and scalable and supports expanding a business.

Electronic Commerce

Living Life on the Internet

Electronic Commerce Links

The personal computer is quickly becoming a household necessity like a stove or a fridge. However, if it is not connected to a worldwide infrastructure that gives you access to abundant information, it is of little value. The primary reason the personal computer has become such an important part of our lives is the Internet. There are literally thousands of ways people use the Internet to perform tasks.

Do you have a personal computer with Internet connectivity in your home? How often do you use it and why? You probably use it all the time to perform tasks ranging from sending e-mails to finding driving directions. So many great sites are available, and all of them can help you accomplish things such as finding movie times, cooking a delicious meal, and seeking medical advice.

In this section we'll provide you with a few key sites you can use to help you live your life, and you can find many more on the Web site that supports this text (www.mcgrawhill.ca/college/haag).

ONLINE MAGAZINES

Every year, people spend an incredible amount of money buying magazines. Many of these magazines are received through the mail and never read, ending up in a giant pile

a giant recycling plant. Do you receive magazines through the mail or buy them while doing your grocery shopping? How much are you paying for them, and do you actually find the time to read them? Did you know that many magazines are available online for free? That's right, free. Save yourself some money by using the Internet to get the latest news and fashion tips instead of buying those costly magazines. Here are just a few of the many hundreds available:

- *Canadian Geographic* (www.canadiangeographic.ca)
- *ChartAttack* (www.chartattack.com)
- *Sports Illustrated* (sportsillustrated.com)
- *Chatelaine* (www.chatelaine.com)
- *Maclean's* (www.macleans.ca)
- *PC Magazine* (www.pcmag.com)
- *TV Guide* (www.tvguide.ca)
- *Popular Mechanics* (www.popularmechanics.com)

Connect to a few of these magazines and try answering the following questions:

A. Does the site contain the most recent issue?

B. Is it easy to view past issues or search for articles on a particular topic?

C. Can you find three additional magazines you enjoy that are not listed above?

D. Are there any additional features in the online version of the magazine that are not available in the paper version?

E. Do you enjoy reading the magazine online better than in print? Why or why not?

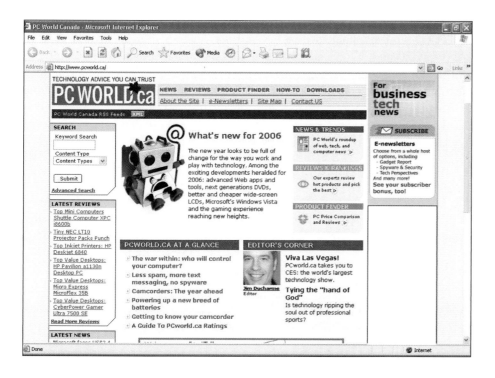

ONLINE MOVIE LISTINGS AND REVIEWS

How often do you get to go to the movies? How many times do you head out to the movies without knowing the theatre location, movie time, or movie rating? How often do you rent movies? Do you wander around the store unable to decide which to rent?

Wasting time and money on a bad movie happens to us all, but there is a way to eliminate this problem: the Internet.

The Internet has a wealth of information regarding movies, including theatre locations, movie times, and movie ratings and reviews. You can also check out detailed movie reviews at the Movie Review Query Engine site (www.mrqe.com). If you are interested in what movies are coming out over the next few months, try the Coming Attractions site (www.cinescape.com/0/devheck_2.asp). You can search for movie times at your local theatres by visiting the Moviefone site (www.movies.aol.com). Lastly, you must visit the Internet Movie Database (www.imdb.com), for tons of information on any movie ever made.

A. Can you find the movies that are currently playing at a theatre near you?

B. Try to research a classic movie such as *Grease* or *Animal House* to find out the movie's rating and the year it was released.

C. Try to locate three new movies that are coming out over the next year.

D. Log on to the Internet Movie Database and search for all the movies made by your favourite actor or actress. Were any movies listed that you had not watched?

E. Log on to the Internet Movie Database and try to research the top ten movies of all time.

COOKING FROM THE INTERNET

Does making a box of Kraft Macaroni and Cheese challenge your cooking skills? Don't worry, help is only a few clicks away. There are hundreds of Web sites that can provide you with recipes, detailed cooking instructions, and nutritional information.

The first stop you should make is the Nutrition Analysis Tools and System (NATS) site (nat.crgq.com). NATS analyzes the foods you eat for various different nutrients and gives you recommendations on the types of food that are missing from your diet. Next, visit Cooking.com (www.cooking.com) for information on everything from cookbooks and cookware to recipes and cooking tips. For those of you interested in healthy meals try Cooking Light (www.cookinglight.com) and those of you interested in gourmet cooking try Good Cooking (www.goodcooking.com).

A. Try to find a recipe for barbequed chicken and mashed potatoes on one of the above sites.

B. Try logging on to the Nutritional Analysis Tool and find out the nutritional value of your last meal.

C. Try to find a Web site that will help you plan a menu for a dinner party of six people.

D. Log on to the gourmet site and see how many different recipes you can find for your favourite food.

E. Log on to Cooking Light and find a few tips on how you can decrease cholesterol in your diet.

 Go to the Online Learning Centre at www.mcgrawhill.ca/college/haag for quizzes, extra content, a searchable glossary, and more! Click on "Electronic Commerce Projects" for links to hundreds of Web sites.

 Go to the text CD-ROM for data files, extra content, and Skills Modules on Microsoft Excel, Microsoft Access, HTML, and e-portfolios.

CHAPTER SIX

Visit
www.mcgrawhill.ca/college/haag

LearningCentre

CASE STUDY:

USING A BUSINESS INTELLIGENCE SOLUTION TO ACHIEVE GREATER FINANCIAL AND OPERATIONAL EFFICIENCIES

Black Photo Corporation (www.blackphoto.com), the largest photographic retailer in Canada, is a wholly owned subsidiary of Fuji Photo Film Canada Inc. It owns more than 180 retail locations specializing in photographic goods and services and on-site photo finishing production. Prominent vendors such as Pentax, Canon, Minolta, and Nikon supply the company. The company had an existing JDA enterprise solution, which did not provide adequate analytics or reporting, with a limited ability to assess inventory, sales margins, and demand trends in each store. "There was a need to see our data differently," says Tim Hammond, senior vice-president of merchandising and marketing at Black. "We have 180 locations, and there was a need to analyze areas like inventory movement and sales margins by store. In addition, there was a need to let our vendors see their inventory movement. I wanted to be able to give them as much information about their products as possible."

Black Photo turned to Intellera (www.intellera. com), a Montreal-based provider of business intelligence and workflow solutions, for an answer to their needs. Intellera was chosen because it understood the retail industry and Black Photo's specific needs, and because of its speed of devel-

opment and implementation. Intellera used its retail sector knowledge, along with Cognos business intelligence applications, to provide Black Photo with a BI solution that was integrated very quickly into the existing JDA database: a "merchandising cube," which was designed in less than 60 days and which helped Black gain detailed exception reporting and analysis in more than 180 stores and the ability to see inventory in 3D perspective. The company could now measure and manage its inventory better. It could also now measure the performance of advertising campaigns in different geographical locations, and developed a flexible business intelligence infrastructure that could facilitate creation of additional "cubes" for other functional areas such as human resources and CRM.

The Intellera solution is used at every level in the company, from CEO to accountant. It has helped Black Photo achieve massive savings in inventory, internal savings as well as vendor savings. Black's vendors are now well informed about their inventory and play a proactive role in inventory management. Today, they use the Intellera solution to understand Black's needs better and can make recommendations based on direct information. This has strengthened the vendor relationship with Black.

In sum, Black Photo Corporation has successfully used a quality BI solution to reduce costs, handle business data and inventory more efficiently, and manage its supply chain better.[1]

Introduction

People in business everywhere regularly make decisions as complex as those outlined in the opening Case Study. Information technology can help in the decision-making process, regardless of whether you're running a hospital or a small retailing business.

The big winners in tomorrow's business race will be those organizations, according to *Management Review*, that are "big of brain and small of mass."[2] For example, with a small number of employees, the company Adtrack is able to track millions of records (in a data warehouse) of information pertaining to newspaper and magazine ads. These people perform complex tasks to provide newspapers and ad agencies with information on their relative position against competitors.[3,4]

For many years, computers have been crunching numbers faster and more accurately than people can. A computer can unerringly calculate a payroll for 1000 people in the time it takes a pencil to fall from your desk to the floor. Because of IT, knowledge workers have been freed of much of the drudgery of manually handling day-to-day transactions. And now IT power is augmenting brainpower and thought processes in ways previously seen only in science fiction. In some cases, IT power is actually *replacing* human brainpower to a limited degree.

Businesses, like individuals, use brainpower to make decisions, some big, some small, some relatively simple, and some very complex. As an effective knowledge worker, you'll have to make decisions on issues such as whether to expand the workforce, extend business hours, use different raw materials, or start a new product line. IT can help you in most, if not all, of these decisions. The extended brainpower that IT offers you as a decision maker comes in the form of decision support systems and artificial intelligence.

Whether to use a decision support system (there are several variations) or some form of artificial intelligence depends on the type of decision you have to make and how you plan to go about making it. So let's first look at different types of decisions and the process you go through to make a decision. Then we'll discuss decision support systems and artificial intelligence—IT brainpower (see Figure 6.1).

Decisions, Decisions, Decisions

You make many decisions every day from the simplest to the very complex. For example, you may want to made a decision on what mozzarella cheese to buy on the basis of cost. Contrast that decision with the one where you try to decide which job offer to take. Choosing the right job is definitely more complex, because it has multiple decision criteria, not all of which are quantifiable. Therefore, it's much more difficult to select the "best" of the alternatives.

Decision making is one of the most significant and important activities in business. Organizations devote vast resources of time and money to the process. In this section,

Figure 6.1

The Two Categories of Computer-Aided Decision Support

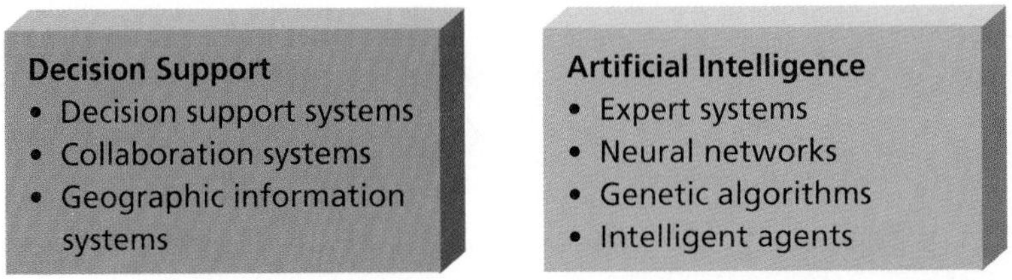

Decision Support
- Decision support systems
- Collaboration systems
- Geographic information systems

Artificial Intelligence
- Expert systems
- Neural networks
- Genetic algorithms
- Intelligent agents

we'll consider the phases of decision making and different decision types to help you better understand how IT can benefit that process.

HOW YOU MAKE A DECISION

In business, decision making has four distinct phases (see Figure 6.2):[5]

- **Intelligence** *(find what to fix).* Find or recognize a problem, need, or opportunity (also called the diagnostic phase of decision making). The intelligence phase involves detecting and interpreting signs that indicate a situation which needs your attention. These "signs" come in many forms: consistent customer requests for new-product features, the threat of new competition, declining sales, rising costs, an offer from a company to handle your distribution needs, and so on.
- **Design** *(find fixes).* Consider possible ways of solving the problem, filling the need, or taking advantage of the opportunity. In this phase, you develop all the possible solutions you can.
- **Choice** *(pick a fix).* Examine and weigh the merits of each solution, estimate the consequences of each, and choose the best one (which may be to do nothing at all). The "best" solution may depend on such factors as cost, ease of implementation, staffing requirements, and timing. This is the prescriptive phase of decision making—it's the stage at which a course of action is prescribed.
- **Implementation** *(apply the fix).* Carry out the chosen solution, monitor the results, and make adjustments as necessary. Simply implementing a solution is seldom enough. Your chosen solution will always need fine-tuning, especially for complex problems or changing environments.

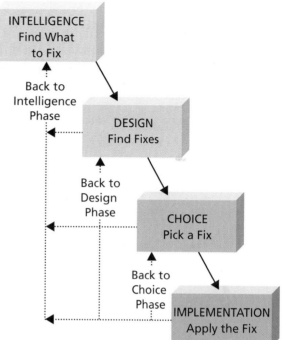

Figure 6.2

Four Phases of Decision Making

These four phases are not necessarily linear—you'll often find it useful or necessary to cycle back to an earlier phase. When choosing an alternative in the choice phase, for example, you might become aware of another possible solution. Then you would go back to the design phase, include the newly found solution, return to the choice phase, and compare the new solution to the others you generated.

TYPES OF DECISIONS YOU FACE

It's pretty clear that deciding which cheese to buy when you want the cheapest is a decision with a simple comparison that leads to a correct answer. Thus it is an example of a structured decision, whereas choosing the right job is an example of a decision with nonstructured and structured elements. That is, some parts are quantifiable and some are not.

A **structured decision** involves processing a certain kind of information in a specified way so that you will always get the right answer. No "feel" or intuition is necessary. These are the kinds of decisions that you can program—if you use a certain set of inputs and process them in a precise way, you'll arrive at the correct result. Calculating gross pay for hourly workers is an example. If hours worked is less than or equal to 40, then gross pay is equal to hours times rate of pay. If hours worked is greater than 40, then gross pay is equal to 40 times rate of pay plus time-and-a-half for every hour over 40. You can easily automate these types of structured decisions with IT.

Figure 6.3

Viewing Structured Versus Nonstructured Decision Making as a Continuum

WHAT JOB DO I TAKE?

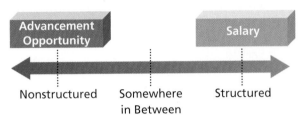

A **nonstructured decision** is one for which there may be several "right" answers and there is no precise way to get a right answer. No rules or criteria exist that guarantee you a good solution. Deciding whether to introduce a new product line, employ a new marketing campaign, or change the corporate image are all examples of decisions with nonstructured elements.

In reality, most decisions fall somewhere between structured and nonstructured, and are referred to as **semistructured**. The job choice decision is an example (see Figure 6.3). In choosing the right job, the salary part of the decision is structured, whereas the other criteria involve nonstructured aspects (e.g., your perception of which job has the best advancement opportunity). Stock market investment analysis is another example of "somewhere in-between" because you can calculate financial ratios and use past performance indicators. However, you still have to consider nonstructured aspects of the companies, such as projected prime interest rate, unemployment rates, and competition.

Another way to view decisions is by the frequency with which the decision has to be made. The decision as to which job to take is the sort of decision you don't make on a regular basis—this is a nonrecurring, or ad hoc, decision. On the other hand, determining pay for hourly employees is a routine decision that businesses face periodically. Therefore determining gross pay for hourly employees is a recurring decision.

A **recurring decision** is one that happens repeatedly, and often periodically, whether weekly, monthly, quarterly, or yearly. You will usually use the same set of rules each time. When you calculate pay for hourly employees, the calculation is always the same regardless of the employee or time period. A **nonrecurring**, or **ad hoc**, **decision** is one that you make infrequently (perhaps only once) and you may even have different criteria for determining the best solution each time. A company merger is an example. These don't happen often—although they are becoming more frequent. And if the managers of a company need to make the merger decision more than once, they will most likely have to evaluate a different set of criteria each time. The criteria depend on the needs of the companies considering the merger, the comparability of their products and services, their debt structure, and so on.

Decision Support Systems

**Skills Module 1
Decision Analysis—
Excel**

In Chapter 4, you saw how data mining can help you make business decisions by giving you the ability to slice and dice your way through massive amounts of information. Actually, a data warehouse with data mining tools is a form of decision support. The term "decision support system," used broadly, means any computerized system that helps you make decisions. However, there's also a more restrictive definition. It's rather like the term "medicine"—it can mean the whole health care industry or it can mean cough syrup, depending on the context.

Narrowly defined, a **decision support system (DSS)** is a highly flexible and interactive IT system designed to support decision making when the problem is not structured. A DSS is an alliance between you, the decision maker, and specialized support provided by IT (see Figure 6.4). IT brings speed, vast amounts of information, and sophisticated processing capabilities to help you create information useful in making a decision. You bring know-how in the form of your experience, intuition, judgment, and knowledge of the relevant factors. IT provides great power, but you—as the decision maker—must know what kinds of questions to ask of the information and how to

What You Bring	Advantages of a DSS	What IT Brings
Experience	Increased productivity	Speed
Intuition	Increased understanding	Information
Judgment	Increased speed	Processing capabilities
Knowledge	Increased flexibility	
	Reduced problem complexity	
	Reduced cost	

Figure 6.4

The Alliance Between You and a Decision Support System

process the information to get those questions answered. In fact, the primary objective of a DSS is to improve your effectiveness as a decision maker by providing you with assistance that will complement your insights. This union of your know-how and IT power makes you better able to respond to changes in the marketplace and to manage resources in the most effective and efficient ways possible. Following are some examples of the varied applications of DSSs:

- A national insurance company using a DSS to analyze its risk exposure when insuring drivers who had histories of driving under the influence. The DSS revealed that married male homeowners in their 40s with one DUI conviction were rarely repeat offenders. By lowering its rates to this group the company increased it market share without increasing its exposure.[6]
- The Canadian National Railway regularly tests the rails its trains ride on to prevent accidents. Worn-out or defective rails result in hundreds of derailments every year, so it's important to address the problem. Using a decision support system to schedule rail testing, CN decreased its rail-caused derailments, while other railroad companies had a 16 percent rise in such accidents.[7]
- Customer relationship management (CRM) is an important part of any successful company's strategy. Decision support is an important part of CRM. On Bay Street, retail brokerage companies analyze customers' behaviors and goals with decision support which highlights opportunities and alerts brokers to developing problems.[8]

COMPONENTS OF A DECISION SUPPORT SYSTEM

DSSs vary greatly in application and complexity, but they all share specific features. A typical DSS has three components (see Figure 6.5): data management, model management, and user interface management.

Before we look at these three components individually, let's get a quick overview of how they work together. When you begin your analysis, you tell the DSS, using the user interface management component, which model (in the model management component) to use on what information (in the data management component). The model requests the information from the data management component, analyzes that information, and sends the result to the user interface management component, which in turn passes the results back to you (see Figure 6.5). Here's an example of a decision support system at the clothing business Lands' End:

→ **Skills Module 1 Decision Analysis— Excel**

- *Model management.* The DSS at Lands' End has to have models to analyze information. The models create new information that decision makers need to plan

Figure 6.5

Components of a Decision Support System

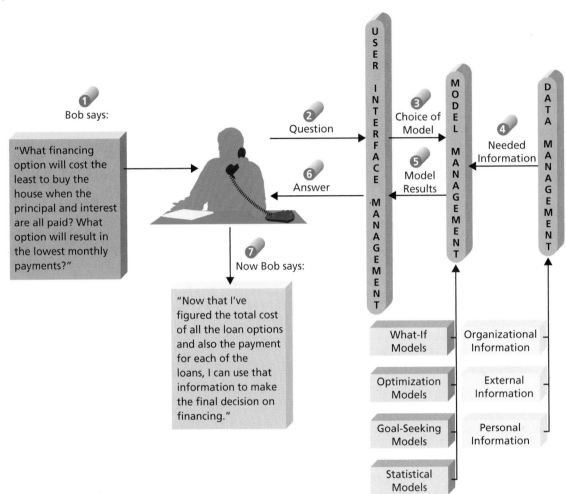

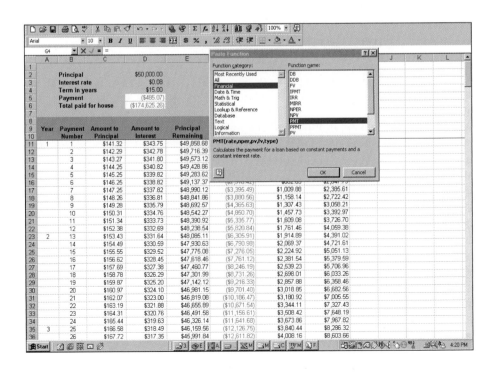

product lines and inventory levels. For example, Lands' End uses a statistical model called regression analysis to determine trends in customer buying patterns and forecasting models to predict sales levels.

- *Data management.* The DSS's data management component stores Lands' End's customer and product information. In addition to this organizational information, the company also needs external information, such as demographic and industry and style trend information.
- *User interface management.* A user interface enables Lands' End decision makers to access information and specify the models they want to use to create the information they need.

Now we'll examine the three DSS components in more general terms.

MODEL MANAGEMENT COMPONENT The **model management** component consists of both the DSS models and the DSS model management system. A model is a representation of some event, fact, or situation. Businesses use models to represent variables and their relationships. For example, you would use a statistical model called analysis of variance to determine whether newspaper, TV, and billboard advertising are equally effective in increasing sales. DSSs help in various decision-making situations by utilizing models that allow you to analyze information in many different ways. The models you use in a DSS depend on the decision you're making and, consequently, the kind of analysis you require. For example, you would use what-if analysis to see what effect the change of one or more variables will have on other variables, or optimization to find the most profitable solution given operating restrictions and limited resources. You can use spreadsheet software such as Excel to create a simple DSS for what-if analysis. Figure 6.5 has an example of a spreadsheet DSS you might build to compare how much you'd pay for a house at different interest rates and payback periods.

The model management system stores and maintains the DSS's models. Its function of managing models is similar to that of a database management system. The model management component can't select the best model for you to use for a particular problem—that requires your expertise—but it can help you create and manipulate models quickly and easily.

DATA MANAGEMENT COMPONENT The *data management* component performs the function of storing and maintaining the information that you want your DSS to use. The data management component, therefore, consists of both the DSS information and the DSS database management system. The information you use in your DSS comes from one or more of three sources:

- *Organizational information.* You may want to use virtually any information available in the organization for your DSS. You can design your DSS to access this information directly from your company's databases and data warehouses.
- *External information.* Some decisions require input from external sources of information. Various branches of the federal government, S&P/TSX, and the Internet, to mention just a few, can provide additional information for use with a DSS.
- *Personal information.* You can incorporate your own insights and experience—your personal information—into your DSS.

USER INTERFACE MANAGEMENT COMPONENT The *user interface management* component allows you to communicate with the DSS. It consists of the user interface and the user interface management system. This is the component that allows you to combine your know-how with the storage and processing capabilities of the computer. The **user interface** is the part of the system you see—through it you

WHICH & WHY?

Are you having difficulty deciding where to advertise? Having trouble choosing a particular health care plan for your employees? Or simply where to go on vacation? Canadian software developer Arlington Software Corp. from Vancouver (www.arlingsoft.com) may not have the solution but certainly promises to help you find one.

The company has developed Which & Why, a decision support system priced at about $350 designed to accelerate and improve managers' decision making. Peter Strum, a senior partner with Deloitte & Touche in Ottawa, while helping a Canadian federal government department select a prime contractor, noted that "using Which & Why reduced the time to complete the project from four months to one month … the product enabled 15 people with various goals to reach a clear, rational decision." According to Dave Lobley, manager

of Arlington Software's Eastern region, the software's strength is that it "guides users through a series of steps, resulting in a carefully thought-out decision." Users are presented with a blank screen on the right called a "model tree" and a "note pad" on the left. All the factors that could possibly affect your decision are typed into the note pad. This includes, for example, such as "contractor's ability to finish project in 10 weeks" and "cost of project should not surpass $2 million dollars." The more important factors are retained and dragged into the model tree while those deemed as extraneous are discarded into the "trash." The DSS then asks the user to rate each of the factors in the tree according to importance. Once all the factors are rated, you simply click on the "build a model" button for a tally of the ratings and analysis of the alternatives under consideration.[9]

---

enter information, commands, and models. If you have a DSS with a poorly designed user interface—if it's too rigid or too cumbersome to use—you simply won't use it no matter what its capabilities. The best user interface uses your terminology and methods and is flexible, consistent, simple, and adaptable.

Collaboration Systems

Toronto Hydro has 650,000 customers, 1700 employees, and five corporate offices. As you can imagine, the company gets and sends a lot of e-mail messages. The volume was 100 megabytes per day in 1999 and had increased to more than a gigabyte a day by 2002.

E-mail is a simple form of a collaboration system. A **collaboration system** or **collaboration software** is software that allows people to work together (see Figure 6.6). E-mail is, of course, vital to survival, but for many companies it's no longer enough. In fact, almost 60 percent of companies surveyed by *InformationWeek* in February 2002 said that they intended to increase their collaboration initiatives in the near future. Collaboration software takes many forms with many combinations of features with varying degrees of complexity.

ENTERPRISE-WIDE COLLABORATION

Toronto Hydro, for example, found it needed employees also to have access to each other's calendars, group scheduling, imaging, automated workflow, task and document management, message management, as well as e-mail. For these tasks the company now uses Lotus Notes.[10] Microsoft has a comparable product called Exchange, which allows integration with Access, Excel, Word, and even Visual Basic.

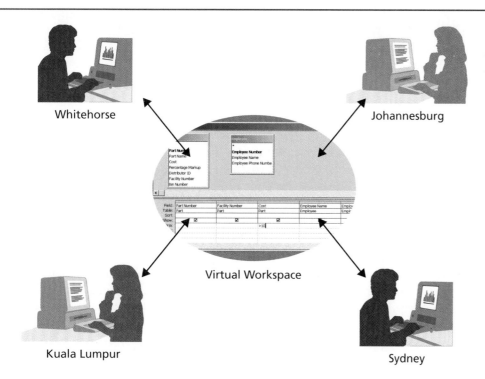

Figure 6.6
Collaboration Software
Connects People

Whitehorse

Johannesburg

Virtual Workspace

Kuala Lumpur

Sydney

Like the Toronto utility company, many companies first use e-mail and then move on to integrated collaboration systems like Lotus Notes or Exchange. After that, they may need to migrate to more sophisticated collaboration systems that incorporate tele-, video- and Web conferencing in real time, and may even include project management and workflow automation. For example, Ford gets parts for vehicles from places as far apart as France and Singapore, so coordinating ordering, shipping, and delivery with production is very complex, particularly in a just-in-time environment. Electronic collaboration and information sharing are important for any business. But the task becomes particularly critical the more geographically scattered employees, customers, and suppliers are.

SUPPLY CHAIN COLLABORATION

As you already saw in Chapter 2, a supply chain includes the paths reaching out to all of the suppliers of parts and services to a company. It consists not only of a company's suppliers, but of its suppliers' suppliers as well. Supply chain management means working with your suppliers and distributors in all phases of planning, production, and distribution. This involves the routine sharing of information to reduce inventories and improve cash flow.

You might want your suppliers to be able to add or change information. Boeing is a case in point. The company conducts the whole design process for its 777 jets online. All plans, schedules, orders, confirmations, and so on, are online and available to engineers, customers, maintenance staff, project managers, and suppliers all over the world. Changing from physical models and paper blueprints with fax, phone, and travel has cut the time for delivery of a plane from three years to less than 12 months. So Boeing reaps the twin benefits of happier customers and a tripling in its production rate.[11]

You might want to share information with clients too. So you could set up a collaboration system whereby your customers can access information, but can't change or delete it. Ogilvy & Mather, the company that handles advertising for IBM, Ford, and American Express, among others, does this. Ogilvy & Mather has a collaboration system that lets clients view images, text, and multimedia files.[12]

WEB-BASED COLLABORATION

One of the major application areas of collaboration systems is in e-commerce. As you'll see in Chapter 7, e-commerce is simply traditional business in a new form. It's conducted in cyberspace, but is still based on relationships, which means people working together. Web-based collaboration tools use the power of the Internet to enable people to work together effectively and efficiently.

Web-based collaboration software can be wide-open sharing of information on the Internet where anyone can access it, like Lands' End Live where anyone with Web access can interact with representatives of the company. Or it can be a special virtual workspace with access restricted to a select few. For example, CareGroup HealthCare System, a network in six hospitals, uses a collaboration system to permit doctors tending newborns, especially babies that are at risk. While the baby must stay in the hospital, a private Web page, accessible only to the neonatal centre at the hospital and the parents, is set up so that the parents can find out about the baby anytime. The hospital staff put information onto the Web site about feeding, weight, and medical care along with digital photos of the baby. When the new baby goes home, the parents can hold videoconferences with hospital staff so that they can keep a close watch on the baby's progress.[13,14]

Another example of a by-invitation-only virtual workspace is at Intel, the maker of the Pentium chip. More than half of Intel's direct material suppliers are in Asia, so the Internet is a great way for the company to speed up communication and information access. But Intel doesn't necessarily want everyone in the world to be able to snoop into company information. So Intel's suppliers can use passwords to access Intel's demand forecasts, engineering plans, orders, and invoices. Suppliers get demand, inventory, and receipt information automatically from the factory without human intervention. Intel plans to eventually make the company completely electronic.[15]

PEER-TO-PEER COLLABORATION   Groove and NextPage are both examples of a special kind of information-sharing software called peer-to-peer collaboration software. It's based on the same principle as Napster, that is, the ability to communicate in real time and share documents between peers without going through a central server. The peer-to-peer file-sharing feature in the collaboration software is combined with the ability to collaboratively create and edit documents, and to send and receive text and voice messages.

Here's an example of how it might work. Let's say you're a representative working at FastTrucks, a company that ships perishable goods all over the country. One of your customers is PotatoSupply, a PEI-based company that grows and distributes potatoes. You're both using the Groove collaboration system. One day a truck filled to the brim with potatoes and other perishables is headed through Niagara Falls—but so is a major winter storm. To avert disaster in the form of rotting potatoes and a stranded truck, you could go online and bring up the virtual workspace that you share with your PotatoSupply counterpart. From there you could check on the potato company's current and past shipments and can access records on routing plans and other pertinent information. This is the file-sharing part of the operation. You could then contact your counterpart at PotatoSupply and negotiate a new route, saving the potatoes and the day.[16]

COLLABORATION TO FIND CURES

Projects that require collaboration between different departments in a company use collaboration software that goes beyond e-mail, instant messaging, and calendar management. Such software would include workflow management, project management, and other tools that improve the efficiently of work processes.

GlaxoSmithKline, a British pharmaceutical company, is a case in point. The company spends $4 billion a year on research, has 4000 researchers whose work is stored in more than a dozen databases in various formats. There are separate databases for chemical and biological information and another for the specimen inventory. In 2001, the company set up an Intranet collaboration system that searches all the company databases and even goes out onto the Web to find any and all research done on a given molecule. By reducing the cost of finding information, the company can spend more time and money developing new medicines.[17]

Geographic Information Systems

Suppose you've decided to go on a two-week vacation that will include camping, sightseeing, and mall touring in Edmonton (after all, Edmonton boasts the largest shopping mall in the world—the West Edmonton Mall). What maps should you buy? Some will show roads for travelling from one place to another; others will show campgrounds in the province; others will pinpoint historic landmarks; still others will detail hotels around the West Edmonton Mall and the locations of the hundreds of stores in the mall.

To get a truly comprehensive picture of your proposed vacation, you'd consolidate the information by redrawing all the maps into a single map. But what about a business that needs to analyze different maps with geographic, demographic, highway, and other information?

Fortunately there's a special type of DSS for just this kind of problem—it's called a geographic information system. A **geographic information system (GIS)** is a decision support system designed specifically to work with spatial information—any information that can be shown in map form, such as roads, the distribution of bald eagle populations, sewer systems, and the layout of electrical lines.

Today GISs are helping businesses perform such tasks as:

- Identifying the best site to locate a branch office based on number of households in a neighbourhood
- Targeting pockets of potential customers in a particular market area
- Repositioning promotions and advertising on the basis of sales
- Determining the optimal location of a new distribution outlet

When businesses combine textual information and spatial information, they are creating a new type of information called *business geography*. GISs are well suited to storing, retrieving, and analyzing business geography to support the decision-making process.

A GIS is actually a combination of sophisticated graphics and database technology. Using a GIS, you can logically link textual and spatial information. For example, you could gather geographic information about the distribution of customers who buy yachts (spatial information). You could also gather information about their colour preferences (textual information) and link it to the spatial information. Then, using queries similar to those illustrated in Chapter 4, you could analyze both the spatial and

Figure 6.7

Geographic Information Systems

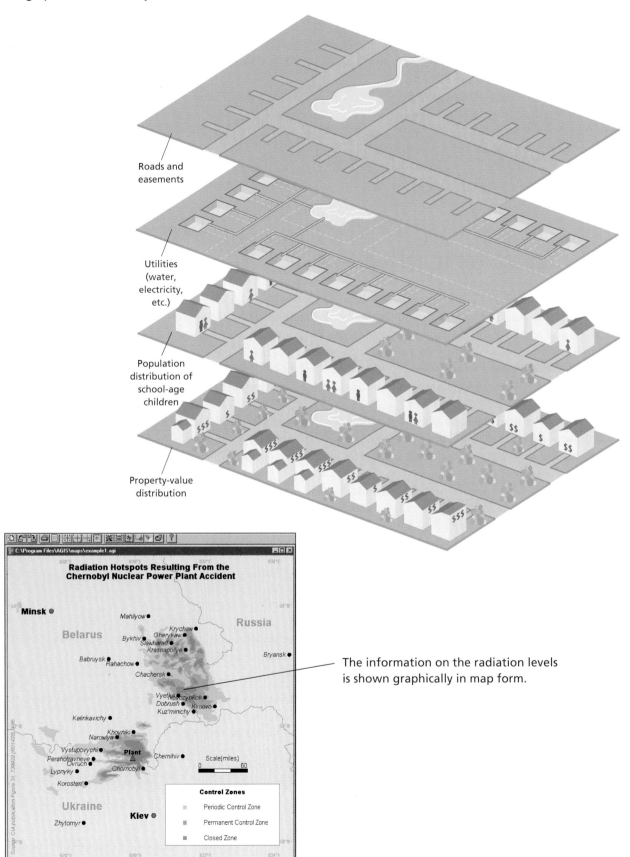

Roads and easements

Utilities (water, electricity, etc.)

Population distribution of school-age children

Property-value distribution

The information on the radiation levels is shown graphically in map form.

the textual information, generating output in the form of maps, graphs, or numeric tables. Some GISs let you load thousands of rows of information from a spreadsheet.

A GIS database represents information thematically. That means that a GIS map is composed of many separate, overlapping information layers, each of which has its own theme. For example, the first layer might be roads, the next might be utilities (water, electricity, etc.), the third school-age children, and the fourth homes within a certain price range (see Figure 6.7). This feature of a GIS, to show map information and attribute information as layers, distinguishes a GIS from other decision support system. Studies show that how information is presented significantly impacts the effectiveness and efficiency of the decision-making process.[18]

Figure 6.8 shows a mobile GIS called ArcPad developed by ESRI Canada, a Canadian owned company specializing in GIS products and services. ArcPad operates on Windows CE palm-size computers. It downloads data via a TCP/IP connection such as a wireless LAN, cellular phone, or wireless modem. It has layering features allowing the user to toggle the display of street lights, roads, rail stops, etc.

Here is another example of GISs in use. Clean Harbor Inc. is the company that hauled away the potentially anthrax-tainted debris from the offices of NCB during the anthrax scare toward the end of 2001. Since hazardous waste removal is such a dangerous job, the company had to keep track for the shipment every minute. Clean Harbor used software that incorporated a GIS map and GPS information to watch the trucks along their journey.[19]

Figure 6.8
ArcPad

Artificial Intelligence

DSSs and GISs are IT systems that augment business brainpower. IT can further expand business brainpower by means of artificial intelligence—the techniques and software that enable computers to mimic human behaviour in various ways. Financial analysts use a variety of artificial intelligence systems to manage assets, invest in the stock market, and perform other financial operations.[20] Hospitals use artificial intelligence in many capacities, from scheduling staff, to assigning beds to patients, to diagnosing and treating illness. Many government agencies use artificial intelligence, including the Canada Customs and Revenue Agency (CCRA) and the armed forces. Credit card companies use artificial intelligence to detect credit card fraud, and insurance companies use artificial intelligence to ferret out fraudulent claims.[21] Artificial intelligence lends itself to tasks as diverse as airline ticket pricing, food preparation, oil exploration, and child protection. It is widely used in the insurance, meteorology, engineering, and aerospace industries and by the military.

Artificial intelligence (AI) is the science of making machines imitate human thinking and behaviour. For example, an *expert system* is an AI system that makes computers capable of reasoning through a problem to reach a conclusion. We use the process of reasoning to find out, from what we already know, something that we don't know.

ROBOTS TO THE RESCUE

High-temperature gas samples are invaluable in volcanology, yet scientists are regularly killed attempting to obtain them. Developed by the Carnegie Mellon University Field Robotics Center, the Dante II tethered walking robot explored Mt. Spurr in Alaska, connected by satellite and Internet to the field team. The spider-like robot collected data samples and sent back live video from eight cameras to the scientists, safely away from the heated gases of the active volcano. Though Dante II, like its predecessor, Dante I, lost its footing on the volcano wall and fell to the floor of the crater, it continued to send back video footage. So, while the robot was irreparably damaged during the trek, the project was considered a success.

In the future, robots will have artificial intelligence software to enable them to find their way around rubble or difficult terrain independently without cords.

Search and rescue are not the only applications of robots. You've probably seen RoboMower, Sony's Aibo and Honda's competing Asimo, which are consumer robots. Here are some others.

- The Pentagon has a robot that delivers mail in an automated truck that follows a wire in the floor to move from office to office. As it enters each office, the robot calls the occupants to come and pick up mail.
- For many years the food service industry has used robots to prepare pizza, tacos, and other tasty morsels. Robots also pour drinks and transport food to conveyer belts ready for delivery to customers. Some in the food service industry are predicting that, in the not-too-distant future when better and more sophisticated software that includes wireless and video capabilities is incorporated into robots, a single employee will remotely service multiple robots.
- In London, there's a restaurant that has a robot waiter delivering drinks to customers. The software enables the robot to know the location of different tables.[22,23]

Today computers can see, hear, smell, and, what is important for business, think—in a manner of speaking. Robots are a well-known form of AI. A **robot** is a mechanical device equipped with simulated human senses and the capability of taking action on its own (in contrast to a mechanical device such as an automobile which requires direction from the driver for its every action). Robots are in use in many industries. For example, Piedmont Hospital's Pharmacy Dosage Dispenser is a robotic prescription-filling system. Using barcode technology, the Dispenser receives medication orders online, retrieves prepackaged doses of drugs, and sends them to hospital patients.[24] One of the most exciting new areas of research in robotics is the development of microrobots that can be introduced into human veins and arteries to perform surgery.

Seventy percent of the top 500 companies use artificial intelligence as part of decision support, and the sale of artificial intelligence software is rapidly approaching the $1 billion mark. The artificial intelligence systems that businesses use most can be classified into the following major categories:

- *Expert systems*, which reason through problems and offer advice in the form of a conclusion or recommendation
- *Neural networks*, which can be "trained" to recognize patterns
- *Genetic algorithms*, which can generate increasingly better solutions to problems by generating many, many solutions, choosing the best ones, and using those to generate even better solutions

- *Intelligent agents*, which are adaptive systems that work independently, carrying out specific, repetitive, or predictable tasks

Expert Systems

Suppose you own a real estate business, and you generate over 40 percent of your revenue from appraising commercial real estate. Consider further that only one person in your firm is capable of performing these appraisals. What if that person were to quit? How do you replace that expertise? How fast can you find someone else? How much business would you lose if it took you a month to find a suitable replacement?

In business, people are valuable because they perform important business tasks. Many of these business tasks require expertise, and people often carry expertise in their heads—and often that's the only place it can be found in the organization. AI can provide you with an expert system that can capture expertise, thus making it available to those who are not experts so that they can use it, either to solve a problem or to learn how to solve a problem.

An **expert system**, also called a **knowledge-based system**, is an artificial intelligence system that applies reasoning capabilities to reach a conclusion. Expert systems are excellent for diagnostic and prescriptive problems. Diagnostic problems are those requiring an answer to the question "What's wrong?" and correspond to the intelligence phase of decision making. Prescriptive problems are those that require an answer to the question "What to do?" and correspond to the choice phase of decision making.

An expert system is usually built for a specific application area called a *domain*. You can find expert systems in the following domains:

- *Accounting*. For auditing, tax planning, management consulting, and training
- *Medicine*. To prescribe antibiotics where many considerations must be taken into account (such as the patient's medical history, the source of the infection, and the price of available drugs)
- *Process control*. For example, to control offset lithographic printing
- *Human resources management*. To help personnel managers determine whether they are in compliance with an array of federal employment laws
- *Financial management*. To identify delinquency-prone accounts in the loan departments of banks
- *Production*. To guide the manufacture of all sorts of products, such as aircraft parts
- *Forestry management*. To help with harvesting timber on forest lands

A DSS sometimes incorporates expert systems, but an expert system is fundamentally different from a DSS. To use a DSS, you must have considerable knowledge or expertise about the situation with which you're dealing. As you saw earlier in this chapter, a DSS *assists* you in making decisions. That means that you must know how to reason through the problem. You must know which questions to ask, how to get the answers, and how to proceed to the next step. However, when you use an expert system, the know-how is in the system—you need only provide the expert system with the facts and symptoms of the problem for which you need an answer. The know-how that actually solves the problem came from someone else—an expert in the field. What

PLEASE SEND ALL APPLICATIONS TO THE EXPERT SYSTEM

Companies that hire a lot of hourly workers sometimes use an expert system or some other form of artificial intelligence to sort through the list of candidates and help managers identify the employees who are the best qualified and will stay the longest. Blockbuster, Target, and Universal Studios use a system called Unicru which was developed by psychologists (domain experts) to identify the best applicants.

Applicants sit at a computer and spend a half an hour answering questions, after which a report is sent to the hiring manager with a recommendation of no, maybe, or yes. "Yes" usually results in an interview, "maybe" is accompanied by suggestions on what follow-up questions to ask, and "no" usually results in the application being sent to the recycle bin.

The system has helped Blockbuster cut the time it takes to hire someone from two weeks to 72 hours. The system has also resulted in a reduction in the turnover rate for its users by up to 30 percent, which is very important since the turnover rate in this kind of job can be up to 150 percent per year.

Here's a sample of the type of questions the system asks:

- *True or false?* I was meant to work at Target.
- *True or false?* Slow people irritate me.
- *True or false?* A lot of people do annoying things.
- *True or false?* I like a job that's quiet and predictable.
- *True or false?* I can smile and chat with anyone.
- *True or false?* I am good at taking charge.
- *True or false?* I'd rather do things my way than follow the rules.

When a vice-president of Macy's West was testing the Unicru system, it told him he wasn't qualified to be a clerk in his own store. He was outraged until a Unicru executive explained that with his drive, ambition, and salary requirements, he'd be frustrated and bored to death and would soon quit. The VP had forgotten the difference between being able to do a job and being a good match for the position.[25]

does it mean to have expertise? When someone has expertise in a given subject, that person not only knows a lot of facts about the topic, but also can apply that knowledge to analyze and make judgments about related topics. It's this human expertise that an expert system captures.

Let's look at a very simple expert system that would tell a driver what to do when approaching a traffic light. Dealing with traffic lights is the type of problem to which an expert system is well suited. It is a recurring problem, and to solve it you follow a well-defined set of steps. You've probably gone through the following mental question-and-answer session millions of times without even realizing it (see Figure 6.9).

When you approach a green traffic light, you go on through. If the light is red, you try to stop. If you're unable to stop, and if traffic is approaching from either side, you'll probably be in trouble. Similarly, if the light is yellow, you may be able to make it through the intersection before the light turns red. If not, you will again be faced with the problem of approaching traffic.

Let's say that you know very little about what to do when you come to a traffic light, but you know that there are experts in the field. You want to capture their expertise in an expert system so that you can refer to it whenever the traffic-light situation arises. To gain an understanding of what's involved in the creation and use of an expert system, let's now consider the components of an expert system individually with the traffic-light example in mind.

COMPONENTS OF AN EXPERT SYSTEM

An expert system, like any IT system, combines information, people, and IT components:

Information Types	People	IT Components
Domain expertise	Domain expert	Knowledge base
"Why?" information	Knowledge engineer	Knowledge acquisition
Problem facts	Knowledge worker	Inference engine
		User interface
		Explanation module

These components and their relationships are shown in Figure 6.9, which includes the screen shown at right.

INFORMATION TYPES The traffic-light domain expertise is the core of the expert system, because it's the set of problem-solving steps—the reasoning process that will solve the problem. You'll also want to ask the expert system how it reached its conclusion, or why it asked you a question. The *"Why?" information* included in the expert system allows it to give you the answers. It's information provided by the expert—the traffic expert in our example. With the domain expertise and the "Why?" information, the expert system is now ready to solve traffic-light problems. So now you need to enter the *problem-facts*, the specifics of your traffic-light situation. Problem facts are the symptoms of and assertions about your problem. You'll enter these problem facts as answers to the expert system's questions during your consultation.

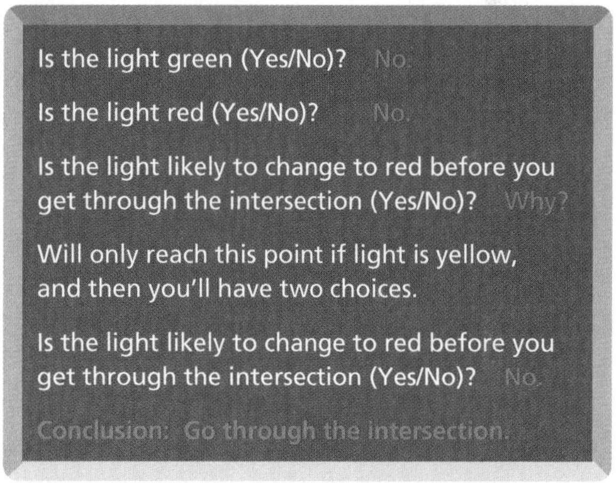

Is the light green (Yes/No)?   No.

Is the light red (Yes/No)?   No.

Is the light likely to change to red before you get through the intersection (Yes/No)?   Why?

Will only reach this point if light is yellow, and then you'll have two choices.

Is the light likely to change to red before you get through the intersection (Yes/No)?   No.

Conclusion: Go through the intersection.

Figure 6.9
Traffic-Light Expert System Rules

Rule	Symptom or Fact	Yes	No	Explanation
1	Is the light green?	Go through the intersection.	Go to Rule 2.	Should be safe if light is green. If not, need more information.
2	Is the light red?	Go to Rule 4.	Go to Rule 3.	Should stop, may not be able to.
3	Is the light likely to change to red before you get through the intersection?	Go to Rule 4.	Go through the intersection.	Will only reach this point if light is yellow, then you'll have two choices.
4	Can you stop before entering the intersection?	Stop.	Go to Rule 5.	Should stop, but there may be a problem if you can't.
5	Is traffic approaching from either side?	Prepare to crash.	Go through the intersection.	Unless the intersection is clear of traffic, you're likely to crash.

PEOPLE Three separate roles must be filled in the development and use of an expert system. The first is that of the domain expert, who knows how to solve the problem. The **domain expert** provides the **domain expertise** in the form of problem-solving strategies. In our traffic-light expert system, the domain expert could be an official from the department of motor vehicles. This official, turned domain expert, would also be able to indicate where to gather further domain expertise, and might direct you to the local police station or give you a booklet with the rules of the road. Eventually, the combination of these sources will produce the five steps that you saw in Figure 6.9.

The domain expert usually works with an IT specialist, a **knowledge engineer**, who formulates the domain expertise into an expert system. In this case, the knowledge engineer might consider it best to represent the five steps in the form of rules, making a **rule-based expert system**. The knowledge engineer will see to it that the rules are in the correct order and that the system works properly.

The knowledge worker or user—that's you—will then apply the expert system to the problem of what to do when approaching a traffic light. When you face the traffic-light problem, you would run a *consultation* (see Figure 6.9) and provide the expert system with the problem facts. You would answer the questions as they appear on the screen, with the expert system applying the appropriate rules and asking you more questions. This process continues until the expert system presents you with a conclusion (telling you what to do) or indicates that it can't reach a conclusion (telling you that it doesn't know what you should do).

IT COMPONENTS When the knowledge engineer has converted the domain expertise into rules, the **knowledge base** stores the rules of the expert system (see Figure 6.10). All the rules must be in place before a consultation, because the expert system won't be able to offer a conclusion in a situation for which it has no rules. For example, if the traffic light is broken and has been replaced by a four-way stop sign, the expert system, as it stands, would not be able to reach a conclusion. The knowledge engineer could, of course, go back to the domain expert and enter rules about four-way stops. The knowledge engineer uses the **knowledge acquisition** component of the expert system to enter the traffic-light rules. The domain expertise for the rules can come from many sources, including human experts, books, organizational databases, data warehouses, internal reports, diagrams, and so on.

The **inference engine** is the part of the expert system that takes your problem facts and searches the knowledge base for rules that fit. This process is called *inferencing*. The inference engine organizes and controls the rules—it "reasons" through your problem to reach a conclusion. It delivers its conclusion or recommendation on the basis of (1) the problem facts of your specific traffic light situation and (2) the rules that came from the

Figure 6.10
Developing and Using an Expert System

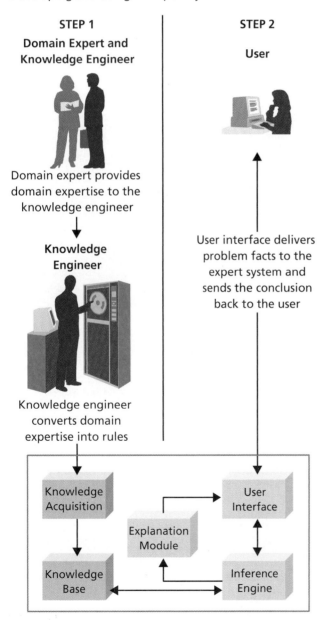

TRAFFIC LIGHTS REVISITED

Create a table similar to the one in Figure 6.9 to extend the traffic-light expert system. Include the following situations in the table:

1. There is a wreck in the middle of the intersection.
2. You are turning left at the intersection.

3. You are turning right at the intersection.
4. A pedestrian is crossing in front of you.
5. A dog has wandered into the intersection.
6. A ball belonging to children playing near the intersection has rolled into the street.
7. The car in front of you has stalled.

domain expert about traffic-light procedures in general. The **user interface** is the part of the expert system that you use to run a consultation. Through the user interface, the expert system asks you questions, and you enter problem facts by answering the questions. In the traffic-light expert system, you would enter "yes" or "no." These answers are used by the inference engine to solve the problem.

The domain expert supplies the "Why?" information, which is entered by the knowledge engineer into the **explanation module**, where it is stored. During a consultation, you—as the knowledge worker or user—can ask why a question was posed and how the expert system reached its conclusion. If you're using the expert system as a training tool, then you'll be very interested in how it solved the problem.

In Figure 6.10 you can clearly see the distinction between the development and use of an expert system. The domain expert and the knowledge engineer develop the expert system, then the knowledge worker can apply the expert system to a particular set of circumstances.

WHAT EXPERT SYSTEMS CAN AND CAN'T DO

An expert system uses IT to capture and apply human expertise. For problems with clear rules and procedures, expert systems work very well and can provide your company with great advantages. An expert system can:

- Handle massive amounts of information
- Reduce errors
- Aggregate information from various sources
- Improve customer service
- Provide consistency in decision making
- Provide new information
- Decrease personnel time spent on tasks
- Reduce cost

You can, however, run into trouble in building and using an expert system:

1. Transferring domain expertise to the expert system is sometimes difficult, because domain experts cannot always explain how they know what they know. Often, experts are not aware of their complete reasoning processes. Experience has given them a feel for the problem, and they "just know."
2. Even if the domain expert can explain the whole reasoning process, automating that process may be impossible. The process may be too complex, requiring an excessive number of rules, or it may be too vague or imprecise. In using an

expert system, keep in mind that it can solve only the problems for which it was designed. It cannot deal with inconsistency or a newly encountered problem situation. An expert system can't learn from previous experience and can't apply previously acquired expertise to new problems the way humans can.

3. An expert system has no common sense or judgment. One of the early expert systems built into an F-16 fighter plane allowed the pilot to retract the landing gear while the plane was still on the ground and to jettison bombs while the plane was flying upside down, both highly dangerous actions.

Neural Networks

Suppose you see a breed of dog you've never encountered before. Would you know it's a dog? For that matter, would you know it's an animal? Probably so—for all of the above. You would know, because you've learned by example. You've seen lots of living things, have learned to classify them, and so can recognize a dog when you see one. A neural network simulates this human ability to classify things without taking prescribed steps leading to the solution. A **neural network** (often called an **artificial neural network** or **ANN**) is an artificial intelligence system that is capable of finding and differentiating patterns. Your brain has learned to consider many factors in combination to recognize and differentiate objects. And this is also the case with a neural network. A neural network can learn by example and can adapt to new concepts and knowledge. Neural networks are widely used for visual pattern and speech recognition systems. If you've used a PDA that deciphered your handwriting, it was probably a neural network that analyzed the characters you wrote.[26]

Neural networks are useful to a variety of other situations too. For example, bomb detection systems in airports use neural networks that sense trace elements in the air indicating the presence of explosives. Some police departments use neural networks to identify corruption within their ranks.[27] In medicine, neural networks check 50 million electrocardiograms per year, check for drug interactions, and detect anomalies in tissue samples that may signify the onset of cancer and other diseases. Neural networks can detect heart attacks and even differentiate between the subtly different symptoms of heart attacks in men and women.[28,29,30] In business, neural networks are very popular for securities trading, fraud detection, real estate appraisal, evaluating loan applications, and target marketing, to mention a few. Neural networks are even used to control machinery, adjust temperature settings, and identify malfunctioning machinery.

Neural networks are most useful for identification, classification, and prediction when a vast amount of information is available. By examining hundreds, or even thousands of examples, a neural network detects important relationships and patterns in the information. For example, if you provide a neural network with the details of numerous credit card transactions and tell it which ones are fraudulent, eventually it will learn to identify suspicious transaction patterns.

Here are some examples of the uses of neural networks:

- Many banks and financial institutions use neural networks. For example, Citibank uses neural networks to find opportunities in financial markets.[31] By carefully examining historical stock market data with neural network software, Citibank financial managers learn of interesting coincidences or small anomalies (called market inefficiencies). For example, it could be that whenever IBM stock goes up, so does Unisys stock. Or it might be that the Canadian dollar is selling for 1 cent less in Japan than it is in Canada. These snippets of information can make a big difference to Citibank's bottom line in a very competitive financial market.

CAUTION! THE NEURAL NETWORK IS WATCHING YOU

Neural networks are used in all sorts of situations where a pattern of conditions or behaviour signals an event, either past or future. For example, there's a neural network that predicts what play a football team is likely to run under a particular set of circumstances.

Mostly, when financial institutions use neural networks for fraud detection, they're looking for certain signals, things that are outside the usual usage pattern of the customer. Sometimes, it's the characteristics of the use of the financial instrument itself that trip the alarm.

For example, many credit card companies send their customers convenience cheques. They encourage card holders to transfer balances from other accounts, and allow you to pay for purchases when the merchant won't accept that credit card. However, convenience cheques are ripe for theft. First, they're easier to steal or counterfeit than credit cards. Second, they're often available in trash cans (tear or shred your convenience cheques if you don't want to use them!). Third, they're easy to order under a false name. Fourth, it's easy for thieves to open a chequing account with a convenience cheque. Fifth, people heading into bankruptcy sometimes use convenience cheques to cover their financial problems.

Neural networks use certain flags to spot possible convenience cheque fraud. For example, if the cheque is written for an unusually large sum, or if multiple cheques are written out of sequence, there might be a problem. If a card holder hasn't used convenience cheques before, or if a particular cheque doesn't fit the card holder's spending patterns, there might be a problem. Another red flag is a higher-than-normal use of automated inquiries to cheque balances followed by several convenience cheques being submitted for payment.[32,33]

- Police use neural network software to fight crime. With crime reports as input, the system detects and maps local crime patterns. Police say that with this system they can better predict crime trends, improve patrol assignments, and develop better crime prevention programs.[34]
- A mail order company has six million people on its customer list. To determine which customers were and were not likely to order from its catalogue, it recently switched to neural network software. The company finds that the new software is more effective and expects to generate millions of dollars by fine-tuning its mailing lists.[35]
- Fraud detection is one of the areas in which neural networks are used the most. Visa, MasterCard, and many other credit card companies use a neural network to spot peculiarities in individual accounts. MasterCard estimates neural networks save them over $50 million annually.[36]
- Many insurance companies along with compensation funds and other carriers use neural network software to identify fraud. The system searches for patterns in billing charges, laboratory tests, and frequency of office visits. A claim for which the diagnosis was a sprained ankle and which included an electrocardiogram would be flagged for the account manager.[37]
- FleetBoston Financial Corp. uses a neural network to watch transactions with customers. The neural network can detect patterns that may indicate a customer's growing dissatisfaction with the company. The neural network looks for signs like a decrease in the number of transactions or in the account balance of one of Fleet's high-value customers.[38]

All of the above situations have pattern recognition in common. They all require identification and/or classification, which may then be used to predict a finding or

HOW WOULD YOU CLASSIFY PEOPLE?

Some people have suggested that neural networks could be applied to people to indicate how likely they are to develop disease or even become criminals. The idea is to input a child's personal characteristics, demographics, and genealogy into a neural network and it will classify that youngster as being at risk for a disease or aberrant behaviour.

Choose either susceptibility to disease or to criminal behaviour, discuss it with your group, and make the following lists, explaining why you chose each:

1. What personal characteristics would be useful?
2. What demographics factors would strongly influence a person's future?
3. What inherited characteristics can predict a child's future?

Would such classification on a large scale be legal? Would it be ethical? Would it be effective? Why or why not?

---

outcome. Neural networks are often called predictive systems since they can see patterns in huge volumes of information.

TYPES OF NEURAL NETWORKS

There are two basic types of neural networks; the one you use depends on the problem you're facing. The difference between them is in how the "learning" is done.

The **self-organizing neural network** finds patterns and relationships in vast amounts of data by itself. If you have a lot of experimental data, and you're looking for commonalties, you'd use this type. Self-organizing neural networks often form part of data mining tools for data warehouses (see Chapter 4 for more information on data warehouses and data mining).

A **back-propagation neural network**, on the other hand, is a neural network trained by someone. You'd "teach" the neural network the same way you would a child. That is, you'd show the neural network multiple examples of a dog, a cat, a donkey, etc. until it could correctly identify the animal by itself.

INSIDE A NEURAL NETWORK

Neural networks are so called because they attempt to mimic the structure and functioning of the human brain. Conceptually, neural networks consist of three layers of virtual nerve cells, or neurons. There's an input layer and an output layer and between them are one or more hidden layers. The input and output layers are connected to the middle layer(s) by connections of various strengths called *weights* (see Figure 6.11). If you were to train a neural network to recognize a "good" stock portfolio, you would input many, many examples of good and bad portfolios, telling the neural network which was which. As the neural network is learning to differentiate between good and bad, the weights change. The flow of information to the output layer also changes. After you have fed the system enough examples, the neural network will be able to recognize and classify portfolios and the weights will stabilize so that future portfolios will consistently be correctly classified.

So, you may be asking, how is a neural network different from an expert system, since both can take input and produce an answer as to which group the input belongs to? An expert system, as we saw, can also classify—it asks questions and, on the basis

Figure 6.11

The Layers of a Neural Network

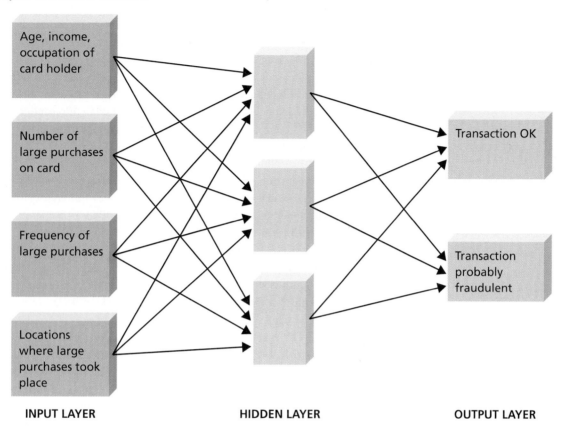

Age, income, occupation of card holder		Transaction OK
Number of large purchases on card		
Frequency of large purchases		Transaction probably fraudulent
Locations where large purchases took place		
INPUT LAYER	**HIDDEN LAYER**	**OUTPUT LAYER**

of the answers, can diagnose or prescribe. The difference is that an expert system does not adjust by itself and is too rigid in its application of the rules. For example, if a credit card fraud detection expert system had a rule that said to flag a purchase over a certain amount on certain types of account, the expert system would flag a transaction that was even one penny over. A neural network, on the other hand, would learn the spending behaviour of card holders and would be better able to evaluate whether deviations were large enough to be queried or not. A neural network can even adjust to situations not explicitly used in training. For example, if when the neural network was learning, mortgage rates were between 6 percent and 10 percent, the system could interpolate if the rate dropped to 5 percent.

Neural networks have many advantages:

- They can learn and adjust to new circumstances on their own.
- They lend themselves to massive parallel processing.
- They can function without complete or well-structured information.
- They can cope with huge volumes of information with many dependent variables.
- They can analyze nonlinear relationships in information and have been called fancy regression analysis systems.

The biggest problem with neural networks to date has been the fact that the hidden layers are "hidden." That is, you can't see how the neural network is learning and how the neurons are interacting. Newer neural networks no longer hide the middle layers. With these systems you can manually adjust the weights or connections, giving you more flexibility and control.

Genetic Algorithms

Have you ever wondered how chefs around the world create great recipes? For example, how did the Chinese discover that cashew nuts and chicken taste good when combined? How did Mexican chefs arrive at combining tomatoes, onions, cilantro, and other spices to create pica de gallo? All those great recipes came about through *evolutionary processes*. Someone decided to put together a few ingredients and taste the result. Undoubtedly, many of those combinations resulted in unpalatable concoctions that were quickly discarded. Others were tasty enough to warrant further experimentation of combinations.

Today significant research in AI is devoted to creating software capable of following similar trial-and-error process leading to the evolution of a good result. A **genetic algorithm** is an artificial intelligence system that mimics the evolutionary, survival-of-the-fittest process to generate increasingly better solutions to a problem. In other words, a genetic algorithm is an optimizing system—it finds the combination of inputs that give the best outputs.

Here's an example. Suppose you were trying to decide what to put into your stock portfolio. You have countless stocks to choose from and a limited amount of money to invest. You might decide that you'd like to start with 20 stocks and you want a portfolio growth rate of 7.5 percent.

Probably you'd start by examining historical information on the stocks. You would take some number of stocks and combine them, 20 at a time, to see what happens with each grouping. If you wanted to choose from a pool of 30 stocks, you would have to examine 30,045,015 different combinations. For a 40-stock pool, the number of combinations rises to 137,846,500,000. It would be an impossibly time-consuming, not to mention numbingly tedious, task to look at this many combinations and evaluate your overall return for each one. However, this is just the sort of repetitive number crunching task at which computers excel.

So instead of a pencil, paper, and calculator, you might use a genetic algorithm. You could input the appropriate information on the stocks, like the number of years the company has been in business, the performance of the stock over the last five years, price to earnings ratios, and other information.

You would also have to tell the genetic algorithm your exact "success" criteria. For example, you might use a growth rate in the company over the last year of at least 10 percent, a presence in the marketplace going back at least three years, a connection to the computer industry, etc. The genetic algorithm would simply combine and recombine stocks eliminating any combinations that don't fit your criteria and continuing to the next iteration with the acceptable combinations—those that give an aggregate growth rate of at least 7.5 percent while aiming for as high a growth rate as possible.

Genetic algorithms use three concepts of evolution:

- **Selection** or survival of the fittest. The key to selection is to give preference to better outcomes.
- **Crossover** or combining portions of good outcomes in the hope of creating an even better outcome.
- **Mutation** or randomly trying combinations and evaluating the success (or failure) of the outcome.

Genetic algorithms are best suited to decision-making environments in which thousands, or perhaps millions, of solutions are possible. Genetic algorithms can find

THE EVOLUTION OF FARMING EQUIPMENT

There are an almost infinite number of possible combinations possible for features on a car. This is true for many products, as Deere, a company that makes agricultural equipment, knows all too well. Deere's customers demand all sorts of variations in planters. These different combinations of features make creating a good manufacturing schedule by hand all but impossible. But Deere found that genetic algorithm software not only makes the task manageable, but can compute the best schedule that offers the easiest and fastest way to utilize the production line to optimize production.

The initial stages of the huge project were very expensive, but the software gave the company a way to meet customer demand quickly and to gain competitive advantage. It worked so well for Deere that the company's supplier, Auburn Consolidated Industries, is also using it and Deere is reaping the benefits of improved supply chain management.

As always, technology alone is not the answer. To benefit significantly from technology, the production and business processes have to be efficient and effective.[39]

and evaluate solutions intelligently and can get through many more possibilities more thoroughly and faster than a human can. As you might imagine, businesses face decision-making environments for all sorts of problems like engineering design, computer graphics, strategies for game playing—anything, in fact, that requires optimization techniques. Here are some other examples:

- Genetic algorithms are used by business executives to help them decide which combination of projects a firm should invest in, taking complicated tax considerations into account.
- They're used by investment companies to help in trading choices and decisions.
- In any garment that you buy, the fabric alone accounts for between 35 percent and 40 percent of the selling price. So, when cutting out the fabric to make the garment, it's important that there be as little waste as possible. Genetic algorithms are used to solve this problem of laying out the pieces of the garment and cutting fabric in a way that leaves as little waste as possible.[40]
- US West uses a genetic algorithm to determine the optimal configuration of fibre optic cable in a network that may include as many as 100,000 connection points. By using selection, crossover, and mutation, the genetic algorithm can generate and evaluate millions of cable configurations and select the one that uses the least amount of cable. At US West, this process used to take an experienced design engineer almost two months. US West's genetic algorithm can solve the problem in two days and saves the company $1 million to $10 million each time it's used.[41]

Genetic algorithms are good for these types of problems because they use selection, crossover, and mutation as methods of exploring countless solutions and the respective worth of each.

You have to tell the genetic algorithm what constitutes a "good" solution. That could be low cost, high return, etc., since many solutions are useless or absurd. If you created a genetic algorithm to make bread, for example, it might try to boil flour to create moistness. That obviously won't work, so the genetic algorithm would simply throw away that solution and try something else. Other solutions would eventually be good, and some of them would even be wonderful.

BE A GENETIC ALGORITHM AND PUT NAILS IN BOXES

This project involves packaging nails so that you make the most profit possible (this is a profit-maximizing problem). Say you have five types of nails and can make as many as you need of each. These are: 4", 3.5", 3", 2.5", 2", and 1.5". The cost of making each type of nail depends on how big it is. Those cost and selling prices are listed in the table below along with the weights. The nails will be sold in boxes of up to 30 nails. There must be no more than 10, but no less than 5, of each of three types of nails in each box. The nails in each box should weigh no more than 20 ounces. You're looking for the combination with the highest profit using trial and error.

A spreadsheet would be helpful in completing this project. You'll most likely find that you identify some promising paths to follow right away and will concentrate on those to reach the best one.

Nail	Weight	Cost	Selling Price
4"	1 oz	4 cents	8 cents
3.5"	0.85 oz	3.5 cents	6 cents
3"	0.7 oz	3 cents	5 cents
2.5"	0.5 oz	2.5 cents	4 cents
2"	0.25 oz	2 cents	3 cents
1.5"	0.1 oz	1.5 cents	2 cents

Intelligent Agents

Do you have a favourite restaurant? Is there someone there who knows you and remembers that you like Italian dressing, but not croutons, on your salad, and ice cream and a slice of cheddar cheese on your apple pie? Does this person familiar with your tastes put a glass of diet cola on your favourite table when you come in the door? If so, he or she has the qualities that artificial intelligence scientists are working on incorporating into intelligent agents. An **intelligent agent** is software that assists you, or acts on your behalf, in performing repetitive computer-related tasks. Future intelligent agents will most likely be autonomous, acting independently, and will learn and adapt to changing circumstances.

You may not realize it, but you're probably already familiar with a primitive type of intelligent agent—the shifty-eyed paper clip that pops itself up when you're using Word. For example, if your document looks as if it is going to be a business letter—that is, you type in a date, name, and address—the animated paper clip will offer helpful suggestions on how to proceed. Another example of a primitive intelligent agent is the software on Amazon.ca's Web site that suggests books to you on the basis of your previous purchases and those of people who bought the books you did.

You can find hundreds of intelligent agents, or *bots*, for a wide variety of tasks. The BotSpot and SmartBots Web sites at www.botspot.com and www.smartbots.com are good places to look for the different types of agents available.

Essentially there are four types of intelligent agents:

- Buyer agents or shopping bots
- User or personal agents
- Monitoring-and-surveillance agents
- Data mining agents

BUYER AGENTS

Buyer agents travel around a network (very likely the Internet) finding information and bringing it back to you. Buyer agents are also called shopping bots. These agents search the Internet for goods and services that you need and bring you back the information.

A **buyer agent** or **shopping bot** is an intelligent agent on a Web site that helps you, the customer, find products and services you want. Shopping bots work very efficiently for commodity products such as CDs, books, electronic components, and other one-size-fits-all products.

Shopping bots make money by selling advertising space, special promotions in cooperation with merchants, or click-through fees, which are payments to the site that provided the link to the merchant site. Some shopping bots give preference to certain sites for a financial consideration. The people who run shopping bot sites have two competing objectives. They want to present as many listings as possible to the consumer in the most useful way, but they also want to make money doing it.[42]

The popular Yahoo! Shopping Web site (ca.shopping.yahoo.com) is a general shopping bot that spans a wide range of categories including apparel, computers, flowers and gifts, music, health and beauty, and sports (see Figure 6.12).

You may have encountered a shopping bot without having specifically requested its services. For example, Amazon.com will offer you a list of books that you might like to buy on the basis of what you're buying now and what you have bought in the past. The Amazon site uses a shopping bot to provide this service. As you saw in Chapter 2, Amazon's agent uses **collaborative filtering**, which consists of matching each customer with a group of users who have similar tastes and presenting choices common in that group.

Figure 6.12

Yahoo! Shopping Bot Site

You can tell the shopping bot what you're looking for and it will find lots of sources for you.

Collaborative filtering is only one of many techniques that predict your preferences. Here are three more currently being used or considered for use at online shopping sites:

- **Profile filtering** requires that you choose terms or enter keywords. This provides a more personal picture of you and your preferences.
- **Psychographic filtering** anticipates your preferences on the basis of the answers you give to a questionnaire. This method is also more personal than collaborative filtering.
- **Adaptive filtering** asks you to rate products or situations and also monitors your actions over time to find out what you like and dislike.[43]

Collaborative filtering, although it can be quite effective, has two big disadvantages. First, since this method bases your future choices on past purchases of the group to which it deems you to belong, it usually won't offer new or obscure products that might be just what you want. Second, the Web site needs vast amounts of information to be able to use collaborative filtering in the first place. This puts the method out of reach for smaller businesses.

Given these drawbacks, shopping bot designers are experimenting with incorporating the other three methods into shopping agents. Profile filtering, psychographic filtering, and adaptive filtering tend to discover more personal traits of individuals, and therefore if applied well can better anticipate what you'd like to buy.

USER AGENTS

User agents (sometimes called **personal agents**) are intelligent agents that take action on your behalf. In this category belong those intelligent agents that already perform, or will shortly perform, the following tasks:

- Check your e-mail, sort it according to priority (your priority), and alert you when good stuff comes through—like college acceptance letters.
- Play computer games as your opponent or patrol game areas for you.
- Assemble customized news reports for you. There are several versions of these. A CNN Custom News bot will gather news from CNN on the topics you want to read about—and only those.
- Find information for you on the subject of your choice.
- Fill out forms on the Web automatically for you. They even store your information for future reference.
- Scan Web pages looking for and highlighting the text that constitutes the "important" part of the information there.
- "Discuss" topics with you from your deepest fears to sports.

One expanding application of intelligent agent technology is in automating business functions. For example, Mission Hockey, a company that manufacturers and distributes in-line and ice hockey skates and other gear, uses software from Sweden called Movex that has a user agent component. Movex will search a company intranet or extranet to negotiate and make deals with suppliers and distributors. In this case, the intelligent agent is incorporated into an enterprise resource planning system. Enterprise resource planning (or ERP) is a very important concept in today's business world. The term refers to a method of getting and keeping an overview of every part of the business (a bird's-eye view, so to speak), so that production, development, selling, and servicing of goods and services will all be coordinated to contribute to the company's goals and objectives. For more about the concept of ERP, see Chapter 5.

In the future, user agents for personal use will be available for both your wired and your wireless computer devices. Sprint has recently announced an e-assistant that will carry out verbal requests.[44] In the future we'll see personal agents that:

- Interact with the personal agents of colleagues to set up a meeting time
- Incorporate shopping bots and can take you preferences for features on a new car (or anything else) along with a price range and then haggle with car dealers (or their personal agents) to find you the best deal

MONITORING-AND-SURVEILLANCE AGENTS

Monitoring-and-surveillance agents (also called **predictive agents**) are intelligent agents that observe and report on equipment. For example, NASA's Jet Propulsion Laboratory has an agent that monitors inventory, planning, and scheduling equipment ordering to keep costs down.[45] Other monitoring agents work on the manufacturing shop floor, finding equipment problems and locating other machinery that will do the same job.

Monitoring-and-surveillance agents are often used to monitor complex computer networks. Allstate Insurance has a network with thousands of computers. The company uses a network monitoring agent from Computer Associates International called Neugent that watches its huge networks 24 hours a day. Every five seconds, the agent measures 1200 data points and can predict a system crash 45 minutes before it happens. Neugent combines intelligent agent technology with neural network technology to look for patterns of activity or problems. The neural network part can learn what conditions predict a downturn in network efficiency or a slowing of network traffic. Neugent also watches for electronic attacks and can detect them early so that they can be stopped.

Another type of monitoring-and-surveillance agent works on computer networks keeping track of the configuration of each computer connected to the network. It tracks and updates the central configuration database when anything on any computer changes, such as the number or type of disk drives. An important task in managing networks lies in prioritizing traffic and shaping bandwidth. That means sending enough network capacity or bandwidth to the most important tasks over those that are secondary. At a university, for example, processing end-of-semester grades might take precedence over Net surfing.

DATA MINING IN THE BODY SHOP

Have you ever taken a catalogue out of your mailbox and thrown it straight into trash—perhaps even before you brought it into your home? If you're like most people, you probably have. The Body Shop International, like most businesses, knows that. This U.K.-based company would much prefer to send their catalogues only to those who will place orders for products, and so it is using predictive analysis, which is one type of data mining. Data mining involves using technology to find trends and patterns in a vast quantity of information. Predictive analysis consists of forecasting and propensity analysis. Forecasting finds trends and then predicts the future on the basis of those trends. Propensity analysis uses statistical methods such as regression analysis and clustering in combination with neural networks to figure the likelihood that a particular consumer will respond to an offer or buy a product or service. Propensity analysis is also used to predict what customers are most likely to default on a loan or payment plan.

Using data mining, the Body Shop was able to cut in half the number of catalogues it sent out in 2001 after identifying a new 120,000 customers from its Web, store, and customer database. And, not only that, but revenue per catalogue increased 20 percent.

A few years ago, if you wanted to conduct a complex predictive analysis with lots of variables, you'd have to have access to a supercomputer. Today, your desktop computer can do the job.[46]

Some further types of monitoring-and-surveillance agents include:

- Agents that watch your competition and bring back price changes and special offer information
- Agents that monitor Internet sites, discussion groups, mailing lists, and so on, for stock manipulation, insider training, and rumours that might affect stock prices
- Agents that monitor sites for updated information on the topic of your choice
- Agents that watch particular products and bring back price or term changes
- Agents that monitor auction sites for products or prices that you want

DATA MINING AGENTS

A **data mining agent** operates in a data warehouse discovering information. A data warehouse brings together information from lots of different sources. Data mining is the process of looking through the data warehouse to find information that you can use to take action, such as ways to increase sales or keep customers who are considering defecting. Data mining is so called because you have to sift through a lot of information for the gold nuggets that will affect the bottom line. This sort of nugget spotting is similar to what CSIS and the CIA do when they bring together little bits of information from diverse sources and use the overall pattern to spot trouble brewing.

As you learned in Chapter 4, database queries answer questions like "How much did we spend on transportation in March of this year?" Multidimensional analysis is the next step in complexity and answers questions like "How much did we spend on transportation in the southeast during March of the last five years?" Data mining goes deeper and finds answers to questions you may not even have thought to ask like "What else do young men buy on Friday afternoons when they come in to buy diapers?" (The answer, culled by data mining tools, is "beer.")[47]

One of the most common types of data mining is classification, which finds patterns in information and categorizes items into those classes. You may remember that this is just what neural networks do best. So, not surprisingly, neural networks are part

INTELLIGENT AGENTS DO BACKGROUND CHECKS

The Army hires a lot of people who will have access to sensitive and potentially lethal information and hardware and who, therefore, need security clearance. This involves a thorough background check for each soldier, a process which, even with all the resources and experience that the investigators have, can take days or even weeks to complete.

In 2002, the Army started to use intelligent agents to automate the data gathering. The intelligent agent searches through electronic records collecting information. It places all this information in an electronic file and then inspects the contents looking for anything that looks suspicious or might be a precursor to later problems. Such warning signs would be arrests, financial problems, or anything else that could indicate personal weakness exploitable by unauthorized interested parties.

The effects of this electronic investigator have been dramatic. The Army Central Clearance Facility in Fort Meade, MD, can now process a background check in 24 hours, has cleared some of its year-long backlog, and can handle almost one-third more checks per year.[48]

of many data mining tools. And data mining agents are another integral part, since data mining agents search for information in a data warehouse.

A data mining agent may detect a major shift in a trend or a key indicator. It can also detect the presence of new information and alert you. Volkswagen uses an intelligent agent system that acts as an early-warning system about market conditions. If conditions become such that the assumptions underlying the company's strategy are no longer true, the intelligent agent alerts managers.[49] For example, the intelligent agent might see a problem in some part of the country that is or will shortly cause payments to slow down. Having that information early lets managers formulate a plan to protect themselves.

Summary: Student Learning Outcomes Revisited

1. **Define decision support system, list its components, and understand its applications.** A *decision support system (DSS)* is a highly flexible and interactive IT system designed to support decision making when the problem is not structured. It's primarily an analysis tool to support your decision making and you making the final decision. A DSS has three components: data management, model management, and user interface management.

2. **Describe collaboration systems along with their features and uses.** *Collaboration software* is software that allows people to work together. A basic form of collaboration software is e-mail; other forms are instant messaging, calendar management, group scheduling, conferencing of various kinds, and workflow, task, and document management. You would use collaboration software whenever members of a team are separated, whether on different floors of a building or on opposite sides of the globe.

3. **Describe geographic information systems and how they differ from other decision support tools.** A *geographic information system (GIS)* is for the analysis of data viewed in map form. Information is stored in layers which can be overlaid as appropriate. It's the layering and presentation that separates a GIS from other decision support tools.

4. **Define artificial intelligence and list the different types used in business.** Artificial intelligence is the science of making machines

imitate human thinking and behaviour. The types used in business include: expert systems, neural networks, genetic algorithms, and intelligent agents.

5. **Describe expert systems and knowledge-based systems, their components, and the types of problems to which they are applicable.** An *expert system* (or *knowledge-based system*) is an artificial intelligence system that applies reasoning capabilities to reach a conclusion. An expert system ask the user questions and, on the basis of those questions, asks other questions until it has enough information to make a decision or a recommendation. Expert systems are good for diagnostic (what's wrong) and prescriptive (what to do) problems. For example, you could use an expert system to diagnose illness or to figure out why a machine is malfunctioning. And you could use one to determine what to do about the problem.

6. **Define neural networks, their uses, and their strengths and weaknesses.** A *neural network* (also called an *artificial neural network* or *ANN*) is an artificial intelligence system capable of finding and differentiating patterns. Neural networks are good for finding commonalties in situations that have many variables. The greatest strength of a neural network is that it can learn and adapt. Its greatest weakness is that it's not

usually clear how the system reached its result and it's hard, therefore, to verify its solutions.

7. **Define genetic algorithms, the concepts on which they are based, and the types of problems they solve.** A *genetic algorithm* is an artificial intelligence system that mimics the evolutionary, survival-of-the-fittest process to generate increasingly better solutions to a problem. Genetic algorithms borrow the principles of selection, crossover, and mutation from the theory of evolution. These systems are best suited to problems where hundreds or thousands of solutions are possible and you need an optimum solution.

8. **Define intelligent agents, list the four types, and identify the types of problems they solve.** An *intelligent agent* is software that assists you, or acts on your behalf, in performing repetitive computer-related tasks. The four types are:
   - *Buyer agents* (or *shopping bots*) search the Web for products and services.
   - *User agents* (or *personal agents*) take action for you, particularly in repetitive tasks like sorting e-mail.
   - *Monitoring-and-surveillance agents* (or *predictive agents*) track conditions, perhaps on a network, and signal changes or troublesome conditions.
   - *Data mining agents* search data warehouses to discover information.

CLOSING CASE STUDY ONE

USING NEURAL NETWORKS TO CATEGORIZE PEOPLE

Would your banker give you an A, a B, or a C? What about your supermarket? You know you're being graded in your classes, but did you know that you're also being graded by businesses?

Special treatment for certain customers is not new. Airline customers who fly first class have always received preferential treatment, even when flights were cancelled or delayed. You won't find them napping on a stone floor with their backpacks as pillows. This makes business sense to the airlines, since these are the customers who are most profitable.

Although companies have always offered preferential treatment to their more profitable customers, the speed and capacity of computers today is making the

segmenting of customers possible to a degree unheard of just a few years ago. Part of the reason for this is neural networks. Using neural network software, businesses now have the ability to look for patterns in their customer information and classify customers into according to how they affect the company's bottom line and thus to gauge whether it's worth the trouble to make them happy.

BANKS

Some banks use software that categorizes people into red, green, and yellow depending on the customer's history and value to the bank. Customers who are "green" might get better credit card rates than customers who are "red" and are judged to add less to the bank's bottom line.

Say you called the bank that issued you your credit card and said that you didn't want to pay the annual fee anymore. The bank could look at your credit card activity and decide whether it's more profitable to the bank to waive your fee rather than risk your not using the credit card anymore.

CREDIT CARD COMPANIES

Visa has saved millions of dollars using neural network software to spot fraud and to determine which of their customers might default or go bankrupt. Neural networks are good at spotting patterns, and if your profile looks like that of people who have defaulted, you'll be tossed into that category.

ROYAL BANK OF CANADA

On a monthly basis, Toronto-based Royal Bank of Canada segments its ten million customers according to credit risk, current and future profitability, demographics (i.e., whether they are young or seniors approaching retirement), channel preference (i.e., call centres, branches, or the Internet), and propensity to purchase other products. The bank's customer segmentation practice has worked so well that it has helped increase the company's response rate to marketing campaigns and sales programs to as high as 30 percent while the banking industry's average remains close to 3 percent.

SUPPLIERS

Neural network classifying software can be applied to finding the best suppliers too. Weyerhaeuser Corporation's door-factory executives have software to rank suppliers and distributors based on price, speed of delivery, and innovation. Using this information Weyerhaeuser doubled its sales and increased its return on net assets from 2 to 24 percent.

MOVIES

Even the movie business is getting in on the act. Twentieth Century Fox slices and dices its information in its databases to determine the most popular movies, actors, and plots in certain theatres, cities, and areas of the country. The aim is to show movies in those areas that will add the most to the bottom line. The result

may be that people in certain areas will not get the chance to see certain movies.

There was a time when certain neighbourhoods or geographic regions were "redlined." That meant that banks and other businesses wouldn't deal with anyone who lived there. Some people think that this sort of market segmentation is a new form of redlining. Do you? The following are some questions for you to answer regarding this practice.[50]

Questions

1. A neural network learns to recognize patterns on the basis of past information. One set of people is judged by the behaviour of another. Is this fair or reliable? How accurate is it for a business to predict the future behaviour of customers on the basis of historic information? Don't people change? Have you ever changed your behaviour in the course of your life?

2. Customers are not likely ever to see the information that companies are using to pigeonhole them. Even the company executives may not know what criteria the neural network uses. How important are the assumptions underlying the software (i.e., the facts that the neural network are given about customers)? Even the IT specialists who design neural networks can't vouch for their accuracy or specify exactly how the neural network reaches its conclusions. Is this safe for businesses? What are the possible business consequences of using neural networks without assurances of their reliability?

3. Businesses can use segmenting to suggest products and services to you, or if you request it, to prevent your getting junk mail you don't want. Is that good? Would receiving wanted information or avoiding junk mail be worth the price of being categorized?

4. Say you run a business that supplies medical equipment—wheelchairs, hospital beds, heating packs (not prescription drugs). You're trying to determine which customers you should give preferential treatment to. What assumptions or variables would you use (e.g., age, income, and so on) to segment your customer population?

5. Do you think that this segmentation practice is fair? First consider the business stockholders, then consider the customers. Does it matter

whether it's fair or not? Why or why not? Should there be laws against it, or laws controlling it, or none at all? Explain and justify your answer.

6. Does the practice make business sense? If you owned stock in a company, how would you feel about this practice? Do you think you should get better treatment if you're a better customer? Do you think people who are not such good customers should get the same deal that you

get? Would it make any difference whether the company collected the information and did the neural network analysis itself, or bought the information or the whole package from a third party?

7. Is this the same as redlining, or is it OK because it looks at behaviour and classifies people rather than assuming characteristics on the basis of membership in a particular group?

CLOSING CASE STUDY TWO

DECISION SUPPORT AND ARTIFICIAL INTELLIGENCE IN HEALTH CARE

Good health care is based largely on good information. Information technology helps with diagnosing illness and treating it. It also aids research in identifying and finding cures for illness. Here are two examples of the use of information technology in health care.

WIRELESS HOME CARE IN NEWFOUNDLAND

In 2001, a pilot project was launched in St. John's, Newfoundland. A revolutionary home care delivery system was developed by AdActus Care Technologies Inc., a Canadian company located in Nova Scotia. The system consists of equipping nurses from the city's Health and Community Services with handheld computers for home visits giving them the ability to capture timely, high-quality data in the course of providing care in the patent's home. Overall, it aims to eliminate the time, effort, and risk of error in documenting visits after the fact.

Highly portable Palm Pilots enable nurses to connect to a packet digital wireless network to receive their daily download which includes appointments for the day, the details of the care to be provided for each patient, patient demographics and current medication, whether the patient has allergies and his/her treatment history. Downloads include "a complete set of protocols for each step of the care prescribed to that patient," explains Keith Sheppard of Collaborative Network Technologies, a St. John's company which helped develop the system. "When they get their

download, it comes with a complete set of protocols for each step of the care prescribed for that patient. ... When a bandage has to be checked, for example, it then steps the nurse through examining and describing the wound. Ticked off with the Palm Pilot at each step, the nurse also notes any vital signs or other patient readings taken," adds Sheppard. The handheld also tallies all the syringes, rubber gloves, and other supplies used during daily visits. When each visit ends, nurses need simply reconnect to the network and quickly upload any information about the visit back to the central database without having to physically travel back to the clinic. "You automatically end up with a complete, time-stamped record of all the activities undertaken with the patient," says Sheppard. With the new system, errors in information collection and analysis have been reduced dramatically. All in all, St. John's Health and Community Services is very pleased with the new system.[51]

TECHNOLOGY ENABLES BETTER HEALTH CARE AT SUNNYBROOK

In 2001, MedcomSoft Inc. announced that a Toronto hospital, the Sunnybrook & Women's College Health Sciences Centre, would test their new electronic patient-record software. By using the new system, a physician can now document his or her encounter with a patient as it happens, share this information with colleagues, and even streamline the entire treatment process from initial testing to diagnosis and billing. The system, called MedWorks, was designed to tap into the Medcin database developed by Medicomp Systems Inc. of Chantilly, VA—an extensive database containing more than 200,000 data elements, including symptoms (e.g., "persistent cough" or "blurred vision"), tests, diagnoses and therapies. Each of the data elements is connected via 68 million interrelationships making the system "intelligent." During a consultation, it prompts the physician to answer several questions thereby improving diagnosis speed and accuracy. According to MedcomSoft's president and CEO Dr. Sami Aita, health care professionals can document a patient encounter in 1.5 minutes rather than the typical 15 minutes it used to take using traditional patient record software. The gain in productivity comes from the system's ability to automatically display a series of pop-up choices which can be quickly checked using a stylus or on a keyboard that a physician can use to drill through and quickly create a record of an encounter. Another advantage is that the database is non-static. It is being thoroughly updated every six months, providing physicians with the latest diagnoses and therapies.

A powerful feature of the system is its ability to do outcomes analysis; information over multiple encounters can be loaded into the data warehouse, helping health care managers select the best medical treatments early on, further reducing costs. Moreover, because the encounter information is collected in data form (as opposed to text), it can be easily manipulated, aggregated, graphed, processed, and analyzed. This is significant, according to Dr. Aita, as it allows administrators and other health care professionals to "mine" the data for a range of purposes, including drug utilization evaluation, epidemiological analyses, best-practices assessment, and of course cost/benefit analyses based on outcomes. "We can verify the outcome of various therapies, so we understand whether we're doing the right thing." Moreover, one of the most appreciated features of the MedWorks system is that physicians can customize it. Rather than searching through all 200,000 pieces of information in the database, templates are made for various specialties, such as orthopedics, surgery, critical care, etc.[52]

Questions

1. The two cases had essentially the same goals—to track symptoms, treatment, and outcomes—that require the collection and maintenance of a huge amount of qualitative and quantitative information. What type of software would you recommend for storing this information so that it can be easily accessed and analyzed? What sort of software query tools would you suggest?

2. Would there be a role for a geographic information system help in either of these examples? How could it be useful? Are there extreme cases, perhaps natural disasters, where a GIS would be useful?

3. How could a neural network help the Newfoundland nurses to generate the information it needs? Would it be advisable to automate the medication process for routine illnesses by connecting the pattern recognition abilities of a neural network to a robot that dispenses pills and letting medical staff deal with more complicated cases? Why? Why not?

4. An expert system is designed to ask questions, and then ask more questions based on the answers to the previous questions. Isn't that what medical specialists do when they're diagnosing your illness? Would you, therefore, like to dispense with visiting a doctor and just buy a medical expert system that you could install on your home computer and consult when you don't feel well? Why? Why not?

5. What sort of collaboration might be helpful for the Newfoundland nurses and the doctors at Sunnybrook? What situations can you envisage where a video or a Web conference would be helpful?

6. For both cases, describe tasks that the various types of artificial intelligence software would lend themselves to and state specifically what tasks each AI system is suited to.

7. Part of quality assurance in any organization is the identification and correction of things that went wrong and ways in which processes can be improved. It's no different in health care—errors are inevitable. However, it's part of the mission of health care workers to keep these errors as small and as infrequent as possible. How could a decision support system help in the implementation of safer procedures? What part could expert systems, neural networks, and intelligent agents play?

Key Terms and Concepts

ad hoc decision, 202
adaptive filtering, 226
artificial intelligence (AI), 211
artificial neural network
    (ANN), 218
back-propagation neural
    network, 220
buyer agent, 225
choice, 201
collaboration software, 206
collaboration system, 206
collaborative filtering, 225
crossover, 222
data mining agent, 228
decision support system (DSS), 202
design, 201
domain expert, 216
domain expertise, 216
expert system, 213

explanation module, 217
genetic algorithm, 222
geographic information system
    (GIS), 209
implementation, 201
inference engine, 216
intelligence, 201
intelligent agent, 224
knowledge acquisition, 216
knowledge base, 216
knowledge-based system, 213
knowledge engineer, 216
model management, 205
monitoring-and-surveillance
    agent, 227
mutation, 222
neural network (artificial neural
    network, ANN), 218

nonrecurring decision
    (ad hoc decision), 202
nonstructured decision, 202
personal agent, 226
predictive agent, 227
profile filtering, 226
psychographic filtering, 226
recurring decision, 202
robot, 212
rule-based expert system, 216
selection, 222
self-organizing neural
    network, 220
semistructured decision, 202
shopping bot, 225
structured decision, 201
user agent, 226
user interface, 205

Short-Answer Questions

1. What are the four types of decisions discussed in this chapter? Give an example of each.

2. What is a DSS? Describe its components.

3. What sort of a system would you use if you wanted to work with your suppliers electronically?

4. What are three of the features that collaborative software might have?

5. What is a geographic information system used for?

6. How is information represented in a geographic information system?

7. What is artificial intelligence? Name the artificial intelligence systems used widely in business.

8. What are the components of an expert system?

9. What three concepts of evolution are used by the genetic algorithm?

10. What are intelligent agents? What tasks can they perform?

11. What do shopping bots do?

12. What do monitoring-and-surveillance agents do?

Assignments and Exercises

1. **COLLABORATIVE WORK.** In a group of two or more students, collaborate on a project to make a list of 100 videos or music CDs. Classify the videos or CDs into groups. For example, if you choose movies, you categories might be adventure, comedy, classic, horror, musicals, etc. All communication about the project must be electronically communicated (but not by phone). You could use e-mail, set up a Web site, use a chat room, or a collaboration e-room, if your university has that facility. Print out a copy of all correspondence on the project and put the correspondence together in a folder in chronological order.

    What this task very different from collaborating face-to-face with your partners? In what ways was it better, in what ways worse? What additional problems or advantages would you expect if the person or people you're working with were in a different hemisphere?

2. **CHOOSE A FINANCING OPTION.** Using a spreadsheet (e.g., Excel), evaluate your options for a $12,000 car. Compare the payments (use the =pmt function in Excel), the total amount of interest, and the total you'll pay for the car under the following four options:

   a. 3 years at 0% interest
   b. 2 years at 1.99% annual percent rate (APR)
   c. 4 years at 5% APR
   d. 6 years at 6% APR

   What other considerations would you take into account, were you to buy a new car? Are there considerations other than the interest rate, and the other parts that can be calculated? What are they? How is a car different from other purchases, like CDs or TV sets or computers?

3. **WHICH SOFTWARE WOULD YOU USE?** Which type or types, of computer-aided decision support software would you use for each of the following situations? Note why you think that those you choose are appropriate. The decision support alternatives are:

   - Decision support system
   - Collaboration software
   - Geographic information system
   - Expert system
   - Genetic algorithm
   - Intelligent agent

Problem	Type of Decision Support
Marketing executives on two continents want to develop a new pricing structure for products.	
A financial expert is trying to find a way to predict when customers are about to take their business elsewhere.	
Filling out a short tax form.	
Determining the fastest route for package delivery to 23 different addresses in a city.	
Deciding where to spend advertising dollars (TV, radio, newspaper, direct mail, e-mail).	
Keeping track of competitors' prices for comparable goods and services.	

4. **FIND SOME NEURAL NETWORKS.** Go to the Internet and find three neural network software packages. Make a short report on the three you find. Be sure to include in your report the following:

   - The applications (finance, manufacturing accounting, fraud detection, etc.)
   - Whether the product is free or, if not, how much it costs (if you can determine this)
   - The operating system required to run the software
   - Any special hardware or software requirements listed

   Do any of those sites explain how the neural network works? Did you have to register to get information?

5. **WHAT SHOULD THE MUSIC STORE OWNER DO?** A music store owner wants to have enough of the hottest CDs in stock so that people who come in to buy a particular CD won't be disappointed—and the store won't lose the profit. CDs that are not sold within a certain length of time go onto the sale table where they may

have to be sold at cost, if they sell at all. She wants to design a decision support system to try and predict how many copies she should purchase and what information will she need.

List some of the considerations that would go into such a system. Here are a couple to start you off:

- The population of the target market
- Sales for particular types of music in similar markets

Discussion Questions

1. Some experts claim that if a business gets 52 percent of its decisions right, it will be successful. Would using a decision support system guarantee better results? Why or why not? What does the quality of any decision depend on? Do you think it matters what type of decisions are included in this 52 percent? For example, would getting the right type of paper clips be as influential a decision as deciding where to locate the business? Can you think of a situation where the type of paper clip matters a great deal?

2. Early systems researchers called expert systems "experts in a box." Today, in most situations, people who consult expert systems use them as assistants in specific tasks and not to totally replace human experts. What sorts of tasks would you feel comfortable about having expert systems accomplish without much human intervention? What sorts of tasks would you not be comfortable having expert systems handle independently? Give examples. The first famous expert system, called MYCIN, was developed to diagnose blood diseases. Would you be comfortable consulting an expert system instead of a live doctor when you're ill? Why or why not? If you knew that expert system "doctors" diagnose illness correctly five times as often as human doctors, would this change your answer? Why or why not?

3. Consider the topic of data warehouses in Chapter 3. In the future, AI systems will be increasingly applied to data warehouse processing. Which AI systems do you think might be helpful? For which tasks, or situations, might they best be applied? Do you think that AI systems will someday play a greater role in the design of databases and data warehouses? Why or why not?

4. Consider the differences and similarities among the four AI techniques discussed in this chapter. Name some problems that might be amenable to more than one type of AI system.

Say you had a Web site and sold baseballs. What types of AI systems could you use to generate information that would be useful to you in deciding what direction to take your company in the future? Say you were pretty successful at selling baseballs. Would you expect to have the amount of information on customers that, say, Wal-Mart has? Why or why not?

5. AI systems are relatively new approaches to solving business problems. What are the difficulties with new IT approaches in general? For each of the systems we discussed, identify some advantages and disadvantages of AI systems over traditional business processes. Say you were selling specialty teas both in traditional retail stores and on the Internet. Would you use the same type of AI systems for each part of your business? In what way would you use them or why would you not? Is there a place for decision support and artificial intelligence techniques in small specialty businesses? In what way would decision support be value adding? Can you think of how a DSS or an AI system would be value-reducing (in terms of Porter's value chain theory)? What do you see as the major differences between running a mammoth concern and a small specialty business?

6. Neural networks recognize and categorize patterns. If someone were to have a neural network that could scan information on all aspects of your life, where would that neural network potentially be able to find information about you? Consider confidential (doctor's office) as well as publicly available (department of motor vehicles) information.

7. What type of AI systems could your school use to help with registration? Intelligent agents find vast amounts of information very quickly. Neural networks can classify patterns instantaneously. What sort of information might your school administration be able to generate using these (or other AI systems) with all of its student information?

8. Would you be comfortable with your institution allowing a third party (like a credit card company) access to student information? Would it make a difference if there were no identifying information included—if only aggregate or summary information were available to the third party? If this third party got student information (names and all), what sort of AI techniques could it use to generate support for decision making? What sort of third-party companies (apart from credit card companies) would like to be able to get student lists from lots of higher education institutions? Identify ten types of businesses that might be interested in such lists. If these third parties were to get personal information on you, would you like there to be restrictions on what they can and can't do with it? If so, what restrictions would you like to see?

Electronic Commerce

Finding Investment Opportunities on the Internet

When you buy stock in a company, you're betting on the success of that firm. Sometimes that bet is a good one, and sometimes it's not. Finding a company that's a good bet involves lots of research. To further complicate matters, some people prefer investing in large, safe companies, whereas others prefer the higher return of a small, more risky firm. So how do you make sense of all the options? Well, now you have access to financial information that professional investors use to evaluate stocks. The Internet brings together information-hungry investors with companies that have been anxiously looking to reach out to investors online. Over 900 companies now offer investment information on the World Wide Web, and the number is increasing rapidly. Remember, though, you must proceed with caution. Do your best to verify the source of any information.

Electronic Commerce Links

You'll find many links on the Web site that supports this textbook (www.mcgraw hill.ca/college/haag) and select "Electronic Commerce Projects").

LEARNING ABOUT INVESTING

Investing can be as simple as finding a company that performs well financially and buying some of their stock. Or, if you want to spread your investment over a number of stocks and you don't want to personally select each stock, you can invest in a mutual fund. Of course there are thousands of mutual funds with all types of investment objectives. So, any way you go, you must pick your investment wisely. To help you get up to speed quickly, you'll find many helpful Web sites on the Internet.

For starters, you might explore Advice for Investors (www.fin-info.com). Click on their "Publications" link. Alternatively, go to eNorthern (www.enorthern.com) and click the menu on Brokerage/Education/Investor Learning Centre.

Find three investment reference sites and explore what information is available, and answer the following questions.

A. Is the site designed for first-time investors or those who are more experienced?

B. Can you search for a specific topic?

C. Are specific stocks or mutual funds reviewed or evaluated?

D. Does the site provide direct links to brokerage or stock quoting sites?

E. Is a forum for submitting questions available? If so, are frequently asked questions (FAQs) posted?

F. Who sponsors the site? Does it seem as if the sponsor is using the site to advertise its own products or services?

G. Can you download reference documents to read later?

RESEARCHING THE COMPANY BEHIND THE STOCK

One excellent way to pick a stock investment is to research the company behind that stock. Focusing on items such as sales revenues and profits to pick a stock is called *fundamental research*. So you might choose to invest in Hughes stock because you've discovered their sales revenues have been climbing steadily for the last three years. Or you might initially consider buying some Disney stock but change your mind when you find that Euro Disney revenues have been below expectations.

Now that you're ready to research a stock investment, connect to four different company sites. You can find your own or go to the Web site that supports this text (www.mcgrawhill.ca/college/haag) where you will find a list of many other company sites. As you connect to the four sites, look up each company's financials and answer the questions that follow. You'll probably want to include at least two companies with which you are familiar and two that are new to you. In addition to reviewing company financials, look around each company site and see to what degree the site is investor-oriented.

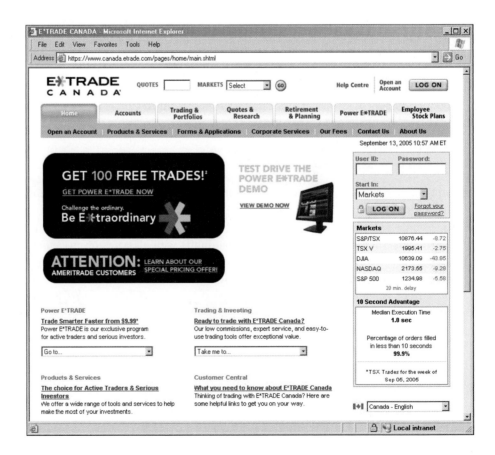

A. Do all the company sites offer financial information?

B. Is the information targeted at investors? How can you tell?

C. Can you download financial information to your computer and use it in a spreadsheet?

D. Can you download the company's annual report? Is it a full-colour version?

E. Does the site provide direct links to e-mail addresses for requesting additional information?

F. Do the companies provide comparisons to others in their industry?

G. Does the site provide stock quotes as well as financials?

H. Can you search the site for financials-related information such as press releases?

I. Was there a charge for retrieving the financial information?

FINDING OTHER SOURCES OF COMPANY FINANCIALS

Searching for a company's financials may be a bit more difficult than you may have first imagined. First you must determine the Internet address for the company either by guessing the address and typing it in or using one of the many search engines available. Both of these methods are fraught with error. For example, if you guessed that "www.amex.com" was the address for American Express you'd be wrong. And even if you did guess a company's address, many companies don't provide their financials on their company-sponsored Web site. You'll find that many company Web sites lack information for investors.

The reason many companies don't provide financials on their Web sites is that they view the primary purpose of their sites as reaching consumers, not investors. So many companies elect to post their financials on a financial provider site or simply let investors view the company's submissions to the Securities and Exchange Commission at the SEC's Web site.

Pick three providers of financial information, access their Web sites, and answer the following questions.

A. Is there a charge for retrieving the information?

B. Do you have a choice about the information's format?

C. Are companies listed alphabetically?

D. Does the site offer more than just annual reports?

E. Are there direct links from the site to the desired company's page?

F. Can you find more companies at the site than by searching for individual company Web pages?

G. How many companies are available on each Web site?

H. Are the represented companies mostly large and established or small and relatively unknown?

MAKING TRADES ONLINE

If you want to invest in securities, you might do what a lot of people do, go to a stockbroker. However, many of the same services offered by stockbrokers are now available on the Internet.

Virtually all of the stockbrokers with offices you can visit have Web sites that support online investing and more. These services include account information, financial planning, and online investing services. Before we go online to look at some of these stockbrokers we should be sure we understand the difference between a full-service brokerage house and a discount brokerage house. As the names imply, the full-service brokerage offers many more services than the discount brokerage. And it's important to understand that the price for many of these services is built into the fees to buy and sell stocks and mutual funds. So you pay for having these services available even if you don't use them at a full-service brokerage.

Let's venture online and see what the various brokerages have to offer us. Find three brokerages on the Web, examine what it takes to conduct an online investment transaction, and answer the following questions:

A. Must you already have an investment account with the brokerage to purchase stocks or mutual funds?

B. Which sites are full-service brokerages and which are discount brokerages? How can you tell?

C. Is online research available? Is it free?

D. Can you retrieve stock price quotes for free?

E. If you already have an account with the brokerage, do they offer special services for these customers? What kinds of services are offered?

F. Is the site aimed at experienced investors or new investors?

G. If you are investing for the first time, would you feel comfortable using online investing? Why or why not?

RETRIEVING STOCK QUOTES

Once you find the right stock to buy, you'll be asking yourself, "How much will this stock cost me?" Stocks and mutual funds are both offered by the share and so you can easily buy as much or as little of the stock or mutual fund as you like. Still, some individual shares are priced in the hundreds or thousands of dollars and that alone might make the purchase undesirable to you.

In addition to pricing individual shares to assess the affordability of an investment, you'll probably want to see how the price has varied over time. Even though most financial advisors will tell you that historical price variations provide no indication of future performance, most everyone uses price history to get a feel for whether the investment is trading at all-time highs or lows. So finding a chart of a stock price online might be helpful when making your purchase.

And even after you've made your purchase, you'll probably want to follow how your investment is doing. The thrill of realizing a "paper profit" is enough to keep many investors checking their investments daily. Of course, realizing a "paper loss" can be equally disappointing. And even if daily tracking isn't for you, you'll certainly want to check on your investments regularly and doing so online can be quick and painless.

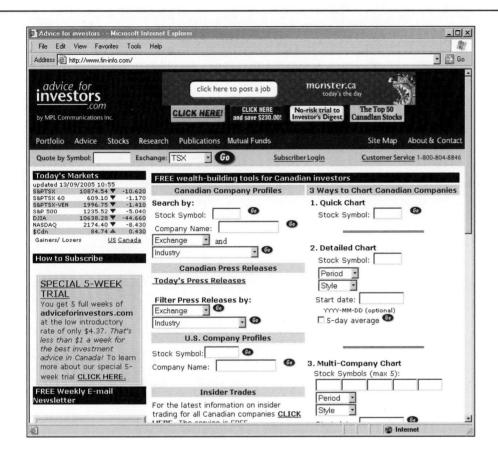

Pick three stock-quoting services, examine what it takes to retrieve a stock or mutual fund quote, and answer the following questions:

A. Are the quotes provided free of charge or for a fee?

B. Does the site require a "ticker" symbol (the abbreviation used by experienced investors) or can you type in a company name?

C. Are the quotes "real-time" or are they "delayed" (15–20 minutes old)?

D. Does the site require registration?

E. Are historical prices available?

F. Are price charts available? Can you customize the chart display?

G. Can you create and save a personal portfolio of stocks?

Go to the Online Learning Centre at www.mcgrawhill.ca/college/haag for quizzes, extra content, a searchable glossary, and more! Click on "Electronic Commerce Projects" for links to hundreds of Web sites.

Go to the text CD-ROM for data files, extra content, and Skills Modules on Microsoft Excel, Microsoft Access, HTML, and e-portfolios.

EXTENDED LEARNING MODULE B

COMPUTER HARDWARE AND SOFTWARE

Student Learning Outcomes

By the end of this Module, students will be able to:

1. Define information technology (IT) and its two basic categories hardware and software.

2. Describe categories of computers by size.

3. Compare the roles of personal productivity, vertical market, and horizontal market software.

4. Describe the roles of operating system and utility software as components of system software.

5. Define the purposes of the six major categories of hardware.

Introduction

In this Module, we cover the basics of computer hardware and software, including terminology, characteristics of various devices, and how everything works together to create a complete and usable computer system. If you've had a previous computing concepts course, this material will be a quick, solid review for you. If this is your first real exposure to hardware and software technologies, you'll definitely learn a great deal from this Module.

Information technology (IT) is any computer-based tool that people use to work with information and support the information and information-processing needs of an organization. So information technology (IT) is the Internet, a personal computer, a cell phone that can access the Web, a personal digital assistant you use for note-taking and appointment scheduling, presentation software you use to create a slideshow, a printer, a joystick or game pad for playing video games . . . the list is almost endless.

All of these technologies help you perform specific information processing tasks. For example, a printer allows you to create a paper version of a document, the Internet connects you to people all over the world, a floppy disk allows you to store information for use a later time, and word processing software helps you create letters, memos, and term papers.

So do you need all of these various technologies? Yes and no. As you'll read throughout this Module, there are categories of both hardware and software. More than likely, you'll need some sort of technology within each category. But you certainly won't need every single piece of available technology.

A Quick Tour of Technology

There are two basic categories of technology. **Hardware** is the physical devices that make up a computer (often referred to as a *computer system*). **Software** is the set of instructions that your hardware executes to carry out a specific task for you. If you create a graph, you would use various hardware devices such as a keyboard to enter information and a monitor to see the graph, and you would use software such Microsoft Excel, the most popular spreadsheet software.

All hardware falls into one of six categories—here's a quick summary (see Figure B.1):

- An *input device* is a tool you use to capture information and commands.
- An *output device* is a tool you use to see, hear, or otherwise receive the results of your information processing requests.
- A **storage device** is a tool you use to store information for use at a later time.
- The *central processing unit (CPU)* is the actual hardware that interprets and executes the software instructions and coordinates how all the other hardware devices work together. *RAM*, or *random access memory*, is temporary storage that holds the information you're working with, the application software you're using, and the operating system software you're using.
- A **telecommunications device** is a tool you use to send information to and receive it from another person or location.
- *Connecting devices* include such things as parallel ports into which you would connect a printer and connector cords to connect your printer to the parallel port.

There are two main types of software—application and system. **Application software** is the software that enables you to solve specific problems or perform specific

Figure B.1
Six Categories of Computer Hardware

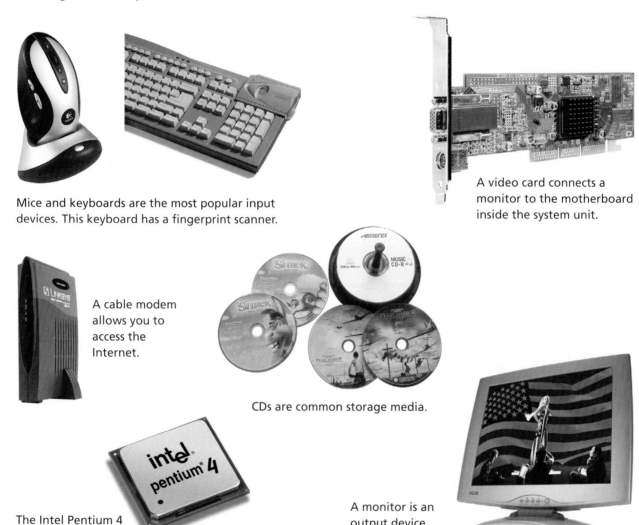

Mice and keyboards are the most popular input devices. This keyboard has a fingerprint scanner.

A video card connects a monitor to the motherboard inside the system unit.

A cable modem allows you to access the Internet.

CDs are common storage media.

The Intel Pentium 4 is a CPU.

A monitor is an output device.

tasks (see Figure B.2). Microsoft PowerPoint, for example, can help you create slides for a presentation, so it's application software. From an organizational perspective, payroll software, collaborative software such as videoconferencing (within groupware), and inventory management software are all examples of application software.

System software handles tasks specific to technology management and coordinates the interaction of all technology devices. System software includes both operating system software and utility software. **Operating system software** is system software that controls your application software and manages how your hardware devices work together. Popular personal operating system software includes Microsoft Windows XP, Microsoft Windows 2000 Me, Mac OS (for Apple computers), and Linux (an open source operating system). There are also operating systems for networks (Microsoft Windows NT is an example), operating systems for personal digital assistants (Windows CE is an example), and operating systems for just about every other type of technology configuration.

Utility software is software that provides additional functionality to your operating system. Utility software includes antivirus software, screensavers, disk optimization software, uninstaller software (for properly removing unwanted software), and a host

Figure B.2

Print Shop and Excel Are Application Software Tools

Pareto chart of the Excel information. A Pareto chart graphically summarizes and displays the relative importance of numeric values.

With Excel you can manipulate numeric and label information. You can also create various types of charts and graphs with the numerical values.

of others. Just because utility software provides "additional" functionality doesn't mean that this type of software is optional. For example, antivirus software protects you from deadly computer viruses that can be very bad for your computer. You definitely need antivirus software.

So ends of our quick tour of technology. In the remainder of this Module we'll explore categories of computers by size, software in more detail, hardware in more detail, and finally how all technology components work together to perform a specific task for you.

Categories of Computers by Size

Computers come in different shapes, sizes, and colours. Some are small enough that you can carry them around with you, while others are the size of a telephone booth. Size in some way equates to power and speed, and thus price.

PERSONAL DIGITAL ASSISTANTS (PDAS)

A **personal digital assistant (PDA)** is a small, handheld computer that helps you surf the Web and perform simple tasks such as note-taking, calendaring, appointment

Figure B.3
PDAs, Desktops, Tablet PCs, and Notebooks

Notebooks are fully functional portable personal computers.

Convertible tablet PCs have screens that swivel and lie flat on top of the system unit.

Some desktops are built especially for gaming.

PDAs are small handheld computers.

scheduling, and maintaining an address book (see Figure B.3). The PDA screen is touch-sensitive, allowing you to directly write on the screen with the screen capturing what you're writing. PDAs today cost from $200 to $500.

A **tablet PC** is a pen-based computer that provides the screen capabilities of a PDA with the functional capabilities of a notebook or desktop computer. Like PDAs, tablet PCs allow you to handwrite notes on the screen with a digital pen or stylus and touch the screen to perform functions such as clicking on a link to visit a Web site. They come in two forms—convertible and slate.

Convertible tablet PCs look like notebook computers, with a screen that you lift into position and a full keyboard and touchpad underneath. You can swivel the screen and lay it flat on the keyboard, converting it into a tablet. *Slate tablet PCs* have no integrated physical keyboard, so that the tablet is the entire computer, but if you also buy a docking station you can connect a keyboard and mouse.

NOTEBOOK COMPUTERS

A **notebook computer** is a fully functional computer designed for you to carry around and run on battery power. Notebooks come equipped with all the technology to meet your personal needs and weigh as little as four pounds. If you need a fully functional computer in a variety of places—home, work, school, and/or on the road—then a notebook may be just the answer. Notebook computers range in price from about $800 to several thousand dollars.

DESKTOP COMPUTERS

A **desktop computer** is the most popular choice for personal computing needs. You can choose a desktop with a horizontal system box (the box is where the CPU, RAM, and storage devices are held) and place a monitor on top of it or choose one with a vertical system box (called a tower) that you usually place on the floor near your work area. Desktops range in price from a little less than $500 to several thousand dollars. Dollar for dollar, a desktop is faster and more powerful than a notebook with comparable characteristics.

Which you need—a PDA, notebook, or desktop computer—is a function of your needs. PDAs offer great portability and allow you to keep a calendar, send and receive e-mail, take short notes, and even access the Web. But they certainly can't help you write a term paper, build a Web site, or create a complex graph with statistical software. For any of those tasks, you would need either a notebook or desktop computer.

So there's another question. Say you need a computer that supports full word processing, spreadsheet, presentation, Web site development, and some other capabilities. Should you buy a notebook or a desktop? In short, you need to decide *where* you'll need your computer. If you need to use your computer at home and at school (or perhaps at work), then you should buy a notebook computer because it is in fact portable. But, if you think you might want a notebook because it would be nice to take it with you on vacation, think again. Do you really want to sit in your hotel room and work on your computer instead of having fun on the beach? Probably not.

MINICOMPUTERS, MAINFRAME COMPUTERS, AND SUPERCOMPUTERS

PDAs, notebooks, and desktop computers are designed to meet your personal information processing needs. In business, however, many people often need to access and use the same computer simultaneously. In this case, businesses need computing technologies that multiple people can access and use at the same time. Computers of this type include minicomputers, mainframe computers, and supercomputers (see Figure B.4).

A **minicomputer** (sometimes called a **mid-range computer**) is designed to meet the computing needs of several people simultaneously in a small to medium-size business environment. Minicomputers are more powerful than desktop computers but also cost more, ranging in price from $5000 to several hundred thousand dollars. Businesses often use minicomputers as servers, either for creating a Web presence or as an internal computer on which shared information and software is placed. For this reason, minicomputers are well suited for business environments in which people need to share information, processing power, and/or certain peripheral devices such as high-quality, fast laser printers.

A **mainframe computer** (sometimes just called a **mainframe**) is designed to meet the computing needs of hundreds of people in a large business environment. They are a step up from minicomputers in size, power, capability, and cost. Mainframes can easily cost in excess of $1 million. With processing speeds greater than a trillion instructions per second (as against a typical desktop which can process only about 2.5 billion instructions per second), mainframes can easily handle the processing requests of hundreds of people simultaneously.

The fastest, most powerful, and most expensive type of computer is the **supercomputer**. Organizations such as NASA that are heavily involved in research and

Figure B.4
Minicomputers, Mainframes, and Supercomputers

Minicomputers are well suited for small to medium-size businesses.

Mainframe computers support the information-processing tasks of large businesses.

Supercomputers are very expensive and fast number-crunching machines. They are usually scalable, meaning that you get as many units as you need and they work together on your processing tasks.

"number crunching" employ supercomputers because of the speed with which they can process information. Other large, customer-oriented businesses such as General Motors and Bell Canada employ supercomputers just to handle customer information and transaction processing.

How much do you really need to know about the technical specifics (CPU speed, storage disk capacity, and so on), prices, and capabilities of minicomputers, mainframe computers, and supercomputers? Not much, unless you plan to major in information technology. As a typical and well-informed knowledge worker you really only need to know what we've stated above. What you should definitely concentrate on, though, is the technical specifics, prices, and capabilities of PDAs, notebooks, and desktop computers. These will be your companions for your entire business career. Learn and know them well.

Software—Your Intellectual Interface

The most important tool in your technology tool set is software. Software contains the instructions that your hardware executes to perform an information processing task for you. Software is really your *intellectual interface*, designed to automate processing tasks that you would undertake with your mind. Without software, your computer is just a very expensive doorstop. As we've stated before, there are two categories of software—application and system.

APPLICATION SOFTWARE

Application software is the software you use to meet your specific information processing needs, including payroll, customer relationship management, project management, training, word processing, and many, many others.

PERSONAL PRODUCTIVITY SOFTWARE **Personal productivity software** helps you perform personal tasks—such as writing a memo, creating a graph, and creating a slide presentation—that you might do even if you didn't use a computer. You're probably already familiar with some personal productivity software tools, including Microsoft Word and Excel, Netscape Communicator or Internet Explorer, and Quicken (personal finance software).

In fact, we have Modules in this text that help you learn how to use two of these tools—Skills Module 1 (for Microsoft Excel, spreadsheet software) and Skills Module 2 (for Microsoft Access, database management system software). Figure B.5 describes the ten major categories of personal productivity software and includes some of the more popular packages within each.

→ **Skills Module 1**
Decision Analysis—
Excel

Skills Module 2
Database Design—
Access

VERTICAL AND HORIZONTAL MARKET SOFTWARE While performing organizational processes in your career, you'll also frequently use two other categories of application software—vertical market software and horizontal market software.

Figure B.5

Categories of Personal Productivity Software

Category	Examples*
Word processing. Helps you create papers, letter, memos, and other basic documents.	• Microsoft Word • Corel WordPerfect
Spreadsheet. Helps you work primarily with numbers, including performing calculations and creating graphs.	• Microsoft Excel • LotusIBM Lotus 1-2-3
Presentation. Helps you create and edit information that will appear in electronic slides.	• Corel Presentations • LotusIBM Freelance Graphics
Desktop publishing. Extends word processing software by including design and formatting techniques to enhance the layout and appearance of a document.	• Microsoft Publisher • Quark QuarkXPress
Personal information management (PIM). Helps you create and maintain (1) to-do lists, (2) appointments and calenders, and (3) points of contact.	• Corel Central • LotusIBM Organizer
Personal finance. Helps you maintain your chequebook, prepare a budget, track investments, monitor your credit card balances, and pay bills electronically.	• Quicken Quicken • Microsoft Money
Web authoring. Helps you design and develop Web sites and pages that you publish on the web.	• Microsoft FrontPage • LotusIBM FastSite
Graphics. Helps you create and edit photos and art.	• Microsoft PhotoDraw • Kodak Imaging for Windows
Communications. Helps you communicate with other people.	• Microsoft Outlook • Internet Explorer
Database management system (DBMS). Helps you specify the logical organization for a database and access and use the information within a database.	• Microsoft Access • FileMaker FileMaker Pro

*Publisher name given first.

BUYING PERSONAL PRODUCTIVITY SOFTWARE SUITES

When you buy personal productivity software, we recommend that you do so in the form of a suite. A **software suite (suite)** is a group of various applications that comes from the same software publisher and costs less than buying all the software individually.

In this project, your team has two tasks. First, research the most popular personal productivity software suites. These include Microsoft Office, Corel WordPerfect Office, and Lotus SmartSuite. For each, identify which specific software pieces falls into the ten categories of personal productivity software listed earlier. Then try to find information that describes the market share of each suite.

Second, choose one suite and determine the price for each individual application in it. Now do a price comparison. How much cheaper is the entire suite? Can you think of a situation in which someone would buy the individual pieces as opposed to the entire suite? If so, please describe it.

Vertical market software is application software that is unique to a particular industry. For example, the health care industry has a variety of application software unique to it, including radiology software, patient-scheduling software, nursing allocation software, and pharmaceutical software. This type of software is written with a specific industry in mind; health care industry patient-scheduling software, for example, wouldn't work for scheduling hair and manicure appointments in a beauty salon.

Horizontal market software is application software general enough to be suitable for use in a variety of industries. Examples are software used for the following purposes:

- Inventory management
- Payroll
- Accounts receivable
- Billing
- Invoice processing
- Human resources management

The above functions (and many others) are very similar, if not identical, in many different industries.

If you think about it, personal productivity software is actually a type of horizontal market software in that it is general enough to be suitable for use in a variety of industries. For example, no matter in which industry you work, you need basic word processing software for creating memos, business plans, and other basic documents. There are, however, some key differences between personal productivity software and horizontal and vertical market software. First is the issue of price. You can buy a full suite of personal productivity software for less than $400. In contrast, some individual horizontal and vertical market software packages may cost as much as $500,000 or more. Second is the issue of customizability. When you purchase personal productivity software, you cannot change the way it works. That is, you're buying the right to use it but not to change how it operates. With horizontal and vertical market software you may in fact also be able to purchase the right to change the way the software works. So, if you find a payroll software package that fits most of your organizational needs, you can buy the software and the right to change the operation of the software so that it meets 100 percent of your needs. This is a very common business practice when purchasing and using horizontal and vertical market software.

In Chapter 3 we discussed how organizations go about developing software unique to their particular needs, including how organizations can and do purchase vertical and horizontal market software and then customize that software.

SYSTEM SOFTWARE

System software is software that controls how your various technology tools work together as you use your application software to perform specific information processing tasks. It includes two basic categories—operating system and utility.

OPERATING SYSTEM SOFTWARE   As mentioned above, operating system software is system software that controls your application software and manages how your hardware devices work together. For example, while using Excel to create a graph, if you choose to print the graph, your operating system software would take over, ensuring that you have a printer attached and that the printer has paper (and notifying you if it doesn't), and sending your graph to the printer along with instructions about how to print it.

Your operating system software also supports a variety of useful features, one of which is multitasking. **Multitasking** allows you to work with more than one piece of software at a time. Suppose you wanted to create a graph in Excel and insert it into a word processing document (see Figure B.6). With multitasking, you can have both pieces of application software open at the same time, and even see both on the screen. So, when you complete the creation of your graph, you can easily copy and paste it into your word processing document without having to go through a series of steps to exit the spreadsheet software and start your word processor.

Within operating system software, there are different types for personal environments and for organizational environments that support many simultaneous users (these are called *network operating systems* or *NOSs*, and we explore some of these in

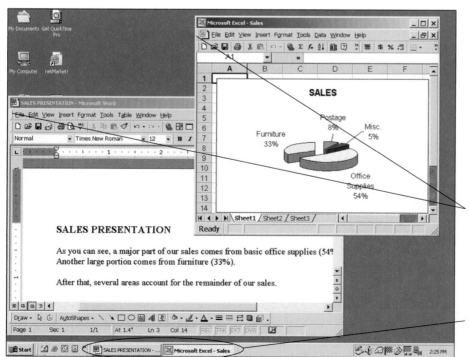

Figure B.6

Most Operating Systems Support Multitasking

Multitasking allows you to work with more than one piece of software at a time.

The taskbar area tells you what software you're currently working with.

EVALUATING UTILITY SOFTWARE SUITES

Just as you can purchase personal productivity software suites that contain many pieces of software, you can also purchase utility software suites. In the table below, we've included the three most popular utility software suites—McAfee Office Pro, Norton System-Works, and Ontrack SystemSuite.

As a team, do some research and determine what major pieces of software are included in each. As you do, fill in the table.

Now, pick a particular utility suite and visit its Web site. What is the process for updating your software? Is it free? How often does the site recommend that you update your utility software?

	McAfee Office Pro	Norton SystemWorks	Ontrack SystemSuite
Utility Software Pieces:			

greater detail in Extended Learning Module D). Popular personal operating systems include:

- **Microsoft Windows XP Home**. Microsoft's latest upgrade to Windows 2000 Me, with enhanced features for allowing multiple people to use the same computer
- **Microsoft Windows XP Professional (Windows XP Pro)**. Microsoft's latest upgrade to Windows 2000 Pro
- **Mac OS**. The operating system for today's Apple computers
- **Linux**. An open source operating system that provides a rich operating environment for high-end workstations and network servers

If you're considering purchasing a notebook computer that you'll use extensively at school connected to a network there, we recommend that you contact your school's technology support department to determine which operating system is best for you.

UTILITY SOFTWARE Utility software adds additional functionality to your operating system. A simple example is that of screensaver software (which is probably also a part of your operating system). Most importantly, utility software includes **antivirus software**—utility software that scans for and can destroy viruses in your RAM and on your storage devices. Viruses are everywhere today, with 200 to 300 new ones surfacing each month. Some are benign—they might merely cause your screen to go blank (or something on that order) but do not corrupt your information. Others are deadly, often reformatting your hard disk or altering the contents of your files. You definitely need antivirus software to combat them. We talk much more about this vitally important topic, including denial-of-service attacks, in Chapter 9.

Other types of utility software include:

- **Crash-proof software**. Utility software that helps you save information if your system crashes and you're forced to turn it off and then back on again
- **Uninstaller software**. Utility software you can use to remove software from your hard disk that you no longer want
- **Disk optimization software**. Utility software that organizes your information on your hard disk in the most efficient way

We would once again state that utility software is not optional just because it is meant to add functionality to your computer. You definitely need utility software. The four specific pieces we described above are just a few of the many you'll find in a utility software suite.

Hardware—Your Physical Interface

To properly understand the significant role of your hardware (the physical components of your computer), it helps to know something about how your computer works differently from you. You work with information in the form of characters (A–Z, a–z, and special ones such as an asterisk) and numbers (0–9). Computers, on the other hand, work in terms of bits and bytes. Basically, computers use electricity to function, and electrical pulses have two states: on and off.

A **binary digit (bit)** is the smallest unit of information that your computer can process. A bit can either be a 1 (on) or a 0 (off). The challenge from a technological point of view is to be able to represent all our characters, special symbols, and numbers in binary form. Using ASCII is one way to do this. **ASCII (American Standard Code for Information Interchange)** is the coding system most personal computers use to represent, process, and store information. In ASCII, a group of eight bits represents one natural language character and is called a **byte**.

For example, if you were to type the word "COOL" on the keyboard, your keyboard (a hardware device) would change it into four bytes—one for each character—that would look like the following used by other parts of your computer (see also Figure B.7):

01000011	01001111	01001111	01001100
C	O	O	L

This grouping of 1s and 0s is then used throughout the rest of your computer, as it travels from one device to another, is stored on a storage device, and is processed by your CPU.

There are three important conclusions that you should draw from the previous discussion. First, your hardware works with information in a different form (although with the same meaning) than you do. You work with characters, special symbols, and the numbers 0–9. Your computer, on the other hand, represents all these in binary form, a collection of unique 1s and 0s. Second, the term "byte" is the bridge between people and a computer. A computer can store one character, special symbol, or number in the form of a byte. One byte is essentially one character. So a floppy disk with a storage capacity of 1.44 megabytes can hold approximately 1.44 million characters of information.

Figure B.7

Representations of Information As It Moves Through Your Computer

Finally, a primary role of your input and output devices (such as a keyboard and monitor) is to convert information from one form to another, either from how you understand information to bits and bytes (the role of input devices) or from computer-stored bits and bytes to a form you understand (the role of output devices). All other hardware internally works with information in the form of bits and bytes.

COMMON INPUT DEVICES

An **input device** is a tool you use to capture information and commands. You can, for example, use a keyboard to type in information and use a mouse to point and click on buttons and icons. And, as we have just stated, input devices are responsible for converting your representation of information (the letter "C" for example) into a form that the rest of your computer can work with (01000011).

Within almost any complete technology environment, you'll find numerous input devices, some of which have more suitable applications in a business setting than in a personal setting. Some common input devices include (see Figure B.8):

- **Keyboard**. Today's most popular input technology
- **Point-of-sale (POS)**. For capturing information at the point of a transaction, typically in a retail environment
- **Microphone**. For capturing live sounds such as a dog barking or your voice (for automatic speech recognition)
- **Mouse**. Today's most popular "pointing" input device
- **Trackball**. An upside-down, stationary mouse in which you move the ball instead of the device (mainly for notebooks)
- **Pointing stick**. Small rubberlike pointing device that causes the pointer to move on the screen as you apply directional pressure (popular on notebooks)
- **Touch pad**. Another form of a stationary mouse on which you move your finger to cause the pointer on the screen to move (also popular on notebooks)
- **Touch screen**. Special screen that lets you use your finger to point at and touch a particular function you want to perform
- **Barcode reader**. Captures information that exists in the form of vertical bars whose width and distance apart determine a number
- **Optical mark recognition (OMR)**. Detects the presence or absence of a mark in a predetermined place (popular for multiple-choice exams)

Figure B.8

Popular Input Devices

- **Scanner**. Used to convert information that exists in visible form into electronic form:
  - **Image scanner**. Captures images, photos, text, and artwork that already exist on paper
  - **Barcode scanner**. Reads information that is in the form of vertical bars whose width and spacing represent digits; often used in point-of-sale (POS) systems in the retail environment
  - **Optical mark reader**. Detects the presence or absence of a mark in a predetermined spot on the page; often used to read true/false and multiple-choice exam answers
  - **Optical character reader**. Reads characters that appear on a page or sales tag; often used in point-of-sale (POS) systems in the retail environment
  - **Biometric scanner**. Scans some human physical attribute, such as a fingerprint or iris, to identify persons for security purposes
  - **Digital camera**. Captures images as a series of 1s and 0s; a **digital still camera** captures still images in varying resolutions, while a **digital video camera** captures video digitally
  - **Webcam**. Captures digital video to upload to the Web; often live, or updated regularly

COMMON OUTPUT DEVICES

An **output device** is a tool you use to see, hear, or otherwise accept the results of your information processing requests. Among output devices, printers and monitors are the most common, but you'll also usually find speakers and even plotters (special printers

  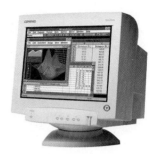

that draw output on a page) being used. And output devices are responsible for converting computer-stored information into a form that you can understand.

MONITORS Monitors come in two varieties—CRT or flat-panel display (see Figure B.9). **CRTs** are monitors that look like television sets, while **flat-panel displays** are thin, lightweight monitors and take up much less space than CRTs. When considering monitors as an output device, you need to think about monitor size, viewable screen size, resolution, monitor type, and dot pitch.

Monitor size determines how large your entire monitor is, measured diagonally from corner to corner. Monitor size, especially for CRTs, gives you some idea of the amount of space your monitor will require. However, the size that really is of interest to you is viewable screen size, often expressed as *VIS* or *viewable inch screen*. Viewable screen size tells you the size of your screen, which is measured diagonally from corner to corner and always smaller than monitor size. Viewable screen size tells you the size of the screen on which you will see things. So a monitor with a 17" VIS has a screen on which you will see things that measures 17 inches diagonally (1 inch = 2.54 centimetres).

The **resolution of a screen** is the number of *pixels* it has. Pixels (picture elements) are the dots that make up an image on your screen. For example, a monitor with a resolution given as 1024 × 768 has 1024 pixels horizontally and 768 vertically. The number of dots varies with the type of monitor you have, but larger numbers (of pixels) provide more clear and crisp screen images than smaller ones. Monitor types range from basic VGA (with a resolution of 640 × 480) to QXGA (with a resolution of 2048 × 1536). QXGA monitors obviously cost the most and provide the clearest images.

Dot pitch is the distance between the centres of a pair of like-coloured pixels. So a monitor with a 0.24 millimetre dot pitch (0.24 millimetres between pair of like-coloured pixels) is better than one with a 0.28 millimetre dot pitch because the dots are smaller and closer together, giving you a better-quality image.

PRINTERS Printers are another common type of output device, creating output on paper. A printer's sharpness and clarity depends on its resolution. The **resolution of a printer** is the number of dots per inch (dpi) it produces, which is the same principle as resolution in monitors. The more dots per inch, the better the image, and usually the more costly the printer.

Most high-end personal printers have a resolution of 1200 × 1200 dpi or better. Multiplying these numbers gives you 1,440,000 dots per square inch. Also, printers that have the same number of dots per inch both vertically and horizontally give you a better-quality image.

FINDING A PRINTER TO MEET YOUR NEEDS

A printer for a personal environment is definitely a "personal choice." Some people care only about print quality for mainly words and numbers. Others may want a personal printer that creates high-quality colour images. Whatever the case, you need to choose a printer carefully.

As you think about buying a printer, do so first in terms of quality and speed. Once you've considered those two aspects, find one inkjet, one laser, and one multifunction printer that will meet your needs. Compare them now on price and capability. Which would you choose and why?

Finally, check out some complete computer systems that you can buy at a local computer store. Do they include a printer for free? If so, would getting this printer for free encourage you to purchase the system? Why or why not?

Common types of printers are:

- **Inkjet printers**. Make images by forcing ink droplets through nozzles (see Figure B.10). Standard inkjet printers use four colours—black, cyan (blue), magenta (purplish pink), and yellow. Some inkjet printers produce high-quality images and are often advertised as photo printers. These have six colours (a second shade of magenta and of cyan).
- **Laser printers**. Form images using an electrostatic process, the same way a photocopier works. Laser printers are more expensive than inkjet printers but do provide higher-quality images. Most common personal laser printers only print in black and white. You can buy high-end colour laser printers, but be ready to spend a lot more money.
- **Multifunction printers**. Scan, copy, and fax, as well as print. These are becoming quite popular in the personal technology arena, mainly because they cost less than if you bought separate tools (printer, scanner, copier, and fax machine). Multifunction printers can be either inkjet or laser, the latter being more expensive and providing better quality.

Figure B.10

Printers Are Also Common Output Devices

CHARACTERISTICS OF CPUs AND RAM

Together, your CPU and RAM make up the real brains of your computer. As well, your CPU will largely determine the price of your system. The **central processing unit (CPU)** is the actual hardware that interprets and executes the software instructions and coordinates how all the other hardware devices work together. **RAM**, or **random access memory**, is temporary storage that holds the information you're working with, the application software you're using, and the operating system software you're using.

The CPU is often referred to as a microprocessor or a CPU chip. The dominant manufacturers of CPUs today include Intel (with its Celeron and Pentium lines for personal computers) and AMD (with its Athlon series). The most helpful information when comparing CPUs is their relative speeds.

CPU speed is usually quoted in **megahertz (MHz)**, which is millions of CPU cycles per second, and **gigahertz (GHz)**, which is billions of CPU cycles per second. The number of CPU cycles per second determines how fast a CPU carries out the

Figure B.11

Your CPU and RAM at Work

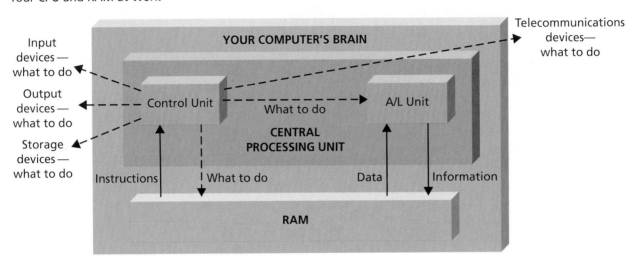

software instructions—more cycles per second means faster processing. And, as you might expect, faster CPUs cost more than their slower counterparts.

A CPU contains two primary parts—the control unit and the arithmetic/logic unit (see Figure B.11). The **control unit** interprets software instructions and tells the other hardware devices what to do, on the basis of the software instructions. The **arithmetic/logic unit (A/L unit)** performs all arithmetic operations (e.g., addition and subtraction) and all logical operations (such as sorting and comparing numbers).

These two units perform very different functions. The control unit actually gets another instruction from RAM which contains your software (this is called a *retrieve*). It then interprets the instruction, decides what each other device must do, and finally tells each device what to do (this is called *decoding*). The A/L unit, on the other hand, responds to the control unit and does whatever it dictates, performing either an arithmetic or a logic operation (this called an *execution*). At the end of this Module, we'll take you through a small program that demonstrates all these steps at work.

RAM is a sort of chalkboard your CPU uses while it processes information and software instructions. That is why we refer to RAM as "temporary." When you turn off your computer, everything in RAM is wiped clean. That's also why people (and your operating system) will always tell you to save your work before shutting down your computer. So, while you type in a term paper using word processing software, the contents of your term paper (that appear on your screen) are actually stored in RAM. When you perform a save function, the contents are copied from RAM to your designated storage device.

RAM capacity is expressed in bytes, megabytes being the most common unit of measurement. A **megabyte (MB or M or meg)** is roughly one million bytes. So, if your computer has 256 MB of RAM, your RAM can hold roughly 256 million characters of information and software instructions. RAM is cheap compared to most other parts of your computer, so don't hesitate to buy as much as you need.

COMMON STORAGE DEVICES

As opposed to RAM, which is temporary, storage devices don't lose their contents when you turn off your computer. Although we use the term "permanent" for storage devices, most do give you the ability to change your information or erase it altogether.

When considering which storage device(s) are best, you should ask (1) whether you need to be able to update the information on the storage device and (2) how much information you have to store.

Some storage devices, such as a hard disk, offer you easy update capabilities and a large storage capacity. Others, such as floppy disks, offer you easy update capabilities but with limited storage capacities. Still others, such as CD-ROM, offer no update capabilities but do posses large storage capacities. When we talk about storage device capacities, we still measure it in terms of bytes, megabytes, gigabytes, and terabytes. A **gigabyte (GB** or **gig)** is roughly one billion characters. A **terabyte (TB)** is roughly one trillion bytes. Most standard desktops today have a hard disk with storage capacity in excess of 20 GB. And hard disks (sometimes called *hard disk packs*) for large organizational computer systems can hold in excess of 100 TB of information. To give you some idea of these capacities, consider that a typical double-spaced page of pure text is roughly 2000 characters. So a 20 GB (20 gigabyte or 20-billion-character) hard disk can hold approximately 10,000,000 pages of text.

Common storage devices include (see Figure B.12):

- **Floppy disk.** Great for portability of information and ease of updating but holds only 1.44 MB of information.
- **High-capacity floppy disk.** Great for portability and ease of updating and hold between 100 MB and 250 MB of information; examples are Superdisks and Zip disks are examples.
- **Hard disk.** Rests within your system box and offers both ease of updating and great storage capacity.
- **CD-ROM.** Optical or laser disc that offers no updating capabilities with about 800 MB of storage capacity. Most software today comes on CD-ROM.
- **CD-R (compact disc—recordable).** Optical or laser disc that offers one-time writing capability with about 800 MB of storage capacity.
- **CD-RW (compact disc—rewritable).** Offers unlimited writing and updating capabilities on the CD.
- **DVD-ROM.** Optical or laser disc that offers no updating capabilities with upwards of 17 GB of storage capacity. The trend is now for rental movies to be on DVD.
- **DVD-R.** Optical or laser disc that offers one-time writing capability with upwards of 17 GB of storage capacity.

Figure B.12

Common Storage Devices

- **DVD-RW**, **DVD-RAM**, or **DVD+RW** (all different names by different manufacturers). Optical or laser disc that offers unlimited writing and updating capabilities on the DVD.
- **Flash memory**. This comes in two varieties. A *flash memory device* plugs directly into the USB port on your computer and is small enough to fit on a key ring. A *flash memory card* (which is laminated inside a small piece of plastic) has to be inserted into a reader, which in turn plugs into the USB port. Flash memory cards provide high-capacity storage.

TELECOMMUNICATIONS DEVICES

Telecommunications is the most dynamic, changing, exciting, and technically complicated aspect of MIS and IT today. Telecommunications basically describes our ability to be *connected*, to almost anyone, anywhere, and at any time. Because this topic is so vast, we've devoted all of Extended Learning Module E to it. Here, we want to just introduce you to the basics of telecommunications and its associated technologies, by focusing on your personal needs while at home.

Telecommunications enables the concept of a network. A **network** is two or more computers connected so that they can communicate with each other and possibly share information, software, peripheral devices, and/or processing power. A simple example of a network is two computers connected to the same printer. The most well-known (and complicated) example of a network is the millions of computers connected all over the world that make up the Internet.

Let's talk about how you would connect to the Internet from home. First, you need some sort of modem that will serve as a connection from your home computer to another network, that is, the Internet. There are many types of modems, including:

- A telephone modem
- Digital subscriber line (DSL) modem
- A cable modem
- A satellite modem

In Extended Learning Module E, we cover DSL, cable, and satellite modems in more detail. Here, we focus on the **telephone modem**—a device that connects your computer to your phone line so that you can access another computer or network (see Figure B.13). If you use your standard telephone line for connecting to a network, a telephone modem is necessary because it acts as a converter of sorts. Your computer (and the network you're connecting to) work in terms of digital signals, while a standard telephone line works in terms of analog signals. Digital signals are discrete with each signal representing a bit (either 0 or 1). Think of analog signals as being "wavy." So your modem must convert the digital signals of your computer into analog signals that can be sent across the telephone line (this conversion process is called *modulation*). At the other end, another modem (similar to yours) translates the analog signals into digital signals which can then be used by the other computer or network (this conversion process is called *demodulation*). So, modems *mo*dulate and *dem*odulate signals, hence the term.

When you type information on a Web form to order a product, that information starts in digital form within your computer. When you hit the Submit button, your modem converts that information to analog form and sends it on its way through your telephone line. At the other end, another modem converts it back to digital form, which allows a server computer to process your request. Then the server prepares its response in digital form and sends it through a modem which converts it to analog form. When the information reaches you, your modem first converts it to digital form so your computer can display it to you.

Figure B.13

The Role of a Telephone Modem

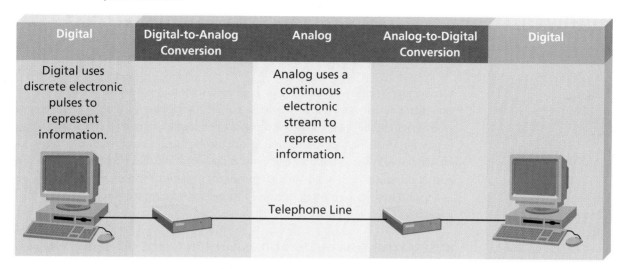

Digital	Digital-to-Analog Conversion	Analog	Analog-to-Digital Conversion	Digital

Digital uses discrete electronic pulses to represent information.

Analog uses a continuous electronic stream to represent information.

Telephone Line

As you may recall, whenever you use your computer for any task, you need both hardware and software. For telecommunications, your hardware—in our example of connecting to the Internet—is a modem. You also need communications software, specifically:

- **Connectivity software**, which enables you to use your computer to "dial up" or connect to another computer
- **Web browser software**, which enables you to surf the Web
- Probably **e-mail software** (short for **electronic mail software**), which enables you to electronically communicate with other people by sending and receiving e-mail

For example, if you want to connect to your school so that you could surf the Web and send and receive e-mail, you would first use connectivity software to dial up your school's computer (see Figure B.14). Once you are connected to your school's computer, you can use Web browser software to surf the Web or e-mail software (such as Microsoft Outlook in Figure B.15) to send and receive e-mail.

Figure B.14

Connecting with Connectivity Software

Figure B.15

Microsoft Outlook Is E-Mail Software

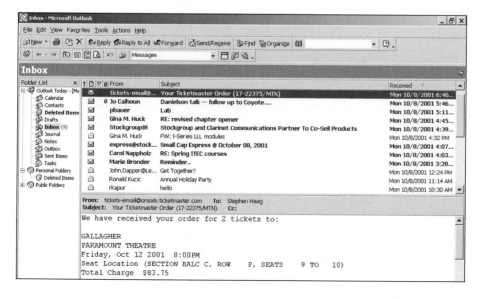

Again, this is a very brief introduction to telecommunications and focuses on only using your home computer and a telephone modem to connect to your school so you can get to the Internet. We encourage you to read Extended Learning Module E for a more complete discussion of networks and telecommunications devices.

CONNECTING DEVICES

Connecting devices enable all your hardware to communicate with each other. For example, you use a connector, called a parallel connector, to plug your printer into your system box. When you do, you're plugging it into a parallel port connected to an expansion card. That card is connected to the expansion bus (via an expansion slot) which moves information between various devices and RAM. The expansion bus is a part of the larger system bus, which moves information between the RAM and CPU and to and from various other devices. That may seem like an awful lot of technical jargon, so let's break it down a bit.

BUSES, EXPANSION SLOTS, AND EXPANSION CARDS   The **system bus** consists of the electronic pathways which move information between basic components on the motherboard, including between your CPU and RAM (see Figure B.16). A part of the system bus is called the **expansion bus**, which moves information from your CPU and RAM to all of your other hardware devices such as your microphone and printer. So, there's actually only one common "highway" that connects all of your hardware.

Along the expansion bus, you'll find expansion slots. An **expansion slot** is a long, skinny socket on the motherboard into which you insert an expansion card. An **expansion card** is a circuit board that you insert into an expansion slot. Expansion cards include such things as video cards (for your monitor), sound cards (for your speakers and microphone), and modem cards (obviously for your modem). Each expansion card contains one or more ports (which we'll soon discuss further) into which you plug a connector (which we'll also discuss soon) connected to some other hardware device such as a printer.

Figure B.16

Buses, Expansion Slots, and Expansion Cards

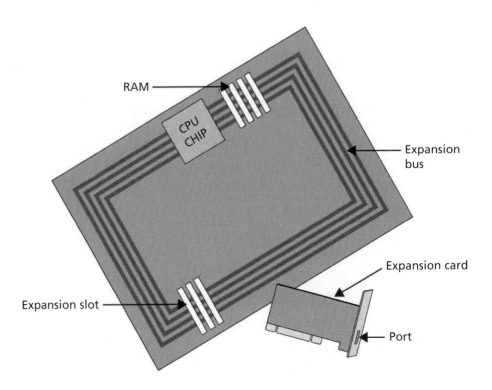

When you buy a complete computer system, it comes already equipped with the expansion cards inserted into the expansion slots. All you have to do is plug the appropriate connectors into the right ports. If, however, you decide to buy a new monitor and want increased video capacity, you may have to remove your old expansion card and insert a new one.

PORTS AND CONNECTORS Different hardware devices require different kinds of ports and connectors. **Ports** are simply the plug-ins found on the outside of your system box (usually in the back) into which you plug a connector (see Figure B.17). Popular connectors include:

- **USB (universal serial bus).** These are becoming the most popular means of connecting devices to a computer. Most standard desktops today have at least two USB ports, and most standard notebooks have at least one.

Figure B.17

Ports and Connectors

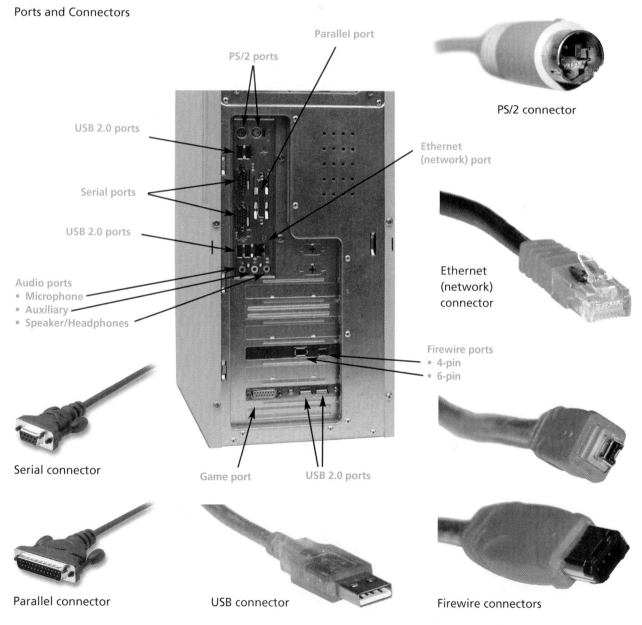

PS/2 ports
Parallel port
USB 2.0 ports
Serial ports
USB 2.0 ports
Audio ports
• Microphone
• Auxiliary
• Speaker/Headphones
Ethernet (network) port
Firewire ports
• 4-pin
• 6-pin
Game port
USB 2.0 ports
Serial connector

PS/2 connector

Ethernet (network) connector

Parallel connector

USB connector

Firewire connectors

- **Serial connector**. Usually has 9 holes but may have 25, which fit into the corresponding number of pins in the port. Serial connectors are often most used for monitors and certain types of modems.
- **Parallel connector**. Has 25 pins, which fit into the corresponding holes in the port. Most printers use parallel connectors.

WIRELESS CONNECTIONS Wireless devices transfer and receive information in the form of either infrared or radio waves. Different types of waves have different frequencies. The three types of wireless connections most frequently used in personal and business computer environments are:

- **Infrared**, also called **IR** or **IrDA** (Infrared Data Association), uses infrared light, which has a frequency below what the eye can see. It is used for TV remotes and other devices that operate over short, obstacle-free distances.
- **Bluetooth** uses short-range radio waves over distances of up to 9 metres. It is used for such purposes as wirelessly connecting a cell phone or PDA to a computer.
- **WiFi (wireless fidelity)** uses radio waves for connection over distances up to about 91 metres, usually in a network environment. WiFi may also called IEEE 802.11A, B, or G, each of which is a unique type.

Now that you've seen what's under the hood and what it takes to connect everything together, let's see how your computer processes a piece of application software.

The Complete Computer at Work

As we explore a simple example of how your computer processes a piece of application software, remember first that no matter what you want to do with your computer, you need both hardware and software. For our example, let's suppose that you have an icon on your Windows desktop for a special program that you use frequently. That program allows you to enter two numbers and then it displays the result of adding the two numbers together. Of course, we realize that you would never use such a piece of software, but it suits our illustration just fine.

When you double-click on that icon, your mouse sends that command to your CPU. Using the operating system instructions which reside in your internal memory (RAM), your control unit (inside your CPU) determines that you want to launch and use a program. So your control unit determines the path to that program and sends a message to your hard disk. That message includes where the program is located on your hard disk and instructions that tell your hard disk to get it and transfer it to your RAM. Then your control unit tells your RAM to hold the program for processing.

With that stage set, let's look at the software as well as what happens on your screen. The software is shown in Figure B.18 and what appears on your screen is shown in Figure B.19. Looking at Figure B.18, you can see the program contains six lines of code. The first is line 10, the last is line 60. Below, we list each line of code and the corresponding series of internal instructions that your computer must perform.

10 CLS

10.1 Your control unit must first send a message to your RAM telling it to pass the first line of code (fetch).

10.2 Your control unit interprets the line of code and determines what each hardware device needs to do (decode).

```
10    CLS
20    PRINT "Please enter two numbers"
30    INPUT A, B
40    C = A + B
50    PRINT "The result is: "; C
60    STOP
```

10.3 Your control unit sends a message to your screen, telling your screen to build a small window with no contents (execution).

20 PRINT "Please enter two numbers"

20.1 Your control unit sends a message to your RAM telling it to pass the next line of code (fetch).

20.2 Your control unit interprets the line of code (which is a display function) and determines what each hardware device needs to do (decode).

20.3 Your control unit takes what is between quotes (*Please enter two numbers*), passes it to your screen, and tells your screen to display it (execute).

30 INPUT A, B

30.1 Your control unit sends a message to your RAM telling it to pass the next line of code (fetch).

30.2 Your control unit interprets the line of code (which is a data entry function) and determines what each hardware device needs to do (decode).

Figure B.19

What Appears on Your Screen

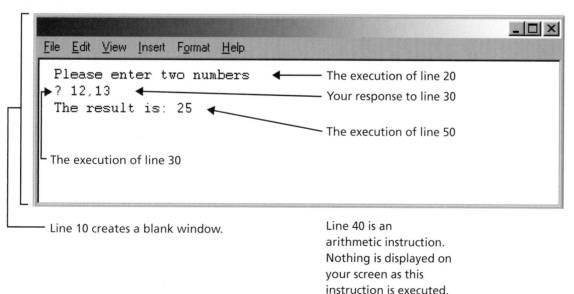

Line 10 creates a blank window.

Line 40 is an arithmetic instruction. Nothing is displayed on your screen as this instruction is executed.

30.3 Your control unit sends a message to your screen telling it to display a question mark (execute).

30.4 Your control unit sends a message to your keyboard telling it to accept two numbers and pass those to RAM (another execute).

30.5 Your control unit sends a message to your RAM telling it to accept two numbers from your keyboard and store them in memory positions A and B (another execute—beginning to get the idea?).

40 C = A + B

40.1 Your control unit sends a message to your RAM telling to pass the next line of code (fetch).

40.2 Your control unit interprets the line of code (which is an arithmetic function) and determines what each hardware device needs to do (decode).

40.3 Your control unit sends a message to RAM telling it to pass the contents of A and B to your A/L unit (execute).

40.4 Your control unit sends a message to your A/L unit telling it to accept the two numbers from RAM, add the two numbers, and pass the result back to RAM (another execute).

40.5 Your control unit sends a message to your RAM to accept the result from the A/L unit, and store the result in memory position C.

50 PRINT "The result is: "; C

50.1 Your control unit sends a message to your RAM telling it to pass the next line of code (fetch).

50.2 Your control unit interprets the line of code (which is another display function) and determines what each hardware device needs to do (decode).

50.3 Your control units sends a message to your RAM telling it to pass the contents of memory position C to your screen.

50.4 Your control units sends a message to your screen telling it to display the text between the quotes (*The result is:*) and the content of memory position C that was passed to it by RAM (execute).

60 STOP

60.1 Your control unit sends a message to your RAM telling it to pass the next line of code (fetch).

60.2 Your control unit interprets the line of code (which is a termination function) and determines what each hardware device needs to do (decode).

60.3 Your control unit sends out a broadcast message telling each hardware device to "stand down" and await further instructions (execute).

That is a very realistic example of what goes on inside your computer while you use software. What is amazing is that most software packages include millions of lines of code and require that buttons, images, and icons appear on the screen.

Summary: Student Learning Outcomes Revisited

1. **Define information technology (IT) and its two basic categories—hardware and software.** *Information technology (IT)* is any computer-based tool that people use to work with information and support the information and information processing needs of an organization. IT includes cell phones, PDAs, software such as spreadsheet software, and a printer. *Hardware* is the physical devices that make up a computer (often referred to as a computer system). *Software* is the set of instructions that your hardware executes to carry out a specific task for you.

2. **Describe categories of computers by size.** Categories of computers by size include personal digital assistants, notebook computers, desktop computers, minicomputers, mainframe computers, and supercomputers. A *personal digital assistant (PDA)* is a small handheld computer that helps you surf the Web and perform simple tasks such as note-taking, calendaring, appointment scheduling, and maintaining an address book. A notebook computer is a fully functional computer designed for you to carry around and run on battery power. A *desktop computer* is the most popular choice for personal computing needs. These three are all computers designed to for use by one person. A *minicomputer (mid-range computer)* is designed to meet the computing needs of several people simultaneously in a small to medium-size business environment. A *mainframe computer (mainframe)* is a computer designed to meet the computing needs of hundreds of people in a large business environment. A *supercomputer* is the fastest, most powerful, and most expensive type of computer. In the order given, PDAs are the smallest, least powerful, and least expensive while supercomputers are the largest, most powerful, and most expensive.

3. **Compare the roles of personal productivity, vertical market, and horizontal market software.** *Personal productivity software* helps you perform personal tasks—such as writing a memo, creating a graph, and creating a slide presentation—that you can usually do even if you don't own a computer. *Vertical market software* is application software that is unique to a particular industry. *Horizontal market software* is application software that is general enough to be suitable for use in a variety of industries. Personal productivity software is very inexpensive when compared to both vertical market and horizontal market software. With personal productivity software, you do not obtain the right to change the way the software works. If you buy vertical market or horizontal market software, you can often buy the right to change the way the software works.

4. **Describe the roles of operating system and utility software as components of system software.** *System software* handles tasks specific to technology management and coordinates the interaction of all technology devices. Within system software, you will find operating system software and utility software. *Operating system software* is system software that controls your application software and manages how your hardware devices work together. So operating system software really enables you to use your computer to run application software. *Utility software* is software that adds additional functionality to your operating system. It includes such utilities as antivirus software, screensavers, crash-proof software, uninstaller software, and disk optimization. Although these would be considered "additional" functionality, you need utility software, especially antivirus software.

5. **Define the purposes of the six major categories of hardware.** The six major categories of hardware include:
   - *Input devices.* Help you capture information and commands and convert information in a form you understand into a form your computer can understand
   - *Output devices.* Help you see, hear, or otherwise accept the results of your information processing requests and convert information in a form your computer understands into a form that you can understand
   - *CPU and RAM.* The real brains of your computer that execute software instructions (CPU) and hold the information, application software, and operating system software you're working with (RAM)
   - *Storage devices.* Help you store information for use at a later time
   - *Telecommunications devices.* Help you send information to and receive it from another person or location
   - *Connecting devices.* Help you connect all your hardware devices to each other

Key Terms and Concepts

antivirus software, 252
application software, 243
arithmetic/logic unit (A/L unit), 258
ASCII (American Standard Code for Information Interchange), 253
barcode reader, 254
barcode scanner, 255
binary digit (bit), 253
biometric scanner, 255
Bluetooth, 264
byte, 253
CD-R (compact disc—recordable), 259
CD-ROM, 259
CD-RW (compact disc—rewritable), 259
central processing unit (CPU), 257
connectivity software, 261
control unit, 258
crash-proof software, 253
CRT, 256
desktop computer, 247
digital camera, 255
digital still camera, 255
digital video camera, 255
disk optimization software, 253
dot pitch, 256
DVD-R, 259
DVD-ROM, 259
DVD-RW, DVD-RAM, DVD+RW, 260
e-mail (electronic mail) software, 261
expansion bus, 262
expansion card, 262
expansion slot, 262
flash memory, 260

flat-panel display, 256
floppy disk, 259
gigabyte (GB or gig), 259
gigahertz (GHz), 257
hard disk, 259
hardware, 243
high-capacity floppy disk, 259
horizontal market software, 250
image scanner, 255
information technology, 243
infrared (or IR or IrDA), 264
inkjet printer, 257
input device, 254
keyboard, 254
laser printer, 257
Linux, 252
Mac OS, 252
mainframe computer (mainframe), 247
megabyte (MB or M or meg), 258
megahertz (MHz), 257
microphone, 254
Microsoft Windows XP Home, 252
Microsoft Windows XP Professional (Windows XP Pro), 252
minicomputer (mid-range computer), 247
mouse, 254
multifunction printer, 257
multitasking, 251
network, 260
notebook computer, 246
operating system software, 244
optical character reader, 255
optical mark reader, 255

optical mark recognition (OMR), 254
output device, 255
parallel connector, 264
personal digital assistant (PDA), 245
personal productivity software, 249
pointing stick, 254
point-of-sale (POS), 254
port, 263
RAM (random access memory), 257
resolution of a printer, 256
resolution of a screen, 256
scanner, 255
serial connector, 264
software, 243
software suite (suite), 250
storage device, 243
supercomputer, 247
system bus, 262
system software, 244
tablet PC, 246
telecommunications device, 243
telephone modem, 260
terabyte (TB), 259
touch pad, 254
touch screen, 254
trackball, 254
uninstaller software, 253
USB (universal serial bus), 263
utility software, 244
vertical market software, 250
Web browser software, 261
webcam, 255
WiFi (wireless fidelity), 264

Short-Answer Questions

1. What are the two categories of information technology (IT)?

2. What are the six categories of hardware?

3. What is the difference between application and system software?

4. What are the four categories of computers by size? Which is the least expensive? Which is the most powerful?

5. Dollar for dollar with comparable characteristics, which is faster and more powerful—a desktop computer or notebook computer?

6. What are the major categories of personal productivity software?

7. What is the difference between vertical market and horizontal market software?

8. How is personal productivity software a type of horizontal market software? How is personal productivity software not a type of horizontal market software?

9. What are some of the personal operating systems on the market today?

10. Why is antivirus software important today?

11. What do the terms *bits* and *bytes* mean?

12. What are some popular pointing input devices for notebook computers?

13. How are resolution of a screen and resolution of a printer different and how are they similar?

14. What is the relationship between a megabyte, a gigabyte, and a terabyte?

15. What are the major types of storage devices? How do they compare in terms of updating capabilities and amount of storage?

16. What communications software do you typically need to use the Internet?

17. What is the role of expansion slots, expansion cards, ports, and connectors?

Assignments and Exercises

1. **CUSTOMIZING A COMPUTER PURCHASE.** One of the great things about the Web is the number of e-tailers that are now online offering you a variety of products and services. One such e-tailer is Dell, which allows you to customize and buy a computer. Connect to Dell's site (www.dell.ca). Go to the portion of Dell's site that allows you to customize either a notebook or a desktop computer. First, choose an already-prepared system and note its price and capability in terms of CPU speed, RAM size, monitor quality, and storage capacity. Now, customize that system to increase CPU speed, add more RAM, increase monitor size and quality, and add more storage capacity. What's the difference in price between the two? Which system is more in your price range? Which system has the speed and capacity you need?

2. **UNDERSTANDING THE COMPLEXITY OF SOFTWARE.** Software instructions, such as those in Figure B.18, must be provided to a computer in great detail and with excruciating accuracy. For example, you can easily change line 40 to read C = A + B + 1. If you did, your computer would follow it exactly and always arrive at the wrong result. To understand how detailed you must be, pick a partner for this project and imagine you are standing in a kitchen. The task for one of you is to write down all the instructions necessary to make a peanut butter and jelly sandwich. When complete, have the other person follow those instructions exactly. How successful was the second person in making the sandwich? Did your instructions include every single step? What did you leave out?

3. **WEB-ENABLED CELL PHONES AND WEB COMPUTERS.** When categorizing computers by size for personal needs, we focused on PDAs, notebook computers, and desktop computers. There are several other variations, including Web-enabled cell phones that include instant text messaging and Web computers. For this project, you'll need a group of four people, split into two groups of two. Have the first group research Web-enabled cell phones, their capabilities, and their costs. Have that group make a purchase recommendation based on price and capability. Have the second group do the same for Web computers. What's your vision of the future? Will we ever get rid of clunky notebooks and desktops in favour of more portable and cheaper devices such as Web-enabled cell phones and Web computers? Why or why not?

4. **ADDING MEDIA TO A PRESENTATION.** We certainly live in a "multimedia" society, in which it's often easy to present and receive information using a variety of media. Presentation tools such as Microsoft's PowerPoint can help you easily build presentations that include audio, animation, and video. And this may help you get a better grade. Using your preferred presentation software, document the steps necessary to add a short audio or video clip to a presentation. How does the representation of the clip appear on a slide? How can you initiate it? Does your presentation software include any clips that you can insert or do you have to record your own? Now, try recording a short audio clip. What steps must you perform?

5. **OPERATING SYSTEM SOFTWARE FOR PDAs.** The personal digital assistant (PDA) market is a ferocious, dynamic, and uncertain one. One of the uncertainties is what operating system for PDAs will become the dominant one. For notebooks and desktops right now, you're pretty well limited to the Microsoft family unless you buy an Apple computer (in which case your operating system is Mac OS) or you want to venture into using Linux (which we wouldn't recommend for most people). Do some research on the more popular PDAs available today. What are the different operating systems? What different functionality do they offer? Are they compatible with each other? Take a guess—which one will come out on top?

6. **TYPES OF MONITORS AND THEIR QUALITY.** The monitor you buy will greatly affect your productivity. If you get a high-resolution, large-screen monitor, you'll see the screen content better than if you get a low-resolution, small-screen monitor. One factor in this is the monitor type. Seven major types are available today— HDTV, QXGA, SVGA, SXGA, UXGA, VGA, and XGA. Do a little research on them. Rank them from best to worst in terms of resolution. Also, determine a price for each.

EXTENDED LEARNING MODULE C

DESIGNING DATABASES AND ENTITY-RELATIONSHIP DIAGRAMMING

Student Learning Outcomes

By the end of this Module, students will be able to:

1. Identify how databases and spreadsheets are both similar and different.

2. List and describe the four steps in designing and building a relational database.

3. Define the concepts of entity class, primary key, instance, and foreign key.

4. Given a small operating environment, build an entity-relationship (E-R) diagram.

5. List and describe the steps in normalization.

6. Describe the process of creating an intersection relation to remove a many-to-many relationship.

Introduction

As you learned in Chapter 4, databases are quite powerful and can aid your organization in both transaction and analytical processing. But you must carefully design and build a database for it to be effective. Relational databases are similar to spreadsheets in that you maintain information in two-dimensional files. In a spreadsheet, you put information in a cell (the intersection of a row and a column). To use the information, you must know the row number and column character. For example, cell C4 is in column C and row 4.

Databases are somewhat similar. You still create rows and columns of information. However, you don't need to know the physical location of the information you want to see or use. For example, in a spreadsheet, if cell C4 contained sales for Able Electronics (one of your customers), you would reference its physical location (C4). In a database, you would simply indicate that you want *sales* for *Able Electronics.* The physical location of the information is irrelevant. That's why we say that a **database** is a collection of information that you organize and access according to the logical structure of that information.

So you do need to design your databases carefully for effective utilization. In this Module, we'll take you through the process of designing and building a relational database, the most popular of all database types. A **relational database** uses a series of logically related two-dimensional tables or files to store information in the form of a database. There are well-defined rules to follow, and you need to be aware of them.

As far as implementation is concerned, you then just choose the DBMS package of your choice, define the tables or files, determine the relationships among them, and start entering information. We do not deal with the actual implementation in this Module. However, in Extended Learning Module G, we will show you how to implement a database using Microsoft Access.

Once you've implemented your database, you can then change the information as you wish, add rows of information (and delete others), add new tables, and use simple but powerful reporting and querying tools to extract the exact information you need.

Designing and Building a Relational Database

Using a database amounts to more than just using various DBMS tools. You must also know *how* to actually design and build a database. So let's take a look at how you would go about designing a database. The four primary steps include

1. Defining entity classes and primary keys.
2. Defining relationships among entity classes.
3. Defining information (fields) for each relation (the term *relation* is often used to refer to a file while designing a database).
4. Using a data definition language to create your database.

Let's continue with the example database we introduced you to in Chapter 4. Let us call the company Solomon Enterprises. Solomon Enterprises specializes in providing concrete to commercial builders and individual home owners in the greater Toronto area. In Figure 4.3 in Chapter 4, we provided a graphical depiction of some of the tables in the database, including *Part, Distributor, Facility,* and *Employee.* As you recall, an order is created when a customer calls in for the delivery of a certain concrete type. Once the concrete is mixed, Solomon has an employee drive the truck to the customer's location. That illustrates how you can use a database in support of your customer relationship management initiative and order processing function.

In this Module, we want to design and model the supply chain management side for the company. Figure C.1 contains a supply chain management report that Solomon frequently generates. Let's make some observations.

- Solomon provides five concrete types: 1—home foundation and walkways; 2—commercial foundation and infrastructure; 3—premier speckled (with gravel); 4—premier marble; 5—premier shell.

Figure C.1

A Supply Chain Management Report for Solomon Enterprises

Concrete		Raw Material					Supplier	
SOLOMON ENTERPRISES								
Supply Report Ending October 14, 2005								
Type	**Name**	**ID**	**Name**	**Unit**	**QOH**		**ID**	**Name**
1	Home	B	Cement paste	1	400		412	Wesley Enterprises
		C	Sand	2	1200		444	Juniper Sand & Gravel
		A	Water	1.5	9999		999	N/A
			TOTAL:	4.5				
2	Comm	B	Cement paste	1	400		412	Wesley Enterprises
		C	Sand	2	1200		444	Juniper Sand & Gravel
		A	Water	1	9999		999	N/A
			TOTAL:	4				
3	Speckled	B	Cement paste	1	400		412	Wesley Enterprises
		C	Sand	2	1200		444	Juniper Sand & Gravel
		A	Water	1.5	9999		999	N/A
		D	Gravel	3	200		444	Juniper Sand & Gravel
			TOTAL:	7.5				
4	Marble	B	Cement paste	1	400		412	Wesley Enterprises
		C	Sand	2	1200		444	Juniper Sand & Gravel
		A	Water	1.5	9999		999	N/A
		E	Marble	2	100		499	A&J Brothers
			TOTAL:	6.5				
5	Shell	B	Cement paste	1	400		412	Wesley Enterprises
		C	Sand	2	1200		444	Juniper Sand & Gravel
		A	Water	1.5	9999		999	N/A
		F	Shell	2.5	25		499	A&J Brothers
			TOTAL:	7				

- Solomon uses six raw materials: A—water; B—cement paste; C—sand; D—gravel; E—marble; F—shell.
- Mixing instructions are for a cubic yard. For example, one cubic yard of commercial concrete requires 1 part cement paste, 2 parts sand, and 1 part water. The terms "part" and "unit" are synonymous.
- Some raw materials are used in several concrete types. Any given concrete type requires several raw materials.
- QOH (quantity on hand) denotes the amount of inventory for a given raw material.
- Suppliers provide raw materials. For a given raw material, Solomon uses only one supplier. A given supplier can provide many different raw materials.
- QOH and supplier information are not tracked for water (for obvious reasons). However, Solomon places the value 9999 in the QOH for water and uses 999 for the ID of the supplier.

When you begin to think about designing a database application, you first need to capture your *business rules*—statements concerning the information you need to work with and the relationships within the information. Such rules will help you define the correct structure of your database. From the report in Figure C.1 and the observations above, we derived the following business rules:

1. A given concrete type will have many raw materials in it.
2. A given raw material may appear in many types of concrete.
3. Each raw material has one and only one supplier.
4. A supplier may provide many raw materials. Although not displayed in Figure C.1, Solomon may have a supplier in its database that doesn't currently provide any raw materials.

STEP 1: DEFINING ENTITY CLASSES AND PRIMARY KEYS

The first step in designing a relational database is to define the various entity classes and the primary keys that uniquely define each record or instance within each entity class. An **entity class** is a concept—typically people, places, or things—about which you wish to store information and that you can identify with a unique key (called a primary key). A **primary key** is a field (or group of fields in some cases) that uniquely describes each record. Within the context of database design, we often refer to a record as an instance. An **instance** is an occurrence of an entity class that can be uniquely described with a primary key.

From the supply chain management report in Figure C.1, you can easily identify the entity classes of *Concrete Type, Raw Material,* and *Supplier.* Now, you have to identify their primary keys. For most entity classes, you cannot use names as primary keys, because duplicate names can exist. For example, your school provides you with a unique student ID and uses that ID as your primary key instead of your name (because other students may have the same name as you).

From the report, you can see that the entity class *Concrete Type* includes two pieces of information—*Concrete Type* and a name or *Type Description.* Although *Type Description* is unique, the logical choice for the primary key is *Concrete Type* (e.g., 1 for home, 2 for commercial, and so on). Notice that the primary key name is the same as the entity class name. This is perfectly acceptable; if it is a potential point of confusion for you, change the primary key name to something like *Concrete Type ID* or *Concrete Type Identifier.* For our purposes, we'll use *Concrete Type* as the primary key name.

DEFINING ENTITY CLASSES AND PRIMARY KEYS

Learning how to design a relational database really requires that you roll up your sleeves and practise, practise, practise. To help with this, you'll be designing a relational database that might be used at your school while we go carefully through the process of designing the relational database for Solomon Enterprises' supply chain management function. Below is a description of a hypothetical relational database that might be used at your school.

In conjunction with taking an introductory computer concepts course, your school has decided to test the idea of offering weekend seminars to cover the basics of the Internet and the Web. Initially, your school will offer two such seminars: Web101—The Basics of the Web and Internet; and Web205—Building a Web Site. Web101 will have five different sections, and Web205 will have four different sections.

Although they are not required to, students can enroll in one or both seminars. The seminars are held for eight hours on a single day. There is no cost associated with taking the seminars. One teacher, from a pool of qualified teachers, will be assigned to each section of each seminar. Some teachers will obviously not be assigned to teach any sections, and some teachers may be assigned to several different sections.

Finally, the system should track the final grades assigned to each student. One more thing. Your school is simply testing this idea in this particular term. So don't worry about the term (e.g., Fall, Winter, Spring, or Summer) or the year.

For this particular scenario, you are to create a simple two-column table that lists all the entity classes in the left column and their associated primary keys in the right column. Finally, record as many business rules as you can find provided in the description.

If you consider *Raw Material* as an entity class, you'll find several pieces of information, including *Raw Material ID, Raw Material Name,* and *QOH.* The logical choice for a primary key here is *Raw Material ID* (e.g., A for water, B for cement paste, and so on). Although *Raw Material Name* is unique, we still suggest that you not use names.

Likewise, if you consider *Supplier* as an entity class, you'll find two pieces of information: *Supplier ID* and *Supplier Name.* Again, we recommend that you use *Supplier ID* as the primary key.

STEP 2: DEFINING RELATIONSHIPS AMONG THE ENTITY CLASSES

The next step in designing a relational database is to define the relationships among the entity classes. To help you do this, we'll use an **entity-relationship (E-R) diagram** —a graphical method of representing entity classes and their relationships. An E-R diagram includes five basic symbols:

1. A rectangle to denote an entity class
2. A dotted line connecting entity classes to denote a relationship
3. A | to denote a single relationship
4. A 0 to denote a zero or optional relationship
5. A crow's foot (shown as <) to denote a multiple relationship

To use these symbols, you must first decide among which entity classes relationships exist. If you determine that two particular entity classes have a relationship, you

Figure C.2

An Entity-Relationship (E-R) Diagram

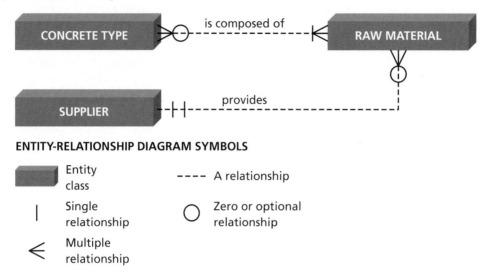

ENTITY-RELATIONSHIP DIAGRAM SYMBOLS

▬	Entity class	----	A relationship
│	Single relationship	○	Zero or optional relationship
≺	Multiple relationship		

simply draw a dotted line to connect them and then write some sort of verb that describes the relationship.

In Figure C.2, you can see the E-R diagram for the supply chain management side of Solomon's database. To determine where the relationships exist, simply ask some questions and review your business rules. For example, is there a relationship between concrete type and raw material? The answer is yes, because raw materials are used in mixing the various concrete types. Likewise, the raw materials are provided by suppliers (another relationship). However, there is no logical relationship between concrete type and supplier. So we drew dotted lines between *Concrete Type* and *Raw Material* and between *Raw Material* and *Supplier*. We then added some verbs to describe the relationships. For example, a *Concrete Type* is composed of *Raw Material,* and a *Supplier* provides a *Raw Material*.

It should also make sense (both business and logical) when you read the relationships in reverse. To do this, simply flip the location of the nouns in the sentence and change the verb accordingly. For example:

- *Concrete Type–Raw Material:* A *Concrete Type* is composed of *Raw Material*.
- *Raw Material–Concrete Type:* A *Raw Material* is used to create a *Concrete Type*.
- *Supplier–Raw Material:* A *Supplier* provides a *Raw Material*.
- *Raw Material–Supplier:* A *Raw Material* is provided by a *Supplier*.

Each of the preceding statements makes logical sense, follows the relationships we identify in Figure C.2, and reflects the business rules listed earlier. Again, we stress the importance of using business rules. Technology (databases, in this instance) is a set of tools that you use to process information. So your implementations of technology should match the way your business works. If you always start by defining business rules and using them as guides, your technology implementations will most likely mirror how your business works. And that's the way it should be.

DEFINING RELATIONSHIPS AMONG ENTITY CLASSES

Let's continue exploring how to design a relational database for your school and its offering of weekend seminars. If your group correctly completed the tasks in the preceding Team Work exercise, you know that there are four entity classes. They include (along with their primary keys):

Entity Class	Primary Key
Seminar	Seminar 3-character identifier and number (e.g., Web101 and Web205)
Seminar Section	Seminar 3-character identifier, number, and section number (e.g., Web101-1 through Web101-5 and Web205-1 through Web205-4)
Student	Student ID (whatever your school happens to use)
Qualified Teacher	Teacher ID (your school may use social insurance number)

Now your task is to define among which of those entity classes relationships exist and then write some verbs that describe each relationship just as we did in Figure C.2. We've drawn rectangles for each of the four entity classes. Connect the rectangles with dotted lines where relationships exist and write the appropriate verbs to describe the relationships.

Seminar

Seminar Section

Qualified Teacher

Student

Figure C.3

Reading an Entity-Relationship (E-R) Diagram

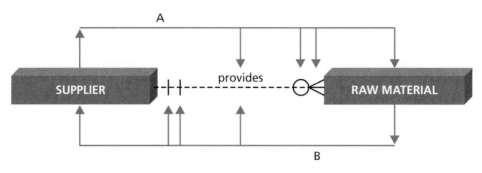

Once you determine that a relationship does exist, you must then determine the numerical nature of the relationship, what we refer to as "minimum and maximum cardinality." To describe this, you use a | to denote a single relationship, a 0 to denote a zero or optional relationship, and/or a crow's foot (<) to denote a multiple relationship. By way of illustration, let's consider the portion of your E-R diagram in Figure C.3. To help you read the symbols and diagram, we've added coloured lines and arrows. Following the line marked A, you would read the E-R diagram as:

> "A *Supplier* may not provide any *Raw Material* (denoted with the 0) but may provide more than one *Raw Material* (denoted with the crow's foot)."

So that part of the E-R diagram states that the logical relationship between *Supplier* and *Raw Material* is that a *Supplier* may provide no *Raw Material* currently in inventory, but if it does, may provide more than one *Raw Material* currently in inventory. This is exactly what business rule 4 states.

Following the coloured line marked B, you would read the E-R diagram as:

> "A *Raw Material* must be provided by a *Supplier* and can only be provided by one *Supplier*."

That statement again reinforces business rule 4.

Similarly, you can also develop statements that describe the numerical relationships between *Concrete Type* and *Raw Material* based on that part of the E-R diagram in Figure C.2. Those numerical relationships would be as follows:

- A *Concrete Type* is composed of more than one *Raw Material* and must be composed of at least one *Raw Material*.
- A *Raw Material* can be used to create more than one *Concrete Type* but is not required to be used to create any *Concrete Type*.

Again, these statements reinforce business rules 1 and 2.

To properly develop the numerical relationships (cardinality) among entity classes, you must clearly understand the business situation at hand. That's why it's so important to write down all the business rules.

DEFINING THE CARDINALITY AMONG ENTITY CLASSES

As we continue with the design of the relational database at your school, it's time to define the cardinality among the entity classes. If you correctly completed the Team Work project earlier, the relationships among the entity classes are as follows:

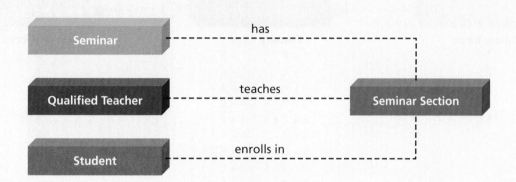

Your task is to create the numerical relationships by adding the symbols of l, O, and crow's foot in the appropriate places. Once you do, complete the table that follows by providing a narrative description of each numerical relationship.

Relationship	Narrative Description
Seminar–Seminar Section	
Seminar Section–Seminar	
Qualified Teacher–Seminar Section	
Seminar Section–Qualified Teacher	
Student–Seminar Section	
Seminar Section–Student	

Figure C.4

Creating an Intersection Relation to Remove a Many-to-Many Relationship

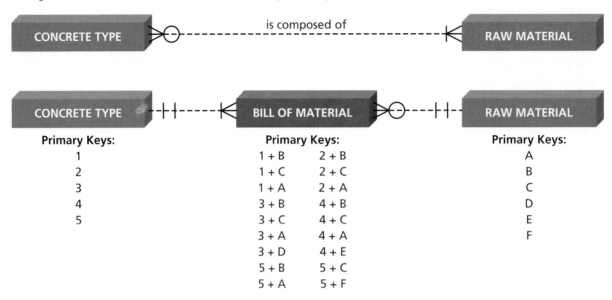

CONCRETE TYPE			BILL OF MATERIAL			RAW MATERIAL
Primary Keys:			**Primary Keys:**			**Primary Keys:**
1			1 + B	2 + B		A
2			1 + C	2 + C		B
3			1 + A	2 + A		C
4			3 + B	4 + B		D
5			3 + C	4 + C		E
			3 + A	4 + A		F
			3 + D	4 + E		
			5 + B	5 + C		
			5 + A	5 + F		

After developing the initial E-R diagram, it's time to begin **normalization**—a process of assuring that a relational database structure can be implemented as a series of two-dimensional relations (remember: relations are the same as files or tables). The complete normalization process is extensive and quite necessary for developing organizationwide databases. For our purposes, we will focus on the following three rules of normalization:

1. Eliminate repeating groups or many-to-many relationships.
2. Ensure that every field in a relation depends only on the primary key for that relation.
3. Remove all derived fields from the relations.

The first rule states that no repeating groups or many-to-many relationships can exist among the entity classes. You can find these many-to-many relationships by simply looking at your E-R diagram and noting any relationships that have a crow's foot at each end. If you look back at Figure C.2, you'll see that a crow's foot is on each end of the relationship between *Concrete Type* and *Raw Material*. Let's look at how to eliminate it.

In Figure C.4, we've developed the appropriate relationships between *Concrete Type* and *Raw Material* by removing the many-to-many relationship. Notice that we started with the original portion of the E-R diagram and created a new relation between *Concrete Type* and *Raw Material* called *Bill of Material*, which is an intersection relation. An **intersection relation** (sometimes called a **composite relation**) is a relation you create to eliminate a many-to-many relationship. It's called an intersection relation because it represents an intersection of the primary keys between the first two relations. That is, an intersection relation will have a **composite primary key** that consists of the primary key fields from the two intersecting relations. The primary key fields from the two original relations now become **foreign keys** in the intersection relation—primary keys of one file (relation) that appear in another file (relation). When combined, these two foreign keys make up the composite primary key for the intersection relation.

Figure C.5

The Completed E-R Diagram for the Supply Chain Management Side of Solomon's Database

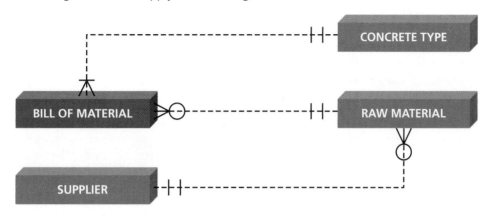

For Solomon's supply chain management portion of its database, the intersection relation *Bill of Material* represents the combination of raw materials that go into each concrete type. Here is how you would read the relationships between *Concrete Type* and *Bill of Material* and *Raw Material* and *Bill of Material* (see Figure C.5):

- *Concrete Type–Bill of Material*

  From left to right: A *Concrete Type* can have multiple listings of *Raw Material* in *Bill of Material* and must have a listing of *Raw Material* in *Bill of Material*.

  From right to left: A *Concrete Type* found in *Bill of Material* must be found and can be found only one time in *Concrete Type*.

- *Raw Material–Bill of Material*

  From left to right: A *Raw Material* can be found in many *Bill of Material* listings but may not be found in any *Bill of Material* listing.

  From right to left: A *Raw Material* found in *Bill of Material* must be found and can be found only one time in *Raw Material*.

If you compare the E-R diagram in Figure C.5 to the E-R diagram in Figure C.2, you'll notice that they are very similar. The only difference is that the E-R diagram in Figure C.5 contains an intersection relation to eliminate the many-to-many relationship between *Concrete Type* and *Raw Material*.

And removing many-to-many relationships is the most difficult aspect when designing the appropriate structure of a relational database. If you do find such a relationship, here are some guidelines for creating an intersection relation:

1. Just as we did in Figure C.4, start by drawing the part of the E-R diagram that contains a many-to-many relationship at the top of a piece of paper.
2. Underneath each relation for which the many-to-many relationship exists, write down some of the primary keys.
3. Create a new E-R diagram (showing no cardinality) with the original two relations at each end and a new one (the intersection relation) in the middle.
4. Underneath the intersection relation, write down some of the composite primary keys (these will be composed of the primary keys from the other two relations).
5. Create a meaningful name (e.g., *Bill of Material*) for the intersection relation.
6. Move the minimum cardinality appearing next to the left relation just to the right of the intersection relation.

CREATING AN INTERSECTION RELATION

Back to work on the project for your school. If you completed the Team Work project given earlier, you are now able to identify a many-to-many relationship between *Student* and *Seminar Section.* That is, a given *Seminar Section* may have many *Students,* and a given *Student* can enroll in many different *Seminar Sections* (two, to be exact). So that portion of your E-R diagram looks like this:

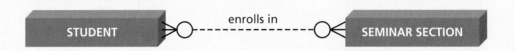

Your task is to eliminate the above many-to-many relationship by creating an intersection relation. As you do, we would encourage you to follow the guidelines given on this page and the previous. What did you name the intersection relation? What does the completed E-R diagram look like?

7. Move the minimum cardinality appearing next to the right relation just to the left of the intersection relation.
8. The maximum cardinality on both sides of the intersection relations will always be "many" (the crow's foot).
9. As a general rule, the new minimum and maximum cardinalities for the two original relations will be one and one.

As we have stated, removing many-to-many relationships is the most difficult aspect of structuring a relational database. The business world is full of such relationships. Let's walk through another example.

Assume that Solomon sometimes has to use more than one truck to make a delivery of concrete to a customer. That is, what if—given that a truck can carry at most 8 cubic yards of concrete—Triple A Homes asks for 12 cubic yards of premier marble for a given delivery. In that case, Solomon would have two choices for modelling and storing multiple trucks for the order. First, it could create two separate orders, one for 8 cubic yards of premier marble concrete and the other for 4 cubic yards of premier marble concrete. That option doesn't make business sense—when a customer places an order, the entire order should be contained in only *one* order, not two.

The second choice—the correct one—is to have the ability to specify multiple trucks on a single order. In that case, Solomon would have a many-to-many relationship between *Order* and *Truck.* That is, the revised business rule would be that an *Order* can have multiple *Trucks* assigned to make the delivery and a *Truck* can be assigned to make a delivery on multiple *Orders.*

But it doesn't stop there. Solomon may wish to sometimes send two employees in one truck to deliver one order of concrete. Then, Solomon would need the ability to specify more than one employee per delivery truck.

As you can see, the business world is complex and full of many-to-many relationships. If you can master the art and science of eliminating them in a database environment, you will have created a substantial career opportunity for yourself.

STEP 3: DEFINING INFORMATION (FIELDS) FOR EACH RELATION

Once you've completed steps 1 and 2, you must define the various pieces of information that each relation will contain. Your goal in this step is to make sure that the information in each relation is indeed in the correct relation and that the information cannot be derived from other information—the second and third rules of normalization.

In Figure C.6, we've developed a view of the relational database for Solomon based on the new E-R diagram with the intersection relation. To make sure that each piece of information is in the correct relation, look at each and ask, "Does this piece of information depend only on the primary key for this relation?" If the answer is yes, the information is in the correct relation. If the answer is no, the information is in the wrong relation.

Let's consider the *Raw Material* relation. The primary key is *Raw Material ID*, so each piece of information must depend only on *Raw Material ID*. Does *Raw Material Name* depend on *Raw Material ID*? Yes, because the name of a raw material depends on that particular raw material (as does *QOH*, quantity on hand). Does *Supplier ID* depend only on *Raw Material ID*? Yes, because the particular supplier providing a raw material depends on which raw material you're describing. In fact, *Supplier ID* in the *Raw Material* relation is a foreign key. That is, it is a primary key of one relation (*Supplier*) that appears in another relation (*Raw Material*).

What about *Supplier Name* in the *Raw Material* relation? Does it depend only on *Raw Material ID*? The answer here is no. *Supplier Name* depends only on *Supplier ID*. So the question becomes "In which relation should *Supplier Name* appear?" The answer is in the *Supplier* relation, because *Supplier Name* depends on the primary key (*Supplier ID*) for that relation. Therefore, *Supplier Name* should appear in the *Supplier* relation (as it does) and not in the *Raw Material* relation.

Now take a look at the intersection relation *Bill of Material*. Notice that it includes the field *Unit*. *Unit* is located in this relation because it depends on two things: the concrete type you're describing and the raw material in it. So *Unit* does depend completely on the composite primary key of *Concrete Type* + *Raw Material ID* in the *Bill of Material* relation.

If you follow this line of questioning for each relation, you'll find that all other fields are in their correct relations. Now you have to look at each field to see whether you can derive it from other information. If you can, the derived information should not be stored in your database. When we speak of "derived" in this instance, we're referring to information that you can mathematically derive: counts, totals, averages, and the like. Currently, you are storing the raw material total (*Raw Material Total*) in the *Concrete Type* relation. Can you derive that information from other information? The answer is yes—all you have to do is sum the *Units* in the *Bill of Material* relation for a given *Concrete Type*. So you should not store *Raw Material Total* in your database (anywhere).

Once you've completed step 3, you've completely and correctly defined the structure of your database and identified the information each relation should contain. Figure C.7 shows your database and the information in each relation. Notice that we have removed *Supplier Name* from the *Raw Material* relation and removed *Raw Material Total* from the *Concrete Type* relation.

Figure C.6

A First Look at the Relations for the Supply Chain Management Side of Solomon's Database

CONCRETE TYPE RELATION

Concrete Type	Type Description	Raw Material Total
1	Home foundation and walkways	4.5
2	Commercial foundation and infrastructure	4
3	Premier speckled (with smooth gravel aggregate)	7.5
4	Premier marble (with crushed marble aggregate)	6.5
5	Premier shell (with shell aggregate)	7

RAW MATERIAL RELATION

Raw Material ID	Raw Material Name	QOH	Supplier ID	Supplier Name
A	Water	9999	999	N/A
B	Cement paste	400	412	Wesley Enterprises
C	Sand	1200	499	A&J Brothers
D	Gravel	200	499	A&J Brothers
E	Marble	100	444	Juniper Sand & Gravel
F	Shell	25	444	Juniper Sand & Gravel

SUPPLIER RELATION

Supplier ID	Supplier Name
412	Wesley Enterprises
499	A&J Brothers
444	Juniper Sand & Gravel
999	N/A

BILL OF MATERIAL RELATION

Concrete Type	Raw Material ID	Unit
1	B	1
1	C	2
1	A	1.5
2	B	1
2	C	2
2	A	1
3	B	1
3	C	2
3	A	1.5
3	D	3
4	B	1
4	C	2
4	A	1.5
4	E	2
5	B	1
5	C	2
5	A	1.5
5	F	2.5

Unit belongs in this relation because it depends on a combination of how much of a given raw material (*Raw Material ID*) goes into each type of concrete type (*Concrete Type*).

Figure C.7

The Correct Structure of the Supply Chain Management Side of Solomon's

CONCRETE TYPE RELATION

Concrete Type	Type Description
1	Home foundation and walkways
2	Commercial foundation and infrastructure
3	Premier speckled (with smooth gravel aggregate)
4	Premier marble (with crushed marble aggregate)
5	Premier shell (with shell aggregate)

RAW MATERIAL RELATION

Raw Material ID	Raw Material Name	QOH	Supplier ID
A	Water	9999	999
B	Cement paste	400	412
C	Sand	1200	444
D	Gravel	200	444
E	Marble	100	499
F	Shell	25	499

SUPPLIER RELATION

Supplier ID	Supplier Name
412	Wesley Enterprises
499	A&J Brothers
444	Juniper Sand & Gravel
999	N/A

BILL OF MATERIAL RELATION

Concrete Type	Raw Material ID	Unit
1	B	1
1	C	2
1	A	1.5
2	B	1
2	C	2
2	A	1
3	B	1
3	C	2
3	A	1.5
3	D	3
4	B	1
4	C	2
4	A	1.5
4	E	2
5	B	1
5	C	2
5	A	1.5
5	F	2.5

Unit belongs in this relation because it depends on a combination of how much of a given raw material (*Raw Material ID*) goes into each type of concrete type (*Concrete Type*).

CREATING THE FINAL STRUCTURE FOR YOUR SCHOOL

Now it's time for you to fly solo and try a task by yourself. If your group successfully completed the earlier Team Work project, you should have a relational database model with five relations: *Seminar, Seminar Section, Student, Qualified Teacher,* and *Seminar Section Class Roll.* The first four you identified early on. The last one is the result of eliminating the many-to-many relationship between *Seminar Section* and *Student.* We named this intersection relation *Seminar Section Class Roll.* We did so because it represents a list of students enrolling in all of the sections. If you group those students by section, then you get class rolls.

Your task is to complete a table for each relation. We've provided a sample table below. That is, you must first fill in the column headings by identifying what information belongs in each relation. Be sure to follow steps 2 and 3 of normalization. Then, we encourage you to add in some actual data entries.

A word of caution. You could easily identify hundreds of pieces of information that need to be present in this database. For *Qualified Teacher,* for example, you could include birth date, rank, office hours, phone number, e-mail address, office location, employment starting date, and many more. Here, simply identify no more than five key pieces of information for each relation. And, by all means, identify the primary and foreign keys for each relation.

Seminar Relation

STEP 4: USING A DATA DEFINITION LANGUAGE TO CREATE YOUR DATABASE

The final step in developing a relational database is to take the structure you created in steps 1 and 3 and use a data definition language to actually create the relations. Data definition languages are found within a database management system. A **database management system (DBMS)** helps you specify the logical organization for a database and access and use the information within the database. To use a data definition language, you need the data dictionary for your complete database. Recall from Chapter 4 that the **data dictionary** contains the logical structure for the information in a database. Throughout this Module and in the first part of Chapter 4, we provided you with the overall structure of the company's complete database, including the relations of *Order, Truck, Customer, Employee, Concrete Type, Raw Material, Supplier,* and *Bill of Material.*

This is the point at which we'll end this Extended Learning Module. But you shouldn't stop learning. We've written Extended Learning Module G to take you through the process of using a data definition language in Access to create the database for Solomon Enterprises. To help you implement this database, we've provided its complete structure and data dictionary on the Web site that supports this text (www.mcgrawhill.ca/college/haag, select "Solomon Enterprises").

Summary: Student Learning Outcomes Revisited

1. **Identify how databases and spreadsheets are both similar and different.** Databases and spreadsheets are similar in that they both store information in two-dimensional files. They are different in one key aspect: physical versus logical. Spreadsheets require that you know the physical location of information, by row number and column character. Databases, on the other hand, require that you know logically what information you want. For example, in a database environment you could easily request total sales for Able Electronics, and you would receive that information. In a spreadsheet, you would have to know the physical location—by row number and column character—of that information.

2. **List and describe the four steps in designing and building a relational database.** The four steps in designing and building a relational database include

   1. Defining entity classes and primary keys
   2. Defining relationships among entity classes
   3. Defining information (fields) for each relation
   4. Using a data definition language to create your database

3. **Define the concepts of entity class, primary key, instance, and foreign key.** An *entity class* is a concept—typically people, places, or things— about which you wish to store information and that you can identify with a unique key (called a primary key). A *primary key* is a field (or group of fields in some cases) that uniquely describes each record. Within the context of database design, we often refer to a record as an instance. An *instance* is an occurrence of an entity class that can be uniquely described. To provide logical relationships among various entity classes, you use *foreign keys*—primary keys of one file (relation) that also appear in another file (relation).

4. **Given a small operating environment, build an entity-relationship (E-R) diagram.** Building an entity-relationship (E-R) diagram starts with knowing and understanding the business rules that govern the situation. These rules will help you identify entity classes, primary keys, and relationships. You then follow the process of normalization, eliminating many-to-many relationships, assuring that each field is in the correct relation, and removing any derived fields.

5. **List and describe the steps in normalization.** *Normalization* is the process of assuring that a relational database structure can be implemented as a series of two-dimensional tables. The normalization steps include

   1. Eliminate repeating groups or many-to-many relationships.
   2. Assure that each field in a relation depends only on the primary key for that relation.
   3. Remove all derived fields from the relations.

6. **Describe the process of creating an intersection relation to remove a many-to-many relationship.** To create an intersection relation to remove a many-to-many relationship, follow these steps:

   1. Draw the part of the E-R diagram that contains a many-to-many relationship.
   2. Create a new E-R diagram with the original two relations at each end and a new one (the intersection relation) in the middle.
   3. Create a meaningful name for the intersection relation.
   4. Move the minimum cardinality appearing next to the left relation just to the right of the intersection relation.
   5. Move the minimum cardinality appearing next to the right relation just to the left of the intersection relation.
   6. The maximum cardinality on both sides of the intersection relation will always be "many."
   7. As a general rule, the new minimum and maximum cardinalities for the two original relations will be one and one.

Key Terms and Concepts

composite primary key, 280
database, 272
database management system
    (DBMS), 286
data dictionary, 286

entity class, 274
entity-relationship (E-R)
    diagram, 275
foreign key, 280
instance, 274

intersection relation (composite
    relation), 280
normalization, 280
primary key, 274
relational database, 272

Short-Answer Questions

1. How are relational databases and spreadsheets both similar and different?

2. What is a database?

3. What are the four steps in designing and building a relational database?

4. What are some examples of entity classes at your school?

5. What is the role of a primary key?

6. What is an entity-relationship (E-R) diagram?

7. How do business rules help you define minimum and maximum cardinality?

8. What is normalization?

9. What are the three major rules of normalization?

10. What is an intersection relation? Why is it important in designing a relational database?

11. Why must you remove derived information from a database?

12. What is a database management system (DBMS)?

Assignments and Exercises

1. **DEFINING ENTITY CLASSES FOR THE MUSIC INDUSTRY.** The music industry tracks and uses all sorts of information related to numerous entity classes. Find a music CD and carefully review the entire contents of the jacket. List as many entity classes as you can find (for just that CD). Now, go to a music store and pick out a CD for a completely different music genre and read its jacket. Did you find any new entity classes? If so, what are they?

2. **DEFINING BUSINESS RULES FOR A VIDEO RENTAL STORE.** Think about how your local video rental store works. There are many customers, renting many videos, and many videos sit on the shelves unrented. Customers can rent many videos at one time. And some videos are so popular that the video rental store keeps many copies. Write down all the various business rules that define how a video rental store works with respect to entity classes and their relationships.

3. **CREATING AN E-R DIAGRAM FOR A VIDEO RENTAL STORE.** After completing assignment 2 above, draw the initial E-R diagram according to the rules you defined. Don't worry about going through the process of normalization at this point. Simply identify the appropriate relationships among the entity classes and define the minimum and maximum cardinality of each relationship. By the way, how many many-to-many relationships did you define?

4. **ELIMINATING A MANY-TO-MANY RELATIONSHIP.** Consider the following situation. At a small auto parts store, customers can buy many parts. And the same part can be bought by many different customers. That's an example of a many-to-many relationship. How would you eliminate it? What would you call the intersection relation? This one is particularly tough: You'll have to actually create two intersection relations to model this correctly.

5. **DEFINING THE CARDINALITY AMONG TWO ENTITY CLASSES.** Consider the two entity classes of *Student* and *Advisor* at your school. How would you build an E-R diagram to show the relationship between these two entity classes? What are the minimum and the maximum cardinality of the relationship?

EXTENDED LEARNING MODULE D

DECISION ANALYSIS WITH SPREADSHEET SOFTWARE

Student Learning Outcomes

By the end of this Module, students will be able to:

1. Define a list and list definition table within the context of spreadsheet software, and describe the importance of each.

2. Compare and contrast the AutoFilter function and the Custom AutoFilter function in spreadsheet software.

3. Describe the purpose of using conditional formatting.

4. Define a pivot table and describe how you can use it to view summarized information by dimension.

Introduction

As you read in Chapter 6, technology can and does play a vitally important role in both supporting decision making and, in some instances, actually making decisions or recommendations. In this Module, we'll focus on decision-making support, by exploring many of the advanced and productive features of Microsoft Excel.

Microsoft Excel is spreadsheet software that allows you to work with any kind of information, with each individual piece of information located in a cell. A cell is the intersection of a row and a column, and is uniquely identified by its column character and row number. In Figure D.1 you can see a simple workbook (the terms *workbook* and *spreadsheet* are used interchangeably). It shows the number of customers by region (North, South, East, and West) and by "rent" versus "own."

There are a total of 487 customers (cell D9), of which 262 own a home (cell B9) and 225 rent (cell C9). Within this workbook, you can easily see some interesting information. For example, there are 148 customers in the East region while only 98 live in the South region. By region and ownership status, 82 own a home in the East region while only 47 rent in the South region.

Of course, now the question becomes "How is that information helpful?" Well, it depends on the nature of your decision-making task. If you believe that homeowners spend more money than those who rent and want to target advertising to the largest region, the information in Figure D.1 might be helpful. Then again, it might not be. It could very well be that homeowners actually spend less than customers who rent. And perhaps you generate more sales in regions with a lower number of customers.

Let's see how spreadsheet software can help you make better decisions. As we do, we'll introduce you to some spreadsheet features, including AutoFilter, conditional formatting, and pivot tables. Our goal here is not to provide great detail on how each of these work, but rather what's most important about each in supporting your

Figure D.1

Number of Customers by Region and Rent Versus Own

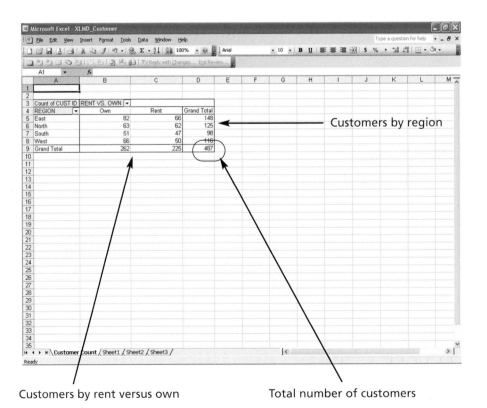

Customers by region

Customers by rent versus own   Total number of customers

decision-making tasks. After completing this Module, you'll definitely be able to use all features in their basic forms. We recommend that you continue to explore them in detail.

Lists

What we showed in Figure D.1 was a *pivot table*—a spreadsheet function that summarizes information by category. In our case, it summarized information by region and rent versus own. To create a pivot table (and use many of the other features we'll discuss in this Module), you have to first build a list. You should work along with us on this. Connect to the Web site that supports this text (www.mcgrawhill.ca/college/haag and select XLM/D). There, you can download the file called XLMD_Customer.xls.

A **list** is a collection of information arranged in columns and rows in which each column displays one particular type of information. In spreadsheet software, a list possesses the following characteristics:

1. Each column has only one type of information.
2. The first row in the list contains the labels or column headings.
3. The list does not contain any blank rows.
4. The list is bordered on all four sides by blank rows and blank columns (it may not have a blank line above it, if it starts in the first row).

Take a look at the workbook in Figure D.2. It contains detailed information about our customers. In fact, we used this very list to generate the pivot table in Figure D.1.

First, notice that each column contains only one type of information: column A contains *CUST ID*, column B contains *REGION*, and so on. Second, notice that the first row (row 1) contains the labels or column headings. Third, if you scroll down

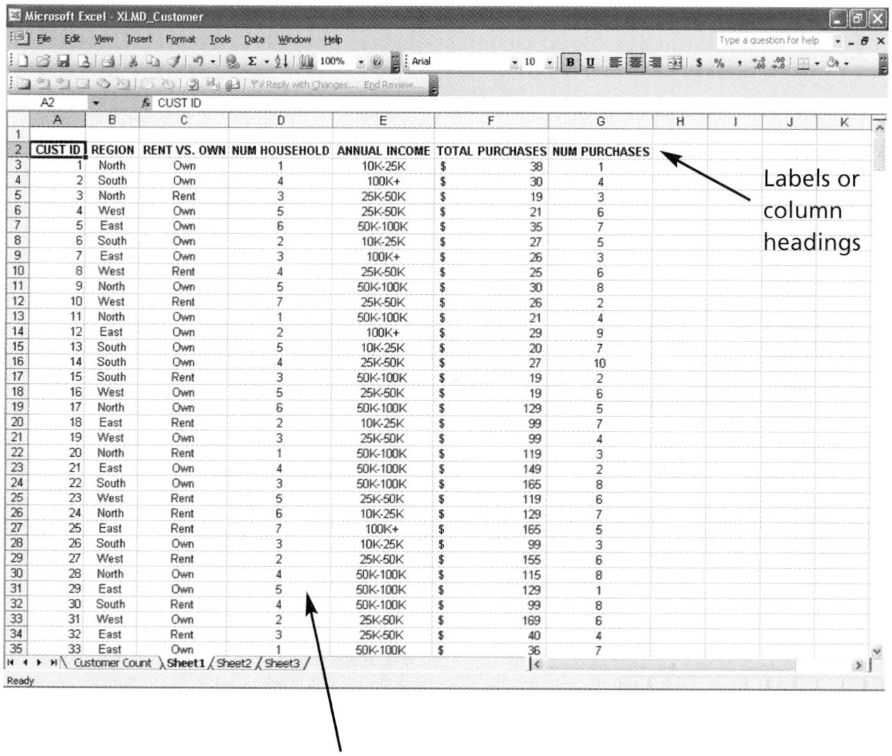

Figure D.2

The Complete List of Customers

Labels or column headings

Each column has only one type of information.

completely through the list, you'll notice that there are 487 customers and there are no blank rows. Finally, notice that the list is bordered on all sides (except the top) by blank rows and columns. So this is a list according to the four characteristics we listed.

We're going to be working extensively with this list throughout this Module, so let's take a little time to explore the information in it. The columns of information include:

A. *CUST ID*. A unique ID for each customer
B. *REGION*. The region in which the customer lives (North, South, East, or West)
C. *RENT VS. OWN*. Whether the customer rents or owns a home
D. *NUM HOUSEHOLD*. The number of family members in the household
E. *ANNUAL INCOME*. The total combined annual income of all family members
F. *TOTAL PURCHASES*. The dollar total of all purchases made by the customer within the past six months
G. *NUM PURCHASES*. A count of all purchases made by the customer within the past six months

What we listed above is called a **list definition table**, a description of a list by column. List definition tables are important. If you can create one just as we did, you can create a list in a workbook with the appropriate characteristics. If you can't, you may not be able to use many of the features we're about to show you.

With the good solid list in place, you're now ready to start exploring many of the decision support features in Excel. Let's assume that you work for our hypothetical retail company and have been asked to perform the following tasks to aid in various decisions:

1. Show all information for only customers who live in the North region.
2. Show all information for only customers who (a) live in the North region, (b) own their homes, and (c) have only one household member.
3. Show all information for customers who have at least 4 household members.
4. Show all information for customers who (a) have spent less than $20 or (b) more than $100.
5. Show all information for all customers highlighting those customers who have spent more than $100.
6. Provide a two-dimensional table that counts the number of customers by the categories of *REGION* and *RENT VS. OWN*.
7. Provide a two-dimensional table that both (a) counts the number of customers and (b) sums the *TOTAL PURCHASES* of customers by the categories of *REGION* and *RENT VS. OWN*.
8. Provide a three-dimensional table that counts the number of customers by the categories of *REGION*, *RENT VS. OWN*, and *NUM HOUSEHOLD*.

Basic AutoFilter

Working with small lists that can be displayed in their entirety on a screen is seldom a problem. With a small list you can see the entire domain of information without scrolling up or down. But our list is much larger, containing 487 customers, so you have to scroll through it to see all the information. If you were looking for specific information, such as all the customers in the North region (your first task in the list above), you could sort using the *REGION* column but you still get all the information (not to mention that customers in the North would come after the customers in the East region, alphabetically).

To quickly create smaller lists out of a much larger list, you can use the **AutoFilter function**, which filters a list and allows you to hide all the rows in a list except those

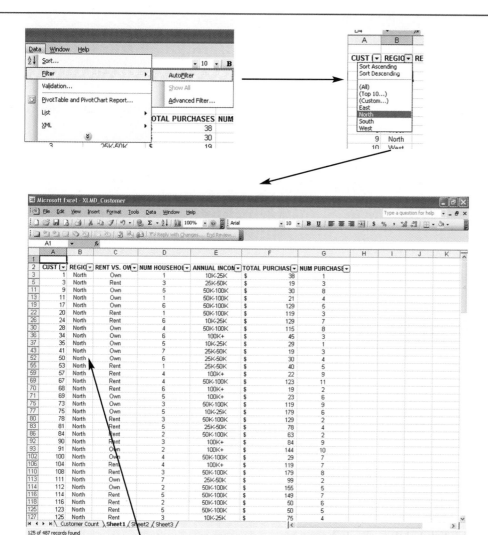

Shows only customers in the North *REGION.*

that match criteria you specify. To filter a list with the AutoFilter function, perform the
following steps (see Figure D.3):

1. Click in any cell within the list.
2. From the menu bar, click on Data, point at Filter, and click on AutoFilter.

Once you complete those two steps, Excel will show list box arrows next to each label
or column heading. Now, all you have to do is click on the appropriate list box arrow
and select the type of filtering you want. In Figure D.3, you can see that we clicked on
the *REGION* list arrow box and chose North. Excel then presented us with a filtered
list of only those customers in the North region. Our list is still quite long, but it does
show only customers in the North. To turn off the AutoFilter function, from the menu
bar, click on Data, point at Filter, and click on AutoFilter.

With the AutoFilter function, you're not limited to working with just one column.
In Figure D.3, we filtered using the *REGION* column. Now, what if you want a filtered
list of those customers in the North who own a home and have only one household
member (your second task in the list)? That's easy. Click in the *RENT VS. OWN* list
arrow box and choose Own. Then, click in the *NUM HOUSEHOLD* list arrow box
and choose 1. That will show you the complete list (4 to be exact) of customers in the
North who own a home and have only one household family member (see Figure D.4).

ON YOUR OWN

LISTS, LIST DEFINITION TABLES, AND USING AUTOFILTER

Now it's your turn to practise using the basic AutoFilter function on a list. Go to the Web site that supports this text (www.mcgrawhill.ca/college/haag), select XLM/D, and download the file called XLMD_Customer2.xls. Take a moment and review the information in that workbook.

First, in the table below, create the list definition for it just as we did earlier.

Now perform the following AutoFilter exercises:

1. Show only those customers in the state of California.

2. Show only those customers whose type of business is nonprofit.

3. Show only those customers in the retail business sector.

4. Show only those customers in Texas whose type of business is government.

5. Show only those customers in the manufacturing business sector.

Column Name	Description

Figure D.4

A List Generated with Three Filters

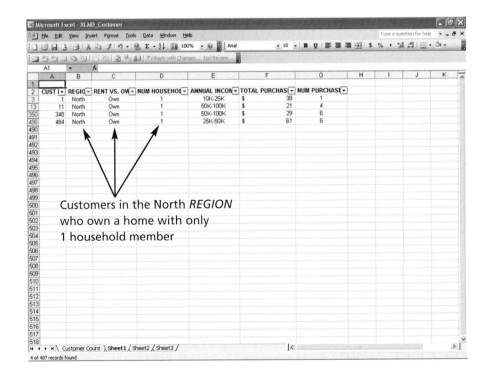

Customers in the North *REGION* who own a home with only 1 household member

Custom AutoFilter

The basic AutoFilter function allows you to create sublists using exact match criteria: *REGION* must be North, *NUM HOUSEHOLD* must be 1, and so forth. But what if you want to know all those customers who have at least four people in their households (your third task in the list)? In that case, you can't use the basic AutoFilter function—you need to use the **Custom AutoFilter function**. This function allows you to hide all the rows in a list except those that match criteria, besides "is equal to," you specify. Let's see how to use Custom AutoFilter.

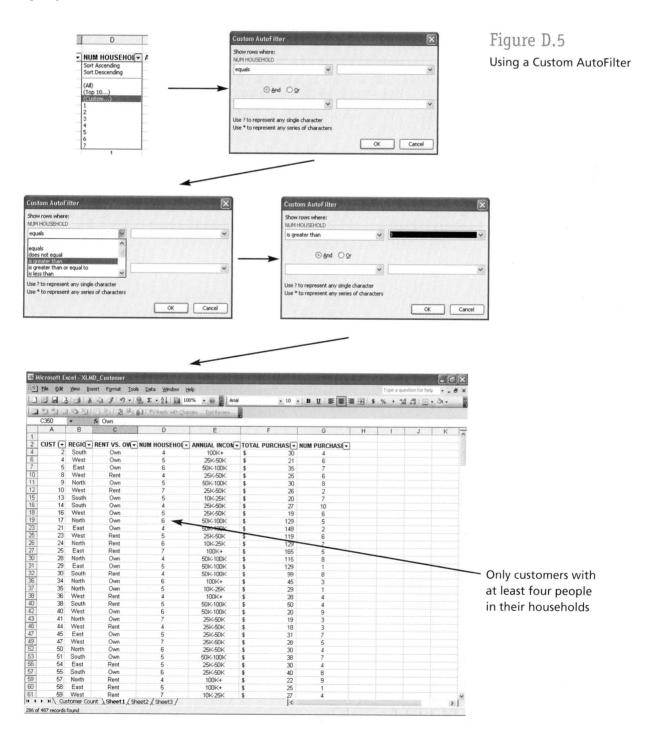

Figure D.5

Using a Custom AutoFilter

Only customers with at least four people in their households

Let's say you want to see a list of all customers who have at least four people in their households. Perform the following steps:

1. Make sure you can see the entire list with the AutoFilter function turned on.
2. Click on the *NUM HOUSEHOLD* list arrow box.
3. Select (Custom . . .)

What you'll then see is a Custom AutoFilter box (the top right box in Figure D.5). For the top-left entry field, click on its pull-down arrow and select Is Greater Than. For the top-right entry box, click on its pull-down arrow and select 3 (or type the number 3 directly into the box). Now all you have to do is click on OK. Excel does the rest and shows you the appropriate list of customers with at least four people in their households.

You should notice in Figure D.5 that the Custom AutoFilter box allows you to enter two criteria for creating a filtered list. So you can easily create a Custom Auto-Filter that answers the following question: What customers have spent less than $20 or more than $100 in the past six months (your fourth task in the list)? In Figure D.6, we've shown you how to do that along with the result.

Figure D.6

Using a Custom AutoFilter with Multiple Criteria

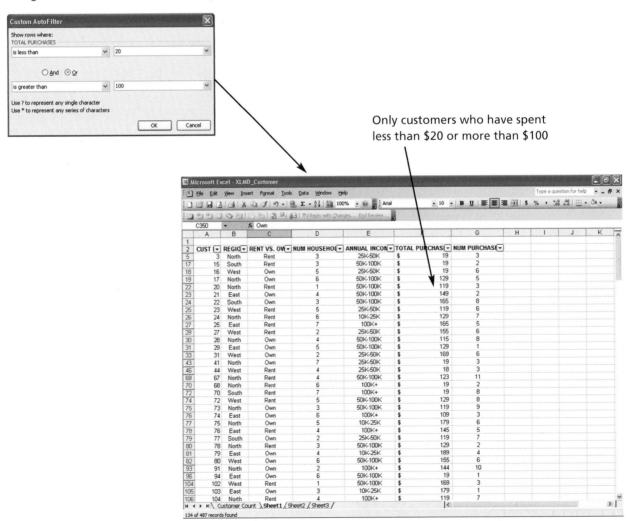

Only customers who have spent less than $20 or more than $100

USING CUSTOM AUTOFILTERS

Now it's your turn to practise using the Custom AutoFilter function on a list. Go to the Web site that supports this text (www.mcgrawhill.ca/college/haag), select XLM/D, and download the file XLMD_Customer2.xls (the same one you used previously for the On Your Own project). Now perform the following Custom AutoFilter exercises:

1. Show only those customers who have more than 100 employees.

2. Show only those customers who have fewer than 100 employees.

3. Show only those customers who have at least 50 employees but no more than 100 employees.

4. Show only those customers in Tennessee who have fewer than 10 employees.

Conditional Formatting

When you use AutoFilter (either basic or custom), in a way you're highlighting information you want to see by basically hiding the other information you don't. As an alternative, you might want to highlight certain information while still being able to see all the other information. If so, you can use **conditional formatting**, which highlights all information that meets some criteria you specify.

For example, what if you still wanted to be able to scroll through the entire list of customers but also wanted to have all *TOTAL PURCHASES* greater than $100 highlighted (your fifth task in the list). This is a simple process in Excel (see Figure D.7):

1. Select the entire *TOTAL PURCHASES* column (move the pointer over the F column identifier and click once).
2. From the menu bar, click on Format and then click on Conditional Formatting.

You will then see a Conditional Formatting box (as shown in the middle-left of the figure).

Now click on the pull-down arrow for the field second from the left and click on Greater Than. In the field on the right, enter 100. Finally, you need to select the conditional formatting for the information. To do so, click on the Format button. You will then see a Format Cells box. Across the top, you'll see tabs for Font, Border, and Patterns.

In our example, we clicked on the Patterns tab, chose the colour red, and clicked on OK. Excel returned us to the Conditional Formatting box, at which time we clicked on the OK button. As you can see in Figure D.8, Excel left the list intact and highlighted all cells in the *TOTAL PURCHASES* column in which the value exceeded $100.

To remove conditional formatting, first highlight the entire column again. Second, from the menu bar, click on Format and click on Conditional Formatting. Third, click on the Delete button in the Conditional Formatting box. Fourth, select Condition 1 in the Delete Conditional Format box. Finally, click on OK in the Delete Conditional Format box, and click on OK in the Conditional Format box.

Figure D.7

The Steps in Applying Conditional Formatting to Highlight Information

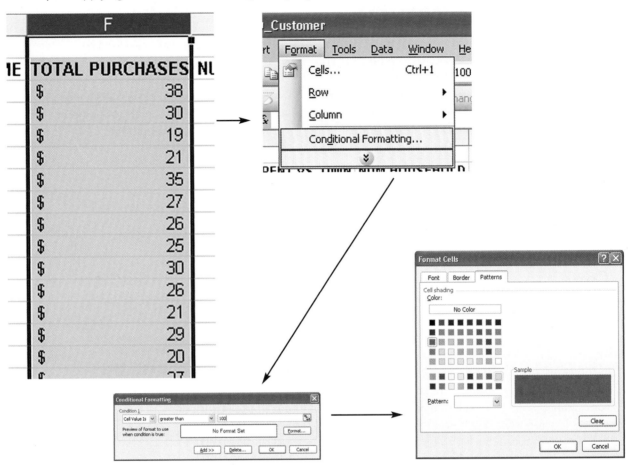

Figure D.8

The Result of Applying Conditional Formatting

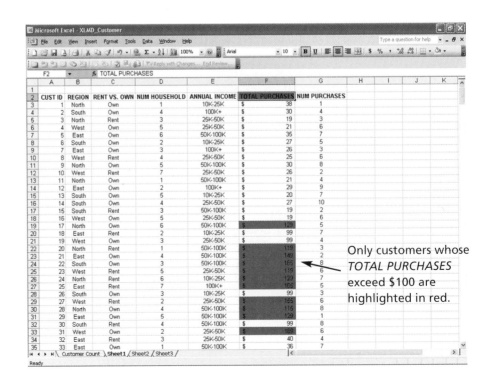

Only customers whose *TOTAL PURCHASES* exceed $100 are highlighted in red.

CONDITIONAL FORMATTING

On the Web site that supports this text (www.mcgraw hill.ca/college/haag and select XLMD), we've provided a workbook titled XLMD_Production.xls. It contains information concerning batches of products produced. Each batch is produced using only one machine by one employee. For each batch, a batch size is provided as well as the number of defective products produced in the batch.

Highlight the following by applying conditional formatting:

1. All batches made by Employee 1111.
2. All batches for which the number of defective products is greater than 10.
3. All batches for which the batch size is greater than 1000.
4. All batches for Product 10.

Pivot Tables

Now, let's return to our original pivot table in Figure D.1. Formally defined, a **pivot table** enables you to group and summarize information. That's just what we did in Figure D.1. We created a two-dimensional pivot table that displayed a count of customers by *REGION* and by *RENT VS. OWN* (your sixth task in the list). Of all the Excel decision-support features we demonstrate in this Module, pivot tables take the most steps to create, but they also tend to yield highly valuable information.

Figure D.9

The First Steps in Creating a Two-Dimensional Pivot Table

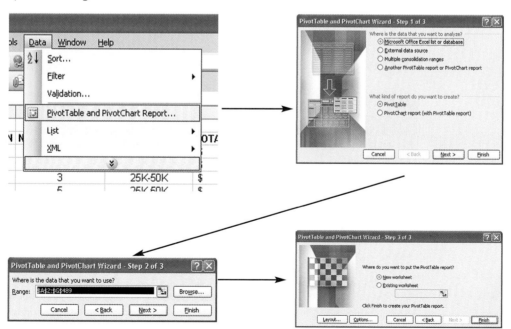

To create a two-dimensional pivot table, first ensure that your list has no conditional formatting and that you do not have the AutoFilter function turned on. To create any two-dimensional pivot table, follow these four steps (and see Figure D.9):

1. From the menu bar, click on Data and PivotTable and PivotChart Report.
2. In the Step 1 of 3 box, click on Next.
3. In the Step 2 of 3 box, click on Next.
4. In the Step 3 of 3 box, click on Finish.

What you will then see is the skeletal structure of a pivot table as shown in Figure D.10.

Figure D.10

The Skeletal Structure of a Pivot Table and the Pivot Table Toolbar

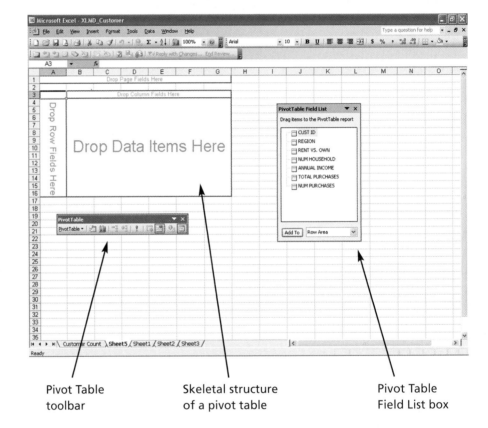

Pivot Table toolbar

Skeletal structure of a pivot table

Pivot Table Field List box

BUTTON NAME	PURPOSE
PivotTable	Drop-down that displays shortcut menu of pivot table commands
Format Report	Displays a list of pivot table report styles
Chart Wizard	Creates a chart sheet from a pivot table
MapPoint	Creates map from PivotTable data
Hide Detail	Hides detail lines of a pivot table field
Show Detail	Reveals detail lines of a pivot table field
Refresh Data	Updates a pivot table
Include Hidden Items in Total	Items you have hidden are still counted in the PivotTable totals
Always Display Items	Controls when Excel goes to an external data source to determine a pivot table value
Field Settings	Opens the PivotTable field dialog box containing options you can apply to the selected pivot table field
Hide/Show Field Test	Toggles between hiding and displaying the field list

To provide a brief explanation of what we've done so far, let's examine the three dialog boxes in Figure D.9. The first box allows you to choose the location of the information from which you want to build a pivot table. We wanted to use an Excel list so we accepted the default. The first box also gives you the ability to choose between creating a pivot table or a pivot table chart. We wanted a pivot table, so we accepted the default.

The second box allows you to choose a range of information from which to build a pivot table. The default is the entire list, which we accepted. Finally, the third box allows you to specify a location for the pivot table. The default is a new worksheet, which we accepted. At some point in time, you should explore the various other options.

What you see in Figure D.10 takes some more explaining. In the upper left portion is the skeletal structure of the pivot table. To the right, you can see the Pivot Table Field List box. It includes a list of all the labels or column headings we have in the list.

Near the bottom left, you can see the Pivot Table toolbar. It includes numerous buttons for different functions. The primary one of interest to us now is the Field Settings button, the second button from the right in the toolbar. Figure D.10 lists and explains all the buttons in the Pivot Table toolbar.

What you do now is to drag and drop the appropriate labels or columns headings from the Pivot Table Field List box into the appropriate areas of the pivot table itself.

Recall that we are attempting to build a two-dimensional pivot table that looks like the one in Figure D.1. So, you know that the row information is by *REGION*. To achieve this, drag the *REGION* label from the Pivot Table Field List box to the pivot table and drop it into the area marked "Drop Row Fields Here" (see Figure D.11). You also know that the column information is by *RENT VS. OWN*. So drag that label from the Pivot Table Field List box and drop it into the area marked "Drop Column Fields Here."

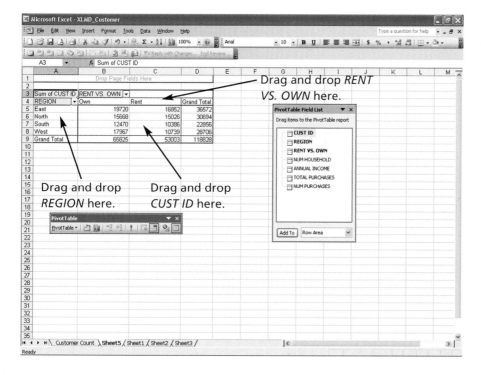

Figure D.11

Creating a Pivot Table by Dragging and Dropping Information

Figure D.12

The Pivot Table with the Information You Want

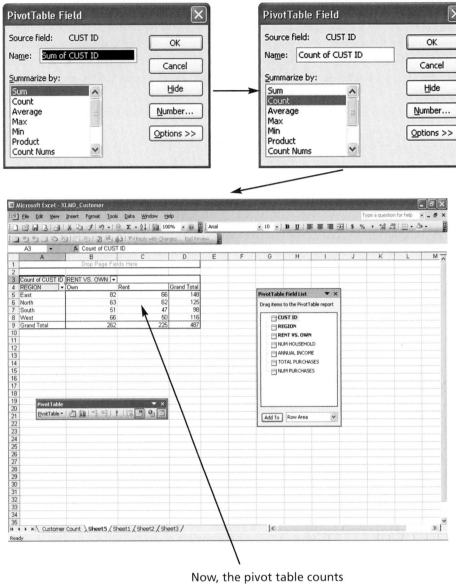

Now, the pivot table counts the number of customers.

Finally, you need to place something in the main area of the pivot table that will enable you to count customers by region and rent versus own. The simplest way to achieve this is to drag *CUST ID* from the Pivot Table Field List box and drop it into the area marked "Drop Data Items Here." What you will then have is a pivot table that looks like the screen in Figure D.11, which is not at all what we want. Why?

When you drop information into the main area of a pivot table, the default aggregation or summarization is by summation. You don't want to sum customer IDs—that doesn't make any sense. What you want to do is count them. To change this, perform the following steps (see Figure D.12):

1. Click on the Field Settings button in the Pivot Table toolbar.
2. In the PivotTable Field box, click on Count in the Summarize By list.
3. Click on OK.

The final screen in Figure D.12 shows the correct information.

CREATING A TWO-DIMENSIONAL PIVOT TABLE

Let's return to our workbook containing production information (XLMD_Production.xls). Using it, create separate pivot tables that show:

- The number of different machines used to produce each product
- The number of defective products produced by employee by product

- The total number of products produced by each employee
- The total number of products produced by each employee as well as the total number of defective products produced by each employee

We now have a pivot table that shows a count of customers by *REGION* and *RENT VS. OWN*. But depending on what decision you're trying to make, that may not be enough information. What else might be helpful? Again, depending on the decision, it might be helpful to also know the total of all purchases by *REGION* and *RENT VS. OWN* (your seventh task in the list). If so, you don't need to create another pivot table. You can simply add the field *TOTAL PURCHASES* to the main area of the pivot table. To do so, drag that label from the Pivot Table Field List box and drop it into the main area of the pivot table. Figure D.13 shows the result.

Is the information helpful? Again, it depends on the decision you're trying to make. But adding another piece of information to the main area of a pivot table is easy, and it does illustrate the true productivity of spreadsheet software.

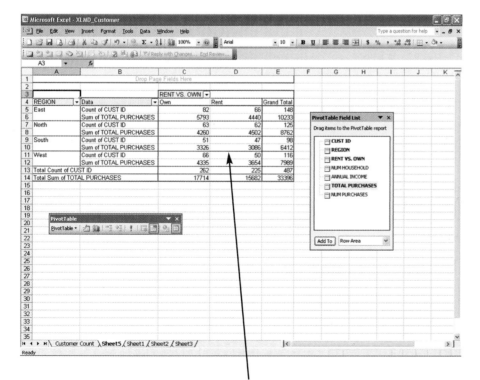

Figure D.13

An Added Field of Information to a Pivot Table

Drag and drop *TOTAL PURCHASES* here to obtain a summary of another dimension of information.

Your final task in the list is to create a three-dimensional pivot table that counts the number of customers by the categories of *REGION, RENT VS. OWN,* and *NUM HOUSEHOLD.* The result will look similar to the two-dimensional pivot table in Figure D.13 with two exceptions. First, you will not include the sum of *TOTAL PURCHASES* in the main area of the pivot table. Second, you will add depth to the pivot table, making it three-dimensional. In short, you do this by dragging the *NUM HOUSEHOLD* label from the Pivot Table Field List box to the pivot table and dropping it into the area marked "Drop Page Fields Here."

In Figure D.14, you can see in the upper left screen that we created a two-dimensional pivot table showing a count of customers by *REGION* and *RENT VS. OWN.* This is the same two-dimensional pivot table we created in Figure D.12. To add depth to the pivot table, we dragged the *NUM HOUSEHOLD* label from the Pivot Table Field List box to the pivot table and dropped it into the area marked "Drop Page Fields Here." Notice that the new pivot table (the lower right screen in Figure D.14) still looks like a two-dimensional pivot table and provides the same information in the main area of the pivot table. That's because the default display for a three-dimensional pivot table is to show all summarized information for the depth. You can tell this because to the right of *NUM HOUSEHOLD* in cell A1 is the word "All."

Figure D.14

Creating a Three-Dimensional Pivot Table

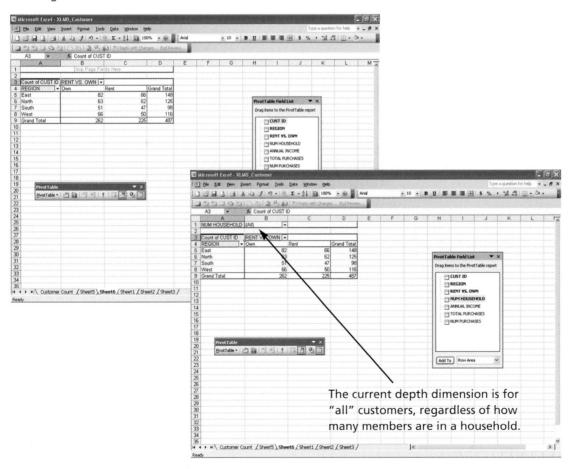

The current depth dimension is for "all" customers, regardless of how many members are in a household.

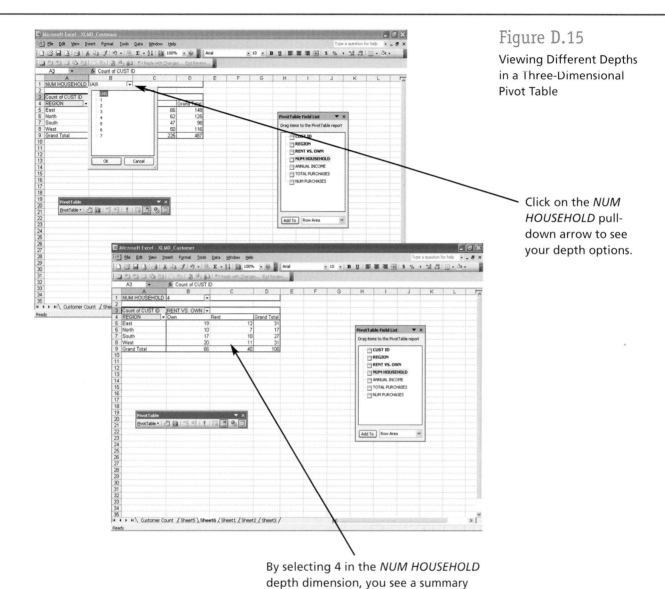

Figure D.15

Viewing Different Depths
in a Three-Dimensional
Pivot Table

Click on the *NUM
HOUSEHOLD* pull-
down arrow to see
your depth options.

By selecting 4 in the *NUM HOUSEHOLD*
depth dimension, you see a summary
of customers for only that criterion.

To view the count of your customers according to specific values for *NUM HOUSEHOLD,* simply click on the list box arrow immediately to the right of the word "All" as we did in the top screen in Figure D.15. You then click on the value you want in *NUM HOUSEHOLD* for displaying the count of customers for that value by *REGION* and *RENT VS. OWN.* We clicked on 4 and then OK. The bottom screen in Figure D.15 shows the result. It shows some interesting information that might help you make a decision. For example, in the West region there are 20 customers who own their homes and only 11 who rent their homes. Furthermore, across all regions there are 66 customers who own their homes and only 40 who rent. Again, is this helpful information? That depends on the decision you're trying to make.

The three-dimensional pivot table feature in Excel is a powerful one. If you recall our discussions of data warehouses in Chapter 4, you can actually build a data warehouse with rows, columns, and layers by simply creating a three-dimensional pivot table in Excel. By selecting different values for the page (depth) field, you are actually bringing layers of information to the front.

Back to Decision Support

Let's take a break from the computer for a moment and discuss what we've just demonstrated within the context of decision support. After all, you don't need to learn the various tools of spreadsheet software just "because they are there." You should learn them because they will be beneficial to you.

In general, the spreadsheet features we've just shown you give you the ability to look at vast amounts of information quickly. Indeed, our customer workbook contained information on 487 customers. Can you imagine trying to summarize or aggregate information on 48,700 customers without the use of spreadsheet software? Even creating simple totals and subtotals would be a daunting task.

AUTOFILTER

The AutoFilter function (either basic or custom) helps you quickly create a view of a partial list of information. The basic AutoFilter function creates a partial list based on exact match criteria, while the custom AutoFilter function allows you to specify ranges (e.g., greater than, less than, and so on).

The purpose of the AutoFilter function is really to help you quickly focus on only the information that's important to you by "hiding" the information that isn't. It's rather like having a very good search engine that only gives you a list of useful articles to help you write a term paper.

CONDITIONAL FORMATTING

Conditional formatting maintains the view of the entire list of information but highlights key pieces of information that you may be looking for. This gives you the ability to see the entire list of information but quickly draws your attention to specific information.

PIVOT TABLE

A pivot table (either two- or three-dimensional) helps you quickly aggregate or summarize information by *dimension*. This gives you a nice overview of the information without bogging you down in any of the details.

Further, a pivot table can help you see relationships in the information. If you look back at the pivot table in Figure D.13, you can see the relationship between the number of customers and their total purchases within *REGION* and *RENT VS. OWN*. These types of relationships can certainly be insightful.

Can any of these tools or functions make a decision for you? Definitely not. But they can help you make that decision. That's why spreadsheet software is often called *decision support* software.

Summary: Student Learning Outcomes Revisited

1. **Define a list and list definition table within the context of spreadsheet software, and describe the importance of each.** A *list* is a collection of information arranged in columns and rows in which each column displays one particular type of information. A *list definition table* is a description of a list by column. Lists are important within the context of spreadsheet software because they enable you to use such spreadsheet features as AutoFilter, conditional formatting, and pivot tables. Creating a list definition table is important because it requires you to adhere to the necessary rules for creating a list.

2. **Compare and contrast the AutoFilter function and the Custom AutoFilter function in spreadsheet software.** The *AutoFilter function* filters a list and allows you to hide all the rows in a list except those that match specific criteria you specify. The *Custom AutoFilter function* allows you to hide all the rows in a list except those that match criteria, besides "is equal to," you specify. So, the basic AutoFilter function makes use of "is equal to" as the criteria, while the Custom AutoFilter function allows you to use other criteria such as greater than, less than, and so on.

3. **Describe the purpose of using conditional formatting.** *Conditional formatting* highlights the information in a cell that meets some criteria you specify. So, conditional formatting allows you to view the entire list while having certain information called to your attention.

4. **Define a pivot table and describe how you can use it to view summarized information by dimension.** A *pivot table* enables you to group and summarize information. When creating a pivot table, you create dimensions of information by specifying how information is to be summarized by dimension. You define the dimensions by dragging and dropping information labels or column headings into the row, column, and page areas of a pivot table.

Key Terms and Concepts

AutoFilter function, 292
conditional formatting, 297

Custom AutoFilter function, 295
list, 291

list definition table, 292
pivot table, 299

Assignments and Exercises

1. **WHAT PRODUCTION PROBLEMS DO YOU HAVE?** Throughout this Module, you've been practising some spreadsheet features using XLMD_Production.xls. Its list definition table is as follows:

   A. *BATCH.* A unique number that identifies each batch or group of products produced
   B. *PRODUCT.* A unique number that identifies each product
   C. *MACHINE.* A unique number that identifies each machine on which products are produced
   D. *EMPLOYEE.* A unique number that identifies each employee producing products
   E. *BATCH SIZE.* The number of products produced in a given batch
   F. *NUM DEFECTIVE.* The number of defective products produced in a given batch

   It seems you have some real problems. There are an unacceptable number of defective products being produced. Your task is to use some combination of AutoFilter, conditional formatting, and pivot tables to illustrate where the problems seem to be concentrated, perhaps by product, by employee, by machine, or even by batch size. On the basis of your analysis, recommend how to correct the problems.

2. **EVALUATING TOTAL PURCHASES AND ANNUAL INCOME.** Using XLMD_Customer.xls, create a pivot table that illustrates the relationship between *TOTAL PURCHASES* and *ANNUAL INCOME*. What trends do you see in the information? Suppose your task is to concentrate marketing efforts and resources. On which annual income level would you concentrate? Why? If you were the marketing manager, what additional information would be helpful as you make your decision? Where would you be able to obtain such information?

3. **FINDING OUT INFORMATION ABOUT YOUR EMPLOYEES.** Suppose you own a small business and have a workbook with the following list:

   A. *ID*. Unique employee's identification number
   B. *First Name*. Employee's first name
   C. *Last Name*. Employee's last name
   D. *Department*. Employee's department
   E. *Title*. Employee's job title
   F. *Salary*. Employee's annual salary
   G. *Hire Date*. Date employee was hired
   H. *Birth Date*. Employee's birthday
   I. *Gender*. Female (F) or male (M)
   J. *Clearance*. N (none), C (confidential), S (secret), or TS (top secret)

   You can obtain this workbook from the Web site that supports this text (www.mcgrawhill.ca/college/haag and select XLM/D). Its filename is XLMD_Employee.xls. Perform the following tasks:

   a. Create a pivot table that shows average salary by gender within department.
   b. Create a pivot table that shows the number of employees by clearance.
   c. Use conditional formatting to highlight those employees in the Engineering department.
   d. Use conditional formatting to highlight those employees who have no clearance (none).
   e. Use basic AutoFilter to show only those employees who have top secret clearance (TS).
   f. Use Custom AutoFilter to show only those employees who earn more than $50,000.

4. **EXPLORING INFORMATION AT B&B TRAVEL.** Benjamin Travis and Brady Austin are co-owners of B&B Travel Consultants, a medium-size business in Vancouver with several branch offices. B&B specializes in selling cruise packages. Ben and Brady maintain a workbook that contains the following list for each cruise package sale:

   A. *LOCATION #*. A unique number that identifies which office location recorded the sale
   B. *TRAVEL AGENT #*. A unique number that identifies which travel consultant recorded the sale
   C. *CRUISE LINE*. The name of the cruise line for which the package was sold
   D. *TOTAL PACKAGE PRICE*. The price charged to the customer for the package
   E. *COMMISSION*. The amount of money B&B made from the sale of the package

   Ben and Brady have decided to scale back their operations. They're looking to you for help. The workbook name is XLMD_Travel.xls, and you can find it on the Web site that supports this text at www.mcgrawhill.ca/college/haag (select XLM/D). Using AutoFilter, conditional formatting, and pivot tables, prepare a short report that answers each of the following questions and illustrates the justification for your answers:

   a. Which, if any, location should be closed?
   b. Which, if any, travel consultants should be downsized?
   c. On which cruise lines should B&B focus its sales efforts?

5. **CREATE A LIST FOR A BOOKSTORE.** Suppose that you're the manager for your school's bookstore. Your task is to create a list in a workbook that contains information about the textbooks it sells. In addition to tracking price, first author name, and publisher, identify five other pieces of information for each textbook. For this list, first provide a list definition table. Second, enter some information for 20 textbooks. Third, illustrate the use of the basic AutoFilter function, the Custom AutoFilter function, conditional formatting, and pivot tables. Finally, address how your bookstore might be able to use this information to support its decision-making tasks.

EXTENDED LEARNING MODULE E

NETWORK BASICS

Student Learning Outcomes

By the end of this Module, students will be able to:

1. Identify and describe the four basic concepts on which networks are built.

2. List the components you need to set up a small peer-to-peer network at home.

3. Compare and contrast the various Internet connection possibilities.

4. Describe client/server business networks from a business and physical point of view.

5. Define local area networks (LANs), municipal area networks (MANs), wireless local area networks (WLANs), and wide area networks (WANs).

6. Compare and contrast the types of communications media.

Taking Advantage of the CD

When you're surfing the Web, accessing software on your school's server, sending e-mail, or letting your roommate use his/her computer to access the files on your computer, your computer is part of a network. A **computer network** (which we simply refer to as a network) is two or more computers connected so that they can communicate with each other and share information, software, peripheral devices, and/or processing power. Many networks have dozens, hundreds, or even thousands of computers.

Networks come in all sizes from two computers connected to share a printer, to the Internet, which is the largest network on the planet, joining millions of computers of all kinds all over the world. In between are business networks, which vary in size from a dozen or fewer computers to many thousands.

Some networks are extremely complex with perhaps thousands of computers connected together. These networks require highly skilled professionals to keep them up and running. However, regardless of their size, some basic principles apply to all networks:

1. Every computer on a network must have a network interface (either as an expansion card or integrated into the motherboard or through software for a modem) that provides the entrance or doorway for information traffic to and from other computers.
2. A network usually has at least one connecting device (such a hub or a router) that ties the computers on the network together and acts as a switchboard for passing information.
3. There must be communications media like cables or radio waves connecting network hardware devices. The communications media transport information around the network between computers and the connecting device(s).
4. Every computer must have software that supports the movement of information in and out of it. This might be modem software and/or a network operating system.

We definitely believe that it's worth your time and energy to pop in the CD and read this Module. Like the Modules in your text, it includes Team Work and On Your Own projects and great end-of-Module Assignments and Exercises. In it, you'll learn many things including:

- How to build a peer-to-peer network at home or in your dorm with network cards, cabling, and a network connecting device
- Five ways to connect to the Internet:
  - Phone line and dial-up modem
  - Phone line and digital subscriber line (DSL) modem
  - Cable TV line and cable modem
  - Satellite dish and satellite modem
  - Wireless access points
- How to add wireless access to a network
- Client/server networks from a business point of view
- Client/server networks from a physical point of view
- What differentiates LANs, MANs, WLANs, and WANs
- The types of telecommunications media that networks use

EXTENDED LEARNING MODULE F

OBJECT-ORIENTED TECHNOLOGIES

Student Learning Outcomes

By the end of this Module, students will be able to:

1. Explain the primary difference between the traditional technology approach and the object-oriented technology approach.

2. List and describe the five primary object-oriented concepts.

3. Explain how classes and objects are related.

4. Describe the three fundamental principles of object-oriented technologies.

5. List and describe two types of object-oriented technologies.

Taking Advantage of the CD

The explosion of object-oriented technologies is radically changing the way businesses view information and develop information systems. Object-oriented technologies are everywhere in the business world today. It's difficult to find a business or IT department that isn't using them. Every single Fortune 500 company is using some type. System developers everywhere are quickly learning how to write software in object-oriented programming languages, create databases using object-oriented database management systems, and design new systems using object-oriented analysis and design techniques. The race to learn and understand the special concepts of this field began many years ago and is still going strong.

Extended Learning Module F, found on the CD that accompanies this text, provides an easily understandable explanation of object-oriented technologies. Like the Modules in your text, it includes Team Work and On Your Own projects and end-of-Module Assignments and Exercises.

One of the primary goals of this Module is to introduce you to the object-oriented approach for developing information systems. By taking a look at the traditional technology approach for developing such systems, you'll quickly understand the advantages of the object-oriented approach. The *object-oriented (OO) approach* combines information and procedures into a single view. This statement probably seems a bit confusing but, after reading this Module, it will become crystal-clear. Just remember that the key to understanding the object-oriented approach is to recognize that combining information and procedures is quite different from the traditional technology approach in which information is separated from procedures. Some of the other important object-oriented concepts you'll be introduced to include:

- The *traditional technology approach*, which has two primary views of any system—information and procedures—and keeps these two views separate and distinct at all times
- The five primary concepts of object-oriented technologies:
  1. *Information* as key characteristics stored within a system
  2. A *procedure* that manipulates or changes information
  3. A *class* that contains information and procedures and acts as a template to create objects (instances of a class)
  4. An *object* which is an instance of a class
  5. *Messages* that allow objects to communicate with each other
- The three fundamental principles of object-oriented technologies which are inheritance, encapsulation, and polymorphism
- Several real-world object-oriented examples
- A detailed business case example, Ice Blue Snowboards, Inc., in which you can apply your object-oriented knowledge
- Three types of object-oriented technologies: object-oriented programming languages, object-oriented databases, and object-oriented technologies and client/server environments

Be sure to take advantage of this Module on your CD. You'll be taking a giant leap toward understanding object-oriented concepts. You might already be familiar with a few of the key concepts related to these technologies—information, procedures, classes, objects, or messages. But if you're unfamiliar with these concepts, there's no need to worry, because you'll gain a solid understanding of each in this Module.

EXTENDED LEARNING MODULE G

IMPLEMENTING A DATABASE WITH MICROSOFT ACCESS

Student Learning Outcomes

By the end of this Module, students will be able to:

1. Identify the steps necessary to implement the structure of a relational database using the data definition language provided by Microsoft Access.

2. Demonstrate how to use the data manipulation subsystem in Access to enter and change information in a database and how to query that information.

3. Explain the use of the application generation subsystem in Access to create reports and data entry screens.

In Chapter 4 we discussed the important role that databases play in an organization. We followed that with Extended Learning Module C, in which you learned how to design the correct structure of a relational database. That Module includes four primary steps:

1. Defining entity classes and primary keys
2. Defining relationships among entity classes
3. Defining information (fields) for each relation (the term *relation* is often used to refer to a file while designing a database)
4. Using a data definition language to create your database

In Extended Learning Module C, you followed the process through the first three steps above. In this Module, we'll take you through the fourth step—using a data definition language to create your database—by exploring the use of Microsoft Access, today's most popular personal database management system package (it comes as a standard part of Microsoft Office Professional suite).

You'll find this Extended Learning Module on the CD that accompanies this text. In it, we've included coverage of:

• Creating a simple query using one relation
• Creating an advanced query using more than one relation
• Generating a simple report
• Generating a report with grouping, sorting, and totals
• Creating a data input form

We believe this material is vitally important. As the business world increasingly moves toward empowering employees with technology tools, you'll be better prepared for the job market if you know how to design, implement, and access a database. Module C covered how to design a database, and this one covers how to implement and access a database using Microsoft Access.

If you need proof of the growing importance of databases, just connect to any job database Web site and enter "Microsoft Access" as a search term. We did that at Monster.ca (www.monster.ca) and found over 550 job listings requiring expertise in Microsoft Access. Some of the job titles included:

• Financial Analysis Manager
• Education Administrator
• Logistics Engineer
• Military Intelligence
• Corporate Trust Administrator
• Market Research Analyst
• Medical Finance Coordinator
• Guest Satisfaction Agent
• Training Coordinator
• Data Consumption Analyst
• Project Manager
• Retail Support Analyst
• Quality Engineer
• Reinsurance Accountant

If you look carefully at the above list, you'll see that not a single job title is IT-specific. Rather, the titles represent job openings in such areas as finance, hospitality, logistics, retail sales, medicine, and insurance.

We applaud you for popping in the CD and reading this Module.

SECTION TWO
GROUP PROJECTS

Taking Advantage of the CD

The following group projects are Cases that reflect the concepts and skills you've learned in Section Two: Developing and Using Technology Effectively.

Case 6: Using Relational Technology to Track Projects
Phillips Construction

Case 7: Building a Decision Support System
Creating an Investment Portfolio

Case 8: Outsourcing Information Technology
A&A Software: Creating Forecasts

Case 9: Making the Case with Presentation Software
Information Technology Ethics

Case 10: Should I Buy or Should I Lease?
Decision Support Systems

Case 11: Decision Support System
Breakeven Analysis

Case 12: Financing
Creating a Conventional Mortgage Worksheet

Case 13: Scheduling
Airline Crew Scheduling

SECTION THREE
MOVING ALONG

CHAPTER SEVEN

STUDENT LEARNING OUTCOMES

BY THE END OF THIS CHAPTER, STUDENTS WILL BE ABLE TO:

1. Define and describe the two major e-commerce business models (business-to-business and business-to-consumer) as well as e-commerce and e-business.

2. Summarize Porter's Five Forces Model and how business people can use it to understand the relative attractiveness of an industry.

3. Describe the emerging role of e-marketplaces in B2B e-commerce.

4. Identify the differences and similarities among customers and their perceived value of products and services in the B2B and B2C e-commerce business models.

5. Compare and contrast the development of a marketing mix for customers in the B2B and B2C e-commerce business models.

6. Summarize the various ways of moving money in the world of e-commerce and related issues, including electronic payment systems.

WEB SUPPORT

- Competitive Intelligence

- Storefront Software

- Hosting Services

- Marketing Your Site

Visit
www.mcgrawhill.ca/college/haag

ELECTRONIC COMMERCE
Strategies for the New Economy

CASE STUDY:

IS AMERICA ONLINE (AOL) INCHING TOWARD BECOMING AN INTERNET BANK?

In March 2004, America Online (AOL) launched a streamlined new service for online bill payment. No—it doesn't yet provide the capability to pay online bills directly through AOL, but it does seem to be a step by AOL toward making that a reality.

The service—called AOL Bill Pay—is free to all AOL members and is provided through an alliance with Yodlee.com, Inc. (www.yodlee.com), a company that provides a variety of online personal financial services. After AOL members sign up for the service, they will receive summaries of their online bills via AOL e-mail messages. The messages will include links directly to the business e-commerce Web sites where members can make their payments.

A nice feature of AOL Bill Pay is that it creates a single portal (the AOL account) with only one user ID and one password. Once inside his or her AOL account, an AOL member does not have to enter a new ID and password at any of the e-commerce Web sites.

AOL members can configure AOL Bill Pay to provide alerts in several different forms: e-mail, instant messaging, or a text-based message to a cell phone. The system can also trigger an alert that is more of a warning message when, for example, an AOL member's bank account balance drops below a certain limit or a credit card transaction exceeds a certain amount. It is AOL's hope that its members will see these types of alerts and warnings as value-added services.

AOL Bill Pay connects directly to over 2500 Web sites that offer bill paying over the Internet. If a certain AOL member makes payments to a Web site not on AOL Bill Pay's list, AOL can easily add the site to the list.

Even so, some users may be wary of using such a service. According to Patrick Mahoney, an analyst with The Yankee Group, "Some people may prefer going to individual Web sites instead of having the one-password access to everything." But Patrick does think this is a good business model for AOL. He explains, "Although some companies provide this type of service, the market isn't overcrowded and existing offerings haven't been highly publicized. It's not like AOL is coming into a market with a lot of competition."

Just like in the traditional brick-and-mortar business environment, in the world of e-commerce you must constantly strive to stay ahead of the competition. You have to determine innovative ways to offer products and services that your customers will perceive as adding value. You must constantly evaluate industry segments and competitive spaces to determine if there is a lack of competition where you might enter.

In this chapter you'll explore the world of e-commerce, and we'll introduce you to many "special" considerations to take into account to be successful. Commerce will always be commerce—the buying and selling of products and services. But the "e" brings new challenges and opportunities.[1]

Introduction

You've probably heard the ancient Chinese curse, "May you live in interesting times." It's a curse because it is often easier to live in times that are not so interesting, when things move along pretty much as expected, as they always have. The past ten years of the new economy introduced by the World Wide Web have certainly been interesting. There has been an entrepreneurial frenzy unlike anything the world has ever seen. Fortunes have been made and lost. Dot-com millionaires and billionaires were literally created overnight—many became dot-bomb paupers in about the same amount of time.

What fuelled this frenzy and is still doing so today? It's electronic commerce enabled by information technology. **Electronic commerce (e-commerce)** is commerce, but it is commerce accelerated and enhanced by IT, in particular the Internet. E-commerce enables customers, consumers, and companies to form powerful new relationships that would not be possible without the enabling technologies. E-commerce breaks down business barriers such as time, geography, language, currency, and culture. In a few short hours, you can set up shop on the Internet and be instantly accessible to millions of consumers worldwide. The Internet facilitates commerce because of its awesome ability to move digital information at low cost.

Is there a catch? The answer is both no and yes. It's "no" because it doesn't take much effort to create your own e-commerce Web site. It's "yes" because you still have to follow sound business fundamentals and principles to be successful. Let's not forget that fundamentally it's still all about commerce—businesses and people buying and selling products and services. It is no silver bullet, as some entrepreneurs have found out to their chagrin. You must know your competition; you must have insight into your customers' demographics and buying habits; you must offer your products and services at a superior price or at a superior level of service to beat the competition; you must make a profit.

As illustrated in Figure 7.1, there are four main perspectives for e-commerce: business-to-business (B2B), business-to-consumer (B2C), consumer-to-business (C2B), and consumer-to-consumer (C2C). We'll focus on B2C and B2B in this chapter as they represent the greatest percentage of revenue dollars in e-commerce. Another emerging and important player is governments—we'll focus on the explosion of e-government in Chapter 8.

To succeed in the e-commerce environment, you must develop a strategic position and execute your business operations well. After introducing you to the basics of the B2B and B2C e-commerce perspectives, we'll cover Porter's Five Forces Model, an effective tool for determining the relative attractiveness of an industry and developing

Figure 7.1

Four Perspectives of E-Commerce

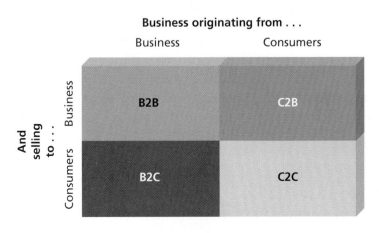

a strategic position. We'll then cover three important e-commerce critical success factors. There are countless others, but these three in particular will help you execute your business operations well.

E-Commerce Business Models

Of all the variations of e-commerce business models to be found operating in the real world today, business-to-business (B2B) is the most lucrative area. Business-to-consumer (B2C) e-commerce, on the other hand, is the most well known in everyday life.

- **Business-to-business (B2B) e-commerce** occurs when a business sells products and services to customers who are primarily other businesses.
- **Business-to-consumer (B2C) e-commerce** occurs when a business sells products and services to customers who are primarily individuals.

So, for example, when Gates Rubber Company sells belts, hoses, and other rubber and synthetic products to General Motors or any other manufacturer that needs those parts, this is B2B e-commerce. B2C e-commerce, on the other hand, is all about the commerce between a business and an individual end consumer—you, for example, when you buy a music CD from Circuit City online at www.circuitcity.com.

B2B e-commerce is where all the money is right now, accounting for approximately 97 percent of all e-commerce revenues. Business organizations have realized that there are tremendous efficiencies and potential savings from innovations in doing business electronically. Businesses can shorten cycle times and reduce costs in the supply chain. They can more effectively reach a wider audience of potential customers (other businesses in this case). Via the Web they can reduce traditional barriers such as time, location, language, and currency. But probably you like most people are more familiar with B2C e-commerce. Have you ever bought something on the Internet? B2C e-commerce is typically what you hear about on television or read about in such periodicals as *PC Magazine* and *Wired*.

It's important for you to understand in which environment your organization operates—either in B2B or in B2C (or perhaps a combination of the two), as there are significant differences. Businesses in one area or the other employ different tactics, electronically speaking. For example, as you can see in Figure 7.2, businesses participating in B2B e-commerce are taking advantage of electronic marketplaces, or e-marketplaces. B2B e-marketplaces are virtual marketplaces in which businesses buy and sell products, share information, and perform other important activities. B2B e-marketplaces include many variations such as vertical e-marketplaces, horizontal e-marketplaces, value-added network providers, and many others.

B2B e-marketplaces represent one of the fastest-growing trends in the B2B e-commerce model. Businesses are increasingly aware that they must create supply chain management systems, drive out costs, create information partnerships with other businesses, and even collaborate with other businesses on new product and service offerings. B2B e-marketplaces offer tremendous efficiencies to businesses for performing all of these tasks.

Consumers, on the other hand, in the B2C e-commerce business model tend to deal directly with a chosen business on the Internet (see Figure 7.3). That is, consumers usually surf the Web evaluating products and services at numerous separate e-commerce Web sites until they eventually choose one distinct site from which to make a purchase. That is not to say that consumers don't have access to or use e-marketplaces. eBay is a good example of an e-marketplace for consumers, where you can buy and sell just about anything you want. As an e-marketplace, eBay brings together many buyers and sellers,

Figure 7.2

What's Happening in the World of E-Commerce?

Top 10 Most Popular Queries from Google and Yahoo! for 2003[3]

Rank	Google	Yahoo!
1	Britney Spears	Kazaa
2	Harry Potter	Harry Potter
3	Matrix	American Idol
4	Shakira	Britney Spears
5	David Beckham	50 Cent
6	50 Cent	Eminem
7	Iraq	WWE
8	Lord of the Rings	Paris Hilton
9	Kobe Bryant	NASCAR
10	Tour de France	Christina Aguilera

E-Mail and Online Advertising Impressions in 2003[2]

Q1—136,600,000

Q2—149,800,000

Q3—172,000,000

Q4—203,800,000 (40% increase over Q1)

Web Usage in Canada[4]

Canadians are among the world's most enthusiastic users of the Internet. According to a 2004–2005 EKOS survey on trends in Internet usage and access:

- 78% of Canadians had used the Internet in the past three months.
- 72% of Canadians had Internet access at home.
- Canadian households with high-speed Internet access now outnumber those with dial-up.
- 44% of Canadians have made purchases online, and 43% do their banking over the Internet.

Top Parent Companies for Home Use, December 2003 (United States)[5]

Parent	Number Homes	Time per Session
Microsoft	87,322,000	01:31:43
Time Warner	77,981,000	04:01:58
Yahoo!	75,639,000	01:45:42
Google	41,561,000	00:16:01
eBay	39,424,000	01:21:52
Amazon	27,557,000	00:20:33
U.S. Government	26,172,000	00:16:00
RealNetworks	24,097,000	00:25:43
Terra Lycos	23,364,000	00:08:30
About-Primedia	20,148,000	00:08:59

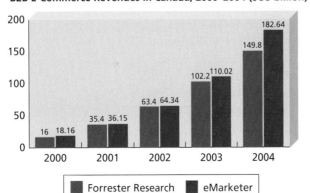

B2B E-Commerce Revenues in Canada, 2000–2004 ($US billion)[6]

Forrester Research / eMarketer

2000: 16 / 18.16
2001: 35.4 / 36.15
2002: 63.4 / 64.34
2003: 102.2 / 110.02
2004: 149.8 / 182.64

Percentage of Online Purchases of Music CDs and DVDs[7]

1997—0.3%

1998—1.1%

1999—2.4%

2000—3.2%

2001—2.9%

2002—3.4%

2003—5%

TELEMEDICINE IN CANADIAN RURAL AREAS

Providing health care to isolated communities across Canada has always been a challenge. For instance, doctors must regularly be flown in from Vancouver Island on a small Bell JetRanger B206 helicopter to provide health care services to the residents of Zeballos, B.C., one of Canada's more remote settlements. This is often stressful and tiring for doctors. Other health care professionals who have actually established residence in rural communities often complain of low morale, isolation, and burnout. On another stop of the flying circuit called Holberg, local nurse Elizabeth Frost is on call 24 hours a day. "I have no replacement here . . . and I get very stressed having no professional colleague to talk to." Yet residents of these communities may still be among the lucky ones. Many rural areas in Canada do not benefit from local service at all. Residents must regularly travel significant distances to consult doctors.

In 1999, while urban centres across Canada boasted a ratio of one doctor for every 200 people, in rural areas the ratio had plummeted to one for every 800, and it was expected that this disparity would become even more pronounced. Not only were rural populations growing because more aging baby boomers chose to retire away from large cities, but provinces were losing rural doctors at an astonishing rate. British Columbia reported an average attrition rate of two country doctors per month. At the time, Dr. Peter Hutten-Czapski of Haileybury, Ontario warned that, at this rate, rural services would likely disappear by 2006.

Today, the provinces are addressing the crisis by increasingly adopting Internet technologies to end rural isolation. In particular, Nova Scotia has been the most aggressive proponent of telemedicine. The province spent $8 million to link its smaller health care facilities to major medical centres in Halifax. Innovations include giving doctors in Halifax the ability to examine patients in rural communities via remote control video camera equipment. Furthermore, small-town physicians across the country are also embracing the Internet. Today, Trina Larsen-Soles, who works in Dryden, 300 kilometres northwest of Thunder Bay, Ontario, heads the Society of Rural Physicians of Canada. The organization, founded in 1993, has flourished in cyberspace, and membership now exceeds 1200. The group sponsors online discussion groups that let rural physicians exchange ideas and share experiences.[8]

Figure 7.3

Business-to-Business and Business-to-Consumer E-Commerce Business Models

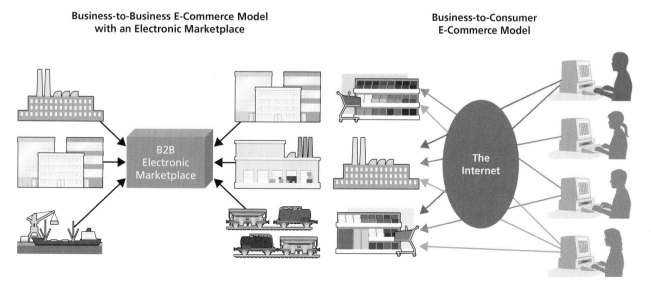

offering chat rooms, discussion boards, and a variety of other consumer-centric services. Although eBay is the most well known of these types of sites, there are other gathering places for individual end consumers such as Epinions.com (www.epinions.com).

The distinction presented in Figure 7.3 is a very important one. If your organization has customers who are primarily other businesses, you need to find the appropriate e-marketplace or e-marketplaces in which to participate. If your organization has customers who are primarily individual end consumers, you need to create a marketing mix that will allow as many potential individual consumers as possible to find your organization while they surf and search the Web.

Porter's Five Forces Model: A Framework for Competitive Advantage

To achieve and sustain a competitive advantage in today's information-based and digital business environment, you must take creative steps in the use of information technology. Michael Porter's framework—called the *Five Forces Model*—has long been accepted as a useful tool for business people to use when thinking about business strategy and the impact of IT. Given that the e-commerce environment is so highly competitive, your ability to create and sustain a competitive advantage is essential.

The **Five Forces Model** helps business people understand the relative attractiveness of an industry and includes the following five forces (see Figure 7.4):

1. Buyer power
2. Supplier power
3. Threat of substitute products or services
4. Threat of new entrants
5. Rivalry among existing competitors

You can use Porter's Five Forces Model to decide to (1) enter a particular industry or (2) expand your operations if you are already in it. Most important, the strategies you develop should then be supported by enabling technologies. It doesn't matter if your organization is operating within B2B, B2C, or a combination of the two; the Five Forces Model can help.

BUYER POWER

Buyer power in the Five Forces Model is high when buyers have many choices from whom to buy, and low when their choices are few. As a provider of products and

Figure 7.4

Michael Porter's Five Forces Model

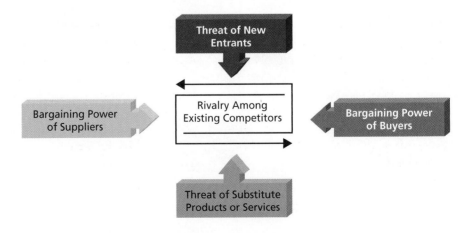

Figure 7.5

Evaluating Buyer and Supplier Power for Your Organization

services, your organization wishes to reduce buyer power. You create a competitive advantage by making it more attractive for customers to buy from you than from your competition. One of the best IT-based examples is the **loyalty programs**, which reward customers based on the amount of business they do with a particular organization. This depends on keeping track of the activity and accounts of many, perhaps millions of customers, which is not practical—or even feasible—without large-scale IT systems. Loyalty programs use IT to reduce buyer power. They are very common in the travel industry (see the discussion in Chapter 2 on frequent flyer programs). Because of the rewards (e.g., free airline tickets, upgrades, and hotel stays) they receive, travellers are more likely to give most of their business to a single organization.

SUPPLIER POWER

Supplier power in the Five Forces Model is high when buyers have few choices from whom to buy, and low when their choices are many. Supplier power is the converse of buyer power: as a supplier organization in a market, you want buyer power to be low and supplier power to be high. In a typical supply chain, however, as we discussed in Chapters 1 and 2 (see Figure 7.5), your organization will probably be both a supplier (to customer organizations) and a customer (of other supplier organizations).

In the case of being a customer of other supplier organizations, you want to increase your buyer power. You can create a competitive advantage by locating alternative supply sources for your organization. IT-enabled B2B e-marketplaces can help you. B2B e-marketplaces are Internet-based services that bring together many buyers and sellers. We'll talk about implementations of e-marketplaces throughout this chapter.

THREAT OF SUBSTITUTE PRODUCTS OR SERVICES

The **threat of substitute products or services** in the Five Forces Model is high when there are many alternatives to a product or service, and low when there are few alternatives from which to choose. Ideally, your organization would like to be a supplier organization in a market in which there are few substitutes for the products and services you offer. Of course, that's seldom possible in any market today, but you can still create a competitive advantage by increasing **switching costs**—costs that make customers reluctant to switch to another product or service supplier. What you need to realize is that a switching cost does not necessarily have to have an actual monetary cost.

As you buy products at Amazon.com over time, for example, the company develops a unique profile of your shopping and purchasing habits through such techniques as collaborative filtering. When you visit their site, products are offered to you that have been tailored to your profile. If you choose to do your shopping elsewhere, there is a switching cost, because the new site you visit will not have a profile of you nor a record of your past purchases. So Amazon.com has reduced the threat of substitute products or services, in a market in which there are many substitutes, by tailoring offerings to you, by creating a "cost" to you to switch to another online retailer.

Switching costs can be real monetary costs too. You've probably been introduced to a switching cost when you signed up for the services of a cell phone provider. All the options and plans sound really great. But there is a serious switching cost in that most cell phone providers require you to sign a long-term contract (as long as two years) in order to receive a free phone or unlimited night and weekend calling minutes. These sorts of switching costs, unfortunately, are sometimes hidden in the fine print.

THREAT OF NEW ENTRANTS

The **threat of new entrants** in the Five Forces Model is high when it is easy for new competitors to enter a market, and low when there are significant entry barriers to entering a market. An **entry barrier** is a product or service feature that customers have come to expect from organizations in a particular industry and that must be offered by an entering organization to compete and survive. Such barriers are erected, then overcome, and then new ones are created.

For example, if you're thinking of starting a bank, you must nowadays offer your customers an array of IT-enabled services, including ATM use, online bill paying and account monitoring, and the like. These are significant IT-based entry barriers to entering the banking market, because you must offer them for free (or for a very small fee). The first bank to offer such services gained a first-mover advantage and established entry barriers, an advantage nullified as other banking competitors developed similar IT-enabling systems.

RIVALRY AMONG EXISTING COMPETITION

The **rivalry among existing competitors** in the Five Forces Model is high when competition is fierce in a market, and low when competition is more complacent. Simply put, competition is more intense in some industries than in others, although the overall trend is toward increased competition in just about every industry.

The retail grocery industry is intensely competitive. While Loblaw's and Provigo in Canada compete in many different ways, essentially they try to beat or match the competition on price. For example, most of them have loyalty programs that give shoppers special discounts. Customers get lower prices while the store gathers valuable business intelligence on buying habits to craft pricing and advertising strategies. In the future, you can expect to see grocery stores using wireless technologies to track customer movement throughout the store and match it to products purchased to determine purchasing sequences.

Since margins are quite low in the grocery retail market, grocers build efficiencies into their supply chains, connecting with their suppliers in IT-enabled information partnerships (as we discussed in Chapter 2). Communicating with suppliers over telecommunications networks rather than using paper-based systems makes the procurement process faster, cheaper, and more accurate. That equates to lower prices for customers—and increased rivalry among existing competitors.

USING PORTER'S MODEL IN AN E-COMMERCE CONTEXT

Porter's Five Forces Model is a valuable tool for considering whether to enter any industry, and that holds true in the e-commerce environment as well. However, the "e"

USING PORTER TO EVALUATE THE MOVIE RENTAL INDUSTRY

One hotly contested and highly competitive industry is the movie rental business. You can rent videos from local video rental stores (usually for a specified number of days), you can order pay-per-view from the comfort of your own home (usually to watch as many times as you want in a given 24-hour period of time), and you can rent videos from the Web at such sites as Netflix (www.netflix.com) and keep the videos as long as you want.

Using Porter's Five Forces Model, evaluate the relative attractiveness of entering the movie rental business. Specifically, answer the following questions and perform the following tasks (and provide the appropriate justification/description for each of your outputs):

1. Is buyer power low or high?
2. Is supplier power low or high?
3. What substitute products and services are perceived as threats?
4. What is the level of threat of new entrants? That is, are the barriers to entry high or low? What are the barriers to entry?
5. What is the level of rivalry among existing competitors? Create a list of the top five competitors in the business.

Finally, what's your overall view of the movie rental business? Is it a good or bad industry to enter? How would you use Porter's Five Forces Model to enter this industry?

---

in e-commerce implies technology, and technology has even further intensified the competition in almost every industry you care to name.

Today it will help you be successful in business if you truly understand the impact technology has on the relative attractiveness of an industry. Without referencing a specific industry or industry segment, consider the following statements as they relate to Porter's Five Forces Model.

- Because of technology, buyer power has increased in most industries. It's now far easier for new suppliers to enter a given industry and for all suppliers to reach more potential buyers. That translates into more options for buyers, thus increasing buyer power.
- Because of technology, the entry barriers into many industries have been lessened. Geographic boundaries of markets are a simple yet effective illustration of this. Previously, many markets were difficult—without the aid of technology—to enter because of their geographic location. Technologies such as the Internet have made it easier to enter these markets in distant or inaccessible areas of the country or world.
- The threat of substitute products or services has increased in most industries because of technology. Again, it's easier now because of technology for suppliers to reach more buyers with either directly competing products and services or substitute products and services.

Those statements may not exactly paint a pretty picture for the competitive landscape of business today, but they do offer a realistic view of just how competitive business is.

So how can your organization be successful in the business world of e-commerce? We have no magic answer, but we can offer you several guidelines by which your organization should operate, which are the focus of the next several sections in this chapter. As you'll see, each guideline has its own unique set of considerations depending on the focus of your e-business efforts, either as the "B" in business-to-consumer e-commerce or the first "B" in business-to-business e-commerce.

THE SERVICE SECTOR

As we discussed with regard to Porter's Five Forces Model, e-commerce can reduce entry barriers in an industry.

Today, the service sector accounts for more than 65 percent of Atlantic Canada's gross domestic product. In New Brunswick alone, almost 90 percent of jobs being created are in the service industry. The Internet has played an important role in economically reinvigorating the region after a slump in the fishery and construction sectors. For instance, E-com Inc. (www.accra.ca), a Moncton-based software developer established in 1995, offers business solutions via the Internet to companies located across three continents.

"For us, e-commerce is a lean and mean way to expand without incurring mega costs," says president Jean Nadeau. Communicating with both buyers and sellers across the Web avoids the time and travel associated with international travel. The company provides Web-based training and support, and "try before you buy" options using live, online software demonstrations. Furthermore, although the company only has ten employees working out of Moncton, E-com deals electronically with more than 35 freelance graphic designers and programmers. "E-commerce gives you access to the best people at the right price, wherever they are," adds Nadeau.[9]

Understand Your Business, Products, Services, and Customers

To be successful in any business, you must be able to define exactly the products and services you provide, who your target customers are, and how your customers perceive the use of your products and services within their business activities (for the B2B model) or in their personal lives (for the B2C model). In order to create strategies that will help you gain a competitive advantage you have to clearly articulate the nature of your products and services, customers, and the value that your customers put on your products and services.

For the moment skip over the traditional notions of developing a mission statement and glitzy marketing brochures. Although both of these are essential, first you need to develop an objective, very down-to-earth understanding of what your business does. The reality is you can't be all things to all customers. You must clearly define (1) your target customers and (2) the value of your products and services as perceived by your customers. Let's look at each in turn.

WHO ARE YOUR CUSTOMERS?

Just like in the brick-and-mortar business world, you must focus your efforts on selling to other businesses, individual end consumers, or some combination of the two. If you were like our example earlier in the chapter, Gates Rubber Company, which produces mostly rubber and synthetic products primarily for sale to the automotive industry and other manufacturers that extensively use such items in the manufacture of other products (such as boats and bicycles), you would almost exclusively focus on the B2B e-commerce model, with other businesses as your target customers. If you were to sell résumé and job placement services to individuals looking for careers, your customers would be individual end consumers. If you wanted to be like Monster.ca (www.monster.ca) and provide an electronic marketplace with services catering to both individuals looking for careers and businesses looking for employees, your customer mix would include both end consumers and businesses. In this case, you'd need to carefully consider both groups of customers, their needs, and the value to them of the products and services you sell.

Many businesses in the travel industry, American Express for example, cater to both businesses and end consumers. As an individual consumer, you may work with American Express to plan and pay for a vacation. At the same time, many businesses use the services of American Express to handle all their travel needs.

Whatever the nature of your business, you must know who your customers are. In the world of e-commerce, that means clearly distinguishing between end consumers (B2C) and other businesses (B2B), even if you target both. As you will see throughout this chapter, individual end consumers and other businesses have dramatically different needs. For some different kinds of products and services needed by B2C and B2B, see Figure 7.6, and the discussion that follows.

WHAT IS THE VALUE OF YOUR PRODUCTS AND SERVICES AS PERCEIVED BY YOUR CUSTOMERS?

If a customer orders a product or service from your organization, it is because that customer perceives some value in what you provide—the customer either *wants* or *needs* your product or service. Here, the distinctions between end consumers and businesses as customers become increasingly important and clearly evident, so let's look at each customer group in turn.

B2C: CONVENIENCE VERSUS SPECIALTY In many respects, you can differentiate between convenience and specialty merchandise (or services) on the basis of price and consumers' frequency of purchase. To end consumers, convenience merchandise is typically lower-priced, but it is something they need, usually on a frequent basis. Nonperishable food items such as cereal are a good example. From organizations such as Peapod (www.peapod.ca), you can easily order food items and have them delivered to your home within 24 hours of making the order or at predetermined time intervals such as weekly. Consumers might pay more for these low-priced items in order to have them "conveniently."

Specialty merchandise might be such things as home stereo systems, computers, name-brand clothing, furniture, and the like. For consumers, these are higher-priced (than convenience merchandise) items, are typically ordered on a less-frequent basis,

Business to Consumer (B2C)	Business to Business (B2B)
• *Convenience.* Low-priced but something needed on a frequent basis	• *Maintenance, repair, and operations (MRO) materials.* Necessary items that do not relate directly to the company's primary business activities
• *Specialty.* Higher-priced, ordered on a less frequent basis, and often requiring customization	• *Direct materials.* Materials used in production in a manufacturing company or put on the shelf for sale in a retail environment
• *Commodity-like.* The same no matter where you buy it	
• *Digital.* The best of all, because of low cost of inventory and shipping	

Figure 7.6

B2C and B2B Products and Services

YOUR PERCEPTION OF PRODUCT AND SERVICE VALUE

Within the B2C e-commerce model, not all consumers are the same. They have, not only different tastes and needs, but also different perceptions of product and service value. Your task is to evaluate the products and services in the table below according to your personal preferences, and to specify (1) your perception of whether each is a convenience or specialty item and (2) whether you require some level of customization for each. Put an X in the appropriate cells for each.

Product/Service	Convenience	Specialty	Customization
Fiction book			
Textbook			
Cell phone			
Internet access			
Job search			
Computer			
Chequing account			
Living space (e.g., apartment)			
Music			
Car stereo			
Home stereo			

and often require some sort of customization or feature specification. For specialty merchandise, consumers will spend more time shopping around for the best deal, not only in terms of price but also in terms of customization, warranty, service, and other after-sales features.

B2C: COMMODITY-LIKE AND DIGITAL In B2C e-commerce, as a general rule, the best merchandise to sell is either commodity-like, digital, or a combination of the two. This enables you to minimize your internal costs, but requires that you be innovative in how you offer your merchandise and attract consumers to your site.

Commodity-like merchandise, to your customers, is the same regardless of where they purchase it, and it is similar to convenience items in that respect. Books are a good example. No matter where you buy a particular book, it is the same. As a business, you compete in a commodity-like environment on the basis of:

- Price
- Ease and speed of delivery
- Ease of ordering
- Your returns policy

Of course, commodity-like business environments are typically easy to enter (i.e., they have low barriers to entry) and thus buyer power is high. Your organization's goals in this type of environment would have to include (1) minimizing price to the end consumer and (2) minimizing your internal costs by creating a tight supply chain management system. You also want to create a "sticky" Web site that not only attracts consumers but also encourages them to return again and again.

Digital merchandise offerings are also important in the B2C e-commerce model. The goal here is to eliminate shipping costs by delivering the digital product over the Internet once a consumer has made a purchase. Music is a good example. Apple's iTunes Web site (www.apple.com/itunes/store) allows you to select the exact song you want, pay for it, and then download it from the Internet. Apple can offer each song for just 99 cents because it has no physical delivery costs and no physical inventory. As this example illustrates, digital products are also advantageous (to the business and the consumer) because they are customizable. That is, customers don't have to purchase an entire music CD—they can pick only the song or songs they want.

B2C: MASS CUSTOMIZATION As we've alluded to, end consumers are often interested in customizing their purchases. In the B2C e-commerce model this is the concept of **mass customization**—the ability of an organization to give its customers the opportunity to tailor its product or service to the customer's specifications. Customization can be appropriate and is a key competitive advantage regardless of customer value perception. For example, Dell Computer (www.dell.ca) is well regarded in its market for being the best at allowing consumers to customize a computer purchase. Music sites now allow you to pick the songs you want instead of an entire CD. Clothing sites allow you to select from among various styles, colours, and size of clothing to fit your needs.

In a B2C environment, you're potentially dealing with millions of different consumers, each with unique tastes and needs. You must support the concept of mass customization.

B2B: MRO VERSUS DIRECT **Maintenance, repair, and operations (MRO) materials** (also called **indirect materials**) are materials that are necessary for running a modern corporation, but that do not relate to the company's primary business activities. MRO materials include everything from ballpoint pens to three-ring binders, repair parts for equipment, and lubricating oils. Thus, B2B MRO materials are similar to convenience and commodity-like items in the B2C e-commerce model.

In their purchases of these materials, however, business customers (B2B) are very different from end consumers (B2C) in many ways. For example, a business because of its volume of MRO materials purchases can bargain with suppliers for a discount (end consumers in the B2C e-commerce model usually don't have this ability). Many businesses may band together to create even more volume and thus demand an even higher discount from a supplier. This practice is known as **demand aggregation**—the combining of purchase requests from multiple buyers into a single large order, which justifies a discount from the business. If your organization is a supplier of MRO materials in the B2B e-commerce model, you will compete mostly on price (including discounts), delivery, and ease of ordering.

Direct materials are those used in production in a manufacturing company or placed on the shelf for sale in a retail environment. So, as opposed to MRO materials, direct materials relate to a company's primary business activities. It is critically important that the customer business receive exactly what is needed in terms of quality, quantity, and the timing of delivery of direct materials.

For direct materials acquisition, some businesses participate in a **reverse auction** (through an electronic marketplace), in which a buyer posts its interest in buying a certain quantity of items with notations concerning quality, specification, and delivery

BEAUTY AND "VALUE" ARE IN THE EYE OF THE BEHOLDER

Customer "value" is an elusive concept. Sometimes it means low price, other times it means high quality, and yet other times it means convenience.

Consider the joint venture offering by JCB Co., Japan's largest credit card issuer, and Fujitsu. The new offering is a cell phone that authenticates the owner of the phone through a fingerprint scanner. As a user of the phone, you can check your JCB account balances and transfer funds. But you don't have to enter a special password or PIN. Instead, you place your finger on the phone's fingerprint scanner and it does the rest.

There is no real competitive advantage to telephone-based banking, as most financial institutions already offer that service. The competitive advantage for JCB and Fujitsu (i.e., customer value) lies in the phone's ability to recognize who you are without requiring you to provide some sort of validation such as a password or PIN.

What's your perception? As a customer, do you agree that there is value in a phone with a fingerprint scanner?[10]

---

timing, and sellers compete for the business by submitting successively lower bids until there is only one seller left. Reverse auctions create tremendous "power" for the buyer because multiple sellers are competing for the same business.

B2B: HORIZONTAL VERSUS VERTICAL As a supplier to other businesses, you also need to understand whether you are selling in a horizontal or vertical e-marketplace (see Figure 7.7). An **electronic marketplace (e-marketplace)** is an interactive business providing a central market space where multiple buyers and suppliers can engage in e-commerce and/or other e-commerce business activities. E-marketplaces feature a variety of implementations, including value-added network providers (which we'll discuss later in this chapter), horizontal e-marketplaces, and vertical e-marketplaces. A

Figure 7.7
Horizontal and Vertical B2B Electronic Marketplace

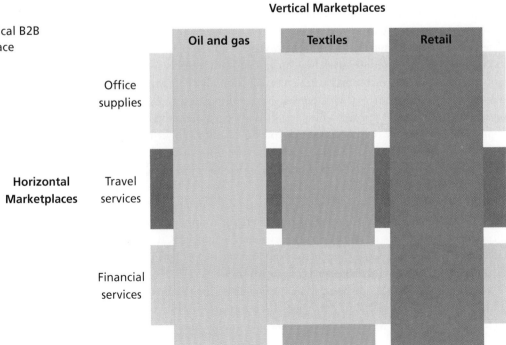

Vertical Marketplaces

Oil and gas   Textiles   Retail

Office supplies

Horizontal Marketplaces   Travel services

Financial services

WHAT ABOUT B2C E-BUSINESS?

The Canadian government plans to make Canada the most connected nation in the world, which might become a reality. In 2003, approximately 73 percent of Canadians were connected, which put Canada at the head of other G7 countries such as the United States and the United Kingdom.

The rapid increase in users is being mirrored by the ever-growing percentage of Canadian households who are purchasing online, which hit 44 percent in 2004. However, the report warned that while the number of Canadians buying online continued to grow, many Canadian companies were not capitalizing on this.

Canadian retail presence over the Internet is actually diminishing, particularly for SMEs.

David Conklin and Marc Trudeau at the School of Business Administration at the University of Western Ontario have suggested that several factors are to blame, including a significant difference in business culture between Canada and the United States. Canadian business leaders tend to be more risk-averse and do not fully appreciate the Internet's potential; they also warn that the future does not look particularly bright. Higher salaries and lower taxes in the United States are leading to an exodus of Canadian entrepreneurial talent. So a danger facing Canadian e-tailers and all Canadian e-commerce companies is that American firms will increasingly look north as a land of e-opportunity. In fact, many U.S. companies, such as E*TRADE, are already setting up subsidiaries in Canada.

As a future graduate from a Canadian university and potential e-entrepreneur, what initiatives do you suggest the Canadian government and our business community take to stimulate Canadian retail presence online?[11]

horizontal e-marketplace is an electronic marketplace that connects buyers and sellers across many industries, primarily for MRO materials commerce. Again, MRO materials include a broad of range of both products and services including office supplies, travel, shipping, and some financial services. Because horizontal e-marketplaces support MRO materials commerce, much of our previous discussion on B2B e-commerce for MRO materials holds true here.

A vertical e-marketplace is an electronic marketplace that connects buyers and sellers in a given industry (e.g., oil and gas, textiles, and retail). Covisint (www.covis int.com) is a good example. Covisint provides a B2B e-marketplace in the automotive industry where buyers and sellers specific to that industry conduct commerce in products and services, share mission-critical information for the development of products and parts, collaborate on new ideas, and deploy infrastructure applications that enable the seamless communication of each other's proprietary IT systems.

To summarize, we would offer you the following for understanding your business, products, services, and customers.

Business to Consumer
- Exhibits greatly varying demographics, lifestyles, wants, and needs.
- Distinctions of products and services are by convenience versus specialty.
- Works best for commodity-like and digital products and services.
- Includes mass customization in some instances.

Business to Business
- Distinctions of products and services are by maintenance, repair, and operations (MRO) materials versus direct materials.
- Includes demand aggregation and negotiation capabilities on the part of businesses as customers.
- Supports e-marketplaces, including horizontal e-marketplaces (primarily for MRO materials) and vertical e-marketplaces (specific to a given industry).

333

Find Customers and Establish Relationships

The most important preselling activity in commerce is finding and reaching your customers and establishing a relationship with them—otherwise you can't make a sale. People generally refer to this as *marketing*; there are added considerations to keep in mind about marketing in e-commerce that can create a competitive advantage for you.

BUSINESS TO CONSUMER

With almost one billion people on the Internet, you'd think it would be easy to find and attract customers to your B2C e-commerce site. But that's not necessarily true, because all your competition is trying to do the same thing—drive customers to their Web site and encourage them to make a purchase.

Here, you need to determine your appropriate **marketing mix**—the set of marketing tools that your organization will use to pursue its marketing objectives in reaching and attracting potential customers. In B2C e-commerce, your marketing mix will probably include some or all of the following: registering with search engines, online ads, viral marketing, and affiliate programs.

Many Web surfers use *search engines* to find information and products and services. While some search engines will include your site for free (FreeSearch.com at www.freesearch.ca is an example), almost all the popular search engines such as Yahoo! and Google require you to pay a fee. Most of these sites will guarantee that your site appears in the top portion of a search list for an additional fee.

Online ads (often called **banner ads**) are small advertisements that appear on other sites (see Figure 7.8). Variations include pop-up and pop-under ads. A **pop-up ad** is a small Web page containing an advertisement that appears on your screen apart from the current Web site loaded into your browser. A **pop-under ad** is a form of a pop-up

Figure 7.8

An Online Ad at Cnet.com

Banner ad for Sony

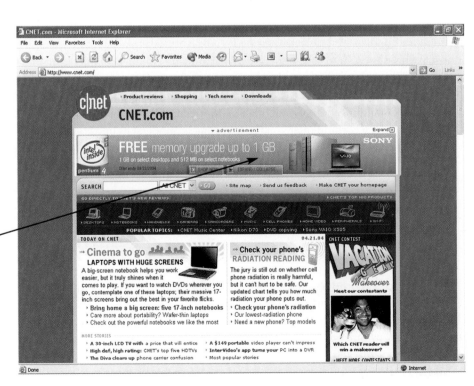

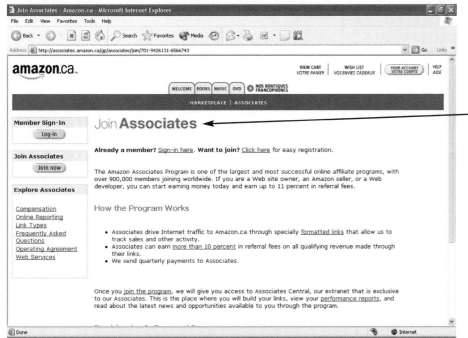

Figure 7.9

Amazon.ca's Affiliate Program Is Called *Associates*

As an Amazon Associate, you can earn up to 10% for referrals.

ad that you do not see until you close your current browser window. A word of caution here: most people don't mind banner ads because they appear as a part of the site they're visiting; however, most people consider pop-up and pop-under ads to be very annoying.

Viral marketing encourages users of a product or service supplied by a B2C e-commerce business to encourage friends to join in as well. Blue Mountain Arts (www.bluemountain.ca) is a good example. When you use Blue Mountain to send an e-birthday card (or some other type of card), the intended recipient will receive an e-mail directing him or her to Blue Mountain's site. Once the recipient views the card, Blue Mountain provides a link so that person can send you a card in return. Of course, Blue Mountain charges for each card sent, so it makes money both ways.

An **affiliate program** is an arrangement made between two e-commerce sites that directs viewers from one site to the other. Amazon.ca is the most well-known creator of an affiliate program. If you become an Amazon associate, your e-commerce Web site would direct viewers to Amazon's site for certain purchases. If a sale results, Amazon will pay you a fee, which is usually a percentage of the sale (see Figure 7.9). Likewise, you can pay another site to direct traffic to yours, which may be through an online ad. In some instances, affiliate programs create relationships such that a payment is made for each click-through. A **click-through** is counted whenever a person who visits a site clicks on an ad and is taken to the site of the advertiser.

In general, you want your marketing mix to drive as many potential customers as possible to have a look at your B2C e-commerce offerings. From there, however, you need to focus on your **conversion rate**, the percentage of potential customers who visit your site who actually buy something. So while total views or *hits* to your e-commerce Web site is important, obviously your conversion rate is even more so.

BUSINESS TO BUSINESS

Finding and attracting customers to your B2B e-commerce site is much different. Businesses—customers in the B2B model—don't usually find products and services by surfing the Web or using search engines. Instead, business customers prefer to actively

A GLOBAL PARTNERSHIP TO CREATE GLOBAL PARTNERING OPPORTUNITIES

In March 2004, Business Commerce Limited, the Hong Kong subsidiary of Global eXchange Services, and ChinaECNet announced a new business partnership that will establish a B2B electronic marketplace named "e-Hub." e-Hub will connect China-based electronics manufacturers with other China-based manufacturers and international customers and suppliers as well.

ChinaECNet is China's leading digital media and e-commerce network, focused mainly on the electronic manufacturing industry. It represents a joint venture between the China Centre for Industry Information Development, Avnet Inc., and Global Techmart.

Global eXchange Services provides one of the largest B2B e-commerce business networks in the world, supporting over 1 billion transactions annually among over 100,000 trading partners.

e-Hub will provide buyers and sellers with a standards-based transaction environment that will ultimately lead to more efficient and effective sourcing, purchasing, and tracking of inventory. According to Gou Zhongwen, vice-minister of China's Ministry of Information Industry, "Strengthening the electronics supply chain and material information management is an important step toward utilizing advanced information technology to reform and improve the manufacturing supply and distribution of electronics enterprises." As Wayne Chao, chairman and CEO of ChinaECNET, further explains, "We anticipate that the e-Hub will be China's premier procurement and logistic data exchange platform to connect Chinese electronics OEMs with other Chinese manufacturers of all sizes, and as importantly, with international customers and suppliers. This will greatly help the Chinese OEM market improve material management efficiency and overcome the challenges caused by the rapid globalization of the Chinese electronics industry."

Sometimes, you build partnerships with other businesses specifically so you can support e-commerce activities among other businesses that also want to build partnerships. In the case of Global eXchange Services and ChinaECNET, their partnership will enable other businesses to create partnerships.[12]

participate in e-marketplaces to find suppliers. Within an e-marketplace, an organization can participate in a reverse auction to find a supplier, as we discussed earlier.

Moreover, an organization can search an e-marketplace for suitable suppliers and then enter into negotiations outside the e-marketplace. This happens for organizations needing to purchase millions of dollars in inventory, parts, or raw materials, and it occurs for organizations wanting to establish a long-term relationship with just one supplier.

Relationships among businesses in B2B are very important. These relationships, characterized by trust and continuity, extend into the IT realm. In the B2B e-commerce business model, you must provide a level of integration of your IT systems with those of your business partners. Once a formal business relationship has been established, the goal is to use IT to streamline the ordering and procurement processes to create tight supply chain management systems and drive out cost, so your IT systems have to work closely together.

To summarize, for marketing, or finding customers and creating relationships with them in e-commerce:

Business to Consumer
- Marketing mix is designed to drive potential customers to a Web site.
- Includes registering with a search engine, online ads, viral marketing, and affiliate programs.
- Focuses on conversion rates as a method of measuring success.

DEVELOPING A MARKETING MIX STRATEGY FOR MONSTER.COM

Monster.com (www.monster.ca in Canada) is a premier service provider in the job placement industry. It exhibits both a B2B e-commerce business model because it provides services for organizations seeking employees and a B2C e-commerce business model because it provides services to individuals hoping to find jobs.

You've been hired by Monster.com to create a marketing mix strategy. Your tasks are many. Complete the table below by filling in the appropriate information. If you feel it is not in the best interests of Monster.com to advertise in a certain media, leave that part of the table blank.

	B2B	B2C
Television Advertising		
• What type of TV station(s)?		
• What type of shows?		
• What time of day?		
Newspaper Advertising		
• What day of the week?		
• What section of the newspaper?		
Internet Advertising		
• What sites for online ads?		
• What sites for affiliate programs?		
• What types of viral marketing?		
Other Advertising		
• Anything not listed in the above three categories		

Business to Business

- Occurs frequently in an e-marketplace.
- Still requires the formal establishment of business relationships that include trust and continuity.
- Requires some level of IT system integration between you and your customer.
- Includes negotiations for pricing, quality, specifications, and delivery timing.
- Doesn't usually include a marketing mix that broadly and generically reaches all businesses that might be potential customers.

Move Money Easily and Securely

In the world of e-commerce, you must create IT systems that enable your customers (other businesses or end consumers) to pay electronically, easily, and securely for their purchases. Of course, you can still accept credit cards as the form of payment just like in the brick-and-mortar world, but credit card payments are really an electronic form of payment.

BUSINESS-TO-CONSUMER PAYMENT SYSTEMS

Your customers in the business-to-consumer e-commerce model will most often pay for products and services using credit cards, smart cards, financial cybermediaries, electronic checks, and electronic bill presentment and payment (EBPP) (and also smart cards in some instances).

- **Financial cybermediary**. An Internet-based company that makes it easy for one person to pay another person or organization over the Internet. PayPal (www.paypal.com) is the best-known example of a financial cybermediary (see Figure 7.10). You create a PayPal account by logging on to the PayPal Web site and providing it with personal, credit card, and banking information. When you want to send money, you go to the PayPal site and enter the amount of money you want to send and provide information for either the person or organization you want to send the money to. You can also accumulate money in your personal PayPal account by accepting money from other people. You can transfer the money to one of your banking accounts, use it for other purposes, send the funds to someone else, or just leave it there for awhile.
- **Electronic cheque**. A mechanism for sending money from your chequing or savings account to another person or organization. There are many implementations of electronic cheques, the most prominent being online banking.
- **Electronic bill presentment and payment (EBPP)**. A system that sends bills (usually to end consumers) over the Internet and provides an easy-to-use mechanism (such as clicking on a button) to pay for them if the amount looks correct. EBPP systems are available through local banks or online services such as CheckFree (www.checkfree.com) and Quicken (www.quicken.com/banking_ and_credit).
- **Smart card**. A plastic card the size of a credit card that contains an embedded chip on which digital information can be stored and updated. The chip, in this case, can contain information about how much money you have. When you swipe your card to pay for a purchase, the swiping device deducts the purchase amount from the amount you have stored on the chip. Some debit cards are implementations of the smart card concept.

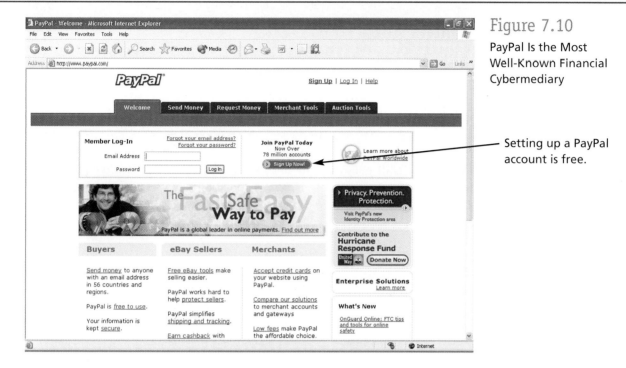

Figure 7.10

PayPal Is the Most Well-Known Financial Cybermediary

Setting up a PayPal account is free.

The entire payment process encompasses more than accepting a form of payment. It also includes determining the shipping address for your customer. You can create a competitive advantage by having a way of asking each customer only once for his or her delivery information and storing it—thus creating a switching cost, because when your customer makes another purchase, you can simply ask him or her to verify the delivery information and not have to provide it all over again. One implementation of this is called a digital wallet. A **digital wallet** is both software and information—the software provides security for the transaction and the information includes payment information (e.g., the credit card number and expiration date) and delivery information. Digital wallets can be stored on either the client side or the server side. A *client-side digital wallet* is one that you create and keep on your computer; you can then use it at a variety of e-commerce Web sites. Most browsers such as Internet Explorer and Netscape Communicator support your ability to create this type of digital wallet. A *server-side digital wallet* (sometimes referred to as a *thin wallet*) is one that an organization creates for and about you and maintains on its server. Many credit card issuers use this type of digital wallet to verify your credit card transactions.

All of this is significant because your customers in the B2C e-commerce model exhibit some common characteristics when paying for your products and services:

- They tend to make numerous purchases for small amounts.
- They pay for each transaction individually.
- Each transaction must be validated.

BUSINESS-TO-BUSINESS PAYMENT SYSTEMS

Payments for products and services in the business-to-business e-commerce model are usually much different from those in the business-to-consumer e-commerce model. In B2B e-commerce, your customers tend to make very large purchases and will not pay using a credit card or a financial cybermediary such as PayPal. Instead, other businesses will want to pay (1) through financial EDI and (2) often in large, aggregated amounts encompassing many purchases.

SPOOFING EBAY CUSTOMERS TO GET CREDIT CARD INFORMATION

When you register as a user at eBay, you set up a personal account that includes your shipping information and important financial information such as your credit card number. At any time, you can log in with eBay and change your personal and financial information. These are necessary aspects of creating the world's largest online auction e-marketplace.

But there is a drawback. Now thieves are trying to steal your credit card information, not by looking through your trash for a credit card statement or by monitoring your electronic communications but rather by pretending to be eBay.

It's called **spoofing**—the forging of the return address on an e-mail so that the e-mail message appears to come from someone other than the actual sender. The thief will send you an e-mail that looks like one coming from eBay. The message will instruct you to do something in order to keep your eBay account active, like clicking on a link that will take you to a page so you can update your credit card information.

In reality, you'll be taken to a site that looks very much like eBay but isn't eBay at all. When you type in your credit card information, things will go bad in a big way and in a big hurry. The thief now has your credit card information and can use it online.

Sometimes, thieves simply ask you to enter your eBay user ID and password on a fictitious site. Then, they have that information and can log into your eBay account and take your information that way.

It's up to you to protect your most personal and confidential information.

ELECTRONIC DATA INTERCHANGE In the B2B model, another business wants to order products and services from your organization via **electronic data interchange (EDI)**, the direct computer-to-computer transfer of transaction information contained in standard business documents, such as invoices and purchase orders, in a standard format. Your organization can implement EDI-facilitated transactions in many ways; one of the more prominent is a B2B e-marketplace that supports EDI through a value-added network. Global eXchange Services (GXS at www.gxs.com) is one such B2B e-marketplace. (We introduced you to GXS in the previous Global Perspectives box.)

GXS, formerly known as General Electric (GE) Information Services, supports one of the largest B2B e-marketplaces in the world with more than 100,000 trading businesses processing 1 billion transactions annually and accounting for over $1 trillion in products and services. GXS focuses on providing value-added network capabilities primarily to supply chain management activities. Figure 7.11 illustrates how General Motors, Ford, and Gates Rubber Company might use GXS's services to support electronic data interchange. In this case, General Motors and Ford would submit orders to Gates through GXS's value-added network (VAN). The VAN supports electronic catalogues (from which orders are placed), EDI-based transactions (the actual orders), security measures such as encryption (which we'll discuss in a moment), and EDI mail boxes (similar to your personal e-mail box). When GM sends an order, for example, to Gates, the order waits in Gates's EDI mail box for processing. Once the order is processed, Gates sends an order confirmation back through the VAN to GM's mailbox.

FINANCIAL ELECTRONIC DATA INTERCHANGE Thereafter, at some predetermined time, Gates would create an invoice totalling many of the orders and purchases from GM. That invoice would be sent through the VAN much like the orders them-

Figure 7.11

How Value-Added Network Providers Support EDI

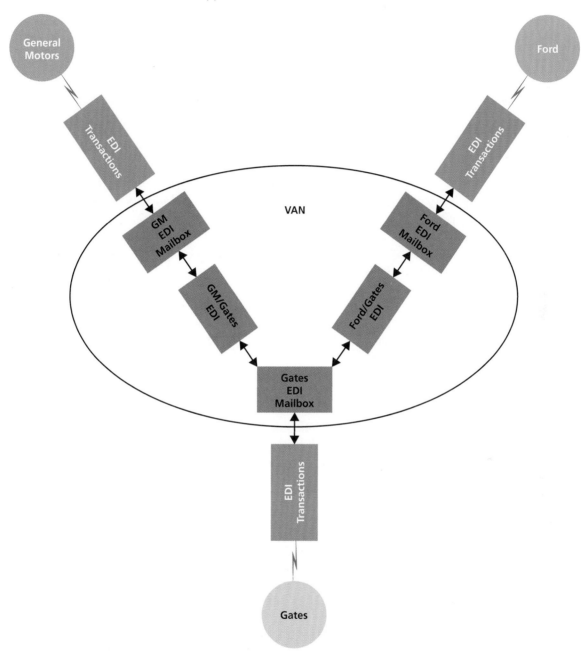

selves. When the invoice was accepted and approved by GM, GM would make a financial EDI payment to Gates. **Financial EDI (financial electronic data interchange)** is an electronic process used primarily within the business-to-business e-commerce model for the payment of purchases. The actual reconciliation of the funds may occur through a bank or an automated clearing house (ACH) support site such as National Cash Management System (www.ach-eft-ncms.com).

As you can see, B2B transactions among businesses are much more involved and complex than B2C transactions between a business and an end consumer such as yourself. Most notably, business-to-business transactions require a level of system integration between the businesses. Considering our previous example in Figure 7.11,

Gates's order fulfillment and processing systems would have to be integrated with similar systems at GM and Ford. That is to say, Gates's order fulfillment and processing systems would have to be able to accept and process EDI-based and standardized electronic order records. GM and Ford would have to have similar systems to create EDI-based and standardized electronic order records. In doing so, costs for order processing among all businesses are minimized, as the orders can be handled electronically, without paper and without much human intervention.

SECURITY: THE PERVADING CONCERN

Regardless of whether your customers are other businesses or end consumers, they are all greatly concerned about the security of their transactions. This includes all aspects of electronic information, but focuses mainly on the information associated with payments (e.g., a credit card number) and the payments themselves, that is, the "electronic money." Here, you need to consider such issues as encryption, *secure sockets layers*, and *secure electronic transactions*. This is by no means an exhaustive list, but it is representative of the broad field of security within electronic commerce.

ENCRYPTION **Encryption** scrambles the contents of a file so that you can't read it without having the right decryption key. Encryption can be achieved in many ways: by scrambling letters in a known way, replacing letters with other letters or perhaps numbers, and other ways.

Some encryption technologies use multiple keys. In this instance, you would be using **public key encryption (PKE)**—an encryption system that uses two keys: a public key that everyone can have and a private key for only the recipient (see Figure 7.12). When implementing security using multiple keys, your organization provides the public key to all its customers (end consumers and other businesses). The customers use the public key to encrypt their information and send it along the Internet. When it arrives at its destination, your organization would use the private key to unscramble the encrypted information.

SECURE SOCKETS LAYERS A **secure sockets layer (SSL)** (1) creates a secure and private connection between a Web client computer and a Web server computer, (2) encrypts the information, and (3) then sends the information over the Internet.

Figure 7.12

Public Key Encryption (PKE) System

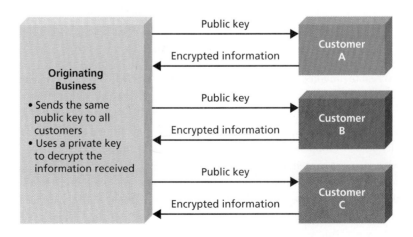

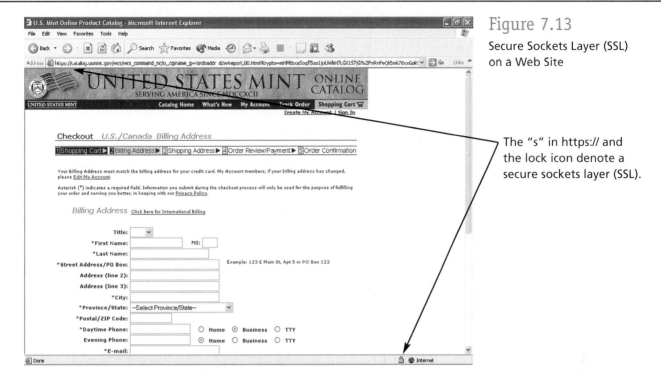

Figure 7.13

Secure Sockets Layer (SSL)
on a Web Site

The "s" in https:// and
the lock icon denote a
secure sockets layer (SSL).

SSLs do provide good security for transferring information and are used widely by
B2C e-commerce Web sites. As an end consumer, you can tell your information is
being transferred via SSL if you see either (1) the Web site address starts with https://
(notice the inclusion of the "s") as opposed to just http:// or (2) the presence of a lock
icon in the bottom portion of your Web browser window (see Figure 7.13).

SECURE ELECTRONIC TRANSACTIONS A **secure electronic transaction (SET)** is
a transmission security method that ensures transactions are *legitimate* as well as
secure. Much like an SSL, an SET encrypts information before sending it over the
Internet. Taking it one step further, an SET enables you, as a merchant, to verify a customer's identity by securely transmitting credit card information to the business that
issued the credit card for verification. SETs are endorsed by major e-commerce players including MasterCard, American Express, Visa, Netscape, and Microsoft.

To summarize:

Business to Consumer
- Methods include credit cards, financial cybermediaries, electronic cheques, electronic bill presentment and payment (EBPP), smart cards, and digital wallets.
- Consumers make numerous individual purchases for small amounts that must
  each be validated.

Business to Business
- The use of electronic data interchange (EDI) facilitates the ordering process.
- Value-added network providers are used for EDI and financial EDI.
- Financial EDI is used for payment of purchases.

Both Business to Consumer and Business to Business
- Security is an overriding concern.
- Security is provided by the use of encryption, secure sockets layers (SSLs), and
  secure electronic transactions (SETs).

DEFINING YOUR B2C E-COMMERCE BUSINESS

It's now time for you to gather everything you've learned in this chapter and use it to create the overall strategy for a B2C e-commerce business. As a group, you are to define a B2C e-commerce business you wish to operate. It can be anything from selling tutoring services to offering music on the Web. First, you need to clearly define your customers according to their demographics and lifestyles. Next, define your products/services according to your customers' perception of their value. Third, define the best marketing mix to reach your customers. Finally, evaluate your new e-commerce business in light of Porter's Five Forces Model. Complete the table below with this information.

Your B2C e-commerce business (provide a one-paragraph description):	
Your customers (provide their demographics and lifestyles):	
Your customers' perception of value (discussion of convenience versus specialty, commodity-like, digital, and extent of needed customization):	
Your marketing mix (where you will advertise, when, etc.):	
Porter's Five Forces Model (describe your competitive space according to each of the five forces):	

Summary: Student Learning Outcomes Revisited

1. **Define and describe the two major e-commerce business models (business-to-business and business-to-consumer), as well as e-commerce and e-business.** *Business to business (B2B) e-commerce* occurs when a business sells products and services to customers who are primarily other businesses. B2B e-commerce is all about the commerce interactions among two or more businesses. *Business-to-consumer (B2C) e-commerce* occurs when a business sells products and services to customers who are primarily individuals. B2C e-commerce is all about the commerce interactions among a business and an end consumer.

2. **Summarize Porter's Five Forces Model and how business people can use it to understand the relative attractiveness of an industry.** Porter's *Five Forces Model* helps business people understand the relative attractiveness of an industry and includes the following five forces:

   a. *Buyer power.* High when buyers have many choices from whom to buy, and low when their choices are few.

   b. *Supplier power.* High when buyers have few choices from whom to buy, and low when their choices are many.

   c. *Threat of substitute products and services.* High when there are many alternatives to a product or service, and low when there are few alternatives from which to choose.

   d. *Threat of new entrants.* High when it is easy for new competitors to enter a market, and low when there are significant entry barriers to entering a market.

   e. *Rivalry among existing competitors.* High when competition is fierce in a market, and low when competition is more complacent.

3. **Describe the emerging role of e-marketplaces in B2B e-commerce.** An *electronic marketplace (e-marketplace)* is an interactive business providing a central market space where multiple buyers and suppliers can engage in e-commerce and/or other e-commerce business activities, such as sharing mission-critical information for the development of products and parts, collaborating on new ideas, and deploying infrastructure applications. Two variations of B2B e-marketplaces include horizontal and vertical e-marketplaces. A *horizontal e-marketplace* is an electronic marketplace that connects buyers and sellers across many industries, primarily for MRO materials commerce. A *vertical marketplace* is an electronic marketplace that connects buyers and sellers in a given industry (e.g., oil and gas, textiles, and retail).

4. **Identify the differences and similarities among customers and their perceived value of products and services in the B2B and B2C e-commerce business models.** Customers in the B2C e-commerce business model are end consumers. They (1) exhibit greatly varying demographics, lifestyles, wants, and needs, (2) distinguish products and services by convenience versus specialty, (3) often shop for commodity-like and digital products, and (4) sometimes require a level of *mass customization* to get exactly what they want. Customers in the B2B e-commerce business model are other businesses. They (1) distinguish products and services by *maintenance, repair, and operations (MRO) materials* versus *direct materials*, (2) aggregate demand to create negotiations for volume discounts on large purchases, and (3) most often perform e-commerce activities within an e-marketplace.

5. **Compare and contrast the development of a marketing mix for customers in the B2B and B2C e-commerce business models.** A *marketing mix* is the set of marketing tools that your organization will use to pursue its marketing objectives in reaching and attracting potential customers. In B2B e-commerce, marketing mixes do not usually include broad and generic strategies that reach all potential businesses. Instead, marketing often occurs within the context of an e-marketplace. Once a contact has been made between businesses, the development of the relationship is still formal and often includes negotiations for pricing, quality, specifications, and delivery timing.

   In B2C e-commerce, a marketing mix will include some or all of the following:

   a. Registering your site with a search engine.

   b. *Online ads* (small advertisements that appear on other sites), including *pop-up ads* (small Web pages containing an advertisement that appear on your screen apart from the current Web site loaded into your browser) and *pop-under ads* (a form of a pop-up ad that you do not see until you close your current browser session).

c. *Viral marketing*, which encourages users of a product or service supplied by a B2C e-commerce business to encourage friends to join in as well.

d. *Affiliate program*, an arrangement made between two e-commerce sites that directs viewers from one site to the other.

6. **Summarize the various ways of moving money in the world of e-commerce and related issues, including electronic payment systems.** B2C e-commerce payment systems most commonly include credit cards, *financial cybermediaries* (such as PayPal), *electronic cheques* (online bank-ing being an implementation), *electronic bill presentment and payment (EBPP)*, *smart cards* (credit card with an embedded computer chip on which digital information can be stored and updated), and *digital wallets* (software and instructions for completing a transaction). In the B2B e-commerce business model, financial EDI is the norm. *Financial EDI* is an electronic process used primarily within the business-to-business e-commerce business model for the payment of purchases. Security for the electronic transfer of funds is an overriding concern. Techniques such as *encryption*, *public key encryption (PKE)*, *secure sockets layers (SSLs)*, and *secure electronic trans-actions (SETs)* all address this issue of security.

CLOSING CASE STUDY ONE

WHEN YOU'RE BIG, YOU CAN BE YOUR OWN B2B E-MARKETPLACE

Business-to-business (B2B) e-marketplaces are the growing trend in the B2B e-commerce business model. Businesses from all industries and countries can gather, perform commerce functions, share mission-critical information, and deploy infrastructure applications that allow those organizations to tie their internal systems to each other.

But some companies—the largest ones—don't have to play in the generic B2B e-marketplaces. Instead, they can build their own and literally require that their suppliers participate. Once such company is Volkswagen AG. Its B2B e-marketplace is called VWgroupsupply.com (www.vwgroupsupply.com).

Volkswagen AG offers eight brands of automobiles—Volkswagen (passenger), Volkswagen Commercial Vehicles, Audi, Bentley, Bugatti, Lamborghini, Seat, and Skoda. In 2003, Volkswagen spent almost 60 billion euros, or approximately $77 billion, on components, automotive parts, and MRO materials for its manufacturing operations. When you spend that much money with your suppliers, you can open and run your own B2B e-marketplace.

VWgroupsupply.com handles 90 percent of Volkswagen global purchases. Almost all request for quotes, contract negotiations, catalogue updating and buying, purchase-order management, vehicle program man-agement, and payments are handled electronically and online through VWgroupsupply.com.

Gains in efficiency and productivity coupled with materials cost reductions have been tremendous. The cost savings alone generated over the last three years were more than 100 million euros, or approximately $127 million.

Volkswagen requires that each of its 5500 suppliers use VWgroupsupply.com for any interactions. Suppliers place product and pricing catalogues on the system, respond to requests for quotes, and collaborate with Volkswagen engineers on new product designs, all in the safe and secure environment of Volkswagen's proprietary B2B e-marketplace.

By requiring its suppliers to interact with Volkswagen in the e-marketplace, purchasing agents no longer have to spend valuable time searching for information and pricing. Volkswagen has, in essence, created a system that brings the necessary information to the purchasing agents. This new system within VWgroupsupply.com is called iPAD, or Internal Purchasing Agent Desk.

Prior to the implementation of iPAD, purchasing agents entering a purchase order for a vehicle front module had to use numerous separate systems to complete the process. They had to retrieve information from a supplier system and its database, query information in Volkswagen's internal parts information system, obtain information from a request-for-quotes database, enter information into a contract-negotiation transcript system, and interact with several other systems and databases. In all, the purchasing agent had to log into and use seven separate systems. Analysis revealed that Volkswagen purchasing agents were spending 70 percent of their time finding, retrieving, analyzing, validating, and moving information. This took away valuable time from such tasks as negotiating better prices with suppliers.

Using a form of an integrated collaboration environment, or ICE, which we discussed in Chapter 2, purchasing agents now participate in a simple three-step process. First, iPAD captures and sends a business event to the purchasing agent, such as the need to order vehicle front modules. Second, iPAD attaches to that communication other necessary information such as information about potential suppliers, their costs, and other forms of analysis and descriptive information. Finally, iPAD sends the corresponding business processes and work flows to be completed electronically.

It works much like a digital dashboard, which we also introduced you to in Chapter 2. When purchasing agents log on to the iPAD portal in the morning, they receive a customized Web page with announcements, business alerts, analyses, and digital workflows to be completed. The purchasing agents can set out immediately to complete the tasks for the day, without having to spend 70 percent of their time finding, retrieving, and analyzing information. iPAD even customizes the Web page according to the purchasing agent's native language, something very necessary for a global manufacturer of automobiles with more than 2000 purchasing agents worldwide.[13]

Questions

1. Volkswagen operates its own proprietary B2B e-marketplace in which its suppliers participate. What are the disadvantages to Volkswagen of not using a generic B2B e-marketplace with even more suppliers? What are the advantages to Volkswagen of developing and using its own proprietary B2B e-marketplace?

2. When Volkswagen needs a new part design, it uses VWsupplygroup.com to get its suppliers involved in the design process early. This creates a tremendous amount of interorganizational collaboration. What are the advantages to the suppliers and to Volkswagen in doing so?

3. How is Volkswagen's VWgroupsupply.com B2B e-marketplace an example of a vertical e-marketplace implementation? How is it an example of a horizontal e-marketplace implementation? Why is it necessary that Volkswagen combine both of these e-marketplaces into one e-marketplace? What would be the drawbacks to creating two different e-marketplaces—one for suppliers of direct materials and one for suppliers of MRO materials?

4. In Chapter 2, we alluded to four challenges to successful supply chain management. Pick two of those and discuss how VWgroupsupply.com helps Volkswagen address them. Is there one in the list not specifically discussed in this case? If so, which is it? Postulate how Volkswagen has successfully met that challenge as well.

5. To make effective purchasing decisions, Volkswagen's purchasing agents need business intelligence. What kind of business intelligence does iPAD provide to purchasing agents for carrying out their tasks? What additional kinds of business intelligence not discussed in this case could Volkswagen's purchasing agents take advantage of to make more effective decisions?

6. IPAD manages the workflow for purchasing agents. Describe how iPAD manages this process including information provided, steps to be executed, and the presentation of information.

CLOSING CASE STUDY TWO

TOTING THE E-COMMERCE LINE WITH EBAGS

For a true e-commerce success story you don't have to look any further than eBags (www.ebags.com). While many pure-play e-commerce Web sites have fallen by the wayside, eBags is not only surviving, it is thriving. It is the world's leading online provider of bags and accessories for all lifestyles. With 180 brands and over 8000 products, eBags has sold more than 2.5 million bags since its launch in March 1999. It carries a complete line of premium and popular brands, including Samsonite, JanSport, The North Face, Liz Claiborne, and Adidas. You can buy anything from backpacks and carry-ons to computer cases and handbags at extremely competitive prices from its Web site.

eBags has received several awards for excellence in online retailing, among them:

- Circle of Excellence Platinum Award, Bizrate.com
- Web Site of the Year, *Catalog Age Magazine*
- Email Marketer of the Year, ClickZ.MessageMedia
- Marketer of the Year, Colorado AMA
- Rocky Mountain Portal Award
- Gold Peak Catalog, Colorado AMA
- Entrepreneur of the Year—Rocky Mountain Region, Ernst and Young
- E-Commerce Initiative Award of Merit, Colorado Software and Internet Association
- Best of Show, eTravel World Awards
- 50 Essential Web Sites, Condé Nast Traveler

A good part of the reason for eBags's success is its commitment to providing each customer with superior service, 24 hours a day, 365 days a year. eBags provides customers with the ability to contact customer service representatives for personal assistance by telephone or e-mail and also provides convenient, real-time UPS order tracking. According to Jon Nordmark, CEO of eBags.com, "From a customer perspective, we've spent a great deal of time developing pioneering ways to guide our shoppers to the bags and accessories that enhance their lifestyles through function and fashion."

Although you would never know it, this superior customer service is not provided by eBags employees. For the past several years, eBags has outsourced both the handling of phone orders and customer service calls to Finali Corporation (www.finali.com). "The call

centre is often the only human contact customers have with our brand," says eBags CEO Jon Nordmark. "By maintaining a call centre staff that can think on its feet, Finali delivers real value to our customers and a measurable return on our call centre investment."

Typically, the conversion rate of inbound customer calls to sales at the call centre has been about 25 percent. But during the 2001 holiday season, special training and incentives for Finali call centre reps servicing the eBags Web site helped raise that number to 44 percent. In addition, the average size of orders placed through the call centre hit $100, topping the average Web order of just over $75. The increased conversion rates and order size meant that for every dollar eBags spent with Finali, Finali generated $3.79 in sales.

eBags' many online services also distinguish it from the rest of the online marketplace. eBags' Laptop Finder searches for compatible laptop cases by brand and model number of your computer. And eBags' Airline Approved Carry-On Finder will show you all the carry-on bags that fit in each airline's overhead bins. eBags has also tightly integrated its systems with those of UPS to provide accurate estimated arrival dates and free returns.

eBags announced profits for the first time in December 2001, posting 5.4 percent earnings before interest, taxes, depreciation, and amortization. "Part of that achievement was due to smart outsourcing like the call centre," says eBags CFO Eliot Cobb. As of early 2004, eBags had posted seven consecutive profitable quarters.[14]

Questions

1. According to Porter's Five Forces Model, how would you characterize the competitive space in which eBags operates according to buyer power, supplier power, threat of substitute products or services, threat of new entrants, and rivalry among existing competitors? You may have to do some research on the Web to determine what other e-commerce Web sites sell similar products. Pick one of Porter's five forces and describe what steps eBags has undertaken to shift that force in a positive way in its direction.

2. In our discussions of customers and their perceptions of value, we noted that customers tend to categorize products and services as either convenience or specialty. How would you characterize what eBags provides—convenience, specialty, or perhaps a combination of the two? Justify your answer.

3. We also noted in this chapter that commodity-like and digital products work extremely well within the B2C e-commerce business model. eBags sells products that are neither. How can it be so successful without selling these types of products?

4. How would you describe the majority of eBags' customers (end consumers)? What sort of demographics would you like to know about eBags' customers if you were an eBags employee?

5. Given that eBags' customers are end consumers, and on the basis of your answer to question 4, what sort of marketing mix would you recommend for eBags? If you specify creating affiliate programs, identify the types of Web sites with which to enter into an affiliate program.

6. What innovative steps could eBags employ to offer mass customization to its customers? Do you think this would have any measurable positive effect on sales? Why or why not?

7. What sort of payment options does eBags accept? You may have to visit its Web site to determine this. Should eBags consider broadening the payment options it accepts? Why or why not?

Key Terms and Concepts

affiliate program, 335
business-to-business (B2B) e-commerce, 322
business-to-consumer (B2C) e-commerce, 321
buyer power, 324
click-through, 335
conversion rate, 335
demand aggregation, 331
digital wallet, 339
direct materials, 331
electronic bill presentment and payment (EBPP), 338
electronic cheque, 338
electronic commerce (e-commerce), 320
electronic data interchange (EDI), 340

electronic marketplace (e-marketplace), 332
encryption, 342
entry barrier, 326
financial cybermediary, 338
financial EDI (financial electronic data interchange), 341
Five Forces Model, 324
horizontal e-marketplace, 333
loyalty program, 325
maintenance, repair, and operations (MRO) materials (indirect materials), 331
marketing mix, 334
mass customization, 331
online ad (banner ad), 334
pop-under ad, 334

pop-up ad, 334
public key encryption (PKE), 342
reverse auction, 331
rivalry among existing competitors, 326
secure electronic transaction (SET), 343
secure sockets layer (SSL), 342
smart card, 338
spoofing, 340
supplier power, 325
switching costs, 325
threat of new entrants, 326
threat of substitute products or services, 325
vertical e-marketplace, 333
viral marketing, 335

Short-Answer Questions

1. What is electronic commerce? What are the four main perspectives for e-commerce?

2. What is the Five Forces Model? What are the "five forces" of that model?

3. How is a loyalty program an example of reducing buyer power?

4. How can you use a B2B e-marketplace to reduce your dependency on a particular supplier?

5. What are switching costs?

6. What are entry barriers?

7. How do convenience and specialty items differ in the B2C e-commerce business model?

8. Why do commodity-like and digital items sell well in the B2C e-commerce business model?

9. What is mass customization?

10. What are maintenance, repair, and operations (MRO) materials?

11. What is demand aggregation?

12. What are direct materials?

13. How does a reverse auction work?

14. How are vertical and horizontal e-marketplaces different?

15. What is spoofing?

16. What can a marketing mix include for a B2C e-commerce business?

17. How do pop-up and pop-under ads differ?

18. What is a conversion rate?

19. What are the major types of B2C e-commerce payment systems?

20. What is the difference between a client-side digital wallet and a server-side digital wallet?

21. What is financial EDI?

22. How does public key encryption work?

23. How are secure sockets layers (SSLs) and secure electronic transactions (SETs) different? How are they the same?

Assignments and Exercises

1. **PORTER'S FIVE FORCES MODEL AND YOUR SCHOOL.** To illustrate the use of Porter's Five Forces Model, let's apply it to your school. Assume that you are a school administrator and want to use Porter's Five Forces Model for evaluating your business program's competitive position in the marketplace. Is buyer power low or high? What are some options other than your school's program that students could choose? Is supplier power low or high? Who are your school's suppliers? Is the threat of substitute products or services low or high? What are possible substitutes to getting an education? Is the threat of new entrants low or high? What entry barriers exist? Is the rivalry among existing competition low or high? Who are your school's competitors?

2. **DEALING WITH THE GREAT DIGITAL DIVIDE.** The great digital divide addresses the concerns of many people that the world is becoming one marked by the "haves" and "have nots" with respect to technology—that is, the traditional notion of a "Third World" is now also being defined by the extent to which a country has access to and uses technology. Find out what, if anything, the United Nations is doing about this issue and express an opinion on whether you believe its efforts will be successful. Determine if there are organizations such as private companies or foundations that have the digital divide high on their agendas. For any such organizations you find, evaluate their efforts and express an opinion on whether they will be successful. Finally, search for a less developed country that is making significant local efforts to deal with the digital divide. If you can't find one, prepare a list of the countries you reviewed and briefly describe the conditions in one of them with respect to technology.

3. **RESEARCHING A BUSINESS-TO-BUSINESS E-MARKETPLACE.** Biz2Biz (www.biz2biz.com/marketplace) is a B2B e-marketplace. Connect to its site and do some looking around. What sort of marketing services does it provide through its Biz2BizCommunication program? What sort of services does it provide for creating and maintaining an electronic catalog? If you owned a business and wanted to join, what process would you have to go through? How much does it cost your organization to join Biz2Biz? What buyer tools does Biz2Biz provide its membership?

4. **DEVELOPING M-COMMERCE SCENARIOS FOR GPS CELL PHONES.** Soon, cell phones will be equipped with GPS chips that enable users to be located to within a geographical location about the size of a tennis court. The primary purpose for installing GPS chips in phones is to enable emergency services to locate a cell phone user. For example, if you dial an emergency assistance number (911 in the United States) from your home now, it is possible for a computer system to use your home telephone number to access a database and

obtain your address. This could be very useful in situations in which you were unable to give address information to the emergency operator for some reason. The problem with trying to do the same thing with present-day cell phones is that you could be calling from anywhere, and that is the problem GPS-enabled cell phones are intended to overcome.

As you might imagine, marketers have been monitoring this development with great interest because GPS phones will support m-commerce, which we discussed in Chapter 1. When the new cell phones become available, marketers visualize scenarios where they will know who you are (by your telephone number) and where you are (by the GPS chip). One possible way they could use this information, for example, is to give you a call when you are walking past their shop in the mall to let you know of a special sale on items they know you would be interested in buying. Of course, retailers would have to possess IT systems that would permit them to craft such personalized offers, and you would have had to give them permission to call you.

Find out what at least three e-commerce marketers are saying about personalized marketing using GPS-equipped cell phones and prepare an analysis of how the phones will be likely to be used when the technology is widely available.

5. **FINDING THE MOST POPULAR B2C E-COMMERCE SITES.** Connect to the Web and do some research to find the most popular B2C e-commerce Web sites in terms of number of hits or views per month. What are the sites? Which of the sites in some way or another supports the concept of an e-marketplace where end consumers can gather?

Discussion Questions

1. In what ways can shopping over the Internet be more convenient for consumers? In what ways can it be less convenient? List at least five products you would have no hesitation buying over the Internet, five products you might want to think about a bit before buying, and five products you would never consider buying over the Internet. Justify your reasons in each case.

2. In your opinion, according to Porter's Five Forces Model, has competition increased or decreased overall as a result of the Internet and e-commerce? Specifically address each of the five forces in Porter's model.

3. Why is the ability to change prices instantaneously considered an advantage for e-commerce Web sites? When might the use of personalized pricing be a disadvantage for an e-commerce Web site?

4. There have been a string of e-commerce Web sites running out of cash, not being able to attract more money from investors, and going out of business as a result. What are some of the main reasons this happened?

5. Under what circumstances would it be appropriate to consider using viral marketing? See if you can think of an organization with an online presence that might benefit from viral marketing but is not

currently using it. It could be your school, for example, or it could be an organization you are involved with. How would you suggest the organization go about using viral marketing in order for it to achieve the desired results? What are some of the other marketing techniques available for an e-commerce Web site to use? Why is it important to consider a mix of techniques rather than just relying on a single one?

6. Describe the services provided by value-added networks that make it easier for companies to exchange EDI transactions with each other. What are the pros and cons of using value-added networks for B2B e-commerce? Why don't more companies use the Internet for EDI since it is much cheaper than using a value-added network? Assume that you work for a telecommunications company that operates a value-added network (AT&T or GXS). What sort of strategies would you encourage your company to explore to deal with the possibility of losing considerable amounts of revenues as your customers leave you in favour of using other Internet-based services?

7. What are the advantages and disadvantages of B2B marketplaces for buyers? For sellers? How could a supplier company play on the relationships that it has with a long-standing customer to avoid

getting pulled into a reverse auction in an open B2B marketplace? Why do some observers say that B2B marketplaces can be risky ventures?

8. Throughout this chapter, we've illuminated numerous differences between end consumers and businesses as customers. Review those differences and then write down the three you consider most significant. Discuss those three. For the differences that you did not choose as the three most important, be prepared to justify your decision.

9. In this chapter, we discussed using such technologies as B2B e-marketplaces to create tighter

supply chain managements, thereby driving out costs. If you refer back to Chapter 2, you'll recall that another major business initiative is customer relationship management (CRM). How can B2C e-commerce businesses use the Internet to further enhance their CRM initiatives? How can B2B e-commerce businesses use the Internet to further enhance their CRM initiatives? Does it become easier or harder to maintain relationships with customers as businesses move toward more "electronic" commerce? Why?

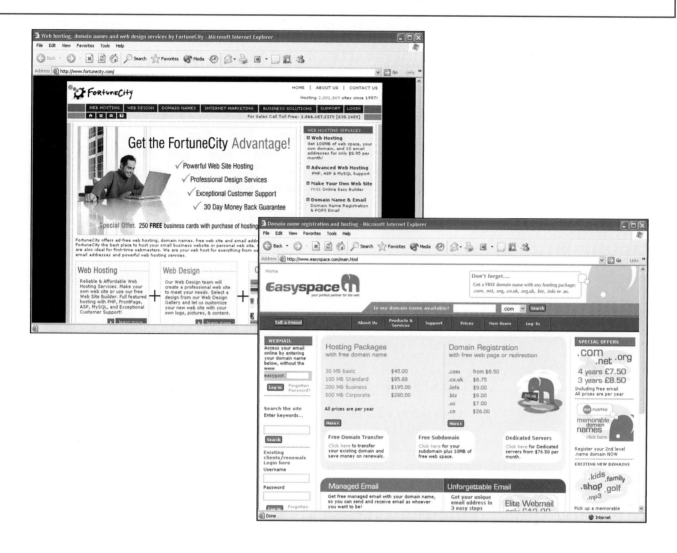

Electronic Commerce

Getting Your Business on the Internet

Let's say you've decided it might be fun (and profitable) to establish a retail-oriented Internet-based business. You can use the one your team created in the previous Team Work project if it's appropriate or you can create a new one. You know that many such e-commerce businesses don't make it, but you'd like to be one that is successful. There are a lot of resources on the Internet that can help you with the tasks of selecting the right business in the first place, getting the site up and running, deciding who should host your site, marketing your site, understanding privacy issues, and obtaining the funds you need to pay your expenses until your business begins to show a profit. On the Web site that supports this text (www.mcgrawhill.ca/college/haag), select "Electronic Commerce Projects"), we've provided direct links to many useful Web sites. These are a great starting point for completing this project. We also encourage you to search the Internet for others.

→ **Electronic Commerce Links**

COMPETITIVE INTELLIGENCE

The first thing you need is an idea for the business. What would you like to sell? A product or a service? Make sure you have expertise, or something special to offer. After you've come up with a candidate, it's time to see how much competition is out there and what they're up to. One of the things many new business owners fail to do is to see how many competitors there are before they launch their business. You may find there are too many and that they would be tough competition for you (review Porter's Five Forces Model). Or you may find that there are few competitors and the ones who are out there aren't doing a terrific job.

Seek out and look at some of the Web sites of businesses in the competitive space you're thinking of entering. As you do, answer the following questions:

A. How many sites did you find that are offering the same product or service you're planning to offer?

B. How many are in your country and how many are in other countries?

C. Did you come across a site from another country that has a unique approach that you did not see on any of the sites in your own country?

STOREFRONT SOFTWARE

If you decide to sell products, there is software that you can use to make it easy to create a Web site. There are many software products for you to choose from. Some will cost you a lot of money, but others are free. FreeMerchant.com, for example, has a Basic Store for $9.95 per month, a Bronze Package for $24.95 per month, a Silver Package for $49.95 per month, and a Gold Package for $99.95 per month. What you get in each of these packages is listed in detail on the FreeMerchant.com Web site (www.freemerchant.com). Since there are many options to choose from, it would be worth your while to do a little research to see if you can find an article that compares current versions of storefront software. A site like ZDNet.com (www.zdnet.com) would be a good place to start your search. Build up a list of features that you will need for your e-commerce site, and then compare your needs with the features offered by the various software packages. They all sound good when you read about them on the vendors' Web sites so be sure you take a "test drive" of the software before you sign up.

Another possibility would be to sign up for a shopping mall. Find your way to Amazon.com's zShops or Yahoo!Store and see what you think of these alternatives. Finally, you'll need a way for your customers to pay you for what they buy. This involves getting a merchant account which permits you to accept credit cards. Most of the storefront sites will explain how merchant accounts work and will help you get a merchant account (see www.bigstep.com, for example).

A. What features have you decided your storefront software must provide?

B. How have you evaluated the pros and cons of using a storefront software package versus the options offered by Amazon.ca and Yahoo!?

C. See if you can track down users of software options you are considering. Send them an e-mail and ask them what they like and dislike. You may be surprised at their answers.

HOSTING SERVICES

You've got some options here. You can decide to acquire the necessary computer and communications hardware and software to manage your own technical infrastructure, or you can let a specialist firm do it for you. Unless you're really into the technical side of things, it's probably better to work with a firm that specializes in it. They are called *Web hosting services* and there are plenty of them around. Cost, reliability, security, and customer service are some of the criteria you might use in selecting a hosting service. If you're planning to have your business located in a country with poor telecommunications services, don't forget that you can choose a hosting service located in a country with a more reliable telecommunications infrastructure, anywhere in the world. Some companies provide directories that make it easy for you to find and compare prices and features of Web hosting companies, sort of like shopping malls for Web hosting services. An example of such a company is FindYourHosting.com (www.findyourhosting.com). Take a look at its site to see some of the options available. As you consider Web hosting services, answer the following questions:

A. Compare the costs of the various hosting services. Were you able to find one that seems to be within your budget?

B. How can you evaluate the reliability of the various Web hosting services?

C. How can you evaluate the quality of a Web hosting company's customer service? What do you have a right to expect in the way of customer service and also security?

MARKETING YOUR SITE

In this chapter, we discussed several options for marketing a Web site: registering with search engines, online ads, viral marketing, and affiliate programs. Deciding on the marketing mix that will be most effective and still permit you to stay within a reasonable budget will be critical to the success of your venture. You may want to consider employing an Internet marketing consultant to help you lay out a marketing plan. One, AdDesigner.com (www.addesigner.com), even offers some free services. Also, you may want to see what marketing services your storefront software or Web hosting service may offer. As you consider how to market your site, answer the following questions.

A. How have you defined your target market? What people will be most interested in your product or service?

B. Which of the available marketing techniques have you selected as most appropriate to market your site? Why have you selected this particular marketing mix?

C. What have you decided about using the services of a marketing consultant? How did you justify your decision?

Go to the Online Learning Centre at www.mcgrawhill.ca/college/haag for quizzes, extra content, a searchable glossary, and more! Click on "Electronic Commerce Projects" for links to hundreds of Web sites.

Go to the text CD-ROM for data files, extra content, and Skills Modules on Microsoft Excel, Microsoft Access, HTML, and e-portfolios.

CHAPTER EIGHT

STUDENT LEARNING OUTCOMES

BY THE END OF THIS CHAPTER, STUDENTS WILL BE ABLE TO:

1. Describe the emerging trends and technologies that will have an impact on the changing Internet.

2. Compare and contrast the various types of technologies that are emerging as we move toward physiological interaction with technology.

3. Understand technological innovations and trends that will increase portability and mobility.

4. Describe the coming C2C explosion and the broadening of e-government as they relate to the rebirth of e-commerce.

WEB SUPPORT

- MBA Programs

- Specialized MBA Programs

- Graduate School Information and Tips

- Tele-education (Distance Learning)

Visit
www.mcgrawhill.ca/college/haag

LearningCentre

CASE STUDY:

THE FUTURE: TECHNOLOGY OUT, PRINGLES IN

You might hold a future technological innovation in your hand right now if you were eating Pringles. It's true. In 2002, i-sec, a security company in England, built a wireless antenna from a Pringles can, attached it to a computer, and then drove around London's financial district. Because of the particular construction of the can (a long tube with aluminum-type material inside), i-sec employees were able to detect and attach to over two-thirds of the wireless networks in that financial district. More alarming, they were then able to break into the networks because there was no security.

In a rich neighbourhood in New York, hackers used a Pringles can antenna and drove around the neighbourhood during the late night hours trying to detect home wireless networks. When they found one, they stopped and spray-painted a small dot on the curb in front of the house. On a later date, the hackers drove around (in the middle of the day) in a construction van, stopped at every marked house, and attempted to break into the wireless network. If they were successful (and many times they were), they were able to steal bank account numbers, passwords, and other personal and sensitive information.

Technology of the future will take on many forms, with a can of Pringles being an extreme example. Some of the more plausible and helpful coming technological innovations include:

- Digital cash that you can use on the Internet just like folding cash without a credit card or traditional money transfer.
- Renting personal productivity software from an application service provider for only a few pennies while you use your PDA.
- CAVEs that recreate 3D likenesses of people so you believe they are in the room with you.
- Biometrics that will use your physiological characteristics (such as your iris scan) to determine your identity and perhaps even tell if you have low blood sugar.
- Biochips that will help blind people regain some of their sight.

The list is really endless. In this chapter, we want to introduce you to several such upcoming technological innovations. The primary focus of the chapter isn't just on the technology, however, but on what future technologies will enable you to do. Equally important, we want you to think about the societal ramifications of these technologies. As we've emphasized throughout this book, technology is important but how you choose to use it is far more important.

By the way, some schools now teach hacking with a Pringles can. One such school is Intense School, which provides CEH (Certified Ethical Hacker) Certification courses. There, you can learn the right way to use an empty Pringles can.[1,2]

Introduction

Technology is changing every day. But even more important than simply staying up with the changes in technology, you need to think about how those changes will affect your life. It's often fun to read and learn about "leading- and bleeding-edge" technologies. It is something that we would encourage you to do. The consequences of those technology changes, however, may have an impact on all our lives more far reaching than you can imagine.

In this final chapter, we will take a look at several leading- and bleeding-edge technologies, including speech recognition, biometrics, implant chips, and digital cash. These new technologies can and will impact your personal and business life. Technology for the sake of technology is never a good thing and can even be counterproductive. Using technology appropriately to enhance your personal life and to move your organization toward its strategic initiatives, on the other hand, are always both good things.

This has been both an exciting and a challenging chapter for us to write. The excitement is in the opportunity to talk with you about some emerging technological innovations. The challenge has been not to spotlight the technologies themselves overmuch, but rather to help you focus on how those technologies will affect your life.

So, as you read this chapter, have fun but don't get caught up exclusively in the technology advances themselves that are on the horizon. Instead, try to envision how those new technologies will change the things that you do and the way you do them, both from a personal and organizational perspective. As throughout this book, we remind you always to consider how to make new technology relevant and productive for you.

To introduce you to just a few of the many new technologies on the horizon, we've chosen those that we believe will have the greatest impact. We present those emerging technologies within the context of four important trends (see Figure 8.1).

Figure 8.1

Emerging Trends and Technologies

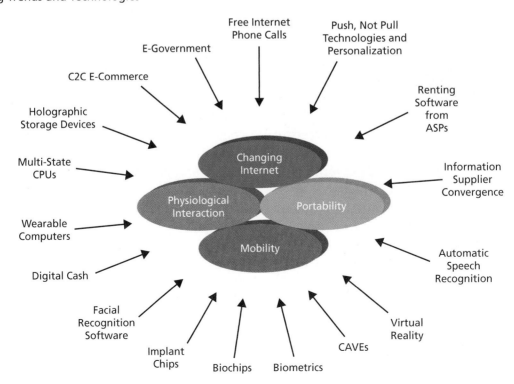

The Changing Internet

Without a doubt, the most explosive and visible aspect of technology is the Internet. Over the next several years, you will witness an unbelievable number of changes with respect to the Internet. You'll see the emergence of many new Internet-based trends and Internet-based technologies. Among those will be free Internet phone calls, push (not pull) technologies and personalization, renting personal productivity software from application service providers, information supplier convergence, and digital cash (which we'll discuss in a later section).

FREE INTERNET PHONE CALLS

Right now, true "free" Internet-based phone calls all over the world are not possible. That will soon come. But you can now use the Internet and your computer to make phone calls, with many of the phone calls you make costing as little as 2.9 cents per minute to many places around the globe.

One such company offering Internet phone calls is Voicenet (www.voicenet.com). To use Voicenet, you connect first to its Web site and download and install some simple software (see Figure 8.2). You also pick a user name and password. You can then use your computer's equipment—microphone and speakers—to make a phone call to anyone, even if they have a cell phone. You can also connect a standard telephone to your computer and use it in conjunction with Voicenet's service.

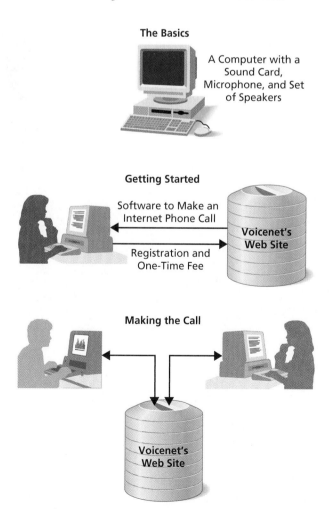

The Basics

A Computer with a Sound Card, Microphone, and Set of Speakers

Getting Started

Software to Make an Internet Phone Call

Voicenet's Web Site

Registration and One-Time Fee

Making the Call

Voicenet's Web Site

Figure 8.2

Making an Internet Phone Call

Internet phone calling will certainly impact every part of your life. You will have greater mobility with your technology and your telephone-calling system. We believe it will eventually greatly reduce your telephone bill. It will increase customer service over the Web, because companies will be able to communicate with you using a "traditional" phone call while you visit their Web sites and consider products and services to purchase.

PUSH, NOT PULL TECHNOLOGIES AND PERSONALIZATION

We live in a *pull* technology environment. That is, you look for, request, and find what you want. On the Internet, for example, you visit a specific site and request information, services, and products. So you're literally "pulling" what you want. Future emphasis will be on *push* technologies. In a **push technology** environment, businesses and organizations come to you with information, services, and product offerings based on your profile. This isn't spam or mass e-mailings.

For example, in some parts of the country you can subscribe to a cell service that pushes information to you in the form of video rental information. Whenever you pass near a video store, your cell phone (which is GPS-enabled) triggers a computer within the video store that evaluates your rental history to see if any new videos have arrived that you might be interested in viewing. In this case, the system generates a personal data warehouse of rental history—including dimensions for the day of the week, the time of the day, and video categories—concerning you and then evaluates information in the smaller cubes (see Figure 8.3). The evaluation seeks to affirm that (1) you usually rent videos on that particular day, (2) you usually rent videos during that time of that day, and (3) there is a distinct video category from which you rent videos during that time of the day. If so, the system then checks to see if there are any movies in that category that you haven't rented and that it hasn't previously contacted you about.

Figure 8.3

Tracking What You Want When You Want It with a Data Warehouse

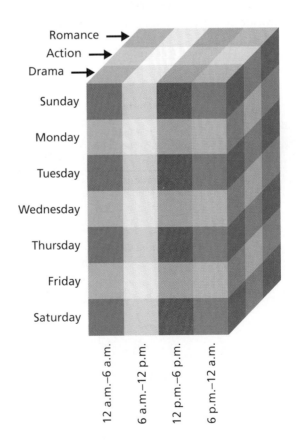

If so, the video store computer will call your cell phone with a message concerning a new release. It will also give you street-by-street directions to the video store and hold the video for you. If the video store doesn't have any new releases that might interest you, you won't receive a phone call.

You might also someday receive a personalized pizza delivery message on your television as you start to watch a ball game. The message might say, "We'll deliver your favourite sausage and mushroom pizza to your doorstep before the game begins. On your remote control, press the *order now* button."

Of course, situations such as these rely on IT's ability to store vast amounts of information about you. Technologies such as databases and data warehouses will definitely play an important role in the development of push technologies that do more than just push spam and mass e-mail. In the instance of the pizza delivery message on your television, a local pizza store would have determined that you like sausage and mushroom pizza and that you order it most often while watching a ball game.

RENTING SOFTWARE FROM APPLICATION SERVICE PROVIDERS

As more technology choices become available to you (smart phones, PDAs, tablet PCs, and the like), you'll probably opt to use many different devices to satisfy your computing needs. As technology becomes increasingly small, you may not have the capacity necessary on every device to store all your software needs. This has given rise to the notion of renting personal productivity software instead of buying it. Many businesses—as you learned in previous chapters—now do rent some software instead of buying it and installing it on every single technology device within the organization. Those businesses are using an application service provider (ASP), or some variation of one.

Let's focus for a moment on your personal use of an ASP (see Figure 8.4). In the future, ASPs will provide personal productivity software for you to use (for a fee, perhaps $0.25 per session) and storage so you can store your files on their Web servers as opposed to your personal technologies.

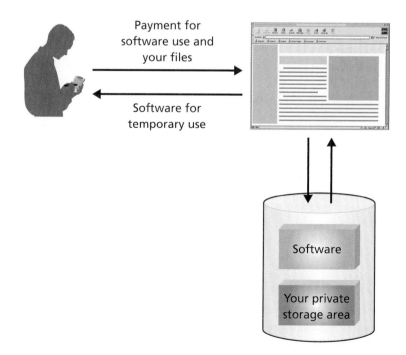

Payment for software use and your files

Software for temporary use

Software

Your private storage area

Figure 8.4

Renting Personal Productivity Software from an Application Service Provider (ASP)

THE FUTURE OF INFORMATION SUPPLIER CONVERGENCE

Information supplier convergence, through the process of mergers and acquisitions (M&A), seems to be an already foregone conclusion in the business world. Cable TV providers are acquiring telephone service providers, and vice versa. Internet conglomerates, such as America Online, are merging with entertainment giants such as Time Warner. Other information conglomerates are composed of TV stations, newspapers, radio stations, and countless other types of information suppliers.

What will be interesting to see is the M&A deals that occur within the next several years. Here are a few possibilities as predicted by Erick Schonfeld and On Malik in a recent issue of *Business 2.0* magazine. Which do you think will become a reality?

- AT&T Wireless and Cingular—creating a company with over 40 million wireless users
- Apple and Roxio—you know Apple; Roxio provides the most popular CD- and DVD-burning software
- Yahoo! and Overture—you know Yahoo!; Overture is one of the largest paid-search providers on the Internet
- Yahoo!, Overture, and Diller's Interactive—see previous bullet; Diller's is the parent company of Citysearch, Expedia, the Home Shopping Network, Hotels.com, Match.com, and Ticketmaster[3]

For example, you may be in an airport and need to build a spreadsheet with your PDA. Your PDA, however, may not have a complete version of Excel. So, you would use your PDA to connect to the Internet and a personal ASP. With your PDA, you would then use the personal ASP's Excel software to create your spreadsheet and save it on the ASP's Web server. When you finally get back to the office, you would use your computer there, connect to the same ASP, and retrieve your spreadsheet and save it on your computer.

There are many issues you'll have to consider when determining whether or not to use a personal ASP, with privacy and reliability definitely being important ones. If all your information is on a Web-based server, it will be easier for someone to gain access to it (for the wrong reasons) than if you stored all your information on your home or office computer. When considering reliability, you need to think about what happens if the personal ASP's Web site goes down. How will you perform your work? In spite of many potential drawbacks, we believe personal ASPs will become a part of your everyday life in the future.

INFORMATION SUPPLIER CONVERGENCE

You'll notice many benefits when we see the convergence of information suppliers. "Information suppliers" provide you with magazines, newspapers, Internet access, telephone service, cable TV, books, business news, and many other types of information. For example, as you read in the opening case study in Chapter 7, America Online is now providing its customers with bill payment information and reminders. Right now, you probably receive information products and services from numerous suppliers. It's difficult therefore for any one of them to help you organize and filter information, because it's coming from so many sources.

You may already be suffering from the information glut of the information age. You may receive hundreds of e-mails, text messages, and phone calls each day. Moreover, when faced with a business problem or opportunity you may have too *much* information, and may suffer from "analysis paralysis," which can occur because you simply have too much information to analyze and you never really get around to actually

WHERE SHOULD THE DECISION REST?

In the future, you can also expect to see a movement toward intellectual computing, a step beyond artificial intelligence (review Chapter 6) in which computers will learn, become increasingly smarter, and take over many decision-making tasks for you.

The degree to which you allow a computer to take over a decision-making task is often a function of the decision being made. For example, most inventory management systems are very good at determining what quantities of a given product line to reorder. If the system orders too many, no real harm is done because excess inventory just sits on the shelf. If not enough is ordered, the business will simply experience a stockout for a given period of time.

On the other hand, you should never let a computer system tell you how much dosage of a given medicine to give a patient without first verifying the recommendation. The wrong dosage—either too much or too little—can have catastrophic and detrimental effects on the patient, potentially leading to serious illness and even death.

List three decisions in the business world that can be largely left to a computer, and list three that should definitely not be. Do not use the examples given in this chapter.

---

solving the problem or taking advantage of the opportunity, or at least not as optimally as you might with better focus. Information filtering in the future will be key.

When you start to receive the majority of your information from a single supplier, you'll notice a greater ability to filter the information. For example, if you receive your newspaper from the same organization that provides you Internet access, that organization could determine your preferences and provide you with a personal portal and a customized electronic newspaper tailored to just the topics you want to read about. For example, if the organization operated a worldwide news source it would search the international news and provide you news content appropriate to your interests.

You may already be seeing this convergence happen. Perhaps your cable TV provider is also your telephone service provider. Perhaps you use an information service on the Web that delivers daily articles to you according to your reading preferences. That information service is probably gathering information from numerous other news services, filtering it, and providing only what you want.

Physiological Interaction

Right now, your primary physical interfaces to your computer include a keyboard, mouse, monitor, and printer (basically, your input and output devices). These are physical devices, not physiological. Physiological interfaces capture and utilize your real body characteristics, such as your breath, your voice, your height and weight, and even the iris in your eye. Physiological innovations include automatic speech recognition, virtual reality, cave automatic virtual environments, and biometrics, along with many others.

AUTOMATIC SPEECH RECOGNITION

The most common and well-known example of the broader consideration of biometrics is automatic speech recognition (ASR). One of the Canadian leaders in biometrics is Diaphonics Incorporated of Halifax, Nova Scotia (www.diaphonics.com), a developer of speech recognition and voice security technologies. Diaphonics enables companies to automate and improve interaction with customers over the telephone. With voice biometrics that verify the identity of callers, companies using this software can enable customers to conduct secure, automated self-service transactions over any phone by giving simple, natural voice commands. An **automatic speech recognition (ASR)** system not only captures spoken words but also distinguishes word groupings to form sentences. To do this, an ASR system follows three steps:

1. **Feature analysis**. The system captures your words as your speak into a microphone, eliminates any background noise, and converts the digital signals of your speech into phonemes (syllables).
2. **Pattern classification**. The system matches your spoken phonemes to a phoneme sequence stored in an acoustic model database. For example, if your phoneme was "dü," the system would match it to the words "do" and "due."
3. **Language processing**. The system attempts to make sense of what you're saying by comparing the word phonemes generated in step 2 with a language model database. For example, if you were asking a question and started with the phoneme "dü," the system would determine that the appropriate word is "do" and not "due."

ASR is certainly now taking its place in computing environments. Manulife Canada, for instance, has adopted speech recognition to address the problem of an increasing number of "dropouts"—customers who hang up because they'd rather speak to a live operator than push a sequence of buttons on a touchtone telephone. "We knew we were either going to have to hire more service reps so people could speak to a live operator or change the way that customers obtained their information," says former chief strategy officer Kendall Kay. After "speech-enabling" high-service transaction areas including fund rebalance and interaccount transfers, "we've received positive feedback from our customers. . . . We feel that this system is a business driver because it deals with a customer satisfaction level. People want access to know what their money is doing," says Kay.[4] Visit the Web site that supports this text (www.mcgrawhill.ca/college/haag) to learn more about ASR systems.

VIRTUAL REALITY

On the horizon (and in some instances here today) is a new technology that will virtually place you in any experience you desire. That new technology is **virtual reality**—a three-dimensional computer simulation in which you actively and physically participate.

NASA, for instance, used virtual reality to train its astronauts to operate the Canadarm (developed by Spar Aerospace Limited) to catch and repair the Hubble Space Telescope. Rather than being one of NASA's great and most ambitious accomplishments, deployment of the telescope initially turned out to be of its most embarrassing moments. The main mirror was too flat by 1/50th the width of a human hair. This is all it took to create a huge defect in terms of optics. To correct the problem, astronauts had to use the Canadarm, a remotely operated appendage that can be used on board any space shuttle and designed to perform a variety of missions, to grab the 12.7 tonne satellite and place it on a rotating service platform at the rear of space shuttle *Endeavour*'s cargo bay in order to repair it. Before the mission, the crew extensively trained for over 400 hours, a procedure that included space walks in deep-water tanks and the use of virtual reality simulators to make sure they would perform all the necessary repairs quickly and thoroughly.[5]

RESEARCH IN MOTION'S BLACKBERRY DEVICE SUCCESS STORY

Research in Motion (www.rim.net), founded in 1984 and headquartered in Waterloo, Ontario, has been one of the most successful Canadian companies in the Internet appliance market. In 1999, RIM received the "Product of the Year Award" in the Mobile Computing category from *InfoWorld* magazine for the simple setup and deployment, ease of use, and superior product functionality of its two-way e-mail pager called BlackBerry.

This cigarette-pack-sized wireless device was the first to offer users both e-mail and organizer capabilities. The initial popularity of the device lay in its ability to check e-mail anywhere anytime. In 2004, RIM, along with wireless partner T-Mobile, introduced its newest gizmo in the BlackBerry line, the BlackBerry 7100t,

which is much more phone-like than its predecessors. While still including the "qwerty" keyboard that makes it possible for thumb typists to peck out e-mails and text messages, it now also incorporates Bluetooth for connecting wirelessly to a headset or car kit, a speakerphone, a large colour screen, and a photo album and can operate abroad.

It is because of close attention to what customers wanted and continuous innovation that the BlackBerry user base has grown to 3 million people and the little device now accounts for 80 percent of the company's quarterly sales revenue. RIM has also more than doubled its employee base and has more than 200 students as co-ops and interns working for them.[6]

In a virtual reality system, you make use of special input and output devices that capture your physiological movements and send physiological responses back to you. These include a:

- **Glove**. An input device that captures and records the shape and movement of your hand and fingers and the strength of the movements
- **Headset**. A combined input and output device that (1) captures and records the movement of your head and (2) contains a screen that covers your entire field of vision and displays various views of an environment on the basis of your movements
- **Walker**. An input device that captures and records the movement of your feet as you walk or turn in different directions

APPLICATIONS OF VIRTUAL REALITY Virtual reality applications are popping up everywhere, sometimes in odd places. The most common applications are found in the entertainment industry. There are a number of virtual reality games on the market, including downhill Olympic skiing, racecar driving, golf, air combat, and marksmanship. Other applications include:

- *Matsushita Electric Works*. You design your kitchen in virtual reality and then choose the appliances you want and even request colour changes.
- *Volvo*. For demonstrating the safety features of its cars.
- *Airlines*. To train pilots how to handle adverse weather conditions.
- *Motorola*. To train assembly-line workers in the steps of manufacturing a new product.[7]
- *Health care*. To train doctors how to perform surgery using virtual cadavers.[8]

Let's consider the potential ramifications of virtual reality and how you might someday interact with your computer. New virtual reality systems include aroma-producing devices and devices that secrete fluid through a mouthpiece that you have in your mouth. So, you could virtually experience a Hawaiian luau. The aroma-producing device would generate various smells and the mouthpiece would secrete a fluid that tastes like pineapple or roasted pig. If you were using virtual reality to surf big waves, the mouthpiece would secrete a fluid that tastes like salt water.

Those examples are the "fun" uses of virtual reality. In business, building contractors would use virtual reality to show a new building and the location of fire exits. Managers may be able to experience how a proposed "downsizing" effort would affect productivity. The possibilities are virtually limitless.

CAVE AUTOMATIC VIRTUAL ENVIRONMENTS

A **CAVE (cave automatic virtual environment)** is a special 3D virtual reality room that can display images of other people and objects located in other CAVEs all over the world. CAVEs are **holographic devices**, devices that create, capture, and/or display images in true three-dimensional form. If you watch any of the *Star Trek* movies, you'll see an example of a holographic device called the holodeck.

In working form, you would enter a CAVE room. At the same time, someone else would enter another CAVE room in another location (see Figure 8.5). Numerous digital video cameras would capture the likenesses of both participants and recreate and send those images to the other CAVEs. Then, you and the other person could see and carry on a normal conversation with each other, and you would feel as if that other person were in the same room with you.

Current CAVE research is also working on the challenges of having other physical objects in the room. For example, if you sat on a couch in your CAVE, the couch would capture the indentation you made in it and pass it to the couch in the other CAVE. That couch would respond by constricting a mesh of rubber inside it so that your indentation would also appear there. And what about playing catch? Which person would have the virtual ball and which person would have the real ball? The answer is that both would have a virtual ball. When throwing it, the CAVE would capture your arm movement to determine the speed, arc, and direction of the ball. That information would be transmitted to the other CAVE, and it would use that information to make the virtual ball fly through the air accordingly.

Unlike virtual reality, you don't need any special gear in a CAVE. Let your imagination run wild and think about the potential applications of CAVEs. An unhappy customer could call a business to complain. Within seconds, a customer service representative would not answer the phone but rather appear in the room with the unhappy customer. That's an example of great customer service. Your teacher might never attend your class. Instead the teacher would enter a CAVE and have his or her image broadcast

Figure 8.5

CAVEs (Cave Automatic Virtual Environments)

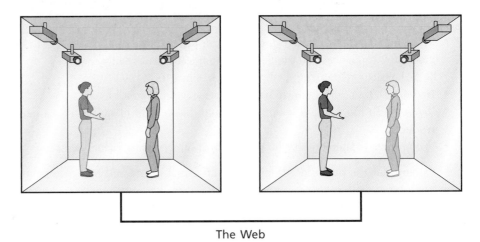

The Web

FINDING APPLICATIONS OF VIRTUAL REALITY

Virtual reality is quickly taking its place in the technology world. In our discussion of it, we listed several well-known applications of it.

Your task is twofold in this project. First, search the Web for more applications of virtual reality. Find at least three and provide a brief description of each. Only one of these applications can be in the area of entertainment. That is, you cannot use more than one game-oriented application of virtual reality.

Second, identify five potential applications for virtual reality. For each application, describe how virtual reality would be used and why it would be beneficial. Each of these potential applications must relate to the use of virtual reality by an organization. As you describe each application, list the type of organization or industry that would use it.

into the classroom. You might not really be in class either but rather a holographic likeness of you. Are CAVEs a realistic possibility? The answer is definitely yes. We believe that CAVEs are the successor to virtual reality. So virtual reality may not be a long-term technological innovation, but rather a stepping-stone to the more advanced CAVE. Whatever the case, CAVEs will not only significantly alter how you interact with your computer (can you imagine the thrill of video games in a CAVE?), they will even more significantly alter how you interact with other people. With CAVE technologies, you can visit your friends and relatives on a daily basis no matter where they live. You may even have television shows and movies piped into your home CAVE.

BIOMETRICS

Biometrics is the use of physiological characteristics—such as your fingerprint, the blood vessels in the iris of your eye, the sound of your voice, or perhaps even your breath—to provide identification. That's the strict and narrow definition, but biometrics is beginning to encompass more than just identification. Consider these real-world applications in place today (see Figure 8.6):

- *Internet-enabled toilets.* These toilets use your physiological output to capture readings (e.g., white-cell count, red-cell count, sodium level, sugar level, the presence of certain types of drugs, etc.) and send that information via the Internet to your doctor's computer. Your doctor's computer can then analyze that information to determine if you're getting sick or perhaps using the wrong type of medication. Of course, you have to plug an Internet-enabled toilet into both an electrical outlet and an Internet connection. Internet-enabled toilets are finding their way into assisted-care living facilities in which older people need 24-hour monitoring of their physiological characteristics.
- *Custom shoes.* Several shoe stores, especially those that offer fine Italian leather shoes, no longer carry any inventory. When you select a shoe style you like, you place your bare feet into a box that scans the shape of your feet. That information is then used to make a custom pair of shoes for you. It works extremely well if your feet are slightly different from each other in size or shape (as is the case with most people).
- *Custom wedding gowns.* Following the custom-fit shoe idea, many bridal boutiques now do the same thing for wedding dresses. Once the bride chooses the style she likes, she steps into a small room that scans her entire body. That information is used to create a wedding dress that fits perfectly.

Figure 8.6

Custom-Fit Clothes Through Biometrics

- *Custom bathrobes.* Some high-end spa resorts now actually have patrons walk through a body-scanning device upon check-in. The scanning device measures the patron's body characteristics and then sends that information to a sewing and fabricating facility that automatically creates a custom-fit bathrobe. Some of these same spa resorts are using the readings from Internet-enabled toilets to design nutritionally optimal meal selections for patrons.

BIOMETRIC SECURITY The best form of security for personal identification encompasses three aspects:

1. What you know
2. What you have
3. Who you are

The first—*what you know*—is something like a password, something that everyone can create and has. The second—*what you have*—is something like a card such as an ATM card you use at an ATM (in conjunction with your password, what you know). Unfortunately, most personal identification security systems stop there. That is, they do not include *who you are*, which is some form of a biometric.

It's no wonder crimes like identity theft are spiralling out of control. Without much effort, a thief can steal your password (often through social engineering) and steal what you have. For the latter, the thief doesn't actually have to steal your physical card; he or she simply has to copy the information on it. However, stealing a biometric—such as your fingerprint or iris scan—is much more difficult.

Many banks are currently converting ATMs to the use of biometrics, specifically an iris scan, as the third level of personal identification security. When you open an account and request ATM use, the bank will issue you an ATM card (you pick the password). The bank will also scan your iris and create a unique 512-byte representation of the scan. To use an ATM, you must insert your card, type in your password, and allow the machine to scan your iris. The ATM uses all three forms of identification to match you to your account. You can then perform whatever transaction you wish.

Some private schools for young children now require parents and guardians to submit to iris scans. Once the scan is captured and the person is verified as a parent or guardian, the information is entered into a security database. Then, when the parent or guardian comes to the school to pick up a child, his or her iris scan is compared to the one stored in the database. Parents and guardians cannot, under any circumstances, take a child from the school without first going through verification via an iris scan.

INTEGRATING BIOMETRIC PROCESSING AND TRANSACTION PROCESSING

Once society accepts the use of biometrics for security and identification purposes, organizations of all types will be able to add another dimension of business intelligence to their data warehouses—that dimension will capture and record changes in physiological characteristics (see Figure 8.7).

Consider, as a hypothetical example, a woman using an ATM—equipped with iris scanning capabilities—to withdraw cash. Current research suggests that it might be possible to use an iris scan to determine not only that a woman is pregnant but also the sex of the unborn child. (That is a very true statement.) When the woman has her iris scanned, the bank might be able to tell that she is pregnant and expecting a boy. When the woman receives her cash and receipt, the receipt would have a coupon printed on the back for 10 percent off any purchase at Babies "Я" Us. Furthermore, the ATM would generate another receipt that says "buy blue."

The key here is for you to consider that transaction processing systems (TPSs) of the future will be integrated with biometric processing systems (BPSs). The TPS will capture and process the "events" of the transaction—when, by whom, where, and so on. The BPS will capture and process the physiological characteristics of the person performing the transaction. Those physiological characteristics may include the presence of alcohol or illegal drugs, hair loss, weight gain, low blood sugar, vitamin deficiencies, cataracts, and yes—even pregnancy.

When businesses start to gather this type of intelligence, you can leave it to your imagination to envision what will happen. For example, because of the noted pregnancy in our previous example of the woman using an ATM, the bank might offer financing for a minivan, evaluate the size of the family's home and perhaps offer special financing for a second mortgage so another room can be added, or establish a tuition account for the child and place $25 in it. These possibilities will further intensify competition in almost all industries.

OTHER BIOMETRICS AND BIOMETRIC DEVICES Biometrics is a "hot topic" in research circles right now. Although we haven't the space to discuss them all, you might want to watch for these:

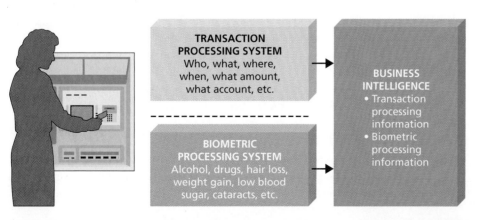

Figure 8.7

Integrating Biometric and Transaction Processing to Create Business Intelligence

FACIAL RECOGNITION SOFTWARE AT AIRPORTS AROUND THE WORLD

Airport security is now a must. And most airports and airlines are no longer relying on government-issued forms of identification for determining who should and who should not be allowed on a plane. Instead, they're relying on facial recognition software such as FaceIt, a joint-venture product of ARINC and Visionics Corporation. FaceIt creates a digital map of a person's face and compares it to a database that contains the facial images of unwanted fliers and known terrorists.

Facial recognition software plays an important role in the use of biometrics for providing and authenticating identification. FaceIt's ARGUS system can handle an unlimited number of video cameras capturing facial images and comparing them to a database that is also unlimited in size. To learn more about FaceIt, visit ARINC at www.arinc.com and Visionics at www.visionics.a.se.

Facial recognition software has made great strides over the past couple of years. Consider these facts:

- Tests conducted in 2002 showed a 50 percent reduction in error rates over those conducted in 2000.
- In determining if a person is who he or she claims to be, the best facial recognition systems yield a 90 percent verification rate, with only a 1 percent false-acceptance rate.
- Males are still easier to identify than females.
- Older people are still easier to identify than younger people.[9]

- **Biochip.** A technology chip that can perform a variety of physiological functions when inserted into the human body. Biochips have been proven in some cases to block pain for people who suffer severe spinal injuries, help paralyzed people regain some portion of their motor skills, and help partially blind people see better.
- **Implant chip.** A technology-enabled microchip implanted into the human body that stores important information about you (such as your identification and medical history) and that may be GPS-enabled to offer a method of tracking.
- **Facial recognition software.** Software that provides identification by evaluating facial characteristics (see the Global Perspectives box here).

Whatever becomes a reality in the field of biometrics promises to forever change your life and how you interact with technology.

Increasing Portability and Mobility

Portability and mobility go hand in hand. *Portability*, in this instance, refers to how easy it is for you to carry around your technology. *Mobility* is much broader and encompasses what you have the ability to do with your technology while carrying it around. For example, PDAs are very portable; they weigh less than a kilogram and easily fit in your pocket or purse. However, your mobility may be limited with a PDA. That is, while you can manage your schedule, take some notes, and even use e-mail with a PDA, you certainly can't generate spreadsheets with elaborate graphs. You want technology that is no more intrusive than your wallet or purse. Ideally, your watch would really be a powerful computer system with speech and holographic capabilities (it may happen someday). If your watch is a powerful computer system, then it maximizes your mobility.

It goes without saying that to achieve maximum portability and mobility we'll need completely wireless communications. This is a vast and dynamically changing field.

We won't delve into it here, but we will need it for portability and mobility. You can learn more about wireless communications in Extended Learning Module E.

To further advance the portability and mobility of technology, you can expect to find digital cash, wearable computers, multi-state CPUs, and holographic storage devices in the future.

DIGITAL CASH

When the digital economy arrives, so must digital money. Coins and folding cash have little or no value themselves; they are representations of value. They became the standard on which the economy works because it's much easier to pay for products and services with them than it is to use gold and silver or some other precious metal. **Digital cash** (also called **electronic cash** or **e-cash**) is an electronic representation of cash.

To use digital cash, you must first purchase it from an electronic bank (see Figure 8.8). You can do this by sending real cash in the mail, using a debit or credit card, or actually opening an account with the electronic bank and requesting that an amount of digital cash be deducted from your balance and sent to you. Whatever the case, the electronic bank will electronically send you your digital cash files. For example, you could request $100 in digital cash in $20 increments. What you would end up with is five digital cash files, each representing $20 on your hard disk.

Now all you have to do is find a product or service on the Internet you want to buy. You would send the merchant the appropriate number of digital cash files to equal the purchase amount. The merchant could then use those digital cash files to buy other merchandise or return it to the electronic bank for real money.

The concept seems quite simple when you think about it. The implementation, however, has turned out to be extremely difficult for many reasons:

- If your system crashes and your digital cash files are wiped clean, you've lost your money. It's rather like losing your wallet. The electronic bank will not replace the files.

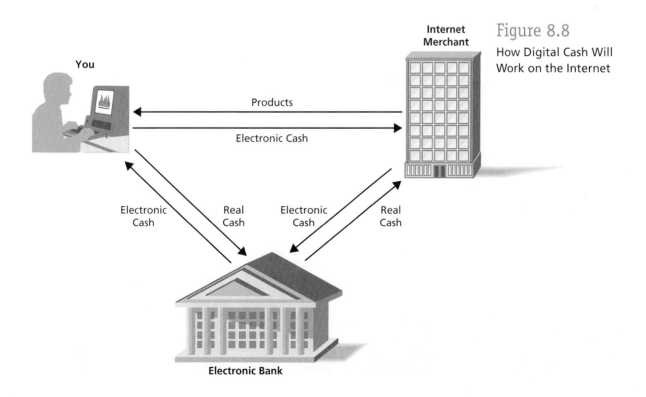

Figure 8.8

How Digital Cash Will Work on the Internet

- There is no standard for how digital cash should look, so a digital cash file from one electronic bank may not look like digital cash from another electronic bank. That makes many merchants very hesitant to accept digital cash.
- Digital cash makes money laundering easy. Because none of your personal information travels with the digital cash when you use it to make a purchase, it's extremely difficult to tell where it came from. So illegally obtained cash can be easily exchanged for digital cash.
- Digital cash travels across the vast Internet and is susceptible to being stolen. Digital information (which includes digital cash) is easy to steal and hard to trace. This may be the single biggest obstacle to the widespread use of digital cash.

In spite of the above challenges and many others, digital cash is destined to take its place as a standard technology. The real question is how soon.

WEARABLE COMPUTERS

Focusing on portability now, let's turn our attention to wearable computers. A **wearable computer** is a fully equipped one that you wear as a piece of clothing or attached to a piece of clothing similarly to how you would carry your cell phone.

In reality, wearable computers are not some far-fetched cutting-edge technology that will take years to arrive. Today, Charmed Technologies and Xybernaut® (to name just a few) are already manufacturing and selling wearable computers (see Figure 8.9). The leader in this area is Xybernaut (www.xybernaut.com) with its many lines of wearable computers designed for manufacturing environments, disaster areas, and even children at school.

For schoolchildren, Xybernaut offers XyberKids, a fully functional computer in the form of a pen-based flat-panel display that can be easily held in hand or set on a desk along with a lightweight backpack for carrying the other computer components such as the system unit and hard disk. At the time we wrote this text, Xybernaut's XyberKids computer included a 500 MHz processor; 128 MB RAM expandable to

Figure 8.9
Wearable Computers

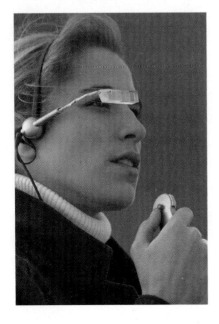

256 MB; 1 GB Compact Flash card; Compact Flash, USB, and Firewire ports; an 800 × 600 colour SVGA flat-panel display with a 21.3 centimetre viewable screen; and an onscreen keyboard and built-in handwriting recognition. What's really nice is that the technology components in the backpack (i.e., everything but the flat-panel display) weigh less than half a kilogram total.

Again, the focus of wearable computers is portability first and mobility second. Right now, wearable computers are very nonintrusive (portability). But they do have limited processing capabilities, so your mobility is limited. You can certainly expect that to change very soon. As technology increases in capability and decreases in price and size, wearable computers will offer you as much processing capability (mobility) as a standard desktop or notebook computer.

Let your imagination run wild again. Imagine carrying and using your wearable computer as if it were a cell phone. You would have high-speed wireless access to the Internet. You could use one eye to view your headset and work on a spreadsheet application while using your other eye to watch a baseball game. No matter where you were or what you were doing, you could still use your wearable computer to write term papers, send and receive e-mail, buy products on the Internet (m-commerce using micro-payments or digital cash, which we'll discuss in a moment), or just have fun surfing the Web.

MULTI-STATE CPUs AND HOLOGRAPHIC STORAGE DEVICES

To increase portability and mobility, technology will have to become increasingly faster and capable of storing more information in exceedingly smaller spaces. Multi-state CPUs and holographic storage devices are two technological innovations on the horizon that promise to help in those areas.

Right now, CPUs are binary-state, capable of working only with information represented by a 1 or a 0. That greatly slows processing. What we really need to increase speed are CPUs that are multi-state. **Multi-state CPUs** work with information represented in more than just two states, probably ten states with each state representing a digit between 0 and 9. When multi-state CPUs do become a reality, your computer will no longer have to go through many of the processes associated with translating characters into binary and then reversing the translation process later. This will make them much faster. Of course, the true goal is to create multi-state CPUs that can also handle letters and special characters without converting them to their binary equivalents.

Again, right now, storage devices store information on a two-dimensional surface, but research in the holographic realm will change that, and **holographic storage devices** will store information on a storage medium that is composed of 3D crystal-like objects with many sides or faces (see Figure 8.10). This is similar in concept to

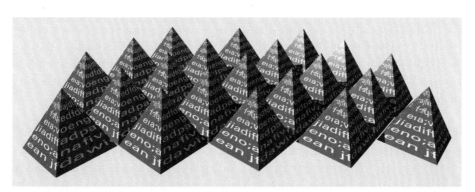

Figure 8.10

3D Crystal-Like Objects in a Holographic Storage Device

small cards that you may have seen which change the picture or image as you view the cards from different angles.

If and when holographic storage devices do become a reality, you may be able to store an entire set of encyclopedias on a single crystal that may have as many as several hundred faces. Think how small technology will become then.

Rebirth of E-Commerce

In the late twentieth century and into the first years of the new century, e-commerce was highly touted as the next big business frontier. Venture capitalists and individuals alike poured literally trillions of dollars into dot-com businesses. Most of those dot-coms had no idea what they were doing and could very seldom show a clear and reasonable path to profitability (P2P). Of course, the e-commerce balloon popped in the middle of the year 2000 and you know the rest of the story.

But e-commerce as a business principle survived, although the dot-coms that failed to implement it correctly did not and became "dot-bombs." Over the next ten years or so we will see a strong resurgence in the e-commerce area, this time by companies backed by sound business principles and clear paths to profitability. As you witness this, you'll see some interesting trends, including the explosion of consumer-to-consumer (C2C) e-commerce and the broadening of e-government.

EXPLOSION OF C2C E-COMMERCE

Of all the types of private-sector e-commerce activities—B2B, B2C, C2C, C2B, and the government venues—the least amount of revenue dollars right now is in the C2C (consumer-to-consumer) space. But we expect that to change rather dramatically in the next several years. **Consumer-to-consumer (C2C) e-commerce** occurs when an individual sells products and services to customers who are primarily other individuals. eBay is a good example. It's really just an e-marketplace in which consumers buy and sell products from and to each other. eBay doesn't guarantee the quality or authenticity of any products or services sold in its auction format. It simply provides a convenient mechanism for allowing consumers to gather and buy and sell products and services.

But consider the impacts of push technologies, m-commerce, digital cash, wearable computers, and even GPS-enabled implant chips. You could drive around your neighbourhood in search of garage sales, for example. As you neared one, your GPS-enabled implant chip would trigger someone's personal computer that would call you on your cell phone and notify you what they have for sale and even provide you with driving directions. Once you arrived at the sale and found something to buy, you could make a digital cash transfer with your cell phone or PDA.

Far beyond garage sales, someday you may be able to create and store a C2C Web site on a personal digital assistant (PDA). People would access your PDA, view the products you have to sell, and then make digital cash payments. Throughout the day, your PDA would constantly update your inventory records and notify you instantly of any stockouts. At the end of the day, your PDA would show you all the necessary delivery and shipping information.

These are not far-fetched ideas. Right now, we think in terms of setting up e-commerce Web sites and hosting them on Web server computers. That will change someday, and your home computer, wearable computer, or even PDA will become a server computer that hosts your Web site and includes all the necessary e-commerce software. When that happens, expect C2C e-commerce to explode.

BUYING SODA WITH A CELL PHONE

In many countries in Europe, especially in Scandinavian countries, you can't find a slot on a vending machine to insert money to buy a soda. No, it's not because the sodas are free or because there's an extremely high criminal and vandalism rate. But you have to buy the soda with your cell phone.

On the soda machine is a telephone number that you call. When you do, the telephone call automatically triggers the soda machine so you can make a selection. The best part is that the cost of the soda is charged to your cell phone bill. No more trying to find the right change when the "CORRECT CHANGE" message is blinking. No more trying to get the creases out of a dollar bill. You simply charge the cost of the soda to your cell phone. Of course, at the end of every month you still have to pay for it, but it is indeed convenient.

This is an example of how B2C (business-to-consumer) e-commerce is beginning to incorporate nontraditional computing technologies. Within the context of C2C (consumer-to-consumer) e-commerce, this example should help you expand your mind and think of endless wild possibilities for selling products and services to other consumers.

Could you set up some sort of product-selling business that requires consumers to use a cell phone to charge the cost of the product to their cell phone bill? If you answer no, our next question to you is: Have you actually contacted an ISP and cell phone service provider to determine that you can't do it? How would you answer that question?

C2C e-commerce will require that everyone "think outside the box" or "beyond your ears" as we like to put it. Don't rule out any idea, no matter how strange or far-fetched. Thomas Watson, CEO and Chairman of IBM in 1943, stated, "I think there is a world market for maybe five computers." He was definitely wrong and, to some extent, narrow-minded in his futuristic views. Don't make the same mistake.

BROADENING OF E-GOVERNMENT

In Chapter 7, we briefly alluded to the fact that the major players in e-commerce include businesses (B), consumers (C), and the government (G). Within the electronic government (e-government) arena, there are four primary focuses (see Figure 8.11).

1. **Government to government (G2G**, also called **intra-G2G)**. The electronic commerce activities performed within a single nation's government focusing on vertical integration (local, city, provincial, and federal) and horizontal integration (within or among the various departments). If you consider the Canadian government, a vertical integration example would include Environment Canada interacting with local, city, and provincial government entities for the enforcement and monitoring of environmentally focused legislation and statutes. A horizontal integration example would include the interaction and information transfer between a branch of the military and Veterans Affairs Canada when military personnel retire.
2. **Government to business (G2B)**. The electronic commerce activities performed between a government and its business partners for such purposes as purchasing direct and MRO materials, soliciting bids for work, and accepting bids for work.
3. **Government to consumer (G2C)**. The electronic commerce activities performed between a government and its citizens or consumers including paying taxes, registering vehicles, and providing information and services.
4. **International government to government (inter-G2G)**. The electronic commerce activities performed between two or more governments including providing foreign aid.

375

Figure 8.11

The Primary Focuses of E-Government

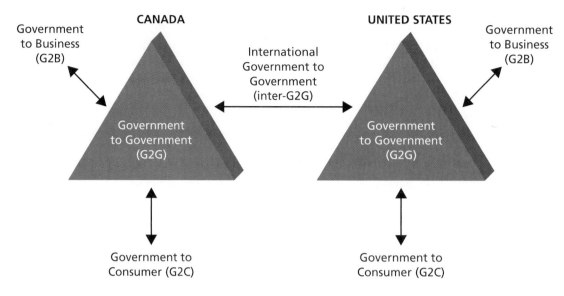

You should take an interest in e-government for two reasons. First, many e-government applications have a direct impact on your personal and business life. You already use G2C to submit your tax forms electronically to the Canada Revenue Agency. Many governmental agencies are also using G2B to send out and accept bids at work. They simply refuse to work with businesses that cannot perform this electronic commerce activity. Second, there are substantial career opportunities in the e-government arena. Consider that the U.S. federal government is the single largest acquirer and user of information technology and related services (see Figure 8.12). In 2002, the U.S. federal government spent just over $46 billion on IT and related services. Almost 25 percent of that $46 billion went to internal staffing, which is essentially IT personnel. So there are substantial career opportunities in e-government. Even if you only want to work as an IT consultant to a government, notice in Figure 8.12 that over 25 percent of U.S. federal government IT dollars went to professional services ($7.8 billion) and outsourcing ($6.4 billion). Current estimates have IT spending increasing at a rate of 10 percent annually for the next several years.

Figure 8.12

How the U.S. Federal Government Spends Its IT Dollars ($46 Billion in 2002)[10]

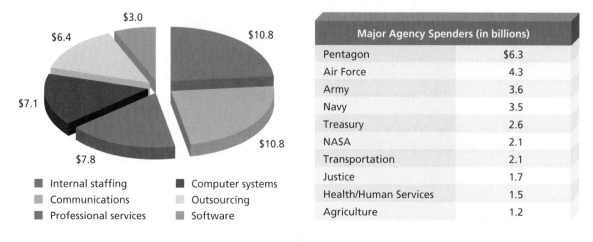

Major Agency Spenders (in billions)	
Pentagon	$6.3
Air Force	4.3
Army	3.6
Navy	3.5
Treasury	2.6
NASA	2.1
Transportation	2.1
Justice	1.7
Health/Human Services	1.5
Agriculture	1.2

Pie chart values: $3.0, $6.4, $7.1, $7.8, $10.8, $10.8

- Internal staffing
- Communications
- Professional services
- Computer systems
- Outsourcing
- Software

HOW MANY COMPUTERS DO YOU RELY ON IN A WEEK?

Technology is certainly a necessity in today's society. If computers and computer systems go down, trains stop running, airline flights are delayed, and stoplights may not work. Your everyday life depends on the use of computers. According to one study, the average American relies on approximately 264 computers every day.

You won't have to think long or hard to come up with a list of computers that you depend on in your everyday life—that's your task for this project. Your team is to develop a list of computers that you rely on in a week's time. Did you recently go to the movies? If so, you relied on the computer that issued your ticket, the cash register computer that totalled your concession bill, and the computer that showed the movie. (No—most movie theatres don't show movies from rolls of film anymore.)

As you create your list, critically evaluate the importance of each computer. Although it might be a nuisance to have the computer go down that's showing you a movie, it's much more critical that other computers in your life be working all the time, without fail.

In Figure 8.12 you can also see the allocation of IT dollars across the major spending agencies. Defence and the armed forces are at the top, followed by the Treasury Department (it accepts and distributes all government monies), NASA (heavily involved in research), and then a series of more socially oriented agencies such as Health and Human Services and Agriculture. (The table in the figure, because it includes only 2002 data, does not show the positioning of the Homeland Security Department, which has an IT budget of approximately $3 billion.)

The goal of the federal government right now is to become a true **click-and-mortar** enterprise—an organization that has a presence in the physical world, that is, buildings you can visit and representatives you can talk to, and also a presence in the virtual world, that is, Web sites with which you can interact at all levels and in all areas.

Most Important Considerations

Throughout this chapter, we've discussed some key emerging trends and technologies. They certainly are exciting and promise that the future will be different and dynamic, to say the least. We have suggested that you anticipate these changes and how they will affect you personally and in your career.

As we close this chapter (and perhaps your studies in this course), let's take a close look at five key topics. Each is a culmination in some way of the material you've learned in this course. Each is inescapable in that it will happen and you must deal with it. Finally, each is vitally important and reaches far beyond the technologies that either necessitate or support it. For you, these last few pages are a chance to reflect on what you've learned and to place that knowledge within the bigger picture.

THE NECESSITY OF TECHNOLOGY

Like it or not, technology is a necessity today. It's hard to imagine a world without it. Just as we need electricity to function on an everyday basis, we need technology as well.

Of course, that doesn't mean you should adopt technology just for the sake of the technology or because it sounds fun. Rather, you need to carefully evaluate each technology and determine if it will make you more productive, enhance your personal life,

VIRTUAL REALITY SIMPLIFIES PATIENT'S WORLD

Imagine a world in which the colour blue feels like sandpaper, the only furniture you can sit on must be green, or the sound of a pin dropping on the floor sounds like the cracking of thunder. Fortunately, most of us can't, but that's the real world for a person with autism. Autism is a disease that interferes with the development of the part of the brain that processes sensory perceptions. So autistic people may feel sandpaper grinding across their skin when they see a colour or they may be unable to correlate objects, such as chairs, barstools, couches, and love seats (all items on which you can sit).

For autistic people, the world is a mishmash of objects that make no sense to them when they have to deal with them all at once. That makes teaching autistic people very difficult. For example, if you place two differently coloured chairs in front of an autistic person and tell him or her that they are both chairs, that person may become confused and disoriented.

A simple world is the best world for individuals suffering from autism. Unfortunately, the real world is not so simple. So Dorothy Strickland and many others are researching ways to use virtual reality to teach people with autism. In a virtual reality simulation, researchers can eliminate all forms of background noise, colours, and objects, except those that they want the autistic person to focus on. As the autistic person becomes comfortable with the virtual reality simulation, new objects or colours can be introduced without the usual adverse effects.

Technology is really great—it can help an organization gain a competitive advantage in the marketplace or help you get a job in the future. But the greatest uses of technology may never make anyone rich; instead those uses will help many mentally and physically challenged individuals cope with daily life.[11]

enrich your learning, or move your organization in the direction of its strategic goals and initiatives.

Technology is not a panacea. If you throw technology at a business process that doesn't work correctly, the result will be that you'll perform that process incorrectly millions of times faster per second. At the same time, you can ill afford to ignore technology when it really will help you and your organization become more efficient, effective, and innovative.

CLOSING THE GREAT DIGITAL DIVIDE

We must, as a human race, completely eliminate the great digital divide. As we hinted in Chapter 7, the *great digital divide* addresses the concerns of many people that the world is becoming one marked by the "haves" and "have nots" with respect to technology. That is, the traditional notion of a *Third World economy* is now being defined by the extent to which a country has access to and uses technology.

The power of technology needs to be realized on a worldwide scale. We cannot afford to have any technology-challenged nation or culture (within reason). If you live and work in a technology-rich country, don't keep it to yourself. When possible, take it to other countries by creating international business partnerships and strategic alliances. The world will benefit greatly from your efforts.

TECHNOLOGY FOR THE BETTERMENT OF SOCIETY

Life isn't just about making money. As you approach the development and use of technological innovations (or even standard technologies), think in terms of the betterment

NECESSITY, CONVENIENCE, AND PRIVACY

As you consider your own use of technology, it's important that you consider that use within the context of necessity, convenience, and your own privacy. You really have two questions to answer:

1. *Necessity*. If you truly need technology to perform a personal task, how much of your personal privacy are you willing to forgo?
2. *Convenience*. If you can use technology to make your life more convenient (but your use of it isn't an absolute necessity), how much of your personal privacy are you willing to forgo?

Regarding question 1, provide your answer on a scale of 1 to 5. A 1 represents the fact that you would relinquish all your privacy to use technology that is a necessity. A 5 represents the fact that you would not relinquish any privacy even if it meant not being able to use a technology that was a necessity.

Regarding question 2, also provide your answer on a scale of 1 to 5. A 1 represents the fact that you would relinquish all your privacy in exchange for using technologies that would make your life more convenient. A 5 represents the fact that you would not relinquish any of your privacy even if it meant not being able to use a technology that made your life more convenient.

Compare your answers with those of several classmates. How do your answers compare to everyone else's?

of people and society in general. (Making money and helping people often go hand in hand, in fact.)

Medical research is performing marvellous work in the use of technology to treat ailments and cure diseases. But if these efforts are purely profit-driven, we may never wholly realize the fruits of them. For example, therapists are using virtual reality to teach autistic people to cope with increasingly complex situations (see the Global Perspectives box). We know for a fact that this use of technology isn't making anyone a lot of money. But it isn't always about making money. It's about helping people who face daily challenges far greater than ours. You're fortunate to be in an environment of learning. Give back when you have the chance.

EXCHANGING PRIVACY FOR CONVENIENCE

On a personal level, you need to consider how much of your personal privacy you're giving up in exchange for convenience. The extreme example is GPS-enabled implant chips. The convenience is knowing where you are and being able to get directions to your destination. But you're obviously giving up some privacy. Is this okay? Convenience takes on many forms. When you use a discount card at a grocery store to take advantage of sales, that grocery store then tracks your purchasing history in great detail. You can bet that the grocery store will use that information to sell you more tailored products.

It really is a tradeoff. In today's technology-based world, you give up privacy when you register for sweepstakes on certain Web sites. You give up privacy just surfing the Web because tracking software monitors your activities. Even when you click on a banner ad, the Web site you go to knows where you came from. Although such tradeoffs may seem insignificant, small ones can add up to a big one over time.

Because you are very much a part of this trend, it's often hard to see the big picture and understand that every day you're giving up just a little more privacy in exchange for a little more convenience. Don't ever think that organizations won't use the information they're capturing about you. They're capturing it so they can use it. Of course, much of it will be used to better serve you as a customer, but some of it may not.

ETHICS, ETHICS, ETHICS

As our final note to you, we cannot stress enough again the importance of ethics as they guide your behaviour toward other people in your career. We realize that business is business and that businesses need to make money to survive. But the recent scandals involving Enron and others in the corporate world should be a reminder of how important your personal ethical compass is to you. Success shouldn't come to the detriment of other people. It's quite possible to be very ethical and very successful. That's our challenge to you.

Summary: Student Learning Outcomes Revisited

1. **Describe the emerging trends and technologies that will have an impact on the changing Internet.** The Internet is the single most visible aspect of technology and is changing every day. In the future, you can expect to see a number of emerging trends and technologies including:
   - *Free Internet phone calls.* Using your computer and Internet connection to make phone calls over the Internet
   - *Push technology.* When businesses and organizations come to you with information, services, and product offerings based on your profile
   - *Personalization.* The tailoring of products and services to your needs
   - *Renting software from ASPs.* Especially while using portable devices such as PDAs to work with various types of personal productivity software
   - *Information supplier convergence.* The mergers and acquisition processes that will combine many information suppliers into one may help you organize and filter information

2. **Compare and contrast the various types of technologies that are emerging as we move toward physiological interaction with technology.** Emerging technologies in the area of physiological interaction include:
   - *Automatic speech recognition (ASR).* A system that not only captures spoken words but also distinguishes word groupings to form sentences
   - *Virtual reality.* A three-dimensional computer simulation in which you actively and physically participate

   - *Cave automatic virtual environments (CAVEs).* Holographic devices that create, capture, and/or display images in true three-dimensional form
   - *Biometrics.* The use of physiological characteristics—such as your fingerprint, the blood vessels in the iris of your eye, the sound of your voice, or perhaps even your breath—to provide identification

3. **Understand technological innovations and trends that will increase portability and mobility.** Technological innovations that will focus on increasing portability and mobility include:
   - *Digital cash.* An electronic representation of cash
   - *Wearable computers.* Fully equipped computers that you wear as a piece of clothing or attached to a piece of clothing similar to the way you would carry your cell phone on your belt
   - *Multi-state CPUs.* Work with information represented in more than just two states, probably ten states, each representing a digit between 0 and 9
   - *Holographic storage devices.* Devices that store information on a storage medium made up of 3D crystal-like objects with many sides or faces

4. **Describe the coming C2C explosion and the broadening of e-government as they relate to the rebirth of e-commerce.** Consumer-to-consumer e-commerce currently generates the least revenue in the e-commerce space. However, with the advancement of portable and mobile technologies, you can expect to see a tremendous increase

in the activity and revenue of C2C e-commerce. The broadening of e-government will come in four forms:

- **Government to government.** The electronic commerce activities performed within a single nation's government focusing on vertical integration and horizontal integration
- **Government to business.** The electronic commerce activities performed between a government and its business partners for such purposes as purchasing direct and MRO mate-

rials, soliciting bids for work, and accepting bids for work

- **Government to consumer.** The electronic commerce activities performed between a government and its citizens or consumers including paying taxes, registering vehicles, and providing information and services
- **International government to government.** The electronic commerce activities performed between two or more governments including foreign aid

---

CLOSING CASE STUDY ONE

WILDSEED—A CELL PHONE FOR EVERY FASHION

U.S. manufacturers of cell phones and providers of cell phone service are heavily targeting one select group of customers—teenagers. In the United States, only about 38 percent of all teenagers have cell phones, as against over 80 percent in most European countries and some Asian countries. Providers and manufacturers know that there is plenty of room to grow in the teenage market, not only because 62 percent don't currently have cell phones but also because teenagers are very quick to embrace and use new technologies. Those same companies know that teenagers aren't as frugal with money and tend to spend much more time talking on a cell phone than adults.

Of course, cell phones aren't really new technologies, but what you can do with them is. Motorola, for example, manufactures a model with FM radio capability (XM radio may not be far behind). Samsung and many others offer cell phone service that includes AOL Instant Messenger (with audio and limited video). Most providers offer phones with cameras and multimedia messaging.

One of the leaders in this dynamic and changing industry is Wildseed. It regularly holds focus groups just for teenagers. Wildseed has determined that teenagers have three cell phone concerns:

1. *Visual appeal.* A cell phone should make a fashion statement. Teenagers also believe that cell phones should be a statement of individuality ("I want a cell phone that doesn't look like anyone else's").
2. *Functionality.* A cell phone should do more than just support phone-calling capabilities.

3. *Price.* Long-term calling plans are not the way to go.

VISUAL APPEAL

Wildseed has tested numerous designs on teenagers. One cell phone holder was designed to be worn like a garter belt, and it flopped in a big way. According to one young man in the focus group, "Is a guy supposed to wear that?" And a young girl in the focus group commented, "It looks like something for a prostitute." But Wildseed did hit upon a good idea. It now manufactures "smart skins," covers with an embedded computer chip. According to what the teenager is wearing, he or she can quickly change the design of the face plate. While skateboarding one day, for example, a young man might change his to a splashy rendition of hard colours such as red, yellow, and green. Teenagers can also choose from among music-oriented themes according to their favourite artist.

FUNCTIONALITY

Cell phones are certainly no longer devices just for talking. Most have e-mail capabilities and support surfing the Web. Those are no longer a competitive advantage for any cell phone manufacturer. Wildseed tried a couple of new ideas on teenage focus groups; the first failed and the second met with great success. The first additional functionality was a cell phone that supported Morse code. No one liked that, because no one knew how to send and interpret Morse code. Additionally, teenage girls stated they would have a problem because their long fingernails made it difficult to type. The second function was "airtexting." Using an airtexting-enabled cell phone, you type in a brief message (e.g., "Call me") and then wave your cell phone back and forth in the air. Blinking red lights on the cell phone are synchronized to display the message in the air. That way, someone across the room can receive your message without having to use a cell phone. You may have seen airtexting clocks that have an arm that moves back and forth through the air and seems to suspend the time and day in the air. As one young lady put it, "That's tight."

PRICE

Price is a major drawback for most teenagers, not necessarily the per-minute charge but rather the long-term contract that must be signed. In the United States, as opposed to most other countries, you must typically sign a six-month or one-year contract for cell phone service. That excludes many teenagers, because they have to get their parents to co-sign. Unfortunately, Wildseed is a phone manufacturer and not a service provider.[12]

Questions

1. The role and purpose of cell phones have certainly changed over the past few years. Not too long ago, business professionals were the only ones to use such phones. Now, over one in three teenagers in the United States have one, and about 99 percent of them don't use the phones for business. Are cell phones becoming a technology of convenience and not of necessity? If people use them just for the convenience of communicating anywhere at anytime, are they really a necessity? On the other hand, if you use a cell phone as your primary mode of communication, is it no longer just a convenience?

2. Airtexting sounds like a good idea. From across a room, you'll be able to easily send someone a short message without using your minutes or having the other person's cell phone ring. But you are giving up some privacy. If you airtext your message, everyone in the room will be able to see it. Are you willing to give up some amount of privacy to use an airtexting feature? Why or why not? What about while sitting in a classroom? Should you be able to airtext a message in the middle of class? Does your school have a policy requiring you to turn off your cell phone when entering a classroom? If so, should this policy apply to airtexting? Why or why not?

3. Functionality is very important for cell phones. What types of functionality does your cell phone support beyond making and receiving phone calls? If you could design the "perfect" cell phone, what additional functionality would you include?

4. Do you foresee a day when cell phones will be the standard phone and we'll simply do away with land-based phone lines? It's probably going to happen. If cell phones do become the standard, how will you access the Internet from home?

CLOSING CASE STUDY TWO

STADIUMS OF THE FUTURE

There are several industries that always seem to be the leaders in using technological innovations. The movie industry, for example, quickly embraced the use of 3D technologies and animation to create such movie series as *Shrek, Terminator,* and *The Matrix,* all blockbusters in part because of their use of technological innovations. The movie industry is even exploring how to create and use virtual actors and actresses. Real people may no longer be used in movies; instead, likenesses of them will be computer-generated and -controlled.

Another, related industry always on the forefront of the use of new technologies is professional sports. It may not be an industry that immediately pops into your mind in this regard, but that industry must strive daily to attract and retain large audiences (just check out the salaries many professional athletes make and you'll understand why). The professional sports industry wants your business in one of two ways: either you watch a sporting event on television or you attend a sporting event in person. For the latter, sports franchises are building some unbelievable arenas and stadiums that make use of technological innovations. Consider these technology-based activities for you in the stadium of the future.

ORDER AND PAY FOR FOOD AND BEVERAGES AT YOUR SEAT

In future stadiums, you won't have to catch the attention of a stadium vendor selling popcorn, beverages, and hot dogs. Instead, you'll use a small keypad at your seat to view a menu and order exactly what you want. You'll use the same keypad to pay for your order by swiping your credit card. Your order will be transmitted to a kitchen where it's made and then given to a runner who will deliver it to you.

WATCH REPLAYS ON A PRIVATE SCREEN

Your seat will also have a private screen that folds down and within your arm rest. At any point during the game, you can unfold the screen and view replays. You'll be able to choose from among a variety of camera angles from which to see the replay, and you'll be able to use a zooming function to see the entire field or just a portion of it.

VIEW HOLOGRAPHIC REPLAYS SUSPENDED IN THE AIR

Ideally, you'll be able to watch replays not on a flat two-dimensional screen but rather suspended in the air in front of you as a holographic image. These images will be completely three-dimensional, allowing you to turn them at different angles to view the replay from different perspectives. Many people believe that much of the audience will opt to watch an entire game in this fashion as opposed to through binoculars.

PARTICIPATE IN REAL-TIME INTERVIEWS WITH PLAYERS

Almost all player interviews occur after the game is over and are primarily viewed by people watching a game on television. In a future stadium, you'll be able to request and participate in a real-time interview with a player during the game. For example, after a player makes a great catch in a baseball game to end the

inning, you'll be able to interview that player and ask him or her how the catch was made.

VIEW STATISTICS ON ANY PLAYER

You'll also be able to use your screen and keypad to pull up any statistics you might want to view. These could include career statistics for a specific player, season statistics for a specific team, current game statistics for a specific player, and even records within a particular sport. You'll even be able to request that this type of information be presented in graphical form perhaps accompanied by an audio analysis provided by a sports or statistics expert.

VIEW SCORES AND HIGHLIGHTS OF OTHER GAMES

You certainly won't have to wait for a stadium to display scores and highlights of other games on a hanging big-screen monitor. You'll be able to view scores and highlights of other games at the press of a button. You'll even be able to attend one game and watch another completely on your screen.

SEND MESSAGES TO PEOPLE IN THE STADIUM

If you buy tickets the day before a sports event, it's often difficult to get a group of tickets all in the same area. If you can't get tickets all together, then you miss out on some of the fun associated with attending a sports event with friends. That won't be a problem in future stadiums. You'll soon be able to use videoconferencing software to communicate with any other person in the stadium.

Questions

1. Will this type of stadium of the future further widen the "digital divide"? It makes sense that people who don't have enough money to buy personal technologies will also not have enough money to attend sporting events. Will that group of people fall further behind because they can't take advantage of technological innovations in the stadium of the future? Or is this use of technology one of convenience and not of necessity?

2. How do you think players will react to being interviewed during the middle of a game? Can you think of some professional athletes who

would not want to do this? Can you think of some professional athletes who would want to do this? Many governing bodies of professional sports such as the NBA and NFL require that athletes be available before and after the game for interviews. Should those same governing bodies require that athletes be available during games for interviews? Why or why not?

3. Do you believe that stadiums of the future will encourage more people to attend sports events? Why or why not? Right now, you can sit at home, watch picture-in-picture to see multiple games,

and change channels to see yet other games. And let's not forget that these stadiums of the future will be extremely expensive to build and maintain, so you can expect ticket prices to go up as well.

4. In this chapter, we introduced you to several leading-edge and bleeding-edge technologies. Which of those that we didn't highlight in this case study do you believe could be used to enhance the experience of attending a sporting event? How would you use them? Would the use of those technologies further encourage you to attend a sporting event? Why or why not?

Key Terms and Concepts

automatic speech recognition (ASR), 364
biochip, 370
biometrics, 367
CAVE (cave automatic virtual environment), 366
click-and-mortar, 377
consumer-to-consumer (C2C) e-commerce, 374
digital cash (electronic cash, e-cash), 371

facial recognition software, 370
feature analysis, 364
glove, 365
government to business (G2B), 375
government to consumer (G2C), 375
government to government (G2G, intra-G2G), 375
headset, 365
holographic device, 366

holographic storage device, 373
implant chip, 370
international government to government (inter-G2G), 375
language processing, 364
multi-state CPU, 373
pattern classification, 364
push technology, 360
virtual reality, 364
walker, 365
wearable computer, 372

Short-Answer Questions

1. How will free Internet phone calls work?

2. What is a push technology environment?

3. How will push technologies support personalization?

4. Why may you someday rent personal productivity software from an ASP?

5. What is the concept of information supplier convergence?

6. What is the role of physiological interfaces?

7. What are the three steps in automatic speech recognition?

8. What is virtual reality?

9. What type of special input and output devices does virtual reality make use of?

10. What are CAVEs?

11. What are some examples of biometric applications?

12. How will biometrics aid in providing security and identification?

13. What is the function of a biochip?

14. What is the role of an implant chip?

15. How will digital cash someday work on the Internet?

16. What is a wearable computer?

17. How do multi-state CPUs differ from today's standard CPUs?

18. Why will holographic storage devices be able to store more information than today's storage devices?

19. Why will we see an explosion of C2C e-commerce?

20. What are the four primary focuses of e-government?

21. What is the great digital divide?

Assignments and Exercises _____

1. **SELLING THE IDEA OF IMPLANT CHIPS AT YOUR SCHOOL.** Let's assume for a moment that your team is in favour of using implant chips that contain vitally important information such as identification and medical information. Your task is to put together a sales presentation to your school that would require all students obtain implant chips. Within your presentation, include the following:

   A. The school-related information that each implant chip would contain
   B. The nonschool-related information that each implant chip would contain
   C. The processes within your school that would use the information on the implant chips
   D. The benefits your school would realize by requiring implant chips
   E. The benefits students would realize by having implant chips

   Your presentation should be no more than five minutes, so it must be a powerful selling presentation.

2. **RESEARCHING WEARABLE COMPUTERS.** One of the leading-edge manufacturers of wearable computers is Xybernaut. Connect to its Web site at www.xybernaut.com and research its various lines of wearable computers. What are the names of the lines of Xybernaut's wearable computers? What are their CPU speeds? How much RAM do they include? What functions can you perform with them? What sort of technology devices (e.g., wireless Internet access) can you add to each line? Is there any line advanced enough and cheap enough that you would consider buying one? Why or why not?

3. **FINDING A GOOD AUTOMATIC SPEECH RECOGNITION SYSTEM.** Research the Web for automatic speech recognition (ASR) systems. Make a list of the ones you find. What are the prices of each? Are they speaker-independent or speaker-dependent? Do they support continuous speech recognition or discrete speech recognition? What sort of add-on vocabularies can you purchase? How comfortable would you feel speaking the contents of a term paper as opposed to typing it? Would you have to be more or less organized to use speech recognition as opposed to typing? Why?

4. **UNDERSTANDING THE RELATIONSHIPS BETWEEN TRENDS AND TECHNOLOGICAL INNOVATIONS.** In this chapter, we presented you with numerous key technologies and how they relate to six important trends. (See Figure 8.1 at the beginning of this chapter for the list of technologies and trends.) For each trend, identify all the technologies presented in this chapter that can have an impact. For each technology that you do identify, provide a short discussion of how it might have an impact.

5. **LEARNING ABOUT E-GOVERNMENT.** Visit the Web site for Government Computer News (GCN) at www.gcn.com. GCN is a periodical devoted to the use of technology within various governmental agencies in the United States. Click on some of the "hot topics" listed on the left side of the screen. Pick a couple of articles that detail how a government agency is using some type of technology. Now, prepare a short report for your class on the differences between two groups—governments and for-profit businesses. Your report should show how each uses technology to achieve some type of "competitive advantage."

6. **RESEARCHING INTELLIGENT HOME APPLIANCES.** Visit a local appliance store in your area and find three home appliances that contain some sort of intelligence (i.e., an embedded computer chip that takes over some of the functionality and decision making). For each appliance, prepare a short report that includes the following information:

   • A description and price for the intelligent home appliance
   • The "intelligent" features of the appliance
   • How those features make the appliance better than the nonintelligent version

Discussion Questions _____

1. There is currently legislation pending that would make it illegal for people to use a cell phone while driving a car. The reason is that society has already noticed a significant increase in the number of traffic accidents in which one of the drivers involved in the accident was using a cell phone. Think beyond that for a moment and include wearable computers. As this new technology becomes more widely available, isn't it possible for someone to be driving a car while using a computer? Should the government enact legislation to prevent it? Why or why not?

2. In a push technology environment, businesses and organizations will come to you with information, services, and product offerings based on your profile. How is a push technology environment different from mass mailings and spam? Is it an invasion of your privacy to have organizations calling you on your cell phone every time you come near a store? Why or why not? Should you be able to "opt in" or "opt out" of these offerings? Is this really any different from someone leaving a flyer at your house or on your car while it's parked in a parking lot?

3. There are three steps in automatic speech recognition (ASR): feature analysis, pattern classification, and language processing. Which of those three steps is the most challenging for a computer to perform? Why? Which of those three steps is the least challenging for a computer to perform? Why? If ASR systems are to become automatic speech understanding systems, which step must undergo the greatest improvement in its capabilities? Why?

4. Much debate surrounds the use of biometrics. Many people like it because biometrics can provide identification and increase security. Others see it as a tremendous invasion of privacy. Just as you read in this chapter, a bank—by using biometric identification—may be able to tell if a woman is pregnant. So the greatest challenge to overcome is not technological but societal. What needs to happen for society to accept the use of biometrics? How long will it be before society accepts the use of biometrics? In what year do you believe the federal government will begin requiring a biometric of every newborn child?

5. Digital cash is destined to greatly impact the use of coins and folding cash. What sort of future do you foresee if we do away completely with traditional forms of currency and just use electronic forms? Will this help eliminate the digital divide, or will the digital divide provide a barrier to the widespread use of electronic forms of payment? Justify your answer.

6. What are the ethical dilemmas associated with using facial recognition software? Is the use of this type of software really any different from a store asking to see your driver's licence when you use your credit card? Why or why not? Should the government be able to put digital video cameras on every street corner and use facial recognition software to monitor your movements? Why or why not?

7. When (and if) CAVEs become a common reality, you'll be able to visit your family and friends whenever you want no matter where they live. What sort of impact will this have on the travel industry? If you can see your relatives in a CAVE as often as you want, will you be more or less inclined to buy a plane ticket and visit them in person? Why or why not?

Electronic Commerce

Continuing Your Education Through the Internet

To be perfectly honest, it's a dog-eat-dog world out there. The competitive landscape of business is more intense than it has ever been. And that competitiveness spills into your personal life. Many of you are in school right now to get an education to better compete in the job market. But many knowledge workers are finding out that an undergraduate degree is simply not enough to compete in the business world, and so they wish to acquire more education.

→ **Electronic Commerce Links**

Just like businesses, graduate schools (and all schools in general) are using the Internet as a way to communicate information to you. Many of these schools are even offering you online courses through the Internet to further your education.

MBA PROGRAMS

Many of you will undoubtedly choose to continue your education by obtaining an MBA. And you probably should. The market for the best business positions is extremely competitive, with hiring organizations seeking individuals who can speak more than one language, have job experience, and have extended their educational endeavours beyond just getting an undergraduate degree.

Each year, the *Financial Times* ranks the top business schools in the nation. On the Web site that supports this text, you'll find a list of the sites for some of the top 50 business schools in the nation.

Choose a couple of different business schools from the list of 50, visit their Web sites, and answer the following questions for each:

A. What business school did you choose?

B. Does that school offer a graduate program in your area of interest?

C. Can you apply online?

D. Does the site list tuition and fee costs?

E. Does the site contain a list of the graduate courses offered in your area of interest?

SPECIALIZED MBA PROGRAMS

In the previous section, you explored a few of the top 50 business schools in the nation. Those schools were ranked irrespective of any specialization, focusing rather on overall academic reputation. The *Financial Times* also compiles an annual list of the best business schools in ten specializations: accounting, entrepreneurship, finance, health services administration, management information systems, international business, general business, marketing, nonprofit organizations, and production/operations. If you're interested in a specialized MBA, you should consider viewing schools in these lists.

Choose at least three schools that offer a specialization in your area of interest and visit their Web sites. Then rank those three schools according to your first, second, and third choices. What factors did you consider? Was cost an overriding concern? Before you began your analysis, did you already have a preconceived notion of the best school? Did you change your mind once you visited the schools' sites?

GRADUATE SCHOOL INFORMATION AND TIPS

Before you begin your decision-making process concerning which graduate school to attend, you should gather a variety of material. For example, obtaining a directory of universities (both domestic and international) would be helpful. Perhaps even more importantly, you should ask yourself several questions. Are you ready for graduate school? Why are you considering going to graduate school? How do you determine which school is best for you according to such issues as price, location, and area of specialization?

Many of these questions are very personal to you. For example, we can't help you determine if you're really ready for graduate school or answer why you're considering going to graduate school. But what we can do is point you toward some valuable resources on the Internet to help you answer some of your questions and find a wealth of information relating to universities. On the Web site that supports this text, we've included many links to those types of sites.

At your leisure, we recommend that you connect to several of these sites and see what they have to offer. Some simply provide a list of universities, whereas others may be particularly useful as you make that all-important decision.

TELE-EDUCATION (DISTANCE LEARNING)

Throughout this text, you've explored the concept of 24/7 connectivity through information technology. Using IT (part of which is the Internet), organizations today are sending out telecommuting employees, and medical and health facilities are establishing telemedicine practices.

Tele-education, which goes by a number of names including e-education, distance learning, distributed learning, and online learning, enables you to get an education without "going" to school. Quite literally, you can enroll in a school on the East Coast and live in Vancouver, enjoying great winter skiing. Using various forms of IT (video-conferencing, e-mail, chat rooms, and the Internet), you can take courses from schools all over the world. Some of those schools even offer complete degree programs via IT.

Connect to at least five of these sites and explore the possibilities of tele-education. As you do, consider these issues:

A. Can you just take courses or enroll in a complete degree program?

B. What is the cost of tele-education?

C. What process do you go through to enroll in a tele-education program?

D. How would you feel about staying at home instead of going to class?

E. How do tele-education programs foster interactivity between students and teachers?

Go to the Online Learning Centre at www.mcgrawhill.ca/college/haag for quizzes, extra content, a searchable glossary, and more! Click on "Electronic Commerce Projects" for links to hundreds of Web sites.

Go to the text CD-ROM for data files, extra content, and Skills Modules on Microsoft Excel, Microsoft Access, HTML, and e-portfolios.

CHAPTER NINE

STUDENT LEARNING OUTCOMES

BY THE END OF THIS CHAPTER, STUDENTS WILL BE ABLE TO:

1. Describe two ways in which information is valuable to business.

2. Define ethics and describe the two factors that affect how you make a decision concerning an ethical issue.

3. Define and describe intellectual property, copyright, the Fair Use Doctrine, and pirated and counterfeit software.

4. Understand privacy and describe ways in which it can be threatened.

5. Describe the ways in which companies are vulnerable to computer attacks.

6. Compare risk management and risk assessment and describe the seven security measures that companies can take to protect their information.

7. Understand what a disaster recovery plan is and list the six components it should cover.

WEB SUPPORT

- Transportation

- Road Conditions and Maps

- Lodging

- One-Stop Travel Sites

- Destination Information

Visit
www.mcgrawhill.ca/college/haag

LearningCentre

CASE STUDY:

THEY KNOW ABOUT 96 PERCENT OF AMERICAN HOUSEHOLDS

There's a company in Little Rock, Arkansas, called Acxiom, that handles consumer information, mainly for marketing purposes. That is, Acxiom stores and analyzes information, both its own and its clients'. Acxiom gets the information it sells from many sources, including the three major credit bureaus (TransUnion, Equifax Inc., and Experian Inc.). Nine of the country's ten largest credit card issuers are clients along with many other high-profile financial companies in the banking and insurance industries. Forty percent of Acxiom's revenue comes from banking alone.

The company's inventory includes 20 billion records on consumers that include names, addresses, social security numbers, and public-record information. In fact, Acxiom has a data-base with information on about 110 million Americans, or 96 percent of U.S. households. The company categorizes consumers into one of 70 lifestyle clusters that include such groups as "Rolling Stones," "Single City Struggles," and "Timeless Elders." In any given year, about 33 percent of the people in the database move from one cluster to another when they change their lives in some significant way, as when they get married, have children, or retire.

Acxiom was one of the first companies to use grid-based computing "enabling data analysis, modelling and applications at previously un-achievable speed—and with a lowered cost," according to Charles Morgan, Chairman and CEO of Acxiom. With so much information belonging to so many clients, it made sense to have a very scalable and flexible system.

To help clients react quickly to changing market conditions, Acxiom offers hundreds of lists.

One of these is a daily updated "pre-movers file" which lists people who are about to change residences. Another list is of people who use credit cards, and the list is sorted in order of frequency of use. A further list is sorted according to the square-footage of consumers' homes. This type of information helps companies selling goods and services to target their customers and develop solid marketing strategies.

For example, Capital One Financial Corporation, a financial services company based in Virginia, spent $290 million (about 14 percent of its revenue) on marketing for the last quarter of 2003. The company sends out about 1 billion pieces of mail every year that largely consist of advertising intended to entice consumers to sign up for credit cards. Acxiom's information and analysis help Capital One send credit card solicitations only to those who are likely to want another credit card.

Another service that Acxiom provides is the merging of huge databases. The merger of Bank One and J. P. Morgan is a case in point. Both companies had huge, independent databases, and merging such mountains of information is Acxiom's specialty. First the information must be cleaned (called "data hygiene" in the industry), that is, duplicate records must be identified and combined. Acxiom also adds records from its own database to those of its clients, complementing and completing the clients' customer information.

To support these information services, Acxiom has thousands of servers and storage units. Some clients request that their information be kept separate, and so Acxiom supplies a locked room for that purpose. Another client company wants its information stored underground and far away from Acxiom's main site and, again, Acxiom fills the need.[1,2,3,4]

Introduction

As you've already learned, the three components of an IT system are information technology, information, and knowledge workers. Most of what you've seen in previous chapters has dealt with IT and how it stores and processes information.

In this chapter we're going to concentrate on information—its use, ownership, role, and protection. The best environment for handling information is one that has stability without stagnation and change without chaos.

To handle information in a responsible way, you must understand (see Figure 9.1):

- The importance of ethics in the ownership and use of information
- People's need for privacy
- The value of information to the organization
- Threats to information and how to protect against them (security)
- The need to plan for the worst-case scenario (disaster recovery)

The most important part of any IT system is the people who use it and are affected by it. How people treat each other has always been important, but in an electronic age, with huge computer power at our fingertips, we can affect more people's lives in more ways than ever before. How we act toward each other, and this includes how we view and handle information, is largely determined by our ethics.

You don't have to look far to see examples of questionable computer use:

- Employees search organizational databases for information they want on celebrities and friends.
- Organizations collect, buy, and use information and don't check the validity or accuracy of that information.
- Information system developers build systems that are hard to test completely and put them on the market before they work properly. A few years ago, the developers of an incubator thermostat control program didn't test it fully, and two infants died as a result.[5]
- People copy, use, and distribute software they have no right to.
- People create and spread viruses that cause a lot of trouble for people using and maintaining IT systems.
- People break into computer systems and steal passwords, information, and proprietary information.
- Employees destroy or steal proprietary schematics, sketches, customer lists, and reports from their employers.

Figure 9.1

Chapter Overview

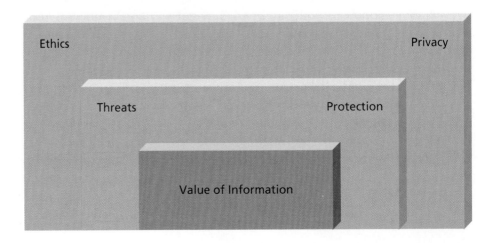

• People snoop on each other and read each other's e-mail and other private documents.

Ethics

Ethical people have integrity. They're people you can definitely trust. They're people who are just as enthusiastic about the rights of others as they are about their own rights. They have a strong sense of what's fair and right and what isn't. But even the most ethical people sometimes face difficult choices.

Ethics are the principles and standards that guide our behaviour toward other people. Acting ethically means behaving in a principled fashion and treating other people with respect and dignity. It's simple to say, but not so simple to do since some situations are complex or ambiguous. The important role of ethics in our lives has long been recognized. As far back as 44 B.C., Cicero said that ethics are indispensable to anyone who wants to have a good career. Having said that, Cicero, along with some of the greatest minds over the centuries, struggled with what the rules of ethics should be.

Our ethics, rooted in our history, culture, and religions, remain the same over time at important levels, but our sense of ethics shifts over time and from culture to culture. In this electronic age there's a new dimension in the ethics debate—the amount of information that we can collect and store, and the speed with which we can access and process that information.

TWO FACTORS THAT DETERMINE HOW YOU DECIDE ETHICAL ISSUES

How you collect, store, access, and distribute information depends to a large extent on your sense of ethics—what you perceive as right and wrong. Two factors affect how you make your decision when you're faced with an ethical dilemma (see Figure 9.2). The first is your basic ethical structure, which you developed as you grew up. The

Figure 9.2
Your Ethical Structure

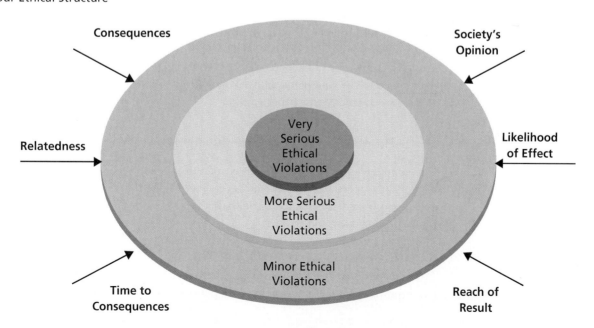

second is the set of practical circumstances involved in the decision that you're trying to make—that is, all the shades of grey in what are rarely black-or-white decisions.

Your ethical structure and the ethical challenges you'll face exist at several levels.[6] At the outside level are things that most people wouldn't consider bad, taking a couple of paper clips or sending an occasional personal e-mail on company time. Do these things really matter? At the middle level are more significant ethical challenges. One example might be accessing personnel records for personal reasons. Could there ever be personal reasons so compelling that you would not feel ethical discomfort doing this? Reading someone else's e-mail might be another "middle" example. At the innermost ethical level are ethical violations that you'd surely consider very serious: embezzling funds or selling company records to a competitor. And yet, over time, your ethical structure can change so that even such acts as these seem less unethical. For example, if everyone around you is accessing confidential records for their own purposes, in time you might come to think it's no big deal. And this might spell big trouble for you.

The practical circumstances surrounding your decision always influence you in an ethical dilemma.[7] It would be nice if every decision were crystal-clear and considerations such as these needn't be taken into account, but decisions are seldom so easy.

1. *Consequences.* How much or how little benefit or harm will come from a particular decision?
2. *Society's opinion.* What is your perception of what society really thinks of your intended action?
3. *Likelihood of effect.* What is the probability of the harm or benefit that will occur if you take the action?
4. *Time to consequences.* What length of time will it take for the benefit or harm to take effect?
5. *Relatedness.* How much do you identify with the person or persons who will receive the benefit or suffer the harm?
6. *Reach of result.* How many people will be affected by your action?

Let's hope your basic sense of right and wrong will steer you in the right direction, but no matter what your sense of ethics is or how strong it is, such practical aspects of the situation may affect you as you make your decision, perhaps unduly, perhaps quite justifiably. Ethical dilemmas usually arise, not out of simple situations, but from a clash between competing goals, responsibilities, and loyalties. Ethical decisions are complex judgments that balance rewards for yourself and others against responsibilities to yourself and others. Inevitably, your decision process is influenced by uncertainty about the magnitude of the outcome, by your estimate of the importance of the situation, sometimes by your perception of conflicting "right reactions," and more than one socially acceptable "correct" decision.

GUIDELINES FOR ETHICAL COMPUTER SYSTEM USE

Central to the ethical use of computers and information are the issues of ownership, responsibility, personal privacy, and access (see Figure 9.3).[8] And just to make it all more complicated, different countries have different views on personal privacy, copyrights, pornography, and so on.

Ownership embodies the rights to information and intellectual property. *Responsibility* deals with who is accountable for the accuracy and completeness of information. *Personal privacy*, which we will examine in more detail shortly, addresses the question of who owns personal information (the people who collect it or the people about

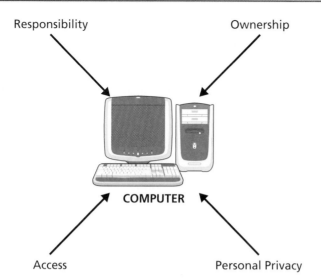

Figure 9.3

Ethical Dimensions of
Information

whom it's collected)? *Access* deals with who can use, view, store, and process what
information.

It's sometimes tough to decide what to do since there are few hard-and-fast rules.
Knowing the law doesn't even help because what's legal is not always ethical and vice
versa. In Figure 9.4 you see the four quadrants of ethical and legal behaviour. You're
pretty safe if you can manage to stay in quadrant I.

So what do you do then if you're faced with a choice that is not perfectly ethically
clear? If you feel you are in an ethical quandary—you probably are. If you find you're
giving the situation a whole lot of thought, the situation very likely deserves it. You
may wish to talk to a friend, a teacher, a supervisor, or a mentor. Know that we're all
faced with such dilemmas, they are real, and they have consequences. And there *is* a
line that you shouldn't cross.

Let's look at an example. Say your organization is developing a decision support
system (DSS) to help formulate treatments for an infectious disease. Other companies
in the industry are working on similar projects. The first system on the market will
most likely reap huge profits. You may know that your DSS doesn't yet work properly—it's good, but not yet totally reliable. But you're feeling extreme pressure from
your boss to get the system onto the market immediately. You're worried about the
harm that might come to a patient because of your DSS; but, on the other hand, it does
work well most of the time. Is it up to you or not? You have a family to support and student loans to repay. And you like being employed. Can you hold out and get more
information on the system's reliability? What do you do? Where can you get help?

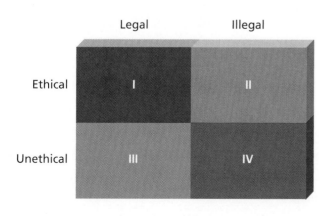

You can certainly ask questions about what you're being asked to do—and you should. Sometimes legitimate actions look unethical, but if you find out more about the situation, you might find that it's perfectly all right. For instance, in the case above, management may be planning to leave out the dubious part of the system or warn customers that it has a problem. But, you must keep digging until you're very sure and comfortable with what you're being asked to do. If you really believe that what you're expected to do is wrong, you'll have to say so to your boss and be prepared to quit if you have to. But first, explain what you think is so bad and couch it in terms of the company's future and reputation if at all possible. Be sure and think also of your own future and reputation, many Enron employees wish they had taken a firm stand when they had the chance.[9]

Your company may well have an office or person (sometimes called an "ombudsman") whose job it is to give advice on work-related ethical dilemmas. Many companies do. Failing that, you could look up your company's code of ethics. If you can't find that or don't think it's taken seriously in your place of work, you can check your profession's ethical code. The ACM, for example, has a code of ethics for IT employees.

Another source of help is the Computer Ethics Institute (www.brook.edu/its/cei/cei_hp.htm). This organization has developed the "Ten Commandments of Computer Ethics" to help guide you in the general direction of ethical computer use (see Figure 9.5).

1. *Don't use a computer to harm other people.* This one is the bedrock for all the others.
2. *Don't interfere with other people's computer work.* This includes the small sins like sending frivolous e-mail, to the big ones, like spreading viruses, and the really big ones like electronic stalking.
3. *Don't snoop around in other people's computer files.* This means you shouldn't access another person's computer files unless expressly authorized to do so.
4. *Don't use a computer to steal.* This one's pretty obvious.
5. *Don't use a computer to bear false witness.* This means you shouldn't spread rumors and spoof your address (change the sender portion of the e-mail to

Figure 9.5

Computer Ethics Institute

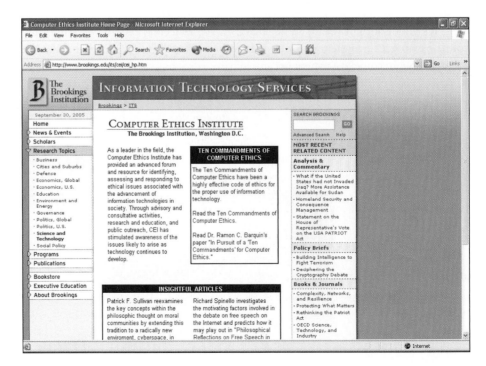

make it look like it came from someone other than you). It's much easier to lie and cause trouble when you're not using your real name.

6. *Don't copy or use proprietary software for which you have not paid.* Buying one copy of a game and copying it for all your friends is both illegal and unethical. This also applies to shareware (software you can try before you buy).

7. *Don't use other people's computer resources without authorization or proper compensation.* This includes using company time and resources to surf the Web, send e-mail, print large volumes of material, and work on your own private projects.

8. *Don't appropriate other people's intellectual output.* This includes taking and using images, text, music off the Web without permission and it certainly includes claiming material as your own that came from someone else.

9. *Always think about the social consequences of the IT system you're involved in.* Even if you're not a programmer or a systems analyst, you may be supervising a project that involves a computer system.

10. *Always use a computer in ways that ensure consideration and respect for your fellow humans.* People are entitled to the same respect and consideration whether your contact with them is in the "brick" or the "click" world.

INTELLECTUAL PROPERTY

An ethical issue you will almost certainly encounter is one related to the use or copying of proprietary software. Will you take care to do the right thing? Software is a type of intellectual property. **Intellectual property** is intangible creative work that is embodied in physical form.[10] Music, novels, paintings, and sculptures are all examples of intellectual property. So also are your company's product sketches and schematics and other proprietary documents. These documents, along with music, novels, and so on, are worth much more than the physical form in which they are delivered. For example, a single Sarah McLachlan song is worth far more than the CD it's purchased on. It's also an example of intellectual property that is covered by copyright law.

Copyright law protects authorship of literary and dramatic works, musical and theatrical compositions, and works of art. **Copyright** is the legal protection afforded an expression of an idea, such as a song, video game, and some types of proprietary documents. Having a copyright means that no one can use your song or video game without your permission. As a form of intellectual property, software is usually protected by copyright law, although sometimes it falls under patent law, which protects an idea, such as the design of a sewing machine or an industrial pump valve.

Copyright law doesn't forbid the use of intellectual property completely. It has some notable exceptions. For example, a TV program could show your video game without your permission. This would be an example of the use of copyrighted material for the creation of new material, that is, the TV program. And that's legal; it falls under the Fair Use Doctrine. The **Fair Use Doctrine** says that you may use copyrighted material in certain situations—for example, in the creation of new work or, within certain limits, for teaching purposes. One limit is on the amount of the copyrighted material you may use. Generally, the determining factor in copyright disputes is whether the copyright holder has been or is likely to be denied income because of the infringement. Courts will consider factors such as how much of the work was used and how, and when and on what basis the decision was made to use it.

Remember that copyright infringement is *illegal*. That means it's illegal, outside of a fair use situation, to simply copy a copyrighted picture, text, or anything else without permission, whether the copyrighted material is on the Internet or not. In particular, it's illegal to copy copyrighted software. But there's one exception to that rule. You

WHAT PRICE AN IDEA?

A patent protects a form of intellectual property. A patent applies to the implementation of an idea, such as how to construct an ergonomic mouse. IBM, the computer industry giant, has for nine years filed more patents with the U.S. Patent and Trademark Office than any other company. In 2001, IBM received 3454 patents. That's almost ten new patents *every* day. IBM has always been proud of its patent record, and it certainly gives stockholders and the public in general the impression that the company is working hard and is producing future technology. However, good press is not the only reason IBM files so many patent applications. There are many other reasons—1.5 billion of them, in fact. That's the number of dollars that IBM got from licensing income in 2001 alone, money the company put back into research and development. Since it's very hard to tell which new technology will ultimately be successful, IBM patents everything, and then licenses out those ideas that other companies want to use.

IBM isn't the only technology company to take patents seriously. Also busy in the technology-patent-generating race are Hewlett-Packard, Lucent Technologies, NEC, and Microsoft. Many other industries are realizing great return on the licensing of patents, too. For example,

- Bayer AG, a German drug company, clears profits of 78 percent after expenses on its intellectual property licensing fees.
- Du Pont revenues from intellectual property were $100 million in 1996 and grew to $450 million in 2001.
- Eastman Kodak even created a separate company, Eastman Chemical's Global Technology Ventures (GTV) to extract value from the company's intellectual assets. Since 1999, the company has made 20 deals worth more than $50 million with a further $100 million in net present value of future earnings.[11,12]

may always make one copy of copyrighted software to keep for backup purposes. When you buy copyrighted software, what you're paying for is the right to use it—and that's all.

How many other copies you may make depends on the copyright agreement that comes with the software package. Some software companies say emphatically that you may not even put the software on more than one computer—even if they're both yours and no one else uses either one. Other companies are a little less strict, and agree to let you put a copy of software on multiple machines—as long as only one person is using that software package at any given time. In this instance, the company considers software to be like a book in that you can have it in different places and you can loan it out, but only one person at a time may use it.

If you copy copyrighted software and give it to another person or persons, you're pirating the software. **Pirated software** is the unauthorized use, duplication, distribution or sale of copyrighted software.[13] Software piracy costs businesses an estimated $12 billion a year in lost revenue. Microsoft gets more than 25,000 reports of software piracy every year, and the company follows up on every one. The biggest losers (in rank order) are the United States, Japan, United Kingdom, Germany, China, France, Canada, Italy, Brazil, and the Netherlands. One in four business applications in the United States is thought to be pirated.[14] In some parts of the world more than 90 percent of business software is pirated. The Software and Information Industry Association (SIIA) and the Business Software Alliance (BSA) say that this means lost jobs, wages, tax revenues, and a potential barrier to success for software startups around the globe.[15]

With the crackdown by software manufacturers and the growing awareness of corporations, illegally copied software is actually declining in businesses. But a new threat is emerging in the form of counterfeit software. **Counterfeit software** is software that is manufactured to look like the real thing and sold as such. Counterfeit software is being sold by sophisticated crime organizations, and sometimes the counterfeit is so perfect that the software even includes a valid certificate of authenticity.[16] The results of counterfeit software are greater than just lost revenue, which in itself is considerable. Many resellers unwittingly buy counterfeit software and then find that they've sold buggy or infected software to their customers. The legitimate manufacturers have to deal with irate customers who believe that their software and its problems came directly from the software company. It's a public-relations nightmare.

Beware when buying software off the Internet. The BSA estimates that there are close to 950,000 Internet sites selling software illegally. If you buy from a shady site you might never receive your software at all. Or you might get counterfeit software that has a virus. You need to be careful when buying software off the Internet. Following are some guidelines.[17]

- Buy only from trustworthy sources. Official manufacturers' sites can often tell you where you can buy the software.
- Make sure to get full details about the company you're buying from (such as name, address, and telephone number). It's a bad sign if the seller is reluctant to divulge this information.
- Find out, before you buy, the site's policy on return, service, and warranty policies. Again, avoid a site that doesn't want to provide you with this information.
- Make sure to print out all pertinent information, such as order numbers, order confirmations, invoices, and receipts, and keep it until after the software proves to be satisfactory.
- An extraordinarily low price is a good tipoff that something is not right.
- Sellers know about consumer's suspicions about very low prices, so be on the watch for ads like "special deals with the manufacturer" and "liquidated inventories." These phrases are designed to make you believe you're getting a good deal and not an illegal one.
- As usual, knowledge is power, so know something about the product you're buying. If you do, it will be easier to recognize a counterfeit.
- The manufacturer will usually be glad to tell you what the package should have in it and may even be able to tell you about the site you're buying from.

Privacy

Privacy is the right to be left alone when you want to be, to have control over your own personal possessions, and not to be observed without your consent. It's the right to be free of unwanted intrusion into your private life. Privacy has several dimensions. Psychologically it's a need for personal space. All of us to a greater or lesser extent need to feel in control of our most personal possessions, and personal information belongs on the list of those possessions. Legally, privacy is necessary for self-protection.[18] If you put the key to your house in a special hiding place in your yard, you want to keep that information private. This information could be abused and cause you grief.

In this section we'll examine some specific areas of privacy—individuals snooping on each other, employers' collection of information about employees, businesses' collection of information about consumers, government collection of personal information, and the issue of privacy in international trade.

AMERICANS ALREADY PREPARING FOR NEW CANADIAN PRIVACY LAW

The Canadian Personal Information Protection and Electronic Documents Act was enacted in January 2001. The new law stipulates that businesses must give guarantees to Canadian citizens regarding the collection and use of their personal information. Companies will now have to get the customer's consent before sharing any customer information with its affiliates or commercial partners.

According to Murray Long, a privacy consultant in Ottawa, this law promises to create "some interesting nightmares" particularly for Canadian affiliates that store their customer information on servers south of the border. Since 2004, American firms with information on Canadian citizens have to enter into contractual agreements that commit them to following Canada's privacy law. This means that multinational companies operating in Canada have to have contracts with anybody who supplies them with any personal information, including their own subsidiaries. Of particular concern to many U.S. companies is the lack of a grandfather clause, which would have exempted customer information collected before the law's enactment. Many companies had already started asking for their customers' consent before they were legally required to do so. Without this consent, companies are not legally allowed to use any customer information even if the data was collected years before.[19]

PRIVACY AND OTHER INDIVIDUALS

Other individuals, like family members, associates, fellow employees, and "hackers" could be electronically invading your privacy. Their motives might be simple curiosity, an attempt to get your password, or to access something they have no right to. Obviously, there are situations in which you're well within your rights to snoop—for example, if you suspect that your child is in electronic contact with someone or something undesirable, or if you think that someone may be using your computer without permission. Hundreds of Web sites are offering programs, collectively referred to as "snoopware," to help you find out.

For general snooping, you can get **key logger**, or **key trapper**, **software**, which records keystrokes and mouse clicks performed at the computer, thus capturing all e-mail, instant messages, chat room exchanges, Web sites visited, applications run, and passwords typed in. Spector Pro is an example of key logger software; from the same software company you can also get eBlaster, which will actually e-mail you activity reports—every 30 minutes, if you'd like. A word of caution: be careful that you're not breaking the law; family members and friends don't have carte blanche to monitor each other.

If you want to disable activity-monitoring programs like Spector Pro, you can get a free program from www.pcworld.com called Privacy Companion, or one called Who's Watching Me from www.trapware.com.

You can at least make sure that your social insurance number, bank account number, passwords, mother's maiden name, and credit card numbers are not stored on your computer for someone to find. Make sure you clear the "Use inline AutoComplete" or similar option in your browser, a feature that starts suggesting the rest of the entry when you type in the first few letters while filling out a form. You can disable it in Internet Explorer from the menu: go Tools/Internet Options/Advanced and clear the check box for "Use inline AutoComplete." Don't forget to click OK when you're done.

Also available for monitoring computer use are screen capture programs that periodically record what's on the screen (they get the information straight from the video

TRACE THE ROUTE OF YOUR JOURNEY TO A WEB SITE

When you send e-mail or visit a Web site, your request for service goes through lots of computers after your own. First, it goes from your computer to the server that's connecting you to the Internet. It may even move between computers within your school or service provider.

The "tracert" function in DOS (which stands for *disk operating system*, the operating system that we used before Windows) allows you to see that journey. To get to DOS, you have to go to the Command Prompt option in Windows, as follows.

1. Click on the Start button.
2. Click on All Programs.
3. Click on Accessories.
4. Click on Command Prompt.

You'll get a DOS window showing a note about the version of Windows you're using and a declaration of Microsoft's copyright. Next comes the C:\ prompt with the name of the folder you're currently in. It will look something like this (the regular text—not the bold here):

DOS is a command-driven user interface—there's no click-and-point capability—so you have to type in commands. At the last greater-than symbol (>) type in the word "tracert" and the address of a Web site (as shown in the boldface).

You'll get a listing (up to 30 hops) of the computers that your message went through to get to its destination. You'll see the number of the hop (1, 2, 3, etc.), the time in milliseconds it took to get there, and the address of each computer it encountered on the way along with the computer's IP address (digits grouped in four sets consisting of one to three digits each—example: 192.168.1.50).

When you're finished, close the window as usual or type "exit" at the prompt.

Try this for your own school and two other Web site addresses. To print out your results, capture the screen with the Print Screen key (usually found on the top right-hand side of your keyboard), then paste it into Word or Paint, and print from there.

```
Microsoft Windows XP [Version 5.1.2600]
<C> Copyright 1985-2001 Microsoft Corp
C:\Documents and Settings\Maeve>tracert www.pittstate.edu
```

card). These don't trap every single screen, just whatever is on the screen when the capturing program activates, but they still give whoever is doing the monitoring a pretty good idea of what the computer user is up to. Other tools for monitoring include packet sniffers (that examine the information passing by) on switches, hubs, or routers (the devices on networks that connect computers to each other), and log analysis tools that keep track of logons, deletions, and so forth.

As you're probably already aware, e-mail is completely insecure. It might as well be written on a postcard for all the privacy it has. Not only that, but every e-mail you send results in at least three or four copies being stored on different computers (see Figure 9.6). If you write an e-mail, it's stored first in the e-mail program in the computer you're using. Second, it's stored on the e-mail server—the computer through which it gets onto the Internet. Third, it's stored on the recipient's computer and may also be archived on the recipient's e-mail server.

Some people like to "encrypt" their e-mail (see fuller discussion below). Lots of products on the market will do this for you, such as ZixMail, CertifiedMail, PrivacyX, and SafeMessage. Disappearing Email gives you a slightly different type of e-mail protection. This software is free and sends a self-destructing message with the e-mail so that the e-mail deletes itself after the period of time you specify. Before the recipient

Figure 9.6

The E-Mail You Send Is Stored on Many Computers

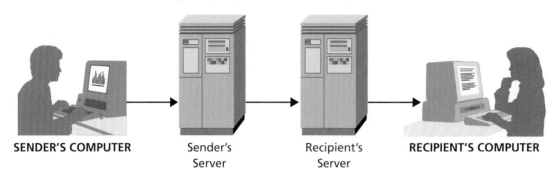

SENDER'S COMPUTER   Sender's
                           Server   Recipient's
                                           Server   RECIPIENT'S COMPUTER

opens the e-mail the Disappearing Email software checks with the Disappearing server that the e-mail hasn't passed its expiration date. However, you can defeat this feature by copying the text and pasting it somewhere else.

IDENTITY THEFT

In Canada, the PhoneBusters National Call Centre received 7629 identity theft complaints by Canadians in 2002, reporting total losses of more than $8.5 million.[20] The Council of Better Business Bureaus in Canada estimates identity theft costs $2.5 billion a year to consumers, banks, credit card firms, stores, and other businesses.[21] Here are some examples of identity theft:

- Dan and Sharon Millar of Hamilton, Ontario, noticed their *TV Guide* didn't arrive at its usual time. As weeks went by, their letters and packages stopped coming altogether. Canada Post then called them and informed them that someone had applied for a change-of-address form, diverting all of the Millars' mail and obtaining their personal information. By the time authorities launched an investigation, someone had applied for and received a credit card in the Millars' name.[22]
- A 42-year-old retired Army captain in Rocky Hill, Connecticut, found that an identity thief had spent $260,000 buying goods and services that included two trucks, a Harley-Davidson motorcycle, and a timeshare vacation home in South Carolina. The victim discovered his problem only when his retirement pay was garnisheed to pay the outstanding bills.
- In New York, members of a pickpocket ring forged the driver's licences of their victims within hours of snatching the women's purses. If you steal someone's purse, your haul usually won't be more than $200, probably much less. On the other hand, if you steal the person's identity, you can net on average between $4000 and $10,000.
- Another crime gang took out $8 million worth of second mortgages on victims' homes. It turned out the source of all the instances of identity theft was a car dealership.

PRIVACY AND EMPLOYEES

Companies need information about their employees and customers to be effective in the marketplace. But people often object to having so many details about their lives available to others. If you're applying for a job, you'll most likely fill out a job application, but that's not the only information a potential employer can get about you. For a small fee, employers, or anyone else, can find out about your credit standing, your telephone usage, your insurance coverage, and many other interesting things. An employer can also get information on what you said on the Internet from companies who collect and collate chat room exchanges. An employer can also ask a job applicant to take drug and psychological tests, the results of which are the property of the company.

After you're hired, your employer can monitor where you go, what you do, what you say, and what you write in e-mails—at least during working hours. One reason that companies monitor employees' e-mail is that they can be sued for what their employees send to each other and to people outside the company. Chevron Corporation and Microsoft have had to settle sexual harassment lawsuits for $2.2 million each because employees sent offensive e-mail. Other companies, such as Dow Chemical Company, Xerox, and Edward Jones, have chosen to take preemptive action by firing people who send or store pornographic or violent e-mail messages.[23]

Another reason employers monitor their workers' use of IT resources is to avoid wasting resources, or "cyberslacking": visiting pornographic sites and news sites, chatting, gaming, trading stocks, participating in auctions, shopping, checking sports scores, or doing anything else not in one's job description. In May 2000, Victoria's Secret had an online fashion show at three o'clock in the afternoon on a weekday. About two million people watched the show, presumably many of them on their companies' computers. One employee watching the show used as much bandwidth as it would take to download the entire *Encyclopaedia Britannica*.[24] So, not only is the employee wasting company time, the employee is also slowing down the work of others.

That about 70 percent of Web traffic occurs during work hours is reason enough for companies to monitor what, and for how long, employees are looking at. Again, various software packages are available to keep track of people's surfing. Some software actually blocks access to certain sites.

To sum up, businesses have good reasons for seeking and storing personal information on employees:

1. They want to hire the best people possible and to avoid being sued for failing to adequately investigate the backgrounds of employees.
2. They want to ensure that staff members are conducting themselves appropriately and not wasting or misusing company resources.
3. They can be held liable for the actions of employees.
4. Financial institutions are even required by law to monitor all communications including e-mail and telephone conversations.

MONITORING TECHNOLOGY Numerous vendors offer software that scans both incoming and outgoing e-mail, looking for specific words or phrases in the subject lines or in the message, and flagging unsolicited ads and newsletters. You can sneak this software onto someone's computer using the "Trojan horse" approach (see below); that is, you can hide it in an innocent-looking e-mail.

Some companies use an approach less invasive than actually reading employees' e-mail. Their e-mail inspection programs just check for a certain level of e-mail to and from the same address. This indicates that there may be a problem and the employee is informed of the situation and asked to remedy it. Then, no intrusive supervisory snooping is necessary.[25]

An employer can track your keyboard activity with a software key logger, just as another individual can (see above). A harder-to-detect alternative is a *hardware* key logger, which captures keystrokes on their journey from the keyboard to the motherboard. These devices can be in the form of a connector on the system-unit end of the cable between the keyboard and the system unit. There's another type you can install into the keyboard that "bugs" it. Both types have enough memory to store about a year's worth of typing. But you have to have access to the bugged computer to be able to see the log of activity. And these devices can't capture anything that's not typed. To defeat them a person can copy the password (or whatever) and paste it into its new location. Although the key logger can tell a copy-and-paste operation was performed, it cannot tell what was copied and pasted.[26]

There is little sympathy in the legal system for private-sector employees who are being monitored. Employers have the legal right to monitor the use of their resources and that includes the time they're paying you for. In contrast to your home, you can have no expectation of privacy when using a company's resources.

PRIVACY AND CONSUMERS

Businesses face a dilemma:

- Customers want businesses to know who they are, but at the same time they want them to leave them alone.
- Customers want businesses to provide what they want, but at the same time they don't want businesses knowing too much about their habits and preferences.
- Customers want businesses to tell them about products and services they might like to have, but they don't want to be inundated with ads.

Like it or not, massive amounts of information are available to businesses. A relatively large Web site may get about 100 million hits per day. The site gets about 200 bytes of information for each hit. That's about 20 gigabytes per day.[27] This level of information load has made electronic customer relationship (eCRM) systems the fastest-growing area of software development. Part of managing customer relationships is personalization. Web sites greeting you by name, and Amazon.com's famous feature telling you that "People who bought this also bought . . ." are examples of personalization, which is made possible by the Web site knowing about you.[28]

Apart from being able to collect its own information about you, a company can readily access consumer information elsewhere. Credit card companies sell information, and so do mailing list companies. Web traffic tracking companies such as DoubleClick follow you (and every other surfer) around the Web and then sell the information about where you went and for how long. DoubleClick can get to know you over time and provide their customers with a profile on you that is highly refined. DoubleClick is also a middleman for companies that want to advertise to surfers. When hired by a company wanting to sell something, DoubleClick identifies people who might be receptive and sends the ad to them as a banner or pop-up ad. Proponents of this practice claim that it's good for the surfer because they get targeted advertising and less unwanted advertising. DoubleClick at first undertook to track consumers without attaching their identity to the information. Then, in 1999, DoubleClick changed its policy and announced that it would henceforth attach consumer names, personal information, and e-mail addresses. Responding to negative consumer reaction, DoubleClick withdrew its proposed change. Interestingly, DoubleClick didn't undertake never to resume the abandoned policy, but only agreed to wait until standards for such activity are in place.[29]

COOKIES: THE ROOT OF ALL EVIL   The basic tool of consumer Web monitoring is the **cookie**—a small file a Web site places on your computer that contains information about you and your Web activities. It can be used for many purposes. For example, it's used to keep ID and password information so that you don't have to go through the

WHAT WOULD YOU DO?

Analyze the following situation. You have access to the sales and customer information in a flower shop. You discover that the boyfriend of a woman you know is sending roses to three other women on a regular basis. The woman you know is on the flower list, but she believes that she's the only woman in his romantic life. You really think you should tell the woman. Your dilemma is that you have a professional responsibility to keep the company's information private. However, you also believe that you have a responsibility to the woman. Do you tell her?

Are there factors that would change your decision? Each team member should individually consider the additional information below, then indicate whether any one or more of these factors would change his or her decision. Form a consensus with your team.

Additional Facts	Yes	No	Why?
1. The woman is your sister.			
2. The man is your brother.			
3. The woman is about to give the man her life savings as a down payment on a house in the belief that they will soon be married.			
4. The woman is already married.			

whole rigmarole every time you log onto a site. It's also used to store the contents of electronic shopping carts, so that the next time you log on, the Web site will be able to see your wish list—and they don't have to store all that information themselves.

A cookie can also be used to track your Web activity. It can monitor and record what sites you visit, how long you stay there, what Web pages you visited, and the sites you came from and go to. This type of cookie is called a *unique* cookie. Some cookies are very temporary and some stay there recording indefinitely.

Apart from the unique cookies above, there are also third-party or *common* cookies that have many privacy advocates disturbed. A common cookie is one that started out as a unique cookie, but the original site sold access to it to a third party such as DoubleClick, that can then change the cookie so that the third party can track the surfer's activity across many sites. The third party collects information about surfers without names or other identifiable personal information. What they usually collect is an IP address and they then link it to a random identifying ID so that the surfer can be identified at other sites. Surveys have shown that the vast majority of people (91 percent) don't like unknown companies gathering the information about them that they provide to the site they interact with.[30]

You have two options if you want to block cookies. First, you can set your browser to reject all cookies, or get your browser to warn you when a site wants to put a cookie on your computer. Second, you can get cookie management software with additional options not available on your browser. For example, CookieCop 3, from *PC Magazine* (www.pcmag.com), will let you accept or reject cookies on a per-site basis. It also allows you to replace banner ads with the image of your choice and to block ads for sites you find offensive. With this or other cookie-stopper software, you can disable

THE JUDGE SAYS "GET PERSONAL" WITH CUSTOMERS

SonicBlue Inc.'s ReplayTV system enables you to record TV shows without the commercials; send programs to other ReplayTV owners over the Internet; and find all the times and stations a particular show is playing and record them without commercials.

When the system was offered, several movie studios and television networks filed suit, claiming that the commercial skipping and the sharing of programming violated copyright law. Before a court case is heard, there is usually a process called "discovery" in which each side must share information with the other. As part of this process, the plaintiff wanted to know exactly how SonicBlue's customers were using ReplayTV. SonicBlue said that the company doesn't collect that information.

Unbelievably, the judge told SonicBlue to write software to monitor all shows that customers watch, every skipped commercial, and all programs they send over the Internet. The order was based on the published privacy policy of SonicBlue, which said that the company may collect audience data. SonicBlue said that it originally planned to collect such information, but decided not to on the basis of the negative reaction from customers that Tivo, ReplayTV's competitor, got when it proposed the same idea.

So SonicBlue found itself in the strange situation of having to go to court to avoid having to collect personal information on its customers—in effect to protect the privacy of its customers. The company filed an appeal and the new judge overturned the previous ruling. However, the original ruling sent shock waves throughout the privacy advocate community.[31]

pop-up windows, and stipulate that certain cookies can stay on your hard drive for the duration of one session only.

SPAM Spam is unsolicited e-mail (electronic junk mail) from businesses that advertise goods and services. Often spam mass mailings advertise pornography, get-rich-quick schemes, and miracle cures. If you haven't been inundated with spam, you're either very lucky or you don't use the Internet much. Spam has become a severe irritant to consumers and a costly matter for businesses, who have to sort through hundreds of e-mail messages every day deleting spam and hoping that they don't delete e-mail messages that are actually legitimate customer orders.

You can get spam filters to block out spam, but spammers are clever about including nonprinting characters in their subject lines and addresses that fool the filters into letting them pass. For example, say a spammer wanted to send out a message about a new weight loss drug called *Off*. The spammer would alter the spelling of the word or add invisible HTML tags so that the subject line would be: O*F*F or O<i></i>F<u></u>F. The HTML tags <i> and <u> would normally italicize and underline text, respectively, and the </i> and </u> would undo the italicizing and bolding, but since there's no text in between the tags do nothing except dupe the filter.

Experts estimate that almost two-thirds of e-mail traffic in 2003 was spam, costing organizations worldwide about $20 billion per year.[32] An individual spammer can send out 80 million or so spams per day. AOL and Microsoft say that their servers block a billion spam messages every day.[33]

One trick that spammers use to collect addresses for spamming is to send out e-mail purporting to add you to a general do-not-spam list if you reply. In fact, what it does is add your e-mail address to the list of "live" ones.

SPYWARE Some companies are really sneaky about getting information from you. For example, the first release of RealNetworks' RealJukebox sent information back to the company about what CDs the people who downloaded the software were playing on that computer. This information collection was going on when the customer wasn't even on the Web.[34]

If you've downloaded a game or other software from the Web for free, you may have noticed that it came with banner ads. These ads are created by **adware**—software to generate ads that installs itself when you install some other (usually free) program. This is a type of **Trojan-horse software**, meaning that it's software you don't want hidden inside software you do want. At installation there's usually a disclaimer saying that by installing the software you are agreeing to accept the adware also. Very few people read the whole agreement, and advertisers count on that. This technique is sometimes called *click-wrap* because it's like the agreement you accept by breaking the shrink wrap on a software box.

Most people don't get upset about pure adware, since they feel it's worth having to view a few ads to get software for free. However, a more insidious extra called **spyware** (also called **sneakware** or **stealthware**) is now being bundled into free downloadable software. Spyware is software that tracks your online movements, mines the information stored on your computer, or uses your computer's processor and storage for some task you know nothing about. For example, unknown to you, your computer may become part of peer-to-peer network operation (called *grid computing*) to solve complicated computer problems—you're paying for the "free" software in CPU cycles. Spyware is fast becoming the hidden cost of free software. Software such as Kazaa Media Desktop and Audiogalaxy, which are the successors to Napster for sharing music and other files online, include spyware. If you download free software and it has banner ads, it's quite possible that it has spyware too. There's usually something in the "I agree" screens about the spyware, but it can be hard to find.[35] Spyware can stay on your computer long after you've uninstalled the original software.

You can detect all kinds of Trojan-horse software with The Cleaner from www.moosoft.com. Also check out www.wilders.org for Trojan First Aid Kit (TFAK). The best-known stealthware blockers are Ad-aware (free from www.lavasoftusa.com) and PestPatrol. These scan your whole computer and offer to any delete spyware programs.

If you want to check out free software for spyware *before* you download it, go to spychecker.com, a site that will tell you if a particular free software includes adware or spyware.

For preventing your computer from automatically communicating over the Internet without your approval, a firewall is good. A very popular software firewall is ZoneAlarm (www.zonelabs.com). It also offers protection from ads and cookies.

Even without spyware, a site can still find out a lot about its visitors from its *Web log*.[36] This is a record consisting of one line of data for every visitor to the site, it is usually stored on the company's server. At the very least, a log file can tell the Web site company:

- What company or ISP you come from
- The amount of time you spent on the site
- The number of pages you viewed
- How you clicked in to the site, that is, from a search engine or some other site, or from your e-mail advertising

The latter three bits of information are collectively called the **clickstream**, which can also include what Web sites you visited, what ads you looked at, and what you bought.

If, as a consumer, you want to protect information about your surfing habits, you can use various software packages to do so. Apart from cookie management software you can avail yourself of **anonymous Web browsing (AWB)** services, which in effect

YOU CAN INSURE AGAINST IDENTITY THEFT

Insurance companies are beginning to cover one of the fastest-growing white-collar crimes—identity theft. Chubb Personal Insurance is one of the first to offer such coverage. Since 1999, Chubb has included $25,000 of coverage for expenses related to identity theft on all its homeowner policies. Travelers Property Casualty was the first in the industry to offer this type of coverage and later added a freestanding policy.

In 2001, almost 12,000 Canadians were victims of identity theft. Take, for example, Dan and Sharon Millar from Hamilton, Ontario. The couple first noticed that their *TV Guide* did not arrive when it should have, the first Tuesday of the month. Over the next few weeks, all mail had simply stopped coming. After contacting Canada Post, the stunned couple discovered that someone had applied for a change of address, diverting all their mail to another address. By the time the whole plot was uncovered, the fraud artist had applied for, received, and used a credit card in the Millars' name. The Millars were not alone. In 2001, Canada Post caught 400 cases of fake address changes, ten times more than in the previous year. Inspector John Sliter of the economic crimes branch of the RCMP says that once someone has acquired your identity, it is actually quite easy to take over financial accounts,

transfer bank balances, apply for loans and credit cards, and purchase items. Often, a social insurance number and a date of birth are all that is needed to assume someone's identity. According to Canada's social insurance registry, there are currently about 1.4 million more social insurance cards in circulation than there are Canadians. According to the Council of Better Business Bureaus in Canada, identity theft accounts for a loss of $2.5 billion a year to Canadian consumers, banks, credit card firms, stores, and other businesses.

Identity theft is the fastest-growing fraud in North America. Consequently, the U.S. Congress has passed the Identity Theft and Assumption Deterrence Act in 1998 making identity theft a federal crime. Convictions carry maximum penalties of 30 years' imprisonment, a fine, and confiscation of any personal property used to perpetrate the crime. In Canada, the penalties are much less severe. Under the Criminal Code of Canada, impersonation *with intent* results in a jail term of up to ten years. The RCMP would like the law to be toughened and unified across Canada. For instance, Inspector Sliter says that one such revision could include passing a law declaring that carrying multiple identities is a prosecutable offence.[37]

hide your identity. Anonymizer (www.anonymizer.com), and other programs like it, route your browsing data through their server and remove all identifying information. AWB services available include disabling pop-up promotions, defeating tracking programs, and erasing your Internet history files. If you don't want to go through an outside server, you can download software like SurfSecret (www.surfsecret.com), a shareware anti-tracking package.

Finally, remember that even if a company promises, and fully intends, to protect its customer information, this may not be possible. Faced with a subpoena, a company will have to relinquish customer records.

PRIVACY AND GOVERNMENT AGENCIES

Government agencies have about 2000 databases containing personal information on individuals.[38] The various branches of government need information to administer entitlement programs, such as social security, welfare, student loans, law enforcement, and so on.

LAW ENFORCEMENT You've often heard about someone's being apprehended for a grievous crime after a routine traffic stop for something like a broken taillight. The arrest most likely ensued because the arresting officer ran a check on the licence plate and driver's licence. The officer probably checked the police database and found the outstanding warrant there. This is how the culprits responsible for the Oklahoma City bombing were caught.

The database of the Canadian Police Information Centre (CPIC), available to police agencies across Canada, holds information on outstanding warrants, missing children, gang members, juvenile delinquents, stolen guns and cars, and so on. CPIC, located in the RCMP headquarters complex in Ottawa, Ontario and in operation since 1972, serves over 60,000 Canadian law enforcement agents. Officers access it from a terminal located in their office or vehicle. CPIC is also linked to more than 400 criminal justice national and international agencies across the planet. One of these is the U.S. National Crime Information Center (NCIC), which has a huge database with information on the criminal records of more than 20 million people. This Canada-U.S. crime fighting partnership has become ever more prevalent with the North American Free Trade agreement (NAFTA). Today, information sharing between Canada and the United States has been routinized by the Automated Canadian/US Police Information Exchange System (ACUPIES) and officers on either side of the border have access to each other's national criminal databases on a 24-hour basis.

It is not surprising that these databases have been abused. Several police departments have found that a significant number of employees illegally snooped for criminal records on people they knew or wanted to know.

WHAT DOES THE LAW SAY ABOUT PRIVACY?

Although the Canadian Privacy Act, implemented on July 1, 1983, was aimed at regulating government record keeping practices as a result of computerization, at the time data mining, direct marketing, and online retailing did not exist. The Act was aimed specifically at making government more accountable for the personal information it held in its databanks. Today, however, countries have recognized that companies can also collect massive amounts of personal information about customers. Hence, protecting citizens from misuse of information in commercial contexts has become important. However, Canada, the United States, and the European Community have not developed a consistent set of laws. Europe's standards are considered the most stringent, followed closely by those of Canada. In effect since 2001, the Canadian privacy law (better known as the Personal Information Protection and Electronic Documents Act, or simply "PIPEDA") mandates as law ten principles adopted in 1996 as voluntary industry standards:

- *Accountability.* Organizations are responsible for the uses of the information they collect. They must ensure its proper handling by third parties with whom they share it.
- *Identifying purposes.* The purposes for which the data is being collected must be identified to Canadian citizens at or before the time the information is collected.
- *Consent.* Consent from Canadian citizens is required for the collection, use, or disclosure of personal information. Exceptions include emergencies, law enforcement, and debt collection.
- *Limiting collection.* It is prohibited to indiscriminately collect information. Only the information necessary to fulfill the purposes that have been identified may be collected.
- *Use, disclosure, and retention limited to what is necessary.* After the personal information collected is no longer required to fulfill the identified purposes, it should be destroyed, erased, or made anonymous.

- *Accuracy.* Collected personal information must be accurate, complete, and up to date.
- *Safeguards.* Collected personal information must be securely protected against unauthorized access, disclosure, copying, use, or modification.
- *Openness.* Organizations' management of personal information must be made open.
- *Individual access.* Canadian citizens must be granted access to their personal information, and be given the ability to correct this information.
- *Compliance challenges.* Canadian citizens will be entitled to challenge organizations on the principles listed above if organizations are noncompliant.

Like the EU's Directive on Protection of Personal Data, the Canadian law applies to its citizens regardless of whether they are inside or outside of Canada. However, although Canada's legislation is similar in many aspects to that of the EU, important differences do exist. Unlike the Directive, which applies to all entities collecting and processing information that could identify a person, Canada's law applies only to personal information collected and disclosed while conducting commercial activities. It does permit the collection and dissemination of personal information without personal consent "for personal and domestic purposes" or for "journalistic, artistic, and literary purposes." Moreover, unlike the EU legislation, the Canadian law exempts names, titles, business addresses, and telephone numbers from its definition of "personal information." Such information can be collected and disseminated freely by companies operating in Canada. Conversely, the U.S. government has traditionally preferred a more hands-off approach to privacy, arguing that private industry should be left alone to self-regulate in this regard. The United States eventually succumbed to EU pressure concerning privacy protection (i.e., the "Safe Harbor" principles—see below). By law, the EU interdicts member countries from conducting transactions involving the transfer of personal information with foreign companies that do not safeguard it in accordance to EU law. Originally, the United States would not offer such guarantees. Through ongoing negotiations, however, the United States has accepted to ensure that EU laws will be respected. Yet, by 2004, U.S. companies will also have to adapt to the Canadian law as well if they want to continue conducting business in Canada—their largest trading partner. Several differences between the Canadian and the European privacy law means that compliance will be difficult not only for U.S. companies but also for Canadian and European companies that decide to operate in all three markets.[39]

PRIVACY AND INTERNATIONAL TRADE

If a customer in Europe buys books from Amazon.com's United Kingdom division, you'd probably be surprised to find out that Amazon may not transfer the customer's credit card information to Amazon in the United States without making sure it is in compliance with **Safe Harbor principles**, a set of rules to which U.S. businesses that want to trade with the EU must adhere. You probably wouldn't think twice about sending customer information, such as a name and address, via e-mail from one part of the company to another. But if you're in a subsidiary in an EU country and the recipient is in the United States you might have a problem.

Canadians do not have this problem when it comes to trading with the EU. The Personal Information Protection and Electronic Documents Act (PIPEDA) received Royal Assent in April 2000 and was adopted into law. Its provisions are being phased in from January 1, 2001 to January 1, 2004. Provinces are being given a three-year grace period to pass their own equivalent privacy laws; afterwards, any province that

WHAT'S YOUR OPINION?

A nationwide survey was conducted by the journal *Marketing Management* on consumer attitudes toward online privacy.[40] It investigated what impact privacy policies have on consumer purchasing behaviour and what consumers considered to be acceptable levels of information gathering.

The questions and responses are listed below. State whether you agree or disagree with the answers and why.

Question	Survey Response	Your Response	
		Yes	No
1. Does your perception of a site's Web privacy affect your willingness to purchase from it?	Depends on the site: 49%		
2. Should a Web site be able to analyze Web traffic on an anonymous aggregate level?	Yes: 75%		
3. Is lack of control over who gets your personal information a strong privacy concern for you?	Yes: 39%		
4. Is spam a strong privacy concern for you?	Yes: 37%		
5. Is it very important to you to be able to access a site's information about you?	Yes: 22%		
6. Would it be acceptable to you if the site protected your privacy, but didn't let you see information about you any time you wished?	Yes: 80%		

does not have its own, equivalent privacy law will be subject to Canada's federal law, PIPEDA. The European Commission has ruled that PIPEDA meets the rigorous standards for data protection.

The EU has very stringent rules about the collection of personal information and has implemented a Directive on Protection of Personal Data, mentioned above. In 1998, the EU set privacy goals and each country had to make laws to achieve those goals according to its own culture and customs. So there are still differences in privacy laws among European countries. In general, the rights granted EU citizens include the consumer's right to:

- Know the marketer's source of information
- Check personal identifiable information for accuracy
- Correct any incorrect information
- Specify that information can't be transferred to a third party without the consumer's consent
- Know the purpose for which the information is being collected

If information can be linked to you—either directly or indirectly—it's personal identifiable information. The list of identifying tags includes names, ID numbers, and unique physical characteristics.[41]

The United States and the European Union began negotiations on the heels of the EU Directive to create Safe Harbor principles for U.S.-based companies to be able to transfer personal information out of European countries. The rules cover every industry and almost all types of personal information. After extensive negotiations, in June 2000 the United States became the first country outside the EU to be recognized as meeting information privacy requirements of EU states.[42] Without this agreement, disruption of the $350 billion in trade between the United States and Europe would have been a distinct possibility.

So for your company, or Amazon.com, to be able to transfer personal information out of EU countries, you'd have to first register with the U.S. Department of Commerce and agree to adhere to the Safe Harbor principles. Although participation is theoretically voluntary, if you transfer personal information without having registered, you're risking punitive action from the U.S. Federal Trade Commission as well as from the European country from which you transferred the information.[43]

See Closing Case Two for more on the European Directive on Protection of Personal Data and the Safe Harbor Agreement.

LAWS ON PRIVACY

Unlike the EU and Canada, the United States doesn't have a comprehensive or consistent set of laws on the use or misuse of information. However, some laws are in place. Two newer examples are the Health Insurance Portability and Accountability Act (HIPAA) and the Financial Service Modernization Act.

The **Health Insurance Portability and Accountability Act** gives the U.S. health care industry until April 14, 2003 to formulate and implement the first set of compliance regulations that require all members of the industry to install policies and procedures to keep patient information confidential. The Act seeks to:

- Limit the release and use of your health information without your consent
- Give you the right to access your medical records and find out who has accessed them
- Overhaul the circumstances under which researchers and others can review medical records
- Release health information on a need-to-know basis
- Allow the disclosure of protected health information for business reasons as long as the recipient undertakes, in writing, to protect the information

Many critics in Canada and the EU consider the U.S. approach to privacy protection still too piecemeal and far behind the curve, often putting the interests of businesses ahead of those of their own citizens. For instance, although HIPAA is a move in the right direction in terms of privacy protection in the U.S. health care industry, by comparison Canada's Personal Information Protection and Electronic Documents Act (PIPEDA) is all-encompassing. It covers all personal data that enters the commercial sphere in all sectors of the economy (see www.privcom.gc.ca for details). In sum, because the Canadian law applies to all industries, it underscores the belief that all Canadians have a fundamental right when it comes to their privacy and that they are not obligated to provide information about themselves. It gives Canadians the right to ask why information requested from them is needed and how it is to be used.

Information

In this section we'll consider the dual roles of information in an organization. Nothing is as universal or versatile as information. What else can you sell or lease to someone else—

and simultaneously retain for yourself? This unique resource called "information" has two functions in an organization: as raw material and as capital (see Figure 9.7).

INFORMATION AS RAW MATERIAL

Raw materials are the components from which a product is made. For example, the raw materials for a chair might be wood, glue, and screws. But almost everything you buy has information as part of the product. If you doubt this, wander through a store and see how many products incorporate absolutely no information. Even bananas have stickers telling you something about their distributor. Of course, the amount of information varies. You get a lot more information if you buy a jet airplane than if you buy a cake mix. Sometimes it's the information that makes a product particularly valuable. Take the example of two identical pairs of sports shoes that were originally made by the same company but sold under different logos. It's very likely that the shoes with the more widely known or prestigious logo will sell for a higher price than those with the lesser logo. The more desirable logo doesn't increase the functional value of the shoes. They're the same shoes! But the information (in this case the logo) proclaims something to the world that the wearer wants to be associated with. For that statement, whatever it is, the customer is prepared to pay extra.

Figure 9.7

Information as Raw Material and Capital

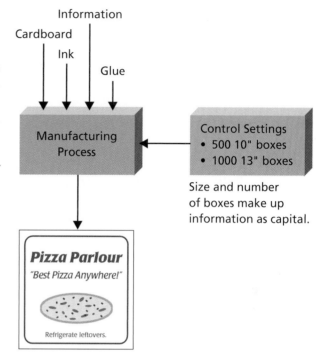

Size and number of boxes make up information as capital.

Information as raw material becomes part of the product.

The most successful companies put the highest value on information. United Parcel Service (UPS) is an example. The company's IT budget is second only to its expenditures on aircraft.[44] This is because UPS is selling not only a shipping service, but also information. You can connect to the UPS Web site and track your package. As UPS Chief Information Officer (CIO) Frank Ergbrick puts it, "A package without information has no value."

General Motors doesn't just sell vehicles. As we've described elsewhere in this text, its Cadillacs feature an option called OnStar that combines a global positioning system (GPS)—which identifies your position anywhere on earth—with networked sensors, a cell phone, and a link to customer support centres. With the OnStar system you can get directions to any destination and even advice on where to dine. OnStar also contributes to your safety. If the car's airbag inflates, the sensor sends a signal to the customer support centre, which tries to contact you on the car phone. If there's no response, the centre uses the GPS component to locate your car, then alerts the nearest emergency service. The OnStar system can help track your car if it's stolen. So a Cadillac is not just a car—it's an IT system on wheels.

INFORMATION AS CAPITAL

Capital is the asset you use to produce a product or service. Buildings, trucks, and machinery are examples of capital. For our chair manufacturer, the capital would be the factory building, the saw, the glue dispenser, screwdrivers, and so on. These items are not part of the chair, but they're necessary to build it. You incur a cost in acquiring capital, and you expect a return on your investment. Additionally, you can sell or lease capital assets.

You can think of information as capital. It's used by companies to provide products and services. Organizations need information to provide what their target market wants. They need information in the form of manufacturing schedules, sales reports, marketing plans, accounting information, and so on.

Information capital is one of the most important and universal types of capital in an organization. Not every company has a building or a truck, but every single one has information. We cannot state the case too strongly; an organization cannot exist without information any more than you can survive without oxygen.

Security

It is estimated that computer sabotage costs businesses somewhere close to $10 billion every year. Companies are increasing their spending on information security services, already having spent more than $4 billion in 2000; this figure is slated to rise to $21 billion by the end of 2005.[45] Hard disks can crash, computer parts can fail, hackers and crackers can gain access and do mischief, thieves engaged in industrial espionage can steal your information, and disgruntled employees or associates can cause damage.

SECURITY AND EMPLOYEES

Most of the press reports are about outside attacks on computer systems, but actually companies are in far more danger of losing money from employee misconduct than they are from that of outsiders. It's a problem that predates computers. A 300-restaurant chain with 30 employees in each location loses, on average, $218 per employee. And then there's the customers. The Cracker Barrel chain is constantly replacing the signature rocking chairs that sit on the porch outside each store, and other restaurants report the taking of salt shakers and silverware as "souvenirs."

But white-collar crime is where the big bucks are lost (see Figure 9.8). White-collar crime in general, from Fortune 100 firms to video stores to construction companies, accounts for about $400 billion every year—and information technology makes it much easier to accomplish and conceal. (Compare that to the $292 billion in the federal defence budget.) In white-collar fraud, the biggest losses are those incurred by management misconduct. Losses caused by managers are quadruple those of other employees, and the median losses are 16 times greater. Take embezzlement, for example. The average cost of a nonmanagerial employee's theft is $60,000, while that for managerial employees is $250,000. The most astonishing aspect of this is that most inside fraud (up to two-thirds) is never reported to the legal authorities, according to the Association of Certified Fraud Examiners (ACFE). A survey by Ernst & Young disclosed that two out of five businesses suffered more than five fraud losses, and fully one-quarter of those resulted in over a loss of over $1 million. The reason most often cited for lack of legal action was fear of damaging the company's reputation or brand name.[46]

Figure 9.8

Statistics on White-Collar Crime

- White-collar crime costs an estimated $400 billion per year.
- Average nonmanagerial embezzlement is $60,000.
- Average managerial embezzlement is $250,000.
- Two-thirds of insider fraud is not reported.
- Of the known losses, one-quarter cost more than $1 million.

Computer-aided fraud includes the old standby crimes like vendor fraud (taking payment for a nonexistent vendor or being paid for goods not delivered), writing payroll cheques to fictitious employees, claiming expense reimbursements for false claims, and so on. In addition, there are newer crimes such as stealing security codes, credit card numbers, and proprietary files. Intellectual property is one of the favourite targets of theft by insiders. In fact, the companies that make surveillance software say that employers are buying and installing the software not so much to monitor employees as to track how intellectual property, like product design sketches, schematics, and so on, are moving around the network.

Fraud examiners have a rule of thumb that in any group of employees, 10 percent are completely honest, 10 percent will steal, and for the remaining 80 percent, it will depend on circumstances. Most theft is committed by people who are strapped for cash, have access to funds that are poorly protected, and perceive a low risk of getting caught.

SECURITY AND COLLABORATION PARTNERS

Computer security used to be an internal matter. It concerned only the company and those who actually used the computers. With the advent of collaboration systems, however, company representatives are gaining access to each other's computer systems. It's very important to be sure that the computer system of the company you're giving access to is as least as secure as yours; otherwise, you'll create a back door into your own system. So now you need to worry about your partners', suppliers', and customers' computer security as well as your own.

Not surprisingly, not having good computer security in place can sour a deal. A large bank was about to close a multimillion-dollar deal with a cheque processing company when the bank's security chief asked the cheque processing company's chief information officer about its security policy. The cheque processing company didn't have one. In fact, it didn't even have the most basic security like firewalls. The deal was put on hold until the security met the bank's standards.[47]

The bank wasn't the only organization worried about the security of its associate companies. Many companies are checking out their suppliers' and other business partners' security before allowing them access to online company information. Goodrich Corporation, an aerospace company, uses collaboration systems so that suppliers can view design drawings. A large portion of Goodrich's $4 billion in annual sales comes from the department of defence. So espionage is a real threat. Goodrich has cut costs dramatically by using collaboration systems with file-sharing capabilities. But, before a supplier can be part of the team, Goodrich checks out the newcomer's security measures. The Goodrich people examine firewalls and encryption, and even how physically secure the information on the system is. Then if everything meets their tough standards, the Goodrich team sets up a detailed procedure to be followed in case there's a security breach. The moral of the story is: if you want to do business with Goodrich, or many other companies, you'd better have a secure computer system.[48]

GRID COMPUTING A new kind of computer infrastructure is beginning to take hold in the business world. **Grid computing** is a way of linking far-flung computers to share CPU power, databases, and database storage via the Internet or a virtual private network. The government is already engaged in grid computing, as evidenced by the National Science Foundation's National Technology Grid and NASA's Information Power Grid. Grid computing software is in development by IBM, Compaq, Sun, and HP. Grid computing includes peer-to-peer file sharing, but it's much more. The core of grid software is its common interface that allows any computer on the grid to tap

TOP TEN DOT-CONS

According to a study following a yearlong investigation with the collaboration of five U.S. agencies and consumer groups from various countries including Canada, the top ten dot-cons are:

- Internet auction fraud
- Internet service provider scams
- Internet Web site design/promotions—Web cramming
- Internet information and adult services—credit card cramming
- Multi-level marketing/pyramid scams
- Business opportunities and work-at-home scams
- Investment schemes and get-rich-quick scams
- Travel/vacation fraud
- Telephone/pay-per-call solicitation frauds (including modem diallers)
- Health care frauds

The most popular scams are advertising computer software and electronic consumer goods at various e-auction sites and taking cashier's cheques or money orders in payment but never delivering the goods. Internet service provider scams consist of sending consumers "rebate" cheques. When the consumer cashes these, he or she is unwittingly agreeing to allow the scammer to be his Internet service provider. Monthly charges on the consumer's telephone bill soon follow. Web cramming involves billing consumers for a Web page they didn't even know they had. Con artists usually target small businesses and not-for-profit organizations with this scam by calling and offering these organizations a "free" Web page. Similarly, credit card cramming includes Web sites which offer visitors to view adult-oriented content for free after leaving their credit card numbers to prove they are over 18. Pyramid schemes promise customers to get rich by recruiting other people to sell particular products and services. Shams also include work-at-home scams that make exaggerated earning claims on the Internet and in print ads to sell "how to" packages over the Internet. Still other deceptions pertain to Web site operators' misleading use of testimonials promising quick riches with little or no risk to consumers. Many consumers have been tricked in this manner into signing up for day trading programs following misrepresentations about their high-risk nature. Some scams also include offering free access to adult material after downloading dialler software which disconnects your modem and then reconnects your computer through international long-distance numbers without your knowledge. The study also warns consumers about Web sites offering luxury trips at very low prices then hitting you with hidden charges after you pay, and unlicensed online pharmacies operating as "cyber-drugstores" but that do not meet regulatory standards, some offering bogus miracle cures for all ills.

As part of this ongoing Internet law enforcement initiative, more than 700 law enforcement and consumer protection officials are being trained in online investigation and law enforcement techniques across 20 different countries including 14 Canadian consumer protection offices. According to Jodie Bernstein, director of the FTC's Bureau of Consumer Protection, "the Internet is revolutionizing the way we gather information, shop and do business. ... This collaboration with law enforcement agencies, industry and consumers will create a climate where e-commerce can be conducted with confidence. We want the dot con artists to know that we're building a consumer protection coalition that spans the globe. We aim to make the Net safe for consumers."[49]

into the CPU power or storage of other available computers. Companies as diverse as Pratt & Whitney, Bristol-Myers Squibb Co., and American Express are using grid computing. Analysts say that it will turn computing power into a utility—the provider will simply send you as much or as little power or storage as you happen to need at that moment.[50]

The issues still to be resolved before grid computing becomes widespread are many and complex, and not least among them is security. Security issues involving computers from multiple locations spans cultural and technical issues ranging from rights of access to data sharing to legal and departmental policies.

WHY DO HACKERS CREATE MALICIOUS CODE?

The answer to why hackers create malicious code in the form of viruses, worms, and denial-of-service attacks (you'll find these attacks on computers discussed further in Extended Learning Module K: Computer Crime and Forensics) is not simple. Some create malware (malicious code that does damage to a computer or a network) because they find a community of hackers where they fit in, because they're bored, because they want revenge, or because they can.

The first example is a 16-year-old, who lives in Austria and writes viruses and worms when he's bored. So far, he has written over 150 such mini-programs. He has even tried his hand at code that automatically creates viruses. He says he doesn't create malware that causes damage because he likes to "be friendly."

In Toronto, Canada, lives our second example, who started writing malware when he found himself out of college with no job (despite having sent out 400 résumés), no friends, and not much family. He had an unsuccessful brush with suicide and then he found the hacker community. Here people were interested in him and what he did and he felt as though he had found a home.

He then decided to turn his new hobby against the people who refused to hire him. He admits that this was an act of revenge to show these companies that they should have hired him since he's probably a much better programmer than whomever they hired instead of him. The point he seems to have missed is that there's more to keeping a job than being a good programmer, and many people would say that the prospective employers had been right about him.

The third example is a young man who lives in Detroit and directs his ire toward another group of hackers who, he believes, stole his code. He created malware that he intended them to steal. The code did no damage; it just had pop-up messages insulting the malware thieves.

Many of the more talented malware writers don't circulate their code themselves. Since it's not illegal to write malware—only to circulate it and cause damage—they make it available so that script kiddies (those who cut and paste, then circulate viruses) can access it. This procedure has been compared to drug dealers who use young teenagers to carry the illegal wares so that they are insulated from direct responsibility. However, it doesn't absolve them from culpability.[51]

SECURITY AND OUTSIDE THREATS

A Computer Security Institute survey of U.S. corporations, government agencies, financial institutions, medical institutions, and universities found that computer systems of 53 percent of them were broken into in 2004. Though only 54 percent of those surveyed put a figure on their losses, the total came to more than $141 million.[52] "There's no Fortune 500 company that hasn't been hacked, I don't care what they tell you," says one hacker.[53] "Hacking" means achieving unauthorized access to computers and computer information. 3Com gets "thousands of attacks a week. From kids to criminals to foreign governments," says David Starr, former CIO.[54] Even Microsoft's computers have been hacked.

The threats from outside are many and varied. Competitors might try to get your customer lists or the prototype for your new project. Kids might be joyriding in cyberspace looking for something interesting to see, steal, or destroy. You might become the victim of a generalized attack such as a virus or worm or a targeted attack such as "denial of service" (see later). If you have something worth stealing or manipulating on your system, there could be people after that too. For example, the online gambling industry is plagued by attacks in which hackers have illicitly gained access to the servers that control the gambling, corrupting games to win millions of dollars.[55] Exploiting well-known system weaknesses accounts for 95 percent of hacker damage; only 5 percent results from breaking into systems in new ways.[56]

People who break into the systems of others are known as **hackers**. They are generally very knowledgeable computer users. They have varying motives. Some just do it for the fun of it. Others (called "hacktivists") have a philosophical or political message they want to share, and still others (called "crackers") are hired guns who break in for a fee. The latter can be a very lucrative undertaking. Some highly skilled crackers charge up to $1 million per job. (See Figure 9.9 for the terminology of hacker types.)

TYPES OF CYBER-CRIME   Cyber-crimes range from electronically breaking and entering to cyberstalking and murder. In October 1999, 21-year-old Amy Boyer was shot and killed outside the building where she worked. Her killer, Liam Youens, had been electronically stalking her for two years. Youens became obsessed with Amy and had even posted a Web site dedicated to her on which he announced his intention to kill her. He got her social security number online, found out where she worked, tracked her down, and shot her, after which he shot himself.

Most cyber-crimes are not as bad as murder, but they can be serious nonetheless. Computer viruses and worms and denial-of-service attacks are the most common types of cyber-crime that companies need to protect themselves against.

A **computer virus** (or simply **virus**) is maliciously created software that spreads from file to file causing annoyance or damage. A virus can be benign or malicious. The benign ones just display a message on the screen or slow the computer down, but don't do any damage. The malicious kind targets a specific application or set of file types and corrupts or destroys them.

Viruses first came on the scene in the 1980s. Today, **worms** are the most prevalent type (see Figure 9.10 for the genealogy of viruses). Worms are viruses that spread themselves, not just from file to file, but from computer to computer via e-mail and other Internet traffic. They don't need your help to spread. They find your e-mail address book, grab the addresses, and send themselves to your contacts, using your e-mail address as the return address.

The "Love Bug" was the first worm to catch the attention of the popular press. It did a lot of damage. Ford Motor Co, H. J. Heinz, Merrill Lynch, AT&T, Capitol Hill, and the British Parliament all fell victim. It's estimated that the Love Bug and its variants affected 300,000 Internet host computers and millions of individual PC users, causing file damage, lost time, and high-cost emergency repairs costing about $8.7 billion.[57,58] Newer versions of worms include Klez, a very rapidly spreading worm, Nimda, and Sircam.

For more information about viruses see Extended Learning Module K, "Computer Crime and Forensics."

A **denial-of-service (DoS) attack** floods a Web site with so many requests for service that it slows down or crashes. The objective is to prevent legitimate customers

Figure 9.9

Hacker Types

- *White-hat hackers* find vulnerabilities in systems and plug the holes. They work at the request of the owners of the computer systems.

- *Black-hat hackers* break into other people's computer systems and may just look around, but they may steal credit card numbers or destroy information.

- *Hacktivists* have philosophical and political reasons for breaking into systems. They often deface a Web site as a protest.

- *Script bunnies*, or *script kiddies*, find hacking code on the Internet and point-and-click their way into systems, causing damage or spreading viruses.

Figure 9.10

The Genealogy of Viruses

- *1980s.* The first viruses were boot-sector viruses that attacked the operating system and spread when people traded floppy disks.

- *1990s.* Macro viruses were all the rage. They spread when people traded e-mail with Word or Excel attachments. The virus was part of the attachment and corrupted the Word or Excel application. Macro viruses needed humans to swap disks or attachments to find new places to infect.

- *2000s.* Polymorphic worms that change their form and are hard to detect started to appear. Viruses such as Klez spoof the return address, making it very difficult to track down the source.

from accessing the target site. E*TRADE, Yahoo!, and Amazon.com have all been victims of this type of attack.

Code Red, first discovered in July 2001, was the first virus to combine the worm's ability to propagate and the denial-of-service attack's ability to bring down a Web site. It broke into servers and used e-mail address lists to send itself to other servers. Then it lay dormant, ready for a signal. The idea was to send the signal to all of the infected servers (millions of them) and make them all try to access the White House Web site at the same time and bring it down. The White House Webmaster foiled the plot by changing the IP address of the site so that the attacks would go to a defunct address.

There are even virus hoaxes, perpetrated by sending out an e-mail about a nonexistent virus threat, and sometimes recommending a protective action that will, in fact, damage one's system. People who get such an alert will usually tell others, who react in the same way. Within companies, the losses from such a prank can be very severe, not least because computer professionals are forced to spend precious time and effort looking for a nonexistent problem.

As well as knowing what viruses can do, you need to know what they can't do. Computer viruses:

- Can't hurt your hardware, such as your monitor or processor
- Can't hurt any files they weren't designed to attack; a virus designed for Microsoft's Outlook generally doesn't infect Qualcomm's Eudora, or any other e-mail application
- Can't infect files on write-protected disks

SECURITY PRECAUTIONS

It has been said that while in years past managers had nightmares about takeover bids, they now have nightmares about teenagers with computers and Internet access. Lloyd's of London says that 70 percent of risk managers see the Internet and e-commerce as the biggest emerging risks in the new century.[59] Due to the ongoing effects of the 9/11 terrorist attacks, which left people and companies feeling more vulnerable than before, most experts expect worldwide security software revenue to rise sharply.[60]

The only really safe computer system is one that is never connected to any other computer and locked away so that almost no one can get to it. In today's business world that's just not practical. Computers are like motor vehicles; they can be used to cause harm unintentionally and maliciously, and just driving one puts you at risk, especially when you're on the road with other cars. However, we still use motor vehicles, but we build in safety features and take precautions to lessen the risk. So it is with computers. The big difference is that security threats in cyberspace are always changing.

GIVE YOUR COMPUTER THE FINGER

If you're an elementary school student in Stockholm, Sweden, and you want to access your course materials, you don't need a password, instead you just need your fingerprints—and it's hard to forget those. The 85,000 students who attend elementary school in Stockholm often forgot their passwords, like lots of people do. And teachers had to issue new passwords every 100 days in keeping with city policy. It was becoming a real burden.

To solve the problem, 25,000 fingerprint scanners were ordered from Bellevue Washington's Saflink Corp. Shortly thereafter, all of the other 120,000 government computers used by city workers were activated by biometrics, smart cards, tokens, or biometrics. The days of the password were over in Stockholm.

Samir Hamouni, manager of the fingerprint project for the city, said that the installation of the fingerprint scanners and software went very fast. The part of the project that took the most time was getting all the fingerprints into the system.[61]

Given the extraordinary importance of information in an organization, it's imperative that companies make their best efforts to protect that information; that is, they should practice risk management. **Risk management** consists of the identification of risks or threats, the implementation of security measures, and the monitoring of those measures for effectiveness. The first step in the process is establishing what the threats are and what parts of the system are vulnerable. This is **risk assessment**: the process of evaluating IT assets, their importance to the organization, and their susceptibility to threats, to measure the risk exposure of these assets. In simple terms, risk assessment asks: (1) What can go wrong? (2) How likely is it to go wrong? and (3) What are the possible consequences if it does go wrong?[62]

Implementing the correct amount and type of security is not an easy matter. Too much security can hamper employees' ability to do their jobs, resulting in decreased revenue. Too little security leaves your organization vulnerable. You need strong enough security to protect your IT systems but not so much that the right people can't access the information they need in a timely fashion. Generally, security consists of a combination of measures such as backup procedures, antivirus software, firewalls, access authorization, encryption, intrusion-detection software, and system auditing.

BACKUPS As always, an ounce of prevention is worth a pound of cure. The easiest and most basic way to prevent loss of information is to make backups of all your information. There's no action you can take that's more rudimentary or essential than making copies of important information methodically and regularly (at least once a week). Employee carelessness and ignorance cause about two-thirds of the financial cost of loss or damaged information.[63] Take the example of one company whose accounting server went down the day that paycheques should have been distributed. The crisis arose during an administration transition. The people who had been temporarily running the system thought that backup occurred automatically. It didn't, so all payroll information was lost. To get the system up and running again, the company had to pay thousands of dollars to consultants to restore the network application, and had to pay four people for 300 hours of overtime to re-enter information. In addition, it cost $48,000 for a disk-recovery company to retrieve the information from the damaged disk drive. And all this trouble and expense could have been avoided if backup procedures had been followed.

Make sure you back up *all* information. It's easy to forget about the information that's not stored in the main computer system or network, such as correspondence and customer information kept only by administrative assistants and receptionists, and private information not kept in the main organizational databases or data warehouses. Your backup schedule should include not only your information, but also your software.

You have several options when backing up information. You can use removable hard disks, a hard disk on another computer, or CD-Rs, CD-RWs, and tapes. Also you should consider where the backups are to be stored:

- *In a safe.* Should you choose to store your backups in a safe, make sure that the safe is not only fireproof, but also heatproof. Mylar disks (like those in zip disks) and CDs suffer damage at temperatures above 52 degrees Celsius. Also remember that water causes damage too, so get a safe that's waterproof.
- *At a different location.* Most experts recommend that you store your backups in a separate building in case the whole building is threatened. Many accounting firms, banks, and other financial institutions send information off the premises at the end of every work day.
- *In a televault.* You can store a copy of your information with a security company that specializes in encrypting and storing backups. This is known as *televaulting*. Several Internet sites offer this service. Many will store backups for individuals too. Sometimes you get a certain amount of space free, perhaps about 20 megabytes, and then you have to pay for any more you need.

ANTIVIRUS SOFTWARE Antivirus software is an absolute must. **Antivirus software** detects and removes or quarantines computer viruses. New viruses are created every day and each new generation is more deadly (or potentially deadly) than the previous ones. When you're looking for virus protection, *PC World* magazine[64] has the following advice. Look for virus protection that finds:

- Viruses on removable media like floppies, CDs, and zip disks, as well as on the hard disk
- Trojan-horse viruses (viruses hiding inside good software) and backdoor programs (viruses that open a way into the network for future attacks)
- Polymorphic viruses and worms, which are sometimes hard for antivirus programs to find because they change their form as they propagate
- Viruses in .zip or compressed files, and even .zip files inside other .zip files.
- Viruses in e-mail attachments

Two final points. First, your antivirus program should be able to get rid of the virus without destroying the software or information it came with. Second, you must update your antivirus software frequently, since new viruses come along every day. Some antivirus sites will automatically send updates to their software.

FIREWALLS A **firewall** is hardware and/or software that protects computers from intruders. The firewall examines every message as it seeks entrance to the network, like a border guard checking passports. Unless the message has the "right" markings, the firewall blocks the way and prevents it from entering. Any competent network administrator will have at least one firewall on the network to keep out unwelcome guests.

ACCESS AUTHORIZATION While firewalls keep outsiders out, they don't necessarily keep insiders out. In other words, unauthorized employees may try to access computers or files. One of the ways companies try to protect computer systems is with authentication systems that check who you are before they let you have access.

CHASING THE BAD GUYS ALL OVER THE WORLD

In Chapter 6 you saw how banks are using artificial intelligence systems to catch fraudulent credit card and cheque transactions. Worldwide a problem just as large is sending large banks back to technology for solutions. Money laundering is always a concern when dealing with wealthy clients and large sums of foreign currency. The International Monetary Fund estimates that $590 billion from criminal and terrorist activities is sent through banks to be "cleaned." And a big bank can spend $15 million a year to meet legal requirements governing antilaundering activities.

Deutsche Bank, the German bank which is the largest in Europe, has developed its own screening system to ferret out money laundering schemes. It creates risk scores for people opening new accounts similar to those that banks assign people applying for loans. The scores are based on past business transactions and other pertinent factors. The information Deutsche Bank uses has been gathered on customers in its 107-country banking system. Since implementation of its system, Deutsche Bank needs only four full-time employees to watch for money laundering instead of the 50 previously required.

The first antilaundering systems simply flagged deposits over a certain amount. But the people doing the laundering figured this out and adjusted their transactions accordingly. The Bank Secrecy Act first obliged banks to report cash transaction of $10,000 or more, but during the 1990s money laundering crimes rose sharply and the U.S. Treasury was getting more reports than agents could read. So the agency created the Financial Crimes Enforcement Network (FinCEN) to counter the increasingly complex transactions. Internationally, FinCEN shares information with other countries and has joined forces with 28 other countries to track money laundering worldwide. In fact, this coalition has threatened to impose sanctions on nations such as Egypt, Nigeria, the Philippines, and Russia for their banking practices.[65]

There are three basic ways of showing your identification: (1) what you know, like a password; (2) what you have, like an ATM card; (3) what you look like (or rather what your fingerprint or your hand's bone structure looks like).

Passwords are very popular and have been used since there were computers. You can password-protect the whole network, a single computer, a folder, or a file. But passwords are not by any means a perfect way to protect a computer system. People forget their passwords, so someone has to get them new passwords or find the old one. Banks spend $15 per call to help customers who forget their passwords. Then if a hacker breaks into the system and steals a password list, everyone has to get a new password. Another bank had to change 5000 passwords in the course of a single month at a cost of $12.50 each.[66]

Which brings us to biometrics, or what you look like. **Biometrics** is the use of some distinguishing physical personal characteristic to authenticate a person's identity. Roughly a dozen different types of biometric devices are available at the moment, fingerprint readers being the most popular. About 44 percent of the biometric systems sold are fingerprint systems. It works just like the law enforcement system where your fingerprint is stored in the database and when you come along, your finger is scanned, and the scan is compared to the entry in the database. If they match, you're in.

Another promising type of biometric system is facial recognition. Wells Fargo is testing a system which uses facial recognition instead of PINs at ATM machines. Many airports are proposing biometric systems to check that passengers are who they say they are. Most envision that the recording of passengers' biological characteristics will be voluntary, so that frequent flyers could sign up, have their physical characteristic scanned, and then forever bypass the long manual clearing process. Chicago's O'Hare airport, the busiest in the world, has been using biometrics for years to authenticate employees' identity.[67]

KEEPING TRACK OF SHOE SALES IS VERY IMPORTANT

Payless ShoeSource, Inc., is North America's largest family footwear retailer. In 2000, Payless sold about $3 billion worth of shoes (average price about $12) at its 4900 stores in Canada, the United States, Puerto Rico, Central America, and Guam.

Shoes are shipped automatically to all stores. The entire system relies on a data centre in Topeka, Kansas. All the data analysis, decision making, and control are based on the information the Topeka data centre collects and stores daily. Payless has a mainframe, several minicomputers, and thousands of PCs. The entire corporate network is controlled from the Topeka data centre. Even if there is a network problem in Taiwan, the people in Topeka handle it. Since Kansas is located in "Tornado Alley," the data centre is underground—all 16,000 square feet of it.

Every night, the data centre polls all the stores, domestic and overseas, for information about their sales for that day. The company has a data warehouse with two years' worth of information on every shoe type and size sold in every store that's available for online analytical processing (OLAP). Since losing this information would be disastrous, Payless has lots of safeguards in place:

- In the event of a problem with AT&T, the phone system will automatically switch to Sprint.
- An array of 120 heavy-duty batteries take over if the power goes down, then a backup generator takes over. There's even a backup generator to the backup generator.
- The data centre also has two backup air conditioning systems in case the original one goes out.
- If fire breaks out, firefighting gas (FM 2000) sprays from the ceiling to suffocate the flames within seconds. If that doesn't work, water sprinklers kick in. But only as a last resort—water isn't good for computer equipment.
- All information is backed up on high-capacity cassette tapes. The company has about 30,000 of these. Every day the tapes are sent off-site by truck.
- Every year all the IT staff practise a disaster drill.

Besides fingerprint and iris scanners, there are also retinal scanners, which check the back of the eye rather than the coloured circular part on the front. Signature checkers activate as you sign your name and check the rhythm, pressure, speed and acceleration of the signature. One system being tested checks the rhythm of your typing, another checks your voice pattern scanners, and still another scans the veins in your hand. Each of these would compare the scan with the stored pattern to see if they match.

ENCRYPTION If you want to protect your messages and files and hide them from prying eyes, you can encrypt them. **Encryption** is the process of scrambling a message so that it can't be read until unscrambled. There are various ways of encrypting. You can switch the order of the characters, replace characters with other characters, or insert or remove characters. All of these methods alter the look of the message, but used alone, each is fairly simple to figure out. So most encryption methods use a combination of methods.

Companies that get sensitive information from customers, such as credit card numbers, need some way of allowing all their customers to use encryption to send the information. But they don't want everyone to be able to decrypt the message, so they might use **public key encryption (PKE)**, an system that uses two keys: a public key that everyone can have and a private key for only the recipient. So if you do online banking, the bank will give you the public key to encrypt the information you send them, but only the bank has the key to decrypt your information. It works rather like wall safe: anyone can lock it (just shut the door and twirl the knob), but only someone with the combination can open it.

DISASTER RECOVERY PLANS: CAN YOU EVER BE PREPARED ENOUGH?

In 1998, a severe ice storm hit parts of Quebec, Ontario, New York, and New England, causing power outages and forcing many businesses to scramble as it affected many computer operations. In some regions, the power failures lasted up to two weeks and forced many businesses to operate with skeleton staffs while relying on generators, move to remote disaster sites, or in many cases shut down completely. Estimated losses were nearly $1 billion in Canada alone.

The storm made many companies realize that IT disasters did not necessarily entail direct physical damage to their computer equipment. Many companies had disaster recovery plans in place and were relying on electricity provided by generators. However, because a majority of roads were closed by fallen trees, broken power lines, and utility poles, many people could not even get to work. The shortage of information technology staff to keep systems running became an unexpected but serious problem. "Most of our problem was just getting people in ..., our technical support came to a screeching halt for a solid week," said Richard Cox, a project manager at Air Canada in Montreal.

Moreover, many businesses were prepared for power outages of no more than a couple of days.

Several relied on uninterruptible power supplies (UPS) and diesel generators, sometimes in combination, to keep their computers running. This strategy had worked well for the Kennebec Valley Health Hospital in Augusta, Maine, where medical staff were able to continue providing normal care. Others were not so lucky. Diesel generators began to break down after a couple of days. At Domco, Inc., located in Farnham, Quebec, generators failed after running for only three days. The company had to quickly switch their IT operations to SunGard Data Systems, Inc.'s disaster recovery site in Philadelphia. However, because all order and shipping applications were centrally managed by the Farnham site, the ice storm had repercussions for Domco's U.S.-based plants, forcing them to shut down computer operations for three days until the hot site became active. Prior to the storm, like many other companies across the region, Domco felt confident that it had a good disaster recovery plan in place. "You can plan for a disaster when a building is destroyed, but we never figured on a disaster where we couldn't communicate with our Farnham offices," said Guy Chamberland, Domco's IT director.[68]

INTRUSION-DETECTION AND SECURITY-AUDITING SOFTWARE Two other types of security software are:

- **Intrusion-detection software**, which looks for people on the network who shouldn't be there or who are acting suspiciously. For example, someone might be trying lots of passwords to gain access. "Honey pots" are a type of intrusion-detection software that create attractive, but nonexistent, targets for hackers. What actually happens is that hackers' keystrokes are recorded instead.
- **Security auditing software**, which checks out your computer or network for weaknesses. The idea is to find out where hackers could get in and to plug up the hole. Many third parties, such as accounting firms or computer security companies, also provide this service.

Disaster Recovery

So far you've seen some of the threats that are out there and the security measures you can take to protect your information and IT system. But what if something catastrophic happens? Annually about 250 natural disasters occur worldwide. This is merely an interesting statistic unless you're bang in the middle of such a disaster—then it's much more than interesting. But natural disasters aren't the only danger on the IT system horizon. Fires, burst water pipes, gas leaks, power outages, and other infrastructure breakdowns can all cause serious damage to your IT system and information. Of the companies hit with a catastrophic loss of computerized records, 43 percent never reopen, 51 percent close within two years, and only 6 percent survive long-term.[69] Since September 11, the prospect of a major disaster has been seen as much more of a real threat than ever before.

To make sure your organization is in that slim 6 percent, you need to be prepared. Banks are required by law to have a **disaster recovery plan**—a detailed plan of what is to be done in the event of a disaster to minimize downtime. General Motors demands that all of its dealers have one.

A good disaster recovery plan will take the following into consideration: customers, facilities, knowledge workers, business information, computer equipment, and communications infrastructure (see Figure 9.11).

- *Customers.* You're more likely to retain the business of people who know what's going on. Customers will be reassured if you inform them what's happening so that they can plan accordingly.
- *Facilities.* You'll most likely need to move operations to another facility if disaster strikes. One option is a **hot site**, a separate and fully equipped facility to which you can move immediately after the disaster and resume business. Hot sites are popular with financial firms, who spend about $300 a year to rent them. The Chubb Contingency Trading Facility, near Wall Street, is one such site. The facility has ten trading rooms with faxes, copy machines, printers, backup generators, 1000 phone lines, a local area network with PCs, and so on.[70] Another alternative is a **cold site**, which doesn't have computer equipment installed, but is ready for the refugee company to move in.

Figure 9.11

Disaster Recovery Plan

- *Knowledge workers.* Disaster recovery usually involves long working days. Before your employees can concentrate on your business, they may have to make arrangements for the care of family members. You may have to make sleeping and eating arrangements for your employees too.
- *Business information.* You've already seen how important it is to back up your business information. Actually, this should be a regular part of daily operations. You'll see its value very clearly during times of disaster.
- *Computer equipment.* Most companies have complex networks with a mixture of software and hardware from various vendors. This makes the networks hard to duplicate for third-party recovery services. So some companies develop their own recovery plan. NationsBank did just that, with 118 software applications running on 77 platforms, with equipment from Digital Equipment, Hewlett-Packard, IBM, Stratus, and Tandem. Although being disaster-ready costs the bank millions of dollars a year, it's still the lesser of two evils.[71]
- *Telecommunications infrastructure.* As the September 11 attacks dramatically demonstrated, communication is one of the most critical factors in dealing with an emergency. Having a backup carrier and enough cell phones for everyone is very important. The most important next step is to be able to move non-voice information around. To do that you need either backup equipment or a hot site.

As the quality of telecommunications improves, with more bandwidth at a lower cost, disaster recovery plans will most likely change, says Bob Roth, disaster recovery coordinator at Payless ShoeSource. In the future, companies will most likely simply mirror all of their information at a second site so that if one goes down, the other can carry on business as usual. Some companies already do this.

Summary: Student Learning Outcomes Revisited

1. **Describe two ways in which information is valuable to business.** Information is valuable as raw material, which uses information as part of the product, and as capital, which is something that goes into the production of goods and services, but which is not actually part of the product.

2. **Define ethics and describe the two factors that affect how you make a decision concerning an ethical issue.** *Ethics* are the principles and standards that guide our behaviour toward other people. How you will decide ethical issues depends on your basic ethical structure and the practical circumstances surrounding your decision.

3. **Define and describe intellectual property, copyright, the Fair Use Doctrine, and pirated and counterfeit software.** *Intellectual property* is intangible creative work that is embodied in physical form. *Copyright* is the legal protection afforded an expression of an idea, such as a song

or a video game. The *Fair Use Doctrine* says that you may use copyrighted material in certain situations. *Pirated software* is illegal copies of copyrighted software made for unauthorized use, duplication, distribution. *Counterfeit software* is software manufactured to look like the real thing and sold as such.

4. **Understand privacy and describe ways in which it can be threatened.** *Privacy* is the right to be left alone when you want to be, to have control over your own personal information, and not to be observed without your consent. Your privacy can be compromised by other individuals snooping on you, by employers monitoring your actions, by businesses who collect information on your needs and preferences and surfing practices, and by various government agencies that collect information on citizens.

5. **Describe the ways in which companies are vulnerable to computer attacks.**

A. Most of the financial loss due to crimes where a computer played a large part is due to employee fraud of various kinds.

B. You give a access to your computer information to collaboration partners who could do damage.

C. Grid computing will mean many computers working together with the potential for information to move between computers when it shouldn't.

D. Hackers and crackers may try to break into computers and steal, destroy, or compromise information.

E. Hackers can spread *computer viruses* or launch *denial-of-service (DoS) attacks* that can cost millions to prevention and cleanup.

6. **Compare risk management and risk assessment and describe the seven security measures that companies can take to protect their information.** *Risk management* consists of the identification of risks or threats, the implementation of security measures, and the monitoring of those measures for effectiveness. *Risk assessment* is the process of evaluation IT assets, their importance to the organization, and their susceptibility to threats, to measure the risk exposure of these assets.

Seven security measures companies can take are:

A. Backups—make sure there is more than one copy of everything.

B. *Antivirus software* detects and removes or quarantines computer viruses. However, to be effective it must be updated regularly and often.

C. A *firewall* is hardware and/or software that protects computers from intruders.

D. Access authorization makes sure that those who have access to information have the authorization to do so with password or biometrics.

E. *Encryption* is the process of scrambling a message so that it can't be read until it's unscrambled again.

F. *Intrusion-detection software* looks for people on the network who shouldn't be there.

G. *Security-auditing software* checks out your computer or network for weaknesses that could be exploited.

7. **Understand what a disaster recovery plan is and list the six components it should cover.** A *disaster security plan* is a detailed plan of what is to be done in the event of a disaster to minimize downtime. A disaster security plan should cover customers, facilities, knowledge workers, business information, computer equipment, and the telecommunications infrastructure.

CLOSING CASE STUDY ONE

BIOMETRIC BORDERS

The movie *Minority Report* chronicled a futuristic world where people are uniquely identifiable by their eyes. A scan of each person's eyes gives or denies them access to rooms, computers, and anything else with restrictions. The movie was a bit far-fetched, with people running a black market in changing eyeballs to help people hide from the authorities. (Why didn't they just change the database entry instead? That would have been much easier, but a lot less dramatic.) However, the idea of using a biological signature is not at all implausible since biometrics is currently being widely used and is expected to gain wider acceptance in the near future.

In fact, the next time you get a new passport, it may incorporate a chip that has your biometric information encoded on it. The reason is that forging documents has become much easier with the advances in computer graphics programs and colour printers. The U.S. Office of Special Investigations (OSI) sent out some agents with such fake documents and found that it was relatively easy to enter the United States from this country, Mexico, and Jamaica, by land, sea, and air.

The task of policing the borders is daunting in that there are 500 million foreigners who enter the country every year and go through identity checkpoints. More than 13 million permanent-resident and border-crossing cards have been issued by the U.S. government. Adding another complication is the fact that there are 27 countries whose citizens do not need visas to enter this country. They will also be expected to have passports that comply with U.S. specifications so that they will also be readable at the border.

In the post-9/11 atmosphere of tightened security, unrestricted border crossing is simply not acceptable. The Department of Homeland Security (DHS) is charged with securing the nation's borders, and as part of this plan, new entry/exit procedures were put in place at the beginning of 2003. An integrated system, using biometrics, which was given another three years, until the end of 2005, to be fully operational, will be used to identify foreign visitors to the United States and reduce the likelihood of terrorists entering the country.

Early in 2003, after 6 million biometric border-crossing cards had been issued, a pilot test conducted at the Canadian border detected more than 250 imposters. The testing started with two biometric identifiers: photographs for facial recognition and fingerprint scans. As people enter and leave the country, their actual fingerprints and facial features are compared to the data on the biometric chip in the passport.

Part of the awesome challenge facing the DHS is the sheer volume of information that has to be catalogued, stored, and retrieved. Current estimates are that it will take about 5 petabytes (that's 5,000,000,000,000,000 characters) of space to store all that information, and this requirement is likely to expand with time. This information must be available on demand—and quickly. The exit information must be matched against the entry information and then be stored so that it can be retrieved the next time the individual enters the country.

IT specialists are still working on providing an extremely fast database system and a very extensive network to accommodate the mammoth task. Some of the more remote border crossings, for example, on the Mexico/United States border, may need wireless access. Then there are the security considerations. The infor-

mation must be kept safe from network intruders and other types of misuse.

The first contracts for equipment to implement the new biometric identity verification system included a $3.5 million agreement to buy 1000 optical-stripe read/write drives with biometric verification systems and a contract for biometric fingerprint scanning technology worth about $27 million.[72,73,74,75]

Questions

1. How do you feel about having your fingerprints, facial features, and perhaps more of your biometric features encoded in documents like your passport? Explain your answer.

2. Would you feel the same way about having biometric information on your driver's licence as on your passport? If so, why? And if not, why not?

3. Is it reasonable to have different requirements for visitors from different nations? Explain your answer. What would you recommend as criteria for deciding which countries fall into what categories?

4. If you've ever been out of the country, you know that there are checkpoints that you go through when returning. These checkpoints vary greatly in the depth of the checks and the time they take. The simplest involves simply walking past the border guards who may or may not ask you your citizenship. The other end of the spectrum requires that you put up with long waits in airports where you have to line up with hundreds of other passengers while each person is questioned and must produce a passport to be scanned. Would you welcome biometric information on passports if it would speed the checkup process and get you through faster, or do you think that the disadvantages of the reduction in privacy outweigh the advantages of better security and faster border processing? Explain your answer.

IS THE SAFE HARBOR SAFE FOR BUSINESSES?

European countries and Australia have passed laws protecting the privacy of name-linked information of consumers. In Europe it's the European Union Directive 95/46/EC, which was adopted in 1998, and in Australia it's the Privacy Amendment Act of 2000. The Australian law says that personal information can be collected only with the consent of the person it's being collected about. The law goes further and forbids transfer of personal information to any other country that does not have privacy protection. The result is that U.S. companies with an Australian subsidiary cannot transfer personal information they have collected to the United States since the country has no privacy protection of this type.

In Europe, the 15 countries that belong to the European Union are supposed to have passed laws by now requiring that personal information can only be collected with the express and unambiguous consent of the person to whom the information applies. And this rule applies to invisible information collection such as the information collected in cookies and details on a person's Web surfing activities.

An individual's information can only be collected without consent under the following circumstances:

1. It's necessary to fulfill a contract.
2. It's necessary to save a life, as when a procedure is necessary on an unconscious person.
3. It's necessary for greater good, such as tax collection.
4. The processing of the information is required by a legal contract.
5. The third party to the information has a lawful right to do so as in an arbitration situation.

Even within these guidelines there is certain "sensitive information" that cannot be asked for. This type of information cannot be processed without specific consent. Such information includes a person's racial or ethnic origin, political and religious affiliations, trade union membership, and sexual preferences. This exception of sensitive information was deemed necessary in the light of hundreds of years of persecution in Europe of one ethnic or religious group or other.

The EU Directive also says that people must be informed when information about them is to be used for direct mailings, and the rules apply any time the information is being processed within the European Union, even if the those who are providing the information are located elsewhere. So why does it matter to U.S. businesses what privacy laws the Europeans choose to have? It matters because it threatens the annual $350 billion trade between the United States and the EU, so the U.S. Department of Commerce and the European Commission has agreed to voluntary, so-called Safe Harbor provisions, which represent a compromise between the strict consumer privacy requirements of Europe and the more relaxed attitude of American law. At its inception, the Safe Harbor agreement was hailed as a great breakthrough and a guarantee that business would indeed continue to thrive.

However, the Safe Harbor agreement no longer seems quite so wonderful, for several reasons. First, it's a voluntary program, and very few companies had signed up for it by the middle of 2001. Second, not all European countries have actually passed laws yet to comply with the Directive. (An EU directive is simply a statement of intent and each member country must enact its own laws to ensure the outcome of the directive.) France, Ireland, and Luxembourg had not passed any such laws by the middle of 2001. Third, some European countries think that the Safe Harbor agreement is much too weak, and is not in keeping with the intent of the Directive. The worry for U.S. companies is that countries such as Sweden might refuse to allow information transfer to countries they deem to be deficient. Fourth, the Safe Harbor agreement may not be enforceable by law, since the FTC doesn't have the authority to protect European consumers' rights within the United States. And finally, EU authorities have the power to intervene in cases of serious violation and suspend the transfer of information to a country until the matter has been resolved.

Questions

1. Imagine, for a moment, that a federal law very similar to the EU Directive were to take effect in

Canada at the beginning of next year. What would the implications be for companies that collect huge amounts of personal information on their customers and clients?

2. Would you like to have stronger privacy laws in this country? If so, what form should they take? If not, do you have any reservations about your personal information being bought and sold like any other commodity? Should there be limits on who can buy what information and for what purposes? If so, what should they be? If not, provide some examples of the advantages of having all personal information available to anyone with the means to acquire it.

3. Strangely enough, the European Union is considering a law that flies squarely in the face of the privacy directive. The proposal is to give border police access to e-mail and Internet use by citizens. The law would mean that police would be able to access any and all e-mail and Internet usage information from ISPs simply by requesting it. No court order would be needed. There would be no restrictions on the amount or type of information that the police could access on people's personal and business lives. What do you think of this law? What do the privacy directive and the proposed law imply about the European attitude toward access to personal information? Who do the European Union see as the abusers of personal information and who are the good guys? Is it the same in the United States? How do the European and American philosophies differ?

4. Do you think Canada should have stricter border laws? At airports the focus tends to be on luggage. Should there be more emphasis on who is travelling? For instance, should everyone, citizens included, be fingerprinted and checked out before they enter or leave the country? If so, would you be prepared to have a special ID card with your fingerprints or some other biometric feature on it to allow you to pass through the checkpoints at ports of entry faster?

Key Terms and Concepts

adware, 407
anonymous Web browsing
  (AWB), 407
antivirus software, 421
biometrics, 422
clickstream, 407
cold site, 425
computer virus, 418
cookie, 409
copyright, 397
counterfeit software, 399
denial-of-service (DoS) attack, 418
disaster recovery plan, 425

encryption, 423
ethics, 393
Fair Use Doctrine, 397
firewall, 421
grid computing, 415
hackers, 418
Health Insurance Portability and
  Accountability Act, 412
hot site, 425
intellectual property, 397
intrusion-detection software, 424
key logger (key trapper)
  software, 400

pirated software, 398
privacy, 399
public key encryption (PKE), 423
risk assessment, 420
risk management, 420
Safe Harbor principles, 410
security auditing software, 424
spam, 406
spyware (sneakware or
  stealthware), 407
Trojan-horse software, 407
virus, 418
worm, 418

Short-Answer Questions

1. What are ethics and how do ethics apply to business?

2. What are the two factors that determine how you decide ethical issues?

3. Six practical circumstances affect how you decide ethical issues. What are they?

4. Describe one exception to the copyright rules.

5. If you buy a CD with software on it, what did you buy?

6. What is pirated software?

7. Are counterfeit software and pirated software the same thing? If not, what is the difference?

8. What does a key logger do?

9. What is spyware?

10. What is grid computing?

11. Is a worm the same as a virus?

12. What is a denial-of-service attack?

13. What does risk management consist of?

14. Why is your security measures important to a partner company?

Assignments and Exercises

1. **HELPING A FRIEND.** Suppose you fully intend to spend the evening working on an Excel assignment due the next day. Then a friend calls. Your friend is stranded miles from home and desperately needs your help. It will take most of the evening to pick up your friend, bring him home, and return to your studying. Not only that, but you're very tired when you get home and just fall into bed.

   The next day your friend, who completed his assignment earlier, suggests you just make a copy of his, put your own name on the cover, and hand it in as your own work. Should you do it? Isn't it only fair that since you helped your friend, your friend should do something about making sure you don't lose points because of your generosity? What if your friend promises not to hand in his or her own work so that you can't be accused of copying? Your friend wrote the assignment and gave it to you so there's no question of copyright infringement.

2. **FIND ANTIVIRUS SOFTWARE.** You've read how important it is to have antivirus software on your computer. Find out what choices are available and what their features and cost are at the following sites:

   - Norton Antivirus (www.symantec.com)
   - McAfee (www.mcafee.com)
   - PC-cillin (www.trendmicro.com)
   - Dr. Solomon Antivirus Toolkit (www.drsolomon.com)
   - Kaspersky Lab Antivirus (www.kaspersky.com)
   - Panda Antivirus (www.panda.com)

3. **FIND OUT WHAT HAPPENED IN CANADA.** In Canada, in March 2001, the government opened up a 90-day comment period so that citizens could voice their opinions on a proposed law concerning cellular phones. The new law would silence cell phones in places where they are a public nuisance, such as restaurants, concert halls, and movie theatres. Essentially, if the law were to pass, it would allowing the jamming of phone signals in such places. This would be a departure from the traditional view on signal jamming. Most countries, including the United States but excluding Israel, prohibit jamming except when public safety would be endangered or when law enforcement or other government agencies find it appropriate. With all this in mind, answer the following questions:

   A. Find out how the citizens of Canada reacted this proposal and whether the law passed.
   B. Would you like to have such a law passed in this country? Why? Or why not?

C. What rights do you have to talk when and where you want to as opposed to the rights of others to be free of noise pollution?

D. What other noisy, intrusive pollution (noise or otherwise) would you like to have outlawed?

4. **FIND OUT ABOUT MONITORING SYSTEMS.** The text lists several monitoring systems, other systems that defeat them, and e-mail encryption programs. Find two more of each of these items:

A. Programs that monitor keyboard activity
B. Programs that detect the keyboard monitoring programs
C. E-mail encryption programs

Discussion Questions

1. When selling antiques, you can usually obtain a higher price for those that have a "provenance," that is, information detailing the origin and history of the object. For example, the property owned by Mrs. Jacqueline Kennedy Onassis and Princess Diana sold for much more than face value. What kinds of products have value over and above a comparable product because of such information? What kind of information makes products valuable? Consider both tangible (resale value) and intangible value (sentimental appeal).

2. Personal cheques that you use to buy merchandise have a standard format. They have only a very few different sizes, and almost no variation in format. Consider what would happen if everyone could create his or her own size, shape, and layout of personal cheque. What would the costs and benefits be to business and the consumer in terms of buying cheques, exchanging them for merchandise, and bank cheque processing?

3. Consider society as a business that takes steps to protect itself from the harm of illegal acts. Discuss the mechanisms and costs that are involved. Examine ways in which our society would be different if no one ever broke a law. Are there ever benefits to our society when people break the law—for example, when they claim that the law itself is unethical or unjust?

4. Many European countries have very strict laws about what you can and can't do with name-linked information. In France, for example, the law stipulates that no information may be saved, electronically or on paper, about a person's religious or political affiliation. Discuss the implications of such laws for an open-information society such as the United States. What kind of information might be appropriate for such laws here, and how would they affect the management of IT systems?

5. Can you access all the IT systems at your college or university? What about payroll or grade information on yourself or others? What kinds of controls has your college or university implemented to prevent the misuse of information?

6. You know that you can't use a Macintosh to access information stored on a disk using a PC (unless you have a PowerPC or special software). What other instances of the lack of interoperability have you experienced personally or heard of? For example, have you used different versions of Power-Point or MS Access that won't work on all the PCs that you have access to?

7. If a major disaster such as a tornado or flood were to strike your college or university in the middle of the semester, who would be impacted and how? Consider all stakeholders.

8. Say you had a small business and you were considering buying expensive ergonomically designed office furniture such as chairs and desks for your knowledge workers. What would the intangible benefits be to your company of having employees who are comfortable?

Electronic Commerce

Making Travel Arrangements on the Internet

It's very likely that in the course of business you'll be expected to travel either within Canada or abroad. You can use the Internet to check out all aspects of your journey, from mode of travel to the shopping opportunities that are available. The Internet can also give you pointers and direction about aspects of the trip you might not even have thought about.

In this section, we've included a number of Web sites related to making travel arrangements on the Internet. On the Web site that supports this text (www.mcgraw hill.ca/college/haag), click on "Electronic Commerce Support," select "Electronic Commerce Project Support," and then select "Making Travel Arrangements on the Internet"). We've provided direct links to all these Web sites as well as many, many more. This is a great starting point for completing this section. We would also encourage you to search the Internet for other sites.

Electronic Commerce Links

TRANSPORTATION

If you're not taking your own transportation—your private jet or your car—you'll have to find flights, buses, trains, and/or rental cars to suit your needs. Let's look at sites where you can get this kind of information.

AIR TRAVEL   Some people are happy to travel with whatever airline provides the flight that fits into their schedule. Others insist on certain airlines, or won't travel on certain airlines. No matter how you feel, the Internet can help you find a flight. On the Internet, you can even get maps of the airports you'll be using. Many airports have sites on the Internet, such as Dallas/Ft. Worth International Airport at Aéroports de Montréal (www.admtl.com). These sites can help you with provisions at the airport for disabled people, among other available services.

The Federal Aviation Authority site (www.faa.gov) has a comprehensive list of airlines all over the world. Find five appropriate Web sites and answer the following questions.

A. Can you make a flight reservation online at this site?

B. If you can book flights, does the site ask you to type in your departure and destination cities, or can you choose from a menu?

C. Again, if you can book flights at this site, rate on a scale of 1 to 10 how difficult it is to get to the flight schedule. That is, how many questions do you have to answer, how many clicks does it take, how much do you have to type in?

D. Is there information on when the lowest fares apply (e.g., three-week advance booking, staying over Saturday night, etc.)?

E. Does the site offer to send you information on special deals via e-mail?

F. Does the site offer information on frequent flier mileage? Can you check your frequent flier account online?

G. Does the site offer you a map of the airports you will be using?

TRAINS AND BUSES   If you want to travel by rail or long-distance bus, you can find many helpful sites. Here is a taste of what's available:

- VIA Rail Canada (www.viarail.ca) has a site that lets you look up train travel times and fares and buy tickets online for train travel in Canada.

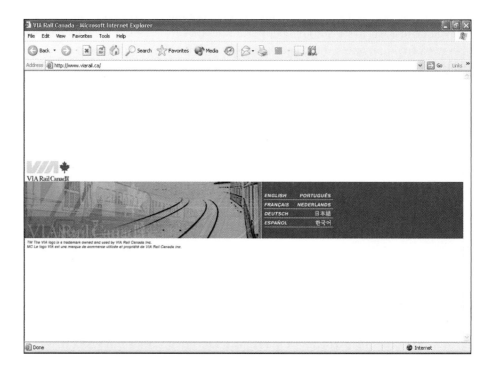

- Rail Europe (www.raileurope.com) offers comprehensive coverage of all modes of travel in Europe, including, of course, rail travel.
- The Orient Express site (www.orient-expresstrains.com) is a great help if you're interested in travelling by rail in Asia or Australia.

Look at two of these sites and see whether you can book tickets online. Do you need a password to see schedules? Incidentally, when you're looking up sites outside the United States, remember that the date is often expressed with the day first, then the month, then the year, so that September 10, 1998, would be 10.9.98 or 10-9-98. Also, most of Europe uses 24-hour time, so that 2:15 p.m. would be 14:15.

RENTAL CARS   When you arrive at your destination, you may need a car. Some sites such as RentalCarGuide's site (www.bnm.com) have information on multiple companies, and all the large car rental companies have sites on the Internet. Find six Web sites that rent cars and answer the following questions.

A. Can you reserve a car at the Web site?

B. Can you search by city?

C. Is there a cancellation penalty? If so, how much?

D. Can you get a list of car types? Does this company rent sports utility vehicles?

E. Are there special weekend rates?

F. What does the site say about collision insurance purchased from that company in addition to your own insurance?

G. Can you get maps from the site?

H. Are special corporate rates specified on the site?

ROAD CONDITIONS AND MAPS

You can generate maps online at several sites. MapQuest (www.mapquest.com) is one of the most popular. Its TripQuest section has city-to-city and turn-by-turn directions, and its Map Shortcuts module gives you a list of cities and countries for which you can get maps. Examine three map sites and answer the following questions.

A. Do these sites all give turn-by-turn driving directions?

B. Will they provide a map of an area without start and end points?

C. Do they have zoom-in and zoom-out capabilities?

D. Can you customize the map, perhaps by inserting a landmark or circling an area?

E. Are hotels, restaurants, etc. marked on the map?

F. If the site offers driving directions, can you specify whether you want the scenic route or the main highways?

LODGING

Hotels, especially the larger chains, usually have Web sites. Here you have access to a wealth of information about rates, amenities, and sometimes even information about the hotel's surroundings. The National Hotel Directory (www.gothotel.com) has lists of a variety of hotels and also trade shows. The Hotel Guide site (hotelguide.net) has information on 60,000 hotels all over the world, and Slow Travel (www.slowtrav.com) has hotel and restaurant reviews. Choose four Web sites and answer the questions below.

A. Can you search for a specific city?

B. Can you book a room online?

C. Can you see a picture of the room on the Internet?

D. Does the site tell you about special deals or promotions?

E. Is there information about perks you can get by staying there frequently?

F. Do you get a discount for booking online?

ONE-STOP TRAVEL SITES

Some travel sites on the Internet allow you to book your entire trip from start to finish, offering a combination of airline, hotel, and other helpful information. Two of the most

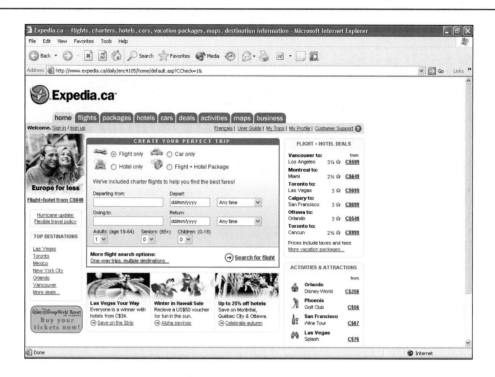

widely used are Microsoft's Expedia (www.expedia.ca) and Preview (www.travel ocity.com). Choose five Web sites and answer the following questions.

A. How many different booking services are offered from this site (airlines, hotels, rental cars, rail travel, etc.)?

B. If the site offers flight booking, how many flight alternatives does it offer? 3? 10? 20? 30? More than 30?

C. Does the site have information on low-cost specials for airlines, hotels, and/or rental cars?

D. Is there a traveller's assistance section?

E. Will the site answer your specific questions?

F. Can you search by destination or company for flights and lodging?

DESTINATION INFORMATION

You might like to know before you get to your destination what restaurants, museums, shows, shopping, and special attractions are available. Many of the sites previously mentioned have this kind of information. MapQuest (www.mapquest.com) is an excellent example of such a site, as are many of the one-stop travel sites.

No matter what your interest or hobby, the Internet has a site for you. You can find sites dedicated to birdwatching, bungee jumping, golf, or anything else that takes your fancy. Many others cater to entertainment events such as concerts. You can find destination information sites on the Web at the following sites:

- Excite's Travel site (travel.excite.com) includes useful software such as a currency converter.
- MyTravelGuide.com (www.mytravelguide.com) includes restaurant reviews among its services.

- Restaurant Row (www.restaurantrow.com) has a list of 100,000 restaurants in 25 countries. You can search by country, city, and cuisine.
- The Open World site (www.openworld.co.uk) includes information on over 1000 hotels worldwide.

Go to the Online Learning Centre at www.mcgrawhill.ca/college/haag for quizzes, extra content, a searchable glossary, and more! Click on "Electronic Commerce Projects" for links to hundreds of Web sites.

Go to the text CD-ROM for data files, extra content, and Skills Modules on Microsoft Excel, Microsoft Access, HTML, and e-portfolios.

EXTENDED LEARNING MODULE H

THE WORLD WIDE WEB AND THE INTERNET

Student Learning Outcomes

By the end of this Module, students will be able to:

1. Define the relationships among Web site, Web site address, domain name, Web page, and uniform resource locator (URL).

2. Explain how to interpret the parts of an address on the Web.

3. Identify the major components and features of Web browser software.

4. Describe the differences between directory and true search engines.

5. Describe the various technologies that make up the Internet.

6. Identify key considerations in choosing an Internet service provider (ISP).

7. Describe the communications software and telecommunications hardware you need to connect to the Internet.

Introduction

Perhaps the most visible and explosive information technology tool is the Internet, and subsequently the World Wide Web (Web). No matter where you look or what you read, someone always seems to be referring to one of the two. On television commercials, you find Web site addresses displayed (such as www.ibm.ca for an IBM commercial or www.toyota.com for a Toyota commercial). In almost every magazine these days, you'll find articles about the Internet because of its growing significance in our society. Most major business publications, such as *Fortune*, *Forbes*, and *Business Week*, devote entire issues each year to the Internet and how to use it for electronic commerce. Of course, many such publications have been carrying articles detailing how and why so many dot-coms failed in recent years (now affectionately referred to as "dot-bombs").

The Internet really is everywhere—and it's here to stay. What's great about the Internet is that it takes only a couple of hours to learn. Once you've read this Module, you should try your hand at the Internet scavenger hunts at the end. You'll be surprised to learn how easy it is to find information on the Internet.

World Wide Web

The **World Wide Web**, or **Web** as you probably know it, is a multimedia-based collection of information, services, and Web sites supported by the Internet. The **Internet** is a vast network of computers that connects millions of people all over the world. Schools, businesses, government agencies, and many others have all connected their internal networks to the Internet, making it truly a large network of networked computers. So the Internet and all its technological infrastructure is really what makes the Web possible. Most people consider the Web and the Internet to be the same. Although there are both subtle and distinct differences between the two, we'll not delve into those differences here.

WEB SITES, ADDRESSES, AND PAGES

As you use the Web, you'll most often be accessing Web sites. A **Web site** is a specific location on the Web where you visit, gather information, and perhaps even order products. Each Web site has a specific Web site address. A **Web site address** is a unique name that identifies a specific site on the Web. Technically, this address is called a domain name. A **domain name** identifies a specific computer on the Web and the main page of the entire site. Most people use the term *Web site address* instead of the technical term *domain name*. For example, the Web site address for *USA Today* is www.usatoday.com (see Figure H.1).

Most Web sites include several and perhaps hundreds of Web pages. A **Web page** is a specific portion of a Web site that deals with a certain topic. The address for a specific Web page is called a URL. A **URL (uniform resource locator)** is an address for a specific Web page or document within a Web site. Most people opt for the common term of *Web page address* when referring to a URL. As you can see in the figure, you can click on the link for "Sports" on the main page for the *USA Today*. By clicking on

Figure H.1

The *USA Today* Web Site and Sports Web Page

Web site address or domain name

Links

that link, you will then be taken to a specific Web page within the *USA Today* Web site. The URL or Web page address for that page is www.usatoday.com/sports/sfront.htm. Links are important. A **link** (the technical name is **hyperlink**) is clickable text or an image that takes you to another page or Web site.

UNDERSTANDING ADDRESSES

When you access a certain Web site or page, you do so with its unique address, such as www.usatoday.com (for our *USA Today* example). Addresses, because they are unique, give you important information about the site or page. Let's consider two different examples (see Figure H.2): Yahoo! (www.yahoo.com) and the University of Technology in Sydney, Australia (www.uts.edu.au).

Most addresses start with "http://www," which stand for *hypertext transfer protocol* (http) and *World Wide Web* (www). The *http://* part is so common now that you don't even have to use it in most cases. The remaining portion of the address is unique for every site or page. If you consider www.yahoo.com, you know that it's the address for Yahoo!. You can also tell it's a commercial organization by the last three letters: com. This three-letter extension can take on many forms and is referred to as the **top-level domain**. Top-level domains include:

- *com*. Commercial or for-profit business
- *coop*. Cooperative
- *edu*. Educational institution
- *gov*. U.S. government agency
- *mil*. U.S. military organization
- *net*. Internet administrative organization
- *org*. Professional or nonprofit organization
- *int*. International treaties organization
- *info*. General information

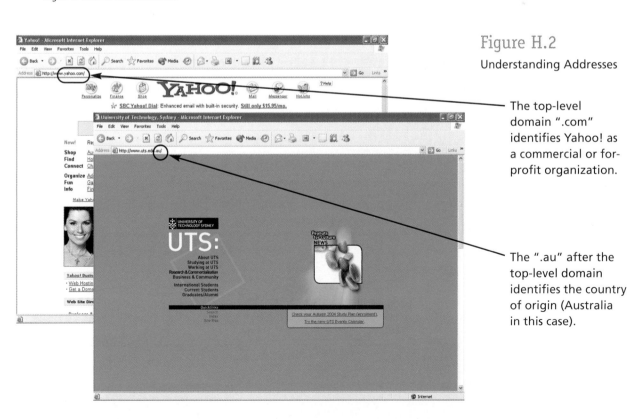

Figure H.2

Understanding Addresses

The top-level domain ".com" identifies Yahoo! as a commercial or for-profit organization.

The ".au" after the top-level domain identifies the country of origin (Australia in this case).

- *biz.* Business
- *museum.* Accredited museum
- *name.* Personal
- *pro.* Accountant, doctor, lawyer, etc.

Some addresses have a two-character extension that follows the top-level domain. In this case, it's to identify the country location of the site. For example, the site address for the University of Technology in Sydney, Australia, is www.uts.edu.au. From that address, you can tell it's for an educational institution (*edu*) located in Australia (*au*).

USING WEB BROWSER SOFTWARE

Web browser software enables you to surf the Web. It is, in fact, the software we used to view sites for the *USA Today*, Yahoo!, and University of Technology in Sydney, Australia. The most popular Web browsers today are Internet Explorer and Netscape Communicator. They are free for you to use; Internet Explorer is standard on most computers today.

To demonstrate how you use Web browser software, let's take a quick tour of Internet Explorer and Netscape Communicator. In Figures H.3 and H.4, you can see we are using Internet Explorer and Netscape Communicator, respectively, to view the Web site for eBay (www.ebay.com). In Figure H.3, you can see the menu bar for Internet Explorer that includes the functions for File, Edit, View, Favorites, Tools, and Help. In Figure H.4, you can see the menu bar for Netscape Communicator that includes the functions of File, Edit, View, Go, Communicator, and Help. Both menu bars are very similar and support the same basic functions. For example, if you click on File in either Internet Explorer or Netscape Communicator, you'll see a pull-down menu that allows you to initiate other actions such as printing the Web site and sending it via e-mail to someone else.

Below the menu bar, you'll find a button bar on both Web browsers that supports more functions. We won't go into any of these in detail here; you can play with them at your leisure. Below the button bar is the Address field for Internet Explorer and the

Figure H.3

Internet Explorer

Menu bar

Button bar

Address field

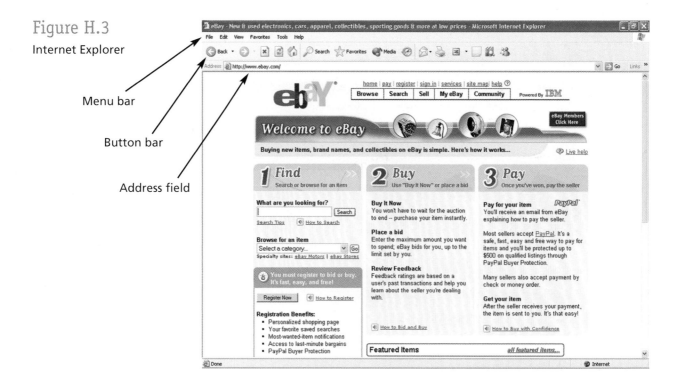

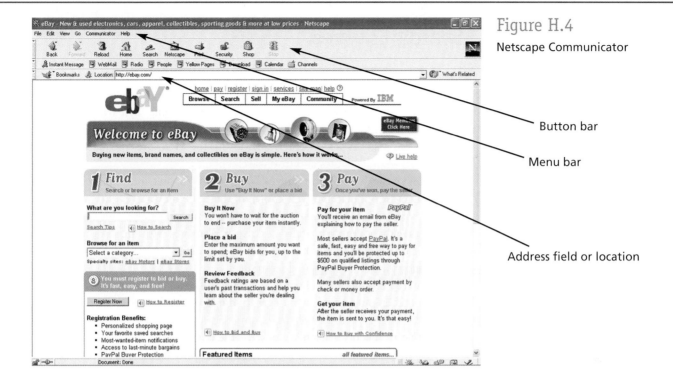

Figure H.4

Netscape Communicator

Button bar

Menu bar

Address field or location

Location field for Netscape Communicator. Both are the same. If you know the address for where you want to go, click in either of these two fields, type in the address, and then hit Enter.

One of the most important features of any Web browser is that you can create and edit a list of your most commonly visited places on the Web. In Internet Explorer, it's called a Favorites list, and in Netscape Communicator it's called a Bookmarks list. So, if you frequently visit eBay, you can save the address in one of these lists while you're viewing it. In Internet Explorer, click on the Favorites button and then Add. In Netscape Communicator, click on the Bookmarks button and then Add Bookmark. Later, when you want to visit eBay, click on the appropriate button (Favorites for Internet Explorer or Bookmarks for Netscape Communicator) and then click on the eBay link. That's all there is to it.

Web browser software is the easiest personal productivity software to learn. Most people find that they need very little instruction and seldom need a book. Just connect to the Web, start the Web browser of your choice, play around for an hour or so, and you'll soon be a Web surfing expert.

It really is quite simple. When you start your Web browser software, you'll first see what is called a *home page*—the Web site that your Web browser automatically connects to and displays when you first start surfing. Once you're there, you can click on any of the links that interest you, or you can type in a new address and go to any other site.

If you're not sure of the exact Web site address, you begin to search for it in one of two ways. The first is to use a search engine, which we'll discuss in the next section. The second is to type in a logical name in the Address field (using Internet Explorer) or the Location field (using Netscape Communicator). For example, if you want to download tax forms from the IRS Web site but don't know the address of the IRS, you can simply type in "IRS" or "internal revenue service" in the Address or Location field. Your Web browser will automatically begin a search for Web sites related to those terms and hopefully will find the right site for you. (In the instance of searching for the IRS, both Internet Explorer and Netscape Communicator do take you to the site you need.)

Search Engines

There will be occasions when you want to find information and services on the Web, but you don't know exactly which site to visit. In this case, you can type in a logical name as we just demonstrated, or you can use a search engine. A **search engine** is a facility on the Web that helps you find sites with the information and/or services you want. There are many types of search engines on the Web, the two most common being directory search engines and true search engines.

A **directory search engine** organizes listings of Web sites into hierarchical lists. Yahoo! is the most popular and well known of these. If you want to find information using a directory search engine, start by selecting a specific category and continually choose subcategories until you arrive at a list of Web sites with the information you want. Because you continually narrow down your selection by choosing subcategories, directory search engines are hierarchical.

A **true search engine** uses software agent technologies to search the Internet for key words and then puts them into indexes. In doing so, true search engines allow you to ask questions or type in key terms as opposed to continually choosing subcategories to arrive at a list of Web sites. Google is the most popular and well-known true search engine.

Let's now consider the task of finding who won the Academy Awards in 2003 to see how directory and true search engines differ.

USING A DIRECTORY SEARCH ENGINE

As we have stated, Yahoo! is the most popular and well-known directory search engine. Figure H.5 shows the sequence of pages (categories) through which you would traverse using Yahoo! to determine who won the Academy Awards in 2003. The sequence of categories includes

- Arts & Humanities
- Awards
- Movies and Film@
- Academy Awards
- 75th Annual Academy Awards

In the final screen you can see a list of Web sites from which you can choose.

There are definite advantages to performing a search in this way. If you look at the next-to-last screen, for example *Academy Awards*, it also includes subcategories for the Academy Awards in each of the last seven years (1996–2002). So you can easily find related information using a directory search engine.

You can also use directory search engines in a different fashion. For example, in the first screen, we could have entered *academy +awards +2003* in the field immediately to the left of the Search button and then clicked on the button. This particular search would yield a list of Web sites very similar to the list we received by choosing subcategories.

Notice that we included plus signs (+) in our key terms list. By doing so, we limited the search to finding just sites that included all three words. That is, the plus sign is interpreted as "and"; leaving it out would imply the word "or" between your key terms. Likewise, if you want to limit a search so that it won't show Web sites that contain certain key words, you would use a minus sign, represented by a hyphen (-); this is interpreted as "not." For example, if you wanted to find Web sites that contain information

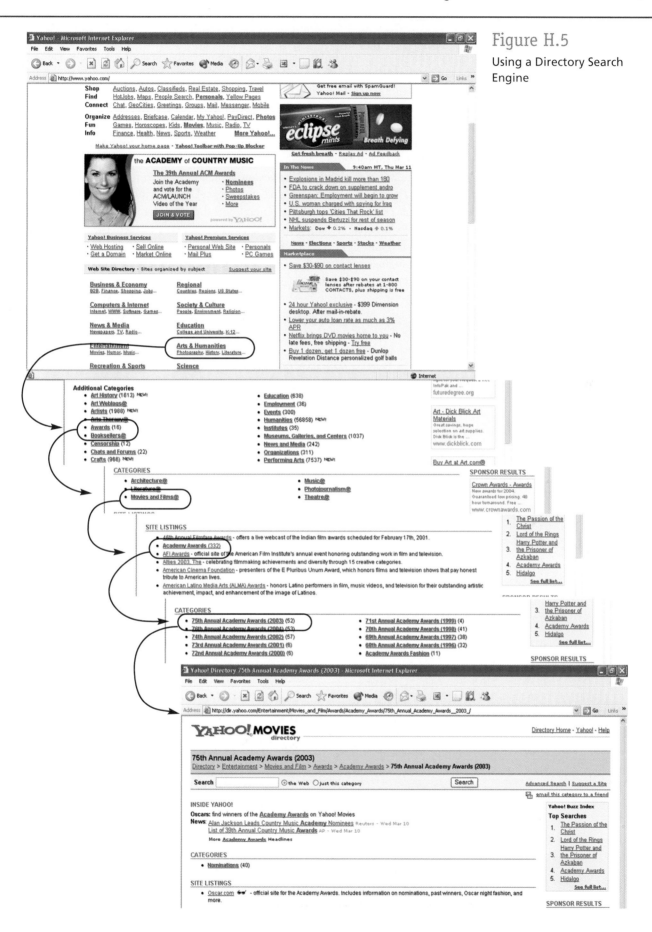

about the Toronto Raptors, you could enter *Toronto +Raptors*. That would probably yield a list of suitable sites, but it might also include sites that include information about watching raptors (the extinct version) in Toronto. You can further refine your search by entering something like *Toronto +Raptors -dinosaur -jurassic*. That search will yield a list of Web sites that have the terms *Toronto* and *Raptors* but will eliminate any sites that have the term *dinosaur* or *jurassic*.

When you use a directory search engine and type in specific terms instead of traversing through subcategories, we definitely recommend that you make use of the plus sign and/or minus sign (hyphen). For example, if you want to find sites about wind tunnels, using *wind tunnel* will return a list of sites related to wind tunnels but also the wind (weather sites) and tunnels in general. On the other hand, *wind +tunnel* will yield a more refined list of sites. We recommend that you complete the Team Work project "Finding and Using Search Engines" that follows. As you do, you'll find that some search engines support advanced and unique capabilities that can help you further refine your search criteria.

USING A TRUE SEARCH ENGINE

Google is the most popular and well-known true search engine. With Google (www.google.ca), you simply ask a question or type in some key terms. For finding out who won the Academy Awards in 2003, we would simply enter *Who won the Academy Awards in 2003* and hit the Google Search button. As you can see in Figure H.6, Google returned a list of possible Web sites.

Both types of search engines are very easy to use. Which you choose is really a function of how you think. Some people think in terms of hierarchical lists while

Figure H.6

Using a True Search Engine

others think in terms of questions. What you'll undoubtedly find is that directory search engines are better in some cases while true search engines are better in others.

Internet Technologies

To best take advantage of everything the Web has to offer, it often helps to understand what's going on behind the Web, that is, the Internet. The Internet is really the enabling structure that makes the Web possible. Without the Web, the Internet still exists and you can still use it. But the reverse is not true. The Internet is the set of underlying technologies that makes the Web possible. The Web is somewhat of a graphical user interface (GUI) that sets on top of the Internet. The Web allows you to click on links to go to other sites, and it allows you to view information in multiple formats.

THE INTERNET BACKBONE

The **Internet backbone** is the major set of connections for computers on the Internet (see Figure H.7). A **network access point (NAP)** is a point on the Internet where several connections converge. At each NAP is at least one computer that simply routes Internet traffic from one place to another (much like an airport where you merely switch planes). These NAPs are owned and maintained by network service providers. A **network service provider (NSP)**, such as MCI or Bell Canada, owns and maintains routing computers at NAPs and even the lines that connect the NAPs to each other. In Figure H.7, you can see that Calgary is a NAP, with lines converging from Vancouver, Edmonton, Chicago, and Toronto.

At any given NAP, an Internet service provider may connect its computer or computers to the Internet. An **Internet service provider (ISP)** is a company that provides individuals, organizations, and businesses access to the Internet. ISPs include AOL, Juno (which is free), and perhaps even your school. In turn, you "dial up" and connect your computer to an ISP computer. So your ISP provides you access to the Internet (and thus the Web) by allowing you to connect your computer to its computer (which is already connected).

If you live in the Moncton area and send an e-mail to someone living near Saskatoon, your e-mail message might travel from Moncton to Montreal, then to Toronto, then to Calgary, then to Edmonton, and finally to Saskatoon. But, no matter—your message will get there. Can you imagine the route that your e-mail message would travel if you were in Moncton sending it to someone in Venice, Italy? One time, it might go west around the world through Australia. The next time, it might go east around the world through Halifax and then on to London, England.

Figure H.7

The Internet Backbone in Canada

LEGEND
——	OC3 (155 Mbps)
——	OC12 (622 Mbps)
——	OC48 (2.5 Gbps)
——	OC192 (10 Gbps)

INTERNET SERVERS

There are many types of computers on the Internet, namely, router (which we've already discussed), client, and server computers (see Figure H.8). The computer that you use to access the Internet and surf the Web is called a *client computer*. Your client computer can be a traditional desktop or notebook computer, a Web or Internet appliance, a PDA, or perhaps even a cell phone.

Internet server computers are computers that provide information and services on the Internet. There are four main types of server computers on the Internet: Web, mail, ftp, and IRC servers. A **Web server** provides information and services to Web surfers. So, when you access www.ebay.ca, you're accessing a Web server (for eBay) with your client computer. Most often, you'll be accessing and using the services of a Web server.

A **mail server** provides e-mail services and accounts. Many times, mail servers are presented to you as a part of a Web server. For example, Hotmail is a free e-mail server

Figure H.8
Servers on the Internet

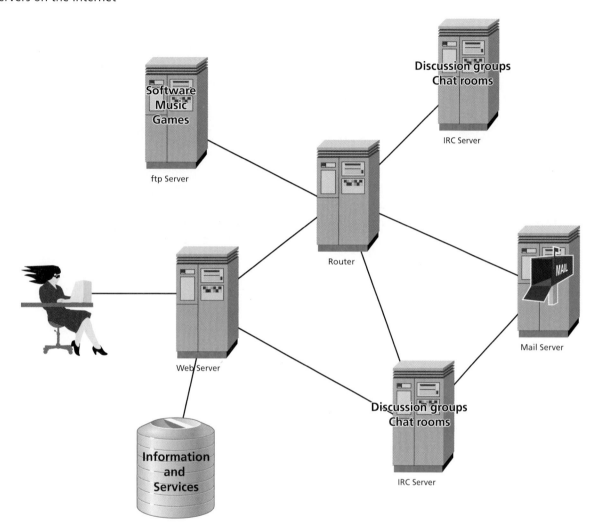

and service provided by MSN. An **ftp (file transfer protocol) server** maintains a collection of files that you can download. These files can include software, screen savers, music files (many in MP3 format), and games. An **IRC (Internet relay chat) server** supports your use of discussion groups and chat rooms. IRC servers are popular hosting computers for sites such as www.epinions.com. There, you can share your opinions about various products and services, and you can also read the reviews written by other people.

COMMUNICATIONS PROTOCOLS

As information moves around the Internet, bouncing among network access points until it finally reaches you, it does so according to various communications protocols. A **communications protocol (protocol)** is a set of rules that every computer follows to transfer information. The most widely used protocols on the Internet include TCP/IP, http, and ftp (and a few others such as PPP, point-to-point protocol, and POP, post office protocol).

    TCP/IP, or **transport control protocol/Internet protocol**, is the primary protocol for transmitting information over the Internet. Whenever any type of information

USING A WEB PORTAL

Most Web browser software is already configured to take you to a certain Web site when you start surfing. For example, Internet Explorer usually starts at the Microsoft Network site (MSN at www.msn.ca). Sites such as MSN, Yahoo!, and the Go Network (www.go.com) are often referred to as Web portals. A **Web portal** is a site that provides a wide range of services, including search engines, free e-mail, chat rooms, discussion boards, and links to hundreds of different sites.

The nice thing about Web portals is that they often let you customize the first page you see. So, you can request a ticker of your favourite stocks, the weather forecast for your area over the next three days, and a list of sites you commonly visit.

In this project, you are to create a customized and personal Web portal at two different places on the Web. We recommend that you do so at one of these sites (although there are many others):

- www.msn.ca
- www.go.com
- www.excite.com
- www.yahoo.ca

As you build each personalized Web portal, answer the following questions:

1. What is the registration process required to build a Web portal?
2. Can you receive a free e-mail account? If so, must you establish it?
3. Can you create categories of your most commonly visited sites?
4. Can you request customized local information for your area? If so, what type of information?
5. How do you adjust your Web browser settings so that it automatically takes you to your Web portal page?

moves over the Internet, it does so according to TCP/IP. **Hypertext transfer protocol (http)** is the communications protocol that supports the movement of information over the Web, essentially from a Web server to you. That's why Web site addresses start with "http://." Most Web browser software today assumes that you want to access a Web site on the Internet. So you don't even have to type in the "http://" if you don't want to.

File transfer protocol (ftp) is the communications protocol that allows you to transfer files of information from one computer to another. When you download a file from an ftp server (using ftp), you're using both TCP/IP (the primary protocol for the Internet) and ftp (the protocol that allows you to download the file). Likewise, when you access a Web site, you're using both TCP/IP and http (because the information you want is Web-based).

Connecting to the Internet

To access the Web (via the Internet), you need an Internet service provider (ISP), as we discussed earlier. ISPs can include your school, your place of work, commercial ISPs such as AOL, and free ISPs such as NetZero. Which you choose is a function of many things.

One of the nice benefits of going to school or being employed is that you often get free Web access through school or your work. All you have to do is connect your home computer to your school's or work's computer (we'll talk about this process in a moment) and you're ready to surf. However, some schools and places of business may restrict where you can go on the Web. And they may even monitor your surfing.

Commercial ISPs charge you a monthly fee, just as your telephone company charges you a monthly fee for phone service. This fee usually ranges from a few dollars a month to about $20. Popular worldwide commercial ISPs include Microsoft (MSN), AOL, CompuServe, and AT&T WorldNet, just to name a few.

Free ISPs are absolutely free, as their names suggest—you don't pay a setup fee, you don't pay a monthly fee, and you usually have unlimited access to the Web. But there are some catches. Many free ISPs do not offer you Web space, as opposed to most commercial ISPs which do. **Web space** is a storage area where you keep your Web site. So if you want to create and maintain a Web site, you may have to choose a commercial ISP over a free ISP (your school probably also offers you Web space). Also when using a free ISP, you will often see banner ads that you can't get rid of. You can move them around and from side to side, but you can't remove them completely from your screen. Technical support is often limited with a free ISP. Some offer only e-mail support, while others do offer phone support but no toll-free number.

In spite of those drawbacks, many people do choose free ISPs over commercial ones, mainly because of cost (remember, $20 per month equals $240 per year). Popular free ISPs include Myfreei (www.access-4-free.com), MSN Internet Access (www.msn.com), and NetZero (www.netzero.net; see Figure H.9). To decide which type of ISP is best for you, ask these questions:

- *Do you need Web space?* If yes, a free ISP may not be the right choice.
- *Is great technical support important?* If yes, then a commercial ISP may be the right choice.
- *Is money a serious consideration?* If yes, then a commercial ISP may not be the right choice.
- *Is privacy important to you?* If yes, then your school or work may not be the right choice.

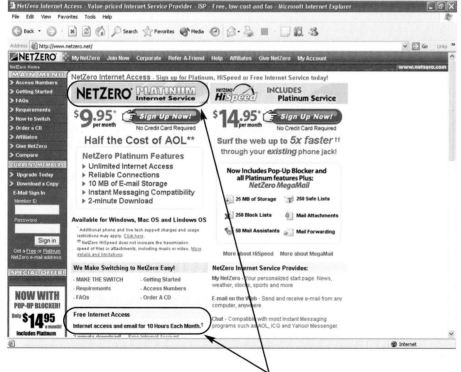

Figure H.9

NetZero, a Popular Free ISP

NetZero, in addition to offering free Internet access, also offers a subscription service with more features.

EVALUATING ISP OPTIONS

Choosing an Internet service provider (ISP) is an important, but not terribly complicated, task. In this project, your group is to evaluate three different ISPs: a well-recognized commercial ISP such as AOL or AT&T World-Net, a free ISP such as NetZero (there are many others), and a local or regional ISP in your area (you may need to look in your phone book to find one of these).

As you evaluate these three different ISPs, do so in terms of (1) price per month, (2) amount of Web space provided, (3) monthly limit of hours you can be connected without paying an additional fee, (4) customer support, and (5) the ability to have e-mail.

Of the three, which would you choose and why?

COMMUNICATIONS SOFTWARE

To access and use the Web, you need communications software, namely:

- **Connectivity software**. Enables you to use your computer to dial up or connect to another computer.
- *Web browser software*. Enables you to surf the Web.
- **E-mail software** (short for **electronic mail software**). Enables you to electronically communicate with other people by sending and receiving e-mail.

Connectivity software is the first and most important item. With it, while using a standard telephone modem, you essentially use your computer (and a phone line) to call up and connect to the server computer of your ISP. Connectivity software is standard on most personal computers today. To use it, you really only need to know the number to call. Then it's a relatively easy process: within Microsoft Windows, click on Start, Programs, Accessories, Communications, Network and Dial-up Connections, and then select Make New Connection (your exact sequence may vary slightly according to which version of Windows you're using).

Alternatively, if you're using connectivity software in conjunction with a high-speed modem connection such as a cable, DSL, or satellite modem (we'll discuss these further in a moment), you don't really "make a call" to connect to your ISP. Instead, you probably have an "always-on" high-speed Internet connection. So, when you turn on your computer, it goes through the process of connecting you to your ISP.

Web browser software and e-mail software are also standard software today. If your school or work is your ISP, then you'll most often be using commercially available Web browser software such as Internet Explorer or Netscape Communicator, and the e-mail software you use will vary according to your school's or work's preference. If you're using a commercial or free ISP, your choice of Web browser software and e-mail software will depend on that particular organization.

Regardless of your choice of ISP, the unique Web browser software and e-mail software provided work in similar fashion. So, if you're used to using Internet Explorer and then choose AOL as your ISP, you will see that AOL has its own Web browser software. It will look different on the screen, but it supports the same functionality (favourites list, moving forward and backward through your list of visited Web sites, and so on). All you have to do is get used to a new interface. Different e-mail software will also look different but support the same functionality.

TELECOMMUNICATIONS HARDWARE

In addition to communications software, you also need some telecommunications hardware to access the Web (again, via the Internet). If you're at school or work, you'll probably be able to connect your computer directly to a network that is then connected to the Internet. This often amounts to simply plugging a network line into your computer and starting your preferred Web browser or e-mail software. We discuss this type of connection to the Internet in more detail in Extended Learning Module E.

If you're connecting from home, you'll need some sort of modem. There are many types, including:

- A **telephone modem (modem)**. A device that connects your computer to your phone line so that you can access another computer or network.
- A **digital subscriber line (DSL)**. A high-speed Internet connection using phone lines, which allows you to use your phone line for voice communication at the same time.
- A **cable modem**. A device that uses your TV cable to deliver an Internet connection.
- A **satellite modem**. A modem that allows you to get Internet access from your satellite dish.

DSL, cable, and satellite modems are among the newest, most expensive, and fastest. They also don't tie up your phone line. If, for example, you're using a basic telephone modem, you can't use your telephone line for voice communications at the same time. A DSL modem on the other hand, for example, basically splits your telephone line so that you can use it simultaneously for voice communications and for connecting to the Internet (see Figure H.10). Even more so, DSL, cable, and satellite modems offer you an "always-on" Internet connection.

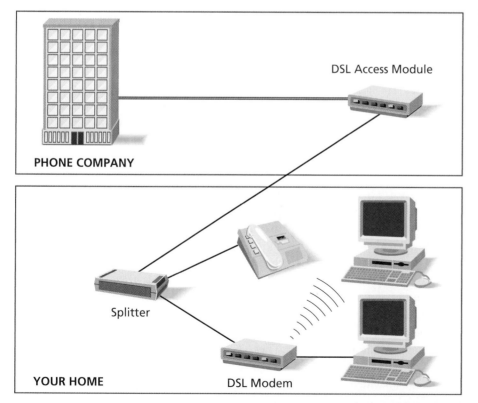

Figure H.10

DSL Modem Connection

With these high-speed Internet connection options, you may also have the ability to connect wirelessly to the modem using a router or other piece of equipment. As you can see in the figure, the DSL modem is wired directly to one computer and wirelessly connected to another computer. This gives you the ability to connect multiple computers to the DSL modem. Again, we'll cover both wired and wireless connections to the Internet in Extended Learning Module E.

The biggest factor in determining your choice of telecommunications hardware (beyond price) may be that of availability. In many areas of the country, phone companies and cable TV service providers do not yet support the use of DSL, cable, and satellite modems. So, you may be limited to just using a basic telephone modem. If some of the other options are available to you, we definitely recommend that you research them.

Summary: Student Learning Outcomes Revisited

1. **Define the relationships among Web site, Web site address, domain name, Web page, and uniform resource locator (URL).** A *Web site* (such as www.usatoday.com for the *USA Today*) is a specific location on the Web where you visit, gather information, and perhaps even order products. A *Web site address* (www.usatoday.com) is a unique name that identifies a specific site on the Web. Technically, a Web site address is called a *domain name*. A *Web page* is a specific portion of a Web site that deals with a certain topic. Technically, the address for a specific Web page is called a *URL (uniform resource locator)*.

2. **Explain how to interpret the parts of an address on the Web.** Most Web site addresses start with *http://www*. Beyond that, the address is unique. The first part (using www.uts.edu.au as an example) provides the name of the organization or Web site (UTS or University of Technology in Sydney). The next part tells the type of organization and is called the *top-level domain*. For UTS, it is "edu," describing it as an educational institution. If something follows after that, it usually provides a country of origin ("au" for UTS which identifies its country of origin as Australia).

3. **Identify the major components and features of Web browser software.** The two most popular Web browsers are Internet Explorer and Netscape Communicator. Each includes a menu bar (with functions such as File, Edit, and View), a button bar (for commonly performed tasks such as printing), and an address or location field into which you can type a Web site address. Web browsers also include capabilities for maintaining a list of commonly visited sites. In Internet Explorer, these are called a *Favorites list*, while Netscape Communicator refers to them as a *Bookmarks list*.

4. **Describe the differences between directory and true search engines.** *Search engines* are facilities on the Web that help you find sites with the information and/or services you want. A *directory search engine* organizes listings of Web sites into hierarchical lists. Using a directory search engine, you start by selecting a specific category and continually refine your search by choosing subsequent subcategories. A *true search engine* uses software agent technologies to search the Internet for key words and then puts them in indexes. You use a true search engine by asking a question or providing key terms.

5. **Describe the various technologies that make up the Internet.** At the heart of the Internet is the *Internet backbone*, the major set of connections for computers on the Internet. A *network access point (NAP)* is a point on the Internet where several connections converge. *Network service providers (NSPs)*, such as MCI or AT&T, own and maintain routing computers at NAPs and even the lines that connect the NAPs to each other. Besides your computer (called a client computer) which you use to access the Internet, there are also four types of *Internet server computers* that provide information and services on the Internet. These include *Web servers* (providing information and services to Web surfers), *mail servers* (providing e-mail services and accounts), *ftp servers* (maintaining a collection of files that you can download), and *IRC servers* (supporting your use

of discussion groups and chat rooms). As information travels from these servers to you, it follows a set of *communications protocols*—sets of rules that every computer follows to transfer information. The most common protocols include *TCP/IP* (the primary protocol for transmitting information), *http* (for supporting the movement of information over the Web), and *ftp* (for allowing you to transfer files of information from one computer to another).

6. **Identify key considerations in choosing an Internet service provider (ISP).** When choosing an ISP—whether it is a commercial ISP, a free ISP, your school, or your work—you need to consider the following:
   - *Web space.* If you want to publish a Web site, your ISP must provide you with Web space.
   - *Technical support.* This can be in the form of e-mail or 24-hour toll-free assistance; or perhaps there is none at all.
   - *Money.* Commercial ISPs are the most expensive, while free ISPs, your school, and your work are free.
   - *Privacy.* Your school or work may monitor your surfing activities.

7. **Describe the communications software and telecommunications hardware you need to connect to the Internet.** Communications software for connecting to the Internet includes *connectivity software* (for dialling up another computer), *Web browser software* (for actually surfing the Web), and *e-mail software* (for electronically communicating with other people). Telecommunications hardware includes the device that you use to physically connect your computer to a network, which may connect through a phone line or cable line. These devices are called modems and include a *telephone modem*, *DSL modem*, *cable modem*, and *satellite modem*.

Key Terms and Concepts

cable modem, 453
communications protocol
    (protocol), 449
connectivity software, 452
digital subscriber line (DSL), 453
directory search engine, 444
domain name, 440
e-mail (electronic mail)
    software, 452
file transfer protocol (ftp), 450
ftp (file transfer protocol) server, 449
hypertext transfer protocol
    (http), 450

Internet, 440
Internet backbone, 447
Internet server computer, 448
Internet service provider (ISP), 447
IRC (internet relay chat) server, 449
link (hyperlink), 441
mail server, 448
network access point (NAP), 447
network service provider (NSP), 447
satellite modem, 453
search engine, 444
TCP/IP (transport control
    protocol/Internet protocol), 449

telephone modem (modem), 453
top-level domain, 441
true search engine, 444
uniform resource locator
    (URL), 440
Web browser software, 442
Web page, 440
Web portal, 450
Web server, 448
Web site, 440
Web site address, 440
Web space, 451
World Wide Web (Web), 440

Short-Answer Questions

1. How do the Web and the Internet differ?

2. What is the relationship between a Web site and a Web page?

3. What is the difference between a directory search engine and a true search engine?

4. How can you use plus signs and minus signs to refine a search?

5. What is the relationship between the Internet backbone, a network access point, and a network service provider?

6. What is the role of an ISP?

7. What are the four major types of servers on the Internet?

8. What are the advantages and disadvantages of choosing a commercial ISP?

9. What communications software do you need to use the Web?

10. What are the four main types of modems you can use to access the Internet while at home?

Assignments and Exercises

For each of the following Internet scavenger hunts, find the answer on the Web. When you do, write down the answer as well as the address where you found it. One restriction: You are not allowed to use encyclopedia sites such as *Encyclopaedia Britannica.*

1. What is the weight of the moon?

Answer: _____

Address: _____

2. Who was the first Canadian billionaire?

Answer: _____

Address: _____

3. Who is Olive Oyl's brother?

Answer: _____

Address: _____

4. Who wrote "It was the worst of times . . ."?

Answer: _____

Address: _____

5. What does the Seine River empty into?

Answer: _____

Address: _____

6. What is a lacrosse ball made of?

Answer: _____

Address: _____

7. Who lives at 39 Stone Canyon Drive?

Answer: _____

Address: _____

8. What is the colour of Mr. Spock's blood?

Answer: _____

Address: _____

9. At what did the Nasdaq stock market close yesterday?

Answer: _____

Address: _____

10. What is the most frequently broken bone in the human body?

Answer: _____

Address: _____

11. What is a pregnant goldfish called?

Answer: _____

Address: _____

12. Who was the first pope to visit Africa?

Answer: _____

Address: _____

13. How many tusks does an Indian rhinoceros have?

Answer: _____

Address: _____

14. What does a pluviometer measure?

Answer: _____

Address: _____

15. What is the fear of the number 13 called?

Answer: _____

Address: _____

16. Which ear can most people hear best with?

Answer: _____

Address: _____

17. Who is the patron saint of England?

Answer: _____

Address: _____

18. What boxer's life story was titled *Raging Bull*?

Answer: _____

Address: _____

19. What was the first domesticated bird?

Answer: _____

Address: _____

20. What is the population of Canada right now?

Answer: _____

Address: _____

EXTENDED LEARNING MODULE I

BUILDING A WEB PAGE WITH HTML

Student Learning Outcomes

By the end of this Module, students will be able to:

1. Define an HTML document and describe its relationship to a Web site.

2. Describe the purpose of tags in hypertext markup language (HTML).

3. Identify the two major sections in an HTML document and describe the content within each.

4. Describe the use of basic formatting tags and heading tags.

5. Describe how to adjust text colour and size within a Web site.

6. Describe how to change the background of a Web site.

7. List the three types of links in a Web site and describe their purposes.

8. Describe how to insert and manipulate images in a Web site.

9. Demonstrate how to insert lists in a Web site.

Taking Advantage of the CD

Creating a Web site . . . everyone seems to be doing it. Businesses create Web sites to sell products and services, provide support information, and conduct marketing activities. Individuals build Web sites for a variety of reasons. Some want a family site. Some want a site for their evening sports leagues. Your instructor has probably built a Web site to support your class. And we've created one to support your use of this text.

Whatever the case, building a basic Web site is actually not that difficult. If you want a site that supports product ordering capabilities, you'll need some specific expertise. But putting up a Web site with just content is simple and easy. In Extended Learning Module I, we'll show you how. You'll find the Module on the CD that accompanies this text. Module I is just like any other Module in this text—it includes Team Work and On Your Own projects and great Assignments and Exercises at the end.

Before we begin, let's discuss several important issues. First, be careful what sort of private personal information you include on your Web site. We definitely recommend that you do not include your social insurance number, your address, or your telephone number. You always need to keep in mind that there are almost 1 billion people on the Internet. Do you really want them to know where you live?

You also need to consider your target audience and their ethics. Having a Web site with profanity and obscene images will offend many people. And, more than likely, your school won't allow you to build a Web site with questionable content. Even more basic than that, you need to consider your target audience and their viewing preferences. For example, if you're building a Web site for school-age children, you'll want to use a lot of bright colours such as red, blue, green, and yellow. If you're targeting college students to advertise concerts and other events, you'll want your Web site to be more edgy and include sharp, contrasting colours (including black).

Just remember this: the most elegant solution is almost always the simplest. Consider eBay. It uses a very simple and elegant presentation of information. The background is basic white. You'll see very little if any flashy movement. You'll hear very little sound. Yet eBay is one of the most visited sites on the Web today, and it's making money.

We definitely believe it's worth your time and energy to pop in the CD and read this Module. You'll learn many things, including:

- How to build and view a Web site on your own computer without connecting to the Web
- How to use a simple text editor to create a Web site
- How to size and position images in your Web site
- How to include e-mail links in your Web site
- How to change the background colour or insert a textured background for your Web site
- How to change the colour and size of text

If you're interested in learning more about what you can do with a Web site, we recommend that you connect to the one that supports this text at www.mcgrawhill.ca/college/haag (and select "XLM-I."). There, we've included more about building a Web site and useful resources on the Web.

EXTENDED LEARNING MODULE J

BUILDING AN E-PORTFOLIO

Student Learning Outcomes

By the end of this Module, students will be able to:

1. Describe the types of electronic résumés and when each is appropriate.

2. Discuss networking strategies you can use during a job search.

3. Explain how self-assessment is valuable to résumé writing.

4. Use the Internet to research career opportunities and potential employers.

5. Develop powerful job search e-portfolio content.

6. Document effective Web site structure and design components.

7. Create a job search e-portfolio Web site and place it on an Internet server.

Taking Advantage of the CD

The electronic job market and online recruiting has been developing for a number of years, and it is still growing fast. Electronic e-portfolios have evolved since the early 1990s to the point now where they have to be cohesive, powerful, and well designed to catch the eye of any potential recruiter. In addition, they have to demonstrate your skills, your education, your professional development, and most importantly, the benefits you would bring to a hiring organization.

If you want to create your own e-portfolio, we can show you how with Extended Learning Module J, which appears on the CD that accompanies this text. Its structure is like that of all Modules in this text with Team Work and On your Own projects as well as many suggestions on how to make your résumé stand out.

Today, e-portfolios are much more than innovative résumés. In education and training contexts, they must be learner-centred and outcomes-based, and as such serve the function of a learning record or transcript. E-portfolios must also be continually updated and used for self-reflective purposes.

The electronic job market makes use of many Internet technologies to recruit employees. With the much broader selection of candidates that this makes possible, employers can screen many more candidates before bringing them in for an interview and can significantly increase the likelihood of finding a good match for their needs. It is thus critical that you capitalize on these technologies that help organizations and potential employees connect and communicate.

Although the basic constituents of your résumé remain the same, and their purpose is still to present your skills and qualifications, how you do so must change in the electronic job market.

If you are interested in learning more, we recommend that you pop in the enclosed Student CD and examine Extended Learning Module J. Also, visit the Web site that supports this text at www.mcgrawhill.ca/college/haag and select "XLM-J."

EXTENDED LEARNING MODULE K
COMPUTER CRIME AND FORENSICS

Student Learning Outcomes

By the end of this Module, students will be able to:

1. Define computer crime and list three types of computer crime that can be perpetrated from inside and three from outside the organization.

2. Identify the seven types of hackers and explain what motivates each group.

3. Define computer forensics and describe the two phases of a forensic investigation.

4. Identify and describe four places on a hard disk where you can find useful information.

5. Identify and describe seven ways of hiding information.

6. Describe two ways in which corporations use computer forensics.

Introduction

Computers play a big part in crime: they're used both to commit and to solve crimes. This should be no surprise, since they're such a big part of almost every other part of our lives. Computers are involved primarily two ways in the commission of a crime or misdeed: as targets and as weapons or tools. A computer or network is a target when someone wants to bring it down or make it malfunction, as in a denial-of-service attack or a computer virus infection. Crimes that use a computer as a weapon or tool would include acts such as changing computer records to commit embezzlement, breaking into a computer system to damage information, and stealing customer lists. See Figure K.1 for examples of computer-related offences that use computers as weapons/tools and targets of crime.

Some crimes are clearly what we'd call computer crimes, such as Web defacing, denial-of-service attacks, and so on. But, as is the case in so many parts of our modern lives, computers are so integrated into crime that it's sometimes hard to separate them out. Here's an example from the case files of Walt Manning, an expert in computer forensic investigation.

A member of a crime syndicate was sprayed with driveby gunfire and was severely wounded. Believing that his services were no longer wanted by his crime gang, he switched sides, agreeing to become a witness for the state. The police secured an isolated intensive-care unit room for him and guarded it heavily, allowing access only to medical staff and those on a very short list of visitors. Because the man was so badly wounded, there was a distinct danger of infection, and since he was allergic to penicillin, the doctor prescribed a synthetic alternative.

One evening, a nurse wheeling a medicine cart went through the police cordon and into the man's room. He injected the patient with penicillin, and the patient died shortly thereafter. An investigation started immediately and the nurse was potentially in big trouble. He insisted that when he looked at the patient's chart on the computer, there was an order there for penicillin. Subsequent examination of the computer records showed no such order. Eventually, it occurred to someone that perhaps a computer forensics expert should look at the computer angle more closely. Having retrieved the backup tapes (nightly backups are standard operating procedure in most places), the expert found evidence that exonerated the nurse. The patient chart had been changed in the computer to indicate penicillin and later changed back to its orig-

Figure K.1

Examples of Computer Crimes That Organizations Need to Defend Against

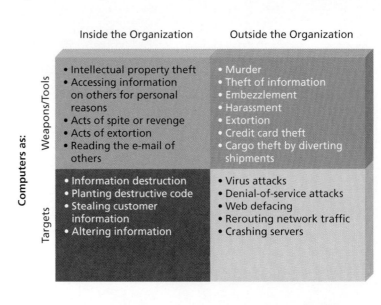

inal form. Examination further revealed the point and time of access, and indicated that the medical record was changed by someone outside the hospital. A hacker had electronically slipped into the hospital's network unnoticed, made the change, and slipped out again—twice.

Most crimes involving a computer are not as lethal as murder, but that doesn't mean they're insignificant. Organizations want to make sure their networks' defences are strong and can prevent their computers from being used for unlawful or unethical acts. That's why so much time, money, and effort goes into security. We discussed that in Chapter 9.

This Module focuses on the sort of threats that computer systems are susceptible to and the examination of electronic evidence. The latter is called computer forensics.

Computer Crime

For our purposes, a **computer crime** is a crime in which a computer, or computers, play a significant part. See Figure K.2 for a list of crimes in which computers, although perhaps not essential, usually play a large part.

In this section we'll focus on crime from the organization's viewpoint. First, we'll examine some of the more high-profile types of computer crime committed against organizations that are perpetrated from the outside. Then we'll discuss the varying motivations of people who commit these acts. Lastly, we'll briefly discuss computer crime within the organization.

OUTSIDE THE ORGANIZATION

Businesses are very concerned about the threat of people breaking into their computers and causing damage. The Computer Security Institute conducted a survey in 2003 to determine the extent of the problem. It found that 82 percent of companies had experienced a virus attack during 2002; 80 percent had uncovered insider abuse of Internet access (costing a total of over $11 million for 251 of the companies); and 45 percent had experienced unauthorized access by insiders. The costs are staggering. In 2003 alone, companies reported a total of over $70 million lost in the theft of

• Illegal gambling
• Forgery
• Money laundering
• Child pornography
• Hate message propagation
• Electronic stalking
• Racketeering
• Fencing stolen goods
• Loan sharking
• Drug trafficking
• Union infiltration

Figure K.2

Crimes in Which Computers Usually Play a Part

proprietary information for 251 companies. Denial-of-service (DoS) attacks for the same group cost over $65 million, and the detection and cleanup of viruses cost over $27 million. The companies further reported that the infection of viruses came, in 86 percent of the cases, from e-mail attachments.[1] To combat these and other attacks, businesses spent about $7.5 billion in 2000 on security software.[2] That market is expected to triple to $21 billion by the end of 2005.

VIRUSES   The term *computer virus* is a generic term for lots of different types of destructive software. A **computer virus** (or **virus**) is software that was written with malicious intent to cause annoyance or damage. Two hundred new ones are developed every day.[3] There are two categories of viruses. The first category comprises benign viruses that display a message or slow down the computer but don't destroy any information.

Malignant viruses belong in the second category. These viruses do damage to your computer system. Some will scramble or delete your files. Others will shut your computer down, or make your Word software malfunction, or damage flash memory in your digital camera so that it won't store pictures anymore until you reformat it. Obviously, these are the viruses that cause IT staff (and everyone else) the most headaches.

The macro virus is one very common type of malignant computer virus. **Macro viruses** spread by binding themselves to software such as Word or Excel. When they infect a computer, they make copies of themselves (replicate) and spread from file to file destroying or changing the file in some way.

This type of virus needs human help to move to another computer. If you have a macro virus on your system and you e-mail an infected document as an attachment, the person who gets the e-mail gets the virus as soon as the infected attachment is opened. When you click on the attachment, Word (or the appropriate program) also loads, thereby setting the executable statements in motion.

Worms are the most prevalent type of malignant virus. A **worm** is a computer virus that replicates and spreads itself, not only from file to file, but from computer to computer via e-mail and other Internet traffic. Worms don't need your help to spread. They find your e-mail address book and help themselves to the addresses, sending themselves to your contacts. The first worm to attract the attention of the popular press was the Love Bug worm, and permutations of it are still out there.

The Love Bug Worm   Released on an unsuspecting world in 2000, the Love Bug worm caused the Massachusetts state government to shut down its e-mail, affecting 20,000 workers. It also caused problems on Capitol Hill and shut down e-mail in the British Parliament building. Companies as diverse as Ford Motor Company, H. J. Heinz, Merrill Lynch & Company, and AT&T were infected.[4] All in all, the Love Bug and its variants affected 300,000 Internet host computers and millions of individual PC users causing file damage, lost time, and high-cost emergency repairs totalling about $8.7 billion.[5,6]

A closer look at the Love Bug worm will give you a general idea of what worms do. The Love Bug arrives in your e-mail as an attachment to an e-mail message. The subject of the e-mail is "I LOVE YOU"—a very alluring message to be sure. The text says to open the attached love letter, the name of which is, appropriately, LOVE LETTER. However, what's attached is anything but love. It's a mean piece of software that is set loose in your computer system as soon as you open the attachment.

The Love Bug has three objectives: to spread itself as far and as fast as it can, to destroy your files, and to gather passwords and other information (see Figure K.3). First, it spreads itself by mailing itself to everyone in your Outlook address book. (A previous worm of the same type named Melissa sent itself only to the first 50 people

Figure K.3

The Love Bug Worm

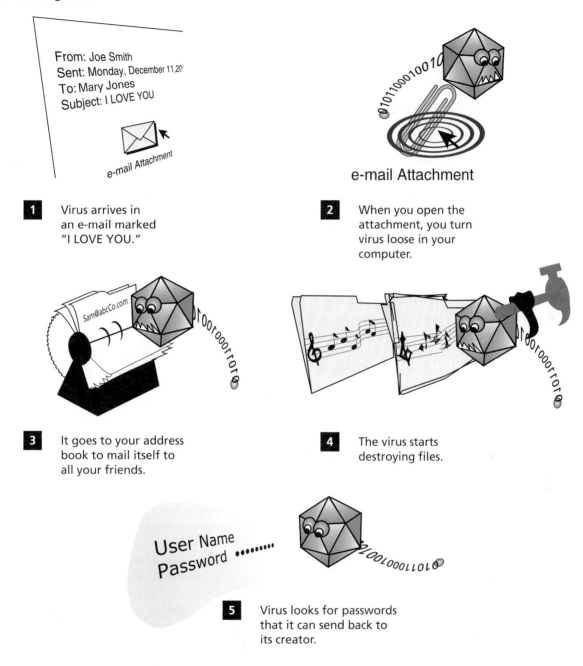

From: Joe Smith
Sent: Monday, December 11,20'
To: Mary Jones
Subject: I LOVE YOU

e-mail Attachment

e-mail Attachment

1 Virus arrives in an e-mail marked "I LOVE YOU."

2 When you open the attachment, you turn virus loose in your computer.

3 It goes to your address book to mail itself to all your friends.

4 The virus starts destroying files.

User Name
Password

5 Virus looks for passwords that it can send back to its creator.

listed in Outlook's address book.) And, as if that weren't enough, it also uses your Internet chat software to spread itself to chat rooms.

Second, the Love Bug locates files on your computer that have certain extensions, .mp3 music files, .jpg picture files, .doc Word files, .xls Excel files, .wav sound files, .html browser files, and many others. Having found these files it wipes them out and puts itself in their place, appending .vbs to the end of the filename. For example, if you had a file called MySong.wav on your hard disk drive, the Love Bug virus would change the name to MySong.wav.vbs after it had done its dirty work.

Before it's done, the Love Bug worm changes your Internet Explorer start page and downloads a program that looks for passwords and network information, sending this information off by e-mail to the virus originator.[7]

There are at least 29 versions of the Love Bug virus. After people were warned not to open the LOVE LETTER attachment, the originators of the virus changed the name to something else. For example, one version is MOTHER'S DAY, and the body of the text says that the receiver has been charged hundreds of dollars for a Mother's Day "diamond special." You have to open the attachment to print the invoice, and then the virus goes into action.

The moral of the story is that you should be very careful about opening an attachment if you're not sure what it is and where it came from. That won't necessarily save you from all virus attacks, but it will certainly help a great deal.

SoBig, Slammer, and Blaster   The year 2003 was called the "worst year ever" for viruses and worms. Among the biggest, in terms of cost and name recognition, were the SoBig virus and the Slammer and Blaster worms.

There are several variations of mass-mailer viruses, but the SoBig virus is probably the best known. On Tuesday, August 19, 2003, the SoBig virus began spreading through networks generating e-mail traffic at levels never seen before. It arrived as an attachment in the victim's inbox with varying subject lines like "Your details," "Your application," and "Wicked screensaver." When the recipient opened the attachment, the virus searched through hard drives for e-mail addresses in document files, cached Web pages, and Microsoft Outlook Express databases. Then it sent out huge numbers of useless e-mail messages. At its peak, security experts estimate that 1 out of every 17 e-mail messages carried the SoBig virus, even more than the Love Bug's 1 in 20. It was estimated that SoBig sent out a mass mailing from infected computers—there were about 100,000 of those—at the rate of one every ten minutes.

Postrini Inc., an e-mail management and screening company, intercepted 1.9 million SoBig e-mails on their way to the company's customers on the first day of the virus's activation. By the next day the volume had increased to 3.5 million.

Whirlpool, a company with $11 billion a year in sales, says that about 95 percent of its sales come through the Internet and that its fast response to protect its 20,000 computers and 800 servers saved the company from suffering much damage. Others weren't so lucky. Experts say that part of the reason that SoBig was so effective was that it incorporated a line in its header that said "X-Scanner: Found to be clean," fooling a popular antivirus application that many Internet service providers use into letting the virus through.

SoBig was preprogrammed to stop replicating itself on September 10, 2003. By that time, it had infected more than five million e-mails. About eight times as many private computers were infected as corporate systems, since organizations moved faster to apply the patch that blocked the destruction.

Two of the many worms that hit networks in 2003 were the Slammer worm that hit in January and the Blaster worm that arrived in August. A worm looks for some flaw, or way to enter a computer, in software (often a Microsoft network operating system product) and sneaks in to do damage. Slammer kept flooding the victim server until its buffer memory was full, then it could trick that computer into sending out thousands of new copies to other servers that were vulnerable. Slammer sent out 55 million bursts of information per second onto the Internet and at that rate it took only ten minutes for the worm to find and invade almost all the vulnerable servers. Microsoft had a patch (a way of plugging the entry point) available on its Web site, but if the network administrators didn't download and apply it, their networks remained vulnerable until they did.

The Blaster worm appeared only 26 days after Microsoft publicized the vulnerability that the worm utilized. Blaster spread like wildfire and among the thousands of companies that were affected were CSX, the third-largest railroad company in North America, Amtrak, the commuter train company, and Air Canada. Passengers and freight in all three organizations experienced delays as their network traffic ground to a halt. Commuter trains in Washington, D.C., were delayed for two hours while IT experts worked feverishly to clean out the worm's effects while Air Canada's phone-reservation system and some check-in processes were slowed down.[8,9,10,11]

Standalone Viruses In any given month, between 200 and 300 viruses are travelling from system to system around the world, seeking a way in to spread mayhem.[12] And they're getting more deadly. Whereas the Love Bug worm was a Visual Basic script virus (i.e., it needed Visual Basic to run), the latest worms can stand alone and run on any computer that can run Win32 programs (Windows 98 or later versions). Examples are SirCam, Nimda, and Klez. Nimda adds JavaScript to every home page on the server it infects, then passes it on to visitors to the site. Viruses of this independent type are very numerous.

The Klez virus is actually a family of worms that introduced a new kind of confusion into the virus business. They spoof e-mail addresses. **Spoofing** is the forging of the return address on an e-mail so that the e-mail message appears to come from someone other than the actual sender. Previous worms went to the recipient from the infected sender's computer and contained the infected person's return e-mail address. The worm found recipient addresses in the infected computer's address book.

Klez goes a step further and uses the address book to randomly find a return address as well as recipient addresses. The result is that people who are not infected with the virus get e-mail from the irate recipients and spend time looking for a virus they may not have. Even worse, some of the virus-laden e-mails look as though they came from a technical support person, leading an unsuspecting victim to open them, believing them to be safe.

Trojan Horse Viruses A type of virus that doesn't replicate is a Trojan horse virus. A **Trojan horse virus** hides inside other software, usually an attachment or download. The principle of any Trojan horse software is that there's software you don't want hidden inside software you do want. For example, Trojan horse software can carry the "ping of death" program that hides in a server until the originators are ready to launch a DoS attack to crash a Web site.

Key-logger software is usually available in Trojan horse form, so that you can hide it in e-mail or other Internet traffic. **Key logger**, or **key trapper**, **software** is a program that, when installed on a computer, records every keystroke and mouse click. Key logger software is used to snoop on people to find out what they're doing on a particular computer. You can find out more in Chapter 9.

Misleading E-mail One type of misleading e-mail is a virus hoax. This is e-mail sent intending to frighten people about a virus threat that is, in fact, bogus. People who get such an alert will usually tell others, who react in the same way. The virus is nonexistent, but the hoax causes people to get scared and lose time and productivity. Within companies the losses can be very severe since computer professionals must spend precious time and effort looking for a nonexistent problem.

Here are some general clues for identifying a virus hoax:[13]

- It urges you to forward it to everyone you know, immediately.
- It describes the awful consequences of not acting immediately.
- It quotes a well-known authority in the computer industry.

These are signs that the e-mail is not meant to help but to cause harm. If you get such an e-mail, delete it immediately.

Another type of misleading e-mail is designed to get people to actually take action that results in setting a virus loose or to do something that will disrupt the functioning of their own computers. The first step is usually to make people believe that they have inadvertently e-mailed a virus to others. They get a message (maybe it purports to come from Microsoft) that they have sent out a virus and that they need to run an attached program or delete a file to fix the problem. They then do what the e-mail says, believing it to be genuine, and furthermore, they e-mail everyone they sent messages to telling them about the problem. The recipients e-mail the people in their address books and so on. Be advised that Microsoft *never* sends out attachments in any official e-mail in a public mass mailing. It's possible that Microsoft may e-mail you warning you of a problem, but it will only indicate where you can download a file to take care of it. Before you delete a file from your computer, which may be an important system file without which your computer can't function, ask someone who knows or check out the various Web sites that keep up with the latest viruses, such as www.symantec.com.

Denial-of-Service Attacks Many organizations have been hit with **denial-of-service (DoS) attacks**, which flood a Web site with so many requests for service that it slows down or crashes. The objective is to prevent legitimate customers from getting into the site to do business. There are several types. A DoS attack can come from a lone computer that tries continuously to access the target computer, or from many, perhaps even thousands, of computers simultaneously. The latter is called a distributed denial-of-service attack and is considerably more devastating.

Distributed Denial-of-Service Attacks **Distributed denial-of-service (DDoS) attacks** come from multiple computers that flood a Web site with so many requests for service that it slows down or crashes. A common type is the Ping of Death, in which thousands of computers try to access a Web site at the same time, overloading it and shutting it down. A ping attack can also bring down the firewall server (the computer that protects the network), giving free access to the intruders. E*TRADE, Amazon.com, and Yahoo!, among others, have been victims of this nasty little game. The process is actually very simple (see Figure K.4).

The plan starts with the hackers planting a program in network servers that aren't protected well enough. Then, on a signal sent to the servers from the attackers, the program activates and each server "pings" every computer. A ping is a standard operation that networks use to check that all computers are functioning properly. It's a sort of roll call for the network computers. The server asks, "Are you there?" and each computer in turn answers, "Yes, I'm here." But the hacker ping is different in that the return address of the are-you-there? message is not the originating server, but the intended victim's server. So on a signal from the hackers, thousands of computers try to access E*TRADE or Amazon.com, to say "Yes, I'm here." The flood of calls overloads the online companies' computers and they can't conduct business.

For many companies, a forced shutdown is embarrassing and costly, but for others it's much more than that. For an online stockbroker, for example, denial-of-service attacks can be disastrous. It may make a huge difference whether you buy shares of stock today or tomorrow. And since stockbrokers need a high level of trust from customers to do business, the effect of having been seen to be so vulnerable is very bad for business.

Combination Worm/DoS Code Red, discovered in 2001, was the first virus that combined a worm and a DoS attack. Code Red attacked servers running a specific type of system software. It used e-mail address books to send itself to lots of computers, and it was very efficient, with the ability to infect as many as 500,000 new servers per day. Its first action was to deface the Web site it infected. Then it went about finding other servers to infect. The last part of the plan was for all the infected servers to attack the White House Web site and shut it down. Having been warned of the

Figure K.4

Distributed Denial-of-Service Attack

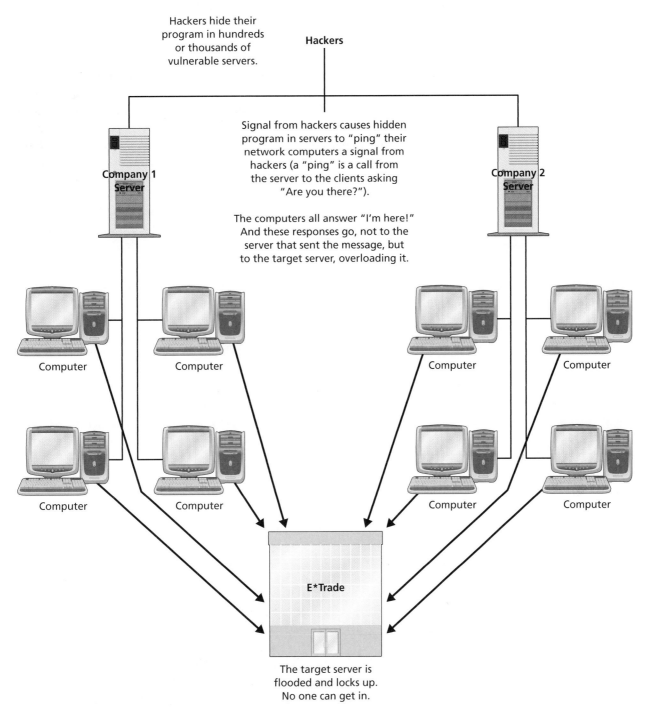

Hackers hide their program in hundreds or thousands of vulnerable servers.

Hackers

Signal from hackers causes hidden program in servers to "ping" their network computers a signal from hackers (a "ping" is a call from the server to the clients asking "Are you there?").

The computers all answer "I'm here!" And these responses go, not to the server that sent the message, but to the target server, overloading it.

Company 1 Server

Company 2 Server

Computer   Computer   Computer   Computer

Computer   Computer   Computer   Computer

E*Trade

The target server is flooded and locks up. No one can get in.

impending attack, the White House changed the IP address of its Web site. Nevertheless, before it was all over, Code Red cost an estimated $2.4 billion in prevention, detection, and cleanup even though it didn't destroy files or otherwise do much damage. This type of attack power is potentially very dangerous.

The Blaster worm in 2003 was also of the combination worm/DoS type. Blaster was programmed to launch a DoS against Microsoft's upgrade page on the Internet on August 16. Microsoft changed the address of its page so that the attempt would fail.

WEB SITE DEFACEMENT   Web site defacement is a favourite sport of some of the people who break into computer systems. They replace the site with a substitute that's neither attractive nor complimentary (see Figure K.5). Or perhaps they convert it to a mostly blank screen with an abusive or obscene message, or to a message reading "So-and-so was here." In essence, it's electronic graffiti, with a keyboard and mouse taking the place of a spraycan.

In 2000, during a flare-up in tensions between Israel and the Palestinians, Israelis defaced the Web sites of Hezbollah and Hamas. In retaliation, Palestinians brought down Israeli government sites and then turned their attention to Web sites of pro-Israeli groups in the United States.

Web site defacement is becoming increasingly popular, and sites accessed by many people worldwide are particular favourites. The USAToday.com Web site was attacked in July 2002, causing the newspaper to shut down the whole site for three hours to fix the problem. The hackers replaced several news stories on the site with bogus stories full of spelling errors. One story said that the Pope had called Christianity "a sham." The phoney stories were on the site for 15 minutes before being spotted.[14]

Figure K.5

The Defacing of the U.S. Department of Justice's Web Site

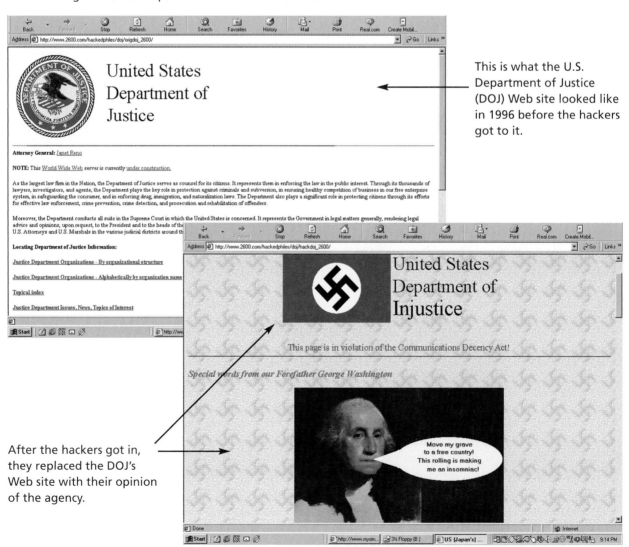

This is what the U.S. Department of Justice (DOJ) Web site looked like in 1996 before the hackers got to it.

After the hackers got in, they replaced the DOJ's Web site with their opinion of the agency.

THE PLAYERS Who's spreading all this havoc? The answer is **hackers**—knowledgeable computer users who use their knowledge to invade other people's computers. There are several categories of hackers, and their labels change over time. The motivation and reasons for hacking are as many and varied as the people who engage in it, as is illustrated in the following discussion.

Thrill-Seeker Hackers **Thrill-seeker hackers** break into computer systems for entertainment. Sometimes, they consider themselves to be the "good guys" since they expose vulnerabilities and some even follow a "hackers' code." Although they break into computers they have no right to access, they may report the security leaks to the victims. Their thrill is in being able to get into someone else's computer. Their reward is usually the admiration of their fellow hackers. There's plenty of information on the Web for those who want to know how to hack into a system—about 2000 sites offer free hacking tools, according to security experts.

White-Hat Hackers The thrill-seeker hackers used to be called white-hat hackers. But lately, the term *white-hat* is being increasingly used to describe the hackers who legitimately, with the knowledge of the owners of the IT system, try to break in to find and fix vulnerable areas of the system. These **white-hat hackers**, or **ethical hackers**, are computer security professionals who are hired by a company to break into a computer system. These hackers are also called counter hackers, or penetration testers.

Black-Hat Hackers **Black-hat hackers** are cyber vandals. They exploit or destroy the information they find, steal passwords, or otherwise cause harm. They deliberately cause trouble for people just for the fun of it. They create viruses, bring down computer systems, and steal or destroy information.

A 16-year-old black-hat hacker was sentenced to detention for six months after he hacked into military and NASA networks. He caused the systems to shut down for three weeks. He intercepted more than 3000 e-mails and stole the names and passwords of 19 defence agency employees. He also downloaded temperature and humidity control software worth $1.7 billion that helps control the environment in the international space station's living quarters.[15]

Crackers **Crackers** are hackers for hire and are the people who engage in electronic corporate espionage. This can be a pretty lucrative undertaking, paying up to $1 million per gig. Typically an espionage job will take about three weeks and may involve unpleasant tasks like dumpster diving to find passwords and other useful information and "social engineering." **Social engineering** is conning your way into acquiring information that you have no right to. Social engineering methods include calling someone in a company and pretending to be a technical support person and getting that person to type in a login and password, sweet-talking an employee to get information, and for difficult jobs, perhaps even setting up a fake office and identity. Often when crackers have accumulated about $500 million, they retire to some country that doesn't have an extradition agreement with the country they cracked in.[16]

Hacktivists **Hacktivists** are hackers who use the Internet to send a political message of some kind. The message can be a call to end world hunger, or it can involve an alteration of a political party's Web site so that it touts another party's candidate. It can be a slogan for a particular cause or some sort of diatribe inserted into a Web site to mock a particular religious or national group.

MAKE UP A GOOD PASSWORD

One way to protect files, folders, entry into stock trading, banking, and other sites is to have a good password. That's the theory anyway. The problem is that most people choose passwords that are easy to remember, and consequently they're easy for others, who perhaps have malevolent intentions, to crack. Others write passwords down, which makes them very accessible to anyone who comes near your desk. Often hackers can get access to a server by way of a legitimate user's ID and password.

Another problem that companies face is that people seem to be unaware of how important it is to keep passwords secret. In a London underground (subway) station, an experiment was conducted in which commuters were offered a cheap pen if they would disclose the password to their company's system. A very large number of people took the deal. Of course, there's no way to know whether they actually gave their real passwords or not, but judging from other studies, it's not unlikely that they did.

ZDNet offers some good advice on picking passwords. You should never pick a password that has a word from any dictionary, or one that is a pet's name or a person's. Instead, you should pick a phrase and use the first letter of each word. Then capitalize some letters and substitute punctuations and digits for others.

For example, the saying "just hang loose, just have fun, you only live once" would become JhL?H6+oLo. If you can remember the mnemonic and your substitutions, you'll certainly have a password that will be hard to break.

To find out about breaking passwords, look on the Web for information about "Jack the Ripper," which is a well-known password-cracking program. Find three more such programs and note whether they're public domain, freeware, shareware, etc. At www.elcom soft.com you'll find all sorts of password crackers for Microsoft and other popular products. The stated purpose of this site is to help you recover lost corporate files. What other "helpful" products do this, and what do other, similar sites have?

Hacktivism, in the form of Web defacement, is becoming a common response to disagreements between nations. When the U.S. military plane made an emergency landing in China and a dispute arose about the return of the crew and plane, U.S. hackers started to attack Chinese Web sites, and Chinese hackers returned the favour, targeting government-related sites.

Cyberterrorists Since September 11, 2001, officials have become increasingly worried about the threat of cyberterrorists. This group of hackers, like the hacktivists, is politically motivated, but its agenda is more sinister. A **cyberterrorist** is one who seeks to cause harm to people or destroy critical systems or information. Possible targets of violent attacks would be air traffic control systems and nuclear power plants, and anything else that could harm the infrastructure of a nation. At a less lethal level, cyberterrorist acts would include shutting down e-mail or even part of the Internet itself, or destroying government records, say on social security benefits or criminals.

However, the FBI and other government agencies are very much aware of the threats they face from computer-based attacks, and have taken steps to protect the infrastructure that supports cyberspace. They can enjoy a reasonable expectation of success, since a computer system is a lot easier to protect than public structures like buildings and bridges.

Script Kiddies **Script kiddies** or **script bunnies** are people who would like to be hackers but don't have much technical expertise. They download click-and-point software that automatically does the hacking for them. An example of this was the young man in Holland who found a virus toolkit on the Web and started the Kournikova worm. It was very similar to the Love Bug worm in that it sent itself to all the people in the Outlook address book. Tens of millions of people got the virus after opening the attachment hoping to see a picture of Anna Kournikova.[17]

The concern about script kiddies, according to the experts, apart from the fact that they can unleash viruses and denial-of-service attacks, is that they can be used by more sinister hackers. These people manipulate the script kiddies, egging them on in chat rooms, encouraging and helping them to be more destructive.

INSIDE THE ORGANIZATION

There are plenty of attacks visited on an organization's computer system from outside the organization but insider fraud and embezzlement are where the big bucks are lost. You can find more information on insider crime in Chapter 9.

Along with the traditional crimes of fraud and other types of theft managers sometimes have to deal with harassment of one employee by another. Chevron Corporation and Microsoft settled sexual harassment lawsuits for $2.2 million each because employees sent offensive e-mail to other employees and management didn't intervene. Other companies such as Dow Chemical Company, Xerox, the New York Times Company, and Edward Jones took preemptive action by firing people who sent or stored pornographic or violent e-mail messages.

But companies have learned to be careful when investigating harassment complaints, as the following example from Walt's case file shows. One company had a complaint from a woman who claimed a male colleague was sending her offensive e-mail. The colleague denied it, but when his computer was checked, the pornographic pictures that the woman claimed she had received from him in e-mails were found. This might have meant his dismissal, but, fortunately, a computer forensics expert was called in. The expert looked beyond the pictures and discovered that the times and dates the e-mails were downloaded and sent corresponded with times the man was out of town. Later, the woman admitted that she had downloaded the pictures and e-mailed them to herself from the man's computer. If the company hadn't been as thorough in its investigation, it could have escaped a harassment lawsuit only to find itself facing a wrongful termination lawsuit.

What exactly did the computer forensics expert do? We'll discuss that in the next two sections.

Computer Forensics

You may remember some of the following recent news stories:

- Federal Bureau of Prisons intern Chandra Levy had not been seen since April 30, 2001. She had used the Internet when making travel plans to return to California and had e-mailed her parents about her travel plans. The police found partly packed suitcases and her wallet and credit cards in her apartment. She was later found dead.
- A search that ended on March 5, 2002, found 339 discarded bodies on the grounds of Tri-State Funeral home in Walker Country. Ray Brent Marsh was formally charged with multiple counts of abusing a corpse and almost two hundred counts of fraud for allegedly taking money for cremations that were not performed and for giving loved ones fake remains. Photos of the dead bodies arranged in lewd poses appeared on the Internet.
- An engineer left Company A and went to Company B. Company A suspected that he had illegally brought intellectual property in the form of designs to his new employer. On his home computer, investigators found evidence that this was true. The engineer claimed that the clock on his home computer had malfunctioned and that the transfer of the designs occurred during the course of his work for Company A. However, his girlfriend's computer and a letter he wrote about the same time exposed this lie.[18]
- A *USA Today* veteran reporter was discovered to have fabricated many of his stories over the period 1993 to 2003. Furthermore, an examination of his company-owned computer revealed pieces that he had written to mislead investigators. This finding indicated consciousness of guilt.[19]

What all of these news stories have in common is the investigative technique that unearthed information—the process of the finding, examining, and analyzing electronic information saved on computer storage media. This process is called *computer forensics*. Many computer forensic investigations involve intellectual property cases, where a company believes that an employee is secretly copying and perhaps selling proprietary information such as schematics, customer lists, financial statements, product designs, or notes on private meetings. Other investigations involve child exploitation domestic disputes, labour relations, and employee misconduct cases. In all such cases, computer forensics is usually the appropriate response strategy.

Computer forensics is the collection, authentication, preservation, and examination of electronic information for presentation in court. Electronic evidence can be found on any type of computer media, such as hard disks, floppy disks, or CDs and also on digital cameras, PDAs, cell phones, and pagers. Computer forensic experts are trained in finding and interpreting electronic evidence to discover or reconstruct computer-related activities.

There are basically two motivations for engaging in computer forensics. The first is to gather and preserve evidence to present in court. The second is to establish what activities have occurred on a computer, often for the purposes of a dispute settlement. You probably know that if you're going to court, you must meet different evidentiary standards for criminal and civil cases. In criminal cases, the standard is "beyond a reasonable doubt." In civil cases, it's the "preponderance of evidence." If you don't have to, and don't want to, involve the legal system, your standard can be lower, perhaps just enough to release someone from employment while reducing the risk of being caught in a wrongful termination lawsuit.

In a well-conducted computer forensics investigation, there are two major phases: (1) collecting, authenticating, and preserving electronic evidence; and (2) analyzing the findings.

THE COLLECTION PHASE

Step one of the collection phase is to get physical access to the computer and related items. Thus, the computer forensic team collects computers, disks, printouts, Post-it notes, and so on and take them back to the lab. This process is similar to what police do when investigating crime in the physical world, collecting hair, clothing fibres, bloodstained articles, papers, and anything else that they think might be useful. The crime investigators usually take these potential clue carriers with them and secure them under lock and key, where only authorized personnel may have access, and even they must sign in and out.

Computer forensic experts use the same kind of protocol. To conduct a thorough investigation, they first take digital photos of the surrounding environment and start developing extensive documentation. Then they start collecting anything that might store information. The hard disk is an obvious place to look, but computer forensic investigators also collect any other media where information might be stored (see Figure K.6). If they can't take a clue source with them, they secure it and create an exact copy of the contents of the original media.

As well as electronic media, investigators collect any other potentially helpful items, especially passwords, for use in case any of the files they come across are encrypted or are otherwise difficult to access. Apparently, a favourite hiding place for passwords that people write down (which you should *not* do) is under the keyboard, so that's the first place investigators look. Then they look in desk drawers and anywhere else that passwords might be, perhaps on Post-it notes or slips of paper. Other helpful items might be printouts and business cards of associates or contacts of the person being investigated.

- Floppy disks
- CDs
- DVDs
- Zip disks
- Backup tapes of other media
- USB mass-storage devices
- Flash memory cards, such as an xD-Picture card, CompactFlash card, or similar storage medium for digital cameras and other devices
- Voice mail
- Electronic calendars
- Scanners
- Photocopiers
- Fax machines

Figure K.6

Where You Might Find Electronic Evidence

Step two of the collection process is to make a forensic image copy of all the information. A **forensic image copy** is an exact copy or snapshot of the contents of an electronic medium. It is sometimes referred to as a bit-stream image copy. To get a forensic image copy, specialized forensic software copies every fragment of information, bit by bit, on every storage medium—every hard disk (if there's more than one), every floppy disk, every CD, every Zip disk. That's usually a lot of stuff. Remember that a CD holds about a half a gigabyte of information, and you can build a hard disk array (several hard disks tied together into one unit) that holds a terabyte (one trillion bytes) or more. It can take a long, long time to copy it all. And the investigator must be able to swear in court that he or she supervised the entire copying process, and that no one and nothing interfered with the evidence. This could mean sitting in the lab literally for days just copying files. Also, many experts advise that the investigator make two copies of everything in case there's a problem later with the first copy.

THE AUTHENTICATION AND PRESERVATION PROCESS To get a forensic image copy of hard disk and other media contents, investigators physically remove the hard disk from the computer. They never turn the suspect computer on, because when the PC is turned on, Windows performs more than 400 changes to files. Access dates change, and so do temporary files, and so on. The hard drive is no longer exactly the same as it was when it was shut down.[20] Thus, opposing counsel could argue that this is not the same hard disk that the suspect used.

Having removed the hard disk, investigators connect it to a special forensic computer that can read files but can't write or rewrite any medium. (They prefer to remove storage devices, but if that's not possible, they copy the contents in place using cables.) Then they use forensic software such as EnCase to extract a forensic image copy of the original medium without changing the files in any way.

How do we know that nothing changed on any disk during the entire investigation, from the time the computer was seized up to the present time? That's the question that opposing counsel will ask the computer forensic expert on the witness stand. So, during the collection phase and later, the analysis phase, the investigators have to make absolutely sure that evidence to be used in a trial could not have been planted, eliminated, contaminated, or altered in any way. This is a basic evidentiary rule for all court proceedings. They have to be able to document a chain of custody and be able to account for the whereabouts and protection of evidence. To help establish a complete chronology of activity, investigators also check the BIOS, which a computer uses to time- and date-stamp files and actions like deleting, updating, and so on.

In a computer forensic investigation, investigators use an authentication process so that they can show sometime in the future—perhaps even two years later—that nothing changed on the hard drive or other storage medium since seizure. They can do this with an **MD5 hash value**, a mathematically generated string of 32 letters and digits that is unique for an individual storage medium at a specific point in time. The MD5 hash value is based on the contents of that medium. Any change in the content changes the MD5 hash value.

A hash value is a seemingly meaningless set of characters. An example of a hash value would be the sum of the ISBNs and the number of pages in all the books on a bookstore shelf. The result, which would be a mixture of ISBN codes and quantities of pages, would be meaningless for anything except identification. If a book, or even a page, were added to or removed from the shelf, the hash total would change, so the contents of the shelf could be shown not to be the same as they were when the hash value was originally computed. Similarly, adding so much as one space in one tiny Word document on a disk will change the MD5 hash value. See Figure K.7 for an example of an MD5 hash value generated by EnCase forensic software.

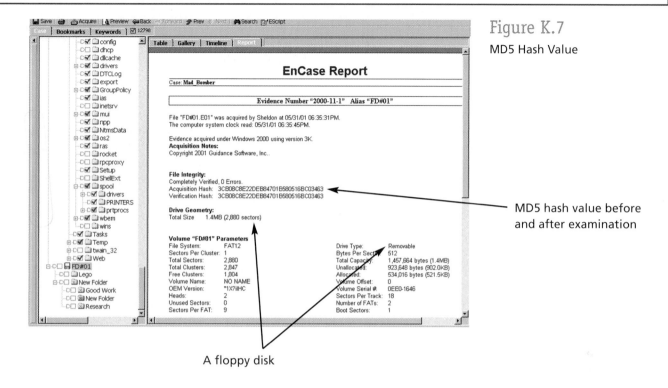

Figure K.7
MD5 Hash Value

A floppy disk

MD5 hash value before and after examination

MD5 hash values are considered very reliable and have become an industry standard accepted by the FBI, the U.S. Marshall Service, and most other law enforcement authorities, as well as private professional firms, as a way of uniquely authenticating a set of contents on a particular storage medium. This confidence in MD5 hash values is based on the fact that the probability of two hard disks with different contents having the same MD5 hash value is 1 in 10 to the 38th power: that's 1 with 38 zeros behind it. This makes the MD5 hash value a sort of DNA or fingerprint for computer media contents. Actually, it's more reliable than those physiological identifiers, since the probability of two sets of hard disk contents resulting in the same MD5 hash value are less than the odds of two individuals' DNA and fingerprints being identical. As an example of this probability, consider that you would have better odds of winning the Powerball lottery 39 times in your lifetime than you would of finding two hard disks with different contents that have matching MD5 hash values.

FORENSIC HARDWARE AND SOFTWARE TOOLS As we've already mentioned, computer forensic experts use special hardware and software to conduct investigations. Usually the computer system has more power than the standard computer on a desktop and much more RAM, as well as much more hard disk capacity. This is to speed up the copying and analysis process. Computer forensic experts are also very careful not to let static electricity cause any damage or changes to magnetic media (like hard disks, zips, and floppies). Therefore they use nonconductive mats under all computer parts, and wear wristbands that connect by wire to the ground of an electrical outlet. And just in case they need a tool, such as a screwdriver, they have a special nonmagnetic set of tools nearby, too.

There are many kinds of software in a computer forensics toolkit, in addition to forensic software, that can help in computer forensic investigations. Quick View Plus, used by many forensic experts, is an example. This is software that will load Word, Excel, image, and many other file formats. If it comes across a file with an .xls extension, which is actually an image and not a spreadsheet file, Quick View will show the file as an image regardless of its extension. That saves the investigator having to try it in multiple programs after loading fails in Excel. Conversions Plus is a package that does the same sort of thing. Other helpful software includes Mailbag Assistant, which reads many e-mail formats, and IrfanView, which is an image viewer that will read most picture files.

For investigations that might be headed toward litigation, computer forensic experts often use EnCase, since it's widely accepted as robust and reliable. EnCase has routinely been judged acceptable by the courts in meeting the legal standard for producing reliable evidence.

THE ANALYSIS PHASE

The second phase of the investigation is the analysis phase when the investigator follows the trail of clues and builds the evidence into a crime story. This is the phase that really tests the skill and experience of the investigators. The analysis phase consists of the recovery and interpretation of the information that's been collected and authenticated. If all the necessary files were there in plain sight with names and extensions indicating their contents, life would be much easier for the forensic investigator, but that's seldom the case. Usually, particularly if those being investigated know that they're doing something wrong, the incriminating files will have been deleted or hidden.

Investigators can recover all of a deleted file pretty easily as long as no new information has been written to the space where the file was. But, they can also recover fragments—perhaps rather large fragments—of files in parts of a disk where new files have been written, but have not completely filled the space where the old file was. With the appropriate software they can recover files or fragments of files from virtually any part of any storage medium (see Figure K.8).

Figure K.8

Some of the Files Recoverable from Storage Media

E-Mail Files
• E-mail messages • Deleted e-mail messages
Program Files and Data Files
• Word (.doc) and backup (.wbk) files • Excel files • Deleted files of all kinds • Files hidden in image and music files • Encrypted files • Compressed files
Web Activity Files
• Web history • Cache files • Cookies
Network Server Files
• Backup e-mail files • Other backup and archived files • System history files • Web log files

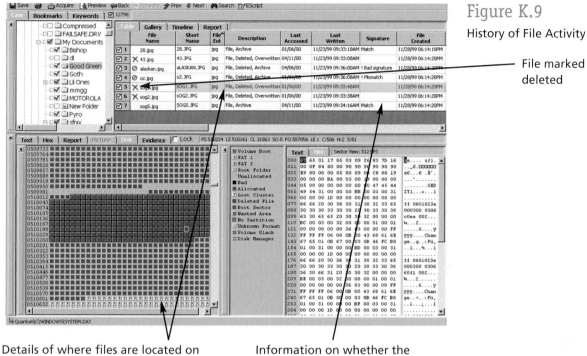

Figure K.9

History of File Activity

File marked as deleted

Details of where files are located on the disk, whether they've been deleted, overwritten, or archived

Information on whether the contents matches the extension or not

Computer forensic programs can pinpoint a file's location on the disk, its creator, the date it was created, the date of last access, and sometimes the date it was deleted, as well as file formatting, and notes embedded or hidden in a document (see Figure K.9).

Also stored on the hard disk is information about where the computer user went on the Web. For example, every graphic image you view on the Internet is copied to your hard disk, usually without your knowledge. In addition, Web servers have information on which computer connected to the Web and when. The same server can also tell you the sites visited by the user of that computer, the date and time of the visits, and the actions of the user at the site. These attributes are useful if the suspect claims to have reached an inappropriate site by accident, since delving deeper into the site implies a deliberate action. And, of course, if a password was required to reach the material in question, you can rest your case. With all the development in computing and investigative techniques, computer forensics experts need a forum to exchange ideas and information. Professional organizations provide such a forum (see Figure K.10).

Recovery and Interpretation

As with all evidence, the analysis of the electronic clues and the assembling of the pieces into a credible and likely scenario of what happened are very important. Much of the information may come from recovered deleted files, currently unused disk space, and deliberately hidden information or files. Some people's e-mail that was recovered to their extreme embarrassment (or worse) but arguably to society's benefit is shown in Figure K.11.

Following is a discussion, not necessarily exhaustive, of places from which computer forensic experts can recover information.

Figure K.10

Professional Organizations and Standards

Professional organizations exist that support computer forensic experts in doing their jobs. The organizations below provide interaction between members who share information, experience, and methods. Such organizations also provide ethical guidelines and certification.

- IACIS (International Association of Computer Investigation Specialists) is open to law enforcement personnel and sets standards and guidelines for computer forensic investigations.
- ACFE (Association of Certified Fraud Examiners) focuses on serving those who investigate fraud. Members include people in law enforcement, auditors, accountants, and computer forensic experts.
- The HTCIA (High Technology Crime Investigation Association) is open to law enforcement and corporate investigators alike and facilitates the sharing of resources among its members.

A group called the Sedona Conference Working Group on Electronic Document Production published *The Sedona Principles: Best Practices, Recommendations & Principles for Addressing Electronic Document Production.* The document, the first draft of which emerged in 2003, is a new set of standards pertaining to properly conducting a computer forensic investigation. These principles were developed by lawyers, consultants, academics, and jurists to address the many issues involved in antitrust suits, intellectual property disputes, and other types of complex litigation.

Figure K.11

Recovered E-mail Messages
(continued on next page)

" . . . something could get screwed up enough . . . and then you are in a world of hurt . . . "

and

"I can only hope the folks . . . are listening . . . "

Excerpts of e-mail traffic that flew back and forth only two days before the February 1, 2003, Columbia shuttle disaster, in which an engineer discussed his misgivings about the possibility of a disaster

One of the "smoking gun" e-mails that helped sink Andersen Consulting and Enron

To: David B. Duncan
Cc: Michael C. Odom@ANDERSEN WO: Richard Corgci@ANDERSEN WO
BCC:
Date: 10/16/2001 08:39 PM
From: Nancy A. Temple
Subject: Re: Press Release draft
Attachments: ATT&ICIQ: 3rd qtr press release memo.doc

Dave - Here are a few suggested comments for consideration.

- I recommend deleting reference to consultation with the legal group and deleting my name on the memo. Reference to the legal group consultation arguably is a waiver of attorney-client privileged advice and if my name is mentioned it increases the chances that I might be a witness, which I prefer to avoid.

- I suggested deleting some language that might suggest we have concluded the release is misleading.

- In light of the "non-recurring" characterization, the lack of any suggestion that this characterization is not in accordance with GAAP, and the lack of income statements in accordance with GAAP, I will consult further within the legal group as to whether we should do anything more to protect ourselves from potential Section 10A issues.

Figure K.11

Recovered E-mail Messages *(continued from previous page)*

From:	Lewinsky, Monica, OSD/PA 833-DC-00009446
To:	Tripp, Linda, , OSD/PA
Subject:	I'm back!
Date:	Wednesday, February 19, 1997 8:09AM
Priority:	High

LRT— Hi, I missed you!!!! I hope you enjoyed your few days of sanity with me gone because I'm back and NOT in good spirits.

1. I have a small present for you. Everything was SOOOOO expensive so I'm sorry it's small.

2. Nice that the Big Creep didn't even try to call me on V-day and he didn't know for sure that I was going back to London.

3. He could have called last night and didn't. He was out of town.

4. Finally, the ????? went away and it was the same night he was gone. ▮▮▮me!!!!

HHHEEELLPPP!!!!

Maybe we can have lunch or meet sometime today cuz I want to give you your present.

Bye...msl

From Monica Lewinsky to Linda Tripp

"oops I haven't beaten anyone so bad in a long time...."

From the arresting officer in the Rodney King beating

From Bill Gates in an intraoffice e-mail about a competitor in the Microsoft antitrust action

" . . . do we have a clear plan on what we want Apple to do to undermine Sun . . . ?"

PLACES TO LOOK FOR USEFUL INFORMATION

Information is written all over a disk, not only when you save a file, but also when you create folders, print documents, repartition the disk, and so on. System and application software alike continually create temporary files resulting in space and file locations being rearranged. Leftover information stays on the disk until another file writes over it, and is often recoverable with forensic software. Next, we'll examine three places where files or file remnants could be: slack space, unallocated disk space, and unused disk space.

DELETED FILES AND SLACK SPACE It's actually not very easy to get rid of electronically stored information completely. A surprising number of people think that if they delete a file it's gone. It's not—at least not immediately, and perhaps never. When you delete a file, all you're actually doing is marking it as deleted in the disk's directory. The actual file contents are not affected *at all* by a delete action.

If you delete a file from a hard disk you usually get a message asking you if you want it in the *Recycle Bin* and then you can recover it simply by using the *Undelete* option. On a removable medium, such as a zip or floppy disk, it's a little harder, but not much. The message you get asks whether you're sure you want to delete the file because it may not be recoverable. Actually that message should read "not as easily recoverable as files in the Recycle Bin," since you can get it back with utility programs such as Norton Utilities, and of course, forensic software.

When you mark a file as deleted, the space is freed up for use by some other file. So another file may shortly be written to that space. However, it's not quite that straightforward. The operating system divides storage space into sectors of bytes or characters. The sectors are grouped into clusters. A file is assigned a whole number of clusters for storage, whether it completely fills the last cluster or not. This storage allocation method usually leaves unused portions of clusters. This is analogous to writing a three-and-one-half-page report. You'd have to use the top half of the fourth page and leave the rest of the page blank. So the fourth page is allocated to the report but not completely used. If the previously stored file (the deleted one) was bigger and used that last part of the space, then the remnants of the deleted file remain and can be recovered using the appropriate software. The space left over from the end of the file to the end of the cluster is called **slack space**, and information left there from previous files can be recovered by forensic software (see Figure K.12).

SYSTEM AND REGISTRY FILES   Operating system files manage the hardware and software of your computer and let your application software access hardware without having to know how all the various types of hardware function. As one of its many functions, the operating system controls virtual memory. Virtual memory is hard disk

Figure K.12

Fragment of E-Mail Found in Slack Space by EnCase

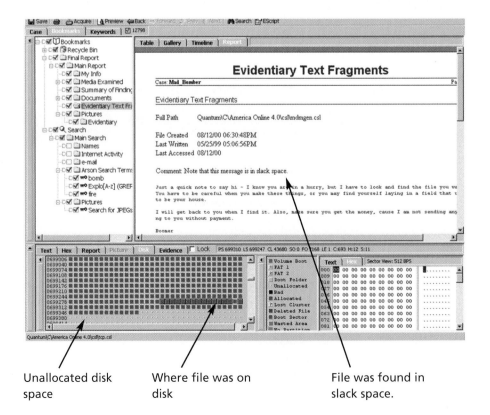

Unallocated disk space

Where file was on disk

File was found in slack space.

space that is used when RAM is full. Details of virtual memory activity are stored in system files. For example, if you have several applications running and you're instant messaging someone, that exchange may be stored on the hard disk without your knowing it simply because there wasn't room for it in RAM.

The Registry is the database that Windows uses to store configuration information. Registry files have information such as preferences for users of the system, settings for the hardware, system software, and installed programs. This information can be very valuable. For example, even if you uninstall a program, remnants of the install process remain in the Registry file. Registry files also contain the MAC (Media Access Control) address, which is a special ID for a computer on a network. When this MAC address is contained in a file, as it is in a Word document, it links that document file to its "owner" computer.

UNALLOCATED DISK SPACE If your hard disk gets a lot of use, it's probable that each sector has had information put into it many times. The operating system is always moving files around, and if you changed a Word file and resaved it, the previous version is marked as deleted and the space becomes unallocated. **Unallocated space** is the set of clusters that has been marked as available to store information, but has not yet received a file, or still contains some or all of a file marked as deleted. Until the new information takes up residence, the old information remains. The bigger the hard disk, the longer it usually takes for old space to be used.

UNUSED DISK SPACE Unused space results from rearranging disk space. For example, when a hard drive is repartitioned, the new partitioning may not use all the space on the hard disk. So, again, those unused portions are not overwritten. The partition table and other operating system information are stored on their own tracks and are not visible under normal circumstances, but may have once stored a Word document. To be able to see the fragments of files tucked away in these tracks the user needs forensic software.

ERASED INFORMATION By now you may be asking whether it's possible to completely erase information from a storage medium. It is possible, but you need to know what you're doing. You can get disk-wiping programs that erase information from a disk by writing nonsense information over the previous contents. Utilities like Norton have this feature. However, erasing a disk takes a lot of time. A 10-gigabyte hard disk (not very big) would take several hours to clean. Even then you're not necessarily safe, for three reasons:

- A single overwrite may not erase the information completely. The Department of Justice recommends that government agencies write over old information seven times to be sure it's completely gone.
- Some programs keep track of what was deleted by whom, and that record is viewable if you know where to look.
- Disk-wiping programs vary greatly in which parts of the hard disk they clean. For most of them, you have to change the settings to reach certain parts of the disk. Some claim to go through the wipe process up to 35 times, but that still doesn't erase the areas that the software isn't set to erase. Also keep in mind that if you're trying to erase information because of some illicit activity, traces may still be left of the information you're trying to discard, and unless you are very careful, you'll leave traces of your attempt to wipe the disk. At the very least, you'll most likely leave a record in the Registry that you installed the wiping program.

WAYS OF HIDING INFORMATION

There are many ways of deliberately hiding information (other than deleting the file) and some are easy to defeat and others are not so easy. Following is a sampling of methods that people use to try to hide files.

RENAME THE FILE The simplest, and most easily detected, way of deliberately hiding a file in Windows is to change the extension of the file. Say you had an Excel file that had calculations you didn't want anyone to know about, you could name the file Space Needle.jpg. Then it would appear in Explorer in the list of files as a .jpeg image file, with the name implying that it's just a vacation photo or something else innocuous.

However, if you try to click on that file, Windows will try to load it with the default .jpg viewer. And, of course, it won't load. What computer forensic experts usually do is load the file into a program that accommodates many file formats. This way, you save a lot of time trying to load the renamed file into lots of different types of software. Even more helpful is a forensic tool like EnCase that actually flags files with extensions that don't match the contents and also show files in their true formats.

MAKE THE INFORMATION INVISIBLE They always say that the best hiding place is in plain sight. A very simple way to hide information inside a file, say a Word document, is to make the information the same colour as the background. This works in Excel and other types of files, too. So if you suspect that something interesting is hidden this way, you could check the size of the file to see if it looks consistent with the contents. Also, software like EnCase is not affected by formatting. So, even white-on-white text will be easily searchable and readable by the forensic investigator.

USE WINDOWS TO HIDE FILES Windows has a utility to hide files of a specific type. You simply open up that drive or folder, choose View, then Options, and hide the files by indicating what extensions you want hidden. If you go through this process, you'll probably see that there's a list of hidden files already on your computer. These are files that have to do with the correct functioning of your computer and to list them would just clutter up Windows Explorer and risk their being changed or deleted by accident. Again, forensic software takes special note of hidden files and flags them for further investigation.

PROTECT THE FILE WITH A PASSWORD Word lets you password-protect files so that when someone tries to open the file a pop-up window asks for the password. Unless you know the password, you won't be able to read the file. Forensic software can view the contents of many file types without opening the file, eliminating the effectiveness of many types of password protection.

ENCRYPT THE FILE Encryption scrambles the contents of a file so that you can't read it without the right decryption key. Often investigators can find the decryption key in a password file or on a bit of paper somewhere around the keyboard. There are also password-cracking programs that will find many passwords very easily (alarmingly easily, in fact). They have dictionaries of words from multiple languages, so whole words from any language are not hard to crack. Some people put a digit or two on the front or back of a word. That doesn't fool password-cracking programs at all.

Sometimes investigators can figure out passwords from knowing something about the person. That's why birthdays, anniversaries, children's or pet's names are not good passwords. Also, since you usually need passwords for lots of reasons and it's hard to remember lots of different random ones, many people use just two or three different passwords. So if investigators find one password, they can try that in multiple places. Also, having one password often offers a clue as to what the other passwords might be. For example, if one password an investigator discovers is a fragment of a nursery rhyme, then the others might be, too.

USE STEGANOGRAPHY **Steganography** is the hiding of information inside other information. Paper money is a good example of steganography. If you hold a dollar bill up to the light you'll see a watermark. The watermark image is hidden inside the other markings on the bill, but can be viewed if you know what to do to see it.

You can electronically hide information using this method. For example, if you want to hide a text file inside an image file, you can use a program called Steganos that does the work for you. Steganos takes nonessential parts of the image and replaces them with the hidden file. "Nonessential" means that these are parts of the picture that you can't see anyway, so changing those to the hidden message makes the message invisible (see Figure K.13). Steganography is a process is similar to file compression, where nonessential information is removed to save space, rather than to hide it.

The FBI and other law enforcement agencies believe that worldwide terrorist networks communicate using steganography. They set up a Web site and find pictures in which they can hide messages. When the message is hidden, the innocent-looking picture goes back up on the Web site. Fellow terrorists can download the picture, and open it with special software. With the correct password, the hidden message appears. Forensic investigators look for clues about steganography by searching for the names of steg programs.

Figure K.13

Steganography Hides a File in an Image

You can't see the parts of the picture that were changed to encode the hidden message. You'll only be able to access the hidden file when you put the right password into a pop-up window.

COMPRESS THE FILE   Compressing a file makes it invisible to keyword searches. To find out what's in it you'll have to decompress it with the right software or use a newer version of EnCase that reads compressed files. This decompression software may be on the hard disk or on another disk somewhere around the suspect's desk. That's why investigators take all media for examination.

Who Needs Computer Forensics Investigators?

Computer forensics is widely used wherever and whenever the investigation of electronically stored files is warranted, such as:

- In the military, both as part of national security intelligence gathering and analysis and for internal investigations of military personnel
- In law enforcement, when the RCMP, provincial investigatory agencies, and local police departments need to gather electronic evidence for criminal investigations
- Inside corporations or not-for-profit organizations, when conducting internal audits, for example, or investigating internal incidents
- In consulting firms that specialize in providing computer forensic services to corporations and law enforcement

Computer forensics experts work both proactively, educating and warning people about possible problems, and reactively, when they're called in to help in response to an incident. The need for such expertise is growing, especially considering that in 1999 it was estimated that 93 percent of all information generated was in digital form.

PROACTIVE COMPUTER FORENSICS EDUCATION FOR PROBLEM PREVENTION

Companies are increasingly providing proactive education for two reasons: first, to educate employees on what to do and not to do with computer resources and why; and second, to teach employees what to do if they suspect wrongdoing, and how not to make things worse by destroying evidence.

People who use computers every day are often not very knowledgeable about what, when, and how information is stored on computers. For example, many corporations have strict policies on how long e-mails will be kept on the system (or in the form of backups). Usually the period of time is about 60 days. You might decide to save your e-mails on your hard disk so that you'll have them indefinitely. This might not be wise, since the reason that companies have this policy is that should the company find itself involved in litigation, all electronic information, including e-mail, may be discoverable. That is, the company may have to hand it over to opposing counsel. The more there is, the more it costs to collect, organize, and deliver it.

In Chapter 9 you saw how much personal information can become public information on the Internet. In the On Your Own project here, you can test what you know about some basic issues that face employees.

The second reason for providing some education in computer forensics has to do with conducting internal investigations properly. Say a company wants to file a complaint with law enforcement about the suspected illegal activity of an employee. Before law enforcement can look into the situation, however, it needs to have sufficient cause

HOW MUCH DO YOU KNOW?

It's been said that what you don't know can't hurt you. That may be true in some circumstances, but not in the cyber world. What you don't know about what happens on your computer can cause you all kinds of trouble. Test your knowledge about what goes on inside your computer. If someone asked you to respond as to the wisdom or foolishness of the following statements, what would you say (include explanations of your answers)?

1. My computer at work is safe, secure, and private.
2. When I delete a file from my hard disk, it's removed from the disk.
3. I'll be safe from any investigators as long as I use a disk-wiping program on my hard disk.
4. Computers store files only when you explicitly save them.
5. As long as I don't save the inappropriate images I view on the Web, no one will ever be the wiser.
6. Sending a joke from my work e-mail will be fine as long as I put a smiley-face emoticon after it.
7. As long as I don't open e-mail attachments I don't recognize, I can't possibly get a virus.

to do so. It can happen that in collecting relevant information the company inadvertently contaminates or destroys the "crime scene." The result may be that law enforcement can't prosecute after all because of lack of evidence.

REACTIVE COMPUTER FORENSICS FOR INCIDENT RESPONSE

Companies need computer forensics, in a reactive mode, to track what employees have been doing with company resources. You saw in Chapter 9 that employees may be using the Internet to such an extent during working hours that their productivity is affected, and the level of personal traffic on the company network may be such that people who are actually working are slowed down. This is just one example of misuse of the company computer system. The evidence of such misappropriation of computer resources can be found on the system itself—on individual client computers and on the servers.

A second reason for reactive computer forensics is changes in laws and government regulations and new laws passed as a consequence of recent corporate crime and misbehaviour, probably the most important being the Sarbanes-Oxley Act of 2002, in the United States. Sarbanes-Oxley requires companies to (1) implement extensive and detailed policies to prevent illegal activity within the company and (2) respond in a timely manner to investigate illegal activity.

The act expressly states that executives must certify that their financial statements are accurate. They will be held criminally liable for fraudulent reporting, removing the insulation that executives previously had of being able to say that they didn't know about misstatements. Sarbanes-Oxley also specifically requires publicly traded companies to provide anonymous hotlines so that employees and others can report suspicious activity.

The provision that suspicious activity must be investigated in a timely manner in many instances automatically requires computer forensics. In earlier litigation, courts have determined that computer-stored evidence is crucial to the proper investigation of alleged corporate fraud. Add to that the fact that delay in investigating alleged wrongdoing meets with severe penalties and that courts impose severe sanctions on those judged guilty of destroying evidence including electronic information.

A DAY IN THE LIFE OF A COMPUTER FORENSICS EXPERT

You may be considering computer forensics as a profession. If so, you're contemplating a vocation that's very demanding but very rewarding. You have to know a lot about computers, and you have to keep learning to keep up with the fast pace of the computer world. You have to have infinite patience and be very detail-oriented. You also have to be good at explaining to lawyers, juries, and other nonexperts how computers work. You have to be able to remain very cool under pressure and think fast since some of the situations you face will be quite adversarial. Lanny Morrow has these qualities.

Lanny is a computer forensics expert with the Forensic and Dispute Consulting division of BKD, LLP, one of the largest accounting firms in the United States. All sorts of organizations, both for-profit and not-for-profit, and legal firms needing detective work done inside computers hire BKD's computer forensics services called Data Probe.

Lanny's cases are many and varied, making his life very interesting. Some cases take a long time and others are resolved pretty fast like the divorce case where the wife believed that her husband was hiding assets and that the records were on their home computer. No one (wife, lawyers, friends) could find anything incriminating on the hard drive or on any other storage medium. But the wife was adamant that the records were there. Lanny was called in. His first step as always was to open up the computer and have a look inside to see if anything in there looked unusual. And there it was—a second hard drive that wasn't plugged in, and was just sitting inside the system unit. When the husband wanted to do his secret accounting, he just opened up the box and swapped hard disk connections, reversing the process when he was done.

Sometimes Lanny can save a reputation, rather than proving wrongdoing, as in the case of the popular schoolteacher. As a lark, some of the teacher's female students, who were using his computer, decided to search for .jpg image files. They found some pornography and were very upset. They told their parents who immediately contacted a lawyer who in turn contacted the school. The school's information technology staff confirmed that there were many pornographic pictures on the computer. The local media picked up the story and, as outrage spread across the community, the teacher was suspended. The teacher then hired a lawyer who called Lanny in to get the facts.

When Lanny investigated the computer, he found that things weren't quite as they seemed. Having looked at the dates and origins of the images and examined their origins, he found that these images had come as pop-ups in e-mails that the teacher had opened, but had only viewed for seconds. The teacher had not gone searching for this material and had not perused it when it arrived in his e-mail. The reason he even saw the pictures was that, instead of looking at the subject line of the e-mails (which, in many cases, specified the nature of the contents) and then choosing which ones to open, he had simply pushed the *Next* button to view his e-mail messages in order of arrival. The teacher was absolved of any wrongdoing and was subsequently reinstated.

A sales representative who changed jobs and was suspected by his former employer of stealing intellectual property didn't fare so well. The suspicious manager viewed all the videotape footage of the former employee coming in and going out of the building without finding anything suspicious. The other possibility was, of course, that the information had been spirited out electronically.

When he started looking into it, Lanny found a trail of where the former employee had been viewing customer lists, product specifications, and other information that he wouldn't have needed in the normal course of doing his job. Interestingly, these files had been accessed during the lunch hour and had left a trail showing that someone had been burning large numbers of files to a CD. The final confirmation was that when the CD copying box had popped up asking the employee whether he wanted to save his CD project to the hard disk, he inadvertently had answered "Yes" so that all the filenames were saved to his hard disk in the *My Documents* folder. Having realized his mistake, the salesman deleted all these filenames to the recycle bin where they were easily retrievable. The manager remarked that the employee had left with a dolly-load of information, not in the physical sense, of course, but with a more modern dolly in the form of a CD.

Summary: Student Learning Outcomes Revisited

1. **Define computer crime and list three types of computer crime that can be perpetrated from inside and three from outside the organization.** *Computer crime* is a crime in which a computer, or computers, played a significant part in its commission. Crimes perpetrated outside the organization include:
   - *Computer viruses*
   - *Denial-of-service (DoS) attacks*
   - Web site defacement
   - *Trojan horse virus*
   Crimes perpetrated inside the organization include:
   - Fraud
   - Embezzlement
   - Harassment

2. **Identify the seven types of hackers and explain what motivates each group.** *Hackers* are knowledgeable computer users who use their knowledge to invade other people's computers. The seven types are:
   - *Thrill-seeker hackers*, who are motivated by the entertainment value of breaking into computers
   - *White-hat hackers*, who are hired by a company to find the vulnerabilities in its network
   - *Black-hat hackers*, who are cyber vandals and cause damage for fun
   - *Crackers*, who are hackers for hire and are the people who engage in electronic corporate espionage
   - *Hacktivists*, who are politically motivated hackers who use the Internet to send a political message of some kind

   - *Cyberterrorists*, who seek to cause harm to people or destroy critical systems or information for political reasons
   - *Script kiddies* or *script bunnies*, who would like to be hackers but don't have much technical expertise

3. **Define computer forensics and describe the two phases of a forensic investigation.** *Computer forensics* is the collection, authentication, preservation, and examination of electronic information for presentation in court. Electronic evidence can be found on any type of computer storage medium. A computer forensic investigation has two phases: (1) collecting, authenticating, and preserving electronic evidence; and (2) analyzing the findings. The collection phase consists of:
   - Getting physical access to the computer and any other items that might be helpful
   - Creating a *forensic image copy* of all storage media
   - Authenticating the forensic image copy by generating an *MD5 hash value*, that, when recalculated at a later date will be the exact same number, as long as nothing at all on the storage medium has changed in any way
   - Using forensic hardware that can read storage media but cannot write to them
   - Using forensic software that can find deleted, hidden, and otherwise hard-to-access information
   The analysis phase consists of:
   - Finding all the information and figuring out what it means
   - Assembling a crime story that fits the information that has been discovered

4. **Identify and describe four places on a hard disk where you can find useful information.** The four places are:
   - *Slack space* which is the space left over from the end of the file to the end of the cluster
   - System and registry files that have lots of information about your hardware, software, and files
   - *Unallocated space*, which is the set of clusters that has been marked as available to store information
   - Unused space that results from actions like repartitioning a disk

5. **Identify and describe seven ways of hiding information.** The seven ways of hiding information are
   - Rename the file to make it look like a different type of file
   - Make information invisible by making it the same colour as the background
   - Use the Windows operating system's hide utility to hide files
   - Protect the file with a password, so that the person who wants to see the file must provide the password
   - *Encrypt* the file, scrambling its contents so you have to have the key to unscramble and read it
   - Use *steganography* to hide a file inside another file
   - Compress the file so that a keyword search can't find it

6. **Describe two ways in which corporations use computer forensics.** Corporations use computer forensics for proactive education and for reactive incident response. Education serves to explain to employees what they should and should not do with computer resources and also how to conduct an internal computer forensic investigation. Incident response involves uncovering employee wrongdoing and preserving the evidence so that action can be taken.

Key Terms and Concepts

black-hat hacker, 471
computer crime, 463
computer forensics, 474
computer virus (virus), 464
cracker, 471
cyberterrorist, 472
denial-of-service (DoS) attack, 468
distributed denial-of-service (DDoS) attack, 468
encryption, 484

forensic image copy, 476
hacker, 471
hacktivist, 471
key logger (key trapper) software, 467
macro virus, 464
MD5 hash value, 476
script kiddie (script bunny), 472
slack space, 482

social engineering, 471
spoofing, 467
steganography, 485
thrill-seeker hacker, 471
Trojan horse virus, 467
unallocated space, 483
white-hat hacker (ethical hacker), 471
worm, 464

Short-Answer Questions

1. In what two ways are computers used in the commission of crimes or misdeeds?

2. What constitutes a computer crime?

3. What kind of software is a computer virus?

4. What differentiates a worm from a macro virus?

5. How does a denial of service attack work?

6. What is the effect of a virus hoax?

7. What is the difference between the Klez family of viruses and previous worms?

8. What is a white-hat hacker?

9. What do crackers do?

10. Is there a difference between a cyberterrorist and a hacktivist? If so, what is it?

11. What is computer forensics?

12. What are the two phases of a computer forensic investigation?

Assignments and Exercises _____

1. **FIND COMPUTER FORENSICS SOFTWARE.** On the Web there are many sites that offer computer forensics software. Find five such software packages and for each one answer the following questions:

   • What does the software do? List five features it advertises.
   • Is the software free? If not, how much does it cost?
   • Is there any indication of the software's target market? If so, what market is it (law enforcement, home use, or something else)?

2. **WHAT EXACTLY ARE THE SEDONA PRINCIPLES?** Figure K.10 mentioned the Sedona Principles. These 14 principles were developed by lawyers, consultants, academics, and jurists to address the many issues involved in antitrust suits, intellectual property disputes, and other types of complex litigation.

   Write a report on the stipulations of the Sedona Principles. Do some research and find out exactly what the Principles suggest. Here's the first one to get you started:

   1. Electronic data and documents are potentially discoverable under Fed.R. Civ. P. 34 or its state-law equivalents. Organizations must properly preserve electronic data and documents that can reasonably be anticipated to be relevant to litigation.

   Be sure to explain in your paper any legal terms, such as "discovery," which appears in the first principle, and "spoliation," in the 14th principle.

3. **THE INTERNATIONAL ANTI-CYBER-CRIME TREATY.** Find out what the provisions of the international anti-cyber-crime treaty are and how they will affect the United States. One of the concerns that will have to be addressed is the issue of whether laws of one country should apply to all. For example, if certain sites are illegal in Saudi Arabia, should they be illegal for all surfers? Or if Germany has a law about hate language, should a German or a Canadian citizen be extradited to stand trial for building a neo-Nazi Web site? What do you think?

4. **DOES THE FOURTH AMENDMENT APPLY TO COMPUTER SEARCH AND SEIZURE?** The U.S. Department of Justice's Computer Crime and Intellectual Property Section has an online manual to guide computer forensics experts through the legal requirements of the search and seizure of electronic information. It's available at www.cybercrime.gov/searchmanual.htm and has a section on "Reasonable Expectation of Privacy." There are four subsections: general principles, reasonable expectation of privacy in computers as storage devices, reasonable expectation of privacy and third-party possession, and private searches. Read and summarize these four subsections.

SECTION THREE

GROUP PROJECTS

Taking Advantage of the CD

The following group projects are Cases that reflect the concepts and skills you've learned in Section Three: Moving Along.

CHAPTER 1

1. R. Hiebeler, Thomas Kelly, and C. Ketteman, *Best Practices: Building Your Business with Customer-Focused Solutions* (New York: Simon & Schuster, 1998).
2. Mortimer Zuckerman, "America's silent revolution," *U.S. News & World Report*, July 18, 1994, p. 90.
3. "Adding speed and intelligence to Celestica's forecasting process," i2 site <www.i2.com/assets/pdf/CC6696EB-8675-4F2A-8C6A75E1D1F0241A.pdf>, accessed December 8, 2005; "Celestica enhances supply chain collaboration with purchase of i2 Technologies' RHYTHM® software," Celestica site <www.celestica.com/index.asp?id=205>, accessed December 8, 2005.
4. Martin Keohan, "The virtual office: impact and implementation," *Business Week*, September 11, 1995, pp. 95–98.
5. EKOS Research Associates Inc., press release, 2001, available <www.ekos.com/admin/press_releases/telework4.pdf>, accessed August 10, 2002; EKOS Research Associates Inc., press release, 1998; available <www.ekos.com/admin/press_releases/nov98.pdf>, accessed August 10, 2002.
6. "Trade update, March 2004," Department of Foreign Affairs and International Trade site <www.dfait-maeci.gc.ca/eet/trade/sot_2004/sot_2004-en.asp#tabc>, accessed December 8, 2005.
7. "SYSTRAN Enterprise," SYSTRAN site <www.systransoft.com/Corporate/Enterprise.html>, accessed November 14, 2002.
8. Brian Dumaine, "What Michael Dell knows that you don't," *Fortune Small Business*, June 3, 2002.
9. Kontzer, Tony, "Brink's gets smarter about learning," *InformationWeek*, December 15, 2003 <www.informationweek.com/story/showArticle.jhtml?articleID=16700281>, accessed December 8, 2005.
10. Marc Peyser and Steve Rhodes, "When e-mail is oops mail," *Newsweek*, October 16, 1995, p. 82.
11. Ernest Kallman and John Grillo, *Ethical Decision Making and Information Technology* (San Francisco: McGraw-Hill, 1993).
12. T. Tripp and M. Gross, "The evolution of an Intranet at Spar Aerospace," *The Courier* (Special Libraries Association—Toronto Chapter), 35(2)(November/December 1997), available <www.sla.org/chapter/ctor/courier/v35/v35n2a8.htm>, accessed August 11, 2002; T. Tripp and M. Gross, "From static Web pages to interactive information delivery," *The Courier* (Special Libraries Association—Toronto Chapter), 35(3)(January/February 1998), available <www.sla.org/chapter/ctor/courier/v35/v35n3a1.htm>, accessed August 11, 2002.
13. ECTACO site <www.ectaco.ca/products/Dictionary-English-French-for-Mobile-Phones>, accessed December 8, 2005.
14. "History," Nokia site <www.nokia.com/aboutnokia/inbrief/history.html>, accessed November 14, 2002.
15. "Losses from identity theft to total $221 billion worldwide," *CIO Magazine*, May 23, 2003, at <www2.cio.com/metrics/2003/metric551.html>, accessed December 8, 2005.

CHAPTER 2

1. Miguel Helft, "Fashion fast forward," *Business 2.0*, May 2002, available <www.business2.com/articles/mag/print/0,1643,39407,FF.html>.
2. S. Beth, D. N. Burt, W. Copacino, C. Gopal, H. L. Lee, R. P. Lynch et al., "Supply chain challenges: building relationships," *Harvard Business Review*, July 2003, pp. 65–73.
3. "Configuring a 500 percent ROI for Dell" [White Paper], i2 site <www.i2.com/customers/hightech_consumer.cfm>, accessed May 5, 2004.
4. Sharron Kahn Luttrel, "Talking turkey with Perdue's CIO—supply chain management," *CIO Magazine*, November 1, 2003 <www.cio.com/archive/110103/tl_scm.html>, accessed June 10, 2004.
5. "VICS—CPFR® Committee," Voluntary Interindustry Commerce Standards Association site <www.vics.org/committees/cpfr>, accessed December 9, 2005.
6. "Gaining recognition for world-class supply chain management," EDB Singapore site, September 1, 2003 <www.edb.gov.sg/edb/sg/en_uk/index/news_room/publications/singapore_investment03/singapore_investment1/gaining_recognition.html>, accessed December 9, 2005.
7. Robert D'Avanzo, "The reward of supply chain excellence," *Orbitz-mag.com*, December 2003, p. 76.
8. S. Beth, D. N. Burt, W. Copacino, C. Gopal, H. L. Lee, R. P. Lynch et al., "Supply chain challenges: building relationships," *Harvard Business Review*, July 2003, pp. 65–73.
9. Deb Navas, "Supply chain software stands tough," *Supply Chain Systems Magazine*, December 2003 <www.scs-mag.com/reader/2003/2003_12/software1203/index.htm>, accessed December 9, 2005.
10. "Websmart 50," *Business Week*, November 24, 2003, p. 96.
11. "Partnering in the fight against cancer," The TDA Group site <tdagroup.com/pdfs/Siebel_AmerCancerSoc.pdf>, accessed December 9, 2005.
12. Peter Koudal, Hau Lee, Barchi Peleg, Paresh Rajwat, and Richard Tully, "General Motors: Building a digital loyalty network through demand and supply chain integration," Deloitte Touche Tohmatsu site <www.deloitte.com/dtt/cda/doc/content/stanfordgmcase.pdf>, accessed December 9, 2005.
13. Roy Schuster, "Nine steps to make the CRM case," CRMIQ 2004, March 12, 2003 <www.crmiq.com/resources/tips/148-CRMIQ_shortcuts.html>, accessed May 5, 2004.
14. Bethune Gordon, "How to create fanatically loyal customers," *Business 2.0*, December 2003, p. 86.
15. Marc L. Songini. "Companies skeptical of CRM success, wary of project rollouts," *Computerworld*, March 4, 2003 <www.computerworld.com/softwaretopics/crm/story/0,10801,79009,00.html>, accessed December 9, 2005.
16. Chris Selland, "Are companies responsible for CRM failures?," *Network World*, July 14, 2003.
17. Alice Dragoon, "Business intelligence gets smart(er)," *CIO Magazine*, September 15, 2003 <www.cio.com/archive/091503/smart.html>, accessed December 9, 2005.
18. Paul Gray, "Business intelligence: a new name or the future of DSS?," in T. Bui, H. Sroka, S. Stanek, and J. Goluchowski (eds.), *DSS in the Uncertainty of the Internet Age* (Katowice, Poland: University of Economics in Katowice, 2003).
19. "IBM and Factiva join forces to transform global content business" [press release], Factiva Press Releases, September 18, 2003

<www.factiva.com/investigative/releases/09182003_ibm.asp?node=menuElem1176>, accessed December 9, 2005.

20. J. Langseth and N. Vivatrat, "Why proactive business intelligence is a hallmark of the real-time enterprise: outward bound," *Intelligent Enterprise*, 5(18)(2003).

21. Claudia Willen, "Airborne opportunities," *Intelligent Enterprise*, 5(2)(January 14, 2002).

22. Paul Gray, "Business intelligence: a new name or the future of DSS?," in T. Bui, H. Sroka, S. Stanek, and J. Goluchowski (eds.), *DSS in the Uncertainty of the Internet Age* (Katowice, Poland: University of Economics in Katowice, 2003).

23. Peter Koudal, Hau Lee, Barchi Peleg, Paresh Rajwat, and Richard Tully, "General Motors: Building a digital loyalty network through demand and supply chain integration," Deloitte Touche Tohmatsu site <www.deloitte.com/dtt/cda/doc/content/stanfordgmcase.pdf>, accessed December 9, 2005.

24. H. Morris, "The 5 principles of high-impact analytics," *DM Review*, 13(4)(2003).

25. Alex Soejarto, "Tough times call for business intelligence services," *VAR-Business*, March 20, 2003, available <www.varbusiness.com/sections/strategy/strategy.asp?ArticleID=40682>, accessed December 9, 2005.

26. K. Rudin and D. Cressy, "Will the real analytics application please stand up?," *DM Review*, 13(3)(2003).

27. D. Stodder, "Enabling the intelligent enterprise: the 2003 Editors' Choice Awards," *Intelligent Enterprise*, 6(2)(2003).

28. "Shell international exploration and production: huge savings through knowledge-sharing," SiteScape site <www.sitescape.com/clients_partners/pdf/shell_nov05.pdf>, accessed January 12, 2006.

29. "The new geography of the IT industry," *The Economist*, July 17, 2003, available <www.economist.com/displaystory.cfm?story_id=1925828>, accessed December 9, 2005.

30. Jon Surmacz, "Collaborate and save: collaboration technology can save big money for the oil and gas industry," *CIO Magazine*, November 5, 2003, available <www2.cio.com/metrics/2003/metric625.html>, accessed December 9, 2005.

31. "LinkedIn in three steps," LinkedIn site <www.linkedin.com/static;jsessionid=CAC221A555830B49D0DF40BA2AE133C5.app01?key=guest_tour>, accessed December 9, 2005.

32. Thomas H. Davenport and Laurence Prusak, *What's the Big Idea? Creating and Capitalizing on the Best Management Thinking* (Boston: Harvard Business School Press: 2003).

33. Y. Malhotra and D. Galletta, "Role of commitment and motivation in knowledge management implementation: theory, conceptualization and measurement of antecedents of success," proceedings of the 36th Hawaii International Conference on System Sciences, January 6–9, 2003, Big Island, HI.

34. "The role of technology in knowledge management," *Internet Strategist*, 1(2)(October 22, 2002), available <www.intranetstrategist.com/xq/asp/sid.0/articleid.CD89216B-8E50-4AB1-9E73-77DFB0DB1D1E/qx/display.htm>, accessed June 10, 2004.

35. "Social networks," *New York Times Magazine*, December 14, 2003, p. 92.

36. "Big Blue's big bet: less tech, more touch," *The New York Times*, January 25, 2004, sec. 3, p. 1.

37. "Tourism—Auberge de La Fontaine," E-Business Case Study, Industry Canada site, June 2004 <strategis.ic.gc.ca/epic/internet/indsib-tour.nsf/en/qq00111e.html>; Bonjour Québec.com (Quebec Ministry of Tourism site) <www.bonjourquebec.com>; "Auberge de La Fontaine bed and breakfast," BedandBreakfast.com <www.bedandbreakfast.com/quebec/auberge-de-la-fontaine.html>. All accessed December 9, 2005.

CHAPTER 3

1. "Global electronics distributor implements Internet EDI, achieving first year cost savings of over $1,200,000: solution pays for itself in less than one month," available <www.adx.com/downloads/files/2/Case_Study_-_Newark_Electronics.pdf>, accessed December 9, 2005.

2. Bruce Abbott, "Requirements set the mark," *InfoWorld*, March 2, 2001 <http://www.infoworld.com/articles/tc/xml/01/03/05/010305tcreqs.html>, accessed December 9, 2005.

3. Microsoft site <www.microsoft.com>.

4. "Business technology optimization," Mercury Interactive site <www.mercuryinteractive.com>, accessed June 11, 2004.

5. Denise Shortt, "The search for schools in IT," *Globe and Mail*, May 10, 2001, available <www.globetechnology.com/woman/archive/20010510.html>, accessed December 9, 2005; "IT and educational leaders team up for a new initiative

in the quest for life-long learning working together to address Canada's skills gap" [news release], *M2 Presswire*, March 29, 2000 <static.highbeam.com/m/m2presswire/march292000/itandeducationalleadersteamupforanewinitiativeinth/index.html>, accessed December 9, 2005; *Vancouver Labour Market Bulletin* (2000/2001), available <www.bc.hrdc-drhc.gc.ca/vancouver/common/lmb_octnov00.pdf>; Michael Martin, "Decrease in IT pay packets persists," *ComputerWorld Canada*, January 5, 2004 <www.itworld.com/Career/1698/040105itpay>, accessed December 9, 2005.

6. Carter Anne Prescott, "Marriott redefines the shared service model," Accenture site <www.accenture.com/Global/Research_and_Insights/Outlook/By_Issue/Y2002/OutlookJournalCaseMarriott.htm>, accessed December 9, 2005.

7. Paul Boutin, "Clearing up *The Confusion*," *Wired Magazine*, October 2003 <www.wired.com/news/culture/0,1284,63050,00.html>, accessed December 9, 2005.

8. Kenn Brown, "Six technologies that will change the world," *Business 2.0*, August 2003, available Mondolithic Studios Inc. site <mondolithic.com/02Gallery17.htm>, accessed December 9, 2005.

9. Joshua Davis, "The graffiti early warning system," *Wired*, 11(10)(October 2003) <wired-vig.wired.com/wired/archive/11.10/start.html?pg=5>, accessed December 9, 2005.

10. Joseph Panettieri, "Lucrative liaisons," *Wired*, December 2003 <www.wired.com>, accessed June 10, 2004.

11. Justin Fox, "Hang-ups in India," *Fortune*, December 22, 2003 <www.fortune.com>, accessed June 10, 2004.

12. "A long-running hit at Canada's National Arts Centre," Compaq Case Studies, January 2001 <www.compaq.com/casestudies/stories/nationalarts/story.html>, accessed November 14, 2002.

13. Anne Fisher, "If all the jobs are going to India, should I move to Bangalore?," *Fortune*, January 12, 2004, available <www.fortune.com/fortune/annie/0,15704,565343,00.html>, accessed December 9, 2005.

CHAPTER 4

1. "Chrysler manages a nationwide supply chain of vendors," IBM site <www-1.ibm.com/industries/automotive/doc/content/casestudy/

283426108.html>, accessed January 19, 2004.

2. Shelley Zulman, "Dressing up data," *Oracle Magazine*, January/February 1995, pp. 46–49.

3. "The chain store age 100," *Chain Store Age*, August 1996, p. 3A.

4. James Cash, "Gaining customer loyalty," *InformationWeek*, April 10, 1995, p. 88.

5. Darrell Dunn, "Fancy footwork moves inventory," *Information-Week*, December 15, 2003 <www.informationweek.com/story/show Article.jhtml?articleID=16700271>, accessed December 9, 2005.

6. Royal Caribbean International Cruise Vacations site <www.royal caribbean.com>.

7. Sami Lais, "Satellite ho!," *Computerworld*, May 29, 2000, pp. 70–71.

8. "Lufthansa boosts customer quality with its COSMIC program," Oracle site <www.oracle.com/customers/profiles/profile9407.html>, accessed December 9, 2005.

9. Gary Anthes, "Car dealer takes the personal out of PCs," *Computerworld*, August 14, 1995, p. 48.

10. Karen Watterson, "A data miner's tools," *BYTE*, October 1995, pp. 91–96.

11. Nikhil Hutheesing, "Surfing with Sega," *Forbes*, November 4, 1996, pp. 350–351.

12. Julia Kling, "OLAP gains fans among data-hungry firms," *Computerworld*, January 8, 1996, pp. 43, 48.

13. "Israel's largest bank strengthens customer relationships with Cognos BI," Cognos site <www.cognos.com/news/release/2003/0115.html>, accessed February 2, 2004.

14. Alice LaPlante, "Big things come in smaller packages," *Computerworld*, June 24, 1996, pp. DW/6–7.

15. "News and events" [press release], Burntsand site, October 31, 2001, available <www.burntsand.com/news_events/2001/oct31_2001.asp>, accessed December 9, 2005.

16. Rosemary Cafasso, "OLAP: who needs it?," *Computerworld*, February 2, 1995, p. 12.

17. Tischelle George, "Big bucks dry up," *InformationWeek*, April 29, 2002 <www.informationweek.com/story/IWK20020426S0005>, accessed December 9, 2005.

18. Ben Phillips, "Ice service's data warehouse goes with the flow," *PC Week*, January 22, 1996, pp. 45–46.

19. Rick Whiting, "Analysis gap," *InformationWeek*, April 22, 2002, available <www.informationweek.com/story/IWK20020418S0007>, accessed December 10, 2005; CIGNA Corporation site <www.cigna.com>.

20. "Red Robin International," Cognos Incorporated site <www.cognos.com/company/success/ss_entertainment.html>, accessed January 13, 2004.

21. "Mining the data of dining," *Nation's Restaurant News*, May 22, 2000, pp. S22–S24.

22. Erika Brown, "Analyze this," *Forbes*, April 1, 2002, pp. 96–98.

CHAPTER 5

1. Xeni Jardin, "Why your next phone call may be online," *Wired*, 12(1)(January 2004), available <www.wired.com/wired/archive/12.01/start.html?pg=8>, accessed December 10, 2005.

2. Sharon Gaudin, "Employee abuse of Internet rampant," *InternetNews*, April 24, 2002 <www.internetnews.com/dev-news/article.php/1015141>, accessed December 10, 2005.

3. Sharon Gaudin, "Employee abuse of Internet rampant," *InternetNews*, April 24, 2002 <www.internetnews.com/dev-news/article.php/1015141>, accessed December 10, 2005.

4. "EAI," *Webopedia* <www.webo pedia.com/TERM/E/EAI.html>, accessed December 10, 2005.

5. Jeff Sweat, "The integrated enterprise," *InformationWeek*, April 26, 1999 <www.informationweek.com/731/eai.htm>, accessed December 10, 2005.

6. "About Gap Inc.," Gap Inc. site <www.gapinc.com/public/About/about.shtml>, accessed December 10, 2005; "The Gap Inc.," Object Management Group's CORBA site, September 17, 2001 <www.corba.org/industries/retail/gap.html>, accessed December 10, 2005.

7. "Forging stronger relationships with customers and partners through content management," Documentum, Inc. site <www.documentum.com/customer_success/success/dow_corning.htm>, accessed December 10, 2005.

8. "Shipping tools: FedEx Ship Manager API," FedEx Canada site <www.fedex.com/ca_english/businesstools/shipapi/?link=4>, accessed December 10, 2005.

9. "Configuring a 500 percent ROI for Dell," i2 Technologies site <www.i2.com/assets/pdf/d8610bf3-d7f1-432d-b9aa6efbc8727186.pdf>.

10. Michael Booth, "The ABCs of ASPs," ebizQ.net, January 28, 2002 <www.ebizq.net/topics/eai/features/1789.html>, accessed December 10, 2005.

11. Lindy Dragstra, "Multrix wins ASPire award for management and operations," Multrix site, January 7, 2002 <www.multrix.com/index.asp?content=/news/releases.asp?reID=17&lang=en>, accessed December 10, 2005.

12. "City of Orlando gives managers immediate access to budget-critical financial information," Oracle Corporation site, April 2002 <www.jdedwards.com/content/enUS/Customer-Customers/orlando.pdf>, accessed October 31, 2002.

13. See also the Obsolete Computer Museum <www.obsoletecomputer museum.org>, accessed December 10, 2005.

14. Eryn Brown, "33 days, 8 campuses, 127 kids and an infinity of gizmos," *Fortune*, June 24, 2002, pp. 126–138.

15. Christopher Null, "How Netflix is fixing Hollywood," *Business 2.0*, July 1, 2003 <www.business2.com/b2/web/articles/0,17863,515760,00.html>, accessed December 10, 2005.

CHAPTER 6

1. "Black's case study," Intellera site <www.intellera.com/blacks.asp>, accessed December 10, 2005; Black Photo Corporation site <www.blackphoto.com>.

2. Kristin Krause, "Airlines feel your pain," *Traffic World*, April 30, 2001, pp. 28–30.

3. Jill Gambon, "A database that 'ads' up," *InformationWeek*, August 7, 1995, pp. 68–69.

4. Roberta Maynard, "Leading the way to effective marketing," *Nation's Business*, October 1996, pp. 10–11.

5. Herbert Simon, *The New Science of Management Decisions*, rev. ed. (Englewood Cliffs, NJ: Prentice Hall, 1977).

6. Steven Kauderer and Amy Kuehl, "Adding value with technology," *Best's Review*, October 2001, p. 130.

7. "M/W planning: it's all in the data," *Railway Age*, January 2001, pp. 60–61.

8. Steven Marlin, Cristina McEachern, and Anthony O'Donnell, "Cross selling starts with CRM system," *Wall Street & Technology*, December 2001, pp. A8–A10.

9. D. K. Taft, "Arlington ships decision tool," *Computer Reseller News*, November 27, 1995, p. 165; M. Pass, "New software packages help you make up your mind, develop company policy, and devise the perfect name," *Inc.*, 1995(3)(Special Bonus Issue): 95.

10. Paul Korzeniowski, "New ways to stay connected," *Utility Business*, January 2000, pp. 58–60.

11. Peter Fingar, "Don't just transact—collaborate," *CIO*, June 1, 2001.

12. Marianne Kolbasuk McGee and Chris Murphy, "Collaboration is about more than squeezing out supply-chain costs," *InformationWeek*, December 10, 2001 <www.informationweek.com/story/IWK20011207S0016>, accessed December 10, 2005.

13. Marianne Kolbasuk McGee and Chris Murphy, "Collaboration is about more than squeezing out supply-chain costs," *InformationWeek*, December 10, 2001 <www.informationweek.com/story/IWK20011207S0016>, accessed December 10, 2005.

14. "PictureTel now shipping SwiftSite II compact videoconferencing system," Findwealth.com site, February 19, 1999 <www.findwealth.com/picturetel-now-shipping-swiftsite-ii-36800pr.html>, accessed December 11, 2005.

15. Marianne Kolbasuk McGee and Chris Murphy, "Collaboration is about more than squeezing out supply-chain costs," *InformationWeek*, December 10, 2001 <www.informationweek.com/story/IWK20011207S0016>, accessed December 10, 2005.

16. "Desktop collaboration software: solution scenarios," Groove Networks, Inc. site, 2002 <www.groove.net/solutions/scenarios>, accessed November 14, 2002.

17. Marianne Kolbasuk McGee and Chris Murphy, "Collaboration is about more than squeezing out supply-chain costs," *InformationWeek*, December 10, 2001 <www.informationweek.com/story/IWK20011207S0016>, accessed December 10, 2005.

18. J. B. Smelcer and E. Carmel, "The effectiveness of difference representations for managerial problem solving: comparing tables and maps," *Decision Sciences*, 1997, pp. 391–420.

19. Bob Brewin, "IT helps waste hauler handle anthrax safely," *Computerworld*, November 12, 2001, p. 8.

20. Amy Dunkin, "The quants may have your numbers," *Business Week*, September 25, 1995, pp. 146–147.

21. Otis Port, "Computers that think are almost here," *Business Week*, July 17, 1995, pp. 68–71.

22. Matthew Axvig, "Cool robot: Dante II: volcano explorer," National Robotics Engineering Consortium site <www.rec.ri.cmu.edu/education/multimedia/l2p2.shtml>, accessed December 11, 2005.

23. Rob Grimes, "Consumer acceptance of robots could signal future use by foodservice," *Nation's Restaurant News*, August 20, 2001, available <www.findarticles.com/cf_0/m3190/34_35/77498093/p1/article.jhtml?term=grimes+%2Brobots>, accessed December 11, 2005.

24. Ann Stuart, "A dose of accuracy," *CIO*, May 15, 1996, pp. 22–24.

25. Alison Overholt, "True or false: you're hiring the right people," *Fast Company*, February 2002, pp. 110–114.

26. Alexx Kay, "Artificial neural networks," *Computerworld*, February 12, 2001, p. 60, available <www.computerworld.com/softwaretopics/software/appdev/story/0,10801,57545,00.html>, accessed December 11, 2005.

27. Alexx Kay, "Artificial neural networks," *Computerworld*, February 12, 2001, p. 60, available <www.computerworld.com/softwaretopics/software/appdev/story/0,10801,57545,00.html>, accessed December 11, 2005.

28. William Perry, "What is neural network software?," *Journal of Systems Management*, September 1994, pp. 12–15.

29. Otis Port, "Diagnoses that cast a wider net," *Business Week*, May 22, 1995, p. 130.

30. William G. Baxt and Joyce Skora, "Prospective validation of artificial neural network trained to identify acute myocardial infarction," *The Lancet*, January 6, 1997, pp. 12–15.

31. Laton McCartney, "Technology for a better bottom line," *InformationWeek*, February 26, 1996, p. 40.

32. Linda Punch and Jason Fargo. "The downside of convenience checks," *Credit Card Management*, November 2000, pp. 78–82.

33. Greg Michlig, "To catch a thief," *Credit Union Management*, January 2001, pp. 48–50.

34. Rick Whiting, "Companies boost sales efforts with predictive analysis," *InformationWeek*, February 25, 2002 <www.informationweek.com/story/IWK20020221S0018>, accessed December 11, 2005.

35. Rick Whiting, "Companies boost sales efforts with predictive analysis," *InformationWeek*, February 25, 2002 <www.informationweek.com/story/IWK20020221S0018>, accessed December 11, 2005.

36. Linda Punch, "Battling credit card fraud," *Bank Management*, March 1993, pp. 18–22.

37. "Cigna, IBM tech tool targets health care fraud," *National Underwriter Property & Casualty-Risk & Benefits*, October 1994, p. 5.

38. Gary H. Anthes, "Picking winners and losers," *Computerworld*, February 18, 2002, p. 34.

39. Patricia E. Moody, "What's next after lean manufacturing?," *Sloan Management Review*, Winter 2001, pp. 12–13.

40. C. L. Hui Patrick, S. F. Ng Frency, and C. C. Chan Keith, "A study of the roll planning of fabric spreading using genetic algorithms," *International Journal of Clothing Science & Technology*, 12(1)(2000): 50–62, available from Emerald Group Publishing Limited site <operatix.emeraldinsight.com/vl=3595504/cl=36/nw=1/rpsv/cgi-bin/linker?ini=emerald&reqidx=/cw/mcb/09556222/v12n1/s4/p50>, accessed December 11, 2005.

41. S. Begley, "Software au naturel," *Newsweek*, May 8, 1995, pp. 70–71.

42. Bernard Baumohl, "Can you really trust those bots?," *Time*, December 11, 2000, p. 80.

43. Nikki Swartz, "App intelligence," *Wireless Review*, September 1, 2001, pp. 8A–10A, available <wirelessreview.com/mag/wireless_app_intelligence_2/index.html>, accessed December 11, 2005.

44. "Virtually helpful," *Telephony Online*, February 11, 2002, p. 56. available <telephonyonline.com/ar/telecom_virtually_helpful>, accessed December 11, 2005.

45. Kevin Dobbs, Sarah Boehle, Donna Goldwasser, Jack Gordon, and David Stamps, "The return of artificial intelligence," *Training*, November 2000, p. 26.

46. Rick Whiting, "Companies boost sales efforts with predictive analysis," *InformationWeek*, February 25, 2002 <www.informationweek.com/story/IWK20020221S0018>, accessed December 11, 2005.

47. Jane Griffin, "OLAP vs. data mining: which one is right for your data warehouse?," dataWarehouse.com, August 22, 2000 <www.datawarehouse.com/article/?articleid=2904>, accessed December 11, 2005.

48. Stephanie Overby, "The new, new intelligence," *CIO Magazine*, January 1, 2003, pp. 82–84, available <www.cio.com/archive/010103/35.html>, accessed December 11, 2005.

49. Howard Wolinsky, "Advisa helps companies get more from their data: helps managers to understand market," *Chicago Sun-Times*, December 20, 2000, p. 81.

50. Marcia Stepanek, "Weblining," *BusinessWeek Online*, April 3, 2000 <www.businessweek.com/2000/00_14/b3675027.htm>.

51. A. Shaw, "From hospitals to home care, wireless improves data collection at point-of-care," *Canadian Healthcare Technology*, April 2002, available <www.canhealth.com/apr02.html>, accessed December 11, 2005.

52. J. Zeidenberg, "Leading hospitals test new health-record software," *Canadian Healthcare Technology*, May 2001, available <www.canhealth.com/may01.html>, accessed December 11, 2005.

CHAPTER 7

1. Juan Carlos Perez, "Update: AOL launches new bill-paying tool," *The Industry Standard*, March 16, 2004 <www.thestandard.com/article.php?story=20040316172813723>, accessed December 17, 2005.

2. Robyn Greenspan, "Online ads, e-marketing on upswing," ClickZ Network site, March 2, 2004 <www.clickz.com/stats/sectors/advertising/article.php/3320671>, accessed December 17, 2005.

3. ClickZ Stats staff, "Top searches of 2003," ClickZ Network site, December 31, 2003 <www.clickz.com/stats/sectors/search_tools/article.php/3293581>, accessed December 17, 2005.

4. "From vision to reality … and beyond," Government On-Line 2005, Government of Canada site <www.gol-ged.gc.ca/rpt2005/rpt03_e.asp>, accessed December 17, 2005.

5. ClickZ Stats staff, "U.S. web usage and traffic, December 2003," ClickZ Network site, January 27, 2004 <www.clickz.com/stats/sectors/traffic_patterns/article.php/5931_3301321>, accessed December 17, 2005.

6. ClickZ Stats staff, "B2B e-commerce headed for trillions," ClickZ Network site, March 6, 2002 <www.clickz.com/stats/sectors/b2b/article.php/986661>, accessed December 18, 2005; Travel Media Association of Canada site <www.travelmedia.ca/content/ontario/rotmanonline.htm>.

7. "2003 consumer profile," Recording Industry Association of America, April 20, 2004 <www.riaa.com/news/marketingdata/pdf/2003consumerprofile.pdf>, accessed December 18, 2005.

8. C. Wood, "A two-tier system," *Maclean's*, 112(23)(June 7, 1999): 32–33.

9. "Innovation through e-commerce: profiles from Atlantic Canada," ACOA site, 2002 <www.acoa.ca/e/business/innovation/ecommerce/ecommprofiles.shtml#6b>, accessed November 14, 2002.

10. Cheryl Rosen, "Passwords are so passé," *Optimize*, 26(December 2003), p. 21, available <www.optimizemag.com/article/showArticle.jhtml?articleId=17701019>, accessed December 18, 2005.

11. Electronic Commerce Branch, Industry Canada, "Household Internet use survey," Industry Canada site, available <e-com.ic.gc.ca/english/research>; 2004–05 EKOS Survey.

12. "Global eXchange Services and ChinaECNet establish B2B exchange for China's $80 billion electronics industry," Global eXchange Services, Inc. site, March 18, 2004 <www.gxs.com/aboutUs_newsEvents_pr_03182004.htm>, accessed December 18, 2005.

13. Martin Hofmann, "VW revs its B2B engine," *Optimize*, March 2004, pp. 22–30.

14. "eBags.com celebrates five years of helping consumers find the perfect bag online," eBags.com site, March 03, 2004 <www.ebags.com/about/index.cfm?Fuseaction=pressitem&release_ID=102>, accessed December 18, 2005.

CHAPTER 8

1. Mark Ward, "Hacking with a Pringles tube," *BBC News*, March 8, 2002 <news.bbc.co.uk/1/hi/sci/tech/1860241.stm>, accessed December 27, 2005.

2. "Professional hacking: CEH boot camp," Vigilar's Intense School site, 2005 <www.vigilar.com/training_professional_hacking.html?mc=ggaw_CEH>, accessed December 27, 2005.

3. Erick Schonfeld and Om Malik, "GULP!" *Business 2.0*, August 2003, pp. 88–95.

4. J. Gallagher, "On the verge of voice commerce," InsuranceTech.com, March 8, 2001 <www.financetech.com/featured/showArticle.jhtml;jsessionid=MU1HZC0T5ZYBUQSNDBCSKH0CJUMEKJVN?articleID=14706221>.

5. Lisa Cavion, "Hubble telescope and the Canadarm," SpaceNet <www.spacenet.on.ca/stories/robotics/hubble>, accessed December 28, 2005.

6. "Success stories: e-mail and more for people on the go," Canada's Innovation Strategy site, Government of Canada, April 23, 2002

<www.innovation.gc.ca/gol/innovation/stories.nsf/vengss/ss01095e.htm>, accessed December 28, 2005; Edward C. Baig, "BlackBerry makes lovely companion, or Sidekick if you will," USATODAY.com, September 9, 2004 <www.usatoday.com/tech/columnist/edwardbaig/2004-09-09-baig_x.htm>, accessed December 28, 2005; TrueContext site <www.truecontext.com/solutions/mow-RIM_BlackBerry.htm>.

7. Nina Adams, "Lessons from the virtual world," *Training*, June 1995, pp. 45–47.

8. Laurie Flynn, "VR and virtual spaces find a niche in real medicine," *New York Times*, June 5, 1995, p. C3.

9. Chabrow, Eric, "Facial-recognition software gives a better picture," *InformationWeek*, March 13, 2003 <www.informationweek.com/story/showArticle.jhtml?articleID=8700238>, accessed December 28, 2005; "Zensys closes over $15 million in funding, launches breakthrough home control technology," *Business Wire*, May 2, 2001 <www.businesswire.com/webbox/bw.050201/211220321.htm>, accessed December 28, 2005.

10. Owen Thomas, "How to sell tech to the Feds," *Business 2.0*, March 2003, pp. 111–112.

11. Bobbie Weikle, "Riding the perfect wave: putting virtual reality to work with disabilities," Articles Archive, *ConnSENSE Bulletin* <www.connsensebulletin.com/weikle.html>, accessed December 28, 2005; Janet McConnaughey, "Virtual reality used to treat autism," *Denver Post*, October 20, 1996, p. 39A.

12. Jennifer Lee, "Youth will be served, wirelessly," May 30, 2002 <tech2.nytimes.com/mem/technology/techreview.html?res=9803EEDE1E3BF933A05760C0A9649C8B63>, accessed December 28, 2005; Monica Soto Ouchi, "Wildseed: a start-up on the cusp of success with teens," *Seattle Times*, January 12, 2004 <seattletimes.nwsource.com/html/businesstechnology/2001834588_ces12.html>, accessed December 28, 2005.

CHAPTER 9

1. Richard Behar, "Never heard of Acxiom? Chances are it's heard of you," *Fortune*, February 23, 2004, pp. 140–48.

2. Josh Herman, "Albany, NY, reflects true test market," *Marketing News*, February 1, 2004, p. 34.

3. "TransUnion teams with Acxiom on anti-fraud tool," *American Banker*, February 23, 2004 <www.acxiom.com/default.aspx?ID=2439&Country_Code=GBR>, accessed December 28, 2005.

4. Jake Bleed, "Acxiom thrives on sorting bank megamergers," *Arkansas Democrat-Gazette*, February 8, 2004 <www.acxiom.com/default.aspx?ID=2421&Country_Code=GBR>, accessed December 28, 2005.

5. Linda Pliagas, "Learning IT right from wrong," *InfoWorld*, September 29, 2000 <www.infoworld.com/articles/ca/xml/00/10/02/001002caethics.xml>, accessed December 28, 2005.

6. Christine Fogliasso and Donald Baack, "The personal impact of ethical decisions: a social penetration theory model," Second Annual Conference on Business Ethics, New York, 1995, sponsored by Vincentian Universities in the United States.

7. T. M. Jones, "Ethical decision-making by individuals in organizations: an issue-contingent model," *Academy of Management Review*, 1991, pp. 366–395.

8. Ernest Kallman and John Grillo, *Ethical Decision-Making and Information Technology* (San Francisco: McGraw-Hill, 1993).

9. Kristin Zhivago, "Et tu, Enron?," *AdWeek Magazines' Technology Marketing*, April 2002, p. 33.

10. Sara Baase, *The Gift of Fire: Social, Legal and Ethical Issues in Computing* (Upper Saddle River, NJ: Prentice-Hall, 1997).

11. Erika Jonietz, "Economic bust patent boom," *Technology Review*, May 2002, pp. 71–72.

12. Tim Stevens, "Cashing in on knowledge," *Industry Week*, May 2002, pp. 39–43.

13. Trevor Moores, "Software piracy: a view from Hong Kong," *Communications of the ACM*, December 2000, pp. 88–93.

14. Moores, "Software piracy."

15. Peter Beruk, "Five years: $59.2 billion lost," Software and Information Industry Association site, May 24, 2000, available <www.siia.net/sharedcontent/press/2000/5-24-00.html>, accessed December 28, 2005.

16. Geoffrey James, "Organized crime and the software biz," *MC Technology Marketing Intelligence*, January 2000, pp. 40–44.

17. James, "Organized crime and the software biz."

18. David Rittenhouse, "Privacy and security on your PC," *ExtremeTech*, May 28, 2002 <www.extremetech.com/article2/0,1697,13921,00.asp>, accessed December 29, 2005.

19. P. Thibodeau, "Canadian privacy law raises ante—complying may place burden on U.S. firms," *Computer World*, December 4, 2000, available <www.computerworld.com/industrytopics/retail/story/0,10801,54674,00.html>, accessed December 29, 2005.

20. "Identity theft," Public Safety and Emergency Preparedness Canada (PSEPC) site, October 25, 2005 <www.sgc.gc.ca/prg/le/bs/consumers-en.asp#1>, accessed December 29, 2005.

21. CBC News staff, "Biggest credit card fraud ring uncovered: Quebec police," CBC News site July 8, 2002 <www.cbc.ca/story/news/national/2002/05/28/Consumers/creditcards_020528.html>, accessed December 29, 2005.

22. CBC News staff, "Mail theft has carriers, customers on guard," CBC News site, March 17, 2002 <cbc.ca/cgi-bin/templates/view.cgi?category=Canada&story=/news/2002/03/16/mail_theft020316>, accessed December 29, 2005.

23. Hall Adams, III, "E-mail monitoring in the workplace: the good, the bad and the ugly," *Defense Counsel Journal*, January 2000, pp. 32–46.

24. Dana Corbin, "Keeping a virtual eye on employees," *Occupational Health & Safety*, November 2000, pp. 24–28.

25. Linda Pliagas, "Learning IT right from wrong," *InfoWorld*, September 29, 2000 <www.infoworld.com/articles/ca/xml/00/10/02/001002caethics.xml>, accessed December 29, 2005.

26. Brett Glass, "Are you being watched?," *PC Magazine*, April 23, 2002, available <www.pcmag.com/article2/0%2C1895%2C2341%2C00.asp>, accessed December 29, 2005.

27. Cassimir Medford, "Know who I am," *PC Magazine*, February 7, 2000, pp. 58–64.

28. Cassimir Medford, "Know who I am."

29. Darren Charters, "Electronic monitoring and privacy issues in business-marketing: the ethics of the DoubleClick experience," *Journal of Business Ethics*, February 2002, pp. 243–254.

30. Mark Naples, "Privacy and cookies," *Target Marketing*, April 2002, pp. 28–30.

31. Frank Hayes, "Assault on privacy," *Computerworld*, May 13, 2002, p. 74.

32. Brad Stone, "Soaking in spam," *Newsweek*, November 24, 2003, pp. 66–69.

33. Julia Angwin, "Elusive spammer sends Web service on a long chase," *Wall Street Journal*, May 7, 2003, pp. A1, A10.

34. Matthew P. Graven, "Leave me alone," *PC Magazine*, January 16, 2001, pp. 151–152.

35. Rachel Konrad and John Borland, "Guess what's in your hard drive?," *ZDNet News*, April 18, 2002 <zdnet.com.com/2100-1104-885792.html>, accessed December 29, 2005.

36. Dara Mirsky, "Tap your Web site's log files to improve CRM," *Customer Inter@ction Solutions*, May 2001, pp. 42–43, available <www.tmcnet.com/call-center/0501/0501estaff.htm>, accessed December 29, 2005.

37. J. Chua, "Identity theft," June Chua personal site, November 7, 2003 <www.junechua.com/web_identity.html>, accessed December 29, 2005.

38. Sara Baase, *The Gift of Fire: Social, Legal and Ethical Issues in Computing* (Upper Saddle River, NJ: Prentice-Hall, 1997).

39. The sources for this whole section were: "Canada enacts broad new privacy law, creating complex interplay with U.S. and EU," June 15, 2000, available <practicalprivacy.org/archive/political_issue_briefs.htm>; M. Gisler, "Canada's new privacy law creates tricky relationship with related EU legislation," WLIA Online (Wireless Location Industry Association) <www.wliaonline.com/publications/canadaprivacy.html>; N. d'Entremont, "Protection of privacy: the hype, the facts, and the government's role," *Government Information in Canada*, 21(2000), available <www.usask.ca/library/gic/21/dentremont.html>, accessed December 29, 2005.

40. Peter Han and Angus Maclaurin, "Do consumers really care about online privacy?," *Marketing Management*, January/February 2002, pp. 35–38.

41. Anna Shimanek, "Do you want milk with those cookies?: complying with the Safe Harbor privacy principles," *Journal of Corporation Law*, Winter 2001, pp. 455–477.

42. Elizabeth De Bony, "EU overwhelmingly approves U.S. data-privacy regulations," *Computerworld*, June 5, 2000, p. 28.

43. Russ Banham, "Share data at your own risk," *World Trade*, November 2000, pp. 60–63.

44. Bruce Caldwell, "We are the business," *InformationWeek*, October 28, 1996, pp. 36–50.

45. "Information security market growing," Nua Internet Surveys site, September 24, 2001 <www.nua.ie/surveys/index.cgi?f=VS&art_id=905357221&rel=true46>, accessed December 29, 2005; John Conley, "Knocking the starch out of white collar crime," *Risk Management*, November 2000, pp. 14–22.

47. George Hulme, "In lockstep on security," *InformationWeek*, March 18, 2002, pp. 38–52, available <www.informationweek.com/story/showArticle.jhtml?articleID=6501441>, accessed December 29, 2005.

48. George Hulme, "In lockstep on security."

49. "Law enforcers target 'top 10' online scams: consumer protection cops from 9 countries, 5 U.S. agencies, and 23 states tackle Internet fraud," Federal Trade Commission site, 2000, available <www.ftc.gov/opa/2000/10/topten.htm>; New Jersey Department of Law and Public Safety, "State targets 'top 10' cyber scams: New Jersey joins consumer protections cops worldwide," New Jersey Department of Law and Public Safety site, October 31, 2000 <www.state.nj.us/lps/ca/press/cyber.htm>, accessed December 29, 2005.

50. Christine Chudnow, "Grid computing," *Computer Technology Review*, April 2002, pp. 35–36.

51. Lisa Meyer, "Security you can live with," *Fortune*, Winter 2002, pp. 94–99.

52. CSI/FBI, Ninth Annual Computer Crime and Security Survey, available Computer Security Institute site <www.gocsi.com>.

53. Deborah Radcliff, "Hackers, terrorists, and spies," *Software Magazine*, October 1997, pp. 36–47.

54. George V. Hulme and Bob Wallace, "Beware cyberattacks," *InformationWeek*, November 13, 2000, pp. 22–24.

55. "Hackers hit lucky streak with Net casinos," USA Today site, September 10, 2001 <www.usatoday.com/life/cyber/tech/2001/09/10/net-gambling-hackers.htm>, accessed December 29, 2005.

56. "Security you can live with: cooperation equals profit," *Fortune Tech Review* <fortune.cnet.com/fortune/0-5937473-7-7720726.html?tag=subdir>, accessed November 11, 2002.

57. "Fast times," *Fortune*, Summer 2000, pp. 35–36.

58. Ron Zemke, "Tech-savvy and people-stupid," *Training*, July 2000, pp. 16–18.

59. Vikki Spencer, "Risk management: danger of the cyber deep," *Canadian Underwriter*, September 2000, pp. 10–14.

60. Lisa Meyer, "Security you can live with?," *Fortune*, Winter 2002, pp. 94–99, available <www.lisameyer.ws/fortune1.html>, accessed December 29, 2005.

61. Deborah Radcliff, "Beyond passwords," *Computerworld*, January 21, 2002, pp. 52–53.

62. Brooke Paul, "How much risk is too much?," *InformationWeek*, November 6, 2000, pp. 116–124.

63. Alison Eastwood, "End-users: the enemy within?," *Computing Canada*, January 4, 1996, p. 41.

64. Robert Luhn, "Eliminate viruses," *PC World*, July 2002, pp. 94–95.

65. John Wagley, "Tech detectives," *Institutional Investor*, August 2001, pp. 18–20.

66. Maura Ammenheuser, "The business case for biometrics," *Bank Systems & Technology*, February 2002, p. 42.

67. "Airlines to offer faster services to attract passengers," *Biometric Digest*, September 1999, available <www.biometricgroup.com/a_bio1/biometric_digest/99sep.pdf>, accessed November 13, 2002.

68. T. Ouellette and T. Hoffman, "Ice storm freezes operations," *Computerworld*, 32(3)(January 19, 1998).

69. Jim Hoffer, "Backing up business," *Health Management Technology*, January 2001, available <www.healthmgttech.com/archives/h0101backing.htm>, accessed December 29, 2005.

70. Stuart Kahan, "Hot sites: the solution when business interruption is fatal," *Practical Accountant*, July 1994, pp. 58–63.

71. Barbara DePompa, "Averting a complete disaster," *InformationWeek*, July 15, 1996 <www.informationweek.com/588/88mtdis.htm>, accessed December 29, 2005.

72. Dan Verton, "IT systems at U.S. borders found lacking," *Computerworld*, March 17, 2003, pp. 1, 16.

73. Dan Verton, "DHS broadens biometrics use for border control," *Computerworld*, October 13, 2003, p. 22.

74. Michael Gips, "Home on the page: www.securitymanagement.com," *Security Management*, May 2003, pp. 24–25.

75. Mitch Betts, "5 petabytes of biometric data," *Computerworld*, November 17, 2003, p. 52.

XLM-K

1. Riva Richmond, "How to find your weak spots," *The Wall Street Journal*, September 29, 2003, p. R3.

2. Marcia Savage, "The white hats: security consultants," *Computer Reseller News*, November 13, 2000, pp. 137–38.

3. Thomas Pack, "Virus protection," *Link-Up*, January/February 2002, p. 25.

4. Jason Meserve, "People around the world bitten by 'Love Bug,'" *Network World*, May 8, 2000, pp. 14, 28.

5. Ron Zemke, "Tech-savvy and people-stupid," *Training*, July 2000, pp. 16–18.

6. Thomas York, "Invasion of privacy? E-mail monitoring is on the rise," *InformationWeek*, February 21, 2000, pp. 142–46.

7. Meserve, "People around the world bitten by 'Love Bug.'"

8. Shane Harris, "SoBig: a look back," *Government Executive*, November 2003, p. 72.

9. Charles Babcock, "Fast-moving virus slams e-mail systems," *InformationWeek*, August 2003, p. 22.

10. Paul Roberts, "The year ahead in security," *InfoWorld*, January 2004, p. 17.

11. David Kirkpatrick, "Taking back the Net," *Fortune*, September 29, 2003, pp. 117–22.

12. Robert Luhn, "Eliminate viruses," *PC World*, July 2002, p. 94.

13. Sara Cox Landolt, "Why the sky isn't falling," *Credit Union Management*, October 2000, pp. 52–54.

14. "Hackers attack *USA Today* web site," *Morning Sun*, July 13, 2002, p. 6.

15. George Hulme, "Vulnerabilities beckon some with a license to hack," *InformationWeek*, October 23, 2000, pp. 186–92.

16. Glenn Bischoff, "Fear of a black hat," *Telephony*, September 3, 2001, pp. 24–29.

17. Janet Kornblum, "Kournikova virus maker: no harm meant," *USA Today*, February 14, 2001, p. 3D.

18. Deborah Radcliff, "Firms increasingly call on cyberforensics teams," CNN.com, January 16, 2002 <archives.cnn.com/2002/TECH/internet/01/16/cyber.sleuthing.idg>, accessed January 12, 2006.

19. "*USA Today* says writer made up part of stories," *Dallas Morning News*, March 20, 2004, p. 11A.

20. Warren G. Kruse and Jay G. Heiser, *Computer Forensics: Incident Response Essentials* (New York: Addison-Wesley, 2002).

GLOSSARY

A

A/L unit See **arithmetic/logic unit**.

ad hoc, or **nonrecurring**, **decision** one that you make infrequently (perhaps only once) and you may even have different criteria for determining the best solution each time.

adaptive filtering asks you to rate products or situations and also monitors your actions over time to find out what you like and dislike.

adware software to generate ads that installs itself on your computer when you download some other (usually free) program from the Web.

affiliate programs arrangements made between e-commerce sites that direct users from one site to the other and by which, if a sale is made as a result, the originating site receives a commission.

AI See **artificial intelligence**.

alliance partner a company that you do business with on a regular business in a cooperative fashion, usually facilitated by IT systems.

American standard code for information interchange See **ASCII**.

analysis phase involves end users and IT specialists working together to gather, understand, and document the business requirements for the proposed system.

ANN See **artificial neural network**.

anonymous Web browsing (AWB) services, which in effect, hide your identity from the Web sites you visit.

antivirus software detects and removes or quarantines computer viruses.

application architects information technology professionals who can design creative technology-based business solutions.

application generation subsystem contains facilities to help you develop transaction-intensive applications.

application service provider (ASP) provides an outsourcing service for businesses software applications.

application software the software that enables you to solve specific problems or perform specific tasks.

arithmetic/logic unit (A/L unit) performs all arithmetic operations (e.g., addition and subtraction) and all logic operations (such as sorting and comparing numbers).

artificial intelligence (AI) the science of making machines imitate human thinking and behaviour.

artificial neural network (ANN) also called a **neural network**, an artificial intelligence system that is capable of finding and differentiating patterns.

ASCII (American standard code for information interchange) the coding system that most personal computers use to represent, process, and store information.

ASCII résumé See **scannable résumé**.

ASP See **application service provider**.

ASR See **automatic speech recognition**.

AutoFilter function filters a list and allows you to hide all the rows in a list except those that match criteria you specify.

automatic speech recognition (ASR) system not only captures spoken words but also distinguishes word groupings to form sentences.

AWB See **anonymous Web browsing**.

B

B2B marketplace an Internet-based service that brings together many buyers and sellers.

B2B See **business-to-business e-commerce**.

B2C See **business-to-consumer e-commerce**.

back office system used to fulfill and support customer orders.

back-propagation neural network a neural network trained by someone.

backup the process of making a copy of the information stored on a computer.

bandwidth or capacity of a communications medium is the amount of information a communications medium can transfer in a given amount of time.

banner ad a small ad on one Web site that advertises the products and services of another business, usually another dot-com.

barcode reader captures information that exists in the form of vertical bars whose width and distance apart determine a number.

barcode scanner reads information that is in the form of vertical bars whose width and spacing represent digits; often used in point-of-sale (POS) systems in the retail environment.

basic formatting tag a HTML tag that allows you to specify formatting for text.

benchmark a set of conditions used to measure how well a product or system functions.

BI See **business intelligence**.

binary digit (bit) the smallest unit of information your computer can process.

biochip an electronic chip that can perform a variety of physiological functions when inserted into the human body: blocking pain, restoring motor skills, improving sight, etc.

biometrics the use of your physical characteristics—such as your fingerprint, the blood vessels in the retina of your eye, the sound of your voice, or perhaps even your breath—to provide identification.

biometric scanner scans some human physical attribute, such as a fingerprint or iris, to identify persons for security purposes.

bit See **binary digit**.

black-hat hackers cyber vandals.

Bluetooth technology provides entirely wireless connections for all kinds of communication devices.

BPR See **business process reengineering**.

broadband high-capacity telecommunications pipeline capable of providing high-speed Internet service.

browser-safe colours 216 colours that can be represented using 8 bits and are visible in all browsers.

business intelligence (BI) knowledge about your own customers, competitors, partners, competitive environment, and internal operations. Business intelligence comes from information.

business intelligence (BI) system the IT applications and tools that support the business intelligence function within an organization.

business process a standardized set of activities that accomplishes a specific task, such as processing a customer's order.

business process reengineering (BPR) the reinventing of processes within a business.

business requirement a detailed knowledge worker request that the system must meet in order to be successful.

business-to-business (B2B) e-commerce the relationship of companies to customers who are primarily other businesses.

business-to-consumer (B2C) e-commerce the relationship of companies to customers who are primarily individuals.

buyer agent or **shopping bot** an intelligent agent on a Web site that helps you, the customer, find the products and services you want.

buyer power is high when buyers have many choices of whom to buy from, and low when their choices are few.

byte a group of eight bits that represents one natural-language character.

C

cable modem a device that uses your TV cable to deliver an Internet connection.

capacity planning determines the future IT infrastructure requirements for new equipment and additional network capacity.

CASE See **computer-aided software engineering tools**.

Cat 5 (or **Category 5**) cable is a better-constructed version of the phone twisted-pair cable.

Category 5 See **Cat 5**.

CAVE (cave automatic virtual environment) a special 3D virtual reality room that can display images of other people and objects located in other CAVEs all over the world.

CD-R (compact disk—recordable) an optical or laser disk with about 800 MB of storage capacity that offers once-only writing capability.

CD-ROM (compact disk—read-only memory) an optical or laser disk with about 800 MB of storage capacity that offers no writing capability. Most software today comes on CD-ROM.

CD-RW (compact disk—rewritable) an optical or laser disk with about 700 MB of storage capacity that offers unlimited writing capabilities.

central processing unit (CPU) the actual hardware that interprets and executes the software instructions and coordinates how all the other hardware devices work together.

chief information officer (CIO) the executive responsible for overseeing an organization's information resources.

choice the third step in the decision-making process, in which you decide on a plan to address the problem or opportunity.

CI See **competitive intelligence**.

CIO See **chief information officer**.

CIS See **customer-integrated system**.

class contains information and procedures and acts as a template to create objects.

click-and-mortar a retailer, such as Nordstrom, that has both an Internet presence and physical stores.

clickstream records information about you during a Web surfing session, such as what Web sites you visited, how long you were there, what ads you looked at, and what you bought.

click-through is counted whenever a person who visits a Web site clicks on an ad and is taken to the site of the advertiser.

client/server network a network in which one or more computers, called servers, provide services to the other computers, called clients.

coax See **coaxial cable**.

coaxial cable (coax) a cable consisting of a central wire surrounded by insulation, a metallic shield, and a final case of insulating material.

cold site a separate facility that does not have any computer equipment, but is a place where the knowledge workers can move after a disaster.

collaboration software software that allows people to work together on a given project or document.

collaboration system a system that is designed specifically to improve the performance of teams by supporting the sharing and flow of information.

collaborative filtering a technique to enable a Web site to support personalization.

collaborative planning, forecasting, and replenishment (CPFR) a concept that encourages and facilitates collaborative processes among members of a supply chain.

collaborative processing enterprise information portal provides knowledge workers with access to workgroup information such as e-mails, reports, meeting minutes, and memos.

collocation what happens when a vendor rents out space and telecommunication equipment to other companies.

communications media the paths, or physical channels, in a network over which information travels.

communications protocol (protocol) a set of rules that every computer follows to transfer information.

communications satellite microwave repeater in space.

communications service provider third party who furnishes the conduit for information.

compact disk—read-only memory See **CD-ROM**.

compact disk—recordable See **CD-R**.

compact disk—rewritable See **CD-RW**.

competitive intelligence (CI) business intelligence focused on the external competitive environment.

composite primary key consists of the primary key fields from the two intersecting relations.

composite relation See **intersection relation**.

computer-aided software engineering (CASE) tools are software suites that automate system development.

computer crime is a crime in which a computer, or computers, plays a significant part.

computer forensics is the gathering, authentication, examination, and analysis of electronic information stored on any type of computer media, such as hard drives, floppy disks, or CDs.

computer network See **network**.

computer virus See **virus**.

conditional formatting highlights the information in a cell that meets some criteria you specify.

connectivity software enables you to use your computer to "dial up" or connect to another computer.

consumer-to-consumer (C2C) e-commerce a type of commerce in which an individual sells products and services to customers who are primarily other individuals.

control unit interprets software instructions and tells the other hardware devices what to do, on the basis of the software instructions.

conversion rate the percentage of customers who visit a Web site who actually buy something.

cookie a small record deposited on your hard disk by a Web site containing information about you.

copyright the legal protection afforded an expression of an idea, such as a song, video game, and some types of proprietary documents.

counterfeit software software that is manufactured to look like the real thing and sold as such.

CPFR See **collaborative planning, forecasting, and replenishment**.

CPU See **central processing unit**.

cracker a hacker for hire who engages in electronic corporate espionage.

crash-proof software utility software that helps you save information if your system crashes and you're forced to turn it off and then back on again.

create, read, update, delete See **CRUD**.

critical success factor (CSF) a factor critical to your organization's success.

CRM See **customer relationship management**.

crossover part of a genetic algorithm in which portions of good outcomes are combined in the hope of creating an even better outcome.

CRT a monitor that looks like a television set.

CRUD (create, read, update, delete) the four primary procedures by which a system can manipulate information.

CSF See **critical success factor**.

culture the collective personality of a nation or society, encompassing language, traditions, currency, religion, history, music, and acceptable behaviour, among other things.

Custom AutoFilter function allows you to hide all the rows in a list except those that match criteria, besides "is equal to," you specify.

customer relationship management (CRM) system uses information about customers to gain insights into their needs, wants, and behaviours in order to serve them better.

customer-integrated system (CIS) an extension of a transaction processing system (TPS) that puts technology in the hands of an organization's customers and allows them to process their own transactions.

cyberterrorist is one who seeks to cause harm to people or destroy critical systems or information.

D

data raw facts that describe a phenomenon.

data administration the function in an organization that plans for, oversees the development of, and monitors the information resource.

data administration subsystem helps you manage the overall database environment by providing facilities for backup and recovery, security management, query optimization, concurrency control, and change management.

database a collection of information that you organize and access according to the logical structure of that information.

database administration the function in an organization that is responsible for the more technical and operational aspects of managing the information contained in organizational databases (which can include data warehouses and data marts).

database management system (DBMS) helps you specify the logical organization for a database and access and use the information within the database.

database-based workflow system stores the document in a central location and automatically asks the knowledge workers to access the document when it's their turn to edit the document.

data cleansing ensures all information is accurate.

data definition subsystem helps you create and maintain the data dictionary and define the structure of the files in a database.

data dictionary contains the logical structure for the information.

data manipulation subsystem helps you add, change, and delete information in a database and mine it for valuable information.

data mart a subset of a data warehouse in which only a focused portion of the data warehouse information is kept.

data mining agent an intelligent agent that operates in a data warehouse discovering information.

data mining tool software tool you use to query information in a data warehouse.

data raw facts that describe a particular phenomenon.

data warehouse a logical collection of information—gathered from many different operational databases—used to create business intelligence that supports business analysis activities and decision-making tasks.

DBMS engine accepts logical requests from the various other DBMS subsystems, con-

verts them into their physical equivalent, and actually accesses the database and data dictionary as they exist on a storage device.

DBMS See **database management system**.

DDoS See **distributed denial-of-service (DDoS) attack**.

decentralized computing an environment in which an organization splits computing power and locates it in functional business areas as well as on the desktops of knowledge workers.

decision support system (DSS) a highly flexible and interactive IT system designed to support decision making when the problem is not structured.

decision-processing enterprise information portal provides knowledge workers with corporate information for making key business decisions.

demand aggregation combines purchase requests from multiple buyers into a single large order which justifies a discount from the business.

denial-of-service (DoS) attack floods a Web site with so many requests for service that it slows down or crashes.

design is the second phase of the decision-making process, in which you consider possible ways of solving the problem, filling the need, or taking advantage of the opportunity.

design phase builds a technical blueprint of how the proposed system will work.

desktop computer the most popular choice for personal computing needs.

development phase takes all of your detailed design documents from the design phase and transforms them into an actual system.

digital camera a camera that captures images as a series of 1s and 0s.

digital cash (also called **electronic cash** or **e-cash**) an electronic representation of cash.

digital dashboard displays key information gathered from several sources on a computer screen in a format tailored to the needs and wants of an individual knowledge worker.

digital economy marked by the electronic movement of all types of information, not limited to numbers, words, graphs, and photos but including physiological information such as voice recognition and synthesization, biometrics (your retina scan and breath for example), and holograms.

digital still camera a digital camera that captures still images in varying resolutions.

digital subscriber line (DSL) enables a high-speed Internet connection using phone lines, and allows you to use your phone for voice communications at the same time.

digital video camera a digital camera that captures video digitally.

digital wallet a combination of software and information, by means of which a customer can make payments electronically. Can be stored either on the client side or on the server side.

direct material a material used in production in a manufacturing company or that is put on the shelf for sale in a retail environment.

directory search engine organizes listings of Web sites into hierarchical lists.

disaster recovery cost curve charts (1) the cost to your organization of the unavailability of information and technology and (2) the cost to your organization of recovering from a disaster over time.

disaster recovery plan a detailed process for recovering information or an IT system in the event of a catastrophic disaster such as a fire or flood.

disk optimization software utility software that organizes your information on your hard disk in the most efficient way.

distributed denial-of-service (DDoS) attack a DoS attack from multiple computers.

distribution chain the path followed from the originator of a product or service to the end consumer.

document management system manages a document through its life cycle.

documentation management system a type of collaboration software (software that allows people to work together) that manages documents through their life cycle: creation, modification, security, approval, distribution, and archiving.

domain expert the person who provides the domain expertise in the form of problem-solving strategies.

domain expertise the set of problem-solving steps; the reasoning process that will solve the problem.

domain name identifies a specific computer on the Web and the main page of the entire site.

DoS See **denial-of-service (DoS) attack**.

dot pitch the distance between the centres of a pair of like-coloured pixels.

DSL See **digital subscriber line (DSL)**.

DSS See **decision support system**.

DVD-R an optical or laser disk with upwards of 17 GB storage capacity that offers once-only writing capability.

DVD-ROM an optical or laser disk with upwards of 17 GB storage capacity that offers no writing capability. The trend is now for rented movies to be on DVD.

DVD-RW, DVD-RAM, or **DVD+RW** (all different names by different manufacturers) an optical or laser disk that offers unlimited writing and updating capabilities on the DVD.

E

EAI middleware See **enterprise application integration middleware**.

EAI See **enterprise application integration**.

EBPP See **electronic bill presentment and payment**.

ebXML a set of technical specifications for business documents built around XML designed to permit enterprises of any size and in any geographical location to conduct business over the Internet.

e-commerce commerce accelerated and enhanced by information technology, in particular the Internet.

EDI See **electronic data interchange**.

e-government the application of e-commerce technologies in governmental agencies.

EIP See **enterprise information portal**.

EIS See **executive information system**.

electronic bill presentment and payment (EBPP) systems send us our bills over the Internet and give us an easy way to pay them if the amount looks correct.

electronic catalogue designed to present products to customers or partners all over the world via the Web.

electronic cheque a mechanism for sending money electronically from a chequing or savings account to another person or organization. One major example is online banking.

electronic commerce See **e-commerce**.

electronic data interchange (EDI) the direct computer-to-computer transfer of transaction information contained in standard business documents, such as invoices and purchase orders, in a standard format.

electronic job market consists of employers using Internet technologies to advertise and screen potential employees.

electronic mail software See **e-mail software**.

electronic marketplace (e-marketplace) an interactive business providing a central market space where multiple buyers and suppliers can engage in e-commerce and/or other e-commerce business activities.

electronic portfolio (e-portfolio) a collection of Web documents used to support a stated purpose such as demonstrating writing, photography, or job skills.

e-mail (electronic mail) software enables you to electronically communicate with other people by sending and receiving e-mail.

e-marketplace See **electronic marketplace**.

encapsulation means information hiding.

encryption scrambles the contents of a file so that you can't read it without having the right decryption key.

end user development See **selfsourcing**.

enterprise application integration (EAI) the process of developing an infrastructure that enables employees to quickly implement new or changing business processes.

enterprise application integration middleware (EAI middleware) allows organizations to develop different levels of integration from the data level to the business-process level.

enterprise information portal (EIP) allows knowledge workers to access company information via a Web interface.

enterprise resource planning (ERP) the method of getting and keeping an overview of every part of the business (a bird's-eye view, so to speak), so that production, development, selling, and servicing of goods and services will all be coordinated to contribute to the company's goals and objectives.

enterprise software a suite of software that includes (1) a set of common business applications, (2) tools for modelling how the entire organization works, and (3) development tools for building applications unique to your organization.

entity class a concept—typically people, places, or things—about which you wish to store information and that you can identify with a unique key (called the primary key).

entity-relationship (E-R) diagram a graphic method of representing entity classes and their relationships.

entry barrier a product or service feature that customers have come to expect from companies in a particular industry.

e-portfolio See **electronic portfolio**.

E-R See **entity-relationship (E-R) diagram**.

ERP See **enterprise resource planning**.

Ethernet card the most common type of network interface card.

ethical (white-hat) hacker a computer security professional hired by a company to purposely break into its computer system.

ethical hacker See **white-hat** (or **ethical**) **hacker**.

ethics the principles and standards that guide our behaviour toward other people.

executive information system (EIS) a highly interactive IT system that allows you to first view highly summarized information and then choose how you would like to see greater detail, which may alert you to potential problems or opportunities.

expandability refers to how easy it is to add features and functions to a system.

expansion bus moves information from your CPU and RAM to all of your other hardware devices such as your microphone and printer.

expansion card a circuit board that you insert into an expansion slot.

expansion slot a long, skinny socket on the motherboard into which you insert an expansion card.

expert system, also called a **knowledge-based system**, an artificial intelligence system that applies reasoning capabilities to reach a conclusion.

explanation module the part of an expert system where they "why" information, supplied by the domain expert, is stored to be accessed by knowledge workers who want to know why the expert systems asked a question or reached a conclusion.

extensible markup language (XML) a coding language for the Web that lets computers interpret the *meaning* of information in Web documents.

external information describes the environment surrounding the organization.

extranet an intranet that is restricted to an organization and certain outsiders, such as customers and suppliers.

F

facial recognition software software that can identify a person by his or her facial characteristics.

Fair Use Doctrine allows you to use copyrighted material in certain situations.

feature analysis the step of ASR in which the system captures your words as your speak into a microphone, eliminates any background noise, and converts the digital signals of your speech in phonemes (syllables).

feature creep occurs when developers add extra features that were not part of the initial requirements.

FEDI See **financial EDI**.

file transfer protocol (ftp) the communications protocol that allows you to transfer files of information from one computer to another.

file transfer protocol (ftp) server a computer that maintains a collection of downloadable files.

financial cybermediaries Internet-based companies that make it easy for one person to pay another person over the Internet.

financial EDI (FEDI) the use of EDI for payments.

firewall hardware and/or software that protects a computer or network from intruders.

Five Forces Model a model developed to determine the relative attractiveness of an industry.

flash memory a rewritable memory chip that retains data without needing a power supply.

flat-panel display thin, lightweight monitor that takes up much less space than a CRT.

floppy disk a storage device that is good for portability of information and ease of updating but holds only 1.44 MB of information.

foreign key a primary key of one file (relation) that appears in another file (relation).

forensic image copy an exact copy or snapshot of the contents of an electronic medium.

front office system the primary interface to customers and sales channels.

ftp See **file transfer protocol**.

G

G2B See **government to business**.

G2C See **government to consumer**.

G2G See **government to government**.

GB See **gigabyte**.

genetic algorithm an artificial intelligence system that mimics the evolutionary, survival-of-the-fittest process to generate increasingly better solutions to a problem.

geographic information system (GIS) a decision support system designed specifically to work with spatial information.

GHz See **gigahertz**.

Gig See **gigabyte**.

gigabyte (**GB** or **Gig**) roughly 1 billion characters.

gigahertz (GHz) the number of billions of CPU cycles per second.

GIS See **geographic information system**.

global digital divide the term used specifically to describe differences in IT access and capabilities between different countries or regions of the world.

global economy one in which customers, businesses, suppliers, distributors, and manufacturers all operate without regard to physical and geographical boundaries.

global positioning system (GPS) a collection of 24 earth-orbiting satellites that continuously transmit radio signals to determine your current longitude, latitude, speed, and direction of movement.

global reach the ability to extend a company's reach to customers anywhere there is an Internet connection, and at a much lower cost.

glove an input device that captures and records the shape and movement of your hand and fingers and the strength of your hand and finger movements.

government to business (G2B) the electronic commerce activities performed between a government and its business partners for such purposes as purchasing direct and indirect materials, soliciting bids for work, and accepting bids for work.

government to consumer (G2C) the electronic commerce activities performed between a government and its citizens or consumers including paying taxes, registering vehicles, and providing information and services.

government to government (G2G, intra-G2G) the electric commerce activities limited to performing electronic commerce activities within a single nation's government focusing on vertical integration (local, city, state, and federal) and horizontal integration (among the various branches and agencies).

GPS See **global positioning system**.

graphical user interface (GUI) the interface to an information system.

grid computing harnesses far-flung computers together by way of the Internet or a virtual private network to share CPU power, databases, and storage.

group document database acts as a powerful storage facility for organizing and managing all documents related to specific teams.

groupware the popular term for the software component that supports the collaborative efforts of a team.

GUI screen design the ability to model the information system screens for an entire system.

GUI See **graphical user interface**.

H

hacker a very knowledgeable person who uses his or her knowledge to invade other people's computers.

hacktivist a politically motivated hacker who uses the Internet to send a political message of some kind.

Handspring, with the Palm, is one of the two major types of PDAs.

hard disk storage device that rests within your system box and offers both ease of updating and great storage capacity.

hardware the physical devices that make up a computer (often referred to as a computer system).

heading tag a HTML tag that makes certain information, such as titles, stand out on your Web site.

headset a combined input and output device that (1) captures and records the movement of your head and (2) contains a screen that covers your entire field of vision and displays various views of an environment based on your movements.

Health Insurance Portability and Accountability Act in the United States, a law that forces the health care industry to install policies and procedures to maintain the confidentiality of patient information.

help desk a group of people who respond to knowledge workers' questions.

hidden job market all those job opportunities that are not advertised; up to 80 percent of new jobs fall into this category.

high-capacity floppy disk storage device that is good for portability and ease of updating and holds between 100 MB and 250 MB of information. Superdisks and Zip disks are examples.

holographic device a device that creates, captures, and/or displays images in true 3D.

holographic storage device a device for electronic storage of information on a medium made up of 3D crystal-like objects with many sides or faces.

home page the main page and entry point of a Web site.

Home Phoneline Networking Alliance See **Home PNA**.

Home PNA (Home Phoneline Networking Alliance) allows you to network your home computers using telephone wiring.

horizontal market software application software that is general enough to be suitable for use in a variety of industries.

horizontal e-marketplace an electronic marketplace that connects buyers and sellers across many industries, primarily for MRO materials commerce.

hot site a separate and fully equipped facility where the company can move immediately after a disaster and resume business.

HTML See **hypertext markup language**.

HTML document a file that contains your Web site content and HTML formatting instructions.

HTML tag specifies the formatting and presentation of information on a Web site.

http See **hypertext transfer protocol**.

hyperlink See **link**.

hypertext markup language (HTML) the language you use to create a Web site.

hypertext transfer protocol (http) the communications protocol that supports the movement of information over the Web, essentially from a Web server to you.

I

ICE See **integrated collaboration environment**.

identity theft pretending to be another person by stealing their personal information, and using the new identity for financial gain or self-concealment.

IEEE 802.11b See **WiFi**.

IG2G See **international government-to-government**.

image scanner captures images, photos, text, and artwork that already exist on paper.

implant chip a technology-enabled microchip implanted into the human body.

implementation the final step in the decision-making process where you put your plan into action.

implementation phase distributes the system to all of the knowledge workers and they begin using the system to perform their everyday jobs.

inference engine the processing component of the expert system. It takes your problem facts and searches the knowledge base for rules that fit your problem facts.

information age a time when knowledge is power.

information data that have a particular meaning within a specific context.

information decomposition breaking down the information and procedures into multiple classes for ease of use and understandability.

information granularity the amount of detail within information.

information technology (IT) any computer-based tool that people use to work with information and support the information and information-processing needs of an organization.

information view includes all of the information stored within a system.

information-literate knowledge workers can define what information they need, know how and where to obtain that information, understand the information once they receive it, and act appropriately on the basis of the information to help the organization achieve the greatest advantage.

infrared (or **IR** or **IrDA**) a wireless communications medium that uses radio waves to transmit signals or information.

Infrared Data Association See **IrDA (Infrared Data Association) port**.

inheritance the ability to define superclass and subclass relationships among classes.

inkjet printer makes images by forcing ink droplets through nozzles.

input device a tool you use to capture information and commands.

insourcing a project means that IT specialists within your organization will develop the system.

instance an occurrence of an entity class that can be uniquely described.

integrated collaboration environment (ICE) the environment in which virtual teams do their work.

integration allows separate systems to communicate directly with each other by automatically exporting data files from one system and importing them into another system.

integration testing verifying that separate systems can work together.

integrity constraints rules that help ensure the quality of the information.

intellectual property intangible creative work that is embodied in physical form.

intelligence the first step in the decision-making process where you find or recognize a problem, need, or opportunity (also called the diagnostic phase of decision making).

intelligent agent software that assists you, or acts on your behalf, in performing repetitive computer-related tasks.

interface any device that calls procedures and can include such things as a keyboard, mouse, and touch screens.

internal information describes specific operational aspects of the organization.

international government-to-government (inter-G2G) the electronic commerce activities performed between two or more governments, including foreign aid.

international virtual private network (international VPN) virtual private networks that depend on services offered by phone companies of various nationalities.

international VPN See **international virtual private network**.

Internet a vast network of computers that connects millions of people all over the world.

Internet backbone the major set of connections for computers on the Internet.

Internet relay chat See **IRC (Internet relay chat) server**.

Internet server computer a computer that provides information and services on the Internet.

Internet service provider (ISP) a company that provides individuals, organizations, and businesses access to the Internet.

Internet telephony a combination of hardware and software that uses the Internet as the medium for transmission of telephone calls in place of traditional telephone networks.

Internet virtual private network a technology that enables establishment of a virtual network over the Internet consisting of a company, its suppliers, and its customers.

interorganizational system (IOS) one that automates the flow of information between organizations to support the planning, design, development, production, and delivery of products and services.

intersection relation (sometimes called **composite relation**) a relation you create to eliminate a many-to-many relationship; represents the intersection of primary keys of two relations.

intranet an internal organizational Internet, guarded against outside access by a special security feature called a firewall (which can be software, hardware, or a combination of the two).

intrusion-detection software looks for people on the network who shouldn't be there or who are acting suspiciously.

IOS See **interorganizational system**.

IRC (Internet relay chat) server supports your use of discussion groups and chat rooms.

IrDA (Infrared Data Association) port a transmitter/receiver for wireless devices that works much like the remote control for a TV set.

ISP See **Internet service provider**.

IT infrastructure includes the hardware, software, and telecommunication equipment that, when combined, provides the underlying foundation to support the organization's goals.

IT See **information technology**.

J

JAD See **joint application development**.

JIT See **just-in-time**.

joint application development (JAD) occurs when knowledge workers and IT specialists meet, sometimes for several days, to define or review the business requirements for the system.

just-in-time (JIT) an approach that produces or delivers a product or service just at the time it is needed by the customer or process.

K

keyboard a computer component that enables input using one's hands; today's most popular input technology.

key logger (or **key trapper**) **software** a program that, when installed on a computer, records every keystroke and mouse click.

key trapper See **key logger software**.

KM system See **knowledge management (KM) system**.

knowledge acquisition the component of the expert system that the knowledge engineer uses to enter the rules.

knowledge base stores the rules of the expert system.

knowledge-based system, also known as an expert system, an artificial intelligence system that applies reasoning capabilities to reach a conclusion.

knowledge engineer the person who formulates the domain expertise into an expert system.

knowledge management (KM) system an IT system that supports the capturing, organization, and dissemination of knowledge (i.e., know-how) throughout an organization.

knowledge worker works with and produces information as a product.

knowledge worker development See **selfsourcing**.

L

LAN See **local area network**.

language processing the step of automatic speech recognition (ASR) in which the system attempts to make sense of what you're saying by comparing the word phonemes generated in the pattern classification step of ASR with a language model database.

laser printer forms images using an electrostatic process, the same way a photocopier works.

last-mile bottleneck problem occurs when information is travelling on the Internet over a very fast line for a certain distance and then comes near your home where it must travel over a slower line.

legacy system a previously built system using older technologies such as mainframe computers and programming languages such as COBOL.

link (hyperlink) clickable text or an image that takes you to another site or page on the Web.

Linux an open-source operating system that provides a rich operating environment for high-end workstations and network servers.

list a collection of information arranged in columns and rows in which each column displays one particular type of information.

list definition table a description of a list by column.

local area network (LAN) a network that covers a limited geographic distance, such as an office, building, or a group of buildings in close proximity to each other.

logical view focuses on how you as a knowledge worker need to arrange and access information to meet your particular business needs.

logistics the set of processes that plans for and controls the efficient and effective transportation and storage of supplies from suppliers to customers.

loyalty program an IT-based rewards system based on the amount of business customers do with an organization, involving keeping track of account activity.

M

M See **megabyte**.

Mac OS the operating system for today's Apple computers.

macro virus spreads by binding itself to software such as Word or Excel.

mailing list a discussion group organized by area of interest; subscribers communicate with other members by means of e-mail.

mail server provides e-mail services and accounts.

mainframe computer (or **mainframe**) a computer designed to meet the computing needs of hundreds of people in a large business environment.

mainframe See **mainframe computer**.

maintenance phase monitors and supports the new system to ensure it continues to meet the business goals.

maintenance, repair, and operations (MRO) materials (indirect materials) materials that are necessary for running a modern corporation, but that do not relate to the company's primary business activities. An example would be ballpoint pens.

MAN See **municipal area network**.

management information system (MIS) deals with the planning for, development, management, and use of information technology tools to help people perform all tasks related to information processing and management.

marketing mix the set of marketing tools that a firm uses to pursue its marketing objectives in the target market.

mass customization when a business gives its customers the opportunity to tailor its product or service to the customer's specifications.

MB See **megabyte**.

m-commerce electronic commerce conducted over a wireless device such as a cell phone or personal digital assistant.

MD5 hash value a mathematically generated number that is unique for each individual storage medium at a specific point in time, because it's based on the contents of that medium.

MDA See **multidimensional analysis**.

Meg See **megabyte**.

megabyte (**MB** or **M** or **Meg**) roughly one million bytes.

megahertz (MHz) the number of millions of CPU cycles per second.

message in object-oriented programming, how objects communicate with each other.

messaging-based workflow system sends work assignments through an e-mail system.

meta tags a part of a Web site text not displayed to users but accessible to browsers and search engines for finding and categorizing Web sites.

MHz See **megahertz**.

micro-payment a technique to facilitate the exchange of small amounts of money for an Internet transaction.

microphone a device that transforms live sounds into electrical signals for the purpose of transmitting or recording sound (necessary, for example, for automatic speech recognition).

Microsoft Windows 2000 Millennium (Windows Me) an operating system for a home computer user with utilities for setting up a home network and performing video, photo, and music editing and cataloguing.

Microsoft Windows 2000 Professional (Windows 2000 Pro) an operating system for people who have a personal computer connected to a network of other computers at work or at school.

Microsoft Windows XP Home Microsoft's latest upgrade to Windows Me, with enhanced features allowing multiple people to use the same computer.

Microsoft Windows XP Professional (Windows XP Pro) Microsoft's latest upgrade to Windows 2000 Pro.

microwave a type of radio transmission used to transmit information.

mid-range computer See **minicomputer**.

minicomputer (sometimes called a **mid-range computer**) designed to meet the computing needs of several people simultaneously in a small to medium-size business environment.

MIS See **management information system**.

model management a component of a decision support system (DSS) that consists of the DSS models and the DSS model management system.

modelling drawing a graphical representation of a design.

modem See **telephone modem**.

monitoring-and-surveillance agents (or **predictive agents**) intelligent agents that observe and report on equipment.

mouse a component enabling computer input by sliding a small unit on a desk surface, which moves a pointer or cursor on the computer screen enabling selection of items or locations; one of today's most popular input devices.

MRO materials See **maintenance, repair, and operations (MRO) materials**.

multidimensional analysis (MDA) tools slice-and-dice techniques that allow you to view multidimensional information from different perspectives.

multifunction printer a printer that scans, copies, and faxes as well as prints.

multimedia (HTML) résumé a résumé that uses a multimedia format and that exists on the Internet for employers to explore at their convenience.

multi-state CPU a CPU that works with information represented in more than just two states—for example, 10, with each state representing a digit between the 0 and 9.

multitasking allows you to work with more than one piece of software at a time.

municipal (metropolitan) area network (MAN) a network that covers a metropolitan area.

mutation part of a genetic algorithm; the process of trying combinations and evaluating the success (or failure) of the outcome.

N

NAP See **network access point**.

network two or more computers connected so that they can communicate with each other and possibly share information, software, peripheral devices, and/or processing power.

network access point (NAP) a point on the Internet where several connections converge.

network hub a device that connects multiple computers into a network.

network interface card (NIC) an expansion card or a PC card (for a notebook computer) that connects your computer to a network and provides the doorway for information to flow in and out.

network service provider (NSP), such as MCI or AT&T, owns and maintains routing computers at NAPs and even the lines that connect the NAPs to each other.

neural network (often called an **artificial neural network** or **ANN**) an artificial intelligence system capable of finding and differentiating patterns.

NIC See **network interface card**.

nonrecurring, or **ad hoc**, **decision** one that you make infrequently (perhaps only once); you may have different criteria for determining the best solution in each case.

nonstructured decision a decision for which there may be several "right" answers and there is no precise way to get a right answer.

normalization a process of assuring that a relational database structure can be implemented as a series of two-dimensional relations.

notebook computer (or **notebook**) a fully functional computer designed for you to carry around and run on battery power.

NSP See **network service provider**.

O

object in object-oriented programming, an instance of a class.

objective information quantifiably describes something that is known.

object-oriented (OO) approach combines information and procedures into a single view.

object-oriented (OO) database works with traditional database information and also complex data types such as diagrams, schematic drawings, video, sound, and text documents.

object-oriented (OO) programming language one used to develop object-oriented systems.

offshore outsourcing in the field of management information systems, using organizations from developing countries to write code and develop systems.

OLAP See **online analytical processing**.

OLTP See **online transaction processing**.

OMR See **optical mark recognition**.

online ad (banner ad) small advertisements that appear on Web sites other than that of the company.

online analytical processing (OLAP) the manipulation of information to support decision making.

online training runs over the Internet or off a CD-ROM.

online transaction processing (OLTP) gathering input information, processing it, and updating existing information to reflect the gathered and processed information.

OO See **object-oriented (OO) approach**.

operating system software system software that controls your application software and manages how your hardware devices work together.

operational database a database that supports OLTP.

operational management manages and directs the day-to-day operations and implementations of the goals and strategies.

optical character reader reads characters that appear on a page or sales tag; often used in point-of-sale (POS) systems in the retail environment.

optical fibre a telecommunications medium that uses a very thin glass or plastic fibre through which pulses of light travel.

optical mark reader detects the presence or absence of a mark in a predetermined spot on the page; often used to read true/false and multiple-choice exam answers.

optical mark recognition (OMR) detects the presence or absence of a mark in a predetermined place (popular for grading multiple-choice exams).

output device a tool you use to see, hear, or otherwise accept the results of your information-processing requests.

outsourcing the delegation of specific work to a third party for a specified length of time, at a specified cost, and at a specified level of service.

P

Palm, with the Handspring, is one of the two major types of PDAs; the other type is PocketPCs.

Palm Operating System (Palm OS) the operating system for Palm and Handspring PDAs.

Palm OS See **Palm Operating System**.

parallel connector one with 25 pins, which fit into the corresponding holes in the port. Most printers use parallel connectors.

parallel implementation using both the old and new system until it is certain that the new system performs correctly.

pattern classification the step of ASR in which the system matches your spoken phonemes to a phoneme sequence stored in an acoustic model database.

PDA See **personal digital assistant**.

PDF See **portable document format**.

PDF résumé See **portable document format résumé**.

peer-to-peer collaboration software permits users to communicate in real time and share files without going through a central server.

peer-to-peer network a network in which a small number of computers share hardware (such as a printer), software and/or information.

performance how quickly an IT system performs a certain process.

personal agent (or **user agent**) an intelligent agent that takes action on your behalf.

personal agent See **user agent**.

personal digital assistant (PDA) a small handheld computer that helps you surf the Web and perform simple tasks such as note-taking, calendaring, appointment scheduling, and maintaining an address book.

personal productivity software helps you perform personal tasks—such as writing a memo, creating a graph, and creating a slide presentation—that you can usually do even if you don't own a computer.

phased implementation implementing a new system in phases (e.g., accounts receivable, then accounts payable), verifying they work correctly before implementing other parts of the system.

physical view deals with how information is physically arranged, stored, and accessed on some type of storage device such as a hard disk.

pilot implementation having only a small group of people use the new system until it works correctly, and then adding the remaining people to the system.

pirated software copyrighted software that undergoes unauthorized use, duplication, distribution or sale.

pivot table an arrangement of information that enables you to group and summarize it.

PKE See **public key encryption**.

plain-text résumé See **scannable résumé**.

planning phase involves determining a solid plan for developing your information system.

plunge implementation discarding an old system completely, and immediately using the new system.

PocketPC one of the two major types of PDAs; the other is the Palm and the Handspring.

Pocket PC OS (or **Windows CE**) the operating system for the PocketPC PDA.

pointing stick small pen-like computer input device that causes the pointer to move on the screen as you apply directional pressure (popular on notebooks).

point-of-sale (POS) the point in time and place of a transaction, typically in a retail environment; often a good point for capturing information.

polymorphism having many forms.

pop-under ad a type of pop-up ad that you do not see until you close your current browser window.

pop-up ad a small Web Page containing an advertisement that appears on your screen outside the site you are viewing.

port the plug-in found on the outside of your system box (usually in the back) into which you plug a connector.

portable document format (PDF) the standard electronic distribution file format for heavily formatted documents such as a presentation résumé because it retains the original document formatting.

portable document format résumé (PDF résumé) a standard electronic distribution résumé typically used for e-mailing.

predictive agent (or **monitoring-and-surveillance agent**) an intelligent agent that observes and reports on equipment.

predictive agents See **monitoring-and-surveillance agents.**

presence awareness a software function that determines whether a user is immediately reachable or not.

primary key a field (or group of fields in some cases) that uniquely describes each record.

privacy the right to be left alone when you want to be, to have control over your own personal possessions, and not to be observed without your consent.

private network the communications media that your organization owns or exclusively leases to connect networks or network components.

procedure manipulates or changes information.

procedure view contains all of the procedures within a system.

profile filtering requires that you choose terms or enter keywords to provide a more personal picture of you and your preferences.

program a set of instructions that, when executed, cause a computer to behave in a certain manner.

programming language the tool developers use to write a program.

project manager an individual who is an expert in project planning and management, defines and develops the project plan, and tracks the plan to ensure all key project milestones are completed on time.

project milestone represents a key date for which you need a certain group of activities performed.

project plan defines the what, when, and who questions of system development including all activities to be performed, the individuals, or resources, who will perform the activities, and the time required to complete each activity.

project scope clearly defines the high-level system requirements.

project scope document a written definition of the scope of a project; usually no longer than a paragraph.

proof-of-concept prototype a prototype you use to prove the technical feasibility of a proposed system.

protocol See **communications protocol.**

prototype a model of a proposed product, service, or system.

prototyping the process of building a model that demonstrates the features of a proposed product, service, or system.

psychographic filtering anticipates your preferences on the basis of the answers you give to a questionnaire.

public key encryption (PKE) an encryption system that uses two keys: a public key that everyone can have and a private key for only the recipient.

public network a network on which your organization competes for time with others.

push technology an environment in which businesses and organizations come to you with information, services, and product offerings based on your profile.

Q

QBE See **query-by-example (QBE) tool.**

query-and-reporting tools tools similar to query-by-example (QBE) tools, SQL, and report generators in the typical database environment.

query-by-example (QBE) tool helps you graphically design the answer to a question.

R

RAM (random access memory) temporary storage that holds the information you're working with, the application software you're using, and the operating system software you're using.

random access memory See **RAM.**

recovery the process of reinstalling the backup information in the event the information was lost.

recurring decision a decision that you have to make repeatedly and often periodically, whether weekly, monthly, quarterly, or yearly.

relation describes each two-dimensional table or file in the relational model.

relational database a database that uses a series of logically related two-dimensional tables or files to store information.

relational database model uses a series of logically related two-dimensional tables or files to store information in the form of a database.

repeater a device that receives a radio signal, strengthens it, and sends it on.

report generator helps you quickly define formats of reports and what information you want to see in a report.

request for proposal (RFP) a formal document that describes in detail your logical requirements for a proposed system and invites outsourcing organizations (vendors) to submit bids for its development.

requirements definition document defines all of the business requirements, prioritizes them in order of business importance and place them in a formal comprehensive document.

resolution of a printer the number of dots per inch (dpi) it produces, which is the same principle as the resolution in monitors.

resolution of a screen the number of pixels it has. Pixels (picture elements) are the dots that make up an image on your screen.

résumé a summary of a person's qualifications for a job—an organized collection of information that will "sell" skills to an employer.

reverse auction the process in which a buyer posts its interest in buying a certain quantity of items, and sellers compete for the business by submitting successively lower bids until there is only one seller left.

RFP See **request for proposal.**

risk assessment is the process of evaluating IT assets, their importance to the organization, and their susceptibility to threats, to measure the risk exposure of these assets.

risk management consists of the identification of risks or threats, the implementation of security measures, and the monitoring of those measures for effectiveness.

rivalry among existing competitors makes an industry less attractive to enter when high and more attractive to enter when low.

robot a mechanical device equipped with simulated human senses and the capability of taking action on its own.

router a device that acts as a smart hub connecting computers into a network, and it also separates your network from any other network it's connected to.

rule-based expert system the type of expert system that expresses the problem-solving process as rules.

S

Safe Harbor principles the set of rules to which U.S. businesses that want to trade with the European Union (EU) must adhere.

sales force automation (SFA) system automatically tracks all of the steps in the sales process.

satellite modem a modem that allows you to get Internet access from a satellite dish.

scalability the ability of an information system to adapt to increased demands on its resources.

scannable résumé (or **ASCII résumé** or **plain-text résumé**) a résumé designed to be evaluated by skills-extraction software and that typically is devoid of text formatting.

scanner a device that captures images, photos, and artwork that already exist on paper.

SCM See **supply chain management**.

scope creep occurs when the scope of a project increases.

script bunny (or **script kiddie**) a person who would like to be a hacker but doesn't have much technical expertise.

script kiddie See **script bunny**.

SDLC See **systems development life cycle**.

search engine a facility on the Web that helps you find sites with the information and/or services you want.

security auditing software checks out your computer or network for potential weaknesses.

secure electronic transaction (SET) the transmission security method that ensures transactions are legitimate as well as secure; an SET encrypts information before sending it over the Internet.

secure sockets layer (SSL) a method of creating a secure and private connection between a Web client computer and a Web server computer, encrypting the information, and sending it over the Internet.

selection part of a genetic algorithm that gives preference to better outcomes.

self-organizing neural network finds, with no human input, patterns and relationships in vast amounts of data.

selfsourcing (also called **knowledge worker development** or **end user development**) the development and support of IT systems by knowledge workers with little or no help from IT specialists.

selling prototype a prototype you use to convince people of the worth of a proposed system.

semistructured decision a decision that is partly structured and partly nonstructured.

serial connector usually has 9 holes but may have 25, which fit into the corresponding number of pins in the port. Serial connectors are often most used for monitors and certain types of modems.

server farm a location that stores a group of servers in a single place.

service level agreement (SLA) defines the specific responsibilities of the service provider and sets the customer expectations.

SFA See **sales force automation**.

shared information an environment in which an organization's information is organized in one central location, allowing anyone to access and use it as they need to.

shopping bot or **buyer agent** an intelligent agent on a Web site that helps you, the customer, find the products and services you want.

sign-off the knowledge workers' actual signatures indicating they approve all of the business requirements.

skill words nouns and adjectives used by organizations to describe job skills which should be woven into the text of applicants' résumés.

SLA See **service level agreement**.

slack space the space left over when a file doesn't completely fill the last cluster of sectors.

smart cards plastic cards the size of a credit card that contain an embedded chip on which digital information can be stored.

sneakware See **spyware**.

social engineering conning your way into acquiring information to which you have no right.

social network system an IT system that links you to people you know and, from there, to people your contacts know.

software the set of instructions that your hardware executes to carry out a specific task for you.

software suite (or simply **suite**) a group of applications sold together by a software company.

spam unsolicited e-mail from a company with whom you have never done business.

spoofing forging the return address on an e-mail so that the e-mail message appears to come from someone other than the actual sender.

spyware (also called **sneakware** or **stealthware**) software that comes hidden in free, downloadable software and tracks your online movements, mines the information stored on your computer, or uses your computer's CPU and storage for some task you know nothing about.

SQL See **structured query language**.

stealthware See **spyware**.

steganography the hiding of information inside other information.

storage device a tool you use to store information for use at a later time.

storyboard a sketch that illustrates the relationships between the pages of a Web site.

strategic management provides an organization with overall direction and guidance.

structure tag a HTML tag that sets up the necessary sections and specifies that the document is indeed an HTML document.

structured decision a decision where processing a certain kind of information in a specified way so that you will always get the right answer.

structured query language (SQL) a standardized fourth-generation query language found in most DBMSs.

subjective information attempts to describe something that is unknown.

suite See **software suite**.

supercomputer the fastest, most powerful, and most expensive type of computer.

supplier power high when buyers have few choices of whom to buy from, and low when there are many choices.

supply chain management (SCM) tracks inventory and information among business processes and across companies.

supply chain management (SCM) system tracks inventory and information among business processes and across companies.

switch a device that connects multiple computers into a network in which multiple communications links can be in operation simultaneously.

switching costs the costs that can make customers reluctant to switch to another product or service.

system bus consists of the electronic pathways which move information between basic components on the motherboard, including between your CPU and RAM.

system software handles tasks specific to technology management and coordinates the interaction of all technology devices.

system testing verifying that the units or pieces of code written for a system function correctly when integrated into the total system.

systems development life cycle (SDLC) a structured step-by-step approach for developing information systems.

T

tablet PC a pen-based computer that provides the screen capabilities of a PDA with the functional capabilities of a notebook or desktop computer.

tactical management develops the goals and strategies outlined by strategic management.

TB See **terabyte**.

TCP/IP (transport control protocol/Internet protocol) the primary protocol for transmitting information over the Internet.

technical architecture defines the hardware, software, and telecommunication equipment required to run the system.

technology-literate knowledge worker a person who knows how and when to apply technology.

telecommunications device a tool you use to send information to and receive it from another person or location.

telecommuting the use of communications technologies (such as the Internet) to work in a place other than a central location.

telephone modem (or **modem**) a device that connects your computer to your phone line so that you can access another computer or network.

terabyte (TB) roughly one trillion bytes.

test condition a detailed step the system must perform along with the expected result of the step.

testing phase verifies that the system works and meets all of the business requirements defined in the analysis phase.

thin client a workstation with a small amount of processing power and costs less than a full-powered workstation.

threat of new entrants high when it is easy for competitors to enter the market and low when it is difficult for competitors to enter the market.

threat of substitute products or services alternatives to using a product or service.

3-tier architecture a type of client/server computing, which contains clients, application servers, and data servers.

thrill-seeker hacker a hacker who breaks into computer systems for entertainment.

top-level domain three-letter extension of a Web site address that identifies its type.

touch pad a kind of stationary mouse on which you move your finger to cause the pointer on the screen to move (popular on notebooks).

touch screen special screen that lets you use your finger to point at and touch a particular function you want to perform.

TPS See **transaction processing system**.

trackball an upside-down, stationary mouse; using it, you move the ball instead of the device (mainly for notebooks).

traditional technology approach has two primary views of any system—information and procedures—and it keeps these two views separate and distinct at all times.

transaction processing system (TPS) processes transactions that occur within an organization.

transnational firm produces and sells products and services in countries all over the world.

transport control protocol/Internet protocol See **TCP/IP**.

Trojan-horse software software you don't want, hidden inside software you do.

Trojan-horse virus a virus that hides inside software, usually an attachment or download.

true search engine uses software agent technologies to search the Internet for keywords and then puts them into indexes.

2-tier architecture the basic type of client/server computing, whose two tiers are the client and server. The server primarily supports data storage or access to peripherals. Most of the system logic and intelligence is located on the client PC. A home network is essentially a 2-tier architecture.

U

UAT See **user acceptance testing**.

unallocated space the set of clusters that have been set aside to store information, but have not yet received a file, or still contain some or all of a file marked as deleted.

uniform resource locator (URL) an address for a specific Web page or document within a Web site.

uninstaller software utility software that you can use to remove software from your hard disk that you no longer want.

unit testing the testing of individual units or pieces of code for a system.

universal serial bus (USB) a connector that allows quick and easy attachment of all kinds of devices to a computer. Most standard desktops today have at least two USB ports, and most standard notebooks have at least one.

URL See **uniform resource locator**.

USB See **universal serial bus**.

user acceptance testing (UAT) determines if the system satisfies the business requirements and enables the knowledge workers to perform their jobs correctly.

user agent (or **personal agent**) an intelligent agent that takes action on your behalf.

user documentation explains the system and how to use it.

user interface the part of a computer program seen by the user, through which information, commands, and models are dealt with.

utility software software that provides additional functionality to your operating system.

V

value-added network (VAN) a semipublic network that provides services beyond the movement of information from one place to another.

VAN See **value-added network**.

vertical e-marketplace an electronic marketplace that connects buyers and sellers in a given industry.

vertical market software application software that is unique to an industry.

view an operation that allows you to see the contents of a database file, make whatever changes you want, perform simple sorting, and query to find the location of specific information.

viral marketing encourages users of a product or service supplied by a B2C company to ask friends to join in as well.

virtual private network (VPN) a public network that promises availability to your organization, but does not provide you with a dedicated line or communications media.

virtual reality a 3D computer simulation in which you actively and physically participate.

virtual team a team whose members are located in varied geographic locations and whose work is supported by specialized ICE software or by more basic collaboration systems.

virtual workplace a technology-enabled workplace with no walls and no boundaries, by which one can work anytime, anyplace, linked to other people and information, wherever they are.

virus (or **computer virus**) software written with the intention to cause annoyance or damage.

VPN See **virtual private network**.

W

walker an input device that captures and records the movement of your feet as you walk or turn in different directions.

WAN See **wide area network**.

wearable computer a fully-equipped computer that you wear as a piece of clothing or attached to a piece of clothing similarly to how you would carry your cell phone on your belt.

Web See **World Wide Web**.

Web browser software enables you to surf the Web.

webcam a digital camera that captures video to upload to the Web; often live, or updated regularly

Web farm either a Web site that has multiple servers, or an ISP that provides Web site outsourcing services using multiple servers.

Web page a specific portion of a Web site that deals with a certain topic.

Web portal a site that provides a wide range of services, including search engines, free e-mail, chat rooms, discussion boards, and links to hundreds of different sites.

Web server provides information and services to Web surfers.

Web site a location on the Web where you visit, gather information, and perhaps even order products.

Web site address a unique name that identifies a site on the Web.

Web space a storage area where you keep your Web site.

white-hat (or **ethical**) **hacker** a computer security professional hired by a company to break into its computer system.

wide area network (WAN) a network that covers large geographic distances, such as a province, a country, or even the entire world.

WiFi (wireless fidelity, also known as **IEEE 802.11b),** a way of transmitting information in wave form that is reasonably fast; often used for notebooks.

Windows 2000 Pro See **Microsoft Windows 2000 Professional.**

Windows CE See **Pocket PC OS.**

Windows Me See **Microsoft Windows 2000 Millennium.**

Windows XP Pro See **Microsoft Windows XP Professional.**

wired communications media transmit information over a closed, connected path.

wireless access point See **wireless network access point.**

wireless communications media transmit information through the air.

wireless fidelity See **WiFi.**

wireless Internet service provider (or **wireless ISP**) does the same job as standard Internet service providers except that you don't need a wired connection for access.

wireless ISP See **wireless Internet service provider.**

wireless local area network (WLAN or **LAWN)** a local area network that uses radio waves rather than wires to transmit information.

wireless network access point (or **wireless access point**) a device that allows computers to access a wired network using radio waves.

workflow defines all of the steps or business rules, from beginning to end, required for a process to run correctly.

workflow system automates business processes.

workgroup support system (WSS) a system designed to support a work team and to enhance group performance and communication of information.

workshop training training that takes place in a classroom-type environment and is led by an instructor.

World Wide Web (or **Web**) a multimedia-based collection of information, services, and Web sites supported by the Internet.

worm a type of virus that spreads itself, not just from file to file, but from computer to computer via e-mail and other Internet traffic.

WSS See **workgroup support system.**

X

XML See **extensible markup language.**

Y

yield management system a specialized kind of decision support system designed to maximize the amount of revenue a function generates.

PHOTO CREDITS

MODULE B

Figure B.1a, page 244, Photo courtesy of Logitech
Figure B.1b, page 244, © Precise Biometrics
Figure B.1c, page 244, © Nance S. Trueworthy
Figure B.1d, page 244, Photo courtesy of Intel Corporation
Figure B.1e, page 244, Image courtesy of KDS USA
Figure B.1f, page 244, Image courtesy of ATI Technologies
Figure B.1g, page 244, © 2004, Courtesy of Linksys
Figure B.3a, page 246, Courtesy of HP
Figure B.3b, page 246, PRNewsFoto / Mindjet LLC / AP / Wide World Photos
Figure B.3c, page 246, Photo courtesy of iBUYPOWER Computer
Figure B.3d, page 246, Courtesy of Dell Inc.
Figure B.4a, page 248, Courtesy of HP
Figure B.4b, page 248, Courtesy of International Business Machines Corporation. Unauthorized use not permitted.
Figure B.4c, page 248, Photo courtesy of Cray Inc.
Figure B.8a, page 255, Courtesy of Epson America
Figure B.8b, page 255, Photo courtesy of Microsof® Corp
Figure B.8c, page 255, © Plantronics, Inc.
FigureB.8d, page 255, PRNewsFoto / Logitech / AP / Wide World Photos
Figure B.8e, page 255, Photo courtesy of Logitech
Figure B.8f, page 255, Photo courtesy of Microsoft® Corp
Figure B.9a, page 256, Photo provided by Samsung Electronics America, Inc.
Figure B.9b, page 256, Photo provided by Samsung Electronics America, Inc.
Figure B.9c, page 256, Courtesy of HP
Figure B.10, page 257, Photo courtesy of GCC Printers

Figure B.12a, page 259, Jazz Disk Photo courtesy of Iomega Corporation
Figure B.12b, page 259, Courtesy of International Business Machines Corporation. Unauthorized use not permitted.
Figure B.12c, page 259, CDs © Nance Trueworthy
Figure B.17a, page 263, Photo by R.D. Cummings, Pittsburg State University
Figure B.17b, page 263, Photo by R.D. Cummings, Pittsburg State University
Figure B.17c, page 263, by R.D. Cummings, Pittsburg State University
Figure B.17d, page 263, by R.D. Cummings, Pittsburg State University
Figure B.17e, page 263, by R.D. Cummings, Pittsburg State University
Figure B.17f, page 263, by R.D. Cummings, Pittsburg State University
Figure B.17g, page 263, by R.D. Cummings, Pittsburg State University
Figure B.17h, page 263, by R.D. Cummings, Pittsburg State University

CHAPTER 8

Figure 8.6a, page 368, Euan Mys/Getty Images
Figure 8.6b, page 368, Andersen Ross/Getty Images
Figure 8.6c, page 368, © Stockbyte
Figure 8.9a, page 372, © Forestier Yves/Corbis Sygma
Figure 8.9b, page 372, Courtesy of Alex Lightman, Charmed Technology
Figure 8.9c, page 372, Courtesy Xybernaut Corporation

INDEX